William Morris
His life and work

JACK LINDSAY

William Morris

HIS LIFE AND WORK

TAPLINGER PUBLISHING COMPANY
New York

HOUSTON PUBLIC LIBRARY

First published in the United States in 1979 by
TAPLINGER PUBLISHING CO., INC.
New York, New York

Library of Congress Cataloging in Publication Data

Lindsay, Jack, 1900-
William Morris: his life and work.

Bibliography: p.
Includes index.
1. Morris, William, 1834-1896. 2. Authors, English
—19th century—Biography. 3. Artists—England—
Biography. 4. Socialists—England—Biography.
I. Title.
PR5083.L5 1979   821'.8 [B]   79-13075
ISBN 0-8008-8339-X

9 8 7 6 5 4 3 2 1

Contents

To Dorothy Garratt

You with a voice that warmly came
from Morris's own world have urged
that I should write this work; and so,
since here it's done, what other name
should stand before it?
                                    Long ago
first under his rich spell I fell
in Guenevere and the Romances.
His medieval light was merged,
thick stained-glass dreaming harmonies,
with bursts from Queensland's fiercest noons
and the bright thunder of her seas.

I wandered down dry gulley-courses
crisscrossing in thin gumtree-shadows
or drowned beneath the dreamtime moons,
enormous, powdered with the heat
of immemorial ghostly dances.

His earthly paradise I entered
and found it with its water-meadows
its Epping dense with hornbeam trees
and trumpets blown by armoured wraiths.

Thus strangely opposites can meet
and turn the same.
Out of the union of dream-forces
the wider fellowship emerged,
duly, long after. Deeply grow
the understructures of our faiths.
Slowly my scattered life was centred
on all the childhood-dream implied,
a lonely dream, the human core.

I merely meant to write your name
with thanks. But see, my thoughts went wide,
back into origins, the far land
from which the underground waters flow,
lost in deep mists, yet close at hand.
A dual task: to explore that past,
yet reach the hilltop whence at last
we view the future's clear expanses.

Jack Lindsay

Foreword

While the number of books on William Morris or some aspect of his work is very large, and has been steadily increasing over the last dozen or so years, there are only three full-scale biographies: those by Mackail (1899), Edward Thompson (1955), and Philip Henderson (1967). Each seems to me to have its virtues. The first is a valuable work, an excellent example of the family-biography; the third is a lively elaboration of the basis that Mackail lays; the second establishes at length the importance of Morris's political career and demolishes various misconceptions which had ruled before its appearance despite the pioneering protest by Page Arnot. There has thus seemed to me to be a place for a work which attempted to draw all the aspects together, made use of the new perspective vigorously provided by Thompson, and brought out the central dynamic which drove the man on through his manifold forms of expression. What I have tried to do here is to keep the man himself always in the forefront, showing both the many and complex changes through which he went, and the deep persisting elements that can be traced back to his childhood experiences.

Anyone working on Morris's life cannot but realise with ever increasing respect the fullness and force of the researches made by Thompson into his political activities, their background, and their great significance. Further, the whole question of Morris's thought and his ceaseless struggle to live out his ideas has been given a new dimension by the detailed study of Paul Meier in *La pensée utopique de William Morris* (1972). Of the many works dealing with Morris as a designer I have found especially illuminating that by Ray Watkinson. Among the many debts that I must acknowledge is that to L. Warwick James for helping me to find out just what happened in the Marlborough College riots (a matter strangely ignored by all writers on Morris); to Dorothy Garratt, daughter of Robert Steele, who has provided material and encouraged me; and to Ken Goodwin for generously putting at my disposal his thorough knowledge of Morris manuscripts, etc. I must add my thanks to R. C. H. Briggs and the William Morris Society that he has so ably helped to develop over the years.

I

Childhood

The years of childhood leave deep marks or patterns of experience on all persons. Such imprints from early years are of much importance in the development of writers and artists, as determining certain aspects of their outlook, the kind of experiences to which they are most responsive, and the general direction of their expression. Not that there is any question of an automatic or mechanical repetition of the original patterns. As the individual grows in character, in range of experience and understanding, new depths of meaning transform the primary content, though an element of continuity remains. In many cases, where little is known of a creative person's early life, we can only guess at the original patterns from the later expressions. But in some cases, such as that of William Morris, we can see to a considerable extent how childhood has provided certain fundamental attitudes or forms of response which keep reasserting themselves throughout life, while taking on new depths and breadths of meaning.

The Morris family was Welsh, of the upper Severn valleys, and William's grandfather was said to have been the first to drop the *Ap* from the surname. A capable and religious businessman, he had settled at Worcester, where he married the daughter of a retired naval surgeon who practised at Nottingham. A second son, William, was born in June 1797; and about 1820, after his father had moved to London, he became clerk in a firm of discount-brokers at 32 Lombard Street. The Harrises of this firm, Quakers, had some family link with the Morrises; and William, when slightly over thirty, was taken in as a partner. Only a small number of firms, with a status near that of the private bank, then carried on as brokers; a firm, once established, was safe from competition and had to be incompetent if it were not to prosper at least mildly.

Soon after becoming a partner William married Emma, youngest daughter of Joseph Shelton, who had been a neighbour at Worcester. The Sheltons had long done well as merchants and landowners; many had entered church or bar. Emma's grandfather had been proctor of the Consistory Court of the Worcester diocese, and his family was musical; two of his sons were singing canons of the local cathedral and Westminster Abbey; a third taught music at Worcester. There was, in fact, a distant link by marriage between Sheltons and Morrises.

William and Emma set up home at the place of business. Two daughters, Emma and Henrietta, were born in 1830 and 1832. In 1833 the family moved to Elm House at Walthamstow overlooking the Lea valley. City-men, going daily to work by stage-coach, had taken to residing in the still rural area. Clay Hill was a lightly rising region pushed over into the flat country from the higher land of Epping Forest, which lay along the skyline to the north-east, with a low timbered valley to the north. The house, plain and comfortable, had been built earlier in the century; the big front lawn held an old mulberry tree and there were shrubberies and kitchen gardens. Here William was born on 24 March 1834; and after him came four more boys and two girls.

He was a weakling in his first years, fed (his mother said) on calves-foot jelly and beef-tea. The Morrises, unlike the Sheltons, do not seem to have been a hardy stock; neither William's father nor his grandfather was long-lived. As he grew, he became unusually strong, but, despite his great energy, he died at the age of sixty-two. Reading came to him easily. 'We never remember his learning regularly to read,' said his sisters, 'though he may have had a few lessons from our governess.' And he himself could not recall the time when he was unable to read. His daughter May tells us:

He used to be very fond of *The Ladder of Learning*, a little book with cuts on yellow paper. At nine years he had read all the Waverley Novels and Marryat's *Peter Simple* and *Midshipman Easy*. He was not taught to write till he was ten, but he remembered being taught to spell, and having to stand on a chair with his shoes off as a punishment for making so many mistakes. In two months he learnt to write well.

His spelling was never good. A mistake over a common word in *Jason* was set and passed, the printer's reader taking it for some oddity; the sheets had to be cancelled and redone.

Mr Morris was doing well in the firm in his own undertakings. In 1840 the family moved across the Forest to Woodford Hall, a spacious Georgian mansion in a park of some fifty acres, set on the highway between Epping and London. The estate included some hundred acres of farmland sloping down to Little Roding; and the Forest was so near that only a fence cut off its glades of beech and hornbeam. Here was 'certainly the biggest hornbeam wood in these islands, and I suppose in the world,' he recalled in the April before his death. 'The said hornbeams were all pollards, being shrouded every four or six years, and were interspersed in many places by holly thickets; and the result was a very curious and characteristic wood, which can be seen nowhere else.' He came to know the whole wood 'yard by yard'. In both his prose and verse hornbeams, impassively solemn even in sunlight, often appear. From the Hall he could see white and ruddy-brown sails moving through the marches along the Thames past the cornfields and pastures; and through a private doorway he could go into the churchyard where stood a small Georgian brick church. In 1888 he told his daughter Jenny:

When we lived at Woodford there were stocks there on a little bit of wayside green in the middle of the village; beside them stood the *cage*, a small shanty of some 12 ft sq: and it was built of brown brick roofed with blue slate. I suppose it had been quite recently in use since its *style* was not earlier than the days of fat George. I remember that I used to look at the two threats of law [and] order with considerable terror, and decidedly preferred to walk on the opposite side of the road; but I never heard of anyone being locked up in the cage or laid by the heels in the stocks.

He always declared himself 'a lover of sad lowland country', of river meadows with brown marshes and lush marigolds, 'the wide green sea of Essex marshlands, with the great domed line of the sky, and the sun shining down in one flood of peaceful light over the long distance'.[1]

He and his brothers were keen anglers, and he kept up his angling throughout his life. They shot too, not regular game, but rabbits and small wildbirds such as redwings and fieldfare in their winter holidays, and were allowed to roast them for supper. Scenes of hunting, roasting and feasting in *Jason* and other works were based on these early activities and the fantasies they bred. A friend who shared this outdoor life with him said later that as a boy he 'knew the names of birds'. May states:

Among William's early playthings was a lamb that squeaked and a model of London Bridge and—the supreme thing—a suit of armour he could get into, and in which he proudly rode his pony among his playmates. He never 'played at trains' or took any interest in mechanical inventions; he never wanted a toy pistol or a gun; at one time the longing of dear delight was to shoot a wood-pigeon with a bow and arrow in the park round Woodford Hall. The open air, the wanderings there and in the Forest, the making-up of stories about everything he met were his chief amusements; he would go off by himself visiting any old ruin or an old church, and it was very early that the sight of ancient buildings began to store his brain with pictures that the prodigious memory called up and used later in life.

The children had their own little gardens, and William always kept a deep love of flowers, of all gardening and farming activities. Later he recalled 'the beautiful hepatica which I used to love when I was a quite little boy'. Again, 'to this day when I smell a may-tree I think of going to bed by daylight'. In *News from Nowhere*, where he maturely sets out the England of his hopes, which he firmly believes will be realised by political struggle, we find a combination that never ceased to excite him: a lovely girl merged with his childhood-imagery of flowers:

One of the girls, the handsome one, who had been scattering little twigs of lavender and sweet-smelling herbs about the floor, came near to listen, and stood behind me with her hand on my shoulder, in which she held some of the plant that I used to call balm: its strong sweet smell brought back to my mind my very early days in the kitchen-garden at Woodford, and the large blue plums which grew on the wall beyond the sweet-herb patch—a connection of memories which all boys will see at once.

There was still a self-contained medieval element in country-houses even as small as the Hall. The Morrises brewed their own beer, made their own butter, baked their own bread. As in the fourteenth century a meal was eaten at high prime, midway between breakfast and dinner, at which the children had cake and cheese with a glass of small-beer—and the cake was 'nicer than anything of the kind he ever tasted since'. Later Morris remarked on *trencher* as meaning a mere flat square board on which the carver put slices of meat.

I have seen the blue-coat-school boys eating off them when I was a little boy, and noticed their devices (with much interest) for banking up a little soup with a potato toft. It seems *our* forefathers when they had flesh-meat, usually boiled it with dough puddings. They ate the puddings first to dull the edge of appetite, then supped the brewis [from cups] & then came to the 'piece de resistance'. This was the custom in country places almost in my young days.

Indeed, all over England, though patchily and in varying degrees, there were survivals of medieval method or procedure, though steadily fading out before the expanding industrialism. Till 1870 hand-harvesting went on in parts of Surrey, and flail-threshing till 1880. The Assize of Bread governed the weight and price of a loaf of bread from 1266 till two years after Morris's birth, even if the bread was often adulterated. Till 1840 there were strenuous efforts in Stamford to carry out the November custom of bull-running as an assertion of local liberty. At the last conflict twenty metropolitan police and forty-three dragoons had to be brought in to aid the ninety local constables. Such examples could be endlessly multiplied. The tension between the bourgeois world and the surviving elements of the medieval system was still real enough in the early half of the nineteenth century.

May tells us how she and Jenny used to listen eagerly to tales of the festivals held at home when their father was a little boy. 'Christmas was fine, but Twelfth Night was always the most entertaining anniversary, with its St George play and all the rest of it. And delicious rum-punch was brewed and given to everyone, children and all—half a tumbler of it!' The mumming-play of death and resurrection was presumably presented by local rustics. We see that when Morris later came to love the medieval world he was in part looking back to his own childhood, with the survivals of old customs and the re-creation of the past in the fantasies of games; at the same time, while imagining himself a knight in armour amid flowers and forests, he was also beginning to take an interest in what of the past he could find intact in old buildings. And his inner life, with its eager reconstructions of a knightly and adventurous world, was already overflowing in the ceaseless telling of stories.

In later years he often spoke of the time 'when I was a little chap', and always with profound contentment. His movement into the desired future of *News from Nowhere* was felt as a return to origins, to his childhood realised on a new level. In 1886 in a lecture he spoke of the best and most useful men as those who never threw off their youthful qualities. In *News*, when Clara says that she feels some miasma of past miseries about the Guest (Morris), her father asks him if he can recall anything of the world he has left which is like what he has found in the new one.

The lovers had turned aside now, and were talking together softly, and not heeding us; so I said, but in a low voice: 'Yes, when I was a happy child on a sunny holiday, and had everything that I could think of.'

'So it is,' said he. 'You remember just now you twitted me with living in the second childhood of the world. You will find it a happy world to live in; you will be happy there—for a while.'

Again I did not like his scarcely veiled threat, and was beginning to trouble myself with trying to remember how I had got amongst this curious people. . . .

The threat of being returned to the divided world of the present is felt like the loss of childhood; it is the loss of the second childhood of the world. A little later: 'I dressed speedily, in a suit of blue laid ready for me, so handsome that I quite blushed when I had got into it, feeling as I did so that excited pleasure of anticipation of a holiday, which, well remembered as it was, I had not felt since I was a boy, new come home for the summer holidays.' Then, 'as we slipped between the lovely summer greenery, I almost felt my youth come back to me, and as if I were on one of those water excursions which I used to enjoy so much in those days when I was too happy to think that there could be much amiss anywhere.' Again, 'I walked upstream a little, watching the light mist curling up from the river till the sun gained power to draw it all away; saw the bleak speckling the water under the willow boughs, whence the tiny flies they fed on were falling in myriads; heard the great chub splashing here and there at some belated moth or other, and felt almost back again in my boyhood.' As the journey up the river nears its end and Ellen shows her strong feeling for him: 'As for me, I felt young again, and strange hopes of my youth were mingling with the pleasure of the present; almost destroying it, and quickening it again into something like pain.' Finally, as they reach their destination, which is Kelmscott Manor transferred into this fantasy-world that is both childhood and the liberated future, he goes into the house and explores it: 'from the roof-covered porch to the strange and quaint garrets amongst the great timbers of the roof', it all 'seemed to be inhabited for the time by children'.

We realise how much his whole hope for the future, for a happy and brotherly world, is linked with his childhood memories—and also how Kelmscott Manor in his later years incarnated for him the sort of life which his childhood had known and imagined. The entry into the house is heralded by Ellen's cry from the deepmost of her heart, which is also the cry of Morris summing all that he had most strongly learned and felt: 'The earth and the growth of it and the life of it! If I could but say or show how I love it!'

Further, he insists that the roots of creativity lie deep in childhood. In *News*, Hammond says:

'It is the child-like part of us that produces works of imagination. When we are children time passes so slow with us that we seem to have time for everything.' He sighed, and then smiled and said: 'At least let us rejoice that we have got back our childhood again. I drink to the days that are!'

'Second childhood,' said I in a low voice. . . .²

The fact that he thus in one sense never outgrew his childhood and never lost the memory of its rooted happiness was what gave him the quality recognised by all who met him in later years as childlike or boyish. A few quotations will drive the point home. Mackail remarks:

'Master of himself and therefore of all near him,' Morris at the same time retained the most childlike simplicity in the expression of his actual thoughts or feelings on any subject, and was as little hampered by false shame as he was guided by convention. In some points he remained an absolute child to the end of his life. If you introduced him to a friend and he had the faintest suspicion that he was there to be shown off, his manners instantly became intolerable. As childlike was another of his characteristics, the constant desire to be in touch with the things he loved.

Yeats noted that the affection he inspired was like that which one felt for children. Compton-Rickett commented on the 'eternal boy' in him.

There was a rough, jovial simple-heartedness about him in all his doings. His culture rode lightly upon him. . . . There was a boyish awkwardness about him too. He tumbled about his friends' rooms with a curious aptitude for knocking things over. This characteristic gave infinite delight to his friends, who were for ever chaffing him. He was a ready butt for good-natured jokes. . . . Boyish in his enthusiasms; boyish in his restless activities; boyish in his friendships; and yet at the back of all this restless ebullience of youth was the stern, steady purpose and clear outlook of the man who has passed through much and felt many things. Though, when all is said, young at heart to the very end, ready to throw his cap into the ring and punch the world on the head—the City World especially—on the least provocation.

Bruce Glasier likens him to a child, though in him 'the trait of childlikeness was the more singular because of the otherwise dominantly manly, self-reliant, and exceedingly manifest practical capacity of the man'—

yet there was ever in him that spontaneity of liking and disliking, that wilfulness and yet tractability, that predisposition at one moment to engage in amusement and frolic, and the next to fall to desperate seriousness, which make unself-conscious childhood such an unfailing source of perturbation and charm. His love of bright colours, and all natural objects and beautiful things; his restless eagerness to be doing something with his hands; his delight in companionship, in art and play, were all part of this elemental freshness of his nature.

Such comments could be multiplied.

We must add that there was also a strongly childish, even infantile, element in the blind tempers that overtook him at some trivial physical obstacle. There are many stories, some of which will come up in our narrative, of the uncontrollable way in which he kicked in doorplates or tore down curtains that annoyed him. Not that we ever hear of him using any kind of violence against people. His black rages were directed against obstructive objects, and were usually brief. They show clearly enough the child who feels hopelessly cornered and shut in (or out) by a power which he resents with all his being, but does not understand. Morris's deep attachment to the garden of enjoyment and the forest of independence had as its counterweight the blind fury he felt at the thwarting power which came between him and these spheres of freedom. We see that from his earliest years there was some interfering hand (presumably that of his mother) which cut him off at times from delights that he deeply desired. We see also the link between this furious infantile reaction and his mature revolt against all the forces that barred men from the earthly paradise, from the full, free, and direct enjoyment of the earth.

In all these attitudes and emotions there was something fiercely idiosyncratic, but there was also an aspect that belonged to a general development going back to the early eighteenth century as the peasantry were uprooted, as cash-values began to dominate, and as the individual felt driven back on himself in a new way. Out of this trend came the phrases 'in the bosom of the family', 'in the bosom of nature', taking the place of the older phrase, 'in the bosom of Mother Church'. Thus the turn to Nature, to the Earth-Mother, involves the finding of a new, and yet more consoling and protective surrogate for the actual mother. As has been remarked of the early eighteenth century, 'Perhaps because they had rejected the mother image at a conscious level, Englishmen were deeply influenced by those echoes of it that rose from their unconscious: while despising as idolaters the papists who prayed to Mary the mother of God, they were able to nestle happily into their own private dreams of womblike homes ringed by gardens and woods and lapping water' (D. Jarrett). In Morris's reactions as a child we then see both the rejection of the mother and her rediscovery on a new level, in a new fullness of satisfaction—a level which in time makes possible a social application and working-out of the conflict.

Morris himself was ready to joke about his accessions of violence. In July 1876 he wrote: 'The news from here is little or none; e.g. that I broke the strings of the Venetian blind in my room last night; that no water came into the cistern on Sunday, and very little yesterday, and so on. Item, I was *not* the man who threw the medicine bottles at the dog last Saturday, and was fined a shilling for that righteous indignation.' May tells us that the two elder sisters were consistently given to rebuking William as a child:

temper

William was often called 'naughty' and 'wicked' for doing all sorts of childish things he could not help doing, such as falling down and grazing his knees. On one occasion he and his two sisters stained their faces with pollen from the tiger-lilies and were much scolded, which he thought very unjust. 'O Willie, you *naughty* boy!' was the constant refrain from the sisters, but most from Henrietta, as Emma was a gentle nature and specially fond of him, and Hennie was more given to 'ruling'.[3]

It must have been the mother, however, who scolded about the pollen, and we may assume that Henrietta was following her example. The nagging prohibitions, working on his impulsive nature, certainly played their part in creating his obsessive rage with obstacles in later life.

The force with which the garden of childhood had entered into his spirit and provided the imagery of a desirable world is shown by many crucial aspects of his work. His decorative designs were essentially an attempt to introduce into life at as many points as possible the forms of flower, leaf, bird, which he had come to love at Elm House and Woodford Hall. Glasier, going into the main rooms at Kelmscott House, felt 'a delightful sense of garden-like freshness and bloom in the room'. Morris's version of the medieval world was of a place where nature in the shape of greenery and flowers appeared as a living aspect of the house. In *John Ball* we read of Will Green's upper room: 'The walls, instead of being panelled, were hung with a coarse loosely-woven stuff of green worsted with birds and trees woven into it. There were flowers in plenty stuck about the room, mostly of the yellow blossoming flag or flower-de-luce, of which I had seen plenty in all the ditches, but in the window near the doors was a pot full of those same white poppies I had seen when I first woke up.' That is, when he woke into his medieval dream. The flowers bless and guard the vision.

In *The Lesser Arts of Life*, 1882, he declared:

To turn our chamber walls into the green woods of the leafy month of June, populous of bird and beast; or a summer garden with man and maid playing round a fountain, or a solemn procession of the mythical warriors and heroes of old; that surely was worth the trouble of doing, and the money that had to be paid for it: that was no languid acquiescence in an upholstery.

And he goes on to link this position with his childhood memories:

How well I remember as a boy my first acquaintance with a room hung with faded greenery at Queen Elizabeth's Lodge, by Chigwell Hatch, in Epping Forest (I wonder what has become of it now), and the impression of romance that it made upon me; a feeling that always comes back on me when I read, as I often do, Sir Walter Scott's *Antiquary*, and come to the description of the green room at Monkbarns, amongst which the novelist has with such exquisite cunning of art embedded the fresh and glittering verse of the summer poet Chaucer; yes, that was more than upholstery, believe me.

Indeed, if we consider his ideas about textile design and of design in general, we feel that he is always thinking in terms of a garden of flowers and foliage. 'The aim should be to combine clearness of form and firmness of structure with the mystery which comes of abundance and richness of detail.' Conversely he says of a garden that it should be both ordered and luxuriant; always there should be a close and living relation between garden and house. In the world of *News from Nowhere* this relation has invaded all aspects of life, including clothes. Clara defends the lovely and bright clothes of the people as an aspect of their return to nature, and the Guest comments, 'I might have guessed that people who were so fond of architecture generally, would not be backward ornamenting themselves; all the more as the shape of their raiment, apart from its colour, was both beautiful and reasonable, veiling the form without either muffling or caricaturing it.'

Lethaby, one of the most intelligent and penetrating of his followers, described his designs:

They stand supreme in modern pattern work, and will necessarily remain supreme until as great a man as Morris again deals with that manner of expression with his *full force* as he did. Even the most formal of his work recalls to us the strong growth of healthy vegetation. . . . Others, more directly, speak in ordered pattern language, of a flower-embroidered field; of willow boughs seen against the sky; of inter-twined jessamine and branching pomegranate, lemon and peach; of a rose-trellised arbour in a garden. . . .

Morris's notion of a regenerated Britain was one in which the garden found its proper place as a dominant factor, redeeming architecture from dead box-shapes and mediating between man and nature in its fullness. On 26 March 1874, having just turned forty, he wrote to Louie Baldwin:

Yet in spite of the round number I don't feel any older than I did in the ancient times of the sunflowers. I very much long to have a spell in the country this spring, but I suppose I hardly shall. . . . Instead of the sweet scents one gets an extra smell of dirt. Surely if people lived some five hundred years instead of threescore and ten they would find some better way of living than in such a sordid loathsome place, but now it seems to be nobody's business to try better things—isn't mine, you see, in spite of all my grumbling—but look, suppose people lived in little communities among gardens and green fields, so that you could be in the country in five minutes' walk, and had few wants, almost no furniture for instance, and no servants, and studied the (difficult) arts of enjoying life, and finding out what they really wanted: then I think one might hope civilisation had really begun.

Thus was born the idea of the Garden City. After turning to socialism he took up the idea again and carried it further; he wanted the whole of England to be a garden where it was not a forest. In *Art and Socialism*, 1884, he wrote:

(a) Our houses must be well built, clean and healthy; (b) there must be abundant garden space in our towns, and our towns must not eat up the fields and natural features of the country; nay I demand that there be left waste places and wilds in it, or romance and poetry—that is Art—will die out amongst us.

In *Town and Country*, 1893, he demanded that each city should become a garden full of splendid houses. (Something of this concept has appeared in the Soviet idea of the *agrogorod*.)[4]

His love of both flowers and old craftwork was strengthened by the strong visual sense which he owned from the outset. He recalled 'a picture of Abraham and Isaac worked in brown worsted', Indian cabinets, 'a carved ivory junk with painted and gilded puppets in it in a glass case'. A copy of

Gerard's *Herbal* helped to clarify his sense of flower-forms, and later he drew on it for craft-designs. We saw that by the age of nine he had read through Scott's novels, with some Marryat stories and many current works; later came Lane's *Arabian Nights*. Scott had a lasting effect, providing the basis from which his historical sense developed, and enabling him at an early phase to correlate his interests. In *The Beauty of Life*, 1880, he discusses the rebirth of a vital literature in England through the forces released explosively by the French Revolution, with Blake and Coleridge representing the new kind of poet. 'With that literature in which romance, that is to say, humanity, was re-born, there sprang up also a feeling for the romance of external nature, which is surely strong in us now, joined with a longing to know something real of the lives of those who have gone before us; of these feelings united you will find the broadest expression in the pages of Walter Scott.' The passage cited about Queen Elizabeth's Lodge shows how the reading of Scott merged with his response to old crafts or buildings to stir his sense of history as something actually lived-through; and he came to feel that Scott had caught a truly popular note, so that characters like Wamba in *Ivanhoe* lead on to the peasants of *John Ball*.

One of the books he read in his childhood was Clara Reeve's *The Old English Baron*, in which two leading characters have the names of William and Emma (the name of his mother as of his favourite elder sister). Emma remembered how they used to read the book together 'in the rabbit warren at Woodford, poring over the enthralling pages till both were wrought up to a state of mind that made them afraid to cross the park to reach home'. The romance, first called *The Champion of Virtue, a Gothic Story*, in 1777, was reissued the next year with the better-known title. It tells how Edmund, reared as a peasant, turns out to be the rightful heir of the Lovels. His father's murderer had handed the estate over to his brother-in-law, who, ignorant of the crime, took a liking to Edmund and reared him in the household. There the second son, William, became Edmund's best friend, and his sister Emma fell in love with him. The facts finally came out and Edmund married Emma.

Certain aspects of the novel had a deep effect on Morris. In an embryonic way we find the pattern of two friends loving the same woman, which was to play a potent part in his life. Edmund, learning of his origin but afraid to speak out openly on his own behalf, woos Emma in the name of a friend (really himself). Later William and Emma guess the truth. Emma says, 'You may depend that I will not dispose of my hand or heart till I know the end of this affair.' William smiles, 'Keep them for Edmund's *friend*: I shall rejoice to see him in the situation to ask them.' Edmund, William, and Emma are shown as closely drawn together. 'Edmund trembled; he leaned upon William's shoulder to support himself. Emma cast her eyes upon him; she saw his emotion and hastened to relieve him.' Brother and sister are depicted in an emotional union with a third person, who claims the sister. The pattern is here simple, but capable of all the complexities of the Guenevere and Iseult stories.

Further, the style of the novel, though rather flat, at one point clearly anticipates the method of dream-sequences which emerges in Morris's early prose-tales: one situation drifts or moves into another unaccountably, with a sense of danger or doom. In varying forms this system of construction reappears throughout Morris's work, finding its supreme form in *John Ball* and *News from Nowhere*.

During his sleep many strange and incoherent dreams arose to his imagination. He thought he received a message from his friend Lord Lovel, to come to him at the castle; that he stood at the gate and received him; that he strove to embrace him, and could not; but that he spoke to this effect: 'Though I have been dead these fifteen years, I still command here, and none can enter these gates without my permission; know that it is I that invite, and bid you welcome; the hopes of my house rest upon you.' Upon this he bade Sir Philip follow him; he led him through many rooms till at last he sunk down, and Sir Philip thought he still followed him till he came in a dark and frightful cave, where he disappeared, and in his stead he beheld a complete suit of armour, stained with blood, which belonged to his friend, and he thought he heard dismal groans from beneath. Presently after that he was hurried away by an invisible hand, and led into a wild heath, where the people were enclosing the ground, and making preparations for two combatants; the trumpet sounded, and a voice called out still louder, 'Forbear! It is not permitted to be revealed till the time is ripe for the event: wait with patience on the decrees of heaven.' He was then transported into his own home, where, going into an unfrequented room, he was again met by his friend, who was living, and in all the bloom of youth, as when he first knew him; he started at the sight and awoke. The sun shone upon his curtains. . . .

We shall have more to say of the significance of dreams and their relation to reality in Morris's scheme of things. For the moment we may note only an early poem, *The Ruined Castle*, where the hauntings, caused by the burial of a murdered woman under a turret stair, are reminiscent of those in *The*

Old English Baron. There was a strong element of fear, we see, in Morris's child-experiences, as well as one of joy. We heard of his fear of the old stocks and the panic of the return home across the park with Emma. (His fits of blind temper were a sort of panic, a sense of being cornered and closed in by hidden and hostile forces.) In the early romance, *Frank's Sealed Letter*, a love-rejection is thus depicted:

I fell there before her feet. I caught the hem of her garment. I buried my face in its folds; madly I strove to convince myself that she was but trying me, that she could not speak for her deep love, that it was a dream only. Oh! how I tried to wake, to find myself, with my heart beating wildly, and the black night round me, lying on my bed; as often, when a child, I used to wake from a dream of lions, and robbers, and ugly deaths, and the devil, to find myself in the dear room, though it was dark, my heart bounding with the fear of pursuit and joy of escape. But no dream breaks now, desperate, desperate, earnest. The dreams have closed round me, and become the dismallest reality, as I often used to fear those other dreams might; the walls of this fact are closed round about me now like the sides of an iron chest, hurrying on down some swift river, with the black waters above, to the measureless, rolling sea. I shall never any more wake to anything like that.

He there expresses just the sort of claustrophobic dream-fear that we would assume to lie behind the blind tempers. It is clear that in his childhood he experienced both deeply satisfying unions (especially with his sister Emma in the garden and the woodland) and crushing periods of exclusion, loneliness, loss of the consoling objects, with a sense of being cooped or closed in.

In the unpublished novel of 1872, written at the crisis of his relations with Janey his wife and Rossetti his close friend, he uses nightmare imagery, linked with his own memories, to tell how the rector (the father of the two protagonists) is confronted with a figure from his guilty past in the dusk:

He rose up from his chair in terror for he really began to think she was a ghost: all the dreadful threatenings of the disbelieved or disregarded creed of which he was the priest flashed across his brain mingled with naif or gross ghost stories read long ago in queer little penny garlands with woodcuts; he put his hand before his face for a moment as if he thought she would be gone when he removed it but she was there facing him at the other end of the room in the gathered dusk—My God Eleanour speak to me he said or are you really a ghost? She understood his base fear, and a smile passed over her face as she came towards him, he could see through the twilight how deadly pale she was.

And just as he, the Guest, enters the blessed land of *News* through a happy fantasy that leads to a picture of the true union of men with one another and with nature, so he is dismissed from it by a nightmare. 'Suddenly I saw as it were a black cloud rolling along to meet me, like a nightmare of my childish days; and for a while I was conscious of nothing else than being in the dark. . . .'

A powerful description of the joy and fear in his dreams may be found in a passage from the 1872 novel where Arthur is waking up, day-dreaming, then deeply dreaming. Here we have the dream-changes learned from Clara Reeves, with the transition from the joy, the sense of security, given by the girl among flowers, to a sense of utter loss and doom. The change of the desired girl into the brother-rival has much significance in the light of the triadic relation which we noted in *The Old English Baron* and which was to play such a key-role in Morris's personal life.

. . . spending the day as though there were no one else in the world; and still he kept beginning over & over again the sort of things she would say to him, the way in which she could kiss him, for still every sweetest way seemed not quite sweet enough, till wearied out at last he fell asleep again just as the eastern sky was beginning to redden, and his waking dream turned into a sleeping one without changing much at first except that it was suffused with a vague excitement and luxury and fear withal that had been almost hope; and he was walking with Clara through meadows not at all like the Leaser meads which yet they both agreed to think were none other than it seemed; they were thickly studded with apple-trees in bloom, and it was moonlight, yet the birds were singing in full chorus; and Clara herself was clad in light fluttering raiment like he had seen on angels in old pictures instead of her usual dress, and she spoke to him in verses in the rhythm of some fragment of old poetry that he had forgotten awake, and so they passed on till as it happens in dreams the landscape changed and there were big blue mountains all about the mead and a rushing stream through it, and suddenly his heart seemed to stop beating for fear and she stopped him and faced him, with fear in her eyes too, and as he tried to speak & could not, she had turned into his brother and they were both quite children again and he thought they had lost themselves & were to die, and the rush of the stream seemed to grow louder & louder, and the wind to rise & howl about the hollows of the mountainside, and presently a horse came galloping past, and then a herd of cows rushed up and then a great flock of sheep seemed to fill up all the valley their endless backs all moving like the sea, and with a sense of something dreadful going to happen he woke panting and gasping with an unuttered cry, and the horror of the dream was so strong in him that at first he seemed to wake into a world of white flame; but as he came fully to himself he saw the broad sun flooding the room, and smiled to himself with returning comfort as he heard the sound of a scythe being whetted outside for the mowing of the piece of grass called the drying ground; and then came the sound of the musical church clock and he counted 7, and the full measure of his happiness came over him.[5]

In an earlier dream Arthur is confronted with horrible images of his obstructive and dreaded father. This dream and the general role of the father in the novel brings us up against the question of Mr Morris, who remains a very shadowy figure. Mackail says: 'On the paternal side of the family there was a marked neurotic and gouty tendency.' By neurotic he doubtless means that Mr Morris suffered from disordered nerves. (A description of 1887 says that 'the neurotic woman is sensitive, zealous, managing'.) In a letter of 16 May 1883, Philip Webb wrote to the ailing Janey: 'Morris has always put aside his nervousness when I asked him to tell me how you were getting on.' Nervousness is not a quality we easily attribute to Morris; but Webb was a subtle and sympathetic observer, who knew both Janey and Morris well, and we cannot disregard his comment. He says that Morris's reticence is based on a nervous strain. Henry James in 1869 noted in Morris 'a nervous restless manner'. Wardle, who worked closely with Morris for so many years, comments on the Merton Abbey system. 'He came down twice or thrice a week in those days. It is noticeable perhaps, in remembering his nervous temperament, that, though he disliked the journey by rail intensely, —underground to Farringdon St. & thence from Ludgate to Merton Abbey, he showed no irritation on arriving. The latter part of the journey perhaps, through the fields was soothing, and then there was the short passage, from the Station through the garden of the Abbey & the prospect of being soon at work, which together may have restored his equilibrium but there remained a certain impetus in his manner, as if he would still go at 20 miles an hour & rather expected everything to keep pace with him. This was I think the effect of the railway journey. I had noticed it in Queen Square if he arrived from a journey.' Note how the passages through the flowers, Wardle thinks, has a quietening effect on his nerves. From early days people noted that Morris seemed inturned, or rather that his whole attention was concentrated on what he was doing or considering, so that he seemed oblivious of persons around and unconcerned with what was regarded as the normal conventions of intercourse. What we meet in all that is not anything egoist or hard; it is in fact a massive direction of energy towards the matter in hand and the nervous strain appears in the blind rages turned on obstructions. Morris may then be said to have inherited a great deal of his father's 'neurotic and gouty tendency' in Mackail's sense.

He himself in 1883 remarked: 'My Father was a business man in the city, and well-to-do; and we lived in the ordinary bourgeois style of comfort; and since we belonged to the evangelical section of the English Church I was brought up in what I should call rich establishmentarian puritanism; a religion which even as a boy I never took to.' Words like Enthusiasm had a derogatory meaning and social reformers like Maurice were not rated true Christians. May adds:

The Morrises were Evangelical, and the children were taught that Unitarians were very bad people and Dissenters not respectable. They were not allowed to mix with any but Quakers, of whom there were many about Walthamstow. All the same, there were High Church books about the house such as Nelson's *Fasts and Festivals*. . . . He used to be taken to a dull church, the parson of which wrote a book called *Bible Readings Simplified*, or some such title. He picked this up later and found it to be as difficult to read as the Bible was easy!

In 1875 (15 November), discouraged with drawing, he said, 'So I keep it up dreading the model day like I used to dread Sunday when I was a little chap.' Clearly the religious ideas and practices of the early years belonged to the sphere of things forbidding and imprisoning, against which he fiercely reacted.

An important event occurred when he was eight years old. His father took him to see Canterbury Cathedral, though whether they went alone together or in a family party is not stated. 'The first great church he saw,' says May; 'and the long nave and great columns and painted glass made an impression on the young mind that lasted all his life. Swift perception and retentive memory were indeed among Heaven's gifts to him: here he was, at the age of eight, so excited by the majesty of the building that in some queer way he took in and registered in his child's brain facts of the famous architecture the significance of which the child could not understand, but which were the beginnings of his store of knowledge of such things.' He thought, he said, 'that the gates of heaven had been opened' to him; but oddly he never seems to have later revisited the site.

On the same holiday he was shown the Minster of Thanet; and fifty years later, without having seen the building since, he described it in some detail.

But we cannot think of his father as having played any conscious role in these initiations of his son. On 31 May 1896 Blunt records in his *Diary*: 'I took him yesterday to see Shipley Church, a fine old Norman tower, injured with restoration. He was very indignant, swearing at the parsons as we walked up the nave: "Beasts! Pigs! Damn their souls!" ' Of the early visit to Canterbury and his first sight of an illuminated manuscript, Morris said, 'These are the first pleasures which I discovered for myself were stronger than anything else I have had in life.' As for the love of beauty, 'I have it naturally, for neither my father nor my mother nor any of my relations had the least idea of it.'

We hear also of his mother taking him to the Isle of Wight, where he was much interested in Black Gang Chine when told that it had been inhabited by pirates. He went up to the firm's offices (now in King William Street) and saw the Lord Mayor's Show; also he went up at times for the day and was 'left till called for'. He used then to amuse himself by watching the tea-dealers opposite making up packets of tea and coffee. In 1881 he spoke of London: 'What a dreadful place I used to think it when I came into it as a boy.' On 24 December 1889 he wrote to his mother: 'Yesterday morning was indeed beautiful, and Jenny went with a friend to the Chiswick Agricultural Gardens, which are still in existence though sadly built up. I remember as clearly as if it were yesterday going with father there when I was quite a little boy, and have never been inside the place since. How the neighbourhood must have altered since then!'[6]

At the age of nine he was sent to a preparatory school in Walthamstow, a couple of miles off; he rode there daily on a pony. A few years later the school moved to George Lane quite close to the Hall. William was at first a day scholar, then a boarder. For a boy so full already of a spirit of independence and used to running wild, the experience of boarding-out must have been very unpleasant, though the nearness to home might have weakened his resistances. His strong reaction to what he felt as the tyranny of education is set out in a letter of 1886–7. He asks: 'How is it possible to protect the immature citizen from the whims of his parents? Are they to be left free to starve his body or warp his mind by all sorts of nonsense; if not, how are they to be restrained?' He argues that in such matters the will of the community has a much stronger right than that of the parents, 'two accidental persons'. The weakness of his argument lies in the fact that he does not define what he means by the will of the community. He is not speaking of socialism; he explicitly states that he is concerned with things as they are, 'in the meantime'. He goes on with a personal statement. 'Putting myself in the position of the immature citizen, I protest against this unfairness. As for myself, being the child of rich parents, it did not weigh heavily on me, because my parents did as all right people do, shook off the responsibility of my education as soon as they could; handing me over first to nurses, then to grooms and gardeners, and then sending me to a school—a boy farm, I should say. In one way or another I learned chiefly one thing from all these— rebellion, to wit. That was good; but, look you, if my parents had been poorer, and had had more character, they would have probably committed the fatal mistake of trying to educate me. I have seen the sad effects of this with the children of some of my friends.'

The argument is confused and seems to concern itself solely with the educational ideas and methods of the Victorian bourgeoisie, large and small; but for this very reason it is all the more illuminating and reveals a very strong resentment towards his parents, despite his pretence of exonerating them. All he really says is that any impersonal kind of education was better than having them interfere directly in his upbringing, and that as a child he reacted against any form of control or direction. May repeats this outlook in saying that 'we were lucky children not to be saddled with parents full of theories— "experimental parents", if I may call them so without disrespect to the elders. I have heard my father speak of the children of X and Y and Z, who were lovingly subjected to experiments in diet or clothing or training or play, as "poor little devils" with real pity in his voice.' He often said: 'Children bring each other up', and 'as one of a large family, he knew it by experience'. In 1886, in *The Society of the Future*, he merely generalised: 'The family of blood-relationship would melt away into that of the community and of humanity.' When he found himself called on to pronounce responsibly on the future of the family, he was always careful to drop all dogmatism, to resist any impulse to argue on the basis of his own experiences, and to insist that any precise forms of relationships in a communist world would be organically worked out, step by step, and would not be laid down by any imposed system. He had learned from his struggles with the anarchists that the sort of freedom he wanted could in no way be achieved by merely throwing off existing constraints or turning the present systems inside out.

In *News* we are merely told that 'families are held together by no bond of coercion, legal or social, but by mutual liking and affection, and everybody is free to come or go as he or she pleases'. And in his lectures he stresses the need for absolute equality in education. 'I want all persons to be educated according to their capacity, not according to the amount of money which their parents happen to have.' Also, he wants to see education linked with productive activity. What emerges from his discussions is a passionate hatred of the existing middle-class system which does its best to stultify children and to kill off all sensuous enjoyments:

What! will, e.g., the family of the times when monopoly is dead be still as it is now in the middle-classes, framed on the model of that of an affectionate and moral tiger to whom all is prey a few yards away from the sanctity of the domestic hearth: Will the body of the woman we love be but an appendage to her property? Shall we try to cram our lightest whim as a holy dogma into our children and be bitterly unhappy when we find that they are growing up to be men and women like ourselves? Will education be a system of cram begun on us when we are four years old, and left off sharply when we are eighteen? Shall we be ashamed of our love and our hunger and our mirth, the joys that accompany procreation of our species, and the keeping of ourselves alive, those joys of desire which make us understand that the beasts too may be happy? Shall we all, in short, as the 'refined' middle-class now do, wear ourselves away in an anxiety to stave off all trouble, emotion, and responsibility, in order that we may have been born for nothing but to be afraid to die?

In 1843, when William was in his ninth year, his father obtained a grant of arms from the Heralds' College: 'Azure, a horse's head erased argent between three horseshoes or, and for crest, on a wreath of the colours, a horse's head couped argent, charged with three horseshoes in chevron sable.' Mr Morris had wanted to signalise his bettered position in the middle-class world. Why the horse was made so prominent is not clear; but William inevitably brooded on the imagery and came to see himself (says Mackail) as in some sense a tribesman of the White Horse. The idea must have been reinforced after he went to Marlborough College, not so far from the White Horse cut on the Berkshire Downs. At Red House later he used tiles and glass that he himself painted with horseheads; and at Kelmscott he made a yearly pilgrimage to the Downs. He was delighted when he found, halfway to the White Horse, in Great Coxwell Church, the two fifteenth-century brasses of William Morys, farmer, and Johane, his wife. Morys was shown in a short gown with pouch at girdle. Once Morris remarked, 'How strange it would be to us if we could be landed in fourteenth-century England; unless we saw the crest of some familiar hill, like that which yet bears upon it a symbol of an English tribe, and from which, looking down on the plain where Alfred was born, I once had many such ponderings.'

The Morris arms thus helped him to feel rooted in the medieval world, in a system of clans or kindreds which the modern world had lost or destroyed —a system which he finally described in his late Germanic romances.[7]

2

Boyhood

The family fortunes had taken a sharp rise upward. In 1844 a company was formed to work copper veins near Tavistock, with a capital of 1,024 shares of £1 each fully paid up. Mr Morris held 172 shares, said to have been assigned to him in part payment of a debt. The lodes proved rich, the working was easy, and the copper fetched £160 a ton. The Morris shares soon rose to the value of some £200,000. Three-quarters of a million tons were got out before the mine was exhausted; the price of copper also fell. But meanwhile Mr Morris had become a rich man and what William inherited carried him along to the days of Red House.

Of events at home between 1844-9 we know very little. Whatever rumours of radical and chartist struggles, and of the revolutions of 1848, reached Woodford must have been wholly in terms of the respectable middle class. (Burne-Jones had been scared by a housemaid with tales of the harrowing deeds of the Chartists in 1839; he had a childhood of restless nights with bad dreams.) Then in 1849 Mr Morris, aged about fifty, died. He had already bought for William a nomination at Marlborough College, founded in 1843, originally for sons of the lesser clergy. For the first time the boy was torn right out of the family bosom, just at the moment of his father's death. These events, coming in the early puberty of a boy with such deep roots in the Woodford world, could not but have had strong effects upon him, strengthening both his attachments to the garden and forest of happy independence and his fears of losing them, of exclusion and confinement.

At the college we see him slowly developing his childhood positions in ways that face out into the great world. Twelve miles from Swindon, Marlborough was set in fine surroundings, in the valley of the Kennet, near Savernake Forest. The Great Western Railway was moving on west of Reading, but the nearest station was at Hungerford, eleven miles away. The Castle Mound, an earthwork, was said to be Merlin's Grave, the name Marlborough interpreted as Merlin's Berg or Rock. The town, on the

Great Bath Road, had been a frequented coaching-centre; the broad street was lined with houses mostly Jacobean, those on the north side with projecting upper storeys. The church of St Peter was perpendicular in style though with Norman pillars and an early black basalt font.

The basis of the school was the Castle Inn, with its ten acres of land, which had been hit by the decay of coach-traffic. In 1843 the Mansion, the White House, was taken over with stables and a few outbuildings, and was turned into dormitories, rooms for masters, a sick-room, a maids' dormitory, and a housekeeper's room. Basement rooms were also used, one probably for the library, for which sums were granted in 1843-4. The boys worked and played in and round the converted stables. At first the number was to be 200, but it soon rose to more than 500. A new schoolroom was needed and the Upper School was built at the back of the three classrooms. Builders were still hard at work just before Morris arrived in February 1849, almost fifteen, with some hundred other new pupils. A box-shaped Porter's Lodge stood at the chapel-side of the entrance gate, with the bell recently rehoused in a small louvered box over the entry to the Lodge. By 1848 there were four Houses, called A, B, C, D, after the lettering in the architect's plan; the old inn became C House.

The college had several new features. The council had wanted to keep charges down; letters from inquiring parents showed worry over the rising cost of living, income-tax, and school-fees. The decision was made to accept boys from lay homes (at first only a third of the whole) and to house all boys inside the college so that an inclusive fee might be charged. Hitherto at such schools the boys had been boarded out at Dames' Houses. Arnold at Rugby had begun to gather his boys under the care of assistants; but it was Marlborough that first took the definite step. So from the start the Mansion was a huge dormitory with classrooms clustering around. A new set of problems came up. Nobody had had experience as a housemaster or knew clearly how to organise such a system. The rapid expansion of the school increased the difficulties.

There were no organised sports, but there were fives' and racquets' courts, and a field where pole-jumping seems to have been the main game, though in 1843 we find football played on most days before lunch. There was much rambling in the countryside, mainly for bird-nesting. From 1850, for some twenty years, there were endless complaints about depredations by the boys, with damage to crops and animals. The boys had to amuse themselves as best they could in the intervals after tea, prep, and chapel.

The buildings round the court were arched, open on the inner side to form a big L-shaped and covered playground. Three or four gas-jets threw a vague light into the darkness of the court, which then had no trees; and the area was under a porter, Pevier, nicknamed Hawk Eye, who had a hard task keeping order. The ill-lit space gave every chance to smokers and stone-throwers; and the gate-sergeants, supposed to superintend, had power only to report offenders. The popular activity was stone-throwing, as in all schools of the gentry in the mid years of the century; it persisted well into the 1870s.

The school year was cut in two: January or February to June, August to December. But entries or departures at times happened at the ends of quarters. Slates and quills were used. The masters had cutlery plated or Albata (German silver) with ivory handles, the boys had handles of horn, the servants handles of stag. There was no set dress, there were no prefects. For boys under the fifth class there was a single big room. Apart from holidays, Morris was to stay on at the college till Christmas 1851.

In the autumn of 1848, while he was in his second term, the family moved to Water House, on the road from Woodford to Tottenham. Now they were only half a mile from their early home on Clay Hill, and they stayed here till 1856. The house was of the same type as the Hall, but on a somewhat smaller scale: a square heavy Georgian building of yellow brick. The square hall was paved with marble flags, from which a broad square staircase, floored and wainscoted with Spanish chestnut, led to a large upper gallery. For several years now, when at home, Morris spent whole days reading in one of the window-seats. Behind was a large lawn, and beyond that a moat some forty feet broad; in its midst was an island planted with a grove of aspens. The water was full of pike and perch, and here the boys bathed, boated, fished, in summer, and skated in winter. The island, fringed with hollies, hawthorns, and chestnuts, was loved by all the children, who spent as much time on it as possible. It must have in part compensated Morris for the loss of the Hall's spacious grounds.

Watson was a gardener's boy at the new house. The family liked him and helped his education. Now and then he was sent to London with £2 to £5 to buy fireworks, which were let off in the grounds. At times the dinner-bell sounded while the boys were cooking in the nursery some bird they had shot, and Watson was left to finish the meal and remove its traces. When Morris met Glasier's mother in Scotland in 1893, he was 'greatly interested when he discovered that she had been brought up at Walthamstow', and he 'inquired about some of the folk he remembered there, particularly a violent old character, Farmer Hitchman'.

On 1 November 1848 Morris wrote from college to his favourite sister Emma. This letter is the first of his writings we possess. He dated it the Feast of All Saints. Under Emma's influence he had grown to have strong High Church sympathies. He was thus able, in alliance with her, to set himself against the evangelical outlook of his parents, but was still far from a secular position. He asked for details of the new house, and ended: 'It is now only 7 weeks to the Holidays, there I go again! Just like me! always harping on the Holidays, I am sure you must think me a great fool to be always thinking about home but I really can't help it I don't think it is my fault for there are such a lot of things I want to do and say and see.'[1]

He had the nickname of Crab: perhaps because of his hard grip, perhaps because he had a way of scuttling off. He certainly kept much to himself. A companion described him as 'a thick-set, strong-looking boy, with a high colour and black curly hair, good-natured and kind, but with a fearful temper'. A keen collector of birds' eggs, he took little share in games, and his restless fingers were already noted. He found relief in ceaseless netting, fastening one end of the net to a desk in the big schoolroom and working on it for hours. He was remembered as 'fond of mooning and talking to himself, and considered a little mad by the other boys. On his walks he invented and poured forth endless stories, vaguely described as "about knights and fairies", in which one adventure rose out of another, and the tale flowed on from day to day over a whole term. The captain of the dormitory, who had a fancy for listening to stories, and exacted them night after night from other boys, found him an inexhaustible source. His gusts of tempers, as violent as they were brief, are what seem to have most impressed him on his contemporaries.'

His strength saved him from bullying. In each schoolroom were only two fires; most boys couldn't get near except in ordeals when they were roasted. Small boys were slung over the bannisters of the upper corridors of A House, or their ears were pierced by pins or even penknives. Complaints were made during these years of tea brewed in tin cans and of flat stale beer served at dinner with bread and butter, of which there was never enough. The boys stamped in their demands for more. One boy tells how he preferred pump-water to the tea or beer. Morris himself told Scheu in 1882:

I went to school at Marlborough College, which was then a new and very rough school. As far as my school instruction went, I think I may fairly say I learned next to nothing there, for indeed next to nothing was taught; but the place is in very beautiful country, thickly scattered over with prehistoric monuments, and I set myself eagerly to studying these and everything else that had any history in it, and so perhaps learned a good deal, especially as there was a good library at the school to which I sometimes had access. I should mention that ever since I could remember I was a great devourer of books.

And later still he told Blunt that 'he was neither high nor low in his form, but always last in arithmetic; hated Cicero and Latin generally, but anything in the way of history attracted him'.

However, he always wrote or spoke deprecatingly of his achievements. All in all, Marlborough seems to have been by far the best school he could have gone to if he had to go to one. A great advantage was the countryside. The weekly whole-holiday in the summer half he spent in Savernake Forest and on the Downs, at times alone, at times with a boy of congenial tastes. He knew Silbury Hill, the long barrows of the ridges above Pewsey Vale, the stone circles of Avebury, the Roman villas at Kennet. 'The royal castle, as it existed in all its splendours in the reign of Henry III,' says Mackail, 'was almost as real to him as the beautiful seventeenth-century building which had replaced it, and which after so many vicissitudes, had become a home of the new school.'

He taught himself much with the aid of the library which was well supplied with works on archaeology and church architecture. In a note of 30 November 1894, with which he sent two Kelmscott Press books, he wrote to the master: 'It is a matter of course that I should feel a deep interest in the fortunes of my old school.' He repeated his debt to the countryside and its monuments, and to 'studying Stukeley in the delightful old library; which was first started in the middle of my school days'. By the time he left school, he knew as much about English archaeology and Gothic as the period could tell him. He was also affected by the High Church character which had come over the college, though no one church party had founded the place. Blore's chapel (now gone) was rising as he arrived; it opened in the autumn with a trained choir which sang the newly discovered Elizabethan church music. Thus the influences of the school and of Emma merged to provide him with something of a coherent basis for his tastes and ideas. What he had learned from Walter Scott was compacted and given a contemporary relevance by his response to the Anglo–Catholic movement; and at the same time his interest in old things, in Gothic and the medieval world, was strongly stimulated and given an added emotional force. Probably he found Pugin's *Contrasts* in the library, a set of paired engravings which ardently underlined the contrasts between the medieval and the modern world, with all the advantages seen to lie with the former.[2]

We have two complete letters he wrote to Emma which enable us to get right inside his mind at this time. The first, of 29 March 1849, describes his confirmation by a bishop. 'We went into Chapel at 8 a.m. all the candidates for confirmation sitting together near the altar the Bishop's charge was received by us all standing it was about 20 minutes long, the Bishop himself is very tall and thin and does not [look] very old though bald at the top of his head his name is Dennison and he is of a high family: the Holy Communion was administered the next day (Sunday). It was administered to every one singly.' He discusses a new surgeon, who comes regularly every morning and evening to Chapel. 'I hope very soon to get a *tremendous* long letter from you dear Emma.' In a postscript he writes about a rabbit that his brother James gave him at home; he has asked James to sell the young ones. 'Do you think there was anything wrong in it will you write and tell me if you think so; (you need not tell anyone of it) the reason I did it was to get a nice fishing rod I did not like to ask Mamma to give me one and what with the other things I did not think I should have enough to buy one otherwise; will you let this part of the letter be private and confidential dear Emma.'

The second letter, of 13 April, is much longer. 'My dearest Emma, I received your dear letter yesterday and I am glad you liked the anthem on Easter Tuesday, we here had the same anthem on Monday and Tuesday as on Sunday it was the first three verses of the 72nd Psalm.' He cites them and goes on:

I certainly thought it was very beautiful though I have never heard it in a Cathedral and like you could not tell how they would sing it there; but a gentleman (one of the boy's fathers) said on the whole our choir sang better than at Salisbury Cathedral; anyhow I thought it very beautiful the first verse was sung by the whole the second began by one treble voice till at last the base took it up again gradually getting deeper and deeper then again the treble voice again and then again the base the third verse was sung entirely by base not very loud but with that kind of emphasis which you would think befitting to such a subject I almost think I liked it better than either of the other two the only fault in the anthem seemed to be to me that it was too short. On Monday I went to Silbury Hill which I think I have told you before is an artificial hill made by the Britons but first I went to a place called Abury where there is a Druidical circle and a Roman entrenchment both which encircle the town originally it was supposed that the stones were in this shape first one large circle then a smaller one inside this and then one in the middle for an altar but a great many in fact most of the stones have been removed so I could [not] tell this. On Tuesday morning I was told of this so I thought I would go there again, I did and then I was able to understand how they had been fixed; I think the biggest stone I could see had about 16 feet out of the ground in height and about 10 feet thick and 12 feet broad the circle and entrenchment altogether is about half a mile; at Abury I also saw a very old church the tower was very pretty indeed it had four little spires on it of the decorated order, and there was a little Porch and inside the porch a beautiful Norman doorway loaded with mouldings the chancel was new and was paved with tesselated pavement this I saw through the Window for I did not know where the sexton's house was so of course I could not get the key, there was a pretty little Parsonage house close by the church. After we had done looking at the lions of Abury which took us about ½ an hour we went through a mud lane down one or two fields and last but not least through what they call here a water meadow up to our knees in water, now perhaps you do not know what a water meadow is as there are none of them in your part of the world, so for your edification I will tell you what a delectable affair a water meadow is to go through; in the first place you must fancy a field cut through with infinity of small streams say about four feet wide each the people to whom the meadow belongs can turn these streams on and off when they like and at this time of the year they are on just before they put the fields up for mowing the grass being very long you cannot see the water till you are in the water and floundering in it except you are above the field luckily the water had not been long when we went through it else we should have been up to our middles in mud, however perhaps now you can imagine a water meadow: after we had scrambled through this meadow we ascended Silbury Hill it is not very high but yet I should think it must have taken an immense long time to have got it together I brought away a little white snail shell as a memento of the place and have got it in my pocket book I came back ½ past 5 the distance was altogether about 14 miles I had been out 3 hours ½ of course Monday and Tuesday were whole holidays. As [you] are going to send me the large cheese perhaps you would let Sarah to make me a good large cake and I should also like some biscuits and will you also send me some paper and postage stamps also my silkworm eggs and if you could get it an Italian pen box for that big box is too big for school. I am very sorry I was not at home with you at Easter but of course that was not to be and it is no good either to you or to me to say any horrid stale arguments about being obliged to go to school for of course we know all about that. Give my best love dearest Emma to all, And believe me Your most affectionate brother William Morris.

We see much of his character already showing up clearly, his pertinacity in what interested him, his historical and antiquarian sense, his capacity for vigorous description. Here such aspects are linked with his strong feeling for Emma and for High Church ritual. The last sentence reveals that, as we would expect, he has put up a hard fight with his mother against being sent away; and he treats Emma as his ally. 'We know all about that.'

A year later the close bond with Emma was ruptured. In May 1850 she married the Rev. Joseph Oldham whom she had known during the years 1845–8 when he was curate at Walthamstow. William, then between eleven and fourteen, would have known him at least casually, but he seems to have had no suspicion of what was happening. In 1850 Oldham was curate of Downe in Kent; so he must have formed the attachment with Emma before he left Walthamstow. Mackail comments: 'Very soon afterwards he was appointed to a living in Derbyshire,' at Clay Cross, 'and William Morris was thus put quite out of reach of his favourite sister. He felt the separation keenly; the brother and sister had been closely intimate in all their thoughts and enthusiasms; and it was to some degree under her influence that the Church was settled on as his own destined profession.' In an unpublished note he added that Morris 'felt deserted after her marriage'.

We may assume that he was not allowed to come home for the marriage. Emma's departure deeply hurt him; it also perhaps confirmed him in his wish to enter the Church, so that he could measure himself up against Oldham. The whole experience left a lasting impression, deeply strengthening the pattern which we noted as latent in *The Old English Baron*: the conflict of two friends for the same girl. Though it was probably not written till a couple of years later, we may here consider the early poem, *The Three Flowers*, which describes a love-trinity. The narrator is called Brother by the girl, who recalls their deep pledge of love, but says that she now has another lover. The latter dies, and then the girl too. The poem is a weak piece, but we need it in full on account of its psychological importance. Childhood memories and a splendour of flowers are entangled with the love-theme, with the consummation of love (here in death).

> Now the crocus is beside me
> In the sweet spring tide of year;
> And the hazelboughs they hide me,
> Daffodillies grow anear.
> Long ago sweet daffodillies
> With their yellow crowned my brow,

That was where the sunny hill is,
In the sun I see them now.
We were children there together
When we sat upon that hill,
In the sunny April weather,
On the flower-covered hill.
There, three flowers grow for ever
On the flower-covered hill;
But two flowers grow together[;]
One, groweth lovely still.
Tiger lilies, tall white lilies,
In the summer grow together;
Gorgeous golden daffodillies
In the spring grow lovely ever.
Yet the daffodils clung round me,
Yet she hung them round my brow;
Yet a child she said she loved me,
Yet I know she loves me now.
He was very noble surely
Very much did I love him,
And they loved each other surely,
Never will this love grow dim.
Yet when there she had been reading,
When with pity she looked on me,
As I stood before her shading
Dreary looked the flowers to me.
Then she rose up in her pity,
While the wind about her played,
In her hand a tiger-lily,
Very lovingly she said;
'Sweet friend do you not remember,
In the summer long ago,
How we children played together
On as sweet a day as now?
How you played at swearing fealty
To a Queen of beauty bright,
Of our vows of love and lealty
In that sunset's golden light?
How you crowned me with white lilies
White as ever snow doth fall,
And three spotted tiger-lilies

Did my royal sceptre call?
How there were no daffodillies
For your head to be a crown
Of his crown of tiger-lilies
Fading as the sun went down?
Past my flowers blew the soft air
To the west your face was turned,
Tenderly wind raised your dark hair
In your face the sunset burned.
We three stood with love between us,
While the swallow overhead
Flew around as he had seen us,
While the clouds the west wind led.
Do you keep your child-love, brother,
As you vowed to keep it then?
Will you love me if another
Be my lover among men?
Earth will not hold us for ever,
On the earth we live not long;
When we live in heaven together
God will make our weak love strong.'
O! my tears fell downward quickly,
Fell, as dropped my head to the ground,
On the daisies there, that thickly
Yellow-centred stood around.
Yet the tears grew very tender;
Through my tears I saw her stand,
Tremblingly I saw the slender
Tiger-lily in her hand.
Last year did I see her lying
Crown of lilies on her head;
Held his hand as he lay dying
Kissed him, as he lay dead.
There they lay, lay dead together
With their hands clasped each in each,
As they sat in summer weather
While above them was the beech.
Round her head a crown of lilies
And a lily in her hand;
Fair white lilies, tiger-lilies,
Round his head and in his hand.

The tiger-lily reminds us of the story told by May about Morris and his two sisters stained with the pollen and scolded for misbehaviour. We may note too the strong sense of outraged possession which vents itself in the revenge-fantasy that kills off the lovers. This deeper meaning is strengthened, not lessened, by the pious idiom that veils the unexplained deaths in a vague effusive sentimentality.

The poem was found by Morris's niece Effie at the back of a drawer belonging to Emma. 'Aunt Emma used to tell me that as a young man Uncle William sent her his poems.' May put the poem second among the juvenilia, suggesting 1854-5 as the date, but the work is certainly much earlier, though if indeed it were to be dated 1854 we should have a yet stronger proof of the extent to which Emma's departure as a married woman disturbed the lad. In some respects it reads technically as a sort of parody of effects that he developed effectively in *The Defence* volume. To show how the emotions of *The Three Flowers* persisted in the 1850s we can take the story *Frank's Sealed Letter*. The hero is driven back frustrated from London to the countryside he loves. He describes lyrically the 'strange balance between joy and sadness' as he walks along a stream making for the River Lea, amid the sounds, colours, scents of the spring. In his heart rises memory. He follows the stream of broad-leaved waterflowers, gathers lush marsh-marigolds—his hand and the yellow flowers making the swift water bubble about them. Walking on with the wet flowers in hand he has a vision of the lost past.

I see a little girl sitting on the grass, beneath the limes in the hot summertide, with eyes fixed on the far away hills, and seeing who knows what there; for the boy by her side is reading to her wondrous stories of knight and lady, and fairy thing, that lived in the ancient days; his voice trembles as he reads.

He reads of Sir Isumbras. The pair talk of the tale and its pictures. The girl bids the boy get some forget-me-nots and white starry flowers. She weaves them into a crown and crowns him as he kneels like a knight in a tournament. Later however the girl leaves him and marries another. The emotion here is one of frank bitterness, not of sentimental forgiveness as in the poem. Indeed Frank-William is described as going off to London as a result of her betrayal; he is determined to prove himself and gain a great name so that she will know what she has discarded. He succeeds and fails. There is a tragic crisscrossing between the man he has become, and the man he might have been as the girl's husband. In a sense then the story is a prophecy of the frustrated side of Morris's life, his failure as lover and husband, which was inextricably tied up with his successful side, his creative achievement as poet, designer, thinker, socialist.

This pattern of experience runs through his whole life, both before and after the roles of Emma and Oldham had been more powerfully taken over by Janey and Rossetti, while he himself vainly loved the wife of his own best friend, Burne-Jones.[3]

Meanwhile, however, his schooldays were cut short by violent events at Marlborough. About mid-October 1851 the story went round that the porter, Pevier, had reported boys for smoking or stone-throwing; reported them, said the headmaster, 'probably not in the best way', whatever that was. Discontent among the boys addicted to stones and tobacco reached the point of provoking a demonstration on Saturday and Sunday night, 19 and 20 October. Windows were broken and passers out in the road were pelted. On Monday there was a 'row about the mischief done', but no steps were taken against offenders. Next day was a Review Holiday. In the evening more stones were thrown. The culprits could not be identified and their misdeeds went on till Pevier himself became the target. So, on the 28th, the school was kept in after dark. On Tuesday there was 'a great row in evening prep', and the three hundred boys who worked in Upper School were kept in 'while Dr Wilkinson investigated cases', of which there seem to have been forty-four. Thirty boys were exonerated; of the others one 'was sent away'.

For a few days there was quiet. Then came 4 November. In the past, fireworks had been allowed or ignored; this year a subscription was raised and a large number of 'crackers and squibs' bought. On the 5th, after tea, fireworks were let off in Upper School out of doors for an hour after 5.30; a few more exploded during evening prep. The weather was fine, with a strong moon; and after chapel more fireworks exploded in the court and continued 'in all the houses throughout the night till 6 a.m.'. In the darkness, with the difficult layout of the Houses, the masters failed to keep order. Next day the headmaster sent three boys home. The diary of a pupil stated: 'Walked up and down under chapel from $5\frac{1}{2}$–$6\frac{1}{2}$ and tea to 7. Fireworks let off from $5\frac{1}{2}$–6. Lots of windows were broken after chapel and some at 3. Played football.' Dr Wilkinson noted: 'much damage to property' and 'life endangered with fear of fire'. One more boy was sent home, but fireworks went on banging between 9 and 10 p.m.

On 7 November a deputation went to the headmaster, who later wrote: 'I have had to reject the prayer of a petition from more than 200 boys.' They were asking for leniency towards the dismissed boys. Dr Wilkinson added, 'The only strange feature of all this business is that the work of the school seems not at all to have been disadvantageously affected.' Seventeen ring-leaders were made out, but only four went away. Things quietened after a notice was posted about the Danger of Velocopedes. But rumours went on multiplying. Wilkinson was embroiled with the council, who suggested, he said, 'without knowing the particulars, that the boys sent away should be restored after Christmas—curiously, the boys here knew two days before the Council that that was to be the resolution'. The senior master Sharpe resigned and the other masters asked Wilkinson 'not to defeat all efforts to maintain authority by restoring any of the dismissed'. However, the boys had been encouraged by the dissension between council and headmaster; a further outburst occurred on 30 November. The diarist writes: 'A great row. Biden's desk broken. Fowler's and Clayton's and Wade's chairs destroyed. Dr W. addressed us after tea and had us in after chapel. 16 boys were named, 9 were flogged, and 2 sent away.' There were seventy-seven names on the list of rioters, with ages ranging from ten to sixteen; one boy was nine, one seventeen, but most were thirteen. Of the accused twenty-five were exonerated, six sent away, and some of the others flogged; most were merely 'reproved'.

The system formulated in 1842 laid down that in cases of expulsion the headmaster should consult the council; perhaps that was why Wilkinson spoke of sending off, not of expelling. But the council may have considered that he had exceeded his powers, despite the abnormal situation. There may however have been some conflicts in religious positions behind the difference of views; and there may have been more points of strain than appeared, as the *Marlburian* of 1851 stated that there were disgruntled persons and they should go to the authorities. The oddity of the situation is underlined by the fact that during the Christmas holidays the doctor wrote to two of the flogged boys with testimonials, adding, 'I am glad you liked the Exhibition.'

The rioters were mostly of the fourth form; only one or two of the fifth. Morris's name does not appear in any list and he does not seem to have played an active part in the troubles; but they must have deeply excited him and left a strong impress. Here he had seen young people getting together against what was felt to be unfair or oppressive controls, and showing considerable solidarity. It is hard to feel much sympathy for the stone-throwers; but as the conflict developed, after the prayer of a petition, the boys must have felt their cause to be worthy. Morris, we saw, later considered children as an oppressed section of humanity; and in the 1886-7 letter he says that his schooldays taught him 'chiefly one thing'—rebellion. He could hardly have made this remark without recalling that he had taken part, albeit passively, in an actual revolt, which must have brought his general emotions of re- sistance to a head. He had seen in action for the first time, however imper- fectly, the principle of fellowship. As he stated in *John Ball*: 'He that waketh in hell and feeleth his heart fail him shall have memory of the merry days of earth, and how that when his heart failed him there he cried on his fellow, and how that fellow heard him and came.'[4]

He did not return to school in 1852, so that the revolt must have appeared as effecting his release from a sojourn that he disliked. His mother decided to keep him at Walthamstow and let him read with a private tutor till thought fit to go up for matriculation. The tutor chosen was the Rev. F. B. Guy, later Canon of St Albans, at this time master of the local Forest School, where he was soon to become head. He took a few private pupils at his house in Hoe Street, and Morris went to him for nearly a year. That they got on well together is shown by the fact that Morris kept up contacts with him in later years. Guy was High Church, and interested in painting and architec- ture, so that his views would have chimed in with those that Morris was developing. He made Morris a fair classical scholar. Among the works they read was Euripides' *Medeia*, which Guy, on reading *Jason* later, felt had provided the germ of that poem.

W. H. Bliss, another of the pupils, recalled many examples of Morris's love of nature and bodily strength. Morris loved single-stick; but a table had to be set between him and his opponent because of his wild rushes. At Water House he and Bliss chased the swans and dragged the moat for perch with a net that Morris had made. They walked and rode almost daily in the forest; and when the other boys went off to London, William stayed true to the greenwood. When they attended the Duke of Wellington's funeral, he rode off on his own to Waltham Abbey. When he was forced to go with the rest of the family to see the Great Exhibition in Hyde Park, he sat down out- side and refused to go in. 'Wonderfully ugly,' he commented. His medievalism had led him to a blunt rejection of Victorian taste and ideas about art, of indeed all the prevailing conventions. He already had the habit of tilting a chair, twisting his legs about it, then suddenly straightening them so that he strained or broke the structure. 'Many of his own Sussex chairs,' says Mackail, 'not in his own house alone, bear to this day the marks of this trick of his.' His voice was a husky shout.

But the straining and breaking of chairs was not a trick; it was an expression of the same sudden intolerable tension, which had to be thrown off, as we find in his blind tempers, in his mad rushes at single-stick.

How did he feel now that he was at home, but without Emma? We can only guess at the loneliness and frustration that now beset him by the depth of his responses as revealed in poems and stories, and by the persistence of the resulting patterns. He must have played to some extent with his younger brothers; but no significant relationship emerged. The almost total lack of any warm or close links with the rest of the family is remarkable in a person so full of fraternal impulses. The end of his loving companionship with Emma seems to have left him with the conviction of exclusion from the family-circle, as if he had given to her all that he had to give there of friendship and communion. He remained a conventionally dutiful son, visiting his mother at her birthdays or Christmas; but in effect the family might have faded out after his departure for Oxford without making much difference to his life. He seems to have kept in touch with Emma for some time, sending her his early poems and paying some visits to her at Clay Cross. But the magical spell of his union with her had been broken, however much the pattern of their earlier happiness in a flowering garden followed by the shock of loss, the fall from the joyous self-sufficiency of childhood's Eden, continued to affect his spirit.

In view of the lack of any meaningful contacts between him and his brothers or sisters in later life, we may as well dispose of them here at the outset. Henrietta, the bossy elder sister, never married; she finally became a Roman Catholic as the result of a visit to Rome with her mother. (In a letter of 1883 William wrote to Jenny, 'The trees in the Tuilleries Gardens have suffered very much even since we were there: it is sad to remember when I first came to Paris and was very high up aloft with aunt Henrietta at Meurice's they were so thick they looked as if you could talk on the tops.' The date of this early visit is hard to make out.) The two younger sisters were Isabella and Alice; the brothers were Hugh, Thomas, Arthur, and Edgar. Isabella, who resembled William in her looks, married a naval officer Gilmore. Widowed after forty years, she trained as a hospital nurse at Guy's and was ostracised by the family as having let them down socially. For twenty years she worked in the south London slums, becoming deaconness and head of the Rochester and Southwark Mission, with her HQ on the north side of Clapham Common. She is commemorated by a plaque in Southwark Cathedral. Alice married a banker, Gill, of Bickham, Devon, who was killed in the hunting field; she then lived at Tunbridge Wells. Hugh became a gentleman-farmer near Southampton and bred Jersey and Guernsey cattle. Thomas went to a German university and showed signs of literary interests, but he joined the Gordon Highlanders. He left three sons and five daughters, one of whom, Effie, made up notes on the family. Arthur became a colonel in the 60th Royal Rifles. William paid a visit to his mother in March 1881 'to see the last of Arthur before he goes to India. Lucky he, that he didn't have to run down hill at Majuba' in the Transvaal, 'though I see that his old battalion seem to have run the fastest and so lost fewest men'. By this time William, with strong anti-imperial views, can only have felt contempt for Thomas and Arthur. In letters written earlier in the month he expresses delight at the Boer gains and the work of the Transvaal Committee. Isabella was the only one who showed something of his dogged unconventional spirit; but by the time she turned to social work, he had no sympathy with merely charitable activities on a religious basis. Arthur later went to China and took part in the sack of Pekin. Edgar, the youngest brother, married and had two sons and daughters; but he lost all his money and worked at Merton Abbey under William. He appears there as a willing assistant with no particular aptitude or character.

When we seek to grasp the deeper meaning of Emma as William's early love we come up against the whole concept, so important for him, of childhood as inhabiting an earthly paradise, from which one is ejected by uncomprehending and tyrannical authority. The neurotic or nerve-wrecked Mr Morris and his well-meaning but conventionally correct wife embodied that authority; but the moment of loss needed to be dramatised in some evocative way. Emma's marriage provided the dramatic interpretation, in a version where no one was to blame. The successful lover (in one sense Morris's double or other self) carries off the girl playmate who incarnates the joys of the flowering paradise. Thus a direct emotion of hatred is avoided, but the anger, driven down, comes out in the fantasy that both intruder and girl die, blessed by the youth whom they have condemned to deprivation. For some time a vague notion of reunion in another world carries on. In *Frank's Sealed Letter*, however, the anger rises up directly, and the attempt of the discarded lover to make his way in the world is a retort and a rebuke to Emma, a desperate expression of misery over the lost paradisiac dream.

In a sense Emma has become a doublet of the mother, the ultimate source of comfort and happiness in early years, who has now sadly become the one that cuts the child off from that source and sends him out into the cold outer world of loneliness.

We can perhaps get nearer to Morris's pattern if we consider the relation of Charles Dickens to his sister Fanny, two years his elder. As children the pair used to sing love-duets together and were emotionally close; then Fanny married and went outside Charles's orbit, dying in 1848. Charles's response was *The Haunted Man*, in which the hero is visited at Christmas by his spirit-double who reminds him of the afflictions that have blighted his life: the death of the sister who had been the one gleam of happiness in his early years and who died thinking only of her brother, and the thoughtless parents who cast him out in a homeless world. This story was followed by *The Child's Dream of a Star*, in which a boy and his sister, devoted to one another, make friends with a star; the sister dies; the disconsolate brother is still linked with her by the light of the star which joins earth and heaven. He grows up and lives out his life, consoled under a succession of bereavements by a renewal of his childhood vision. In his death he returns as a child to his child sister and thanks the heavenly father for the star that has opened to receive all the beloved dead. Dickens told Forster how he and Fanny used to wander in a churchyard looking up at the stars. We cannot here follow out the way in which these deep-rooted attitudes of Dickens determined a great deal of his emotional life and his expression in writing; but we may note the key-roles of his wife's two sisters, first Mary and then Georgina, who meant far more to him than ever his wife did. Mary's death had a shattering effect on him, with all sorts of morbid fancies.

Here then there is the same sense of the sister's death or departure as an exclusion from childhood happiness which is somehow felt as the one stable basis of communion with others. Dickens, in his very different early years, could not dramatise the situation in terms of an earthly paradise which Eve the sister betrays, innocently or wilfully, by turning to a stranger; but the core of the emotion is the same with him as with Morris. The peculiar intensity in both cases can only result from the forms of alienation developing in Victorian bourgeois society, with its exaltation of the family-unit as a bower of domestic bliss, an island of refuge, and with its violent intensification of conflict and competition outside the family. The divisive elements however could not but enter the family from which they were supposed to be banished. Recall Morris's phrase of the affectionate and moral tiger to whom all is prey a few yards away from the sanctity of the domestic hearth. Robert Owen had put the same point in a pamphlet of 1835:

The children within those dens of selfishness and hypocrisy are taught to consider their own little individual family their own world, and that it is the duty and interest of all within that little orb to do whatever they can to promote the advantages of all the legitimate members of it. Within these persons, it is *my* house, *my* estate, *my* children, or *my* husband; *our* estate, and *our* children; or *my* brothers, *my* sisters; and *our* house and property. This family party is trained to consider it quite right, and a superior mode of acting, for each member of it to seek, by all fair means, as almost any means, except *direct* robbery, are termed, to increase the wealth, honour, and privileges of the family, and every individual member of it.

Thus a deep falsity rent the Victorian concept of home; and yet in the home there was also a genuine element of cohesiveness and consolation. The boy, seeking the promised point of stability inside the family, finds it in the sister. A deep and powerful emotion of hope gathers round his union with her; and that union is opposed to the parental systems which in the last resort are felt to coincide with the threatening world. Thus the drama of union and opposition is fought out *inside the family*; and the problem for the brother, become a man outside the family, is to find how he can re-achieve an harmonious union validly in the new situation. Especially to the extent that he fails he is haunted by the ghost of the early relationship. (I may point out that in the two biographies I have written before this of Morris, both men were dominated by early relations with sister or sisters. Courbet, with his rooted family-union which embraced three sisters, never married and could not achieve sexual stability; Cézanne, though he married, was unable to achieve marital happiness and returned to the domination of sister and mother.)

In this situation the sister, as surrogate of the mother, becomes a symbol of both the uniting and the depriving or frustrating elements. The brother in any event cannot marry her, and this ultimate taboo comes to represent the forbidding or exiling force. We may recall how important the theme of brother-and-sister incest was in romantic motifs of rebellion, for example with both Shelley and Byron.

We may put full emphasis on all these factors without saying in any simple way: Morris was in love with Emma, Dickens was in love with Fanny (as later with Mary and Georgina). The situation was far too complex for any such crude formula to explain it. We are concerned with a deep and largely unconscious pattern of union and isolation, of joy and anguish, in which the brother–sister relation provides an important element capable of extended dramatisation. What matters for us with Morris is the revelation of a deep conflict between what he felt to be the sources of joy and satisfaction, and the forces that cut a person away and condemned him to a restless quest for that source. He and Dickens felt these issues so powerfully because in them there was such a strong impulse to deny and resist the forces of distortion and disharmony, to return to the pure source in a way that provided energies for the fuller liberation of what was truly human from the spell of what denied and distorted the human essence. There is no question of reducing their later struggles in a flat way to the childhood pattern. What we must seek to show is how that pattern found new ways of expressing itself, with an ever broadened range of applications, reinterpreting the personal experience in terms of the full social situation.

This account of engrossing brother–sister relationships of the nineteenth century might be much extended by dealing with Wordsworth and his Dorothy, Macaulay and his Hannah, the Brontë girls and their one brother, Elizabeth Barrett and her eldest brother, Charles and Mary Lamb. In extreme cases of romantic revolt a direct incest-element may intrude, as with Shelley and Byron, but that aspect must not be used to cloud or confuse the general pattern we have been exploring. We may note further a link with a poet who at first glance seems as unlike Morris as anyone could possibly be: Baudelaire. He had on the one hand his concept and imagery of *paradis enfantins*, childhood-paradises, which were sources of satisfactions for ever lost to the adult, and on the other hand a conviction, stimulated by the work of Dupont, that all poetry was in essence a utopian protest against injustice, a quest for freedom and happiness. What Morris did was to break through the elements of alienation that still fettered Baudelaire and made him take a passive attitude, and to unite the dream of childhood's lost earthly paradises with the utopian protest—in the end converting the utopian aspect into a truly revolutionary one.

It may be argued that the kind of conflict and contradiction, here indicated, inside the family, has existed in varying degrees at all stages of class-society. That is indeed true. But it gained a new qualitative force in the nineteenth century, begetting its own particular set of deepening and worsening tensions. Hence the *extreme idealisation* of the family in the Victorian world, with its background of the rapidly extending cash-nexus and new forms of exploitation, and with a largely peasant society not so far back in the past. The extreme idealisation of the family came partly from a wish to veil and blur out the brutal facts of the changes going on, partly from a need to provide some kind of counter-values or pretences which would enable men to carry on without being overwhelmed. The usual answer to the new tensions was to strengthen the idealisations, not to face the facts. There seemed no alternative to the dominant processes at work, so that they had somehow to be moralised and deodorised. Socialism could only be visualised in a utopian and unreal form; men had to cling to the belief that somehow a better world would emerge out of increased production. For Morris the problem was to express itself in the play of emotion and realisation round the concept of *hope*, which gradually grew ever more concrete and finally came fully down to the earth of real possibility.[5]

3

Oxford

In June 1852 Morris went to Oxford and passed his matriculation examination at Exeter, a west country college which had links with Marlborough. In the hall next to him was a slight pale lad from King Edward's Grammar School, Birmingham: Edward Burne-Jones, who noticed his name on the Horace paper. Morris was to go into residence after the Long Vacation, but the college was so full that he had to wait till Lent Term, 1853. So he returned to the Rev. Guy and read with him for six months more. During the vacation he was at Alphington in Devon, then came back to Water House for the rest of the year.

Oxford was still medieval in looks, with its towers rising out of meadows and orchards. The Oxford–Didcot line had been opened in June, against the university's wishes, but still had not had much effect. Burne-Jones described the town:

On all sides, except where it touched the railway, the city ended abruptly, as if a wall had been about it, and you came suddenly upon the meadows. There was little brick in the city, it was either grey with stone or yellow with the wash of the pebble-dash in the poorer streets. It was an endless delight to us to wander about the streets, where were still many old houses with wood carving and a little sculpture here and there. The Chapel of Merton College had been lately renovated by Butterfield, and Pollen, a former Fellow of Merton, had painted the roof of it. Many an afternoon we spent in that chapel. Indeed I think the buildings of Merton and the Cloisters of New College were our chief shrines in Oxford.

R. W. Dixon, already up a term, mentions being taken by Morris 'to look at the Tower of Merton'. The strength of Oxford's impact on Morris is shown by the fact that in *News*, when he tried to imagine the dwellings of the future, he turned to memories of the colleges' quadrangles. Previously he had seen only isolated buildings or artworks preserved from the medieval past; at Oxford he could imagine how people had lived in those days.[1]

The findings of a Royal Commission of 1850 give us some idea of the way that undergraduates lived. 'The grosser exhibitions of vice, such as drunkenness and riot, have, in Oxford, as in the higher classes generally, become rare.' But the students were given over to 'sensual vice, gambling in its various forms, and extravagant expenditure'. The town was decorous for the most part, but the villages outside the proctor's jurisdiction were a different matter. Also it was easy to slip up to dissipated London by rail. Students were liable to indulge in ruinously costly furnishings as well as 'the excessive habit of smoking'. Horses could be kept only with the sanction of heads of colleges, but might be hired. The authorities often turned a blind eye, since there were worse pursuits than riding. Both Morris and BJ liked riding, but in quest of old churches, their monuments and brasses, not of village wenches. The Oxford Movement had come and gone, though its effects still lingered, and a liberal reaction had set in, with a small but keen band of Comtists at Wadham.

Morris and BJ had arrived at the end of January 1853 and soon became close friends. Exeter was overfull, so the two had to go into lodgings for the first two terms. No undergraduate was allowed to spend the night out of college, so those with rooms outside were billeted in third rooms of sets belonging to seniors. The college was badly administered, with some students interested in theology or the ancient classics, but the rest taken up with rowing, hunting, drinking, wenching. Only one Fellow at Exeter was concerned about the students. In 1854 a friend of Morris described the system:

As for lectures, I have not ceased to hope that I should learn anything at them which I did not know before. Imagine yourself ushered into a large room comfortably provided with chairs and a large central table. The men take their places round it, and the lecturer, looking up from his easy chair by the fireside, exclaims, 'Will you go on, Mr. —' The approved crib version is then faithfully given, and meanwhile most men are getting, by heart or otherwise, Bohn's translation of the next piece. When No 1 has concluded, the lecturer asks benignly, '*Dum* governs two moods, doesn't it?' 'Yes.'

Morris's tutor is said to have reported that he had 'no special literary tastes or capacity'. BJ says that 'little by little we fed ourselves with the food that fitted us'.

Morris left Oxford with a contempt for its educational system and intellectual pretensions. But he found it a first-rate place for discovering friends with allied tastes and for developing himself through discussion and reading. Within a week he and BJ were inseparable. The latter, now nineteen, was rather tall and very thin, straightly built with wide shoulders, pale, lank hair, high forehead, and wide-set eyes of light grey, radiating energy; his face lighted up when he was moved or interested. He tells us:

We went almost daily walks together. Gloomy disappointment and disillusion were settling down on me in this first term's experience at Oxford. The place was languid and indifferent; scarcely anything was left to shew that it had passed through such an excited time as ended with the secession of Newman. So we compared our thoughts together upon these things and went angry walks together in the afternoons and sat together in the evenings reading. From the first I knew how different he was from all the men I had ever met. He talked with vehemence, and sometimes with violence. I never knew him languid or tired. He was slight in figure in those days; his hair was dark brown and very thick, his nose straight, his eyes hazel-coloured, his mouth exceedingly delicate and beautiful. Before many weeks were past in our first term there were but three or four men in the whole college whom we visited or spoke to. But at Pembroke there was a little Birmingham colony, and with them we consorted when we wanted more company than our own. In a corner of the old quadrangle there, on the ground floor, were the rooms of Faulkner, learned in mathematics and the physical sciences, not so learned in theology, since, in spite of great distinction and University scholarships, he was once plucked because he included Isaiah in the number of the twelve apostles. Dixon, an old school-fellow of mine and the only poet in our school, had rooms at the top of the same staircase, and upon the opposite side of the quadrangle lived Fulford, our senior by about two years, a man then full of energy and enthusiasm. But our common room was invariably Faulkner's, where about nine of the evening Morris and I would often stroll down together, and settle once for all how all people should think.[2]

At Elm House, Woodford Hall, and Water House, Morris had developed his spirit of independence, his enjoyment of garden, forest, old buildings; at Marlborough he saw things in a wider perspective and found himself part of a large community, which finally broke into throes of revolt, but he still lacked the sense of vitally belonging to a group. BJ it was who provided him with a sympathetic group, among which he could talk and develop his ideas, and with which he could feel a community of interests. Faulkner, in particular, was an impressive character, who did much to bring Morris down to firm earth. 'There was about him a special manliness,' says Georgiana, BJ's wife, 'singleness of mind, and fearless honesty. He had great natural skill of hand and sympathy with the executive side of art, but no power of design as far as I know.'

The basis of the group had been Faulkner, Dixon, and Fulford. Fulford was an enthusiastic talker on poetry, on Tennyson and Shelley; Dixon brought Keats in. The main bond was poetry and 'indefinite artistic and literary aspiration', says Dixon, but 'not of a self-seeking character. We all had the notion of doing great things for man: in our own way, however: according to our own will and bent.' Morris seemed at first merely a pleasant garrulous boy, fond of boating with Faulkner, a good fencer and wielder of single-stick.

His fire and impetuosity, great bodily strength, and high temper were soon manifested: and were sometimes astonishing. As, e.g., his habit of beating his own head, dealing himself vigorous blows, to take it out of himself. I think it was he who brought in singlestick. I remember him offering to 'teach the cuts and guards'. But his mental qualities, his intellect also began to be perceived and acknowledged. I remember Faulkner remarking to me, 'How Morris does seem to know things, doesn't he?' And then it struck me that it was so. I observed how decisive he was: how accurate, without any effort or formality: what an extraordinary power of observation lay at the base of many of his casual or incidental remarks, and how many things he knew that were quite out of our way; as, e.g., architecture.

They were keen Tennysonians, admiring all his work up to *Maud* in 1855, 'the last poem that mattered', says Dixon. Two other poets much esteemed were Alexander Smith with his *Life Drama* and Owen Meredith with *The Earl's Return*. In the latter work Morris especially liked the episode of the Earl draining a flagon of wine, then flinging it at the head of him who had brought it. Smith was a leader in what came to be called the Spasmodic School. BJ in a letter of May 1853 mentions the discovery of him. 'He is a very promising poet indeed, and his objective writing is almost incomparable, although his aim is evidently more subjective and metaphysical. There, however, are depths only reached by one—our great Dramatist.' Indeed *The Life Drama* and others of his poems expressed with great power the tumult and stress of the age and the quest for some sort of new way of life which would be adequate to its demands and needs. Dixon recalled Fulford reading *In Memoriam* and Milton.

Morris however had what Dixon calls a 'defiant admiration' of Tennyson, seeing his limitations. He said once, 'Tennyson's Sir Galahad is rather a mild youth,' and he thus apostrophised the hero of Locksley Hall, 'My dear

fellow, if you are going to make that row, get out of the room, that's all.'
So, says Dixon, 'he perceived a certain rowdy, or bullying element that
runs through much of Tennyson's work'. On the other hand, 'he understood
Tennyson's greatness in a manner that we, who were mostly absorbed by
the language, could not share. He understood it as if the poems represented
substantial things that were to be considered out of the poems as well as in
them.' Still, he shared for the moment with the group the belief that no
further development of poetry was possible after Tennyson. Dixon sums up:

At this time, Morris was an aristocrat, and a High Churchman. His manners and
tastes and sympathies were all aristocratic. His countenance was beautiful in
features and expression, particularly in the expression of purity. Occasionally it
had a melancholy look. He had a finely cut mouth, the short upper lip adding greatly
to the purity of expression. I have a vivid recollection of the splendid beauty of his
presence at this time.[3]

In the Long Vacation of 1853 Morris went round looking at churches. BJ
went to London and paid a visit on Morris at Walthamstow, astonished to
find that his friend lived in such a big house, which, compared with his own,
seemed magnificent. Mrs Morris welcomed him, 'and seeing his affection
for her son would willingly have told many stories of his childhood; but at
this Morris chafed so much that the anecdotes had to be deferred'. On their
return to Oxford in October for the Michaelmas Term they both moved into
rooms in college. Morris's rooms were in a small quadrangle called Hell
Quad. 'You passed under an archway called Purgatory from the great
quadrangle to reach it.' The windows looked out on to a small Fellows'
Garden, with a huge chestnut spreading over Brasenose Lane, and on to the
grey stone of the Bodleian Library. (There was a tradition of the old masters
gathering yearly in the guise of chestnut leaves.) BJ arrived late from
Birmingham and had just had his supper when 'Morris came tumbling in
and talked incessantly for the next seven hours or longer'.

     They first studied theology, church history, and archaeology; and Morris
began his lifelong habit of reading aloud to BJ. (He loved reading but hated
being read at.) They went through Sismondi, Gibbon, much of the *Acta
Sanctorum*, many medieval chronicles and Latin poems. They read
Wilberforce's treatises and were affected by his going over to Catholicism
in 1854. They each secretly read *Mores Catholici* by a strong advocate of such
conversions and of medieval ways, Kenelm Digby, and later admitted it to

one another. The group did not discuss religious polemics; the members at Pembroke were Evangelical rather than Anglo-Catholic; and BJ and Morris talked of theological matters only with a few students in Exeter. Morris had read the two volumes of Ruskin's *Modern Painters*; but his and BJ's enthusiasm was even more strongly roused by *The Stones of Venice*, 1853. The chapter on the Nature of Gothic soon became their evangel. Carlyle's *Past and Present* had also much affected them; and a certain social trend in their thinking appears in the fact that, though Anglo-Catholics, they were more interested in Kingsley than in Newman. They were stirred when charges were made against the Rev. F. D. Maurice at King's College, London, such as that he denied the usual meaning of eternal punishment—with the result that he had to leave the college. 'It is a hard question to decide upon, but I am very sorry—for the Christian Socialists,' mused BJ, 'if Maurice and Kingsley are fair examples, must be glorious fellows.' Faulkner certainly played his part in secularising Morris's views. BJ remarked in November 1853: 'Our subjects of private communication and thought this term have been those branches of psychology treating of the affections—a subject which we have elaborated very satisfactorily, in spite of constant interruptions on the part of un-sentimentalists such as Morris and Faulkner.' Fulford had brought up questions of spiritualism and table-turning. He wrote: 'We have fallen at once into our old habits; we assemble nightly in Faulkner's rooms and drink tea as regularly as ever, but the tales from Household Words or scenes from Shakespeare or imitations of the Dons have given place to the japing of a gullible undergraduate with spirit-messages from tables.'

For some time Morris's interest lay rather in Ruskin's powers of evocation than in his social or artistic doctrines. Dixon says: 'He had a mighty singing voice, and chanted rather than read those weltering oceans of eloquence as they have never been given before or since, it is most certain. The description of the Slave Ship, or of Turner's skies, with the burden, "Has Claude given this?" were declaimed by him in a manner that made them seem as if they had been written for no end but that he should hurl them in thunder on the head of the base criminal who had never seen what Turner saw in the sky.' But while he thus read out the eloquent passages, he could not but be stirred by many aspects of the thought.

Fulford's comment on scenes from Shakespeare refers to weekly readings that they gave in one another's rooms. Fulford, BJ, Morris, and Cormell Price (who had come up to Brasenose) were the chief readers. They drew lots for the parts. Dixon recalled Morris as Macbeth and as Touchstone, but most of all as Claudio in the scene with Isabel.

He suddenly raised his voice to a loud and horrified cry at the word 'Isabel', and declaimed the awful following speech, 'Aye, but to die, and go we know not where,' in the same pitch. I never heard anything more overpowering. As an incident not in Shakespeare, I may mention that in the reading of *Troilus and Cressida*, when Thersites ends his catalogue of fools with the remark, 'And Patroclus is a fool positive,' and Patroclus asks, 'Why am I a fool?' Morris exclaimed with intense delight, 'Patroclus wants to know why he is a fool!'

He was also reading Poe, and BJ stresses the tales in which Poe 'exemplifies his notion of analysis and identification with another's thinking'.[4]

Morris was certainly writing poetry through these years, though there is only one case in which we have a definite date for some verses. In 1853 the theme of the Oxford Prize Poem was *The Dedication of the Temple*, and poems had to be sent in by the start of December. Morris composed a poem on this subject, which he sent to his sister Emma, and she alone, observes May, seems to have known of it. It is more than unlikely that Morris would have written the poem later. He must have decided to try his hand at the theme in the latter part of 1853, knowing that he would not be eligible for entry. Written in blank verse (which Morris later detested), the poem is rather flat in rhythm, but has moments of well-observed nature. Though conventional in piety, it refuses to accept the violences of Christians against unbelievers as deeds of holiness. 'Pray, Christians, for the sins of Christian men.' There are occasional vivid touches. The asp crawls over armour, 'his flat head dubbing at the close steel rings'; the waves rise and fall, 'showing the slate-stones lying in the lake, and throwing shadows on them from the sun'. 'Shout for the mailcoat falling back again from the knee slackening underneath its fold.' There is a paean of praise for the north as against the south with its hot dust. The hands of mourning women are restless like Morris's own: they 'twitched at their garments evermore, twisting them into knots'. The style, though hardly distinguished, is yet more mature than that of *The Three Flowers*.[5]

What did Morris get from Ruskin at this phase? His love of the medieval world and its vital craft-basis was certainly strengthened, and the basis for an expansion of his social sense was laid. Ruskin stressed how medieval buildings showed 'the life and liberty of every workman who struck the stone', and how post-Renaissance structures, with their break between architect and craftsman, their set patterns and frigid finish, were 'full of insults to the poor in every line'. Thus the emotions of repulsion which Morris had felt for things like the Great Exhibition were given a full rationale. He also welcomed the attacks on restorations which destroyed the living character of old work; and his slow divorce from the project of becoming a clergyman was speeded up by Ruskin's efforts to separate the medieval craft-virtues from the Catholic Church and to derive them from the workman's status and his pleasure in the work he did. The artistic aspects of the new creed were still uppermost for Morris, but the social aspects could not help but affect him more and more.

The painted roof of Merton Chapel, a new turn in church decoration, helped him to feel what medieval structures had been like in their pristine state; he had also discovered the painted manuscripts of the Bodleian, loving especially an Apocalypse of the thirteenth century. (Forty years later he came to study it with eyes of deepened knowledge.) He went on drawing windows, arches, gables in his books; he even scribbled floriated ornaments in letters. BJ had turned to nature, drawing flowers and leaves in Bagley Wood. 'Of painting we knew nothing.' The only clue they had to early Italian art came from one or two pictures in the Taylorian Museum and the woodcuts to Ruskin's Handbook to the Arena Chapel of Padua. They much admired even a poor copy of Dürer's engraving of the Knight and the Devil in Fouqué's *Sintram*. 1854 saw BJ turning more to art, drawing designs for *The Lady of Shalott*; he was 'beginning to forgive Oxford, and the fidgets of rebellion were over', with increasing perplexities about religion.

From Ruskin's Edinburgh lectures of 1853 (published 1854) they learned of a group of contemporary artists who excited them. 'I was working in my room,' says BJ, 'when Morris ran in one morning bringing the newly published book with him: so everything was put aside until he read it all through to me. And there we first saw about the Pre-Raphaelites, and there I first saw the name of Rossetti. So many a day after that we talked of little else but paintings which we had never seen, and saddened the lives of our Pembroke friends.' But soon afterwards Millais's *Return of the Dove to the Ark* was shown in Wyatt's shop in the High Street. 'And then we knew.' Ruskin had defined the one principle of the new school as that of 'absolute uncompromising truth'. Morris and BJ at last felt that works of the present could equal those of the great past. BJ had introduced Morris to Celtic and Norse tales, showing him Thorpe's *Northern Mythology*. Praising Ruskin, he saw him as 'what the Pre-Raphaelites are in painting, full of devotion, and love for the subject, Insular and Northern in all their affections, giving us the very ideal of Teutonic beauty'.

The bridge from the religious to the secular application of their ideas of self-dedication was found in the project of founding a Brotherhood. This at first took an ecclesiastical form. BJ, rich in personal fantasies, signed himself as Archbishop of Canterbury as early as 1850, then as Cardinal de Byrmingham. On 1 May 1853 he wrote to the amiable Crom (short for Cormel):

10 o'clock, evening. I have just been amusing myself by pouring basons of water on the crowd below from Dixon's garret, such fun, by Jove. Macdonald one of the lapsed!! Good Evans, as —— says, can it be? Poor fellow, I pity him from the innermost recesses of my heart. Don't let that influence you, Crom. Remember, I have set my heart on our founding a Brotherhood. Learn Sir Galahad by heart. He is to be the patron of our Order. I have enlisted one [Morris] in the project up here, heart and soul. You shall have a copy of the canons some day. (Signed) General of the Order of Sir Galahad.

Not long after he wrote, 'We must enlist you in the Crusade and Holy Warfare against the age.' BJ thus appears as the leader at this phase. Crom could recall no such scheme before the Oxford days; and it must have been BJ's close friendship with Morris inside the Pembroke group that made his ideas ferment. He was set on a small conventual society of cleric and lay members working in the heart of London on the lines of Hurrell Froude's Project for the Revival of Religion in Great Towns. In an 1853 letter to Harry Macdonald he argues at length that the spread of 'general knowledge' has made concentration or individuality difficult; but 'we are not here to grumble with the age, but to adapt ourselves to it; the earth is brimming too full of humanity to allow room for asceticism and seclusion, which are necessary conditions of individual advancement'. He clearly felt his conventual system would best combine seclusion and participation.

He was doubtless recalling the small community set up by Newman at Littlemore in 1841. Newman and four or five close friends had lived austerely in a row of poor cottages, with perfect silence observed except during recreation after dinner; the place became a centre for pilgrimages from Oxford. George Edmund Street, architect of revived Gothic, when twenty-six, was absorbed by a scheme for an institution combining college, monastery, workshop, for students of the theory and practice of religious art. He had been living at Oxford since 1852 as architect for the diocese, restoring many churches; he was building the church of SS Philip and James on the northern outskirts for families of married dons, attempting a return to the thirteenth century. Morris must have known of him. Further, there had been the community of Cornelius and Overbeck in Rome a generation earlier, living in a Roman palace under a sort of monastic rule; they had affected painters like Dyce and in some respects led on to the Pre-Raphaelite Brotherhood. We see that community-forms which looked back to medieval society and its art as a protest against bourgeois egoism and disintegration were very much in the air. They appealed to young members of the middle class who wanted to rebel but could not feel the possibility of any political association directed at fundamental change.[6]

In the Long Vacation of 1854 Morris went abroad for the first time. He travelled through Belgium and northern France, seeing the paintings of Van Eyck and Memling, which he found incomparable. And he saw the churches of Amiens, Beauvais, Chartres, Rouen, as well as the Louvre and the Musée Cluny at Paris. Even more than his Essex lowlands he loved the poplar-meadows, the little villages and the waters about the Somme, the long roads; he loved the smell of beeswax, woodsmoke, and onions that greeted him on landing in France. He brought back photographs of Dürer's engravings, increased contempt of would-be classical architecture, and memories of medieval splendours that never left him. Nearly forty years later he wrote of how

I first saw the city of Rouen, then still in its outward aspect a piece of the Middle Ages: no words can tell you how its mingled beauty, history, and romance took hold on me; I can only say that, looking back on my past life, I find it was the greatest pleasure I have ever had: and now it is a pleasure which no one can ever have again: it is lost to the world for ever. At that time I was an undergraduate of Oxford. Though not so astounding, so romantic, or at first sight so mediaeval as the Norman city, Oxford in those days still kept a great deal of its earlier loveliness: and the memory of its grey streets as they then were has been an abiding influence and pleasure in my life.

Through a cholera outbreak term was postponed a week. BJ longed to be back with 'Morris and his glorious little company of martyrs'. But in fact the basis of the monastic ideal was rapidly waning. Men like Crom and Faulkner had much knowledge of the ghastly conditions of life and work in the industrial areas. Crom wrote:

Things were at their worst in the forties and fifties. There was no protection for the millhand or miner—no amusements but prize-fighting, dog-fighting, cock-fighting, and drinking. When a little boy I saw many prize-fights, bestial scenes: at one a combatant was killed. The countryside was going to hell apace. At Birmingham School a considerable section of the upper boys were quite awake to the crying evils of the period; social reform was a common topic of conversation. We were nearly all day-boys, and we could not make short cuts to school without passing through slums of shocking squalor and misery, and often coming across incredible scenes of debauchery and brutality. I remember one Saturday night walking five miles from Birmingham into the Black Country, and in the last three miles I counted more than thirty lying dead drunk on the ground, nearly half of them women.

All the while, too, Morris and BJ were being influenced by expressions and ideas that made monastic schemes seem archaic. We have noted the Christian Socialists; this year Maurice and others started the Working Men's College in London. There was also the Young England Movement, which showed its effect in works like Charlotte Yonge's *The Heir of Redclyffe*. Dixon called that novel 'unquestionably one of the finest books in the world', and thought it the first that seemed to influence Morris. Its hero Guy is a chivalrous young fellow, intensely earnest, devoted to self-culture and social regeneration, planning to improve the lot of his peasantry in the spirit of Young England and seeking ways in which to embody his ideals of love, friendship, piety, honour. He writes an epic on King Arthur, calls his wife Verena, and comforts her on her deathbed with readings from *Sintram*. The period indeed saw a large number of writers and propagandists who looked back to the medieval world in search of cures for the malaises of capitalism. Southey in his *Colloquies* in 1829 had clearly set out the ideas that 'bad as the feudal times were, they were far less injurious than these commercial ones to the kindly and generous feelings of human nature, and far, far more favourable to the principles of honour and integrity'. He contrasted the new depredations with the activities of the medieval outlaw as being 'more intimately connected with the constitution of society, like a chronic and organic disease, and therefore more difficult to cure'. Such positions revealed a deep fear of the working class as an oppressed force that might rise up to disrupt what was accepted as the necessary fabric of society, i.e. private property especially in its landed form. The factory-owners were blamed for having brought about this new dangerous force; and thinkers like Southey, while confusedly mixing praise of King Alfred and Robert

Owen and hoping that somehow 'steam will govern the world' to its betterment, yet kept looking back to monasteries, church fraternities, guilds.

Such attitudes were brought directly into politics by the Young Englanders. Lord John Manners, after hearing a sermon by William Faber in 1838, wrote in his journal, 'We have now virtually pledged ourselves to restore— what? I hardly know—but it is still a glorious attempt.' Then in 1842, the year before *Past and Present*, he stated, 'The mists are rolling away, and the alternative will soon present itself—a Democracy or a Feudalism.' He and his friend George Smythe, now MPs, read More's *Utopia* and visited Lancashire mills; they saw themselves as Jacobites, followers of Burke and Scott. Disraeli realised the chance to turn such positions into support of more conventional Tory programmes. 'The principle of the feudal system was the noblest principle, the grandest, the most magnificent and benevolent that was ever conceived by sage, or ever practised by patriot.' He set before the manufacturers of Manchester the 'stimulating examples of the great merchants of Venice, who were patrons of Titian and Tintoretto . . . and the manufacturers of Flanders.' His novel *Sybil* dramatised these ideas.

We see then that there was nothing unusual in the ideas and projects which haunted young Morris and BJ. The bases from which they began was common ground to the advanced young men of the period, who were aware that something was wrong with the world. What was original was the use that Morris in due time was to make of the shared ideas, the new direction he gave them, and the completeness with which he entered into the situation.

After the Long Vacation the two friends obtained new rooms; now they were next door to one another. 'All day long I have been hurrying about,' wrote BJ, 'seeing after the removal of my property, so that I might not lose half of it. My new rooms are a great improvement.' They were in the section of the college called Old Buildings. 'Tumbly old passages, gable-roofed and pebble-dashed, little dark passages led from the staircase to the sitting-rooms, a couple of steps to go down, a pace or two, and then three steps to go up, and then, inside the rooms, a couple of steps up to a seat in the window, and a couple of steps down into the bedroom—the which was bliss.'

Here they read Chaucer in the evenings and in the days studied illuminated manuscripts. They were eager for old chronicles, anything giving first-hand information about the medieval world. With Harry Macdonald and Crom the Birmingham group was completed. Of Crom BJ says that 'Morris loved him from the first, and was always fond of him and tender about him'. Morris himself went on being 'the most clever glorious fellow in and out of

Oxford', and they were together this term more than ever.[7] *Hard Times* came out this year. The group would certainly have read and discussed it, so Morris must also have taken it in. 'We chatted about life, such as we knew it,' says BJ, 'and about ghosts, which Dixon believed in religiously but Faulkner despised, and many an evening we wound up with a bear-fight, and so at 11, home to Exeter and bed.' The group kept in touch with another Birminghamite, Heeley, at Cambridge. On 18 September Crom's young sister recorded: 'Jones came to tea. He is the most clever and the nicest fellow I ever knew. He says he thinks Fulford will be a "star" and he is sure Morris will be, and I am sure Jones will be, in drawing—he draws splendidly and is inexpressibly splendid.' BJ still hoped to see his community come about. In October he wrote: 'The Monastery, Crom stands a fairer chance than ever of being founded—I know that it will be some day.' He referred to himself as 'Monk as I am and unlettered in the world's etiquette'.

The year 1855 found Morris still keen on fencing, boxing, and single-stick at Maclaren's Gymnasium in Oriel Lane. At single-stick, 'in defence he was unskilful, vehement and iron-handed in attack. I bore for years after discolorations that were due to his relentless onsets.' Maclaren said that his bill for broken sticks and foils equalled those of all the rest of his pupils put together. Morris grew friendly with him, a middle-aged enthusiast, and three or four times a term dined with him and his family at Somertown. With BJ he went to sing plainsong at the morning services at St Thomas's; and the pair, with Dixon and Crom, belonged to the Music Room in Holywell. Other members included Dyce the painter, Street and Woodward, architects, Neale and Palmer, votaries of the Eastern Church. Afternoons were spent on the upper river and among the ruins of Godstow, on expeditions to old churches from Dorchester to Woodstock or in the Wytham and Abingdon woods. Morris's interest in architecture grew ever stronger.

So far he had impressed the rest of the group as an unusual and forceful character, full of a rather undefined promise; but the leadership had lain rather in the hands of Faulkner, Fulford, BJ. Now however he summoned up all his courage and admitted that he wrote poetry. Dixon describes the event:

One night Crom Price and I went to Exeter, and found him with Burne-Jones. As soon as we entered the room, Burne-Jones exclaimed wildly, 'He's a big poet.' 'Who is?' asked we. 'Why, Topsy'—the name we had given him. We sat down and heard Morris read his first poem, the first that he had ever written in his life. It was called 'The Willow and the Red Cliff'. As he read it, I felt that it was something the like of which had never been heard before. It was a thing entirely new: founded on nothing previous: perfectly original, whatever its value, and sounding truly striking and beautiful, extremely decisive and powerful in execution. It must be remembered particularly that it was the first piece of verse that he had ever written: there was no novitiate: and not a trace of influence; and then it will be acknowledged that this was an unprecedented thing. He reached his perfection at once; nothing could have been altered in 'The Willow and the Red Cliff'; and in my judgment, he can scarcely be said to have much exceeded it afterwards in anything that he did. I cannot recollect what took place afterwards, but I expressed my admiration in some way, as we all did; and I remember his remark, 'Well, if this is poetry, it is very easy to write.' From that time onward, for a term or two, he came to my rooms almost every day with a new poem.

The poem was certainly not Morris's first one; he had been writing for some time. And we must allow for the effect of his personality and his way of reading for the enthusiasm the poem evoked. The idiom and method is close to that of *The Three Flowers*, and there are influences both from old balladry and the Spasmodics; but Dixon was right enough in recognising a new voice. The poem begins:

> About the river goes the wind
> And moans through the sad grey willow
> And calls up sadly to my mind
> The heave and swell of the billow.
>
> For the sea heaps up beneath the moon,
> And the river runs down to it.
> It will meet the sea by the red cliff,
> Salt water running through it.
>
> The cliff it rises steep from the sea
> On its top a thorn tree stands,
> With its branches blown away from the sea
> As if praying with outstretched hands. . . .

A woman sits on the cliff, clasping her knee, and sings of her grief, telling the sun that her lover had plighted his troth to her under 'the happy willow tree'. She turns to the sea and lets her hair down, 'and the west wind blew it but wearily'. Singing again, she asks the willow if it still has the ring she hung on a branch when her lover left her. She then throws a picture of the two of them into the sea, and soon after throws herself over the cliff. The poem ends with the image of the golden ring still hanging on the willow-bough.

In March 1855 Morris came of age and had under his control something like £900 a year; the problem of responsibility and choice thus weighed more heavily upon him. During the Easter vacation he wrote to Crom from Walthamstow, including a poem on kisses: the kiss of betrayal by Judas, 'Lover's kiss beneath the moon, With it sorrow cometh soon: Juliet's within the tomb', the kiss given on a deathbed. Christ and his Cross dominate the poem, with stress on love-in-death and union-in-heaven. There is a distinctive quality about the style, rhythm, diction: the meditative note, rambling and slightly clumsy, gives an effect of immediacy.

> 'Twas in Church on Palm Sunday,
> Listening what the priest did say
> Of the kiss that did betray,
>
> That the thought did come to me
> How the olives used to be
> Growing in Gethsamane.
>
> That the thoughts upon me came
> Of the lantern's steady flame,
> Of the softly whispered name. . . .

'Yet I cannot think of love.' He ends the letter with a passage that shows his uncertainties and his isolation at home:

I have been in a horrible state of mind about my writing; for I seem to get more and more imbecile as I go on. Do you know, I don't know what to write to you about; there are no facts here to write about; I have no one to talk to, except to ask for things to eat and drink and clothe myself withal; I have read no new book since I saw you, in fact no books at all.

The other day I went 'a-brassing' near the Thames on the Essex side; I got two remarkable brasses and three or four others that were not remarkable: one was Flemish brass of a knight, date 1370, very small; another a brass (very small, with the legend gone) of a priest in a shroud; I think there are only two other shrouded brasses in England. The Church that this last brass came from was I think one of the prettiest Churches (for a small village Church) that I have ever seen . . . the parson of the parish showed us over this Church; he was very civil and very, very dirty and snuffy, inexpressibly so, I can't give you an idea of his dirt and snuffiness.

In a second letter, a week later, he tells how the poem's idea came to him in church 'as the second lesson was being read: you know the second lesson for Palm Sunday has in it the history of the Betrayal'. We may recall that six years earlier he had written to Emma discussing Easter services. 'It is very foolish, but I have a tenderness for that thing, I was so happy writing it, which I did on Good Friday: it was a lovely day, with a soft warm wind instead of the bitter north-east wind we had had for so long.' He apologises for, and defends, bad rhymes such as soon and tomb. 'You see I must lose the thought, or sacrifice the rhyme to it. I had rather do the latter and take my chance about the music of it.' (In fact the defence of such assonances should point to the muted slow inturned note which they help to maintain and which gives the poem its curious urgency.) He has been stirred by Shelley's *Skylark*: 'Most beautiful poetry, and indeed all beautiful writing makes one feel sad, or indignant, or—do you understand, for I can't make it any clearer; but *The Skylark* makes one feel happy only; I suppose because it is nearly all music, and that it doesn't bring up any thoughts of humanity; but I don't know either.' He was going a-brassing well afield, to Rochester, and to Stoke D'Abernon in Surrey.[8]

Mackail states that less than a month before his death Morris called his first poems imitations of Mrs Browning; but there is nothing of her in *Kisses*. Rather we see the effect of reading Alexander Smith, who at times attained the same sort of faltering direct simplicity:

> One comes shining like a saint,
> But her face I cannot paint,
> For mine eyes and blood grow faint.
> Eyes are dimmed as by a tear,
> Sounds are ringing in mine ear,
> I feel only, she is here.

The element of death-fantasy, strong in *The Three Flowers* and *The Willow and the Red Cliff*, appears again in the other early poem cited by Mackail, *Blanche*:

> Silv'ry birch-trunks rise in air
> And beneath the birch-tree there
> Grows a yellow flower fair.

> Many flowers grow around
> And above me is the sound
> Of the dead leaves on the ground.

He sleeps in the moonlight and has a troubled dream of a white dress flitting by the aspen; Blanche kneels and turns to him, begging to be forgiven; he lifts up her head and says that they will both be dead. 'Let us pray that we may die', may lie in the woods and be raised to heaven where 'mid the angels we may kiss'. Blanche asks to be kissed at once. He kisses her and she dies, lying amid the flowers.

At this stage then Morris's imaginings are essentially morbid and play round a death-wish associated with Emma. Any resolutions are seen as taking place after death, in heaven. However, in May Crom noted that 'our Monastery will come to nought I'm afraid; Smith has changed his views to extreme latitudinarianism, Morris has become questionable in doctrinal points, and Ted is too Catholic to be ordained. He and Morris diverge more and more in views though not in friendship.' The Crimean War had been dragging along, with *The Times* dispatches revealing the awful sufferings of the wounded and the bad conditions of the field hospitals. The group was confirmed in the conviction of a wrong direction having been taken by society. (The effects on sensitive observers came out in *Maud*, in Kingsley's *Two Years After*, in Dickens's *Little Dorrit*.) BJ was so upset that he wanted to take up one of the commissions offered to the university. 'I wanted to go and get killed.' But he was rejected as unfit.

In late May, in the Easter Term, he went to London with Crom for the Royal Academy; Morris was there too. They visited Windus at Tottenham to see his Pre-Raphaelite collection, which included Brown's *The Last of England*. They came away 'strengthened and confirmed'. In the Summer Term they saw Coombe's collection at the Clarendon Press with two works by Hunt and Rossetti's watercolour of Dante drawing Beatrice's head. The idea of a periodical, in place of the foundered Brotherhood, was coming up. Crom and Harry Macdonald had started a magazine at school in Birmingham, which was suppressed. Further, 'we had already fallen in with a copy of *The Germ* containing Rossetti's poem "The Blessed Damozel", and at once he seemed to us the chief figure in the Pre-Raphaelite Brotherhood.' BJ says the idea came first from Dixon. The group decided to draw Heeley in, and at the end of term Morris and BJ went to Cambridge for a week to discuss the venture. In the train they had talked of old French chronicles, and on their first night they went to see 'the little round church'. Morris then travelled to Walthamstow.

A few days later, on 6 July, he wrote to Crom, discussing the magazine which at this phase was called *The Brotherhood*. He had finished a story and reminded Crom that he was to review Mrs Gaskell's *North and South*. He thought Cambridge 'rather a hole of a place' and found Ely 'horribly spoilt with well-meaning restorations, as they facetiously term them', but liked the setting on a hill with green fields, gardens and trees, 'all dotted about with quaint old houses'. Also, he had gone to the Royal Academy, admiring Millais's *Rescue* and sorry at having read Ruskin's pamphlet before seeing Leighton's *Procession of Cimabue*; he was happy at having seen Dürer's *S. Hubert*, and had some engravings of Fra Angelico's works in the Louvre. Georgiana Macdonald, later to marry BJ, had been taken to the Royal Academy by Heeley, and they came on Morris closely examining the *Rescue*. Heeley introduced them, but, she says, 'he looked as if he scarcely saw me. He was very handsome, of an unusual type—the statues of medieval kings often remind me of him—and at that time he wore no moustache, so that the drawing of his mouth, which was his most expressive feature, could be clearly seen. His eyes always seemed to me to take in rather than give out. His hair waved and curled triumphantly.'⁹

This year, 1855, he had been rapidly maturing, finding stronger expression (it seems) in prose than in verse. We need to glance a little more fully at the key influences in this development. In his 1883 account to Scheu he said that he had turned at Oxford to history, especially of the Middle Ages, in part because he was 'under the influence of the High Church or Puseyite school'. This phase did not last long, mainly through the reading of Ruskin; but he was also much affected by the works of Kingsley and got into his head from them 'some socio-political ideas which would have developed probably but for the attractions of art and poetry'. While an undergraduate he found he could write poetry, and 'being intimate with other young men of enthusiastic ideas', he helped to produce a monthly paper 'which was very *young* indeed'. He should however have added the name of Carlyle to his influences; for a seminal work in all the medieval dreamings of this period was his *Past and Present*, 1843, a somewhat idealised account of life in the monastery of St Edmunds Bury of the twelfth century. Carlyle tries to stress the elements of community and man-to-man responsibility in medieval society. Much of what he says is close to the ideas of the Young Englanders, and he wants a chivalry of labour (mill owners) to arise, with permanent or temporary contracts, so that a splendour of God will unfold itself in the factory-world. But what distinguished the work and gave it its great force was its pervasive sense of bourgeois society as held together solely by the cash-nexus.

Cash-payment never was, or could except for a few years be, the union-bond of man to man. Cash never yet paid one man fully his deserts to another; nor could it, nor can it, now or henceforth to the end of the world. . . . We call it a Society; and go about professing openly the totallest separation, isolation. Our life is not a mutual helpfulness; but rather, cloaked under the due laws-of-war, named 'fair competition' and so forth, it is a mutual hostility. We have profoundly forgotten everywhere that *Cash-payment* is not the sole relation of human beings.

The lot of 'the dumb millions born to toil' had never been 'so entirely unbearable' in all history; an England full of wealth was 'dying of inanition'; millions of shirts are turned out that fail to get on to the millions of bare backs. At the same time Carlyle sets out the creed that Work is alone noble. By the work that clears the jungle, sows the field, and builds the city, 'the man is now a man'. However, with the vigour of denunciation that gives him the tone of an Old Testament prophet, he sees work as ultimately the curse laid on man; and he has no doctrine of joy. In all his account of his hero, Abbot Samson, he neglects to mention that he designed the murals and texts for the saint's shrine; art scarcely appears as worth a word.

Here then it was that Ruskin completed the attack on the cash-nexus by stressing the joy of creative activity in the free man. He made this addition without weakening the exposure of the total inhumanity at the heart of a world ruled by the market; indeed he vastly strengthened it. 'The great cry that rises from all our manufacturing cities,' he said in *The Nature of Gothic*, 'louder than the furnace blast, is all in very deed for this,—that we manufacture everything there except man; we blanch cotton, and strengthen steel, and refine sugar, and shape pottery; but to brighten, to strengthen, to refine, or to form a single living spirit, never enters into our estimate of advantages.' In 1892 Morris commented: 'From the time that he wrote this chapter . . . these ethical and political considerations have never been absent from his criticism of art.' This part of his work is that which 'has had the most enduring and beneficial effect on his contemporaries, and will have through them on succeeding generations'.

In his statement on how he became a socialist in *Justice*, 16 June 1894, Morris cited Carlyle and Ruskin as the two great rebels against the

Whiggery of the 'prosperous middle-class men, who in fact, as far as mechanical progress is concerned, have nothing to ask for, if only Socialism would leave them alone to enjoy their plentiful style'. Ruskin, before his days of 'practical Socialism', was his master. 'And, looking back, I cannot help saying, by the way, how deadly dull the world would have been twenty years ago but for Ruskin! It was through him that I learned to give form to my discontent, which I must say was not by any means vague. Apart from the desire to produce beautiful things, the leading passion of my life has been and is hatred of modern civilisation'—that is, of the bourgeois world. Ruskin thus added a positive quality to the jeremiads of Carlyle, who more and more fell back on a call to the Captains of Industry to take charge and carry out his programme. Carlyle wanted the working class obedient and subservient to strong masters of the kind he considered responsible. Ruskin too had his weakness in looking to a master-class, aristocrats or the like, who would enforce a worthy system under which the workers would readily serve; but this aspect of his thought was far less important in his system than was hero worship in Carlyle's, because of his concrete and fully socialised concept of creative work. 'You must either make a tool of the creature, or a man of him.'

Both Carlyle and Ruskin, but especially Ruskin, had a strong sense of the way in which the division of labour divided men, how its fragmentation fragmented them. In *The Nature of Gothic* Ruskin wrote:

We have much studied, and much perfected, of late, the great civilised invention of the division of labour; only we give it a false name. It is not, truly speaking, the labour that is divided; but the men:—Divided into mere segments of men—broken into small fragments and crumbs of life; so that all the little piece of intelligence that is left in a man is not enough to make a pin, or a nail, but exhausts itself in the making the point of a pin or the head of a nail.

Later, in 1883, Morris, making notes for his own use by translating passages from Marx's *Capital* in French, wrote at the top of a sheet: 'It is not only the labour that is divided, subdivided, and portioned out betwixt divers men: it is the man himself who is cut up, and metamorphosed into the automatic spring of an exclusive operation. Karl Marx.' He had followed out Ruskin's deep-probing idea into its full range of applications.[10]

In 1853-5 he was still far from grasping the implications of Carlyle's and Ruskin's thought; but he had started off on the voyage of understanding them, a voyage that had many zigzags and points of confusion, but which in the end brought him out into a stable and dialectically integrated vision of his society. In the summer of 1855 he might well have seemed, however, to be turning away from any consideration of the contemporary issues. He was in fact making one of his detours that in the end, because he persisted in struggling onward, had the effect of strengthening his final realisations and making them all the fuller.

He was writing his short prose-romances. We have already considered *Frank's Sealed Letter*, with its system of dreamlike memories. In others the method of dream-sequence is used, especially in *A Dream*; and even where it is not directly used there is a sort of dream-blurring and transposition of time-relationships, which in *Lindenberg Pool* gains an effect of shock and horror, perhaps influenced by Poe: a revulsion from a world where 'all sacredest things' are made mock of. *The Story of the Unknown Church* merges the Emma-theme with a picture of medieval craft-devotion. The sister of the monk-craftsman loves a deeply admired friend who dies with her at his side; she then herself dies. There is a rich interlacing of flowers and greenery with the tragic moment, with the dream-passage.

After some time (I know not how long), I looked up from his face to the window underneath which he lay; I do not know what time of the day it was, but I know that it was a glorious autumn day, a day soft with melting, golden haze: a vine and a rose grew together, and trailed half across the window, so that I could not see much of the beautiful blue sky, and nothing of town or country beyond; the vine leaves were touched with red here and there, and three overblown roses, light pink roses, hung among them. I remember dwelling on the strange lines the autumn had made in red on one of the gold-green vine leaves, and watching one leaf of one of the overblown roses, expecting it to fall every minute; but as I gazed, and felt disappointed that the rose leaf had not fallen yet, I felt my pain suddenly shoot through me, and I remembered what I had lost; and then came bitter, bitter dreams—dreams which had once made me happy,—dreams of the things I had hoped would be, of the things that would never be now; they came between the fair vine leaves and rose blossoms, and that which lay before the window; they came as before, perfect in colour and form, sweet sounds and shapes.

Thus actuality and dream waver one into the other. The strange effect of dilating and contracting time-vistas is completed by the narrator at the end describing his own death as he finishes carving the effigies and flower-monument of the tomb commemorating the deaths of the lovers. *Svend and his Brethren* has the theme of a girl marrying a man she does not love to save her home-land. The lover arrives at last at the house of the king her husband; he carves her tomb, but refuses to carve one for the king, who says he will then perhaps be his own statue. He dies devotedly clasping the effigy. *Gertha's Lovers* tells of a lovely peasant girl loved by both a king and his close friend; the two men compete in self-sacrifice but the girl chooses the king. In the end the king, killed in battle, comes out of the tree-ring where he has been buried and embraces his wife. 'And they two were together there for hours (talking it seemed), sometimes sitting on the flowers and grass.' At sunset the king vanishes and Gertha lies dead on the flowers with a western wind shaking the aspen-leaves. *Golden Wings* tells of two knights who both fight one another and act together in a good deed, and who love the same girl; at the end the narrator describes his own death. *A Dream* uses at length the full system of dream-transitions to define the partings and comings-together of a pair of lovers. *The Hollow Land* again shows the dream-changes in complex operation. After episodes of violence, Arnald, cornered, leaps into a great hollow land, which stretches out below cliffs. He wakes to hear a girl singing and opens his eyes to behold his beloved. After various tribulations and partings he meets her again. They seek a hollow city in the hollow land; find it with its golden streets and purple shadows, and are themselves transformed, 'winged and garlanded', their faces flashing like stars—'and their faces were like faces we have seen or half-seen in some dream long and long and long ago'. They pass through the gates. 'And before us lay a great space of flowers.'

Even the briefest account brings out how the stories cluster round the Emma-complex of ideas, emotions, imagery. The rivalry of two friends for the same girl, the role of the sister, the death of the girl in the arms of the other man or his death in her arms, the paradisiac garden linked with the love-embrace, the death-union. Here, however, a new theme is attached to the complex: that of medieval art as actively implicated in the theme of love and death, which it commemorates.

We see that Morris, though still haunted by the ideas of the early poems, has made a big advance in his power to objectify the rending conflicts. At the same time he is not unaware of broad social issues. The seeds of later romances such as *The Roots of the Mountain* appear in *Gertha's Lovers* where the people are 'free brave men' whom the 'tyrant kings' rightly fear. In *Svend*, Valdemar is king of a mighty but unhappy people who have achieved many things and made many conquests, but at the cost of inner decay. 'Year by year their serfs, driven like cattle, but worse fed, worse housed, died slowly, scarcely knowing they had souls.' Morris is clearly thinking of Britain:

Should not then their king be proud of such a people, who seemed to help so in carrying on the world to its consummate perfection, which they even hoped their grandchildren would see?

Alas! alas! they were slaves—king and priest, noble and burgher, just as much as the meanest tasked serf, perhaps even more so than he, for they were so willingly, but he unwillingly enough. They could do everything but justice, and truth, and mercy; therefore God's judgments hung over their heads, not fallen yet, but surely to fall one time or other.

Thus the theme of two friends desiring the same girl is linked with that of the struggle for freedom; a band of brave mountaineers in the end triumph over the tyrannous society. *Svend* and *Gertha's Lovers* prefigure Morris's later developments and are of the utmost importance in indicating the lines along which he must develop his art if he is to win self-fulfilment. But the main aspect of the stories is the desperate effort to grasp and understand the hidden forces threatening to disrupt his life from below. The dream-systems reflect the intense pressures which he feels liable to destroy his stability, his effective relations with the outer world. They reflect the difficulties he meets in bringing together purpose and action in his life, in understanding what the upheaval is and how he is to resolve the apparently hopeless conflict of emotions. *Svend* in particular points to the way out, but it was to be many years before he could fully link its pattern of struggle with his grasp of the outer world. Meanwhile the emotional systems that he succeeds in defining reveal how strong are the pressures within, and at the same time give him the ground he needs for his next important step.

We may say that the kind of inner conflict shown in the prose-romances was to go on in his writings till *Love is Enough* and the incomplete novel, round 1871-2, when the Emma-complex was actualised in his relations with Janey and Rossetti. But the intervening years were not wasted. It was because of the prolonged and interlocked resistances that he had to meet and overcome, and because of his unremitting struggle to break through, that he ultimately achieved a stable position, uniting the inner and outer world, with such clarity, breadth, and strength. His violences at single-stick give us the measure of the force with which he felt it necessary to repel the attack of the unknown enemy. With these points in mind we can realise the importance for him of the Ruskinian vision of the medieval world as one where men worked out their salvation by devotion to the art and work in which they expressed their full and undivided selves. Morris had to achieve in himself this medieval condition before he could safely confront the modern world in all its divisive and treacherous involvements. He could not merely discourse about creative happiness and discriminatively admire its products, as Ruskin could; he had to actualise that creativity in his own life and all his activities. Then only could the full consequences of the struggle for the whole man, for the ending of the division of labour and the fragmentation of the worker, be recognised, understood, and acted upon. And because of the ceaseless inner pressures he could not halt at some point of compromise along the way, as other men could. Meanwhile he had to go on dramatising the inner conflict with tales and poems in which a large part was played by the struggle of two men for the same woman: a struggle which was also a sort of brotherly compact and found its resolution in the work of art, the re-achievement of medieval harmonies. In due time the two sides of himself would come together and he would know clearly who the enemy was, who the ally was, what were the aim and the prize, what was the pledge of the whole man.

On 19 July 1855 Morris, BJ and Fulford started off for a walking tour; Crom had been unable to join them. They crossed from Folkestone and went on straight to Abbéville. 'Not that we walked far,' said BJ, 'but started with fine ideas of economy, necessary for me and conceded by him [Morris], who never said whether he had, or had not, money.' They went on to Amiens, where Morris fell lame, 'filling the streets with imprecations on all boot-makers; but he bought a pair of gay carpet-slippers, and in these he walked from Clermont to Beauvais, about 18 miles'. After that they went everywhere by rail or diligence. The only book they had was a copy of Keats. Morris 'knew everything about every place we went to'. He wanted to skirt Paris to get to Chartres, disliking the city streets; but BJ insisted on seeing the Hotel Cluny. 'He had told me that Notre-Dame would be a sight miserable to look at, for the sculptures were half down and lying in careless wrecks under the porches. He was fidgetty in Paris, and after three days we hurried away.' However, they had been delighted to find seven Pre-Raphaelite pictures at the Beaux Arts, 'entirely unappreciated' except Millais's *The Order of Release*.

On 10 August Morris wrote to Crom from Avranches. 'O! the glories of the churches we have seen!' He counted the number on his fingers: nine cathedrals and some twenty-four other churches. From Chartres they decided not to go back via Paris to Rouen by rail, but to strike across country. They left amid rain that veiled the cathedral spires but could not hide their splendour, took the train to Maintenon, then drove to Dreux through a countryside of poplars and aspens, of hedgeless fields of grain, 'the most beautiful fields I ever saw yet', says Morris, 'looking as if they belonged to no man'. They went on to Evreux by rail, where they stayed a short while, eating dinner and gazing on the gorgeous cathedral. The land grew more hilly, with flat valleys, with fruit-trees about the fields, till they reached Louviers, where the noble interior of the church almost startled Morris. 'I have never, either before or since, been so much struck with the difference between the early and late Gothic, and by the greater nobleness of the former.' They went by omnibus some five miles through a valley with the setting sun striking across it, to catch a train for Rouen: 'a nasty, brimstone, noisy, shrieking railway train that cares not twopence for hill or valley, poplar tree or lime tree, corn poppy or blue cornflower . . .'. So they crept into Rouen 'in the most seedy way, seeing actually nothing at all of it till we were driving through it in an omnibus'. They enjoyed the cathedral and bought Thackeray's *Newcomes* in a Tauchnitz edition.

BJ tells of what then happened. 'From there we walked to Caudabec, then by diligence to Havre, on our way to the churches of the Calvados: and it was while walking on the quay at Havre at night that we resolved definitely that we would begin a life of art, and put off our decision no longer—he should be an architect and I a painter. It was a resolve only needing final conclusion; we were bent on that road for the whole past year, and after that night's talk we never hesitated more. That was the most memorable night of my life.'

These trips abroad were typical enough of the period. B. H. Jackson tells us how this same year in September his father took him on a tour that included Abbéville, Amiens, Beauvais, Rouen, Falaise. What he saw gave him the final push into the decision to become an architect. The travelling was done in a diligence. Jackson later entered the office of Gilbert Scott. His account shows how common were the enthusiasms agitating Morris at this time.

When I made my entry as a student, the taste in England was falling back still further and thirteenth-century work was in danger of being deposed to make way for the vigorous transitional work of late twelfth-century date. In France the cult of the thirteenth century had been eloquently preached by M. Viollet-le-Duc, whose lucid literary style and clever though imaginative illustrations had an enormous influence on both sides of the Channel. 'We all crib from Viollet-le-Duc' said William Burges.

While Jackson was sketching the west front of Noyon Cathedral, a rag-and-bone man who had paused by him remarked admiringly, '*Mais oui, c'est du treizième, voyez-vous.*' A fellow student of his (T. Garner, later Bodley's partner) went into raptures over a hansom cab. 'It was so truthful, so—so—so medieval!' St John's Gate at Clerkenwell, once of the Hospitallers, had become a pub, with a signboard recommending its Fine Old Saxon Beer and Medieval Stout.[11]

4

Architect and Artist

Soon after he returned to England, Morris went with BJ to Birmingham, to the little family house on the Bristol Road. 'Wild and jolly as ever', they discussed *Maud*. Most of the Oxford group, plus Heeley, were now living within a few miles of one another, and they met daily. Crom was at Spon Lane, West Bromwich, and the others often went there. They did much reading aloud. Fulford took the lead, while the others gathered round a small oaken table to listen, then to talk, often about the proposed magazine. The diary of Crom's younger sister gives us some glimpses.

Aug. 22. Fan [elder sister] was invited over to Jones' to meet Morris. Fulford also was there. F. says Morris is very handsome. Aug. 23. Fulford, Morris, and Jones came over to tea and supper. Morris *is* very handsome. Aug. 27. Crom, Edward, and Morris went to Dudley Castle: came here to tea and supper, and Fulford later on. Fulford read 'The Palace of Art' 'Vision of Sin' and 'Oenone'. Morris also read, but he is a queer reader. Sept. 2. Edward and Morris came to tea and supper. We had great fun: Morris got so excited once that he punched his own head and threw his arms about frantically.

Crom's diary carries on the story. The group was indignant at Aytoun's hostile review of *Maud* in *Blackwood's*.

Sept. 7. Ted, Top, and Fulford came over to tea and supper. Had much talk with Top about architecture and organisation of labour. Discussed the tone of reviews in general, and 'Blackwood' in particular. It is unanimously agreed that there is to be no shewing off, no quips, no sneers, no lampooning in our Magazine. Sept. 9. Saw Ted and Topsy. Talked chiefly about the review. Politics to be almost eschewed: to be mainly Tales, Poetry, friendly Critiques, and social articles.

During the visit BJ took Morris to a bookshop in New Street where it was still the fashion to drop in and read books from the shelves. He had recently noticed Southey's edition of Malory's *Morte d'Arthur*, but couldn't afford to buy it. Morris at once bought it, and it became one of their most prized possessions. We hear also of a meeting at Heeley's house where Carlyle's *Past and Present* and *French Revolution* were discussed.

After some three weeks Morris left for Malvern, which he found very much spoiled by being made into 'a sort of tea garden for idle people'. The abbey bells rang all day for the fall of Sevastopol; and next day, as he took train for Clay Cross to visit Emma, there were flags everywhere. At Clay Cross, by some error, they hoisted the Russian flag instead of the French. There was only one mild bell here, but it tolled all day. Writing on 29 September to Crom from Walthamstow, Morris said: 'My life is going to become a burden to me, for I am going (beginning from Tuesday next) to read for six hours a day at Livy, Ethics, &c.—please pity me.' The day before, Crom records, 'Wrote to Morris two sheets abusing him roundly for thinking of leaving Oxford.' Some days later Morris replied: 'I am certainly coming back, though I should not have done so if it had not been for my Mother; I don't think even if I get through Greats that I shall take my BA, because they won't allow you not to sign the 39 Articles unless you declare that you are "extra Ecclesiam Anglicanam" which I'm not, and don't intend to be, and I won't sign the 39 Articles. Of course I should like to stay up at Oxford for a much longer time, but (I told you, didn't I?) I am going, if I can, to be an architect, and I am too old already and there is no time to lose, I MUST make haste, it would not do for me, dear Crom, even for the sake of being with you, to be a lazy, aimless, useless, dreaming body all my life long, I have wasted enough time already, God knows; not that I regret having gone to Oxford, how could I?' About the same time he wrote to BJ, who recorded on 6 October that he had got letters from Morris and Dixon, 'both sick of aimless, theoretical lives'.

Mrs Morris could hardly believe the news when Morris told her his decision. The family was filled, says Mackail, with 'disappointment and even consternation'. That Morris would be a clergyman had always been taken for granted. To become even an architect, despite the fact that office work was entailed and the possibility of wealth, was 'to cut oneself away from the staid traditions of respectability'. Morris indeed was so overawed by his mother's reaction that he did not press the matter. He waited till he was back in Oxford, with half the term behind him, before he dared to return to the question. Then he wrote a long letter, which began: 'I am almost afraid you thought me scarcely in earnest when I told you a month or two ago that I did not intend taking Holy Orders; if this is the case I am afraid also that my letter may vex you.' He protested that he did not want idle objectless life, that he wanted to be an architect. He declared that the money spent on his years at Oxford had not been wasted:

if the love of friends faithful and true, friends first seen and loved here, if this love is something priceless, and not to be bought again anywhere and by any means: if moreover by living here and seeing evil and sin in its foulest and coarsest forms, as one does day by day, I have learned to hate any form of sin, and to wish to fight against it, is not this well too? . . . I shall be master of a useful trade; one by which I shall hope to earn money, not altogether precariously, if other things fail. I myself have had to overcome many things in making up my mind to this; it will be rather grievous to my pride and selfwill to have to do just as I am told for three long years, but good for it too, I think; rather grievous to my love of idleness and leisure to have to go through all the drudgery of learning a new trade, but for that rather good.[1]

Henrietta had been much upset by his decision. He asked his mother to tell her that he sympathised with her disappointment. 'You see I do not hope to be great at all in anything, but perhaps I may reasonably hope to be happy in my work, and sometimes when I am idle and doing nothing, pleasant visions go past me of the things that may be.' In a postscript he asked that no one but Henrietta should see the letter. Now it was that he wrote *Frank's Sealed Letter*, which shows a strong fear of going out into the world to make his own way and which bitterly blames the Emma-Mother figure for the rejection that thus exiles him. We must recall that it has been Emma's influence which had turned him to the decision of a church career; now he is renouncing that decision. One factor enabling him to stand up against his mother was certainly his inheritance this year of the mining shares; the dividend per share stood at £56 a year, yielding him an annual income of £900. He was thus well off and no longer had to turn to his mother for money. The dividend remained fairly steady for the next ten years.

He had made up his mind to approach Street already when he wrote to Crom; he repeated his intention to his mother. He had returned to Oxford anxious to get down to work which interested him. On 13 October the group met again. Crom mentions: 'Topsy met me at the station: drove to Dixon's, where were Fulford, Ted, Mac, Hatch, and James Price. Talked about the grind and all topics.' Next day, Sunday, after morning service he went to Morris's rooms, where John Oakley came in, a genial fellow, later a hard-working clergyman in East London, and then Dean of Carlisle and Manchester. In the evening they went to Dixon's and 'talked on a myriad subjects and Ted read some "Yeast" '. BJ in fact was keen to get away and start painting; he admitted, 'Many of us are sadly tired of Oxford I think.' From early 1854 he had been producing designs for one MacLaren; and he and Morris had been much stirred by a Dalziel cut after a Rossetti design in Allingham's *Day and Night Songs*. (Rossetti himself thought the cut poor.) The discussions on the magazine were growing more excited. 'We have such a deal to tell people,' said BJ, 'such a deal of scolding to administer, so many fights to wage and opposition to encounter that our spirits are quite rising with the emergency.' Crom's diary gives some details. 'Nov 6. After Hall to Faulkner's where I helped Top to concoct a letter to the publishers. Nov. 17. Evening to Dixon's: Solemn conclave as to the form, title &c. of the coming Mag. Ultimately decided on 72 pages monthly. Nov. 22. Ground at a prospectus with Top: in the evening to Pembroke and go on with the prospectus, Fulford joining in and doing lion's share.'

Morris gained a pass degree in the Final Schools, and at once arrangements were made to start in Street's office at Oxford; by early December the matter was settled. He had at last set himself to a definite purpose in life: to become an architect who would follow, however humbly, in the footsteps of the Gothic builders he admired.

On 1 January 1856 there appeared *The Oxford and Cambridge Magazine, Conducted by Members of the Two Universities*, under the imprint of Bell and Dalby. It was, however, almost wholly the work of the Oxford group. There were twelve monthly numbers, each of sixty to seventy-two pages, with contents classified as essays, tales, poetry, and notices of books. Morris, who was financing the project, had general control at first, with Dixon keen to help out of his more modest means. But he soon found such jobs as correcting proofs burdensome, and Fulford took over as editor with the second issue, at a salary of £100 a year. He lodged in London with Heeley at 20 Montpellier Square, Brompton Road, and the contributors often met there. Thus BJ tells Crom: 'On Tuesday I dined at Brompton, Topsy and Macdonald were there, five of us together, like old times.' To some extent Fulford pushed his own writings into the magazine, but without his energy the venture would have broken down or carried on less regularly. There was a project of illustrations: but only two photographs of medallion portraits of Carlyle and Tennyson by Woolner were used. BJ did an elaborately jesting drawing (unprinted) for an article by Faulkner on Sanitation.

For the first issue 750 copies, with 250 extra were printed, but there were many presentation copies and the circulation slowly fell off. By December there was a large unsold stock. Hopes, however, were high at first. On 9 January Fulford wrote: 'Ruskin has sent a most jolly note to Jones, promising to write for us when he has time, which won't be at present. But he is very despondent: he thinks people don't want honest criticism; and he has never known an honest journal get on yet.' BJ's own reaction was ecstatic. 'I'm not Ted any longer. I'm not E. C. B. Jones now—I've dropped my personality—I'm a correspondent with RUSKIN.' And he drew himself prostrate at a luminous Ruskin's feet. In the first issue was the first of three articles by Fulford on Tennyson, who acknowledged the copy sent to him. He found 'in such of the articles as I have read, a truthfulness and earnestness very refreshing to me'.

Morris contributed the stories we have discussed and five poems, which show that he had now reached the level of technical development maintained throughout his first volume, *The Defence of Guenevere*. But poems like *Riding Together* or *Pray But One Prayer*, reprinted there, represented his lyrical side; he had not yet gained the power to create the more concentrated dramatic poems. BJ dealt with *The Newcomes* and Ruskin, and printed two stories; Heeley dealt with Kingsley, Macaulay, Sir Philip Sidney, Froude; Fulford with Alexander Smith, *Troilus and Cressida*, and the Crimean War; V. Lushington with Carlyle; Cracroft with Thackeray and Currer Bell (Charlotte Brontë); Crom with Lancashire and *Mary Barton* as well as writing *The Work of Young Men in the Present Age*. Much of the work was earnest and well intentioned, but cloudy. For instance we read:

We have before us a Herculean task to sweep the world clear of work-houses, open sewers, strikes, money-grubbings, over-production, and an ugly infinity of political and religious phantasms; the existence of such things implies an unsettled transitory period—to *what* remains with ourselves.

The 'gospel of social order' embodied in feudalism is approved for its 'completeness and beauty'. Crom in *Mary Barton* addresses the manufacturer: 'There was something more than the mere bond of gold that united the feudal baron, your predecessor, to his dependants.' There are laudatory quotations from *The Nature of Gothic* and from Mill on the division of society into the 'payers of wages and the receivers of them', a system 'neither fit nor capable of indefinite duration'. Froude's *History of*

England was praised for refuting the assumption that 'we are better and better off' than earlier generations. The sixteenth century was seen as a time when the attempt was made to 'bring the production and distribution of wealth under the moral rule right and wrong', when a higher code took in or superseded 'those laws of supply and demand, which we are now taught to regard as the immutable laws of nature'. Morris presumably accepted this sort of position without having thought much about it all apart from opposing medieval and modern values.[2]

Besides Morris's contributions, the only outstanding items were three poems by Rossetti, *The Burden of Nineveh*, the often revised *Blessed Damozel*, and *The Staff and Scrip*. On 11 January we get a glimpse of Morris at work at Walthamstow. 'I am to have a grind about Amiens Cathedral this time, it is poor and inadequate, I cannot help it; it has cost me more trouble than anything I have written yet; I ground at it the other night from nine o'clock till half past four a.m., when the lamp went out, and I had to creep upstairs to bed through the great dark house like a thief.' He seems to have meant to write a series on the churches of northern France, but gave up the project. On 21 January he began his work at Street's office in Beaumont Street and doubtless had his time taken up in adapting himself to his new situation. For the first time he was attempting something like a disciplined existence. His remarks to his mother about fearing 'the drudgery of a new trade' had not been made merely to placate her, for in fact he found it impossible to carry on long under another man's direction. Something of his emotional situation comes out in his comments in the essay he wrote on Browning:

... but now Childe Roland passes straight from our eyes to the place where the true and brave live for ever, and as far as we go, his life flows out triumphantly with that blast he blew. And was it not well to leave us with that snatch of old song ringing through our ears like the very horn-blast that echoed all about the windings of that dismal valley of death? ... In my own heart I think I love this poem the best of all in these volumes.

A comment from the essay on 'Young Men' seems aimed at him and BJ and suggests that the more radically minded of the group thought them too wrapt up in the past. There is need, the writer says, for 'young men of the present age' to meditate on 'social wrongs, their causes, and the best way in which they, each on their several spheres, may help to heal them'. And he adds that the obligation extends even to those 'who love the life of a recluse, and would strive to conjure up images of the Middle Ages as they pore in some quaint Gothic work over the stirring chronicle of the olden days'.

Meanwhile BJ had met Rossetti. Hearing that he taught at the Working Men's College in Great Ormond Street, he went there and learned that for threepence that very evening he could get into the monthly meeting in a room in Great Titchfield Street. He went and sat there, feeling lonely and eating thick bread-and-butter. Furnivall, the man opposite, spoke to him and introduced Vernon Lushington. These others were unsure whether Rossetti would turn up. However, as Maurice was attacking Macaulay's new volume for its treatment of George Fox, Lushington whispered that Rossetti had come in. 'So I saw him for the first time, his face satisfying all my worship.' However, he refused to be introduced. Instead he wrote a long letter to Morris at Walthamstow and went a few nights later to Lushington's rooms. 'And by-and-bye Rossetti came and I was taken up to him and had my first fearful talk with him.' Rossetti tore to pieces someone who spoke disrespectfully of Browning's *Men and Women*. 'I saw my hero could be a tyrant, and I thought it sat finely upon him.' Someone else expressed an interest in metaphysics and was promptly crushed. 'Our host was impelled to ask if Rossetti would have all men painters, and if there should be no other occupation for mankind. Rossetti said stoutly that it was so.' He invited BJ to visit him next day at his studio close to Blackfriars Bridge.

He received me very courteously, and asked much about Morris, one or two of whose poems he knew already, and I think that was our principal subject of talk, for he seemed much interested about him. He showed me many designs for pictures; they tossed about everywhere on the room: the floor at one end was covered with them and with books. No books were on shelves, and I remember long afterwards he said that books were no use to a painter except to prop up models upon in different positions, and that then they might be useful. No one seemed to be in attendance upon him. I stayed long and watched him at work, not knowing till many a day afterwards that this was a thing he greatly hated, and when, for shame, I could stay no longer, I went away, having carefully concealed from him the desire I had to be a painter.

BJ stayed on in London till the second week of February, then went home, stopping at Oxford on the way for five to six days. There was a gathering in Morris's room in St Giles's, in a house opposite St John's: a 'delightful Babel'. Next day they all walked to Summertown, where BJ and Morris called on MacLaren (BJ's patron). There followed a 'glorious evening' at Dixon's; then breakfast 'gay, not to say noisy'. One night 'Oakley and an Oriel man entranced us by music'. BJ missed a train and was seen off by Crom between ten and eleven p.m. on St Valentine's Day. He was back at Oxford for the Easter Term; but almost at once gave up hope of passing his degree till the October Term, and decided to leave. By 6 May he was in London. He sent for Crom, met him at Paddington Station, and took him to meet Morris at the Royal Academy. After some trouble he found lodgings in Chelsea.

Meanwhile Morris went on at Street's, where he had met Philip Webb, the senior clerk, a few years his senior. But at the same time he was drawn into the wider art world. Once again BJ was the leader. He was painting under Rossetti's eye and Morris could not resist slipping up to London on weekends. He arrived on Saturday in time to go and see anything of interest at the moment; then perhaps he went to a play with BJ and Rossetti, after which they all went back to Rossetti's rooms on the embankment at Blackfriars and talked till three or four a.m. All Sunday there was more talk, with Malory readings, in the Chelsea lodgings. Rossetti often looked in during the afternoon. Morris took the first train down to Oxford on Monday morning. All the while Rossetti's ascendancy was being established; Morris felt that he should become a painter. With his restless hands he had no doubt soon started scribbling designs and playing with any materials such as clay that lay around the studio.

On 17 May, Morris wrote to BJ, 'Will you do me a favour, viz. go and nobble that picture called "April Love" [by Arthur Hughes in the Royal Academy] as soon as possible lest anyone else should buy it.' Then one day, says BJ,

whilst I was painting and Topsy was making drawings in Rossetti's studio, there entered the greatest genius that is on earth alive, William Holman Hunt—such a grand-looking fellow, such a splendour of a man, with a great wiry golden beard, and faithful violet eyes—oh, such a man. And Rossetti sat by him and played with his golden beard passing his paint-brush through the hair of it. And all evening through Rossetti talked most gloriously, such talk as I do not believe any man could talk beside him.

On 24 August Madox Brown wrote, 'Yesterday Rossetti brought his ardent admirer Morris of Oxford, who bought my little "Hayfield" for £40.'

Rossetti clearly thought the well-off Morris could do something to support
artists. At this time he was making a study of Morris's head for King David
on the Llandaff triptych. His attitude to Morris is shown by a letter he wrote
some months later. 'You know he is a millionaire and buys pictures. He
bought Hughes's *April Love* and lately several water-colours of mine. . . . I
have three or four more commissions from him. To one of my water-colours,
called *The Blue Closet*, he has written a stunning poem.'[3]

All undergraduates had to shave their moustaches. Now Morris forswore
the razor and never again used it. He disliked unnecessary trouble, and long
hair was affected by artists. His hair, which knew no parting, was so strong
that later he used to let his girls hold on to it while he lifted them up. He
was beginning to take on the appearance by which he was later known: a
massive head, slightly knitted brows, narrow eyelids, heavy underlids, fine
mouth and chin partly veiled by hair, hands broad, fleshy, and rather short.
He managed to stay on for nine months in Street's office. Webb saw him as
'a slim boy like a wonderful bird just out of his shell'. Most of his office time
was taken up in copying a drawing of the doorway of St Augustine's Church,
Canterbury. He found it hard to define the many arch-mouldings, and 'at
last the compass-point nearly bored a hole through the drawing-board'.
The atmosphere was easy. One student stuttered and sang better than he
spoke, so they chanted to him in Gregorian plainsong through rolls of fools-
cap. They all had Ascension Day off if they went to church; Street remarked,
'Some of you, I know, have voices.' He held the architect to be not just a
builder; but also a blacksmith, painter, fabric worker, and designer of
stained glass. He thus helped to inspire both Morris and Webb as well as the
whole arts-and-crafts movement. Both Webb and Morris were keen on
embroidery. Webb was friendly with Agnes Blencowe, who, with Street's
sister, founded the Ladies' Ecclesiastical Embroidery Society. Morris had
had an embroidery frame made (Janey told Mackail) and used worsted dyed
by an old French couple. The experimental piece that he made used to hang
in Red House, its design a repeating pattern of flowering trees with birds
and scrolls, and the motto *If I can*. Janey also stated:

He must have started . . . as early as 1855—he taught me the first principles of
laying the stitches together closely so as to cover the ground smoothly and radiating
them properly—afterwards we studied old pieces & by unpicking, &c. we learnt
much—but it was still uphill work, fascinating but only carried through by his
enormous energy and perseverance.[4]

She is speaking from memory, much later, and seems to have got the date wrong; the year was almost certainly 1856.

Rossetti's influence must have worked against the radical trends of the group and thus have helped Morris's limitation of his interests almost entirely to art, crafts, and poetry. The whole complex of early experiences which we have been analysing gave Morris an extreme fear of emotional suffering, a fear of trusting in the bond that had been betrayed. At this phase he could find relief only inside the circle of young people with similar interests; and having settled on the medieval world as the time when the craft-bond truly united men, he was content with seeing a sort of total opposition between the bourgeois present of division and the medieval past of integrated craft. The present he saw as making wholly for cruelty and ugliness, and he never altogether overcame the repugnance he was thus made to feel for any expressions in art or literature which used the present situation for their material. It seems that it was around 1855 that his attitudes on this point finally crystalised; for a short while before he had been able to appreciate Kingsley, and apparently Mrs Gaskell and Thackeray, as well as Dickens and Scott. Even in 1891 he could not quite accept the artist who dealt directly with the present.

I don't think he has a right, under the circumstances and considering the evasions he is absolutely bound to make, to lay any blame on his brother artist who turns back again to the life of past times; or, who, shall we rather say, since his imagination must have some garb or another, naturally takes the raiment of some period in which the surroundings of life were not ugly but beautiful.

There is a deep weakness in such statements, which we shall later analyse. What are the 'evasions' that the artist realistically treating the bourgeois present 'is absolutely bound to make'? Morris is so sure that art or poetry must deal with the beautiful and the heroic that he feels any definition of the contemporary world, which rises above the photographic level, will tend to certain falsifications or omissions. There is a strength here as well as a weakness, but in the last resort the attitude reveals a fear of coming too close to certain aspects of reality, a fear which in Morris goes back to a deep underlying anxiety, a dread of being forced too directly up against the experience of loss and betrayal—though as a result of the nemesis of such an obsession, he in the end precipitated the dreaded event. The effect then was to turn him on to the quest outside the family, outside the intimate group, for a wider union that would be proof against all loss and betrayal, whatever other difficulties and tribulations it brought upon him. The latter troubles he could bravely bear as long as he felt that the old betrayal-pattern had been overcome.

Rossetti then was in one sense a thoroughly bad influence on Morris, helping to bring him to the point where he could say, 'I can't enter into politico-questions with any interest.' But we can also argue, as was earlier pointed out, that Morris had to concentrate his forces on the aesthetic level before he could dare to confront the existing world with steady accusing eyes and a broadly based conviction in the transformative powers of art and work; and in this sense Rossetti's effect was valuable at the phase between 1856 and 1870. While holding him back at one level, it helped to drive him forward at another.[5]

In view then of the importance of Dante Gabriel Rossetti in Morris's life and development, his role as a sort of anti-Morris, we need to look at him a little more closely. His father Gabriel had arrived in England in 1824 as a political refugee from Italy. A strong patriot, a versifier, an enthusiast about Dante who saw in his poems anti-papal political allegories, he was given to believing that he suffered from persecution and plots; he went through much self-torture and anxiety, and later was afflicted by gout, bronchitis, failing sight. He convinced himself of the existence of a masonic sect, holding Dante's ideas, who had covered the whole field of literature from the early Christians to Milton and Swedenborg. Rossetti recalled vividly the fervent meetings of other refugees in the house. He inherited from his father the notion of Dante's circle as haunted by mysteries and conspiracies, but he reverted to the belief in a symbolism of mystical love for woman, which his father had rejected. When he went to a drawing school in Bloomsbury he showed much vivacity mixed with extreme indolence in acquiring technique or draughtsmanship, sarcastic, full of wayward moods and impulses, afraid of public criticism. At the Academy School he showed the same determination to be an artist mingled with a lack of assiduity. His dominating character emerged and he drew round him a flock of admirers. He began to show much promise as a poet, but his energy as a writer flickered out at the age of twenty-five and stayed dormant for several years. He was long under his mother's strict eye and even feared to buy Shelley's works.

In 1848 he made new friends. He painted awhile in Madox Brown's studio, but couldn't bear his exacting system of work. Then he set himself up in Hunt's studio, paying part of the rent. Hunt drew in Millais, and the Pre-Raphaelite Brotherhood was formed with the addition of the sculptor

Woolner, the sleepy art-student Collinson (who fell in love with Christina), Stephens (who painted nothing), and William Michael Rossetti. Gabriel suggested the term Brotherhood, inspired by his father's ideas and something of the revolutionary air of 1848. Hunt wrote later, 'Like most young men, I was stirred by the spirit of freedom of the passing revolutionary time.' But in some verses by Gabriel the great Chartist demonstration of April was depicted as a futile outburst of lower-class cads. He was however beginning to break from his mother's religiosity. The group among other things discussed the debased taste of the applied arts and the need for a revival of beauty in architecture, furniture, fabrics, and decorations. Gabriel with all his changing moods, his rages and despairs when he came up against his lack of technical resources in art, had considerable intellectual force in talk, and easily took the lead in any group of which he was a member. He painted a *Girlhood of the Virgin Mary*, but put it in an exhibition where one paid for wall-space, annoying Hunt who thought he was trying to get ahead of his friends in showing a work of their new principles.

Gabriel left Hunt's studio without warning, so that Hunt couldn't pay the rent. His aunt persuaded the Marchioness of Bath to buy *The Girlhood* for £60—Gabriel somehow managing to raise the price to £80. He visited Paris, where, while pitying Rubens, Michelangelo, and Delacroix, he vastly admired Flandrin, and wrote a sonnet of high indignation when he saw the can-can. Back at home he roused his group into publishing a magazine, *The Germ*, which appeared early in 1850 and lasted into the spring, helping to fan the antagonisms stirred up by the Royal Academy of that year. The Brotherhood slowly broke up under the shock of attack. Gabriel tried to paint 'from Nature' Dante and Beatrice meeting in the Garden of Eden. Borrowing from mother, brother, aunts, uncles, anyone, he got the handsome young student Deverell to join him in rooms at Red Lion Square. For a while he contemplated becoming a railway telegraphist, emigrating to Australia, or starting an artists' crusade to Jerusalem where Hunt could paint such a realistic Christ that all men would kneel to him. The year 1851 saw a yet more violent series of attacks on Pre-Raphaelitism for blasphemy, tractarianism, French realism, false perspective, antiquated style, affected simplicity, crude colour, caricatures and so on. Patmore interceded with Ruskin, who in May wrote to *The Times* and provided the barely existent school with the common aesthetic they could not find for themselves. He then developed his ideas in the pamphlet which we saw Morris reading at Oxford and which had a strong effect on the public.

Deverell found a striking girl in a milliner's shop while he was shopping with his mother in Leicester Square. This girl became a model for the Brotherhood. She was Lizzie Siddal, tall with red-gold hair and a delicate creamy complexion, six years or so younger than Gabriel. The latter seems to have been so far without sexual experience. Chiaro of his *Hand and Soul* (1849) was clearly based on himself: he regrets his ambitious years of youth, which, given over to art, had no place for women; then he finds 'the fair woman that was his soul'. and knew 'her hair to be the golden veil through which he beheld his dreams'. All his life he was a thorough narcissist. Now, meeting Lizzie, he was to spend twelve years in a tormented love-struggle; wanting to possess her and at the same time looking on her as 'the fair woman that was his soul', unable to give her up and yet refusing to marry her. She in turn, hiding her coarseness and violent temper under an extreme reticence and demureness, became socially acceptable and built up an artistic sensibility of her own, based on that of her lover and yet in its odd minor key releasing something genuinely lost and suffering. Determined to gain recognition as Gabriel's wife, she held out through his long alternation of adoring praises and callous infidelities. In the process she wrecked her health, achieving phases of deathly decline followed by unexplained returns to health. At times she lived in the same rooms as Gabriel, and the strain on them both was extreme. He called her by the infantile name of Guggums, Guggum, Gug; as he worked he went on murmuring 'Guggum . . .'. She at times called him Gug. He too underwent moods of depression, boredom, lethargy, with outbursts of gaiety and expansive energy. Though he had argued with Bell Scott against free love and all 'self-culture' that flourished at the expense of other people, especially women, and denounced 'the egotistical side of the popular English Goetheism of the day', he had now fallen into a need for coarse dissipations as the counterpart of his worship of Lizzie-Beatrice. He coaxed Lizzie on to draw, paint, and versify. He began to find it difficult to sleep. On 3 May 1854 his father died.

That autumn Ruskin drew him into the Working Men's College. Partly through wanting to be in Ruskin's good books, he taught there some years, irregular in appearances, but getting on well with the students in his unconventional way. Ruskin, all his immature chivalry roused by Lizzie, offered to settle £150 a year on her in return for the art works she produced; at the same time he tried to sound Rossetti out on the question of marriage, and offered to buy his paintings up to a certain yearly value, if it would help him to come to a decision. Rossetti was delighted at the money offer, but evaded the marriage issue. Ruskin got Lizzie to go for a while to Oxford to be examined by Dr Acland, but all the latter diagnosed was 'mental power long pent up and lately overtaxed'. He probably meant that she was neurotic. Rossetti, after being paid the first instalments of the pension for both himself and Lizzie, coolly asked for an advance sum on a picture. Brown's second wife, Emma, was a strong partisan of Lizzie and egged her on to assert herself. Ruskin at every visit found Rossetti's rooms at Chatham Place in disorder, and at last managed to get Lizzie off to Paris, where she spent her money on clothes. Gabriel joined her there against Ruskin's wishes, and borrowed from her all the money she'd kept from the allowance. Finally she did go south. The relations between Ruskin and Gabriel steadily deteriorated. Gabriel resented Ruskin's schoolmasterly manners, while Lizzie, abroad, was appealing for money and yet refusing to take Ruskin's advice. She came home in the spring of 1856, after eight months' absence, more resolved than ever to get her own way. There were continual quarrels, with Emma Brown interfering as much as she could. While Lizzie was away, Gabriel had taken up with Alice Miller, Hunt's model for *The Awakened Conscience*. Lizzie, obstreperous, had her own rooms for a while, paid for by Ruskin, at the corner of Charlotte Street, where she was given to shrieking and rolling on the carpet. Gabriel, wearied out, was unable to make up his mind about anything. During this period Morris and BJ had come into his life. Lizzie's absence had enabled him to find much pleasure in these new enthusiastic disciples, who brought with them a revival of artistic discussions.[6]

A July letter shows how Morris was feeling unable to resist Rossetti's magnetic personality:

I have seen Rossetti twice since I saw the last of you; spent almost a whole day with him the last time, last Monday, that was. Hunt came in while we were there, a tallish, slim man with a beautiful red beard, somewhat of a turn-up nose, and deep set dark eyes, a beautiful man. . . . Rossetti says I ought to paint, he says I shall be able; now as he is a very great man, and speaks with authority and not as the scribes, I *must* try. I don't hope much, I must say, yet will try my best—he gave me practical advice on the subject. . . . So I am going to try, not giving up the architecture, but trying if it is possible to get six hours a day for drawing besides office work. One won't get much enjoyment out of life at this rate, I know well, but that don't matter: I have no right to ask for it at all events—love and work, these two things only. . . . I can't enter into politico-social subjects with any interest, for on the whole I see that things are in a muddle, and I have no power or vocation to set them right in ever so little a degree. My work is the embodiment of dreams in one form or another. . . . Yet I shall have enough to do, if I actually master this art of painting: I dare scarcely think failure possible at times, and yet I know in my mind that my chances are slender; I am glad that I am compelled to try anyhow; I was slipping off into a kind of small (very small) Palace of Art. . . . Ned and I are going to live together. I go to London early in August.

Late in the summer Street himself solved the problem by moving his office to London. Morris came up with him and in August he and BJ took rooms in Upper Gordon Street, Bloomsbury, close to Street's office in Montagu Place, to various drawing-schools (given the general name of Gandish's) near Fitzroy Square. For a while he carried on his double life, at the office by day and by night with BJ at a life-school in Newman Street. BJ described the situation:

Topsy and I live together in the quaintest room in all London, hung with brasses of old knights and drawings of Albert Dürer. We know Rossetti now as a daily friend, and we know Browning too, who is the greatest poet alive, and we know Arthur Hughes, and Woolner, and Madox Brown—Madox Brown is a lark! I asked him the other day if I wasn't very old to begin painting, and he said, 'Oh, no! there was a man I knew who began older; by the bye, he cut this throat the other day,' so I ask no more about men who begin late. Topsy will be a painter, he works hard, is prepared to wait twenty years, loves art more and more every day. He has written several poems, exceedingly dramatic—the Brownings, I hear, have spoken very highly of one that was read to them; Rossetti thinks one called 'Rapunzel' is equal to Tennyson: he is now illuminating 'Guendolen' for Georgie. . . . The Mag. is going to smash—let it go! the world is not converted and never will be. It has had stupid things in it lately. I shall not write again for it, no more will Topsy—we cannot do more than one thing at a time, and our hours are too valuable to spend so.

Georgie was Georgiana, sister of Harry Macdonald, to whom BJ had proposed in June. As he couldn't yet marry her, his engagement made no difference to his way of life. Rossetti was getting him odd jobs, but was then shown some of BJ's own designs and at once refused to let him do hack-work such as drawing his *Burd Helen* for a woodcut. Morris's remark about 'love and work, these two things only . . .' suggests that he was at least thinking that he ought to fall in love. Perhaps BJ's engagement and Rossetti's entanglement with Lizzie had made him feel this way, or he may have felt some attraction of which we know nothing. We see that he was moving towards the collection of poems in *The Defence*; but as *Rapunzel* is the only poem mentioned—one that belongs to the earlier fantasy-series rather than to the stronger line to be revealed in his first book—we cannot say how far he had developed. Certainly the example of Browning was helping him; but what he learned from him he fused with his earlier techniques and attitudes, so that he produced a new kind of verse, derived in part from old ballads, medieval poetry and romance, spasmodics like Smith, and Browning with his dramatic approach in *Men and Women*. It seems that the step he had taken in defying his mother and in facing up at last to the question of his place in the world had helped to strengthen and root his work.

At times on Saturday afternoons he and BJ ran down to Oxford to meet old friends, carrying 'the banner of Art and Revolt'. On 25 October Crom noted: 'Ted and Topsy up. To Maclaren's; single-stick with Top. With them before and after hall at Dixon's—then on to Adams' who gave us music. What a difference their coming makes!' Georgiana's young sister had been taken to meet Rossetti as a birthday treat when she was eleven. 'Morris, too, came to love the child very much, and she used to spend whole days with him and Edward in their studio, furnished by them with pencil and paints, working after her own fashion and eagerly drinking in all they said to her and to each other.' The group got together at the end of the Long Vacation, when Heeley was married in Birmingham before going out to India. Morris, BJ, Faulkner, and Fulford were there. Crom's sister Margaret wrote to her absent brother:

I had not seen Morris before; for I was out when he came down last year—I think he is the most splendid fellow! I don't at all wonder at your all loving him so, and his face is really beautiful. Fan thinks he has improved in looks very much lately. I never saw anything like his hair, it is much *greater* than ever it was before, in fact a mass of curls and waves that will soon sweep his shoulders. Edward doesn't look at all well, he is so thin and pale. Fulford was in the most noisy, quizzical humour imaginable, no one could get a word in edgeways for him, and whenever Topsy wanted to say anything he sprang into the middle of the room and flourished his fists till Fulford was silenced. Fulford talked for quite three hours without stopping excepting for Morris' flourishes.

Morris was on good terms with Street. They went together on a visit to the Low Countries in the autumn. The works of art seen there strengthened Morris in his resolve to paint; he also brought back the motto *Als Ich Kanne* of Jan Van Eyck, in the form of *Si Je Puis*. It must have been about this time then that he finished his piece of embroidery.

He and BJ had not stayed long in Upper Gordon Street when Rossetti told them that the rooms he and Deverell had once occupied at 17 Red Lion Square had fallen vacant; he took them along next day and by evening they had decided to rent the place. There were three rooms, now dusty and neglected, on the first floor, with the big one in front looking north, its windows heightened to the ceiling for use as a studio. Behind was a bedroom for BJ, and behind that another small room or powdering-closet for Morris. Here the two men lived till the spring of 1859. The tenants of the house were French feather-dressers, Fauconnier, who carried on their business below.

The removal was made in late November. BJ wrote, 'I think to see me in the midst of a removal is to behold the most abjectly pitiable sight in nature; books, boxes, boots, bedding, baskets, coats, pictures, armour, hats, easels— tumble and rumble and jumble. After all one must confess there is an unideal side to a painter's life—a remark which has received weight in the fact that an exceedingly respectable housekeeper we got has just turned in upon us in the most unequivocal state of intoxication.' Next day they were more settled. 'Topsy has had some furniture (chairs and table) made after his own design; they are as beautiful as mediaeval work, and when we have painted designs of knights and ladies upon them they will be perfect marvels.' He goes on, 'Today we are going to see Ruskin.' And later adds: 'Just come back from being with our hero for four hours—so happy we've been: he is so kind to us, calls us his dear boys and makes us feel like such old friends. To-night he comes down to our rooms to carry off my drawing and shew it to lots of people; to-morrow night he comes again, and every Thursday night the same—isn't it like a dream? think of knowing Ruskin like an equal and being called his dear boys.'

The problem of furnishing the rooms had started Morris off as a designer and decorator. When he and BJ looked round, they couldn't see anything that they wanted to buy from the shops. So Morris drew some rough designs and got a local carpenter to make the things in plain deal. There was to be a large round solid table, then a settle with a long seat below and three cup- boards above. When the two young men reached the house they found all the passages and the staircase choked with blocks of timber. 'I think the measurements had perhaps been given a little wrongly, and that it was bigger altogether than he had ever meant, but set up it was finally, and our studio was one third less in size. Rossetti came. This was always a terrifying moment to the very last. He laughed but approved.' Indeed he set to work himself. On 18 December he wrote to Allingham:

Morris is rather doing the magnificent there and is having some intensely medieval furniture made—tables and chairs like incubi and succubi. He and I have painted the back of a chair with figures and inscriptions in gules and vert and azure, and we are all three going to cover a cabinet with pictures.

A wardrobe was also made, which BJ painted with scenes from Chaucer's *Prioress's Tale* in the spring of 1857. Just before Christmas 1856 Rossetti wrote of Morris that he was quite unrivalled among moderns 'in all illumination and work of that kind'. We may note however that Morris was anticipated by BJ in making designs for manufacture. Rossetti's studio was close to the Temple and to the Whitefriars Works of Powells. The works had been classified as flintglass works and had been prevented by excise regulations, till 1845, from making window-glass. They had already in 1844 tried to get round the regulations by stamping out quarries for church-glass in iron moulds, and had drawn in as adviser Charles Winston, barrister of the Inner Temple, who had made a thorough study of stained glass and was a friend of Hardwick and Woodward, architects. Woodward was also a friend of Rossetti, and the latter drew in several artists to design for the works, including Madox Brown and BJ. In 1856-7 BJ made designs for the dining-hall of Bradfield College. Winston's book, *Ancient Glass*, had been published in 1847, and would have been known in Street's office. It discussed among other things what it called the mosaic system of glass-painting. The designs were to be built up by means of areas of pure colour, which identified themselves with the most important parts of the drawing; defined by the leading, they were to gain a maximum of effect with a minimum of shading or stippling. The book also stressed the need to recognise and use the true nature of one's material, and always to avoid in one medium the imitation of effects proper to another. This idea was prominent also in the teachings of Pugin and Ruskin, and was taken over in time by Morris.[7]

The year 1856 ended with the decease of the magazine, which had outlived its usefulness, and Morris's departure from Street's office.

5

Oxford Union and Jane Burden

Morris now had to key himself up to giving his mother another shock, a shock far worse than the previous one. An architect in her eyes might be a sad come-down from a clergyman, but an artist was a reprobate. 'With characteristic vehemence,' says Mackail, 'he did not prepare her mind for it, but announced it with a nervous suddenness while he and Burne-Jones were on a visit to Walthamstow. She never quite forgave Burne-Jones for what she naturally thought was mainly his doing.' The nervous vehemence must have resulted from the fear and revulsion with which he approached the moment of disclosure. Behind such a fear lay the whole complicated childhood-experience which we have analysed: his turning-away into a private sphere of independence, which was also the world of nature, his deep resentment at the intrusions of authority on this sphere, and the difficulty he felt at treating such intrusions in a rational way. He had taken his decision to become an artist in part no doubt because he was bored with office routine and his minor role under Street, and perhaps in part because he did not see eye to eye with Street in matters of restoration; but the main force at work was the fascination exerted by Rossetti. While he tried for a period of some two years to become a painter, he remained 'moody and irritable; brooded much by himself, and lost for the time a good deal of his old sweetness and affectionateness of manner'. Rossetti's conquest of his mind was complete. When BJ complained that the designs he made in Rossetti's style seemed better than his own, Morris replied with some passion: 'I have got beyond that: I want to imitate Gabriel as much as I can.' He and BJ carried the new gospel to Oxford where those of the group remaining were put to drawing and modelling.

They had gained an odd and delightful maid, Red Lion Mary, plain, with a strong character, an imperturbable air, and some knowledge of poetry. She cooked, mended, read their books and letters, stood behind them and watched them paint. She would have liked to act as model, and, when told she was too short, asked if she'd be any use if she stood on a stool. Rossetti at last put her in as one of the ladies when painting the Florentine meeting of Dante and Beatrice; he also drew her head and gave her the drawing when she married. She made up draperies for the models proper. Her originality, says Georgiana, 'all but equalled that of the young men, and she understood them and their ways thoroughly. Their rough and ready hospitality was seconded by her with unfailing good temper; she cheerfully spread mattresses on the floor for friends who stayed there, and when the mattresses came to an end it was said that she built up beds with boots and portmanteaux. Cleanliness, beyond the limits of the tub, was impossible in Red Lion Square, and hers was not a nature to dash itself against impossibilities.' She listened to the wild exaggerated instructions of her masters or of Rossetti, and knew exactly what it all meant. She gravely took down the notes they dictated to her, such as: 'Mr. Bogie Jones compts: to Mr. Price and begs to inform him expects to be down for Commemoration and that he hopes to meet him, he clean, well shaven, and with a contrite heart.' She also read *Reynolds' Newspaper* to BJ while he worked on Sunday mornings.

Morris' quick temper annoyed her, but she once prettily said, 'though he was so short-tempered, I seemed so necessary to him at all times, and felt myself his man Friday'.... Morris taught her to embroider his designs for hangings, and being in a fever to see how they looked, often made her bring her embroidery frame into the studio so that she might work under his direction—and many a funny conversation took place as she plied her needle and they painted. One day she being in the room, perfectly quiet, neither moving nor speaking, Morris, whose work presumably was going awry, said to her fiercely, 'Mary, be quiet—don't make that insufferable noise,' and she answered 'No, sir; I won't, sir.'

But she sometimes got her own back on him as when she put his watch forward an hour when he was off to Oxford, and 'he remembered to mention it to her' on his return. BJ records the comment: 'I shouldn't think Mr. Morris knows much about women, sir.' 'Why not, Mary?' 'I don't know, sir, but I should think he was such a bear with them.' Once he opened the door after breakfast and roared at her: 'Those six eggs were bad. I have eaten them, but don't let it occur again.' Once when Rossetti was humming a stanza from a version of an oriental legend which amused him, she came into the room; he repeated it as a direct question to her: 'Mary!—Shall the hide of a fierce lion be stretched on frame of wood for a daughter's foot to lie on, stainèd with her father's blood?' She said briskly, 'It shall if you like, sir.'

Rossetti remarked afterwards: 'That's a most remarkable girl, Ned: not one woman in ten would have given an intelligent answer like that to a question.'

Georgiana has one interesting comment about Mary. 'She could be trusted also like a good woman to shew kindness to another woman whose goodness was in abeyance, and could understand the honest goodness of a young man to such a one, and help him to feed and clothe her and get her back to her own people.' So, someone (probably Rossetti) was in the habit of bringing prostitutes in. There was a tendency to reduce the 'social question' on the part of Pre-Raphaelites and others to the question of the fallen woman. Rossetti, after he had taken to picking wenches up, started his never-finished *Found*, with the street-girl discovered in London by the rustic lover of her innocent days, using his own pick-up, Fanny Cornforth, for the model; and the importance of the theme for the Pre-Raphaelites was shown by the long controversy as to who had first got the idea. Rossetti also used the theme in his poem *Jenny*, and Hunt in his painting, *The Awakened Conscience*, in which, with unintended irony, he used his own mistress for the anguished woman.[1]

We hear of Morris rubbing his back against a door like a sheep when bored. To fill in time he had taken up both illuminating and wood-carving. 'I can still see in my mind's eye the long, folded white evening tie which he nailed in loops against his bedroom wall in order to hold his tools.' In June Rossetti mentioned in a letter to Scott that Morris was on his first picture in oils, its theme the recognition of Tristram by the dog in Mark's palace; but he may have been merely wanting to impress the sceptical Scott with the worth of his young friends, and the work may have been only a sketch.

Holidays were generally spent in the Zoological Gardens, Regents Park. Again we see the influence of Rossetti, for whom, as for Christina, the zoo had been a refuge in childhood, leaving him with the desire to collect birds and beasts. Morris liked the big birds, and he used to imitate an eagle, climbing on to a chair, and after a sullen pause coming down with a soft heavy plop. For a while an owl was kept in the Red Lion rooms, despite a feud between it and Rossetti. Evenings often saw the trio at the theatre, watching Robson at the Olympic or Kean at the Princess's in his Shakespearian series (March to July). Morris enjoyed *Richard II* in which there was a dance with medieval music. This was the first early music of a secular kind that he heard. Finally there was the talking from midnight to early morning hours in Rossetti's rooms. We hear nothing of the relation of Lizzie to Morris and BJ at this phase.

Ruskin often visited Red Lion Square. When he first called, he was shown in to BJ (presumably by Mary) with the introduction, 'Your father, sir.' Ruskin had tried to patch things up with Rossetti and Lizzie, but was soon estranged more than ever; in June Lizzie gave up her pension, probably too ill to work and feeling more hostile than ever to Rossetti. In the early Long Vacation Morris went with Rossetti down to Oxford, where the latter wanted to see Benjamin Woodward. A long struggle had been going on as to whether Palladian or Gothic styles should be used for the new university museum, with Gothic at last winning. Woodward's plans, in a style of mixed Rheinish and Venetian Gothic, were now being put into action, and he was also at work on a debating hall for the Union society. This hall, octagonal with apsidal ends, had a narrow gallery all round for books; above the shelves a broad belt of wall was divided into ten bays, pierced by twenty six-foil circular windows and surmounted by an open timber roof. Rossetti got the idea of painting the open space, and Woodward agreed that it should be covered with tempera. He seems to have been talked into the project; Ruskin described him as 'the stillest creature that ever breathed out of an oyster shell'. (Ruskin, before Morris, believed that a designer should be able to carry out practically his own ideas; he built a brickwork column in the museum, though it had later to be redone by ordinary bricklayers. 'Half my power of ascertaining facts of any kind connected with the arts is my stern habit of doing the thing with my own hands till I know its difficulty.' But this stern habit was only carried out very partially.)[2]

Rossetti set to work mobilising his painters. BJ and Morris, then Arthur Hughes, Hungerford Pollen, Spencer Stanhope, Valentine Prinsep, with sculptor Alexander Munro, who was to do a stone relief, after Rossetti's design, for the tympanum over the doorway. When Rossetti called at Little Holland House, Prinsep pleaded inexperience and was told, 'Nonsense, there's a man I know who's never painted anything—his name is Morris— he has undertaken one of the panels and he will do something good you may depend—so you had better come.' Many doubted. Watts gave sardonic advice to Prinsep; Stanhope, knowing Rossetti and his blank ignorance of fresco or any sort of mural painting, prophesied failure. Rossetti on his part made not the least effort to learn anything of the problems involved or to consult someone who knew.

Morris in his enthusiasm was the first to start. BJ put aside his *Blessed Damozel* and joined in. By mid-August the troop were at work, though the surface had not been prepared and the paint went straight on to whitewashed brick, not damp-proof and with the mortar hardly dry. The brick-edges caught the flaking dust; the paint sank in or fell off. Also the dazzle through the windows, two to a bay, was liable to make anything painted almost impossible to distinguish from below. The hall was lit by gasflames in big chandeliers; the smoke and soot went at once on to the paintings. But, says BJ, 'we had no misgivings'; when Rossetti willed a thing, 'it had to be done'.

Morris had taken rooms in 87 High Street, opposite Queen's College; but when the October term began he moved to George Street. The agreement was that the artists would give their work free while the Union paid the cost of lodgings and material (without any idea what that would entail). Indeed the work seems to have started without proper sanction. The question was raised on 27 October, when the treasurer, Charles Bowen of Balliol, admitted irregularity and the subject was let drop. A week later an unanimous motion thanked 'the gentlemen who have kindly and liberally undertaken to decorate the new building', and expressed 'appreciation of the valuable works of art in course of completion'. Rossetti and Hughes were named as at work 'with some of their friends'. Later in term the whole troop were elected honorary members and a loan of £350 sanctioned to meet the cost of the work.

Morris chose the theme of the despised lover: 'How Sir Palomydes loved La Belle Iseult with exceeding great love out of measure, and how she loved not him again but Sir Tristram.' We see again the Emma-motif. Mackail remarks: 'The subject was one for which he felt a singular and almost a morbid attraction, that of the unsuccessful man and despised lover. The motive was the same which he had treated in prose a year before (in *Frank's Sealed Letter*), with many details which were taken directly from his own life.' There was a profusion of flowers in part of the foreground, and Rossetti suggested sarcastically that he should help one of the others out of his difficulties by filling his foreground up with scarlet runners. Despite his inexperience Morris finished first and then turned to the roof, making his design in one day and surprising them all with its beauty and fitness. For the rest of the autumn he worked at the roof over the heads of the others, doing most of the decoration with his own hands. Rossetti's theme, like Morris's, expressed something deep about himself, about his relations with Lizzie (his soul-mate, his Beatrice). His own words for it ran: 'Sir Lancelot prevented by his sin from entering the chapel of the San Grail. He has fallen asleep before the shrine full of angels, and, between him and it, rises in his dream the image of Queen Guenevere, the cause of all. She stands gazing at him with her arms extended in the branches of an apple-tree': a sort of

Eve-Christ. BJ was doing a picture of Nimue luring Merlin, which expressed well enough his fear of sex as a dangerous enchantment, defeating the magician-artist.

The proportions of Morris's picture were odd; the figures were fourteen feet high, with big heads and shoulders coming up above the sunflowers. Rossetti said his Iseult was ugly and sent him to make sketches of a local beauty. The mother refused to let him near her daughter, and on his gloomy return the others welcomed him with a couplet: 'Poor Topsy has gone to make a sketch of Miss Lipscombe, But he can't draw the head, and don't know where the hips come.' Once when he was working clotted with paint in the hall, an intruding don asked him, 'My good man, can you tell me the subject of these pictures?' Morris glared at him through tempera-splashed spectacles. '*Morte d'Arthur!*' he shouted, climbed up a ladder, and was lost to sight amid the tangle of scaffolding.

Val Prinsep later wrote down the whole amusing experience. When he arrived in Oxford he told the cabman to drive him to the Union and was taken to a workhouse. Rossetti invited him to his rooms for the first evening and he punctually turned up.

There I found Rossetti in a plum-coloured frockcoat, and a short square man with spectacles and a vast mop of dark hair. I was cordially received. 'Top,' cried Rossetti, 'let me introduce Van Prinsep.'

'Glad, I'm sure,' answered the man in spectacles, nodding his head, and then he resumed his reading of a large quarto. This was William Morris. Soon after, the door opened, and before it was half opened in glided Burne-Jones. 'Ned,' said Rossetti, who had been absently humming to himself, 'I think you know Prinsep.' The shy figure started forward, the shy face lit up, and I was received with the kindly effusion which was natural to him.

When dinner was over, Rossetti, humming to himself as was his wont, rose from the table and proceeded to curl himself up on the sofa. 'Top,' he said, 'read us one of your grinds.' 'No, Gabriel,' answered Morris, 'you have heard them all.' 'Never mind,' said Rossetti, 'here's Prinsep who has never heard them, and besides, they are devilish good.' 'Very well, old chap,' growled Morris, and having got his book he began to read in a sing-song chant some of the poems afterwards published in his first volume. All the time, he was jiggling about nervously with his watch chain. I was then a very young man and my experience of life was therefore limited, but the effect produced on my mind was so strong that to this day, forty years after, I can still recall the scene: Rossetti on the sofa with large melancholy eyes fixed on Morris, the poet at the table reading and fidgetting with his watch chain, and Burne-Jones working at a pen-and-ink drawing.

He noted as particularly striking the stanzas beginning, 'Gold on her head, and gold on her feet', and 'Swerve to the left, son Roger, he said'. And he adds, 'I confess I returned to the Mitre with my brain in a whirl.' Prinsep himself, strongly built with short fluffy hair, was over six feet tall, aged nineteen. Once he picked BJ up under one arm and carried him up a ladder to the gallery where he painted. The few survivors of the old set joined in the fun, together with new recruits, for instance Birkbeck Hill and Swinburne of Balliol. The latter became so attached that BJ said, 'Now we were four in company and not three.' If they needed models, they sat for one another. Prinsep says that the windows in the painted area were whitened to tone down the light; and the glass was covered with sketches mainly of wombats; 'delightful creature', said Rossetti, 'the most comical little beast'. There were endless jokes amid the popping of soda-water bottles ordered from the Star Hotel on the Union's account. As BJ posed as a knight, Stanhope poured a bucket of dirty water on him from a gallery; BJ poured another on Rossetti as he read a newspaper, saying that he thought he had armour on, though in fact he wore only the helmet together with his usual clothes. In the dark angles of the roof, instead of flowers, they painted little figures of Morris with his legs straddled out as in portraits of Henry VIII to warn him of his fatness.

At some date in October Morris met Jane Burden. After the day's work he, BJ, and Rossetti had gone to the Oxford Theatre. They sat behind two girls, Jane and Elizabeth, daughters of Robert Burden of 65 Holywell Street. (Hughes also was there, says the BJ account, which puts Jane in a box above the artists.) In an effort to make the family respectable, Burden was later described as a livery stable-keeper; but someone who knew him told Mackail that Jane was 'daughter of one of Simmonds' men at the stables in Holywell'. Rossetti, who had long worked out the technique of picking up girls in the character of an artist professionally admiring their charms, talked to the two Burden girls, attracted especially by the elder one, Jane. After some discussions Jane agreed to sit for him and his friends, and she did so while work at the Union went on. She was a tall, large-boned girl with pale ivory face, thick eyebrows, a tower-neck, and much curly black hair. Some people thought she must have gipsy blood, but it has been argued that she was of Cotswold stock going back to pre-Celtic days. Morris made a pencil study of her head and drew her as Iseult on the ship and also as Guenevere.

He was much attracted by her and saw her as an incarnation of medieval beauty; but in doing so he must have been much influenced by Rossetti's conception of that beauty and his comments on her. Once having gained the conviction that she was the perfect image of Iseult-Guenevere, he would have been awed by the difficult silence with which she surrounded herself, probably not because it expressed her own nature, but because she needed it as the only possible defence against the strange gang of admirers now besetting her with compliments. She must have felt wholly out of her depth and had to use all her wits to find a footing in the new world that had opened up incredibly before her. It says much for her native intelligence that she so soon fitted in and was able to hold her own. Though she does not come up clearly into view for a couple of years there is no evidence of gaucheries on her part despite what must have been an almost total lack of education and the sordid milieu of her upbringing. Lizzie, arriving out of the even worse environment of the Elephant and Castle, is another example of a remarkable adaptation of a Victorian working-class girl to the world of middle-class art. Clearly both she and Jane felt the strain, but they expressed it in different ways.

Crom's diary gives no hint of Jane's entry into the world of the artists:

Oct. 17 [day after term started]. Breakfasted with Top at Johnson's in George Street. Rossetti, Hughes, Prinsep, Ted, and Coventry Patmore there. To the Union to see the frescoes. Oct. 18. To Rossetti's—R. painting the Marriage of St. George. Prinsep there; six feet one, 15 stone, not fat, well-built, hair like finest wire, short, curly and seamless—age only 19. Stood for Top for two hours in a dalmatic. Oct. 24. Spent afternoon in daubing in black lines on the Union roof for Topsy. Whist in the evening as usual (at Rossetti's). Oct. 30. Evening at George Street. Rossetti, Ted, Topsy, Hughes, Swan. Faulkner, Bowen of Balliol, Bennet of Univ., Munro, Hill, Prinsep and Stanhope there. Topsy read his grind on Lancelot and Guenevere—very grand. Oct. 31. Stippled and blacklined at Union. Evening at George Street· Rossetti and I versus Top and Faulkner at whist. Madox Brown turned up. Rossetti said that Topsy had the greatest capacity for producing and annexing dirt of any man he had ever met with. Nov. 1. To Hill's, where were Topsy, Ted, Swan, Hatch, Swinburne of Balliol (introduced I think by Hatch) and Faulkner.

About this time Morris went off for a day or two to see the Art Treasures Exhibition in Manchester, staying with Dixon. What interested him were the carved ivories. During his stay he painted a water-colour, *The Soldan's Daughter in the Palace of Glass*, and wrote the poem, *Praise of My Lady*, which we may take to represent his first adoring reactions to Jane Burden.

'My lady seems of ivory'—though he calls her hair yellow, thick, and crisped, not dark. When he and Dixon drove to the station for his departure, they found they had made a mistake; there was no train. 'There was nothing for it but to wait till next day. I was made aware of this by a fearful cry in my ears, and saw Morris "translated": it lasted all the way home; it then vanished in a moment; he was as calm as if it had never been, and began painting in water-colours.' At the Exhibition Ruskin gave his first talks on socialism, *The Political Economy of Art*, published as *A Joy for Ever and its Price in the Market*; but there is no sign that Morris at this Rossetti-dominated phase was at all interested.

We saw the poet Patmore as one of the visitors; he admired Rossetti's colour and wrote a eulogy in the *Saturday Review* at Christmas. Ruskin came a fortnight after Patmore and also expressed pleasure. Madox Brown liked the convivial atmosphere. 'All very jolly here,' he wrote to his Emma at one a.m., but was too hard-up to accept the invitation to stay and help. Hunt too came to have a look at the hall. Now and then Rossetti had to go back to London for a while through pressure of other work as well as worries about Lizzie. He seems soon to have lost interest in the wall-paintings. Prinsep says that while the others worked hard, he never saw Rossetti do more than half an hour's work at his picture all the time.

Morris hated normal social occasions and had to keep on evading the hospitality of Ruskin's friend Dr Acland (nicknamed The Rose of Brazil). Once he sent BJ with apologies that he was ill. Acland at once went round to his rooms and found him eating with Faulkner and playing cribbage at the same time. Morris said that he had recovered, and Acland carried him off. At one dinner-party in George Street Prinsep somehow offended Morris, who, with a tremendous effort of self-control, merely bit his four-pronged fork, leaving it crushed and twisted about. Once when he, Rossetti and Prinsep set off for Christ Church, Rossetti rebuked him for not wearing dress-clothes. Morris borrowed some and rushed along to catch the others up. Rossetti turned on him as he came up and shouted, 'Look at your hair!' On his dark mop was a dab of blue paint. Morris said meekly that he'd go to Faulkner's and get it off. But when they all arrived at Christ Church, Prinsep was amused to see that Rossetti had absent-mindedly worn his old plum-coloured frockcoat and was himself not at all free from paint; but he discreetly said nothing. Crom's sister records Morris turning up on a Sunday night. 'And his hair was so long and he looked so wild that the servant who opened the door would not let him in, thinking he was a burglar.'[3]

The struggle of tackling a large mural space with design and paint, followed by the work on the roof, released something in Morris. No longer restricted to Rossettian schemes of drawing and of easel-painting, he set about work in other fields with more confidence than he had previously shown. He carved a block into a capital of foliage and birds, which Hughes admired; he modelled from clay; he drew and coloured designs for stained glass windows. Crom sat for a clay head; but whenever Morris grew impatient, he smashed it up, so that it was never finished. While he was carving, a splinter struck him in the eye, 'and his language to Dr. Acland, who was called in to look after the injury, was even for him unequalled in force and copiousness'. Also he was writing poems, and if we may judge from Crom's diary, he now entered the full control of his early method. A letter of late 1857 or early 1858 shows Ruskin recommending him to the Keeper of Manuscripts at the British Museum as an illuminator. His 'gift for illumination is I believe as great as any thirteenth-century draughtsman'.

For the models used in the wall-paintings he designed a basinet and a 'great surcoat of ringed mail with a hood of mail and the skirt coming below the knees'. He visited the forge daily, and the encounters with the smith (says BJ) were 'always stubborn and angry as far as I could see'. One afternoon Morris put on the completed basinet. The visor failed to lift, and he bellowed and jumped about in blind fury. When the mailcoat came, he dined in it. The smith also made a sword.

There was much of the adolescent horseplay that the group could not resist. In the morning Rossetti and Pollen used to turn up at eight a.m. to torment BJ and Morris as they lay abed. In a letter BJ tells how he means to cheat them by getting up early. Usually they came 'to ridicule me—and laugh at me, my dear—point the finger of scorn at me, address me by opprobrious names, and finally tear blankets and counterpanes and mattresses and all the other things that cover me, from my enfeebled grasp, and so leave me, to do the same to Topsy'. Rossetti and BJ continually drew caricatures of Morris, who joined in the laughs. Among the themes were his fatness and his chain-fiddling.

On 14 November Crom noted that Rossetti had been called away to Matlock to see Lizzie, who had gone there for a water-cure. She had perhaps heard of Jane and decided on a strategy of illness to draw Rossetti away, while Rossetti may well have been pleased to find a good excuse for leaving the Union. In November too BJ finished his painting and returned exhausted and ill to Red Lion Square, where he lived for the most part on his own till the spring, though he kept visiting Oxford and Morris came almost weekly to London. Jane must have been the main attraction keeping Morris at Oxford.

An amusing anonymous satire on the Union paintings was published late in 1857. The writer has been inspired by a satire on the Pre-Raphaelites composed by one of the superintendents of the Manchester Exhibition: J. B. Waring, who signed himself Tennyson Longfellow Smith. He took part of his title from one of the Manchester guide-books, and he borrowed Waring's way of referring to Ruskin as Mr Buskin. His title ran: *A Peep at the Pictures, and a Catalogue of the Principal Objects of Attraction in the Room of the Oxford Union Society; being an explanation of the gallery of painting, shortly to be opened to the public, with hints for designs suitable to the spaces as yet unoccupied.* He thus described the roof in verse printed as prose:

Here gleams the dragon in the air, there roams a dancing bear; here crocodiles in scaly coats make love to birds with purple throats; and there in vests of brightest green rhinoceroses large are seen; while winking with their weather eye, roll round red hippopotami; and kindly lent in great variety by the Entomological Society blue bees, which honeyed words their trade is, pay court to gray opossum ladies, where mammoth beasts with mammoth wants are kindly fed by ring-tailed ants, while unaccoutred peacocks sing, Mr. B. proffers honey but bears a sting; a black-legged beetle on the turf, a shipwrecked p[h]easant on the surf [serf], a female—blue—without a book, and 'à la Mr. T. P. Cooke', a British lion, and Houndsditch beagle hobnobbing with a Russian eagle, or perched on wings of yellow hue, with eyes of pink, and teeth of blue, protectress of the Union's byrth, a Circe soars 'twixt heaven and earth. . . .[4]

Cooke was an actor in melodrama, known for violently chauvinistic roles. Rossetti, we are told, was infuriated at the satire.

6

Marriage and Red House

In January Rossetti in a letter to Brown mentioned that his patron Plint of Leeds had been in his studio and 'bought Topsy's picture for £75'. Rossetti, who liked bargaining for both himself and his friends, did the negotiating. The picture however was still unfinished when Plint died in 1861; it is now lost, but a pencil study is known. Its theme was Tristram and Iseult, and it has often been confused with the portrait of Jane originally called *Queen Guenevere* (later *La Belle Iseult*). Calling in at Red Lion Square this month, Brown saw BJ and Morris with 'Fanny their model'. Fanny Cornforth here first appears on the scene.

By the spring of 1858 six of the wall-paintings were finished; but after March no more work was done on the project, which had been deserted by its promoter, Rossetti. That month there was published *The Defence of Guenevere* by Morris, printed at the Chiswick Press where four years before the revised Basle type, cut by William Howard, had been used. The book sold badly; Bell and Dalby still had copies years later when they moved to York Street, Covent Garden, and published *Jason*. The dedication ran: 'To my Friend Dante Gabriel Rossetti Painter I dedicate these poems.' *The Spectator* spoke of Morris combining 'the mawkish simplicity of the Cockney school with the prosaic baldness of the worst passages of Tennyson, and the occasional obscurity and affectation of plainness that characterises Browning and his followers'. The *Athenaeum* remarked :'We must call attention to his book of Pre-Raphaelite minstrelsy as to a curiosity which shows how affectation may mislead an earnest man towards the fog-land of Art.' The *Saturday Review* saw the book as Pre-Raphaelite with men and things 'not like anything we ever saw, except in illuminations; but they might, when they did exist, be like Mr. Morris's delineations. Only it is a mercy to have got rid of them.' There were a few friendly notices. *The Tablet* saw 'amazing variety' and 'power everywhere'. Richard Garnett in the *Literary Gazette*, in an unsigned review, saw the link with Rossetti and Browning, but found the writing at times careless, obscure, and affected.

Some individuals realised the merits. J. H. Shorthouse in a lecture at Birmingham, in July 1859, recognised 'the most wonderful reproduction of the tone of thought and feeling of a past age that has been achieved'. Swinburne wrote his admiring views to a friend, who must have objected; for in his next letter he promised to avoid Topsification. Woolner saw 'original ideas and an extraordinary power of entering the far-back old knightly way of looking at things', and Ruskin wrote to Browning that the poems were 'most noble—very, very great indeed—in their own peculiar way'. Browning himself said later that the volume had been his delight ever since he first read it.

The public response then was for the most part hostile or bored. Part of the dislike no doubt came from the association with Rossetti and the Pre-Raphaelites. Morris gained, and never lost, a very low opinion of professional critics. 'To think of a beggar making a living by selling his opinion about other people! and fancy any one paying him for it!' There was indeed a link with Rossetti in some of the poems, and Morris at this time was commissioning water-colours from him: *Burd Ellayne* (heroine of his ballad *Welland River*), *The Tune of the Seven Towers*, *Arthur's Tomb*, and *The Wedding of St George*. Rossetti told Norton in 1858, 'These chivalric, Froissartian themes are quite a passion of mine.' And to Allingham earlier in the year, speaking of *The Blue Closet* (directly based on a water-colour), he added, 'Morris's facility in poeticising puts me in a rage. He has only been writing at all for little more than a year, I believe, and has already poetry enough for a big book.' (Morris of course had been writing for some years.)

But it was the weaker side of the poems that looked to Rossetti. The core was highly original. What matters for Morris is the degree of intensity to which he enters into the life of his medieval characters. He creates a new form, which is at once the climax of the romantic idiom and the transformation into its opposite. The romantic vision, reviving what Keats might call the very 'feel' of medieval life, is merged with a sharp emotional realism. The diction is often archaic, yet its effect is of a casual direct speech wrung-out at the height of an experience that reaches to the depths. The words have almost a stammering slow force as if each of them is being searched for, all but lost, then brought doggedly out. A naïve energy, half-unconscious of itself, is driven by the desperate dramatic moment to fight in a sort of joyous agony for the releasing truth, against a fierce current of resistances. To read these poems aright we must almost give up all the associations of image and rhythm with which we approach poetry, and spell them out with a slow equalising accent—or as near as we can get to that while preserving rhythmic organisation. The inner stress is so acute that the metre gains its particular quality through a faltering meditative intensity, not by any strong intrusion of beat. And this strange tranced energy, with its ignorance of elision and its heaping-up of monosyllables seemed oddly rudimentary to Swinburne. Take the opening lines of the title-poem as an example:

> But knowing now that they would have her speak,
> She threw her wet hair backward from her brow,
> Her hand close to her mouth touching her cheek,
> As though she had had there a shameful blow,
> And feeling it shameful to feel aught but shame
> All through her heart, yet felt her cheek burned so,
> She must a little touch it; like one lame,
> She walked away from Gawaine, with her head
> Still lifted up; and on her cheek of flame
> The tears dried quick; she stopped at last and said:
> 'O knights and lords, it seems but little skill
> To talk of well-known things past now and dead.
> God wot I ought to say, I have done ill. . . .'

Sixty-five iambs and a hundred and twenty words. The inner stress compels the pace and sets the subtle rhythmic curve, with its faint rubato tensions, its long slow swell of passion, suffering, joy. Both the Shakespearian and Miltonic bases are ignored, forgotten, and a new start is gained, which owes something to Morris's love of medieval verse, but is essentially his own creation. Consider the apparent awkwardness of the repetitions: 'Feeling . . . feel . . . felt', or the inner assonances, 'lame . . . away . . . Gawaine'. Try to read, say, 'As though she had had there a shameful blow', according to any previous metrical systems and the words are intolerably clumsy. Read them with a proper wondering weakening of stresses, and they become richly evocative, making us feel the immediate sense of shame, the fever, of Guenevere herself. That is why despite archaisms and moments of conventional diction, these poems mark as definite a crisis in poetic form as the work of Hopkins. They look, in their essential structure, towards the future, not towards the medieval world. Both Morris and Hopkins, in their revulsion against existing society and its forms of expression, turned to medieval bases. Hopkins sought to regenerate the deadened and falsified forms by exploding within the iambic structure the dipodic system of *Piers Plowman* and the dynamic equivalences of his sprung-rhythm; Morris, by discarding post-medieval accretions and relying upon an inturned dramatic urgency.

But even such a radically new turn is sure to have some contemporary roots. I have already pointed out the link of a poem like *Kisses* with the triplets of Alexander Smith. In the same way Smith, in his varied experiments with blank verse, was often feeling for the peculiar simplicity which Morris achieved:

> Could you not find a home within her heart?
> No, no, you are too cold, you never loved.
> —There's nothing colder than a desolate hearth.
> —A desolate hearth! did fire leap on it once.

That is not Yeats, born out of Morris; it is Smith.

The best poems of *The Defence* are those dealing with moments of deep choice, emotional crisis. Guenevere, guilty, facing her accusers and vindicating the triumphant spirit of life that has uttered itself through her; the trapped lovers of the haystack in the floods; Sir Peter Harpdon facing his bitter end; Lancelot and Guenevere meeting in anguish over Arthur's tomb. Treachery, violence, and the defeat of love: there is no idealisation of medieval life here. Rather, we see the poet seeking to bring together what he feels to be the good of that life, its direct and concrete forms of expression, and the inner flaws of division, greed, hate, deceit, which wreck that life. Hence the emotional depth of the poems, the peculiar power by which they live in their own strange yet fully realised moment of space and time, the way in which their Guenevere is the most rounded and convincing image of the queen in all literature. In *The Defence* Morris grasps as a single aspect of her being her guilt and her innocence, her adultery and her single-hearted acceptance of love, so that she mingles an agonised sense of sin with a defiant delight in her deeds, an impulse to confess with an inability to resist the impulse to make the confession a further seductive flaunting of her beauty. And in both her fear and her flaunting there is an all-enveloping naïve conviction of the glory of life that has irresistibly spoken through her.

Morris is able to achieve his new form because his struggle to achieve an imaginative comprehension of medieval life is also a struggle to achieve a way of life in which the medieval values are raised to a new level. In the last resort the poems are not 'literature' but a necessary aspect of the struggle to integrate a new way of life, a new concept of human wholeness. That is why, far as Morris was from any clear views of social and political struggle in 1857–8, his poems already imply the lines on which he will advance.

At the same time we see the Emma-image raised to a new level, partly through Morris's whole development in the Oxford years, partly through his wondering love of Janey. Guenevere, loved by both Lancelot and Arthur and in her strange passionate way faithful in her responses to each man, is Emma-Janey realised in a way that expresses the deep crisis in Morris himself. After a long period of preparation he feels himself driven out into the open, facing a largely unrealised world with his many and complex impulses and energies, unsure of his direction except in so far as he feels the truth of the Ruskinian evangel of joyous work and an allegiance to the systems that beget such work. Yet aware of fettered forces inside himself, and of a harshly inhibiting and enclosing world, which he can grasp only in moments of blind fury or of poetic exaltation. Now he has re-created the Emma-image in terms of Janey. What does that imply for the future? He could not have bluntly asked himself such a question, but he must have felt its pressure in many trepidations, doubts, anxieties.[1]

How far was Rossetti, the future Lancelot to Morris's Arthur, as yet implicated in the situation? No doubt he had been much attracted to Janey as he was to any woman in whom he could imagine his Beatrice incarnated. But he could have been in Oxford near her only for a few weeks before he was called off to Matlock. His later idea that he had been in love with her from the start must have been a fantasy aimed at justifying his treatment of Morris. In May 1858, after his return from Matlock, he was much taken up with persuading the actress Ruth Herbert (Mrs Crabb) to sit for him. She too was tall, but with pale gold hair and ethereal looks to which he paid homage by inscribing round a picture of her: 'Beatrice Helen Guinevere Herbert'.

By February 1858 Morris must have been laying siege to Janey; for on the 17th Swinburne wrote that he liked to think of him 'having that wonderful and most perfect stunner of his to—look at or speak to. The idea of his marrying her is insane. To kiss her feet is the utmost men should dream of doing.' The publication of his poems may have nerved him to propose. What is strange is that neither in Mackail nor in any other source do we hear a word more of her father, while of her mother we know nothing at all. May Morris is silent on her mother's origins. The sister Elizabeth turns up now and then as an embroiderer working for the firm and living with the Morrises in Queen Square. Morris could not bear her. 'She is an accidental person with whom I have nothing to do.' He was alone with her in November 1872, and calls her Poor Bessy. 'I must say it is a shame, she is quite harmless and even good, and one ought not to be irritated with her—but O my God what I have suffered from finding [her] always there at meals and the like!' However, he left her a yearly income of £150. One gathers that she quite lacked Janey's remarkable presence and her feline tact.

The inscription on Rossetti's first pencil study of Janey gives us her age at the time of her encounter with the artists: '*J.B. Aetat. XVII, D.G.R. Oxoniae primo delt. Oct. 1857.*' Prinsep says that Morris's way of wooing her was to sit reading *Barnaby Rudge* to her for hours, while she presumably thought of other things. No doubt she was pleased at such behaviour, which testified to Morris's respect for her. He was attractive to women; we have seen girls like Crom's sisters admiring him with much interest. But we have also seen how Georgiana noted his inability to look at her. Clearly he was rather frightened of girls as such. Not that his personal difficulties came up only with the other sex. Friends observed throughout his life his curious mixture of strong emotional attachment with an element of withdrawal, of *noli me tangere*. While the relationship remained at the level of fun and games, or of serious intellectual argument, he was at ease; what put him out was the problem of a direct and admitted personal relationship. For such a man to speak of love and to maintain a close intimate give-and-take would be excruciatingly hard. He could scarcely have chosen anyone less suitable than a girl like Janey, with her own difficult set of problems. On the other hand he would have found it almost impossible to fall in love with a middle-class girl expecting the conventional responses and reactions. Janey had the virtue of being a working-class girl and yet seeming a remote medieval figure, who could have been a queen. So he could build his fantasy-life afresh around her, withdrawn from all middle-class calculations and constructing his own private island, garden, hall. But the terms of this fantasy-system, satisfying for a while, ensured that the construction would break down after enough strains had come upon it. Cockerell later wrote of Janey: 'She had a charming, unaffected nature and was as responsive to fun as any child.' And Graham Robertson remarked, perhaps with much insight:

I fancy that her mystic beauty must sometimes have weighed rather heavily upon her. Her mind was not formed upon the same tragic lines as her face; she was very simple and could have enjoyed simple pleasures with simple people, but such delights were not for her. She looked like the Delphic Sibyl and had to behave as such. She was Ladye in a Bower, an ensorcelled Princess, a Blessed Damozel, while I feel sure she would have preferred to be a 'bright, chatty, little woman' in request for small theatre parties and afternoons up the river.

If this viewpoint is correct, she was trapped by Morris in a relationship that could not work out happily. Having taken on all the Pre-Raphaelite trappings as a proof of her right to enter the strange and elect world, which must have excited and exalted her incalculably, she could not unbend without seeming to abdicate from that world. Her simpler self could not find the point of contact with the simpler side of Morris, so that they might both meet frankly in the enjoyments that they wanted.

Early in the summer Morris told BJ of the engagement, 'and they both realised that the old days were now at an end'. BJ had fallen badly ill about the time of *The Defence*'s publication. He was carried off by Mrs Prinsep, always kind to artists, to Little Holland House, where he stayed much of the year. Rossetti disapproved of the place as low and liable to harm BJ's health; Morris, because he hated the fashionable world with artistic pretensions. But BJ enjoyed his stay. In June Bell Scott saw the Union paintings and spoke of them as already much defaced. Of Morris's work only Tristram's head above the sunflowers was at all clear. From now on the paintings grew steadily worse.

Red Lion Square remained Morris's London lodgings, but he was mostly at Oxford, in his rooms there or at Summertown with the Maclarens. He still painted hard but with little satisfaction. The Maclarens long recalled the hole he dug in the orchard by wriggling his chair about as he sat at his easel, as well as the power of language he revealed when a gust blew his canvas upside down. At Little Holland House he drew the tree over the garden pond. To his friends he read out Froissart, Monstrelet, Malory. A party he gave with BJ at Red Lion Square is evoked by the invitation to Brown: 'Come tonight and see the chair'—probably the one with a box over it in which Rossetti suggested keeping owls: 'there's a chair, old fellow— such a chair!!!!!! Gabriel and Top hook it tomorrow, so do come. Hughes will come, and a Stunner or two to make melody. Come soon, there's a nice old chap—victuals and squalor at all hours, but come at 6.' A piano was borrowed or hired, and old French songs from Wekerlin's *Echos du Temps Passé* were sung.

We should like to know more of the Stunners who frequented such parties; probably they were the latest models, provided by Rossetti. They certainly did not include girls like Georgiana or Janey. Georgiana gives us an idealised version of the young men:

I wish it were possible to explain the impression made upon me as a young girl, whose experience so far had been quite remote from art, by sudden and close intercourse with those to whom it was the breath of life. The only approach I can make to describing it is by saying that I felt in the presence of a new religion. Their love of beauty did not seem to me unbalanced, but as if it included the whole world and raised the point from which they regarded everything. Human beauty especially was in a way sacred to them, I thought; and of this I received confirmation from a lady whom I had not seen for many years, and who had been in her youth an object of wild enthusiasm and admiration to Rossetti, Morris and Edward. She and I sat and talked for an hour about them and the days when we were all young, and I found that she kept the same feeling that I do about that time—that the men were as good as they were gifted, and unlike any others that we knew. . . . 'I never saw such men,' she said; 'it was being in a new world to be with them. I sat to them and was there with them, and they were different from anyone else I knew. And I was a holy thing to them—I was a holy thing to them.'

There is much truth in the statement, but it points to a callow element which, especially in the case of Rossetti, led to a deep split in the self between the Beatrice-image of the soul-mate (essentially a narcissistic image of oneself as woman) and the real world. The conflict tore Rossetti to pieces; it inhibited BJ's development; and it held Morris in its grip for many years. When he did outgrow it, he was however saddled with a marriage, brought about in the idealising days, which he could not harmonise with his new and more integrated self.

BJ had taken part in the formation of a Hogarth Club (not the same as the later one of that name). 'Stanhope and I thought it would be nice to have a club where we could chatter. But what a mistake I made.' The choice of the name shows that there was still a strong respect for realism among many of the artists drawn around the Pre-Raphaelite idea. The first meeting was in July 1858; the club ended in 1861. It held only two or three shows, to which Rossetti contributed; admission was by card only.[2]

This year, 1858, was that in which Morris truly began as a craftsman. Our image of him as ceaselessly engaged in craft-activity of some sort is so strong that we have to make an effort to realise it was not till 1856 he started at all to find a use for his restless hands. The influence that thus gave an essential release to his creative energies was that of Rossetti. (I assume that Janey was a year out in what she says of his interest in embroidery; she was speaking after his death of a period when she did not yet know him.) Under Street he began attempting to make architectural drawings, but without much success. When he and BJ wanted their own kind of furniture for Red Lion

Square they merely handed some designs or drawings over to a carpenter; and we may conjecture that the more experienced BJ was the one who took the lead. Morris first began seriously using his hands when he obeyed Rossetti and tried to paint; but once he had begun, he was soon able to extend the range of his craft-activities. Turning from the wall-painting at the Union, he found himself at home in making designs for the roof; he designed armour and launched himself into modelling and other craftwork. At last he had found that he was more than a poet, and the Ruskinian message about craft-activities took on a new meaning, far more urgent and concrete. No doubt he began illuminations as soon as he took to drawing and painting, and his aptitude was so great that in a very short time he was a master of the art. If in the earlier years at Oxford he had gone in for any other craftwork than brass-rubbing, we can be sure that we would have heard of it from BJ, Crom, Dixon, or one of the others around him. We must assume then that it was the years 1856–8 which decisively opened the great new fields for his inventive energies. And this fact helps us better to understand why for some years he was now wrapped up in the problems of extending his craft-work and finding its applications.

In August Morris, Webb and Faulkner went for a trip in northern France. They sent a boat over from Oxford and rowed down the Seine from Paris to Rouen. They saw Abbéville on the 17th and Amiens next day. There, aloft in the cathedral tower, Morris spilt out the sovereigns from the satchel where he kept them. Webb says: 'I had to stop them running out of the gargoyles by putting my foot on them.' Then, while the other two were up in the galleries, Morris sat making a drawing in the choir. 'Looking down, we saw him have a struggle with himself and suddenly go away—he had upset his ink bottle all over his drawing.' They moved on to Beauvais and by the 21st were back in Paris, drawing capitals and porch-panels of Notre-Dame, but not going to Sainte Chapelle. After a visit to Chartres, they were on the point of embarking from the *quai du Louvre* when a hole was found in the boat's bottom. Morris was so 'transported' with rage that he rasped the skin off his hand on the bank-parapet. By the time they got away, the bridge was crowded with ribald people. Faulkner used a sail, when there was any wind, on the light boat which had no keel. At Maintes leaks held them up while the boat was tarred. Morris infuriated a lock-keeper in one of the locks so that the man let the water out and left them stranded. At an inn they revived memories of Union days by having a battle with soda-water siphons. Stopping at Château Gaillard, they reached Rouen on 2 September, where they stayed till the 6th, annoyed at seeing the upper part of the cathedral's central spire 'lying hateful on the ground', not yet completed.

During the trip Morris discussed with Webb his plan to build a house of his own, where he could live fitly with his wife. Mainly on the strength of this project, Webb left Street and began practising on his own. Morris went on looking for a good site. In the later autumn he was ill, his friends attributing his condition to a readiness to eat and drink too much or to an unconcern with what it was he ate and drank. There had been a long strain; he was 'languid and subject to strange fluctuations of mood'. A little earlier a friend commented that 'he has lately taken a strong fancy to be human'. He lost all impulse to paint. But during October he went to Paris to buy 'old manuscripts and armour and ironwork and enamel'. The dream of an idyllic earth, of a monastery or art-brotherhood, had now turned into that of a perfect medieval kind of house, a noble and happy enclosure in a dark world, where he would be able to create his own way of life with his wife and their children. Thus all that he prized of his own childhood would be re-achieved with a new force and purity of concentration. After looking at many sites, he chose one at Bexley Heath; and the plans for the house were ready by April 1859.

After the publication of his poems he seems to have tried to carry on with the same method in *Scenes from the Fall of Troy*, using the dramatic method developed especially in *Sir Peter Harpdon's End*. He was attracted by the idea of a group of men fighting gravely and devotedly against hopeless odds. The Trojans' struggle to keep Helen thus became a symbol of the struggle to maintain the image of beauty in a threatening world. He sought to preserve the same kind of faltering intensity in the rhythm as in the best of his published poems, something clumsy and adroit in its effect of an emotion both deeply pondered and spontaneous. But here he was attempting a scheme far more ambitious than anything in *The Defence*: a series of interlocked scenes dealing with a grand epical situation. At some point, probably during 1859, he lost faith in what he was doing. He may have felt that a method, effective for a single scene, became monotonous when repeated many times; but more likely he found that he no longer could enter whole-heartedly into the strenuous heroic material. The full story of that weakening of nerve belongs, however, to the next decade.[3]

1859 opened with Morris thinking much of his marriage and new home. BJ was helping at the Working Men's College, together with Brown, and teaching on his own. In March we glimpse Morris at Oxford. Crom was working at medicine; he, Faulkner, and someone else were reading a French play.

Of course old Charley is just the same as ever, glorious fellow, he never changes—in temper and disposition he couldn't well change for the better. Topsy turned up while I was there and the manner of his turning-up was highly characteristic—very , very Topsian. On Saturday all the Birmingham—or rather all the Set were invited by letter to dine with him on the Sunday at 5 or 5.30. Between 4 and 5 on Sunday he appeared at his lodgings and told them he wanted dinner. They were a little troubled at this, considering the day, but they were aghast when he said he wanted it for half a dozen people. However dinner did at length appear, at about 7 o'clock, and a very good dinner it was. (Fulford)

The marriage took place on 26 April at Oxford in the parish church of St Michael's (recently restored by Street). Faulkner was best man, BJ was there, but not Rossetti, and not Mrs Morris or any member of the family. They must have thoroughly disapproved, and no doubt Morris had no wish for them to meet Janey's family. For 'Robert Burden, groom', signed the register: his one and only appearance that we know of. Dixon officiated and made the mistake of joining the pair as 'William and Mary'; he could not have known Janey at all. Morris was now twenty-five, and she about five years younger. Some thirty years later Morris made Old Hammond in *News* utter the comment: 'Calf love, mistaken for a heroism that shall be life-long, yet waning early into disappointment . . . the unhappiness that comes of man and woman confusing the relations between natural passion, and sentiment, and the friendship which, when things go well, softens the awakening from passing illusions.' It is hard not to believe that he was thinking of his own position at this moment and regretting that there had been so little to soften the awakening.

There was a six-weeks' honeymoon, taking in Paris, Belgium, and the Rhine to Basle. Then the couple returned to London and lived in furnished rooms at 41 Great Ormond Street. Webb, at work on Red House, had set up his office at number 7 in the same street. It was probably now that Georgiana first met Janey. 'Literally I dreamed of her again in the night.'

Meanwhile a committee, appointed by the Oxford Union, after some ineffective communications with Rossetti, took charge of the paintings, and in June, William Riviere, who had left Cheltenham to teach art at Oxford, was engaged to fill three empty bays at £150. Rossetti was seeing a lot of Fanny, who had been a whore operating from the Argyle rooms. With his aid she moved from Dean Street, Soho, to Tennyson Street, Battersea. Boyce records visits to her there with Rossetti and an excursion with her to the zoo. In July Rossetti cajoled him into advancing £40 for an oil portrait of her, probably *Bocca Baciata* (the 'Kissed Mouth' of Boccaccio's sonnet, which 'does not lose its fascination but like the moon renews itself'). Unlike so many prepaid commissions with Rossetti, this one was carried out.[4]

The site for the Morris house was only ten miles from London, and three miles from a railway station, Abbey Wood. It stood on a plateau through which ran the old Watling Road to Dover, near the small village of Upton. The land bought was an orchard and meadow, and the house was built in the orchard, with apple and cherry trees fully grown around it. Three or four cottages near by were known as Hog's Hole, a name that delighted Rossetti. The countryside was of a plain but fertile kind, with woods, orchards, and streams; and Morris liked to think he was close to the route of Chaucer's pilgrims. The house had wide views over the Cray valley. Morris despised any form of box architecture, the product of the age of Gradgrind when designers

could do nothing but produce on the one hand pedantic imitations of classical architecture of the most revolting ugliness, and ridiculous travesties of Gothic buildings, not quite so ugly, but meaner and sillier; and, on the other hand, the utilitarian box with a slate lid which the Anglo-Saxon generally in modern times considers as a good sensible house with no nonsense about it. . . . [But] were the rows of square brown brick boxes which Keats and Shelley had to look at, or the stuccoed villa which enshrined Tennyson's genius, to be the perpetual concomitants of such masters of verbal beauty?

So his own house was meant to adapt late Gothic methods and forms to the needs of the day. Hence the use of plain red brick, the solid and clear structure, the lack of any pretentious or unfunctional decorations.

There were many antecedents. Pugin's Bishop's Palace at Birmingham had been a red-brick building of clear plan and simple detail, containing simple and solid furnishings. Though more Gothic in detail, this house was close to Morris and Webb in spirit. Street and Butterfield had designed town and country rectories which followed the Pugin style of straightforward domestic architecture; and almost all aspects of Red House (the red brick, the brick arches, the lantern of the staircase roof, the grouping of the high red roofs, even the un-Gothic sash-window) could be exemplified from their work. Later Webb developed his own style with no direct Gothic links, but in 1858-9 he was thinking along the lines of Pugin, Street, Butterfield, though his house with its L-form had its own distinctive way of bringing together the previous elements in a massive charm. Red House at the time attracted no particular notice in architectural circles or journals; its role in helping to found modern attitudes was only recognised some decades later when Morris had made his name in many fields.

The gardens, enclosed, were worked out in late medieval style. Georgiana tells us:

In front of the house it was spaced formally into four little square gardens making a big square together; each of the smaller squares had a wattled fence round it with an opening by which one entered, and all over the fence roses grew thickly. The stable, with stalls for two horses, stood in one corner of the garden, end on to the road, and had a kind of younger-brother look with regard to the house.

The garden had long grass-walks, with lilies and sunflowers in mid-summer. Care had been taking in siting the house so that hardly a tree had to be cut down and apples fell into open windows on hot autumn nights. A long wall ran along by the road and big red wooden doors opened into a short winding drive. Vallance, visiting in 1863, found the hall 'grand and severely simple' to eyes used to 'the narrow ugliness of the usual middle-class dwelling'. Dark red tiles covered the floor; on them stood a heavy oak table; and they led to a wide massive oak staircase with treads and risers left exposed, and with no skirting or cupboarding beneath. The big pinnacled newel-posts rose to the open and boldly patterned roof. Exposed too throughout the house were the wooden lintels, beams, brick arches, and the tall open hearth of patterned bricks. The walls of the staircase were meant to be covered with tempera paintings of the siege of Troy, including a huge hero-crowded warship, but these were never done. On the right as one entered was a solid settle-cupboard, designed by Webb, which was painted with scenes from the *Nibelungenlied*. The paintings were never finished, and what was left was filled in with diaper-pattern. To the right, off the hall, was the dining-room with big red wooden dresser and hangings embroidered with designs from Chaucer; the ceiling had a simple stencilled pattern, with holes pierced as guides in repainting. The walls were palely distempered, the sash-windows painted white. To the left off the hall a long gallery led to a back-porch with high windows along one side, in which the stained glass had two small figures by BJ and quarries by Webb and Morris, gay forms of beast and bird. The kitchen, down a passage, had a high window looking west on to the garden (in contrast with the usual way of bundling servants into a basement or concealed wing).

On the first floor the main rooms were the studio and the drawing-room. The walls were carried right up to the roof for extra height, as Pugin had done in his Bishop's Palace. The studio faced south, east, and north, and was full of light. The drawing-room was lit mainly from the north, with a small oriel window on the west to catch the evening sun. As this was a room of special splendour, filled with painting and embroidery, it was probably meant to be sheltered from the sun; Morris said he wanted to make it the most beautiful room in England. (But the house had been worked out in a warm year, and the Victorians in general did not care for the sun. The sunny side of Red House was taken up largely with passages, and so the place was found to be chilly in winter.) The drawing-room had floral designs by Morris and BJ on the ceiling, and BJ started painting the walls with scenes from the romance of Sir Degrevaunt; a frieze below the mottoes, trees, and parrots was by Morris—Rossetti filling the blank labels with a parody of Morris's motto: 'As I can't,' no doubt provoking loud protests from his host. The huge settle had been brought from Red Lion Square, Rossetti painted the *Salutation of Beatrice* on its doors. Webb added the top and ladder as a sort of minstrels' gallery, leading to the loft. Morris's bedroom was hung with dark blue serge embroidered in bright wools by Janey, the effect not unlike that of the later *Daisy* wallpaper. In Red House there was no wallpaper.

The total effect was strange and barbaric to Victorian sensibility. Bell Scott said that 'the adornment had a novel, not to say, startling character, but if one had been told that it was the South Sea Island style of thing one could have believed such to be the case, so bizarre was the execution'. For it was a young man's house and 'genius always rushes to extremes at first'. In the nook of the L outside was the half-quadrangle, its two open sides masked by rose-trellises. In the middle stood a well of brickwork and timber, with steep conical tiled roof. Looking at the house, one saw the simple basic form with constructional effects giving the variety: relieving arches over windows, deep cornice mouldings, the louvre in the high open roof over the staircase, two spacious recessed porches. The tall weather vane had Morris's initials and a horse-head.

In early September, BJ, separated from Georgiana (who had gone with her family to Manchester), went off with Prinsep to Italy. Morris was still much taken up with furnishing his house, his friends helping now and then.

He set about teaching Janey to embroider, and her sister Bessy helped. Though he could use some of the furnishings from Red Lion Square, he again had the problem of having to create his own articles, though now he had the aid of Webb. How he was getting on with his young and unusual wife, we have no clues. But with their peculiar characters there must have been much strain and worry, though perhaps at moments they came close in discussing Red House. In the autumn Rossetti, who was seeing much of Fanny and Annie Miller, started on his Llandaff triptych. He dropped Ruth Herbert as model and asked Janey to sit.

This year there was a scare about an invasion by the French. In July Lord Lyndhurst tried to rouse the country on the strength of some colonels having written to their emperor with a plea to be led against *perfide Albion*. Tennyson wrote *Rifleman Form*, and Woolner told Mrs T. that it was 'like a gun booming of danger fast coming upon us'. Morris joined the Artists Corps of Volunteers, as did Millais, Prinsep, Watts, and W. Richmond (honorary secretary); Ruskin was made Honorary Member. At one time Rossetti at least joined in the drilling. Morris stayed in the corps till 1861. We see then how very far he still was from his later social and political views.[5]

The first six months of 1860 saw Morris still absorbed in the question of Red House and its furnishings. We hear very little about him in any other relation. In February Rossetti finished *Bocca Baciata* for Boyce, who (said Hughes) 'will I expect kiss the dear thing's lips away'. Gabriel was 'certainly looking tremendously well not to say fat'. This was his first oil for nine years and the beginning of his series of exotic females in luxurious settings. But he was also entering the phase of acute inner torment. 'It was remorse at the contrast between his ideal and his real loves,' said the architect J. H. Middleton, 'that preyed on him and destroyed his mind.' At the same time his situation with Lizzie must have been growing ever more wretched, with momentary lulls. His turning to Fanny and other light-loves was both a refuge from her and an act of revenge. She was as obdurate as ever against surrendering to him without marriage; and finally he gave in. They were married on 23 March at Hastings and went off to Paris, which he much disliked. She at once fell ill.

In March a hundred thousand volunteers were enrolled and in June the queen reviewed a large number in Hyde Park. The Artists wore a grey and silver uniform. The French expedition to Syria led to suspicions that an attempt was to be made to break British power in India; and the Suez Canal increased the fears. We have no details of what Morris did; but B. H. Jackson, who had joined the London Scottish Volunteers, drilled on Wimbledon Common in summer and in Westminster Hall in winter, as well as taking part in Grand Field Days and Easter Reviews at Brighton. On 9 June BJ at last married Georgiana. The day was Dante's Day, which they had long decided must be the date. They had £30 and no debts; but, on the 7th, Plint had sent £25 for two drawings. BJ, caught out in the rain, had a bad sore throat; so he and his wife could not go and join the Rossettis in Paris as had been planned. Instead they moved at once into a house in Russell Place, where boys from a Home in Euston Road had made a table after a Webb design and were finishing chairs and a sofa, and where BJ set about painting a deal cupboard with ladies and animals. The Rossettis came home penniless, with Lizzie very ill; Gabriel at once pawned the jewellery that was her wedding present, to help the widow of a journalist friend. Boyce, calling on Fanny, found her 'in a very nervous, critical state'. Finally the two newly married couples met in July at the Wombats Lair in the zoo.

Georgiana thought Lizzie 'as beautiful as imagination poor thing'. The BJs took the Rossettis home. As Lizzie removed her bonnet in the room upstairs, she showed the mass of deep red hair which she wore 'very loosely fastened up so that it fell in soft, heavy wings'. Her complexion looked 'as if a rose tint lay underneath the white skin'. Georgiana, whom Ruskin had described as 'a little country violet with blue eyes & long eyelashes, & as good and sweet as can be', was puzzled at Lizzie's long years of illness 'without ever developing a specific disease'. Janey had already become used to this world. In late July Boyce found Rossetti working at his triptych. 'Morris and his wife (whom he familiarly addresses as Janey) came in.' Lizzie, ill, went off till October to Brighton; and Rossetti took up collecting bric-à-brac. He was getting used to Lizzie's fits of vomiting and patiently attended to her; his isolation made him work hard. A note of hers to Georgie, as we may now call Mrs BJ, ran thus: 'My dear little Georgie,—I hope you intend coming over with Ned to-morrow evening like a sweetmeat, it seems so long since I saw you dear. Janey will be here I hope to meet you. With a willow-pattern dish full of love to you and Ned,—Lizzie.'

At the close of the wet summer the Morrises moved into Red House. Georgie describes how one got there. 'First was the arrival at Abbey Wood Station, a country place in those days, where a thin fresh air full of sweet smells met us as we walked down the platform, and outside was the wagonette sent from Red House to meet us; then a pull up the hill and a swinging drive of three miles of winding road on the higher land until, passing "Hog's Hole" on the left, we stopped at our friend's gate.' The wagonette, designed by Webb, had been built at Bexley. May says, 'It was covered with a tilt like an old-fashioned market-cart, made of American cloth lined with gay chintz hangings: the Morris arms painted on the back. When it was finished, they used to go little jaunts with their friends, and their appearance caused much joy in the neighbourhood where it was thought that they were the advance guard of a travelling show.' The weekends were used for decorating the house and for fun and games, bowls in the garden and bearfights among the men in the drawing-room. Once a scrimmage surged up the steps into the Minstrels' Gallery. Faulkner 'suddenly leapt clear over the parapet into the middle of the floor with an astounding noise; another time he stored windfallen apples in the gallery and defended himself with them against all comers until a well-delivered apple gave Morris a black eye; and then, remembering that Morris had promised to give away one of his sisters at her marriage a day or two afterwards, Edward and Faulkner left him no peace from their anticipations of the discredit his appearance would bring upon the ceremony'.

They told each other riddles. Someone asked, 'Who killed his brother Cain?' Morris fell into the trap and shouted, 'Abel, of course.' Everyone laughed and afterwards he saw the joke; but on returning from the marriage he told how he'd amused the company at breakfast by trying the trick on the parson. 'I asked him "Who killed his brother Abel?" and when of course he said "Cain", I said, "Hah! I knew you'd say that—everyone says it." ' So they all laughed at him more than ever.

Midday dinner was a favourite time for jokes at Morris's expense, as Janey and Georgie were then present 'as eager onlookers of the fun or to take sides for and against'. The men often sent Morris to Coventry for some slight cause and refused to exchange a word with him. At times they even asked Janey if she would communicate with her husband for them. 'But a stranger coming in upon our merriment would never have guessed from the faces of the company who were the teasers and who the teased.' Another joke was to put a tuck in his waistcoat overnight, playing on his fear of getting fat. 'You fellows have been at it again,' he'd say ruefully. But he maintained his good humour. 'It was the most beautiful sight to see Morris coming up from the cellar before dinner, beaming with joy, with his hands full of bottles of wine and others tucked under his arms.'

When night fell, they at times played hide-and-seek all over the house. 'I see,' says Georgie, 'that Edward, leaving the door behind him, has slipped into an unlighted room and disappeared into its black depths for so long that Mrs. Morris, who is the seeker, grows almost terrified. I see her tall figure and her beautiful face as she creeps slowly nearer and nearer to the room where she feels sure he must be, and at last I hear her startled cry and his peal of laughter as he bursts from his hiding-place.' But Janey must have had a boisterous note at times, for once when someone came up behind Morris as he sat on a stool before the fire, and slapped him, he called out, 'Don't do it, Janey,' without turning round. There was a piano in the sitting-room, and in the evenings they sang the old English songs published by Chappell or *Echos du Temps Passé*. Lizzie was at times a guest. She helped at the decorations and appeared 'without word at dinner; rising—gliding away silent and unobserved as she had come—a ghost in the house of the living'. We have a letter of hers from Red House to Rossetti: 'If you can come down here on Saturday evening I shall be glad indeed, I want you to do something to the figure I have been trying to paint on the wall. But I fear I am too blind and sick to see what I am about. Hoping you will not allow Spontock to be too much worried. I remain Your affectionate Lizzie.'

Why was Morris for so long treated as a butt and often submitted to undignified and even painful ordeals? It is not enough to cite his good nature, which never allowed him to be provoked beyond a point. Clearly there was an impulse to find out how far his explosions of temper would go. But the tricks showed considerable insensitivity, an inability to realise the inner instability which caused the outbursts. In the last resort it was the childlike element in him that made the others treat him in such a childish fashion, going much further with him in their pranks than they did with anyone else.[6]

This year Ruskin had published in Thackeray's *Cornhill* the first of three essays (printed in 1862 as *Unto This Last*), in which he made a fundamental attack on the political economy of the day. The essay roused such a fury among the readers that Thackeray had to stop the publication of the next two. 'If we do not crush him,' said a leading article in the *Manchester Examiner*, 2 October 1860, 'his wild words will touch a spring of action in some hearts, and before we are aware, a moral floodgate may fly open and drown us all.' 'Utter imbecility,' wrote one reader. Another, 'The world was not going to be preached to death by a mad governess.' Ruskin had touched the bourgeois to the quick. He made a stark distinction between wealth and riches. 'There is no wealth but Life.' But 'riches is essentially power over men'. He remorselessly drove home the definitions. Bourgeois life was based on an economic abstraction, which was wholly evil. The art of making oneself rich was the art of keeping your neighbour poor.

Buy in the cheapest market?—yes; but what made your market cheap? Charcoal may be cheap among your roof timbers after a fire, and bricks may be cheap in your streets after an earthquake; but fire and earthquake may not therefore be national benefits. Sell in the dearest?—yes, truly; but what made your market dear? You sold your bread well to-day; was it to a dying man who gave his last coin for it, and will never need bread more; or to a rich man who to-morrow will buy your farm over your head; or to a soldier on his way to pillage the bank in which you have put your fortune?

. . . There are many sciences, as well as many arts, of getting rich. Poisoning people of large estates, was one employed largely in the Middle Ages; adulteration of food of people of small estates, is one employed largely now.

On the other hand, 'There is no wealth but Life—Life, including all its powers of love, of joy, and of admiration. That country is the richest which nourishes the greatest number of noble and happy human beings.'

The distinction of wealth and riches thus made was to be of the utmost importance to Morris later; but there is not the least sign that at this time he was aware of the storm that Ruskin had raised. He was taken up with purely personal issues, the actualising of his medieval dream in Red House and the question of what he was going to do with his life. True, his mining shares were still bringing him in about £900 a year; not till 1866 did the drop begin. But he may have heard rumours of a decline and in any case he must have been thinking about money. Red House would have cost a lot and with the breakdown of his hopes of becoming a painter he must have been concerned about the future. He was not living cheaply. Was he to become a mere parasitic aesthete, relying on Red House (largely the work of Webb and other friends) to give him a reason for existence? His first book of poems had done badly, and he seemed now in any event deflated of inspiration.

Hence there arose the idea of the firm as an extension of the activities set going by the needs to furnish Red House. But even in this matter Morris does not seem to have been the originator of the scheme. BJ indeed says that as a result of his falling income 'the idea came to him of beginning a manufactory of all things necessary for the decoration of a house. Webb had already designed some beautiful table glass, made by Powell of Whitefriars, metal candlesticks, and tables for Red House, and I had already designed several windows for churches, so the idea grew of putting our experiences together for the service of the public.' Mackail says that no single person started off the idea. 'It was in a large measure due to Madox Brown; but perhaps even more to Rossetti, who, poet and idealist as he was, had business qualities of a high order, and the eye of the trained financier for anything that had money in it. To Morris himself, who had not yet been forced by business experience into being a businessman, the firm probably meant little more than a definite agreement for co-operation and common work among friends who were also artists.' Watts-Dunton gives us Rossetti's account:

One evening, a lot of us were together, and we got talking about the way in which artists did all kinds of things in olden times, designed every kind of decoration and most kinds of furniture, and someone suggested—as a joke more than anything else—that we should each put down five pounds and form a company. Fivers were blossoms of a rare growth among us in those days, and I won't swear that the table bristled with fivers. Anyway the firm was formed, but of course there was no deed or anything of the kind. In fact, it was a mere playing at business, and Morris was elected manager, not because we ever dreamed he would turn out to be a man of business, but because he was the only one who had time and money to spare. We had no idea whatever of commercial success, but it succeeded almost in our own despite.

Morris's anxiety to do something about his financial position must have been intensified by his discovery that he was soon going to be a father. One day Georgie saw Janey making a baby-shirt and realised that she was pregnant. 'And looking at my friend's face I knew that she had been happy when she made it; but it was a sign of change, and the thought of any change made me sigh. We paid other visits to the Morrises after this, but none quite like it—how could they be?'

We see then a lineal descent from Morris's earthly paradise of childhood to the monastic community of artists, then to the brotherhood of artists in the world, with a narrowing down of the idea into the Red House of his own family and finally an expansion again from the Red House bases into the firm. But in the latter there was a disturbing fusion of Ruskin's notions of wealth and riches. On the one hand there was to be a use of the stored artistic powers of the group for the benefit of mankind, but on the other hand this use was to be in terms of a money-making organisation willy-nilly fighting for its existence in the world of the cash-nexus, of profit.[7]

Photo of William Morris in later years

La Belle Iseult (also called Queen Guinevere) painted by Morris 1858

Kelmscott Manor from the south-east

Red House from the garden

The idea of a revival of the decorative and furnishing arts was not new; it had been set out by Henry Cole and the architects Owen Jones and Matthew Digby Wyatt as well as painter Richard Redgrave. Early as 1847 Cole founded Summerly's Art Manufactures, which carried on for three years until he was taken up with the Great Exhibition of 1851. Cole wanted good painters and sculptors to produce designs for everyday articles so as to 'promote public taste' and raise the low level of Industrial Art at the Exhibition. He founded South Kensington Museum after 1851 to show 'examples of fine workmanship in the applied arts of all times and peoples'. (Brompton Boilers was the slang term for the temporary buildings where the museum began.) Cole founded schools of design in 1857, attached to the museum and hoping to free manufacture from its dependence on the French. One teacher was Christopher Dresser, author of *The Art of Decorative Design*, whose ideas ranged from the odd to the functional. Owen Jones had been superintendent of the works at the Great Exhibition and joint director of decoration for the Crystal Palace, for which he designed the Egyptian, Greek, Roman, and Alhambra Courts after it moved to Sydenham; he published with Wyatt a big *Grammar of Ornament* in 1856, with a predilection for abstract patterns which he insisted must be flat.

Morris made much use of the South Kensington Museum and was in turn helped by it. Lethaby tells us how he once said, 'They talk of building museums for the public, but South Kensington Museum was really got together for about six persons—I am one, and another is a comrade in the room,' Webb.

Organised efforts to link art and industrial design go back to the formation of the Society for the Encouragement of the Arts, Manufactures, and Commerce in 1753. From the first it offered prizes for, and held shows of, inventions and discoveries in chemistry, mechanics, agriculture, and every kind of craft and trade, as well as drawings and designs. But on the art side the concern was almost all with ornament, not with structure and function. A series of shows of manufactured goods was held in London 1828–33, while all over the country literary and philosophical societies or local academies arranged further shows which included industrial products as well as traditional crafts, artworks, curios. In 1843 a Royal Commission dealt with coordinating and centralising the various efforts being made to develop the arts, with Prince Albert as president. He was keen to revive fresco painting. But the rich manufacturers were little interested. In 1835 on the proposal of Ewart, a member from Liverpool, the Commons decided to form a commission to inquire into the state of industry in England and elsewhere. The commission wanted training schools for design with special reference to industrial applications, and asked for museums and galleries open to the public. (In 1836 there was still only the British Museum, charging a shilling for entry; the National Gallery came in 1838.) But the resistance of the industrialists prevented any effect. A school was set up in Somerset House, but it was only a poor elementary art-school. Much stronger in impact was the rebuilding of the House of Commons in perpendicular Gothic by Barry and Pugin. For twelve years (1840–52) there was a veritable school of stone-cutters, woodcarvers, modellers, carpenters, decorators of all kinds in the Westminster workshops. The architects had shown what could be done; but though they developed many good craftsmen, they failed to have any national effect.

In May 1845 the Royal Society of Arts decided to hold periodical shows of industrial products, with prizes for art-manufactures. (Cole's success here, with a silver medal for a tea-service made by Merton, stimulated him to set up his association of artists, designers, and manufacturers to promote domestic goods of high quality.) After a show with 214 items (including pottery, glass, cutlery, silverwork, furniture, wallpaper), visited by some twenty thousand people, the society sought government support for an exhibition on the largest possible scale. Cole and Wyatt, fresh from a similar sort of show at Paris, wanted Britain to surpass the French. Prince Albert blessed the idea; and the Home Secretary in January 1850 accepted the request for a Royal Commission to promote the exhibition. After a year of strenuous preparations the novel hall, later called the Crystal Palace, was built. The opening was on May Day 1851, and cheap excursion tickets enabled workers from all Britain to come and see. The success was vast.

But the rich manufacturers and traders had been little interested, and the nobility saw the whole thing as concerned with trade, not fine art. The manufacturers, hostile to any new ideas, opposed the creation of a state technical school at Marlborough House, to complete that at Somerset House; among other things they wanted a monopoly of the apprenticeship system. Still, the exhibition had a wide impact. Wyatt in *The Industrial Arts of the Century*, dedicated to the prince, gave much space to English contributions. He declared that the era of fumbling and obstruction was over; the need now was for a close link of art and industry, which, using machines and steam-power, and bringing about division of labour, would produce cheap goods in quantity. In fact he showed much bad taste, taking as models the Parisian chintzes with minutely drawn flowers that lacked structure or colour harmonies; and his concept of the use of machines was the opposite of that of Morris. Still the exhibition and such work as that by Wyatt showed the widespread awareness of the problem. As we have seen, many artists had for some time been drawn into designing for industry, though not on a scale or in a way that radically affected the situation. Madox Brown, Hunt, Rossetti, and BJ were examples. Alfred Stevens designed stoves and grates for Hoole and Co., Sheffield; Pugin, furniture, silverware, fabrics; Owen Jones, wallhangings and papers for Crace, a leading furnisher. But essentially such work was art-manufacture, not industrial design.

Generally the standards of mid-Victorian taste were hardly affected. Walter Crane later summarised the situation in the 1850s. The last elements of Empire furniture had faded out, the elegant lines 'had grown gouty and clumsy'. A period of decomposition had set in which prevailed till the end of the Second Empire:

Relics of the period I believe are still to be discovered in the cold shade of remote drawing-rooms, and 'apartments to let', which take the form of big looking-glasses, and machine-lace curtains, and where the furniture is afflicted with curvature of the spine, and dreary lumps of bronze and ormulu repose on marble slabs at every opportunity, where monstrosities of every kind are encouraged under glass shades, while every species of design-debauchery is indulged in upon carpets, curtains, chintzes and wallpapers, and where the antimacassar is made to cover a multitude of sins. . . . The parlour had become a sort of sanctuary veiled in machine-lace, where the lightness of the curtains was compensated for by the massiveness of the poles, and where Berlin wool-work and bead mats flourished.

What was new in the firm then was not the idea, but the particular kind of taste, the modification of the Gothic revival along new lines, which the Red House group brought to the venture.[8]

7

The Firm

On 18 January 1861 Morris wrote to Madox Brown in a laconic tone of extreme happiness: 'My dear Brown, Kid having appeared, Mrs Brown kindly says she will stay till Monday, when you are to come to fetch her, please. I send a list of trains in evening to Abbey Wood met by bus, viz., from London Bridge, 2.20 p.m., 4.20 p.m., and 7.15 p.m. Janey and kid (girl) are both very well.' We see that Emma had come along to help. The girl was named Jane Alice, but later known as Jenny. There was a large gathering for the christening, on a day of windy rain. 'I remember the flapping of the cover of the wagonette and a feeling of hurry-skurry through the weather in the short drive to Bexley Church. The dinner was at a T-shaped table. It must have been at it that I remember Gabriel sitting in a royal manner and munching raisins from a dish in front of him before dessert time. The Marshalls, the Browns, Swinburne, were there. Janey and I went together with a candle to look at the beds strewn about the drawing-room for the men. Swinburne had a sofa; I think P. P. Marshall's was made on the floor.'

That reminiscence must have been by Georgie; but in her own book she mentions that she sat next to Rossetti, 'and noticed that even amidst such merry company he fell silent occasionally and seemed absent in mind. He drank water only, and, after he had helped himself, I asked him if he would give me some, which he did with an instant return to the scene before him, saying at the same time with grave humour in his sonorous voice, "I beg your pardon, Georgie: I had forgotten that you, like myself, are a temperate person." ' He had no doubt been oppressed by Lizzie's presence; she was near her time and Hughes tells us: 'DGR quite cowed by Lizzie who snarled at him.' On 2 May she brought forth a stillborn child. Both she and Rossetti were hard hit. Georgie, calling on her soon after, found her seated in a low chair with the empty cradle on the floor beside her; and she cried out ('with a kind of soft wildness'): 'Hush, Ned, you'll waken it.' Rossetti took to imagining Death as a little child, and later he wanted to adopt May Morris.

All this while steps were being taken to organise the firm of Morris, Marshall, Faulkner and Co. The members were, besides those three, BJ, Rossetti, Madox Brown, Webb. Arthur Hughes was also named in the first prospectus, but he withdrew on the grounds that he lived in the country and 'rather despaired' of the firm ever being set up. All he did for it was the drawing for a part of a window. Peter Paul Marshall, friend of Brown, was a surveyor and sanitary engineer at Tottenham. His inclusion was odd, as all he did were a few designs for furniture and church-decoration, and some cartoons for glass. But clearly Morris wanted to get on quickly and a number of possible persons were consulted. Faulkner decided to leave Oxford. He entered the office of a civil engineer in London, 'where he patiently sat and drew rivets by the thousand in plans for iron bridges—or at least that was the impression we had of his occupation'. Out of office hours he kept the firm's books.

The capital was small. Each member held one share, and on 1 April there was a call of £1 per share. With this sum and an unsecured loan from Morris's mother at Leyton the trading of the first year was based. Morris took over most of 8 Red Lion Square, with the first floor for office showroom, and with the third floor and part of the basement for work-rooms. The lease dated from Lady Day. On the ground floor was a working jeweller. A kiln was installed for firing glass and tiles. As sales increased, some dozen men and boys were regularly employed. The boys came from the Home in Euston Road, the men from Camden Town. The foreman, George Campfield, a glass-painter, had been met at evening classes of the Working Men's College. There were weekly meetings of the partners on Wednesday evening; otherwise Morris and Faulkner were the active managers, each at a salary of £150.

A circular of 11 April described the firm as Fine Art Workmen in Painting, Carving, Furniture, and the Metals.

The growth of Decorative Art in this country, owing to the efforts of English Architects, has now reached a point at which it seems desirable that Artists of reputation should devote their time to it. Although no doubt particular instances of success may be cited, still it must be generally felt that attempts of this kind hitherto have been crude and fragmentary. Up to this time, the want of that supervision, which alone can bring about harmony between the various parts of a successful work, has been increased by the necessarily excessive outlay, consequent on taking one individual artist from his pictorial labours.

The Artists whose names appear above hope by association to do away with this difficulty. Having among their number men of varied qualifications, they will be able to undertake any species of decoration, mural or otherwise, from pictures, properly so-called, down to the consideration of the smallest work susceptible of art beauty. It is anticipated that by such co-operation, the largest amount of what is essentially the artist's work, along with his constant supervision, will be secured at the smallest possible expense, while the work done must necessarily be of a much more complete order, than if any single artist were incidentally employed in the usual manner.

The Artists having for many years been deeply attached to the study of the Decorative Arts of all times and countries, have felt more than most people the want of some one place, where they could either obtain or get produced works of a genuine and beautiful character. They have therefore now established themselves as a firm, for the production, by themselves and under their supervision of—

I. Mural Decoration, either in Pictures or in Pattern Work, or merely in the arrangement of Colours, as applied to dwelling-houses, churches, or public buildings.

II. Carving generally, as applied to Architecture.

III. Stained Glass, especially with reference to its harmony with Mural Decoration.

IV. Metal work in all its branches, including Jewellery.

V. Furniture, either depending for its beauty on its own design, on the application of material hitherto overlooked, or on its conjunction with Figure and Pattern Painting. Under this head is included Embroidery of all kinds, Stamped Leather, and ornamental work in other such materials, besides every article necessary for domestic use.

It is only necessary to state further, that work of all the above classes will be estimated for, and executed in a business-like manner; and it is believed that good decoration, involving rather the luxury of taste rather than the luxury of costliness, will be found to be much less expensive than is generally supposed.

Mackail thought that the document showed 'the slashing hand and imperious accent of Rossetti, now as always contemptuous of all difficulties and not over-scrupulous in accuracy of statement'. But it seems quite a reasonable description of the situation and the part that the firm hoped to play in it. The points about co-operation and the control of all stages in the production of an article expressed precisely the new system that the firm offered. There was no stress on church-work, though clearly in that field lay one of the main chances for the firm. However on 19 April Morris wrote with a circular to his old tutor Guy asking him for a list of clergymen and others, 'to whom it *might* be any use to send a circular'. He claimed that the firm was the one really artistic in its field, 'the others being only glass painters in point of fact (like Clayton & Bell) or else that curious nondescript mixture of clerical tailor and decorator that flourishes in Southampton Street, Strand'. In about a month they hoped to have things on display. Mackail tells us that the first thing sold was some table glass designed by Webb and carried out by Powell. Designs by Webb for furniture and jewellery were being carried out, the first by a near cabinet-maker, Curwen, and the second by the man on the ground floor. Among the helpers were later Albert Moore, William de Morgan, and Simeon Solomon, who made some designs for glass and tiles; Faulkner's two sisters joined him in painting tiles and pottery; Faulkner himself was ready to put his hand to anything and took part in the glass-firing in the basement; Janey and Bessie, with Mrs Wardle and several women under them, did embroidery in cloth and silk; Georgiana also embroidered and painted tiles; Mrs Camperfield helped with altar-cloths. Generally designs for glass were by BJ, Morris, Rossetti, Webb, or Brown. Morris worked at anything and everything, including serge hangings with designs in coloured wool. Each partner was paid for any work he did. In 1862 the payments to Morris were larger than those due to all the others put together. Neither Morris nor Faulkner had had any business experience, and there must have been many mistakes, but all obstacles were overcome in the end by tenacity, devotion, and hard-headed common sense. At the same time we must recognise that the time was more or less ripe for some such venture.

The inevitable response of the trade was a furious and bitter opposition. Every effort was made to kill off the young firm. When L. F. Day as a young man began with Lavers and Barraud, stained-glass makers, he heard of the firm as 'a set of amateurs who are going to teach us the trade'.

The announcement came with the provocation and force of a challenge, and dumbfounded those who read it at the audacity of the venture. . . . Professionals felt themselves aggrieved at the intrusion, as they regarded it, of a body of men whose training had not been strictly commercial into the close premises of their own particular domain; and, had it been possible to form a ring and exclude Messrs Morris, Marshall, Faulkner and Co. from the market, the thing would infallibly have been done. (Vallance)

Morris was still one of the Volunteers, and this year we hear of him on Wimbledon Common where the camp was pitched during the summer. He was said to carry out his duties conscientiously and attend drills regularly.

However he often turned the wrong way at orders 'Left' or 'Right', and he then effusively begged the pardon of the man facing him. When a sergeant-major commanded 'Right about face!' Rossetti was said to have asked, 'Why?' With his first shot he hit the centre of the bull's-eye, but after that he couldn't hit the target at all. Hunt always filled his pocket with screws while cleaning his rifle and then forgot where they were. In June, while BJ and Georgie were on their way one Saturday to Red House and were near London Bridge, they saw crowds running in one direction and guessed that something was on fire. Despite the great heat they too watched the conflagration in Tooley Street. Morris saw the redness in the sky from his tent at Wimbledon. 'I always did hate fireworks,' he wrote later, when mentioning a fire at the works in Islington where his wallpapers were printed, 'especially since I saw Cotton's wharf ablaze some eighteen years ago.'

The BJs often went down to Red House from Saturday afternoon till Monday morning when they returned to London with Morris, who came up daily to the works. Red Lion Square was where the business discussions went on, diversified by talk and games. Brown, who always found names hard to remember, once asked the name of the housekeeper and was told Button. So he went to the top of the stairs and shouted, 'Mrs Penny, will you—' The rest of his call was drowned in the applause. Once when Morris was called away, Faulkner made a booby-trap out of the London Directory and two large copper candlesticks, which were balanced on top of the half-open door. When Morris came back, the things fell on his head.

Bumping and rebounding they rolled to the ground, while Morris yelled with the enraged surprise of startled nerves, and was very near to serious anger, when Faulkner changed everything by holding him up to opprobrium and exclaiming loudly in an injured voice, 'What a bad-tempered fellow you are!' The 'bad-tempered' one stopped his torrent of rage—looked at Faulkner for a second, and then burst into a fit of laughter, which disposed of the matter.

This kind of playing-about with Morris's outbursts is hard to understand.

Lizzie was at Red House in October; and it was probably then she wrote to Gabriel about his pictures going 'at that low price' and asking him to put aside or send on 'the money for those knives, as I do not wish those people to think I am unable to pay for them. The price of the knives is two shillings each.' Gabriel was painting a woman patron in Yorkshire. Before he had returned, Lizzie made one of her abrupt departures without any goodbye, though she had no money at Chatham House. Gabriel wrote to his mother to send her a few pounds. Soon afterwards Emma Brown put her up in Kentish Town. Again Lizzie suddenly disappeared.[1]

In January 1862 a further call of £19 a share was made on the partners, raising the paid-up capital to £140; no more increases were made till the firm was dissolved in 1874. A few hundred pounds more were brought in by loans (supposed to bear 5 per cent) from Morris and his mother. The firm thus had to face the problems of lack of capital, no reserves, and a slow output with an uncertain market. Any attempt to expand was liable to throw the system out of gear. In the first three or four years Morris fed in, little by little, all that he could spare, but with not much appreciable returns. Once or twice the accounts showed a loss for the year; but Morris carried on by sheer doggedness and in time the profits built up. Strictly these were divisible among all the partners, though the whole weight had been borne by Morris and Faulkner. The danger-point when the firm might well have collapsed came in the late 1860s.

Mrs Richmond Richie called in early in 1862:

I perfectly remember going with Val Prinsep one foggy morning to some square, miles away; we came into an empty ground floor room, and Val Prinsep called 'Topsy' very loud, and some one came from above with hair on end and in a non-chalant way began to show one or two of his curios, and to my uninitiated soul, bewildering treasures. I think Morris said the glasses would stand firm when he put them on the table. I bought two tumblers of which Val Prinsep praised the shape. He and Val wrapped them up in paper, and I came away very much amused and interested, with a general impression of sympathetic shyness and shadows and dim green glass.

On 10 February Lizzie committed suicide with an overdose of laudanum. She and Gabriel had been to dine with Swinburne (who much admired her) in Leicester Square. The circumstances are unclear. The pair spent their whole time in a ceaseless tension of quarrels, confusions, and exaltations, with lulls of friendly exhaustion; and this occasion was no exception. Rossetti after taking her home seems to have gone off to the Working Men's College; he may have been angry or merely distracted. Madox Brown destroyed the note that Lizzie left. It was said to run: 'Perhaps you'll be sorry now', or 'My life is so miserable that I wish no more of it', or 'Take care of Harry', her feeble-minded brother. At the inquest there was no reference to the heart-troubles or consumptions mentioned at other times; the verdict was that she had 'by means aforesaid accidentally and casually and by misfortune come to her death'. Whatever Rossetti knew of the facts, he was from now on haunted by the fear of having in effect murdered her. Her death seems a logical enough conclusion to their teasing and hopeless relationship. Rossetti, kindly and long-suffering as he could be, had a deep fear of any claims or responsibilities; Lizzie in her neurotic way wanted some kind of complete union with him that she couldn't define and he couldn't give. He buried his poems with her in a fit of bad conscience. She in her own poems had expressed a vague longing for the blissful marriage that could be realised only in a Fra Angelico heaven:

> How is it in the unknown land?
> Do the dead wander hand in hand?
> Do we clasp dead hands, and quiver
> With an endless joy for ever?
> Is the air filled with sound
> Of spirits circling round and round?
> Are there lakes of endless song
> To rest our tired eyes upon?
> Do tall white angels gaze and wend
> Along the banks where lilies bend?
> Lord, we know not how this may be:
> Good Lord we put our faith in thee—
> O God, remember me.

Such a poem with its deathwish of resentment and fear has a close link with the first poems of Morris, but there is no hint of the struggle by which he brought the imagery more and more down to earth.

On 25 March a second daughter was born to Morris at Red House. The girl was named after the Lady of the Day, Mary, whose Annunciation was then supposed to have occurred. She was always called May.

In April Faulkner wrote to Crom that since Christmas he had been busy with both engineering and the firm. More, Rossetti had given him a woodblock to engrave, 'which I with marvellous boldness, not to say impudence, undertook to do, and by jingo I have done it, and it is published'. The business had been going so well that he meant soon to drop out of engineering so that Morris could devote himself wholly to the art side. The meetings once or twice a fortnight have rather the character of a meeting of the 'Jolly Masons' or the jolly something elses than of a meeting to discuss business. Beginning at 8 for 9 p.m. they open with the relation of anecdotes which have been culled by members of the firm since the last meeting—this store being exhausted, Topsy and Brown will perhaps discuss the relative merits of the art of the thirteenth and fifteenth century, and then perhaps after a few more anecdotes business matters will come up about 10 or 11 o'clock and be furiously discussed till 12, 1, or 2.

The firm was exhibiting at the South Kensington Museum; stained glass had already been sent, with furniture to follow. 'The getting ready of our things first has cost more tribulation and swearing to Topsy than three exhibitions would be worth. I am going down to Topsy's this afternoon and shall try to finish this letter there.' About a fortnight later Faulkner adds a note to say that he couldn't write at Red House, 'the day was so beautiful and there was so much to do in the way of playing bowls and smoking pipes'.

At the International Exhibition that Faulkner mentioned the firm showed many things in the Medieval Court. The exhibition in general stood out as the 'apogee of the High Victorian style of elaborated pastiche'. The firm put in a wall cabinet of Webb's, made by Curwen; the doors were painted by Morris with the legend of St George, parts being in transparent colour over gold and silver; the interior was deep crimson dragons'-blood. Also a gilded bookcase with painted panels of the seven stages in the life of an English family, quite in Victorian taste. There were no tiles, as it was found that one of the judges, Burges, did not like them. Nearly £150 worth of goods were sold. But Rossetti's seven stained-glass panels, *Parable of the Vineyard*, later in a window at Scarborough, seemed so medieval to some exhibitors that they complained, insisting that the firm had put in actual medieval glass touched-up, and wanted them disqualified. These panels got the firm its first commission: to decorate Bodley's new churches at Brighton, Scarborough and Selsley. Another of the firm's items in the show was a big cabinet by J. P. Seddon, painted by Brown, BJ, and Rossetti, with backgrounds by Morris, illustrating episodes in the honeymoon of King René of Anjou (as told in Scott's *Anne of Geierstein*). Such an item was much more extravagant than most of the firm's exhibits. The firm gained two medals and the jury observed that several of their 'pieces of furniture, tapestries &c.' were 'in the style of the Middle Ages. The general forms of the furniture, the arrangement of the tapestry and the character of the details are satisfying to the archaeologist from the exactness of the imitation, at the same time that the general effect is excellent.' The 'tapestries' were in fact embroideries; it was several years before tapestry proper was made. Among the less colourful items were an iron bedstead, a sideboard and washstand by Webb, copper candlesticks (too heavy to carry, said Rossetti), jewellery by Webb, a sofa by Rossetti. The glass and the hangings most impressed the judges, and now, through their connection with advanced architects, the firm managed to get commissions alongside firms like Clayton and Bell, or Heaton, Butler, and Bayne.

The firm had two trends with which to contend. There were the abstract patterns of the Owen school, favoured by the puritanic or evangelical clergy as lacking all idolatrous suggestions; and there was the elaboration of over-worked painting, which dulled and darkened the glass. Glass of the latter kind was strong in the 1862 exhibition; in its naturalism it was liked by persons reacting against Gothic, but even at its best it disregarded the natural qualities of the medium. The firm set itself against both trends. It held fast to Winston's principles, disliking all shading or stippling; and even when powdered effects or flowering details were used, all stress was put on bold patterning, while contrasts were often kept in the lesser motifs, as in the figure of St Agnes (Middleton Cheney, Northants) where the robe is enriched by the diagonal meander of a left twig while the turned-back sleeve has a more geometrical system.

From the outset Morris was working on the principles which he later set out with the clarity brought about by much practice, by long experimentation and all it involved of failure and success:

You may be sure that any decoration is futile, and has fallen into at least the first stage of degradation, when it does not remind you of something beyond itself, of something of which it is but a visible symbol. . . .

I, as a Western man and a picture-lover, must still insist on plenty of meaning in your patterns; I must have unmistakeable suggestions of gardens and fields, and strange trees, boughs, and tendrils, or I can't do with your pattern, but must take the first piece of nonsensework a Kurdish shepherd has woven from tradition and memory; all the more, as even in that there will be some hint of past history. . . .

Those natural forms which are at once most familiar and most delightful to us, as well from association as from beauty, are the best for our purpose. The rose, the lily, the tulip, the oak, the vine, and all the herbs and trees that even we cockneys know about, they will serve our turn.

Thus he decisively rejects abstraction as something which, as soon as it is made an end in itself, leads to impoverishment, monotony, and emptiness: the void that emerges out of the disintegration of human sensibility. And he finds the test of originality in an ever deeper penetration into the essence of the familiar, of the forms out of which mankind has distilled its sense of beauty and enjoyment. What he calls 'outlandishness' he sees as an evasion of the struggle to unite humanity and nature in the most characteristic structures of formative energy.

The aim should be to combine clearness of form and firmness of structure with the mystery which comes of abundance and richness of detail. . . . Do not introduce any lines or objects which cannot be explained by the structure of the pattern; it is just this logical sequence of form, this growth which looks as if . . . it would not have been otherwise, which prevents the eye wearying of the repetition of the pattern. . . . Do not be afraid of large patterns. . . . The geometrical structure of the pattern, which is a necessity in all recurring patterns, should be boldly insisted upon, so as to draw the eye from accidental figures. . . .

Above all things, avoid vagueness; run any risk of failure rather than involve yourselves in a tangle of poor weak lines that people can't make out. Definite form bounded by clear outline is a necessity of all ornament. . . . Rational growth is necessary to all patterns. . . . Take heed in this growth that each member of it be strong and crisp, that the lines do not get thready or flabby or too far from their stock to sprout firmly and vigorously; even where a line ends it should look as if it had plenty of capacity for more growth. . . .

Thus he as decisively rejects naturalism or mere imitation of given forms. Structure and rhythm are always central in the concept of form, in the definition of the image. These elements have their own free field of self-assertion, and this freedom is always dialectically one with the laws of formative development which embrace all manifestations of life, all organisations of matter. Abstraction and naturalism are both forms of disintegration of the vital principle of art, even if they lie at opposite poles, with the dynamic image as the true centre.

In the 1860s Morris would have been hard-put to enunciate the principles in his mind as he was able to do in the 1880s, when his active implication in social and political struggle had helped to clarify for him the nature of energy and its forms of expression; but he was already basing himself upon the principles that later emerged into full consciousness. Behind the urge to find out the laws determining the effective and satisfying pattern (which were also with varying applications the laws inside all art-activity) there was the paradisiac quest we have discussed. Morris was rediscovering the secrets of this childhood-garden of joyous freedom and communion, and applying them to the changing of his society—at first along limited lines of revitalisation, then in ever-broader schemes of renewal.

Brown and Rossetti dropped out as designers after the first years; most of the figures for glass were done by BJ in his lighter style. Mostly they were single figures in pale colours, like the St Cecilia of Christ Church, Oxford. Over the years Morris himself seems to have designed at least a hundred windows, as well as quarries for the background of others. He usually took over the plain uncoloured cartoons (his own and those of others), marked the lead-lines, chose the colours, at times designed the backgrounds. To do all that he needed a full grasp of all the processes of painting and firing the glass, which he achieved by working at the small basement-kiln.[2]

The artists used one another as models, no doubt often getting much fun out of the results. Rossetti in his *Parable*'s small panels, under the great east window of the Crucifixion, showed Morris in the act of dropping a stone on the head of a bailiff, and also included Swinburne. Brown at Scarborough inserted portraits of himself and his Emma, indolent in Eden; Morris showed Janey in green, lying down wreath-crowned, in his window of St Paul at Athens (Selsley); Rossetti put him in profile in his Sermon on the Mount, with Janey as the Magdalen. Domestic stained glass was also made; an example is the Tristram series (1862) for Harden Grange. Morris's love of flowers found prominent expression; thus in a group of heroines by BJ, the Alcestis

is a specially charming figure in a white gown sprinkled with flowers and a coronet all of seed-pearls. The figures are standing among tall-growing flowers against a homely wooden fence, beyond which show a rich grouping of Dido's ships, etc. The flowers, not coloured, show all the delicate invention of the young artists: they are vividly drawn, against a light ground, with the careful accuracy and rhythmic line of the early herbals—a cyclamen, sweet-william, Indian pink, and other delights, among which the exquisite dog-tooth violet, always a favourite with Morris. It is either his hand one sees here or that of Webb: it is hard to say which. There is also here [in the V. and A.] a set of domestic glass of the Greek poets and philosophers by Burne-Jones and some of Morris's music-angels so often used, on lightly-drawn quarries of daisies and sunflowers. (May)

BJ's designs were the most popular, but, apart from the much-used figures of small angels and minstrels, Morris's St Peter, done first for All Saints at

Cambridge, was repeated at least ten times elsewhere. 'This may be significant, for all his figures have certain qualities of strength, weight and stiff dignity, appropriate to their particular subject, which distinguishes them from Madox Brown's more dramatic and Burne-Jones's more elegant designs.'

Morris was especially fascinated by the possibilities of yellow stain:

He used it with tremendous effect not only as a major element in coloured-schemes for draperies, hair and other details of figures, but especially for rendering on glass an equivalent of embroidered and damask designs on costumes. . . . In time the Morris workshop attained an unrivalled mastery in the use of this stain, and was able to produce a range of tints and tones of gold from the palest yellow to the most intense reddish bronze. It was only when experience with this technique had been acquired that some of the glories of the firm's output, like the Cheddleton Angels window of 1869, and the St Cecilia window of 1880, could be produced. But the window which shows most perfectly this minor-pattern aspect of Morris's glass is the Archangels window at King's Walden, Herts (*c.* 1869) where all the figures are from his designs. The figures are covered from head to foot with intricate decorative ornament, and the backgrounds also; but so broad and simple are the main lines of the designs that there can be no question of over-ornamentation. The window is among the greatest successes of modern stained glass: and the credit for it belongs entirely to Morris himself. (Sewter)

On 24 October Rossetti, who had refused to go near Chatham Place since Lizzie's death, took over Tudor House, 16 Cheyne Walk, Chelsea, an old red-brick house with many rooms. He was again close to the Thames, not far from the old wooden Battersea Bridge. Fanny soon installed herself as housekeeper.

1863 saw Morris working ever harder and ever more worried. Among other things he did the Resurrection for the east window of the chancel at Dedworth near Windsor; the other two lights consisted of a Crucifixion by Rossetti and a Nativity by BJ. He also did four of the single figures in panels of clear glass in the east window of Bodley's All Saints, Jesus Lane, Cambridge (1863-6). The pulpit here was painted by Arthur Hughes and Morris stencilled the walls. About this time Morris and Webb designed Bodley's new ceilings at Jesus College Chapel, Morris doing a frieze of angels; he also painted the ceiling of the hall in Queen's College.

Brown had been designing furniture for some time. In 1860 he produced a rush-seated chair of stained oak, which was said to have started off the vogue of green stain in art-furniture. Fifty years later his dressing-table was being copied by commercial firms. Webb's products at this time were mostly of plain oak (often stained green or black) or of oak decorated with paintings, gessowork, and lacquered leather. Morris himself did not design any furniture after his first experiments at Red Lion Square. Generally the firm's distinctive aspect was the solidity of the articles, the way in which they were plainly joiner-made, unlike the degenerated rococo or empire styles of the big commercial firms or the showy flamboyant Gothic of Burges. Morris liked objects to be solid (as in the squat semi-circular chair he had made for himself at Merton Abbey, for stability as he sat weaving) and at the same time to have functional virtue. Things should sit square, not easily break up, yet be light enough to be moved about. Form was related to human proportions and needs. (Her personally did not care for specialised rooms; his ideal remained the old communal hall. He liked to be able to relax, chat, drink if need be in the place where he worked; to study and sleep there as well. Hence the tap-loom he later kept in his bedroom.)

Simple flat forms had for him the advantage that they could be decorated. The idea was not new, but with his strong architectural viewpoint he tended to simplify more than the others, from Pugin to Burges, had done. The decoration had to be part of the flat surface, though it dealt with real objects, not with abstractions. Rossetti, learning in his own off way to subordinate form and colour to the peculiar space-time of his dream world, was useful in providing lines of approach to the styles that Morris felt were required. Morris, though dropping easel-work and the like, continued to find pleasure in painting panels, beams, plasterwork, altar-cloths, hangings, tiles. His early tiles were simple and light in character, freely drawn in blue or grey, and often related to his glass-quarries.

He had entered into a subdued phase. He needed to make many new adaptations of his energies, he was worried over money and the firm's future, and probably Janey was already withdrawing from him. After May's birth she seems to have decided that she wasn't going to have any more children, and she began to move towards the condition of chronic bad health which was so commonly the Victorian lady's refuge. Just before Christmas 1863 Faulkner wrote, 'I grieve to say he has only kicked one panel out of a door for this twelve-month past.' He seems to have largely given up his interest in ideas and in poetry, and to have set himself to become a good craftsman, a good businessman. He must have had to put strong pressure on himself to act the amiable shop-keeper and sell a couple of tumblers to Val Prinsep's friend; such experiences had now become part of the daily texture of his life. To protect himself against what he must have felt as humiliating moments, he had to build up the image of himself as a bluff down-to-earth craftsman, wearing a round hat and a blue blouse, and not bothering about the paint on his hands. 'Light and boisterous chaff among themselves and something like dictatorial irony towards the customers,' wrote William Rossetti (in 1917). Morris, 'as the managing partner, laid down the law and all his clients had to bend or break'. Later, when 'a person of importance' called in at the Oxford Street showrooms and remarked, 'O but, Mr Morris, I thought your colours were subdued!' Morris replied, 'If you want dirt, you can get it in the street.' (We may note however the explanation given by Wardle of this episode: 'Morris was capable of thus trampling on his dead self, more resolutely than any man I have known. Another man & certainly a tradesman would have explained, but Morris's satisfaction with the new dyes was too great to allow him to think any discussion possible and, having himself cast the old makeshift aside, once & for all, he could not bear any reference to them more.')

The system was haphazard. There was no real costing of jobs, no method for controlling and spacing out the flow of work. In the first years design-fees were paid out of the firm's price to clients. In 1862 Rossetti and BJ were paid £5 for a single light; Morris, who subsidised the firm, took £2 less. But back in 1837 Brown had got 16 guineas from Powell for his Transfiguration design. No thought was given to the rate of profit per window or the fact that the designer was not working for the client in the casual way he would work for friends. But it was incompetence and inexperience that had led to the lack of a coherent system in the pricing and costing. (By 1875 he could write to Wardle, 'As to the price per yard named by you the only thing *we* have to consider is the possibility of selling the cloths at a profit.') He wanted to achieve commercial success, even if it was in the craft-side that his heart lay. All these years, Mackail, no doubt with some exaggeration, described him as 'a typical Londoner of the middle class', and even later, when he had become politically hostile to his class, he made no attempt to deny his social origins. 'We of the middle class' were words often on his lips. In these early years he never seems to have had the least compunction about the fact that the money giving him an easy life had been provided by miners working under crushing conditions.[3]

Morris was feeling the strain, as well as the expense, of the continual travelling from Upton to London and back again. Early in 1864, schemes were discussed for removing the workshops to Upton; and Webb worked out plans for further wings to Red House which would make it a full quadrangle. Land was available for the works; and for a while it seemed that the plans would be carried out. The meetings at Red Lion Square went on as usual till the end of the March quarter, when Faulkner went back to Oxford to resume his place as fellow and tutor; he could find no congenial job in London, and he couldn't go on indefinitely being the firm's book-keeper. BJ was working on glass-designs for a series of Chaucer's Good Women; and the firm was helped by the South Kensington Museum buying five panels. The production of wallpapers was now under way. The first designed was the *Daisy* (not the first produced); still rather simple in system it was more complex than the Daisy-tile. The forms were brought out more strongly and more colours added, with a stippled background. Morris held that paper was a poor decorative material and required relief; woven fabrics on the contrary had their own natural richness of texture. *Daisy*, *Trellis*, and *Fruit* (*Pomegranate*) dated from this year; and after them came some seventy more patterns for papers, chintzes, woven cloths in the next thirty years. At the moment Morris's style had a certain naïvety; he was not yet able to make all the elements of a coloured pattern interact and set up a moving interplay, complex and yet unified.

Since 1862 the firm aimed at not merely meeting orders, but also at accumulating a good stock, things which could if necessary be repeated. Stained glass, embroidered hangings, and painted cabinets were too expensive for this purpose; but it was feasible to get a fairly large supply of jewellery, table glass, tiles, glass quarries, small embroideries, light chairs. Woven or printed textiles and wallpapers were important in this expansion, while tapestries and big embroideries maintained prestige and were profitable when sold. As a number of skilled workers were brought in, it was necessary to devise a system that enabled them to keep at work.

This year William de Morgan, who was to play his part later as a potter, first met Morris. He was impressed by the contrast between Morris as salesman and as artist, a contrast which Morris somehow resolved by his passionate absorption in the crafts that the firm practised. 'At my first visit I chiefly recollect his dressing himself in vestments and playing on a regal to illustrate a point in connection with stained glass. As I went home it suddenly crossed my mind as a strange thing that he should, while doing what was trivial and almost grotesque, continue to leave on my memory so strong an impression of his power—he certainly did, somehow.' Mackail remarks that all his diversions left this sort of effect. 'Another friend of his who had been staying a few days with him was asked, after he came away, what they had talked about. He confessed that he could not remember that they had talked of anything but eating: "and yet," he added, "I came away feeling myself enlarged and liberalised".'[4]

This year also Morris came to know F. S. Ellis, bookseller of King Street, Covent Garden, who became his friend and publisher. Swinburne first took him to the shop, and Morris used to call in on his way from work to London Bridge Station. Already he had a thorough knowledge of fifteenth-century printing.

The BJs, the Morrises and the Faulkners holidayed for three weeks at Littlehampton. Georgie speaks of 'Kate's gentle nature, sympathetic, understanding and keen sense of humour'. Mrs F. took over the housekeeping, leaving Georgie and Janey free. 'The evenings were always merry with Red House jokes revived and amplified.' Once Morris threw a pair of broken spectacles out of the window, then couldn't find his second pair. Next morning he searched in the road, with BJ and Faulkner using the occasion to utter 'some words for his good'. One day, while Morris was in London, they devised an elaborate trick. They were accustomed to play whist with a dummy, which Morris took. Now they fixed things so that the dummy seemed to have a splendid hand, but always lost. Janey and Georgie were sent to bed early. At last Morris began to realise something was wrong. 'First came irritation and astonishment, then, as the well-laid scheme revealed itself, shoutings and fury—and finally laughter such as few could equal; while we smiled in our beds at the sound of the distant explosion.'

They all left seeming well, but the BJs took home an infection of scarlet fever. Their boy Phil fell ill. When he was well enough to be left, they rashly visited Red House, but did not carry the infection to May and Jenny. However, on returning home Georgie developed a fever and prematurely bore a second son, who soon died. The family moved to Hastings, and BJ wrote to Morris that he could not now undertake any further expenses so that the plan for living at Upton was at an end. About the same time Morris was deciding that the drive in winter between Red House and Abbey Wood was too strenuous. Late in November, he replied to BJ in a shaky hand, being laid up with rheumatic fever:

As to our palace of art, I confess your letter was a blow to me at first, though hardly an unexpected one—in short I cried, but I have got over it now; of course I see it from your point of view but I like the idea of not giving it up for good even if it is delusive. But now I am only thirty years old; I shan't always have the rheumatism, and we shall have lots of jolly years of invention and lustre plates together I hope. I have been resting and thinking of what you are to do: I really think you must take some sort of house in London—unless indeed you might think of living a little way out and sharing a studio in town: Stanhope and I might join in this you know. There is only one other thing I can think of, which is when you come back from Hastings come and stay with me for a month or two, there is plenty of room for everybody and everything: you can do your work quietly and uninterruptedly: I shall have a good horse by then and Georgie and J. will be able to drive about with the kids jollily, meantime you need not be hurried in taking your new crib.

The B Js moved to 41 Kensington Square, where they lived for two years ten months. Morris had to bring himself to the decision to leave Red House.[5]

The B Js were settled in by the end of January 1865. Morris, recovered from his rheumatics, was found by Agnes Macdonald, 'so nice and kind, pleasanter than ever he was'. Rossetti looked at the new house with the artist Legros; another time Morris arrived with 'a glorious haul of picture books—black letter and engravings'. They played bowls in the small garden. ' "American bowls" too was a game that Edward, Morris, Webb and Faulkner often played in town; dining together at some "pot-house" afterwards and never tired of each other's company.' On 12 April Rossetti had his house-warming party at Chelsea. It had been delayed through the workmen taking too long over the dining-room; and was changed from a dinner-party to an evening reception as Rossetti said there were too many guests for him to feed. Invited were William Rossetti and Bell Scott, the Madox Browns with two daughters, Munro and his wife, Hughes and his wife, Legros 'with his pale, handsome wife', Swinburne and the Morrises. Brown, Georgie noted, had turned grey, at which Emma expressed much vexation when the men were out of the room. He had tried to save cab-fare from Kentish Town by taking a train to Kew, where he, his wife, and girls waited half an hour and then went on to Clapham Junction, but they missed the train and had to wait three-quarters of an hour, then at last they found Chelsea Station so far from Cheyne Walk that they had to take a cab after all, arriving all smiles and quite unruffled.

Georgie also recalled the last party she attended at Brown's place in

Kentish Town. Rossetti and Whistler were there, and Morris with Janey and her sister Bessie. Christina too appeared, 'gently caustic of tongue', while Brown's precocious son Nolly, now ten years old, clung to Faulkner, asking for amusing stories and inquiring of Rossetti 'what he thought Pompeii must have looked like'.

Morris had taken in midsummer 26 Queen Square, his headquarters now for seventeen years. The ground floor was given up to office and show-room. A big ballroom, built at the end of the yard and linked with the house by a wooden gallery, was turned into the main workshop. There was space for more workshops in a small court at the back, and more accommodation when needed could be had in Ormond Yard. With Rossetti now taken up with painting in Chelsea, Faulkner returned to Oxford (though he spent his vacations with his mother and sisters who still lived in the square), and Marshall gone back to his own line of work, Morris was more than ever in charge of the firm. Brown and BJ still made glass-designs, and Webb designed furniture as well as often doing the animals in glass-designs, but all production and a large part of all design-work were in Morris's hands. Gradually he expanded into new spheres, weaving, dyeing, printing on cloth. Cockerell estimated later that in all the fields Morris did some six hundred designs.

But an important new acquisition for the firm was Warrington Taylor as manager. A tall thin man with Roman nose and excitable manner, he was the Roman Catholic son of a Devon squire. For a while he was at Eton with Swinburne, then was sent to be educated in Germany; after losing his money he enlisted in the army. He had had a very varied career, ending as a check-taker at Her Majesty's Theatre, then an opera house.[6] He had a passion for music. Georgie tells us, 'Within a few weeks of his appointment, the rumour spread that he was keeping the accounts of the firm like a dragon, attending to the orders of customers, and actually getting Morris to work at one thing at a time.' A hand like his was needed. The business side was 'still very infirm' (Lethaby). Taylor had his own brand of uncompromising radicalism; for instance he once wrote under an estimate 'to providing a silk and gold altar cloth':

Note.—In consideration of the fact that the above item is a wholly unnecessary and inexcusable extravagance at a time when thousands of poor people in this so-called Christian country are in want of food—additional charge to that set forth above, ten pounds.

So the contract was lost. But in general he was a most exacting and capable manager. He soon began writing strong letters to Webb and Rossetti. His health worsened and he had to live at Hastings, but he still kept his stern eye on the firm's methods and finances.

The upheaval in Morris's life, while increasing his inner tensions and his sense of instability, stimulated afresh his need to write as well as driving him tenaciously into craft-activity. Georgie describes her last visit to Red House in September, 'when on a lovely afternoon Morris and Janey, and Edward and I, took a farewell drive through some of the beautiful little out-of-the-way places that were still to be found in the neighbourhood. Indoors the talk of the men was much about *The Earthly Paradise*, which was to be illustrated by two or three hundred woodcuts, many of them designed and some of them even drawn on the block.' Morris read aloud his poems. Georgie remembered with shame 'often falling asleep to the steady rhythm of the reading voice, or biting my fingers and stabbing myself with pins in order to keep awake'.

The removal to Queen Square came in November. Morris could never bear to go and look at Red House again. He was in fact leaving much more behind than he could have known at the time. With the loss of the dream of re-creating around himself a medieval world he lost also the love of the woman who had been for him the incarnation of the dream. At first there was an effort to continue the weekly dinner in Queen Square, 'and in these evenings,' says Georgie, 'the merriment of our youth was revived for a time, but Janey was now so much out of health that I fear her share of the entertainments was more fatigue than pleasure, and gradually they came to an end. The men never ceased to meet regularly, though, at one house or the other.' The more that Janey became a neurotic invalid and faded out of any active part in Morris's life, the more she appealed to Rossetti and began to appear in his art.

She had been taken from her lowly life in Oxford and made the queen of a rich and easy-going domain, where everything seemed to have been devised to give her a luxurious setting and where she was admired by all the visitors. Then, strong wench as she seems to have been, she bore two children in fairly close succession, and found herself deprived of her domain, pushed into a London house lacking all the spacious distinction of Red House, amid workshops and salesroom. Morris, kindly as he was in all essentials, was not the man to cushion such a descent for her. With his worries and his work-obsessions, the rude boisterous side of his manners could not but have been accentuated. He must have seemed withdrawn and dominating. Liable to throw a badly cooked dinner out of the window, he found it hard to sit still even at table, got up and paced the room like a caged lion. Friends speak of his stormy and exacting company. Janey was not at all equipped to deal with such a character, to understand him, or to fit into his life. In the first years at Red House his temper must have been more equable, and his explosions could be more easily dissipated. But now Janey was right up against him, and at times he must have seemed as frightening as inexplicable. The less they could find any common ground of enjoyment, any shared idiom of intimate exchange, the more she retreated into her refuge of illness, from which she could not be expected to emerge. He, for his part, well meaning and full of goodwill, must have found it hard to sympathise with such a retreat or find the ways of drawing Janey out of it. Rossetti, with his insidious and undemanding adoration, was the diametric opposite of Morris. Flattered by the way she turned to him, he could not help himself striving to console and support her, to win her devotion. Morris, once his humble disciple, was fast becoming the pertinaceous manager of a business that he steadily took over as his own preserve. The element of obsessive concentration which we have noted in Morris from early days could make him seen uninterested in people, disregarding their problems and difficulties. 'In the ordinary concerns of life,' said Mackail, 'he was strangely uncurious of individuals.'

Also, though he was not yet in a position to face the full nature of the world in which he was now a businessman, he felt deeply repelled by it. Until he realised the possibility of real change in the later 1870s, with the culmination of his new hopes in 1882, he could not intellectually confront his world; at most he could express his revulsion and depression in verse. In 1894, looking back, he declared,

Apart from the desire to produce beautiful things, the leading passion of my life has been and is hatred of modern civilisation. . . . The hope of the past times was gone, the struggles of mankind for many ages had produced nothing but this sordid, aimless, ugly confusion; the immediate future seemed to me likely to intensify all the present evils by sweeping away the last survivals of the days before the dull squalor of civilisation had settled down on the world. . . . Was it all to end in a counting-house on the top of a cinder-heap, with Podsnap's drawing-room in the offing? . . . As far as I could tell, scarce anyone seemed to think it worth while to struggle against such a consummation of civilisation.

He could not at this moment pose the question in those terms; but the proof that he was deeply feeling it all is to be found in the poem which he was beginning.[7]

Mackail says that a project of a cycle of verse-tales had 'already been talked over at Red House'. But no beginning was made till after the removal to London. Once he had begun, he threw himself into versifying with all the desperation induced by his inability to face the contradictions of his life, the ultimate bearings of the campaign represented by the firm, the fact that Janey was fast being irredeemably lost. The venture carried him on till 1870 and involved the writing of a poem of 42,000 lines of rhymed verse. Faulkner says that he once wrote 700 lines of *Jason* in a day. May draws attention to the seven great folio volumes of manuscript, fair copy and drafts, and that

some twenty or so other MSS of the single stories exist in one form or another; that the writer was at this time cutting on wood, designing and busy over the hundred and one matters that the head of a personally conducted business has to attend to; that he kept no amanuensis and did all the writing of notes and drafts and fair scripts in his own hand.

He wrote mostly at night or in the small hours of the morning.

He began by attempting to carry on in the dramatic and urgent style of *The Defence*. We have his first version of the prologue. The diction and rhythm indeed lack the tense mastery of the best earlier poems, but they are still akin.

> But in the dead of night I woke,
> And heard a sharp and bitter cry,
> And there saw, struck with a great stroke,
> Lie dead, Sir John of Hedesby. . . .

In the second version the same scene of a night-attack is described in couplets which, though owning some narrative vigour, give up the search for dramatic immediacy:

> But therewithal I woke, and through the night
> Heard shrieks and shouts of clamour of the fight. . . .

Now he had found the style in which he wrote the whole of the vast poem.

Certain gentlemen and mariners of Norway, having considered all they had heard of the Earthly Paradise, set sail to find it, and after many troubles and the lapse of many years came old men to some western land, of which they had never heard;

there they died, when they had dwelt there certain years, much honoured of the strange people,

who are a surviving outpost of the ancient Greek world, though the period is that of the Black Death in Europe. Every month for a year the Wanderers tell their hosts a tale, and the latter tell one in return. In twelve poems on the months Morris intrudes his own personal despair and hopeless hope for the return of love. He abjures all aim of changing the world. 'Why should I strive to set the crooked straight?' Rather, 'forget the spreading of the hideous town', and 'dream of London, small, and white, and clean'. He is himself a 'dreamer of dreams, born out of my due time'. He seeks 'to build a shadowy isle of bliss midmost the beating of the steely sea', in a world 'whose ravening monsters mighty men shall slay, not the idle singer of an empty day'. He is not indeed interested in the characters of the action recounted 'in the sense that the action is in itself either significant or purposeful', and throughout the work there is 'an almost mechanical oscillation between sensuous luxury and horror, melancholy, and despair' (Edward Thompson).

Mackail refers to the fact that in the month-poems 'there is an autobiography so delicate and so outspoken that it must needs be left to speak for itself'. What is lamented is the loss of the marital warmth that he briefly enjoyed with Janey.

> Like a new-wakened man thou art, who tries
> To dream again the dream that made him glad
> When in his arms his loving love he had. . . .
> Change, kindness lost, love left unloved alone;
> Till their despairing sweetness makes thee dream
> Thou once wert loved, if but amidst a dream. . . .

And yet the very title and motive of the poem show that Morris has not departed from the basic patterns in his life which we have been tracing. The loss of Red House and Janey (the dream-house and the wife closely linked and in the last resort fused with it), without a system of ideas that can enable him to stand up against the world of Gradgrind and Podsnap, forces him to feel that the earthly paradise can only be expressed in terms of a backward-looking despair, a sense of ubiquitous loss; there is no way of fighting for it, of actualising it. But it still remains at the core of his being. Nothing else matters. The years of *The Earthly Paradise*, despite their renunciation of struggle, are yet the prerequisite of the deep-going struggle that follows them. He feels that the same forces have deprived him of Red House and of Janey; and so in the end, after he has lost any hope of regaining Janey, he is still left with his hatred of the forces that killed his dream of a personal actualisation of medieval values and forms. The effort to build, furnish, and develop Red House as a centre of a new kind of living is turned into the effort to create and develop the firm, bringing the medieval craft-values to the world in general. But here he is no longer making a love-gift, building a love-dream; he is both trying to find his place in the world of the cash-nexus which he despises, and to affront that world with challenging values—values which, if fully controlling society, would end the cash-nexus altogether. Not till 1882 were all these implications to come out right into the open, but by 1865 Morris had made the first step on the road to the fully realised struggle. *The Earthly Paradise* was necessary to him as a consolation and an encouragement, for all its languors and despairs, if he were to carry on the firm with all his dedicated zeal and vigour.[8]

From the outset Queen Square had been intended for machine as well as hand production. Much material was produced for the firm by trade-printers and weavers. Morris's designs were based both on a close observation of nature and a profound knowledge of the history of the arts. His scholarship, said Webb, 'he was able to assimilate as a foundation for his work, and proceed with *real* originality; thus avoiding the fatal step of imitation'. He knew how to make his patterns spread over the whole field, without making each unit unduly important, and with the formal grid submerged in the flow of movement. Then, as his mastery grew, he often let the repeat assert itself more emphatically (especially when textile effects were in his thought), both where he used meander or ribbon, and where symmetrical systems dominated. To direct observation of plant forms he added his study of the drawings in old herbals. He decided that wallpaper, because of its flatness and its uninteresting texture, needed a slight effect of depth, such as could be gained by having one element developed and expanded over another, with variations of scale and weight as to parts, so that we might feel a major pattern playing over a lesser one.

George Wardle says that he first met Morris while he was still at Red Lion Square; he describes the rather grim atmosphere of the firm's early days:

I went to offer him some drawings I had made of pattern work &c. on the screens

& roofs of churches in Suffolk. I showed him some drawings I had made in Southwold & Blythburgh. He struck me as being overworked. Those were the early days of the firm, business was unremunerative, & perhaps a large share of the work was done by him. If he was writing also at that time he would have had more than his hands full & much anxiety added to the labour. The bad business seemed to have affected Faulkner also. He was then working at tile panels, I think. He had a forpined look which spoke of hard times. I saw also Warrington Taylor, & he being already seriously ill, helped to give the impression of gloomy affairs which I carried away with me.

The year 1866 saw Morris still carrying doggedly on, but seemingly too immersed in business, craftwork, and family worries, to think of other things. Beyond his immediate problems and activities he was concerned only with *The Earthly Paradise*. Here he was lost in his dream world, not striving to bring the dream-system into obdurate dimensions of life as he had in the prose romances. From one angle he had come down right into the lost narcissistic world of Rossetti; but at his most confined and hopeless he never fully surrendered to the passive dream-spell. The very fact that he was writing narrative poems meant that he was to some extent objectifying his experience; the very fact that he was dealing with a group who sought the Earthly Paradise meant that, however the dream might seem a delusion, he was still holding fast to the idea of a quest, a group-quest. Though he had dropped all effort at drama and used the stories and their themes as elaborated symbols of states of mind and heart, his thought and fancy were playing all the while round the old ideas. Restore hope to this cosmos and the old virtues would reassert themselves on a much widened stage.

But meanwhile even Burne-Jones was more political in his outlook than Morris was at this phase. Allingham described him as a People's Man in his diary; and Faulkner was taking interest in the agitation leading up to the Reform Bill of 1867. Warrington Taylor too had his radical views. Rossetti meanwhile was growing worse in health and more inturned; his hydrocele was troubling him and would need medical attention on and off for the rest of his life.[9]

Morris's worries must have been accentuated by the fact that this year saw a commercial panic which brought about the suspension of the Bank Charter on Black Friday, 11 May. His unearned income had begun to shrink; it was now down to £43 a share. In June Rossetti painted Janey in a peacock-blue dress at a table with a glass of roses; long before it was done, he started another of her as La Pia, Dante's ill-starred lady of Siena, who was condemned by her husband to perish among exhalations of the marshy Maremma. At this period Morris at times accompanied her to the studio. In June 1866 Morris, Janey, Webb, and Warrington Taylor went on a tour of north France; Georgie had just borne a daughter, so the BJs couldn't join them. A sketch by BJ shows the four travellers getting sick over the sides of a boat while BJ on the cliffs holds a stiff Georgie across his body.

Morris and BJ were planning an illustrated edition of *The Earthly Paradise*, The Big Book. Five hundred woodcuts were planned, but the project came to nothing. Probably at this phase Morris would not imagine his poems selling. Allingham tells us:

Monday July 30. Kensington Square. Studio, Psyche drawings. Book planned. Morris and lots of stories and pictures.
Wednesday Aug. 1. At dinner William Morris, pleasant, learned about wines and distilling. The Big Story Book, product of Olympus by Ned Jones. Morris and friends intend to engrave the wood-blocks themselves—& M. will publish the book at his own expense. I like Morris much. He is plain-spoken and emphatic, often boisterously, without an atom of irritating manner. He goes about 12.

In August the BJs went to Lymington to be near Allingham, who worked there in the Customs. They made an expedition to Winchester, and Morris came from London to join them. 'And as we waited at the door of our hotel I remember him swinging towards us along the High Street with a look as if he had easily walked all the way. Then we went together over the water meadows to St Cross, and mourned over the "restoration" it was suffering.'

The firm badly needed to expand. Wardle thought it was about 1866 that he came in as draughtsman and bookkeeper and utility-man in general, 'poor Taylor being then about to retire. I found Morris looking better & in good spirits'. Business was now improved, 'but there was not yet a profit, I think'. After this, things went on bettering. 'It was high time for Mr Morris had spent all or nearly all his private means.' Taylor, though ill, was still far from ended. This year he was tackling the situation in glass-work. 'Over £2,000 in glass done. This should have returned at least therefore over £500 profit. You know well enough there was not £200 profit on glass.' He set out the questions that had to be asked and answered to ensure that their glass brought in not only reputation but also the kind of profit it should and which they badly needed. How was the work measured? what were the charges made? were the designs charged for apart from the actual production? and so on.

This year the firm obtained two important commissions. How they got them is not clear; but Cole, director at South Kensington, must have felt favourably towards them. They were asked to do the Green Dining-Room at the museum and to decorate the Armoury and Tapestry Room at St James's Palace. In September they began work at the palace and finished in mid-January 1867. Webb worked out the general plan of work for both palace and museum. His accounts from August 1866 to January 1867 show such details as the following: '3 visits to St James's Palace, measuring; Pattern panels; Enlarging pattern for ceiling of Armoury; do cornice; Redrawing reticulated pattern of panels, Armoury.' Taylor was busy keeping everyone up to mark. He asks Webb: 'What has been settled about the execution of the South Kensington windows: Who is to do them now Campfield is ill? This must be settled at once. *See it done.* E B J ought to have sent in first design by to-day at least. *See to it.* Is the Cambridge window going to hang fire? *See to it.* It ought to go off this week.' And so on and on, with questions and orders.

The firm was now learning to adapt forms from local traditions: for instance the old Sussex chair (as designed by Webb) with its adjustable back or the Sussex type of elbow-chair with rush bottom. Morris was absorbed with his poetry. A visitor at the B Js found him in the parlour nibbing a pen, and after a few words of chat he said, 'Now you see, I'm going to write poetry, so you'll have to cut. I'm sorry, but it can't be helped.' Next Saturday he read what he had written, the story of Psyche. 'I recollect his remarking that it was very hard work writing that sort of thing. I took it he was speaking of the thrashing Psyche gets at the hands of Venus. He really felt for her, and was evidently glad it was over.' Perhaps, however, it was his general state of tension that made him dislike the interruption. Normally he seems not to have minded a chat in the midst of versifying. When Mary De Morgan came on him later writing at a sidetable at Kelmscott Manor, he told her not to go; and when she remarked on his writing poetry, he replied, 'What the devil has that to do with it? Sit down and tell me a tale.'[10]

8

Norse Fortitude

The year 1867 was not very eventful apart from the publication of *The Life and Death of Jason* in June. This story had swollen to such a size that Morris decided to publish it first, on its own. The book had an immediate success, and there were eight editions within the next fifteen years. The critics hailed it. Joseph Knight in the *Sunday Times* saw it as 'one of the most remarkable poems of this or any other age'. The influential *Pall Mall Gazette* found little to cavil at except 'the indifference to manners' shown by Medea in knocking in an unmaidenly way on Jason's door. Henry James in an unsigned notice in the *North American Review* declared that it was some time since he read a work of imagination 'with an enjoyment so unalloyed and so untempered by the desire to protest and to criticise'. Swinburne praised it highly in the *Fortnightly*, seeing in it none of the shortcomings of *The Defence*, though hurt that Morris still ignored elision. In fact the poem lacked character and drama, but showed a mastery of a certain kind of flowing narrative. The dream-element is not directly present, but the shifting of the pictures, lacking as they do any roots in real life, has its dreamy soothing effect, even when the theme is tragic. The conclusion of James's long review explains the great success of the book: 'To the jaded intellects of the present moment, distracted with the strife of creeds and the conflict of theories, it opens a glimpse into a world where they will be called upon neither to choose, to criticise, nor to believe, but simply to feel, to look, and to listen.'

Morris was pleased. 'Naturally I am in good spirits after the puffs,' he wrote on 20 June. Only a week before he had decided that he wouldn't be able to publish *The Earthly Paradise*, 'and was very low'. Now he was keen to get on with it. In the summer he went with his family to Oxford, lodging in Beaumont Street and occasionally going up to London for the day, even then returning with fresh pages of manuscript. (We hear nothing of contacts with Janey's family. Were her parents now dead?) The B Js with their children took some undergraduates' rooms in St Giles; and Faulkner had his mother and sister (probably Kate) with him. The friends went on excursions up and down the river, as commemorated in the poems introducing July and August. Every evening Morris read what he had written, or the men played whist. 'I remember noticing,' says Georgie, 'how beautifully Faulkner shuffled the cards with his beautiful fingers.'[1]

From the summer of this year Rossetti had chronic insomnia as well as nightmares; he suffered much remorse, not only about Lizzie whom he made fresh attempts to glamourise. Fanny provided the main basis of his existence, with the last shred of a romantic element imparted to her in *The Song of the Bower*. Her reign had begun in 1861 and came to an end in 1868, dwindling on till 1870, with Janey and Alexa Wilding having come up as the inspiring models. The house was often dirty and disordered, with many jealous and noisy scenes. Rossetti, with his periodic self-disgust disguised as sardonic humour, tended to be cynical about women, though clinging to his narcissistic ideal. The narcissistic nature of the image was veiled by projecting it as an absolute, as if it existed in its own right, totally cut off from the idealising mind and senses. 'Seek thine ideal anywhere except in thyself. Once fix it there, and the ways of thy real self will matter nothing to thee, whose eyes can rest on the ideal already perfected.' It didn't matter then that the 'real self' was being more and more dosed with whisky.

The BJs were looking for a new house and in November moved to the Grange, Fulham, which was then in a road with old elms, surrounded by fields and market-gardens. The custom was begun of Morris and Webb coming on Sundays. Right to the end Morris came to breakfast and spent the morning in discussions, whenever he could. He went to the house-warming party, 'a very swell affair', according to Brown. But Janey and Rossetti did not come. Morris had meant to stay for the night, but didn't; so he missed being buried in 700 lbs of plaster that fell from the studio ceiling. On 25 November he wrote to his tutor Guy about decorations being done for the chapel in the Forest School at Walthamstow, discouraging the use of mosaic, especially in spiky forms, and stressing that it best suited curved surfaces, domes, and the like. He suggested panelling that could be painted. He seems to have been quite uninterested in the Reform League; and indeed we may say that his interest in the social or political aspects of his themes was far below that he had shown in the prose romances some twelve years before. His unearned income had now fallen to £39 per share.[2]

The year 1868 saw the publication of the first section of *The Earthly Paradise*, the definite coming together of Janey and Rossetti, and Morris's tentative reawakening to social issues. Early in the year the plan of doing the poem in a single volume was given up; the book would have been too bulky and costly. The intention now was to issue two volumes; but the second part turned out to be much longer than the first and was then itself cut in half. On 3 February Morris took the first piece of copy to the printer; the day before he had written thirty-three stanzas of *Pygmalion*. The book appeared at the end of April. Meanwhile Rossetti gave a party to celebrate Janey's sitting for La Pia. 'A great dinner was given in honour of the Topsies,' wrote Brown, 'and we were all warned to appear in *Togs*. However, Morris at the last moment was dispatched to Queen Square to forcibly bring back his partner, Faulkner, thirteen at table being otherwise the mishap.' But no sooner had he gone than it was found out Rossetti had miscounted, 'and there were thirteen without Morris'. It was all 'magnificent and jolly'. On 6 March Rossetti had written to Janey the first of his letters to her that we possess. He politely discusses sittings. 'If I do not hear to the contrary, I will expect you to sit on Friday, & Morris at dinner time. It strikes me as probable that you and Bessie might like to come together, as otherwise she would be left very dull at home.' There was no problem about an extra bedroom, 'as there are several in the house'. This month William Michael Rossetti was much surprised to find that Morris took an 'interest in politics', and that he even held views 'quite in harmony with the democratic sympathies of Jones, Swinburne', and himself. This year Morris's unearned income dropped to £17 per share and kept on falling.

The Earthly Paradise, beginning with the month March, included in its first volume six Greek tales and six medieval (eastern and western). The great success of the work came from the extent to which it appealed to almost every section of the bourgeois public. The *Saturday Review* on 30 May 1869 could find the work perfect for family reading, being 'adapted for conveying to our wives and daughters a refined, although not diluted version of those wonderful creations of Greek fancy which the rougher sex alone is permitted to imbibe at first hand'. And Walter Pater in the *Westminster Review*, October 1868, could praise it highly as the perfect vehicle for escape from the existing world:

Greek poetry, mediaeval or modern poetry, projects above the realities of its time a world in which the forms of things are transfigured. Of that world the new poetry takes possession, and substitutes beyond it another still fainter and more spectral, which is literally an artificial or 'earthly paradise'. It is a finer idea, extracted from what in relation to any actual world is already an ideal.

Note how his term 'artificial paradise' brings out the relation to Baudelaire earlier suggested here. The essay ends with praise of art for art's sake, which frankly professes 'to give nothing but the highest quality to your moments as they pass, and simply for those moments' sake'. *St James's Magazine* again stressed how Morris provided 'one possible means of escape' from 'all that roar of machinery and that bustle about wealth'. The *Saturday Review* noted that 'political economists and scientific men, to whom Shelley is a mystery and Tennyson a vexation of spirit, read "The Earthly Paradise" with admiration'. The advent of the poem, its great success, we may note further, coincided with the triumph of the middle class, which, with the Reform Bill of 1867, had gained all the essential positions that it wanted. On 5 November 1868 John Bright, champion of Free Trade, declared, 'The aristocracy of England which so lately governed the country has abdicated. ... The power which hitherto has ruled over us is shifted.'[3]

The Earthly Paradise as poetry was in much the same dimension as the work done by the firm was as art. The firm's products were steadily becoming acceptable to the more cultivated sections of the middle class. Mrs Humphrey Ward's novel *The Marriage of William Ashe* describes Lady Transmore's house as revealing 'the rising worship of Morris and Burne-Jones'. Her walls 'were covered with the well-known pomegranate or jessamine or sunflower pattern; her hangings were of a mystic greenish blue; her pictures were drawn either from the Italian primitives or their modern followers'. Moncure Conway in his *Travels in South Kensington* (1882) says of Bedford Park: 'The majority of the residents have used the wall-papers and designs of Morris, the draught on whose decorative works has become so serious that a branch of the Bloomsbury establishment will probably become necessary in the vicinity.' The fashionable furnisher Maple, who had made carpets for him from his designs, sold examples behind his back. Morris called on him with Wardle, and Maple said that 'he thought it was fair the sun should shine a little on him also'. Morris was so astounded at his impudence that he merely said, 'Good morning' and left. He himself hated the idea of being fashionable, as he declares in *The Lesser Arts* (1877), and he was very irritated when commercial manufacturers made cheap imitations of his productions. One such wallpaper he described as 'a mangy gherkin on a horse-dung ground'. But just as there were revolutionary potentialities in the work being done by the firm, so were there in the elements coming together to form *The Earthly Paradise*. On the one hand the very flatness of harmonious tone in the poem was a sort of translation of the values and effects of craft-activity. The poem was a tapestry in a real sense, embodying the kind of interrelations of forms and textures that Morris learned at loom and designing-table. On the other hand, the forms and textures, thus released from the accepted conventions of what defined reality in the day's poetry or art, were in fact based in the childhood memories that provided the vital impulse of the paradisiac quest. The poem (like the craft-designs) therefore defined the Earthly Paradise in a far deeper way than could be done by any overt theme, such as that of the Wanderers. Its sensuous essence only needed to gain the further release of a new comprehensive hope, an effective belief that men and society could be truly changed, and the revolutionary poten-tialities would find their outlet. The whole sphere of application would then be changed.

Allingham gives us a glimpse of the dinners at Queen Square:

Wed. May 27. To Queen Square, to dine with Morris and find just alighting Mrs Ned in a gorgeous yellow gown: it is a full dress party! and I in velveteen jacket. Morris, Ned J. (thin), DGR (looking well), Boyce ('has been ill'), F. M. Brown (oldened), Webb, Howell, Mr Wilfrid Heeley, Publisher Ellis and WA, Mrs Morris, Miss Burden, Mrs Ned (gay), Mrs Howell, Mrs Madox Brown (looks young with back to the window), Lucy Brown, Miss Faulkner (I between these), Mrs Ellis, Mrs Heeley (ten ladies). Banquet—'Earthly Paradise' I suggest, and Ned writes this atop of the menu. A storm of talking. I away with DGR about 1; walk first, then cab to Cheyne Walk, in and stay chatting and lounging till 3 in old fashion.

Earlier in the month, on 5 and 7 May, Rossetti had written to Janey, who was at Leyton, about a blue silk dress, a stray dormouse that was caught, his lack of a copy of *The Earthly Paradise*. 'Meanwhile I have attempted some approach to a private Eden by sticking up a big tent in my garden.' Morris in a poem published in August showed the first touch of interest since 1855–6 in a theme of social justice. His ballad *God of the Poor* tells how a good knight by a stratagem deals with a lord who pillages the poor, who 'slew good men and spared the bad'.

BJ was in a bad way. 'This year I did little through illness.' He was suffering from nightmares and a sense of futility:

At present I have evil nights and am most often awake at three, with some four hours of blank time to lie on my back and think over all my days—many and evil they seem—and when I think of the confidence and conceit and blindness and ignorance of ten years ago I don't know whether most to lament that I was ever like that, or that I ever woke out of such a baseless dream.

These evil nights grew worse. He dozed off as the others talked or read; but if they stopped he woke up at once and begged them to go on. The voices gave him a sense of safety. Janey too dreamed a lot; and he and she used to compare notes. Georgie tells of one of Janey's dreams in which she found herself alone in an unknown market-place; an old-fashioned coach drove up, a rickety set of stairs were put to its door, and out came a little old woman with white hair: Georgie. 'And we exchanged doleful greetings, and she said to me, "They are all gone, Georgie"—and we wept together.'

Some time during this year, probably in the later months, BJ had fallen in love with one of the Greek girls whom Rossetti and other artists knew. Rossetti, scared of becoming blind, had been moving around: going to the Leylands at Speke Hall in August, then touring Warwickshire with his assistant Dunn in September, then accepting Bell Scott's invitation to stay at Penkill Castle, Ayrshire, the home of his mistress Alice Boyd. He was afraid of death and discussed suicide, objecting to a posthumous show of his pictures since they failed to satisfy him. He was also thinking of death as well as of bilking creditors with a scheme of making his estate over to his brother; from a Miss Losh he borrowed sums up to £500, as was found out when she died. The Morrises took an autumn holiday at Southwold: an event commemorated in the October stanzas of *The Earthly Paradise*. On his return to London Morris began his studies in Icelandic. Warrington Taylor introduced him to Eirikr Magnusson (who looked remarkably like him). Magnusson tells how he met him in the hall at Queen Square. 'With a manly shake of the hand he said: "I'm glad to see you, come upstairs!" And with a bound he was upstairs and I after him until his study and the second floor was reached.' Morris proposed reading Icelandic with him three times a week, and Magnusson suggested that they start with *Gunnlaug the Worm-tongue*. 'Morris decided from the beginning to leave alone the irksome task of taking regular grammatical exercises.' He said, 'You be my grammar as we go along,' and began at once translating. After going through a passage, Magnusson wrote out a literal version at home and produced it at the next lesson; Morris then made a version in his own style, which was later printed.

Warrington Taylor was pounding away with his efforts to get the firm more businesslike in its whole costing system. May remarks, 'He probably saved the firm from going to pieces through the unpractical ways of its members.' Taylor argued against doing cheap work. 'Morris and I never get hot with one another save on the subject of price. He is nearly always for a low price; seeing the amount of work we do it is absurd, we must have a long price; and it must be considered not so much per foot as so much for painting in glass.' On 3 November Rossetti had returned to Cheyne Walk. He wanted Janey as Pandora opening the chest of evils, 'powers of the impassioned hours prohibited'. But she kept being prostrated, and he had to call on Alexa as understudy while painting *Sibylla Palmifera*. The work was 'held up because poor Mrs Morris has been very ill and unable to sit which threw me out a good deal in my work, besides being a much greater concern to me on her own account'. No doubt he was thinking of her relation to Morris when he painted her as *La Pia* dragged down in health by a callous husband.[4]

About this time we find people realising that something had happened between Janey and Rossetti. Scott, now in London, certainly knew much about the relationship. He wrote on 9 November to Alice Boyd:

Gabriel had not tried painting, nor seen his doctor, nor seen the sweet Lucretia Borgia. I have now come to the conclusion—often when we meet a person in a new place after a few days cessation a new light breaks on one—that the greatest disturbance in his health and temper, and both are extremely different from what they were, is caused by an uncontrollable desire for the possession of the said LB. Letitia was there on Friday to see an Altar Cloth and was the first to inform her of Gabriel's return, he having refrained from going as he understands they are being watched. Even Mrs. Street had spoken to Letitia about Gabriel being so fond of Mrs. Top.

On the 15th the Morrises, Rossetti and others dined with Scott. Scott, describing the event, remarks, 'As to Gabriel he forgets everyone else. When he went down, although it was my part to take Jeanie [Janey], G. got her arm in his in a moment, then abandoned her as hurriedly for the nearest other lady, Morris looking at him all the time.' That last detail helps us to enter into the misery and uncertainty that Morris was feeling throughout this period.

In January 1869 the *Saga of Gunnlaug* appeared in the *Fortnightly*. Morris was turning more and more to Norse tales in preference to Greek legends and medieval romances. BJ was getting in a worse fix than ever and Morris tried to help him. The Victorians were extremely reticent despite their voluminous letter-writing, and if it had not been for Rossetti with his malicious enjoyment of such a situation we should have had no suspicion of this breakdown in BJ's marriage. On 23 January he wrote to Brown: 'Poor Ned's affairs have come to a smash altogether, and he and Topsy, after the most dreadful to-do, started for Rome suddenly, leaving the Greek damsel beating up the quarters of all his friends for him and howling like Cassandra. Georgie stayed behind. I hear to-day however that Top and Ned got no further than Dover, Ned being now so dreadfully ill that they will probably have to return to London.' Marie had insisted on a suicide pact with laudanum in Holland Walk, Kensington; then she did her best to drown herself in the Paddington canal outside Browning's house—'bobbies collaring Ned who was rolling on the stones with her to prevent it, and God knows what else'. (Rossetti adds in a note probably to Howell: 'Janey has stopped her sittings by order during foreign service—just as I supposed.') The scoundrelly Howell, who was much involved in the affairs of Rossetti and Whistler, did his best to cause trouble by taking Marie to meet Georgie at the Grange. When Ned came in and saw her there, he fainted and fell against the mantelpiece. The wound on his forehead left a permanent scar. Georgie in her *Memorials* says hardly anything of the year 1869 except that BJ then painted a water-colour of Circe.

The affair dragged on at least till 1872; for Mackail on 7 December 1897, referring to a letter which Mrs Coronio had lent him, says that he sees it is dated November 1872. 'I had thought MZ was all over by that time, but my chronology is very confused about that very confused & complicated business. How extraordinarily interesting one could make the story, if one were going to die the day before it was published.' The episode has strong bearings on Morris's life; for Georgie must have felt miserable over these years, and he, deserted in a less dramatic way by Janey, cannot but have felt more and more drawn towards her.

In March Henry James called at Queen Square. 'Morris's poetry, you see, is only his sub-trade.' He manufactures 'everything quaint, archaic, pre-Raphaelite—and I may add, exquisite'. The articles are 'of the very last luxury', so that 'his *fabrique* can't be on a very large scale'. He himself 'designs with his own head and hands all the figures and patterns used in his glass and tapestry', that is, embroidery, 'and furthermore works the latter, stitch by stitch, with his own fingers, aided by those of his wife and little girls'. Janey much impressed James.

Oh, my chère, such a wife! Je n'en reviens pas—she haunts me still. A figure cut out of a missal—out of one of Rossetti's or Hunt's pictures—to say this gives but a faint idea of her, because when such an image puts on flesh and blood, it is an apparition of fearful and wonderful intensity. It's hard to say whether she's a grand synthesis of all the Pre-Raphaelite pictures ever made—or they a 'keen analysis' of her—whether she's an original or a copy. In either case she's a wonder. Imagine a tall lean woman in a long dress of some dead purple stuff, guiltless of hoops (or of anything else, I should say) with a mass of crisp black hair heaped into great wavy projections on each of her temples, a thin pale face, a pair of strange, sad, deep, dark Swinburnean eyes, with great thick black oblique brows, joined in the middle and tucking themselves away under her hair, a mouth like the 'Oriana' in our illustrated Tennyson, a long neck, without any collar, and in lieu thereof some dozen strings of outlandish beads—in fine complete. On the wall was a large nearly finished full-length portrait of her by Rossetti, so strange and unreal that if you hadn't seen her you'd pronounce it a distempered vision, but in fact an extremely good likeness.

The picture was probably *The Blue Silk Dress*. James stayed to dinner. After which Morris read from the second series of *The Earthly Paradise*, and Janey, with a bad toothache, lay on the sofa, with her handkerchief over her face. James found it a strange scene: the unusual furniture, Morris reading 'in his flowing antique numbers', and 'in the corner this dark silent medieval woman with her medieval toothache'. He liked Morris. 'He is short, burly, corpulent, very careless and unfinished in his dress,' with 'a very loud voice and a nervous restless manner and a perfectly unaffected and business-like address. His talk indeed is wonderfully to the point and remarkable for clear good sense. He said no one thing that I remember, but I was struck with the very good judgment shown in everything he uttered.'

In April Morris published his version of the *Grettis Saga*. In his effort to keep as close to the actual construction of the original he ends by losing its direct and living tone and by putting oddity in the place of its vividness. In a prefatory sonnet he wrote of the new interest brought by the sagas 'to fill life's void'. He is awakening from the passive dream and becoming interested in people afresh. The sagaman, he says, never relaxes

his grasp of Grettir's character, and he is the same man from beginning to end;

thrust this way and that by circumstances, but little altered by them; unlucky in all things, yet made strong to bear all ill-luck; scornful of the world, yet capable of enjoyment, and determined to make the most of it; not deceived by men's specious ways, but disdaining to cry out because he needs must bear with them.

There he states the ideal he now sets for himself: courage and endurance. For *The Earthly Paradise* he wrote *The Lovers of Gudrun*, in which there is still the old mellifluous smoothness, but also a note of passionate involvement as distinct from harmonious evocation of mood. The theme is once more the love of two friends for the same woman: a theme that appears also in the story of the *Man Who Never Laughed Again*. In 1883, looking back, he said of the sagas: 'The delightful freshness and independence of thought of them, the air of freedom which breathes through, their worship of courage (the great virtue of the human race), their utter unconventionality took my heart by storm.' But why did he turn so strongly to them at this moment? He had already learned something of Norse tales and myths in his Oxford days, but he had not been particularly attracted. He responded now because he was ready for the message of the sagas and deeply needed it. Perhaps he now realised that he had definitely lost Janey to Rossetti and must discard any half-hopes he had had of regaining her. He was losing the unearned income which had done so much to relieve him of anxieties about maintaining his position and keeping his family; but the success of his poems must have done much to restore his self-confidence. The firm was doing well but its affairs were in much confusion and a breakdown was possible. Taylor was hammering home this latter point. Early this year he wrote in his worried way to Webb, noting that during the last twelve months Morris had 'spent just as much over and above his proper income as he did three years ago— ask him what he spent last year—you will be staggered—I know the amount.' And to make sure that Webb would be staggered he appended a statement of the situation. Morris was living at the rate of £1,000 to £1,100 a year. From his dividends he still had got £460; he had drawn £200 from the firm, earned £200 from his publications, and taken £200 from the capital he had invested in the firm. 'He has only £400 capital to draw out of the firm.' So he was sure to run into debt if he didn't change his ways.

We see then that there must have been considerable pressure of anxiety upon him. He felt that unless he made a strenuous effort to stand on his own feet and to take a new grip on his impulses, he would meet disaster in some way. At all costs he had to overcome the more pessimistic and melancholy aspects of *The Earthly Paradise*, which must have now seemed to him a shameful self-indulgence. But his sharp turn was not yet socially-based; he is above all seeking to regain his self-respect. As he told an audience in his socialist days:

Self-restraint was a virtue sure to be thought much of among a people whose religion was practically courage: in all the stories of the North failure is never reckoned a disgrace, but it *is* reckoned a disgrace not to bear it with equanimity, and to wear one's heart on one's sleeve is not well thought of.

The first work which Morris had read with Magnusson was *The Eyrbyggja Saga*, which he finished writing out in illuminated form for Georgie by April 1872; some lines from the *envoi* he first composed define well the phase of transition from the passive dream to a fully active relation of art with life. They also express the hope he was nourishing of yet achieving a true love-relationship (no doubt with Georgie):

> And though this seems so far from me
> Though sunk in dreams I still must be
> Self-made about myself—yet now
> Who knows what out of all may grow;
> Who knows but I myself at last
> May face the truth, with all fear cast
> Clean forth of me: real Love and I
> Set side by side before I die.[5]

Meanwhile Rossetti was being torn with old remorses and the hope of rebirth in a new love. In art he was mainly concerned with Janey as Pandora, the all-gifted, the all-giver, and then as Proserpine, the unhappy wife doomed to spend half the year in darkness with her husband. He asks if Pandora has been made half-divine to infuse 'in Venus' eyes the gaze of Proserpine', and proceeds to build round Janey the imagery of death-in-life, love-in-death, of his later works. On 24 May Scott wrote that he had found him 'in the dumps, not painting on either day, but lounging about the room shouldering everything with his hands in his pockets, because Janey was ill and unable to come'. In early June he wrote two Italian sonnets, which he and his brother suppressed. Here he speaks of the mouth 'which in the hour of reward so often I have kissed', while hearing 'words of divine acquiescence, welcomed with a thousand vows'. He prays that his beloved's kisses with their sacred incense will blot out 'the many old ghosts at last buried', and will fill 'the heavens with the immensity of our love'. In *Dark Lily* (later called *Love-Lily*) he brings out the identity of this love with Pandora, the One Hope hitherto denied him; and at last declares body and soul, passion and worship, to have become one.

But Janey again became prostrate. No doubt she felt her own strain in the situation which had developed. By July she was so bad that Morris decided to take her to the spa at Bad-Ems in Hesse-Nassau; at least he could continue there with his versifying. On 21 July Rossetti wrote to Janey at Cologne, hoping the cloaks he had given her proved useful. He sent a cartoon of Morris reading *The Earthly Paradise*, oblivious of Jane naked in the bath before him. 'The accompanying cartoon may prepare you for the worst— whichever that may be, the 7 tumblers [of spa-water] or the 7 volumes [of the poem].' Of B J Rossetti adds significantly, 'I shall go round to the Greeks tonight and probably see him there.' Six days later he wrote anxiously for news. On 23 July Webb had written, 'Ned & Georgie & Gabriel are part of the family but we look at each other in a kind of rage that the rest are not by— I make a solemn vow that if I ever see you again I will be better, kinder and less selfish, but shall please myself just now by thinking that you would not like me so much if I changed.'

On 31 July Morris wrote to Webb from the Hotel Fortuna. He had been rowing in the river 'in a machine like a butter-boat with a knife and fork for oars', but after a while the water was like a mill-race, he took half an hour to move twenty yards and his hands were blistered. But 'there is a nice green bank on shadow after 5 p.m., just this side of the rapids, and I suppose I shall paddle Janey there pretty often'. Carriages shook her up badly. 'If ("when" I hope) she gets better there are splendid mokes and mules here, whereon she may climb the hills.' The day before Rossetti had written a tender letter to her. He mentions Morris. 'All that concerns you is the all-absorbing question with me, as dear Top will not mind my telling you at this anxious time. The more he loves you, the more he knows that you are too lovely and noble not to be loved.' He is drawn by her absence to make protestations that he had doubtless not so far made to her face. 'I can never tell you how much I am with you at all times. Absence from your sight is what I have long been used to: and no absence can ever make me so far from you again as your presence did for years. For this long inconceivable change, you know now that my thanks must be.' We feel that he had already begun to press her during the sittings and had thus contributed to her collapse, but that he now is more sure of himself and her. On 4 August, sending a cartoon of the Morrises and their German maid, he cries, 'What a joyful hearing it is that you have passed two days almost without pain.' He is expecting to go to Penkill but wants to make sure of being in London at her return.

The day before Webb had written about Gabriel, and supposed that 'Janey in the corner on the sofa is thinking of the "provincial" people she has left behind'. Was he thinking of the provincial girl of working-class origins who had become a grand lady, or was he suggesting that she wasn't so grand after all? Webb had an odd ironic humour. In his previous letter he had asked Morris to see that Janey 'put a female scratch at the end' of his next letter. 'Just to keep me in mind of her finger ends.' He likes to comment on the claws she kept hidden but ready to use.

On 9 August Morris told Webb he was reading *Wilhelm Meister* in Carlyle's translation, but thinks Goethe must have been asleep while writing it. Janey couldn't sit up to write; her back ached if she did so. On 15 August he remarked that it was a month since he had left London. He wanted to get home, kept looking up timetables, and took his pocketbook for scribbling in even on his walks. He found the damp woods 'lonely and dismal', full of enormous ants and slugs, and, of adders as long as his umbrella. Janey added a note:

My finger tips are sound—as you see by this—and fit for much more hard labour—I feel that I have not much else about me that is good for anything—but I have a sort of presentiment (though of course you don't believe in such things) that I may make a rapid turn—and feel myself well all of a sudden—and then I have another presentiment that should this change come all those I now call my friends would also change—and would not be able to stand me.

These words give some idea of the inner struggle which was breaking down her health, or, rather, making her feel the need of a conviction of breakdown.

Rossetti had written on the 10th and 14th. He said that now he knew Janey was on the mend he would go off to Scotland. 'I suppose Topsy is roaring and steaming his way' like a train 'through the Parnassian tunnels and junctions in his usual style now, not without an occasional explosion. Did he remember the couple of blouses he promised me from Lille?' Janey in fact was bored and unable to get out and about. 'She misses,' Morris told Webb, 'a great many little occupations that wear away the day at home.' The doctor advised her to go on to Switzerland; but they had both had enough, said

Morris. Ellis had sent out an article by Austin on Morris and Arnold, in which Morris was praised as supreme for 'the most unvarying sweetness and sustained tenderness of soul'. Austin pointed out that Morris averted his eyes from the realities of the day. 'They are crooked; who shall set them straight? For his part, he will not even try.' He had rejected struggles against the age, 'its vaunted progress, its infinitite vulgar nothings, and has taken refuge in the sleepy region'. Morris replied to Ellis that commercially he should feel grateful and that 'from the critical point of view I think there is so much truth as this in his article, as that we poets of to-day have been a good deal made by those of the Byron and Shelley time.' But he recognised the note of 'tender contempt'. Indeed in his own changing attitudes he must have been somewhat upset by Austin's remark that in turning away from his age he had 'evaded the very conditions in which alone the production of great poetry is possible', so that he was 'the wisely unresisting victim of a rude irreversible current; the serene master of a mean and melancholy time'. Yet Austin was only paraphrasing what Morris had written of himself as the idle singer of an empty day.

On 29 August he wrote to Webb that 'to-day much against the grain I wrote 120 lines but have still got the fidgets'. Rossetti had written from Penkill telling Janey of the picture he wanted to paint of her as Fortune amid 'the symbols of life, death, &c.'. On 30 August he described the glen he frequented, and his 'vain longing for perfectibility', an endless task. 'Topsy will I fear look with utter scorn on this fidgetty fretting over old ground. He is in the right for himself, I know.'[6]

Meanwhile Taylor was still fighting to get order into the firm. Early in July he told Webb:

Memo.—What is absolutely necessary to save the firm from ruin is this: Someone must see the books weekly or fortnightly to see that Morris has not drawn cheques for himself or others, when he has no money due to him—At the present he has still £200 to draw of capital. . . . In his private life he cannot afford more than £6 per week for household expenses and with the present degree of comfort that will only just suffice—therefore he cannot afford to entertain or to feed strangers— what does an extra dinner cost, piece of salmon 5/- leg of mutton 7/6 vegetables 2/- pudding—wine—coals—butter—let him do it as much as he likes if he can only afford it. . . .

Some time this year he also wrote warnings to Morris himself:

You are at it again—you won't have anything like the six years I allotted you two years ago. . . . Two years more will do for you completely—What will your income be this year—What are you spending—How much are you in debt—Under the new bankruptcy act they will sell you up completely—your mines will go to the creditors—so you will have nothing left. You might have had £900 at the bank now can't you manage. . . .

It is clear that he had many angry scenes with Morris, for he writes: 'It's no good your screaming and saying you will shut the bloody shop up. You can't afford to do it any longer. I told you some years ago that it would become indispensable to you. It is evident that you must give up your entertaining. You have not the means to do it.' He protested to Rossetti: 'The personal extravagance of the members used to be spasmodic: it is now confirmed and habitual. WM has grown worse and worse.' While Morris was at Ems, Taylor went on telling Webb that Morris was heading for bankruptcy with his habit of signing cheques for himself drawn on the firm's funds. We see that Morris had got into a state of mind where he couldn't bear to keep detailed weekly accounts; he tried to persuade himself that a small cheque couldn't make much difference. Taylor insisted that after he had used up his last £200 capital, Webb 'must officially for the firm examine the books to see what he is doing—this is our last resource'. The money coming in from his poems at uncertain dates was 'like a "tip" to a schoolboy —and is of no real benefit'. Morris's bad habits, Taylor says, have accumulated during the last eighteen months when he himself has been ill. These warnings and pleas by Taylor did end by having the effect desired. As part of the struggle to regain an inner balance which we see expressed in the turning to the sagas, Morris managed to discipline himself over money.

Early in September the Morrises were back in London. 'No doubt you will take the precaution on your return to London of having proper arrangements made to enable you to take the baths at home,' Rossetti had written on the 7th. Webb was already at work. On the 1st he had drafted and sent out a scheme for sending water down through a flexible pipe wielded by a servant; a cistern was to be put above in the servants' ante-closet. He drew a very fat naked Janey being douched. 'I could not resist giving my recollection of Janey's figure but it wanted Ned to do the subject justice. If Janey does not understand the fat joke on the other side please to explain it—or rather if you *don't* (& I know you *won't*) get Janey to do it.' Rossetti had written that he wanted to celebrate Janey's restoration with a dinner; by the

20th he was himself back in London. Later in September the third volume of *The Earthly Paradise* was ready.

This summer Magnusson had introduced Morris to the *Volsunga Saga*. 'I found him in a state of great excitement, pacing his study. He told me that he had now finished my translation of the "grandest tale that ever was told".' Morris set to work soon on his own version. On the night of 10 October at Highgate Cemetery Lizzie's grave was opened, by a special perm itfrom the Home Office, in the presence of Howell, a solicitor, and a doctor. The manuscript book of poems that Rossetti had put in the coffin was rescued and the doctor took it away to be disinfected. His need to recover the book was somewhat odd. He had a very good memory for his poems, and various people had received copies of many of the poems in the book. Perhaps the sense he now felt of a sort of rebirth through Janey drove him to this action by which he brought back the buried poems into the light. He was vindicating what he felt as the return of his creative energies. In any event it seems around this time, partly as a result of the parting and the reunion, that he definitely surrendered himself to a devoted passion for Janey. Boyce, calling on 26 November, found that he had been trying again at *Found* and working at a *Death of Beatrice*. 'Mrs Morris has been sitting again to him lately.'

The critic in the *Pall Mall Gazette* for December, perhaps Sidney Colvin, while reaffirming the vast popularity of *The Earthly Paradise*, remarked on 'the increased prominence given to passion and emotion', and in particular pointed to *Gudrun* as 'in its intention a half tragic, half epic study of fate and passion'. Swinburne wrote to Morris about the book, and Morris replied, 'I am delighted to have pleased you with the Gudrun. For the rest I am rather painfully conscious myself that the book would have done me more credit if there had been nothing in it but the Gudrun, though I don't think the others are quite the worst things I have done. Yet they are all too long and flabby, damn it?' He goes on about *The Egils Saga* and the *Volsunga*. On the same day he wrote to Norton at some length about the *Volsunga*. 'The scene of the last interview between Sigurd and the despairing and terrible Brynhild touches me more than anything I have ever met with in literature.' He says that he had meditated an epic on the theme, but feels no verse could do it justice. (However, six years later he could not resist writing *Sigurd the Volsung*.)

This year a committee was set up by the Union at Oxford to consider the decaying paintings there. Morris wrote giving details of the works and explaining which had been done by which artist. (Separate negotiations were going on with Rossetti.) He adds, 'In confidence to you I should say that the whole affair was begun and carried out in too piecemeal and unorganised a manner to be a real success—nevertheless it would surely be a pity to destroy some of the pictures, which are really remarkable, and at the worst can do no harm there.' This year also Morris and Webb painted the screen of the organ at Beddington, Surrey.[7]

In letters of early 1870 Rossetti shows himself falling ever deeper under Janey's spell. He revealed a deep need which only she could satisfy, and she could not but have been much moved by his emotional dependence on her. Something of his inner emptiness, his lack of security, must have found its echo in her. He demanded everything; he demanded nothing. And it was this worshipping passivity which drew her to him as a refuge after the noisy entangled world of Morris. On 31 January he wrote to her:

It was so sweet of you to ask me to let you know how I got on, so I write to say I am all right again this morning after the mustard last night. The sight of you going down the dark steps to the cab all alone has plagued me ever since—you looked so lonely. I hope you got home safe & well. Now everything will be dark for me till I can see you again. It puts me in a rage to think that I should have been so knocked up all yesterday as to be such dreadfully dull company. Why should it happen just when you were here?

He thinks he has left his spectacles at her place, and goes on:

For the last two years I have felt distinctly the clearing away of the chilling numbness that surrounded me in the utter want of you; but since then other obstacles have kept steadily on the increase, and it comes too late.

Four days later he wrote to her with a drawing, saying that he felt so badly the need to talk with her.

No one else seems at all alive to me now, and places that are empty of you are empty of all life. And it is so seldom that the dead hours breathe a little and yield your dear voice to me again. I seem to hear it while I write, and to see your eyes speaking as clearly as your voice; and so I would write to you for ever if it were not too bad to keep reminding you of my troubles who have so many of your own. . . . I always reproach myself with the comfort I feel despite all in the thought of you, when that thought never fails to present me also with the recollection of your pain and suffering. But more than all for me, dear Janey, is the fact that you exist, that I can yet look forward to seeing you again, and know for certain that at that moment I shall forget all my own troubles nor even be able to remember yours. You are the noblest and dearest thing that the world has had to show me: and if no loss than the loss of you could have brought me so much bitterness, I would still rather have had this to endure than have missed the fullness of wonder and worship which nothing else could have made known to me.

It seems to him now that he has loved her all the while; but this idea is surely a delusion. No doubt he was much attracted to her from the first and slowly came to admire her more and more in Red House days; and, looking back, he can easily feel that his life would have been different if he had only had her for himself all along. In mid-February his poems went to press, and Morris promised to review the book, which he did in *The Academy*, despite his strong dislike of such tasks. More, he must have realised that some of the poems were addressed to Janey. He had turned to illumination as a craft-release. The fact that he did a *Book of Verse*, *The Eyrbyggia Saga*, and the *Rubaiyat of Omar Khayyam* for Georgie at this junction, brings out clearly enough to whom his thoughts were now continually turning. This work went on from 1870 to late 1872; he also in April 1870 bound up the first draft of *The Lovers of Gudrun* and presented it to Georgie.

In February 1870 Warrington Taylor died, not yet thirty-three years old. He was buried at St Thomas's, Fulham, at the firm's cost, under a stone designed by Webb. George Wardle became manager; he was a member of the dyeing firm, Wardles, whose offices were at Leek in Staffordshire, and was married to Madeleine Smith, who had been the accused in a famous murder-case in Scotland.[8] She had poisoned a lover with arsenic, but escaped conviction. Early in March Rossetti went to Scalands with an American artist and journalist, meaning to work on poems, though he did little. Among his plans was a poem to be called *God's Graal*, which took up the theme of Lancelot on the lines of the painting in the Union (begun shortly before meeting Janey): 'the loss of the Sancgraal by Lancelot—a theme chosen to emphasise the marked superiority of Guinevere over God'. He seems here to be using the triadic theme to praise Janey-Guinevere who has brought him new life by turning from her husband Arthur-Morris. The theme of rebirth-through-love was to come into another poem, *The Harrowing of Hell*: 'as if the redemption wrought by Christ were to be viewed as an elevation of the conception of love from pleasure into passion'.

Stillman used chloral hydrate against insomnia and introduced Rossetti to it. (He had earlier recommended it to Brown, who in turn recommended it to Shields, who was in its grip for some years, and who spoke of 'the death-like stupefaction without restorative power' it produced, 'the suicidal despondency'.) Stillman insisted later that Rossetti was already 'sleepless, excitable and possessed by the monomania of persecution'. The two men agreed to share expenses at Scalands; but Stillman, hard-up, invited no one while Rossetti invited Brown, the Morrises, and others, and lavishly bought things. In the end Stillman had to slip quietly off. Scalands suited Rossetti as he could get over easily to Hastings where Janey had gone with the girls. Morris had to spend much of his time in London, though Rossetti asked him and Janey both to Scalands for a couple of days late in March. 'Top and Janey are here to-day, the former insolently solid—the latter better than when I last saw her at Hastings.' Soon afterwards he writes: 'She and Morris have been in this neighbourhood lately, and are coming again; and I trust the change may prove eventually of some decided benefit to her, as signs of this have already become apparent.' A week later Morris was back in London and Janey seems installed at Scalands, staying on till Rossetti left. A crayon drawing of her he thought 'the best thing I ever did'. On 18 April he told his mother, 'Janey Morris is here and benefiting greatly. Top comes from time to time.' We can date, it seems, to this period the sonnet that begins: 'On this sweet bank your head thrice sweet and dear I lay, and spread your hair on either side,' with his kisses climbing her throat to her mouth. Other sonnets also deal with love-trysts. Yet all the while he was in communication with Fanny.

Meanwhile on the 15th Morris wrote to Janey to say that he had called on Mrs Aglaia Coronio, one of the daughters of Constantine Ionides, Greek merchant and art-patron. The firm decorated the house of Aleco Ionides at Holland Park. Morris was sitting to Watts for his portrait and complained of a bad cold in the head. 'How I do hate Easter, second only to Christmas: however I'm going to Leyton on Monday'—to see his mother. 'My cold makes me stupid today so I will shut up.' On the 25th Rossetti made a one-day visit to London to sign copies of his poems and took Morris to Rule's oyster bar. Morris rather unnecessarily wrote to Janey to tell her. He was again going to see Aglaia and receive 'her bland flatteries' on his way to Ned's that afternoon. 'I so rather wish she wouldn't butter me so, if that isn't ungrateful, so you needn't chaff me as one who can't see the fun of it: I shall certainly come down for a day or two next week and fetch you up when you are ready to be fetched—do you want any more wine?'[9]

The death of Warrington Taylor seems to have shocked Morris into awareness that, with that inquisitorial eye no longer directed at his financial doings,
he would have to take proper charge himself. With the new-found determination that had been partly born out of desperation, he surveyed the situation and took steps to halt the fall of his income. He persuaded the other
partners to add £50 to his salary, grant him 10 per cent of the net annual
profits, and pay his rent, taxes, gas and coals at Queen Square. At the same
time he set himself to watch and control his expenses. We have a pair of lists
in his handwriting calculating his yearly expenses; the totals are £540 and
£500, both half what Taylor had reckoned as his expenditure in 1868. He
had made the first definite step towards the reorganisation of the firm he
carried out in 1874. His 1870 actions were taken just in time, for by 1873 his
mining dividends had faded right out. His economies must have made life
more difficult with Janey; but the need to face without illusions what had
happened to his marriage was an integral part of the struggle going on
inside him; he knew that he had to find a new basis for his life. This year
Dickens died and the Franco-Prussian War broke out; but we know nothing
of his reactions. He seems too enclosed in his own problems to be concerned
much at such events.

Perhaps in part through the success of his poems, Rossetti's health was
better this summer. About this time Gosse saw Janey at Brown's in a long
ivory velvet dress, seated on the model's throne, while Rossetti, 'too stout
for elegance', squatted on a hassock at her feet. Whistler noted at Brown's
'in an inner room, Rossetti and Mrs Morris sitting side by side in state, being
worshipped', with Howell fluttering round them. Francillon tells of Rossetti
at the poet Marston's receptions: 'My most representative recollection of him
is of his sitting beside Mrs Morris, who looked as if she had stepped out of
any one of his pictures, both wrapped in motionless silence as of a world
where souls have no need of words.' Morris, a 'comical figure with the mop
head', was also there now and then. A cousin of William De Morgan remembered Rossetti at a party given by Mrs Virtue Tebbs, 'seated in a corner
feeding Mrs William Morris with strawberries. He was carefully scraping
off the cream, which was bad for her, and then solemnly presenting her the
strawberries in a spoon.'

A story, doubtless invented by Howell, shows at least the way that people
like Whistler talked and sniggered about Morris and Janey. While Rossetti
painted, Janey embroidered a design of his on some hangings. 'Howell—"the
owl" as they called him—hung it up between Mrs Morris's bed and Morris's.

But it was too short, about a foot from the floor, and Howell came to tell Rossetti. What was to be done? It was a foot from the floor, and some night Morris would crawl under! "He would not dare!" Rossetti declared, bringing his fist down on the table with a bang.'[10]

Morris's turn to the north was again expressed by the publication of *The Story of the Volsungs and Niblungs*. But his dropping of the smooth style of *The Earthly Paradise* was not welcomed. G. A. Simcox in *The Academy* for August, commenting on two murders in the story, remarked, 'It is almost too silly to be tragical; and it is hard after all to care for the death's of men who did not care for their own lives. Norse literature, when all is said, must still be left to students. When will the author of *Jason* give us the final perfect English *Odyssey*?'

Janey's health throughout 1870 seems to have been bad; much of the year she was away, recovering from her indefinite ailments. In the autumn she was languishing at Torquay. On 3 October Morris wrote a playful and affectionate letter to her. (She does not seem alone as he ends, 'Goodbye dear child, love to all kinswomen.') 'It was a great relief to know that you are better; I daresay getting home to something more amusing than—well— I send a P.O.O. for £5 drawn by William Morris in favour of Jane do: will that do?' He seems disconcerted and chatters on about a newly papered room; then goes on to the one deeply felt statement that we know from his extant letters to her:

I am quite sure you oughtn't to make the journey alone, poor little dear. As for living, dear, people like you speak about don't know either what life or death means, except for one or two supreme moments of their lives, when something pierces through the crust of dullness and ignorance, and they act for the time as if they were sensitive people. For me I don't think people really want to die because of mental pain, that is if they are imaginative people; they want to live to see the play played out fairly—they have hopes that they are not conscious of—Hilloa! here's cheerful talk for you. I beg your pardon, dear, with all my heart. I am going this afternoon to get a little sentiment out of Aglaia, in case she's in: she is making quite a fine thing of her bookbinding by the way.

We do not know whom he is referring to, but clearly his comments begin to stir his own emotions too deeply and he pulls himself up, aware that he is pleading his own case. Janey came home; then in November she had an attack of sciatica and lumbago and left London again. On 26 November Morris wrote to tell her that he was hard at work over the proofs of

Volume IV of *The Earthly Paradise*. 'I feel rather lost at having done my book.' He felt that he must find 'something serious to do' as soon as he could. He thought of Tristram and Iseult as a theme for a long poem, and perhaps now began the prose romance on the subject, which he left unfinished after a very lengthy introduction. He must have finally realised that he had lost Janey. His thoughts turned more and more to Iceland, the Norse world of fortitude, where 'failure is never reckoned a disgrace' if bravely borne.[11]

Some indication of what he had been feeling can be found in a few of the poems in the collection which he illuminated for Georgie, *A Book of Verse*, and which he never printed.[12] First there is *Lonely Love and Loveless Death*. He asks if it is going, or has already gone for ever, 'The life that seemed round me, The longing I sought? Has it turned to undoing, That constant endeavour To bind love that bound me, To hold all it brought?' He has endured till the pain is intolerable. Then he turns and seems to address Georgie, asking himself: 'If her breath thou wert hearing, What words wouldst thou say?' *Guileful Love* seems to record the failure of his love for Janey. 'Love set me in a flowery garden fair.' (We may note the characteristic garden-setting.) For a while he had no fear of Death, Change, or Eld; then he 'awoke at last, and born again Laid eager hands upon unrest and pain'. Things grew ever better and he knew yet more 'the root and heart of Love'. He knew all fears 'save only one'. Then it seems this one fear came true, for he cries out: 'Where is the fair earth now, where is the sun? Thou didst not say my Love might never move Her eyes, her hands, her lips to bless my love.' It is barely possible that this poem is addressed to Georgie and expresses his regret that she will not give herself up to him; but on the whole it seems more a lament over Janey.

Then there is *Summer Night*. This is quite different in tone and joyfully celebrates a love-tryst. 'O my love, if thou hearest my foot-steps anear Thy very breathing methinks I may hear O my sweet, is it true that we are alone, The grey leaves a-quiver, twixt us and the moon O me, the love, the love in thine eyes, Now the night is a dying as all life dies! Art thou come, swift end of beginning of bliss? O my sweet! O thine eyes, O thy hand, O thy kiss.'

This poem cannot record any experience he ever had with Janey; and when we consider that Morris was never given to writing lyrical verse of a personal kind except when driven to wrestle with his own direct problems, it seems possible that it tells of a summer night when he and Georgie embraced. She at this time, we must recall, was suffering deeply through Ned's affair with Marie Zambaco; and there is no doubt that she and Morris must have come close together, both feeling deserted and in much need of sympathy and consolation. Her letters to Morris have been lost or destroyed; his letters to her which have come down have been carefully chosen and perhaps edited. Certainly she and her son-in-law Mackail have tactfully trimmed and respectabilised her relations with Morris, especially in these years round 1870 when the two of them were brought most intimately and warmly together.

9

Kelmscott and Iceland

1871 was in many ways a crucial year for Morris. The union of Janey and Rossetti was at its climax, and his need to find some way out of the melancholy resignation of *The Earthly Paradise* and the role of upholsterer was extreme. He was still facing the issues almost entirely on a personal level, with no sense of the social situation except in so far as he carried on a general Ruskinian outlook with regard to craft and art. His total lack of response to the Paris Commune, which later meant so much to him, underlines this point. It is with something of a shock that one comes on his poem *The Dark Wood*, in the *Fortnightly Review* in February, amid so many articles, such as those of Frederick Harrison, which seek with passionate seriousness to get inside the French events. That is not to say that the pressures of the social and political situation were not at work on him; he can hardly have failed to glance through the newspapers and such articles as those of Harrison. But he was not yet in a position to move from the purely personal dilemma to the wider issues.

Mackail selects this moment to describe at some length his rages and irritable outbursts.

When 'The Earthly Paradise' was being published 'the men at the shop thought a great deal of it': but if they had been inclined to think meanly of him as a poet, they would in any case have respected and admired the employer whose language was so forcible and copious when things were not going to his mind. In one of his tempers he was capable of almost anything. Once at Red Lion Square he hurled a fifteenth-century folio, which in ordinary circumstances he would hardly have allowed anyone but himself to touch, at the head of an offending workman. It missed the workman and drove a panel out of the workshop door. His 'tempestuous and exacting company', in the phrase of one of his most intimate friends, had something of the quality of an overwhelming natural force; like the north wind, it braced and buffeted in an almost equal measure. He had the incessant restlessness of a wild creature. One of his friends describes him, on the occasion of their first meeting in 1871, as pacing up and down the room like a caged lion. Even at work or at meals he could not sit still for long, but must be continually shifting and fidgeting, getting up to cross the room or look out of the window and then sitting down again. . . . In his gusts of temper he seemed insensible to pain and almost superhuman in his strength: he has been known to drive his head against the wall so as to make a deep dent in the plaster, and bite almost through the woodwork of a window frame. He could lift the heaviest weight in his teeth.

On 11 January this year Rossetti wrote to Miss Losh:

Lately he was known to hang on to the bell-pull at dinner-time for at least 10 minutes; and when one calls on him, one is occasionally informed by the servant from the area that it is no good knocking at the front door, as that will not open since Master last banged it, but one must come round by the back way. So you see Topsy is extant yet, in spite of the fame of Morris.

Morris's remoteness from any revolt against bourgeois values at this phase is brought out by the fact that in this year of the Commune he accepted a place on the directorate of the mining company to which he and his mother had owed their fortune. He even bought a top-hat, though he once remarked, 'You see, one can't go about London in a top-hat, it looks so devilish odd.' (Mackail adds that only in conventional clothes did he look really peculiar.) Yet, deep inside him, his anguish at the situation in which he found himself, an upholsterer who had lost his wife to his best friend, was driving him on to the search for a different way of life. In the March *Academy* he had a poem:

> Ah! shall Winter mend your case:
> Set your teeth the wind to face.
> Beat the snow, tread down the frost!
> All is gained when all is lost.[1]

In March and April his version of the *Saga of Frithiof the Bold* appeared in the *Dark Blue Magazine*. His closeness to Georgie at this moment is shown by doing an illuminated manuscript of the *Eyrbyggia Saga* for her.

When we ask how he was able to accept as he did the relationship of Janey and Rossetti, we must put three factors together: the Victorian fear of any public disclosures of discord and infidelities in the family, Morris's own deep reticence and inability to take a stand on any of the conventional rights of a husband, and his ethic of tolerance and freedom in sexual matters, which, if only arrived at fully later on, was all along an instinctive part of his being. We have seen how the Burne-Joneses were rent by Ned's behaviour with Marie, yet the whole thing was covered up as if it had never happened; Scott Bell's wife accepted his connection with Alice Boyd; Chapman, editor of the *Westminster Review*, lived over his office in the Strand with both wife and mistress, who joined forces to chase off George Eliot. Blunt noted down that Morris with his strong and affectionate heart had centred all his home-emotions on his two children. He was 'a complete fatalist in his attitude towards the conduct of his children and of all human beings where sex was concerned. . . . As to any sort of coercive interference on his part it was inconceivable.' Blunt added, 'One thing only, I think he did not know, much as he had written about it, the love of woman, and that he never cared to discuss.' Blunt had few insights into Morris's character, but he noted well enough his reticence and his inability to coerce. Compton Rickett said of Morris, 'He was the only man I ever came across who seemed absolutely independent of sex considerations.' Here again the mask was mistaken for the reality. Luke Ionides made the same error: 'Women did not seem to count with him.' He tells how he once heard Morris consoling a friend whose woman had left him:

'Think, old fellow,' Morris had said to him, 'how much better it is that she should have left you, than that you should have tired of her, and left her.' I really think he saved his friend's life through his companionship and his help. Though he was a strong man he had the delicate feelings of a tender woman. . . . I would go to him in the depths of misery and after being with him for an hour or two I would leave him feeling absolutely happy. I always compared him with a sea-breeze, which seemed to blow away all one's black vapours.

Morris's remoteness from the Commune shows that he had during these years given up reading Ruskin. If he had been following *Fors Clavigera* he could hardly have failed to be stirred and forced to take some attitudes towards what was happening. Though Ruskin accepted the stories of working-class atrocities, he made the strongest possible denunciation, in Letters VI and VII, of the ruling and exploiting classes:

This cruelty has been done by the kindest of us, and the most honourable; by the delicate women, by the nobly-nurtured men. . . . This robbery has been taught to the hands,—this blasphemy to the lips,—of the lost poor, by the False Prophets who have taken the name of Christ in vain, and leagued themselves with His chief enemy, 'Covetousness, which is idolatry.' Covetousness, lady of Competition and of deadly Care; idol above the altars of Ignoble Victory; builder of streets, in cities of Ignoble Peace. . . .

Occult Theft—Theft which hides even from itself, and is legal, respectable and cowardly—corrupts the body and soul of man, to the last fibre of them. And the guilty Thieves of Europe, the real sources of all deadly war in it, are the Capitalists —that is to say, people who live by percentages on the labour of others; instead of by fair wages for their own. The *Real* war in Europe, of which this fighting in Paris is the Inauguration, is between these and the workman, such as these have made him.

From Georgie's *Memorials* we see that the group discussed the situation and were depressed. 'Last evening was short, and ruffled by politics,' says Ned, 'to which I now bid an everlasting adieu.' Yet at the same time he tried to believe: 'I'm a born rebel, that's my position and utility in the world. I am not, and never was, fitted to belong to any institution.'[2]

Morris had for some time been hoping to find a country-house; no doubt Janey disliked being so closely pushed up against the work of the firm. Also, there was the nuisance of having to find some new place yearly for summer holidays. Early in the spring Morris noticed a Kelmscott Manor House in a house agent's list, which seemed suitable. On 17 May he told Faulkner that he had seen it: 'a heaven on earth; an old stone Elizabethan house like Water Eaton, and such a garden! close down on the river, a boat house and all things handy. I am going there again on Saturday with Rossetti and my wife: Rossetti because he thinks of sharing it with us if the thing looks likely.' The house stood in the meadows of the Upper Thames's backwater, thirty miles from Oxford; lanes led to Lechlade three miles off. At that time the railway reached only to Witney, though later it went on to Lechlade. So at first the way to get to the place was by a long drive through the Berkshire hills from Farringdon, whence came the food for the manor. Morris, who had loved the house at first sight, gained only a deeper attachment over the years. In *News from Nowhere* he happily described the approach by water as the culmination of his journey into the imagined world of communism.

We crossed the road, and my hand raised the latch of a door in the wall, and we stood presently on a stone path which led up to the old house. The garden between the wall and the house was redolent of the June flowers, and the roses were rolling over one another with that delicious superabundance of some small well-tended gardens which at first sight takes away all thought save that of beauty. The black-birds were singing their loudest, the doves were cooing on the roof-ridge, the rooks in the high elm-trees beyond were garrulous among the young leaves, and the swifts wheeled whining about the gables. And the house itself was a fit guardian for all the beauty of this heart of summer.

O me! O me! How I love the earth, and the seaons, and weather and all things that deal with it, and all that grows out of it—as this has done! The earth and the growth of it and the life of it! If I could but say or show how I love it!

The house was a rather low three-storeyed farmhouse with mullioned win-dows and stone slates on the roof; another block had been added at right angles in the seventeenth century. Faulkner joined the visiting party, coming from Oxford; Webb pronounced the structure sound; and Rossetti and Morris agreed to take it jointly, sharing the rent of £60 a year. Morris never owned the place with its 68 acres of closes. As a tenant he did little to the house apart from replacing decayed floorboards with wooden blocks and stone paving; most of his belongings continued to stay in London. The entry was from a porch into a passage with a seventeenth-century oak screen, which seems to have been glazed. Morris attached serge hangings, probably those from Red House. The parlour or panelled room was painted wholly white; it looked out on the garden with clipped hedges. Tudor stairs led up to the second storey, where Morris and Janey had separate bedrooms; a steep ladder-stair went on up to the fine heavy-timbered attic. The tapestry-room had views of clover-meadows and a small elm-crowned hill. In the surrounding country the young Thames wound through level pastures, with low hills not far off; beyond the often-flooded river-meadows the ground rose imperceptibly northwards towards the spurs of the Cotswolds, whence several streams broke to join the Thames. There were a number of charming villages with old churches, often of the thirteenth century: Bibury, Broad-well, Langford, Burford, Great Coxwell. The area, well wooded and fed with streams, was thick with birds, and again and again Morris in his letters speaks of the birdlife. The letters too show with what a loving and scrutinis-ing eye he watched the changes of the seasons and the flowers of the garden.

The house was kept by an old peasant couple, Philip Comely and his wife, frugal and hard working; but Philip always embarrassed Morris by the way he felt impelled to touch his forelock or hat-brim with every word he spoke. His cottage, rented for a shilling a week, had a good and fruitful garden, and served as a sort of lodge to the manor house. We may note how Morris had a peculiar power of giving a legendary or symbolic note to all the houses in which he lived or worked, from the Walthamstow houses on, through the intensity with which he made them parts of his whole outlook, settings for the transformations of the existing world in terms of a steadily realised ideal.[3]

From what followed it is clear that a strong part of the motive in quest for a country house was the desire to find somewhere where Janey and Rossetti could live together without having the eyes of London upon them. How far this was admitted openly among the three of them we cannot say, but at some point Janey or Rossetti must have made the suggestion. Morris, with his incapacity to take a moral stand on such a matter, would have acquiesced. Also he would not have wanted any break or scandal which would have upset his daughters. In *News* he set out his conviction that married people must remain 'free people' and that 'artificial bolstering up of natural human relations is what I object to'. The enforcement of a property contract when the human element had gone was immoral and hateful. He set out these views at length also in a letter to Faulkner of 16 October 1886. But the logic of such views was that when love ended between a man and a woman, and one of them fell in love with someone else, that one should be free to go off with the new choice. That the rejected one should instead proceed to provide a shield for the other two, behind which they might hide from censure, was certainly not part of his principles. Morris took the line he did in the years after 1869 because of the mixture of kindliness, tolerance, and fear of social difficulties, which later developed into his full-blown concept of personal freedom. Clearly the last thing Janey would have wanted to do was to leave Morris and turn openly to Rossetti; and the latter, with the intense respectability and fear of criticism which accompanied his bohemianism, would have been as averse from taking her in at Cheyne Walk.

Mackail then is merely repeating the accepted pretences when he tells us: 'The breakdown in Rossetti's health, which had begun two or three years earlier, was now very marked, and it was hoped that quiet life in a remote country house might do much to restore him to bodily health and relieve his morbid imaginations. For a while he was much more there than Morris, who could not easily be away from London and his work for a long time together.' The fact is that Morris could not bear to be there while Janey and Rossetti were carrying on their idyll. In trying to reject the conventional tyranny of the Victorian husband he had landed himself in a situation compounded of the very lies and hypocrisies against which he was rebelling. Yet at the same time he could not do anything which he felt would let Janey down and destroy the happiness of his girls. So he could not enjoy Kelmscott till in the summer of 1874 Rossetti finally left. 'Not a little to Morris's relief for many reasons,' says Mackail. 'The manor house soon resumed its quietness and simplicity.'

The preparations for taking over the house made it impossible for Janey to move in till early July. Morris had arranged a visit to Iceland so as to be able to escape the miseries of the settling-in. He left London on 6 July, and Rossetti moved to Kelmscott six days later, while Webb proceeded to make additions to the studio in Cheyne Walk. Rossetti liked the place, brought in furniture, and even wrote to Penkill about buying one of their Ayrshire cows. He also introduced dogs, which Morris disliked. Morris didn't believe in animals about the house and hoped that the girls 'would not take to' the dogs, of which there were three in the end. Janey the invalid turned out a good walker when it was a question of going with Gabriel. She 'licks you hollow,' he wrote to Bell Scott, taking 'five or six mile walks without the least difficulty'. He read her Plutarch's *Lives* and Shakespeare, and wondered why the latter didn't write on Pompey, declaimed Browning's *Balaustion's Adventure* till he called it *Exhaustion's Adventure*, and got a set of Scott, also Pepys and Boswell. He was taken up with poems rather than pictures, writing sonnets on a little island—though he had brought a replica of *Beata Beatrix* to finish ('a beastly job, but lucre is lucre') and tried to turn the tapestry-room into a studio. However he found it draughty even in summer and didn't like the old tapestry of Samson. He did drawings of Janey, including one of her asleep over *The Defence of Guenevere*. He laughed when they heard that Morris had been hailed as *skald* in Iceland. Now they had a better name for him than Topsy. There was Skald Morris and Bard Swinburne.

By August he had thirty more sonnets for his *House of Life*, expressing his daily contact with Janey in their love-idyll. With his charm he got on well with the two young girls, 'the most darling little self-amusing machines', finding May especially intelligent and lovely. Indeed he won her over and she wrote of him with warmth till the end, refusing to hear him decried. Once, it seems, he wanted to adopt her. Feeling quite at home, he began inviting down his family and friends. His one fear was that the vulgar and loud-mouthed Fanny would turn up, as indeed she much wanted to do; he kept her off with a mixture of coaxing and command. But he was still not happy. May was struck by his loneliness as he came back from a stroll across the meadows or sat by the studio fire during Janey's absences. 'Indeed we youngsters were more conscious of this element of solitariness in our family life than our elders knew.' Is she there hinting at the girls' awareness of the gap between her father and mother?[4]

Meanwhile Morris had set off for Iceland with Faulkner, Magnusson and W. H. Evans, an army officer keen on fishing and shooting. Evans went on to Leith by sea, but the others left London on 6 July to catch a fortnightly Danish mailboat from Granton. Morris records his divided state of mind. 'This morning my heart failed me, and I felt as if I should have been glad of any accident that had kept me at home; yet now it would have seemed unbearable to sleep in London another night.' On 13 July he first saw the new world, 'a terrible shore indeed: a great mass of dark grey mountains worked into pyramids and shelves, looking as if they had been built and half-ruined'. They rounded a low ragged headland and were in the firth, soon reaching a trading-station with half a dozen wooden roofs, a flagstaff and two schooners at anchor. He was left with a profound impression of challenge, of apocalyptic upheaval, which he put later into his poem on *Iceland First Seen*. On 16 July he wrote to Janey from Reykjavik about leaving the Faroes: 'I have seen nothing out of a dream, so strange as our coming out of the last narrow sound into the Atlantic, and leaving the huge wall of rocks astern in the shadowless midnight twilight: nothing I have ever seen has impressed me so much.' Then at three on a wild morning he glimpsed the island from the *Diana*'s deck: 'very black out to sea, and very bright under a sort of black canopy over Iceland'. Here were the changes and crises of one of his fear-dreams, but now lodged powerfully in waking experience. He was facing his fear and determined to prove himself a man.

His journal records all the details of the journey. They set off on ponies, with guides. 'Most strange and awful the country looked to me.' At Holmr they drank champagne as a stirrup-cup, and the Icelanders turned back. 'And we rode away east into a barren plain,' then on to lava and to a waste of loose large-grained black sand, which changed in its turn into a grass plain again but not smooth this time: all ridged and thrown up into hummocks. Then came boggy ground. When they pitched tents, Morris shot two golden plovers for their supper, but didn't enjoy the killing. He lay awake listening to the plovers' cries, the champing horses, the flapping tents. He cooked the breakfast of bacon and plover, and they rode into the hills. So they went on and on, down to the sea, and over more grey wastes of lava, and steep hills of shale, a milky-white river thick with seals. At Oddi they were pleased that the great recorders of Icelandic lore who had lived there were still remembered. They found the site of Njal's house and were welcomed by the bonder who smiled at the horseplay between Morris and Faulkner. They stared at the three mounds amid ploughed-up marshes and next morning saw the place where the enemy had lain in ambush before burning Njal's house. They rode back along pastures thick with blue gentian and white clover; saw Gunnar's Howe at Lithend. Going up the valley of the Markfleet they passed through endless scenes 'unimaginably strange', with caves 'like the hell-mouths in thirteenth-century illuminations', and a sheep or two grazing on the top of great pillars of rock that looked inaccessible; they investigated a glacier, with spiky white waves against the blue sky, which, close at hand, showed 'great blocks cleft into dismal caves, half blocked with sand and dirt it had ground up, and dribbling wretched white streams'. At last they reached a spot in the bare shale from which they could see the whole length of the mountain:

Surely it was what I 'came out for to see', and yet for the moment I felt cowed, and as if I should never get back again: yet with that came a feeling of exultation too, and I seemed to understand how people under all disadvantages should find their imagination kindle amid such scenes.

They moved on to the Geysir, disgusted at the litter left by tourists who, knowing nothing of the sagas and eddas, came to see geysirs. However they had to stay there four days as Faulkner became ill. They rode off on a bright cold morning, on 29 July, through the wilderness of the firths of the North Sea. They passed through six chilly days of rain and wind amid the black mountains of the waste. As they climbed for the site of the *Grettis Saga*, Morris felt: 'I think it was the most horrible sight of mountains I had the whole journey long.' They explored the cave of Surtshellir, though the dripping water kept putting out their candles; then after three-quarters of an hour they were only halfway to their destination and Morris gave in, staying with Faulkner while the others went on. But they had worse to come, hail and sleet on a highland of bogs where Grettir had dwelt as an outlaw, and a cold grey drift of rain as they went down to where Grettir killed Thorir Redbeard—no sign of life till a swan rose up trumpeting from the lakeside. At last on 6 August they reached the region of the *Laxdaela Saga*. Morris's spirits fell very low. The whole of Iceland seemed mournful.

Setting aside the pleasure of one's animal life, and feeling of adventure; how every place and name marks the death of its short-lived eagerness and glory. . . . But Lord! what littleness and helplessness has taken the place of the old passion and violence that had place here once—and all is unforgotten . . . yet it is an awful place: set aside the hope that the unseen sea gives you here, and the strange threatening change of the spiky mountains beyond the firth, and the rest seems emptiness and nothing else: a piece of turf under your feet and the sky overhead, that's all: whatever solace your life is to have here must come out of yourself or these old stories, not over-hopeful themselves.

Yet this moment of total isolation and bleakness was in the last resort what he had come to find: the need to face himself in a situation where whatever meaning he was to make out of life must come stubbornly out of himself, out of his own depths. After two days at Herdholt they skirted the northern coast, making for home. At Stykkisholme they struck a Danish brigantine making for Liverpool and Morris wrote Janey a letter with a brief account of the journey. He said that he hoped to bring his 'pretty grey pony' to England; and he uses a phrase which shows that he had read the accounts of the Commune. 'The loose stones on the edge of a lava-field is like my idea of a half-ruined Paris barricade.' A week later they reached Grettir's lair on the Fairwood-fells, 'such a dreadful savage place', said Morris that it made him re-visualise Grettir as 'an awful and monstrous being, like one of the early giants of the world'. On 21 August he was maddened by Faulkner's snoring and yelled 'Damn!' Faulkner woke up and they had an acrimonious argument, with Faulkner insisting that Morris had himself done the snoring in a dream. Through a valley of winds they reached the Hill of Laws, the great open-air meeting-place; and Morris excitedly explored it for two days. One more day's riding brought them to Reykjavik, where Morris found eleven letters waiting for him. He read them, 'with not more than the usual amount of disappointment, wondering at people's calmness'. After three days of heavy rain, visiting the museum and dining with the Governor, they set sail on the *Diana*.

On a soft warm grey day, 6 September, the ship came alongside the pier at Grantham. Morris was able to catch the nightmail for London. 'I was curious to see what effect the trees would have on me when day dawned, but they did not have much.' Houses and horses however looked so big for the landscape that it all seemed 'like a scene at a theatre'. He made a brief visit to Kelmscott. On 2 October Rossetti wrote to Scott: 'Morris has been here twice since his return, for a few days at first and just now for a week again.

He is now back in London, and this place will be empty of inmates by the end of this week, I guess. Morris has set to work with a will on a sort of masque called "Love is Enough", which he means to print as a moderate quarto, with woodcuts by Ned Jones and borders by himself, some of which he has already done really beautifully.'⁵

Soon after the return Morris wrote to Georgie's sister, Louisa, married to the ironmaster Baldwin. He was not quite clear how to value the experience of the journey: how much he had forced his reactions. He was about to make a copy of his journal for Georgie (not for his wife). 'I confess to a dread of setting to work on it: it is true that the journey was altogether successful, and that I think I have gained in many ways by it; but it seems such a long way off now, and there is a bit of one's life gone; and the world so much the narrower to me because of it; and when I look over it I am afraid of having to grin sourly at this bit of enthusiasm, and be puzzled at that bit of high spirits; and note here how I refused to acknowledge a disappoint-ment, and there how I pretended not to be weary—and in short—all the rest of it; something in its way like looking at a drawerful of old letters—if anybody ever did venture on such a brave act, which I doubt.' On his second visit to Kelmscott he went via Oxford and bought a boat. He had brought back his Icelandic pony, Mouse. At first he himself rode him about, then the children took over, both riding him—and putting him in a little basket-carriage. He grew enormously fat on the plentiful grass.

Watts-Dunton gives an account of meeting Morris about this time or in the spring of 1872. He was the guest of Rossetti, who warned him that Morris was 'a wonderfully stand-off chap, and generally manages to take against people'. Rossetti described him as like the portraits of Francis I, with blue-grey eyes, 'not quite so small, but not big', with the nose softened a bit and with 'the rose-bloom colour of an English farmer'. Then Morris came riding up on the small pony, 'a figure so broad and square that the breeze at his back, soft and balmy as it was, seemed to be using him as a sail, and blowing both him and the pony towards us'.

When Rossetti introduced me, the manager greeted him with a 'H'm! I thought you were alone.' This did not seem promising. Morris at the time was as proverbial for his exclusiveness as he afterwards became for his expansiveness. Rossetti, however, was irresistible to everybody, and especially to Morris, who saw that he was expected to be agreeable to me, and most agreeable he was, though for at least an hour I could still see the shy look in the corner of her eyes. He invited me to join the fishing, which I did. . . . Not one word passed Morris's lips, as far as I remember . . . which had not some relation to fish and baits. He had come from London for a few hours' fishing, and all the other interests which as soon as he got back to Queen's Square would be absorbing him were forgotten. Instead of watching my float, I could not help watching his face with an amused interest at its absorbed expression, which after a while he began to notice, and then the following little dialogue ensued. . . . 'How old were you when you used to fish in the Ouse?'

'Oh, all sorts of ages; it was at all sorts of times, you know.'

'Well, how young, then?'

'Say ten or twelve.'

'When you got a bite at ten or twelve, did you get as interested, as excited, as I get when I see my float bob?'

'No.'

The way in which he said, 'I thought not,' conveyed a world of disparagement.

Note how Morris is seen as a business manager (no doubt Rossetti's term); also how his criterion for the right sort of responses to the world of nature lies in childhood.

Rossetti left in late autumn, probably because Janey and the girls had gone to London. He had spent what was for him a happy summer, as he showed in sonnets. But the coming of autumn meant the loss of Janey and the fear of separation slowly turns to a sense of frustration. In *Without Her* he defines the loss that he feared. Later he read the sonnet in a sob-choked voice to Hall Caine. Warmed by his close attention, his readings to her and his constant worship, Janey seems to have grown intellectually. When he remarked that the thatched squatting farm-buildings looked as if settled down into a purring state of comfort, she added that they 'seemed as if, were you to stroke them, they would move'. On the other hand Morris's letters to her grow ever more conventional, however amiable and well-meaning; we feel that he had never managed to achieve any real intimacy with her, any warm give-and-take which broke through her enclosed self of silence.[6]

There is a group of his poems in manuscript, written about this time which seem to give us the clues to what he was suffering in his withdrawn and baffled affection. For instance *The Doomed Ship*:

> The doomed ship drives on helpless through the sea,
> All that the mariners may do is done
> And death is left for men to gaze upon,

While side by side two friends sit silently;
Friends once, foes once, and now by death made free
Of Love and Hate, of all things lost or won;
Yet still the wonder of that strife bygone
Clouds all the hope or horror that may be.

Thus, Sorrow, are we sitting side by side
Amid this welter of the grey despair,
Nor have we images of foul or fair
To vex, save of thy kissed face of a bride,
Thy scornful face of tears when I was tried
And failed neath pain I was not made to bear.

In another poem, unfinished, he makes an effort to get inside Janey's mind and understand her rejection. After the sixth line she is speaking:

Why doest thou struggle, strive for victory
Over my heart that loveth thine so well?
When Death shall one day have its will of thee
And to deaf ears thy triumph thou must tell.

Unto deaf ears or unto such as know
The hearts of dead and living wilt thou say:
A childish heart there loved me once, and lo
I took his love and cast his love away.

A childish greedy heart! yet still he clung
So close to me that much he pleased my pride
And soothed a sorrow that about me hung
With glimpses of his love unsatisfied—

And soothed my sorrow—but time soothed it too
Though ever did its aching fill my heart
To which the foolish child still closer grew
Thinking in all I was to have a part.

But now my heart grown silent of its grief
Saw more than kindness in his hungry eyes:
But I must wear a mask of false belief
And feign that nought I knew his miseries.

I wore a mask, because though certainly
I loved him not, yet there was something soft
And sweet to have him ever loving me:
Belike it is I well-nigh loved him oft—

Nigh loved him oft, and needs must grant to him
Some kindness out of all he asked of me
And hoped his love would still hang vague and dim
About my life like half-heard melody.

He knew my heart and over-well knew this
And strove, poor soul, to pleasure me herein;
But yet what might he do some doubtful kiss
Some word, some look might give him hope to win.

Poor hope, poor soul, for he again would come
Thinking to gain yet one more golden step
Toward Love's shrine, and lo the kind speech dumb
The kind look gone, no love upon my lip—

Yes gone, yet not my fault, I knew of love
But my love and not his; how could I tell
That such blind passion in him I should move?
Behold I have loved faithfully and well;

Love of my love so deep and measureless
O lords of the new world this too ye know.

The woman's monologue traces with fine subtlety the veering tensions of her relationship with the rejected lover: his hopes and despairs, the wavering and fitful moments when it seemed to him that love might yet be achieved, the rebuff and the retreat of his wounded sensibility. Note how Morris looks on himself as a child. It is of interest too that in the shifting hesitating rhythms he revives something of the dramatic tensions of *The Defence of Guenevere*. Janey is pleading her case before the bar of his heart as the queen was pleading hers before the accusers; we see the prophetic poem of 1858 coming true in the actual life of the poet.

The most important of these poems has no names. It best makes sense if we read it as addressed to Georgie, with Rossetti as 'the friend' and as 'he', and 'they' as Rossetti and Janey in the last stanzas. The 'great sorrow' would then be no doubt the trouble caused in the Burne-Jones marriage by Maria Zambaco; amid all the breaks and collapses of old relationships, which had seemed so settled, only the bond of Morris and Georgie remains steadfast.

> Alone unhappy by the fire I sat
> And pondered o'er the changing of the days
> And of the death of this good hope and that
> That time agone our hearts to heaven would raise
> Where change and folly lead our wearied feet
> Till face to face this verse and sorrow meet.
>
> I strove to think what like the days would be
> If ere we die we should grow glad again
> But yet no image of felicity
> From out such twice-changed days my heart could gain
> But still on pain I thought, and still on pain
> Of shifts from grief to joy we poets sing
> And of the long days make a little thing.
>
> But grief meseems is like eternity
> While our hearts ache and far-off seems the rest
> If we are not content that all should die
> That we so fondly once unto us pressed
> Unless our love for folly be confessed
> And we stare back with cold and wondering eyes
> On the burnt rags of our fool's paradise.
>
> So I when of the happy days to come
> I strove to think no whit would all avail,
> Rather my thoughts went back to that changed home
> And in mine ears there rang some piteous tale
> And all my heart for very pain did fail
> To think of thine; I cannot bridge the space
> 'Twixt what may be and thy sad weary face.
>
> Ah do you lift your eye-brows in disdain
> Because I dare not pity or come nigh
> To your great sorrow, helpless weak and vain
> E'en as I know myself?—ah rather I
> On you my helper in the darkness cry
> For you alone unchanged now seem to be
> A real thing left of the days sweet to me.

Dreamy the rest has grown now that my lips
Must leave the words unsaid my heart will say
While I grow hot, and o'er the edge there slips
A word that makes me tremble and I stay
With fluttering heart the thoughts that will away.
We meet, we laugh and talk but still is set
A seal o'er things I never can forget.

But must not speak of, still I count the hours
That brings my friend to me, with hungry eyes
I watch him as his feet the staircase mount
Then face to face we sit, a wall of lies
Made hard by fear and faint anxieties
Is drawn between us, and he goes away
And leaves me wishing it were yesterday.

Then when they both are gone, I sit alone
And turning foolish triumph's pages o'er
And think how it would be if they were gone
Not to return, or worse if the time bore
Some seed of hatred in its fiery core
And nought of praise were left to me to gain
But the poor [   ] we talked of as so vain.

If we needed any proof that Morris is here writing of Janey and Rossetti
we have it in the comments jotted on the right-hand margin under flowers
and leaves: 'X tears can come with verse we two are in the same box and need
conceal nothing—don't cast me away—scold me but pardon me What is all
this to me (say you) shame in confessing ones real feelings—' These phrases
perhaps are meant as giving him suggestions for the lines on which to
continue the poem, but above them he has written 'poets unrealities'. The
only reason for writing that would be a sudden fear that someone else would
read the stanzas and consider them all too much 'poet's realities'. If the
verses had been based on mere fantasy, he would never have felt the need
to explain them away. (In November 1872 Morris wrote to Aglaia of Rossetti:
'It is really a farce our meeting when we can help it.') The mood of the poem
chimes in with the many protestations in his letters to Georgie at this time
about his dullness and his hopes that she is not dull or no longer dull.

As a commentary on the poem we may cite a letter from Scott to Alice of
23 October 1871. He tells how he had gone to dine with Morris. The day

before he had asked Rossetti if he would be present, and Rossetti replied no, 'Oh I have another engagement.' Now he learned that the engagement was with Janey at Rossetti's own house. 'Is it not too daring, and altogether inexplicable? Of course I did not ask Morris after his wife, having been warned before that she was at Chelsea.'

We may note that he seems afraid of an open declaration of love for Georgie. But just as several of the poems in *A Book of Verse* might be taken as expressions of his feelings for her, so there is here an implied cry for help, for some love-return. He seems to come closer to a direct statement in a sonnet which praises her for her lack of guile as she beholds 'how my heart doth cling to thy dear heart':

> Yet do I wonder—praise thee as I may
> Or fear to trust thee utterly herein
> Or deem that thou wouldst call my service sin.
> Thou who with love for all thy staff and stay
> Goest great-hearted down the weary way
> Still looking for the new dawn to begin.

Everlasting Spring is a cry for happiness: 'Why was I made for nothing, for my life to pass away For thy kindness as my madness all utterly to die?' Its lyric note of appeal, which maintains an overtone of hope, can hardly have been directed to Janey in these years. 'Alas for the white morning with no hope of touch or kiss!' He must surely have been thinking of Georgie. And again of her in *Three chances and one answer*: 'If thou shouldst say, "One kiss, love, ere the cold The lonely dark, and the sad years grown cold...."' Or of the poem that begins, 'The lips that I have touched no more may speak....' We cannot think of him saying to Janey: 'Thine oft-kissed little hands no more may write The treasured words of comfort and delight....' There is also the sonnet beginning, 'The world perchance to mock and jest would turn My love for thee, and ask what I desire Or with the name of some unholy fire Would name the thing wherewith my heart doth yearn....' Any love for Janey would not be called unholy by the world. The sonnet ends:

> But I now clinging to thy skirt pass through
> The dangerous pleasant place with halfshut eyes
> And with new names I name old miseries
> And turned to hopes are many fears I knew

> And things I spoke as lies are coming true
> Since thou hast shown me where the high heaven lies.

If we may trust the indications of these poems, then, Morris was very close to Georgie during these years and came to love her. But though they certainly consoled one another for the griefs through which they were passing, it is unclear how far the love-making went. It seems that Georgie hesitated on the brink of giving herself to Morris. This reading of the situation is supported by the poem which May printed as *Near but Far Away*, inscribed 'May 11th' and which cannot be addressed to Janey (as it has been taken):

> She wavered, stopped and turned, methought her eyes,
> The deep grey windows of her heart, were wet,
> Methought they softened with a near regret
> To note in mine unspoken miseries:
> And as a prayer from out my heart did rise
> And struggle on my lips in shame's strong net,
> She stayed me, and cried 'Brother!' Our lips met.
> Her hands drew me into Paradise.
> Sweet seemed that kiss till thence her feet were gone,
> Sweet seemed the word she spake, while it might be
> As wordless music—But truth fell on me
> And kiss and word I knew, and, left alone,
> Face to face seemed I to a wall of stone,
> While at my back there beat a boundless sea.

In the manuscript six lines of despair follow: 'Thy love is gone, poor wretch, thou art alone.' He realises that the relationship cannot be sustained. Even if Georgie gave herself to him for a moment at the height of her own misery over Marie Zambaco, as is suggested by the passionate *Thunder in the Garden* in her *Book*, she must have quickly withdrawn and kept Morris's urgencies at bay. With his whole-hearted responses he could never have carried on a discreet adultery as Rossetti could. The deep grey eyes of the sonnet are obviously the eyes of Georgie, not of Janey. Graham Robertson tells us:

Eyes like those of Georgiana Burne-Jones I have never seen before or since, and, through all our long friendship, their direct gaze would always cost me little subconscious heart-searchings, not from fear of criticism or censure, but lest those eyes in their grave wisdom, their crystal purity, should rest upon anything unworthy.

If Janey was the perfect mate for Rossetti—even though he in his self-doubts and his self-destructive impulses could not have been happily married to her or to any woman—Georgie seems the perfect mate for Morris. She owned the qualities which Robertson attributes to her eyes; she had the capacity to throw herself with every fibre of her being into a cause she believed in, as had Morris. Later she took up the cause of the Suffragettes and was pro-Boer; her nephew, Rudyard Kipling, had to rescue her from an angry crowd at Rottingdean. With Ned these qualities of hers were given only a slight chance to develop; at Morris's side we can see her sharing all his enthusiasms and devotions. He and she must have realised this potentiality in their relationship; but the calls of family together with the extreme difficulty of their ever coming together in the Victorian world without quite wrecking themselves socially must have thrust between them in these years.

In the early days at Kelmscott Rossetti wrote a story for a picture to be painted, *The Cup of Cold Water*, which sets out in fantasy-form his version of the fate that bound him to Janey. It is merely his repetition of the triadic pattern we have traced as playing a dynamic part throughout Morris's life. Its importance lies in bringing out how deeply that pattern had bitten into the lives of these people, and how they used it to explain their frustrations and the unresolved conflicts that drove them on.

The young King of a country is hunting one day with a young Knight, his friend; when, feeling thirsty, he stops at a Forester's cottage, and the Forester's daughter brings him a cup of water to drink. Both of them are equally enamoured at once of her unequalled beauty. The King, however, has been affianced from boyhood to a Princess, worthy of all love, and whom he had always believed he loved until undeceived by his new absorbing passion; but the Knight resolved to sacrifice all other considerations to his love, goes again to the Forester's cottage and asks his daughter's hand. He finds the girl has fixed her thoughts on the King, whose rank she does not know. On hearing it she tells her suitor humbly that she must die if such be her fate, but cannot love one another. The Knight goes to the King to tell him all and beg his help; and the two friends then come to an explanation. Ultimately the King goes to the girl and pleads his friend's cause, not disguising his own passion, but saying that as he sacrified himself to honour so should she, at his prayer, accept a noble man who he loves better than all men and whom she will love too. This she does at last.

The fable is in fact a variant of the tale-pattern to be found in Morris's tale, *Gerda's Lovers*, written before he had met either Janey or Rossetti.

In October, we saw, Morris began his poem *Love is Enough*. Here he made his last desperate attempt to express in verse his emotional dilemma, swung between Janey and Georgie, neither of whom, for very different reasons, would have him. He used a fivefold frame: the excitement of a simple plebeian couple at a king's wedding, the wedding itself, the interlude presented at the wedding, the songs of the Music, and the innermost commentary by Love himself. Pharamond, seeking the love he has known in a dream or vision, throws off all the bonds of the world and goes on his endless anguished quest. The desired Azalais could be called Emma, Janey, Georgie; she is the hope of fully satisfying union that Morris now feels will never be his. *Love is Enough* is his final effort to project the paradisiac dream in terms of a merely personal union. There is a strained and even hectic note in the main parts, as if he feels that by some terrific effort of will, an act of abnegation and devotion entirely his own, he can subdue the desired image to his need. 'Because for love's sake, love he cast aside.' He seeks to control the almost-uncontrollable emotion by a display of metrical virtuosity; octosyllabic and pentameter couplets, lyrical anapaestic lines, and four-beat lines with free substitutions which suggest medieval verse. Well might May remark: 'No glimpse of the inner life of Morris was ever vouchsafed even to his closest friends—*secretum meum mihi*. It was a subject on which he never spoke save in *Love is Enough*.'

If we look back at the sonnet, *Near but Far Away*, we find the 'Beloved' addresses Morris as 'Brother' at the climactic moment. It has been argued that here Morris is revealing his unassuaged passion for Emma; but that is untenable. We might say however that his feeling of hopelessness at the moment of closest union (with Georgie?) awakens some sort of recollection of primal pattern of loss and denial. In saying 'Brother' instead of 'Husband' or 'Beloved', Georgie revives the taboo against which there is no appeal, making his exclusion final.

In October came Buchanan's attack on Rossetti in the *Contemporary Review*, 'The Fleshly School of Poetry', under a pseudonym. Buchanan had for some time been on bad terms with Rossetti and his group, in particular resenting the term, 'a poor but pretentious poetaster' which had been applied to him by William Michael. Rossetti attempted at first to treat the matter lightly, mustered his friends for a reply, and tried to find out who the attacker was. His response, 'The Stealthy School of Criticism', in the *Athenaeum* of 16 December, was violent in tone and had to be slightly edited after legal advice was taken, but it was not unbalanced. Underneath, however, he was shaken to the depths. As we have noted, his damn-all bohemianism was linked with an inner uncertainty which made him extremely susceptible to any form of criticism. Superficially he had shown no sign of guilt whatever for his connection with Janey (or with Fanny or anyone else); he carried off the whole situation with his usual air of nonchalant confidence and unconcern, which always daunted Morris and made him incapable of resistance. But what now happened to him revealed how little his apparent attitudes corresponded to his underlying emotions. Soon he was unable to hold down his conviction that he was surrounded by secret implacable enemies.[7]

10

The Heroic Virtues

In February 1872 Morris went to Kelmscott for a fortnight: 'to see spring beginning, a sight I have seen little of for years'. He hadn't been able to get on with *Love is Enough*, 'but I think I have now brought it out of the maze of re-writing and despondency'. The attacks on Rossetti continued, in the *Quarterly Review* and the *Saturday Review*. The writer in the first review, perhaps Courthope, wrote of 'emasculated obscenity' which vainly tried to attach a spiritual meaning to 'the animal passions'. In mid-May Buchanan issued his expanded essay as a pamphlet, denouncing Rossetti for the sin of sensualism that was turning London into 'a great Sodom and Gomorrah waiting for doom'. His style was scurrilous, showing a prurient enjoyment of the passages he pretended to attack. 'Nothing very spicy till we come to Sonnet XXXIX,' and so on, with the conclusion that the *House of Life* was probably the brothel where the poet found Jenny. The *Saturday Review* resumed the attack in a leading article on 1 June. The next night Rossetti tried to emulate Lizzie by committing suicide with an overdose of chloral. For two days he lay stupefied at Dr Hake's house and his friends discussed whether he should be sent to a lunatic asylum. When he had recovered a little he was taken to Brown's place at Fitzroy Square. Janey was deeply upset. She wrote: 'Dear Mr Brown. Have you any fresh news? I had a letter from Mr Scott last [Saturday crossed out] Friday, but have heard nothing since although I have written to him twice. I had such dreadful dreams last night. I can't rest today without trying all means to get news. I am to come back to town on Friday.'

One significant point is that Rossetti's friends who were trying to nurse him back from his shattered and paranoiac condition were all agreed that he must at all costs be kept from Janey, and for some time they warded off her letters. They clearly blamed her, or his relations with her, for his breakdown. How humanely Morris tried to behave is shown by Scott's account:

On Friday afternoon Janey Morris was taken down to see him by her more than amiable husband and he was of course thrown into a miserable state for a while, but all through the fortnight he has really alluded very little to Mrs M. . . . Jones and Morris were the Gabriel yesterday, and Morris offered to go on taking care of him as Brown has done, and let B. get home. Brown however devised a different plan. He proposes Gabriel to go with him to Fitzroy Sqre.

Later on 15 July Janey wrote to Scott:

The question seems to be now as to who Gabriel would endure about him—my opinion is that he would not care to have my husband. Could you find out who he would like? For everyone seems willing to come. You have been talking as to the possibility of his using the house at Kelmscott for a time, but he has said to me so often he never could go there again, that I doubt if he could be persuaded to think of it now—perhaps when he is thoroughly tired by the mountains he may feel more kindly towards it. . . .

When one realises that she must have known quite well that Scott knew all about her relations with Rossetti, one wonders at the abysmal coldness and complacent hypocrisy that lies behind her comments on Morris here. What Scott felt about her is revealed by his use of the name 'Lucretia Borgia' for her.

On 20 June Rossetti was taken to Scotland by Hake, to stay at a house offered by a friend. There he slowly grew better, but still felt surrounded by enemies. Any dog that barked had been set on him; a passing countryman who wished him good-night was trying to insult him. As for the seine-fishers on the coast: 'It is all an allegory of my state. My persecutors are gradually narrowing the net round me until at last it will be drawn tight.' His friends felt that it was necessary to get him away from Janey. When he wrote to her on 11 or 12 August, Dr Hake thought it best to write to her as well, asking her to report any symptoms of delusions in Rossetti's letter and to be very guarded in her reply. On 15 August she replied to William Michael saying that the letter was normal, 'not of a gloomy nature. I have had many from his hand of a far more depressing kind.'

Morris was working on a contemporary novel as well as his poem. In June he sent the manuscript to Louisa Baldwin (who had become a confirmed invalid after bearing her son Stanley). He calls it 'my abortive novel: it is just a specimen of how not to do it . . . 'tis nothing but landscape and sentiment'. Georgie had already seen part of the work. She gave him no hope about it, he says, 'and I have never looked at it since'. We have already noticed the account of dreams in this unfinished work, and the role of the forbidding father. The theme is characteristically the love of two brothers for the same girl. The manuscript breaks off where John is going to join a merchant firm in London after Arthur wins the girl, Clara. The tragic end was clearly to come from the fact that Arthur fails to show Clara the almost frenzied letter which John writes to him, urging him to sieze hold of love at all costs, whatever the consequences. This letter would have presumably roused Clara to awareness that John too passionately loved her. In the account of a journey up the river to an old house (Kelmscott) Morris makes his first attempt at a theme, dear to him, which reached its culmination in *News from Nowhere*; here the trip is linked with the growth of love and the revelation of Clara in all her charm. Clara is an important creation for Morris; she marks the rejection of the languishing or mysterious female of Pre-Raphaelite fancy, the turn to a healthy natural girl full of down-to-earth life and energy. She is the grey-eyed heroine born of Morris's supplanting of Janey by Georgie at the heart of his imagination.

By late September Rossetti had left Scotland and installed himself afresh at Kelmscott. He told his brother: 'But all, I now find by experience depends primarily on my not being deprived of the prospect of the one necessary person.' He soon began making studies of Janey for *Proserpine*. Her nervous condition had been worsened by Rossetti's breakdown. He found her 'very delicate and appallingly unable to walk out compared with her condition last year'.

How did Morris take this return of Rossetti? We get a strange and not easily interpreted glimpse of the tensions among the people at Kelmscott in two letters which Webb wrote to Janey earlier in September before Rossetti arrived. On 2 September he wrote:

Dear Janey, I was very glad to have your letter, because it was written without my asking for it—and I very much wish to have your confidence in my sympathy (if you think it would be worth anything). By 'sympathy' I do not mean to express anything more than to wish that—an old friend should find comfort in liking me, and being liked by me, that no real constraint shd come between us, and as little mistake in expression as possible.

Of course I know the strength of resource in despair, well enough—that is, the willingly cutting one self off from the help of any one, so as to avoid the risk of being deserted by them—but, 'nothing ventured'—you know—well, one must venture in friends help, for such a thing to be possible; and assured friendship is very beautiful, and at times deeply soothing in the mere belief of it—

I send 3 books, not at all knowing whether you have read all or any of them— I've not seen Topsy to ask him—

Very much should I like to come to Kelmscott again, and will try to do so, if you stay much longer—The last visit, on arriving, did give my soul a twist wh. I hope my face did not express, as it was quite unavoidable (in the unfortunate circumstances). . . .

What had he seen? Janey in some paroxysm of despair (as is suggested by the remarks in his second paragraph) or Morris in some paroxysm of rage at the news that Rossetti intended to return? In any event we realise that there was much suffering at Kelmscott. A second letter dated 12 September stresses this point without clarifying just what was going on:

Dear Janey, I thank you for your letter wh. is simple and straightforward to my minds content. I do not think I misunderstood your former letter, for I had no idea that you would think it worth while to tell me a lie, any more than I would really lie to you—There is something in human nature pure and simple, wh. touches me dearly; and when I see any one clinging to the natural part of life, I feel much inclined to become one of their friends. . . . I have always taken a great interest in you, and none the less that time has tossed us all about, and made us play other parts than we set out upon—I see you play yours well and truly under the changes, and I feel most deeply sympathetic on that account—for my own troubles are not so absorbing that I cannot attend to the troubles of those who are wrapt about with the pains of life wh. are not ignoble.

Please believe that I in no way wish to penetrate into sorrows wh. I can in no way relieve. I, from my own self, know the impossibility of other people bearing one's burden.

The remarks about changes make clear that Webb, who always had a soft spot for Janey, was referring to her and Rossetti, and perhaps to Morris and Georgie.[1]

Rossetti did his best to arrange to have Janey without Morris at Kelmscott; and when she went to London he filled the place with visitors, his friends and relations, including such models as Marie Stillman and Alexa Wilding. Christina, with all her stern piety, went to visit him with their mother. On 8 October Morris wrote to Aglaia, 'I have been backwards and forwards to Kelmscott a good deal this summer and autumn; but shall not go there so often now as Gabriel has come there, and talks of staying there permanently:

of course he won't do that, but I suppose he will stay some time: he is quite well and seems very happy.' For himself, 'I suppose I am getting less restless and worried, if at the same time less hopeful, still there is life in me yet I hope.' He was looking, with the aid of the BJs, for a house in west London. On 24 October he was still searching. 'I went down to Kelmscott on Saturday last till Tuesday, and spent most of the time on the river.' But, 'Lord! how dull the evenings were! with William Rossetti also to help us. Janey was looking and feeling much better.' He writes of the birds and the autumnal look in the gardens. 'I shall not be much there now I suppose.' In London he 'had a hardish time of it all alone with Bessy; with whom I seldom exchange any words that is not necessary. What a wearing business it is to live with a person with whom you have nothing whatever to do!' We see that Janey has been all the while at Kelmscott with Rossetti. Aglaia is expected to understand the nature of his fix.

The winter however drove Janey to London. Another letter to Aglaia on 25 November tells more of his situation. 'Janey has just come back from Kelmscott last Saturday, and is very well apparently, and in good spirits certainly.' He says that he is pleased to have her about and renews his complaints about the harmless but insufferable Bessy. He dislikes the prospect of moving, but Wardle needs the whole of the Queen Square house for the works.

When I said there was no cause for my feeling low, I meant that my friends had not changed at all towards me in any way and that there had been no quarreling: and indeed I am afraid it comes from some cowardice or unmanliness in me. One thing wanting ought not to go for so much: nor indeed does it spoil my enjoyment of life always, as I have often told you: to have real friends and some sort of an aim in life is so much, that I ought still to think myself lucky: and often in my better moods I wonder what it is in me that throws me into such rage and despair at other times. I suspect, do you know, that some such moods would have come upon me at times even without this failure.

His 'failure', his lack of 'one thing', can only refer to Janey; and the frank way he discusses the matter shows how everyone in his circle knew the circumstances. He adds to Aglaia: 'Furthermore my intercourse with G. has been a good deal interrupted: not from any coldness of hers, or violence of mine; but from so many untoward nothings.' And goes on:

Another quite selfish business is that Rossetti has set himself down at Kelmscott as if he never meant to go away; and not only does he keep me from that harbour of refuge (because it is really a farce our meeting when we can help it) but also he has all sorts of ways so unsympathetic with the sweet simple old place, that I feel his presence there as a kind of slur on it: this is very unreasonable when one thinks why one took the place, and how this year it has really answered that purpose. . . .

Morris, apart from other matters, could not fit in with Rossetti's way of staying up to three or four in the morning; then lying in a dead sleep till he dragged himself out to a late breakfast and made clever comments on the house's discomforts; finally, after staying in the studio till dusk, going for a walk for his health's sake, dining with the family and then going to the studio, where, says May, they all sat with him. His paranoia was still lurking under his show of ease. When a letter was delivered open by the postman, he sent it back to London and made sure that 'no suspicious symptoms seemed discernible'. Janey spent much time alone with him. Thus, when he invited his brother down in October, he warned him, 'Janey will be sitting to me for the greater part of the day, and I shall not be much at liberty for the light hours.' In November he and Janey both had bad colds. She could not sit for *Proserpine,* so he drew May. He made many studies for *Proserpine* and no less than seven starts on canvas. In a poem about the picture (in both Italian and English) he described his split state: 'Afar from mine own self I seem.' On 11 December he wrote: 'I get on well with work, though much inconvenienced till Janey's return.'[2]

Morris in his discontent told Aglaia that he contemplated another trip to Iceland in 1873; he was working on Icelandic translations. In November *Love is Enough* appeared. Simcox in the *Academy* recognised that something new was happening to Morris:

The charm of the *Earthly Paradise* was that it gave us the picturesqueness of earth with the atmosphere of fairyland; we drifted along a swift current of adventure under a sky heavy with sweet dreams, through which the dew of death fell without dimming the sunshine: we were amused and yet enthralled. In his new work Mr. Morris demands more of the reader; instead of abandoning himself to a passive fascination, he has to be penetrated with a profound and earnest passion: we have to live in the poem, not dream of it.

Late in the year the family moved from Queen Square to Horrington House on the road from Turnham Green to Hammersmith, near Chiswick Lane. Janey described the smallish house in a discontented phrase as 'a very good sort of house for one person to live in, or perhaps two'. Around were market gardens and orchards. Here the Morrises lived some six years. Despite the impact of Iceland and the sagas Morris ended this year without hope, as he told Aglaia. In *Love is Enough* Pharamond, at the height of victory, is haunted by the dream of the unknown beloved. He sets out on his quest and after many mishaps and struggles he finds her; then he is back in his kingdom where a usurper has taken over, but decides not to fight; he returns to seek the dream, the one desired woman, in the far land. Love in his final speech speaks of one who cast everything aside for love and then saw 'Love filched away; the world an adder-den, and all folk foes. . . .' The one desire had grown a poisoned fire. Yet the love did not die, 'but through a dreadful world all changed must move'.

1873 opened with the settling into the new house and further conversions at Queen Square, more workshops being put into the upper floors and the drawing-room becoming a showroom. Morris kept his study and little bedroom there. He told Aglaia on 23 January that at Queen Square 'I have always felt myself like nothing but a lodger.' He was pleased that he could reach the Grange from Horrington House in some half an hour's walk. Next day he took the children to the new place. ' 'Tis a month since I have seen them. Jenny is 12 years old now: bless us, how old I am getting.' He was filling in time with translations (the *Heimskringla*). On 11 February he was feeling more cheerful. The new arrangements meant much more walking, 'which, no doubt, is good for me'. He was beginning to feel cramped by the firm, yet was tied to it.

I should very much like to make the business quite a success, and it can't be, unless I work at it myself. I must say, though I don't call myself money-greedy, a smash on that side would be a terrible nuisance; I have so many serious troubles, pleasures, hopes, and fears, that I have not time on my hands to be ruined and get really poor: above all things it would destroy my freedom of work, which is a dear delight to me. My translations go on apace, but I am doing nothing original: it can't be helped, though sometimes I begin to fear I am losing my invention. You know I very much wish not to fall off in imagination and enthusiasm as I grow older: there have been men who, once upon a time, have done things good or noteworthy, who have got worse with time and have outlived their power; I don't like that at all. On the other hand, all great men that have not died young have done something of their best work when they were getting old.

In his broodings about economic failure we see that even the efforts he had made to grapple with his finances in 1870 had not removed all the sources of worry; he was now thinking on lines that led next year to the reorganisation of the firm. His sense of weakening derives from the fact that with *Love is Enough* he had reached a dead end; he needed to break through into some new dimension. We may note that he speaks of his literary products as his 'work'. In his distracted state he felt that he must return to Iceland. 'If I can only get away in some sort of hope and heart I know it will be the making of me.'

Rossetti spent almost the whole of 1873 at Kelmscott. When Janey had to leave, he invited visitors, including his mother, William, and Christina. He was fatter and had grown a full beard. His sonnets were full of haunting fears. What was the truth about Lizzie? Would he lose Janey?[3]

In April Morris and Burne-Jones went to Italy, though Morris had no enthusiasm for the south. However he enjoyed much of the scenery: such moments as when the train came out of the tunnel and he saw 'from the edge of the mountains the plain of Florence lying below', with 'the beautiful old town of Pistoja within its square walls at the mountains' feet'. In Florence he admired the outside of the Duomo. But he wrote to Webb that he had been 'merchandising for the firm here, rather to Ned's disgust I am afraid'. He had bought some lead-glazed ware and wickered flasks. In Paris he had also done some buying. The large amount of bad restoration depressed him; he had a week of Florence in cold rainy weather, and was not moved by Siena. Burne-Jones found him 'a little disposed to make the worst of things', and they spent only a fortnight in Italy.

Back in England Morris gave the revised transcript of the first Icelandic journey to Georgie, and in July he set off with Faulkner again. They were away for a little more than two months. Apparently Janey had been very ill when he left; for he wrote to her from Reykjavik on 18 July: 'It was a grievous parting for us the other day.' However that very day she had been reunited with Rossetti at Kelmscott, 'looking wonderfully well'. Rossetti was so happy that he started a poem: 'My world, my work, my woman, all my own.' On the boat Morris had met J. H. Middleton, an expert on medieval, Greek and Persian art, and the two became good friends. In Iceland he felt 'quite at home', as if he had never left the place. After ten days spent in traversing land they already knew in south-west, he and Faulkner turned to the more difficult and daunting interior. In his journal Morris does not register such strong responses to the stark landscape and the sagas as the first time; he now knew Icelandic scenery well and could look with more attention at the way people lived on the farms. Still he went to Lithend and roamed about the site of Gunnar's hall; and he kept his keen eye for birds and wild flowers. He usually caught fish for breakfast, which he liked; but the cooking made him feel homesick. Reaching Dettifoss they crossed the northern mountains to a small seaport, then rode more westerly till they arrived in early September at Reykjavik.[4]

Writing to Aglaia on 28 September he said that the journey was a success and had deepened his love for Iceland, though he would be unlikely to go back again. He had been full of longing and unhappiness on the journey out, till he was in the saddle. 'The glorious simplicity of the terrible and tragic, but beautiful land with its well remembered stories of brave men, killed all querulous feeling in me, and have made all the dear faces of wife & children, and love, & friends dearer than ever to me.' We may note how he separated out love from wife and children on the one hand, and friends on the other. Perhaps the reference is to Georgie, in the sense that he could feel whole-heartedly at home and at peace with her as he could not with Janey or any other woman. Janey, who seems to have been happy and well while he was away, now fell ill. She had gone to London; for Webb, at Kelmscott, wrote to her that Morris was expected to turn up for a dinner of roast duck and that he, Webb, would then find out 'who & what your new doctor is'. She had told Webb that she was reading Goethe's *Conversations with Eckermann.*

Morris, in desperation for some work to engross him, had taken up drawing from the model again. On 22 October he wrote to Louie about it. He found the work 'difficult—or impossible', but was doing it for his 'soul's sake chiefly'. He lacked, he said, 'the painter's memory' of forms and he could never see any scene 'with a frame as it were round it, though in my own way I can realise things vividly enough to myself—also I am getting old, hard on 40 Louie'.

Buxton Forman sent his brother's version of Wagner's libretto for *Die Walküre* to Morris, who made no effort to read or understand it. He had decided on unknown grounds that Wagner's theories were 'perfectly abominable' and objected to an epical subject being turned into an opera, 'the most rococo and degraded of all forms of art'. How little he knew Wagner's music is shown by his comment that he is outraged at the idea of a 'sandy-haired German tenor tweedledeeing over the unspeakable woes of Sigurd, which even the simplest words are not typical enough to express!' It was true however that Morris had come to dislike and distrust any elaborated art form, even Shakespeare. He seems never to have heard any Beethoven; the music that appealed to him was all pre-eighteenth century. Anything that could come under the heading of rhetoric repelled him. Still, he was hardly being true to his own principles when he himself later wrote his *Sigurd*.

He wrote to Forman again on 8 December about his Norse translations. He was illuminating works like the *Frithiof Saga*; and the firm this year turned out its first chintz design, *Tulip and Willow*, but Morris disapproved of the job made of it by the leading calico printer of the day (T. Clarkson of Bannister Hall, Preston), and the design was not put on sale till it was printed at his own works in 1889. This year Georgie recorded the last of the old kind of Christmas parties that the group held, with the children of Morris and Poynter and her own. Faulkner and De Morgan were present; they 'enchanted us all with their pranks, in which Morris and Edward Poynter occasionally joined', while Janey, 'placed safely out of the way, watched everything from her sofa'. Perhaps Morris did one of his mimes. May tells us:

My father's dramatic instinct was strong as might be. And his power of mimicry was positively fantastic; he acted with his whole body when he wanted to illustrate some point in a story, and the climax was always admirably rendered. We children rejoiced in the humours of a certain raven that on one of the Icelandic journeys came round the men's tent one night and played all sorts of pranks, which were recounted with the queerest and most vivid raven-expression and raven-voice and action. The mimicry of persons was all the more enjoyable for being quite without a spice of malice or cruelty: there was none of the gibe that wounds, the thought that poisons, in them; it was all sheer fun and enjoyment of the queerness of life.[5]

In February 1874 Rossetti was with Janey at Kelmscott and the children contracted measles. Among his guests in the spring was Nolly Brown, now aged seventeen and author of an immature novel. Nolly went off once in the boat and caused his host anxiety through not coming back till late at night. After he had left for home, Rossetti found that both the boat and a book left in it had been damaged. He wrote to Nolly, who abjectly apologised and promised to make good the damage as soon as he could lay hands on some money. Rossetti replied that he could forget about any payment and would in fact himself be paid £20 if he handed over a painting in his possession. The artist is not named in the printed version of the letter, but he was beyond doubt Morris. Nolly told Rossetti that he could have the picture for nothing. 'Mr —— certainly told me I might have it. (I rather suspect he is hard-up himself at present in which case he might like you to pay the money to him instead.) Anyhow, if the picture really does belong to me, you shall have it.' The comment on Morris's lack of money need not be taken as a bit of irony; in the 60s and 70s Morris was at times in straits and finding it hard to meet the weekly wages of the workers. Nolly had no doubt heard caustic remarks by his father on the running of the firm. Rossetti refused to accept the picture as a gift, and Nolly suggested that Rossetti should give him something of his own in exchange. Rossetti agreed and explained why he wanted Morris's painting. 'My wish to possess the latter is solely as an early portrait of the original, of whom I have made so many studies myself—thus, as long as there is any question of the work becoming mine, please don't touch the figure on any account in the least.' The work was Morris's Oxford painting of Janey known as *Queen Guenevere* or *La Belle Iseult*. We see that he had so little care of it as a token of his early love for Janey that he had let it fall into Nolly's hands; it was Rossetti who saw it as precious.

On 26 March Morris wrote to Louie the letter in which the idea of the Garden City was promulgated and which we discussed in Chapter 1. He ended: 'Sad grumbling—but do you know, I have got to go to a wedding next Tuesday: and it enrages me to think that I lack courage to say, I don't care for either of you, and you neither of you care for me, and I won't waste a day out of my precious life in grinning a company grin at you two.' The marriage (on 31 March) was that of William Rossetti and Lucy Brown. Gabriel refused to attend unless only a few old friends were present. Lucy demurred, but William got his brother along to a breakfast where the only other guests were their mother, Christina, the Madox Browns, Morris and Janey. This month, March, Morris had begun to illuminate the *Odes of Horace* on vellum and was planning to work on his own *Cupid and Psyche*. Towards the end of the year he began a *Virgil*.

He now decided that he had stood enough of Rossetti and that he would oust him from Kelmscott. On 16 April he wrote:

My dear Gabriel, I send herewith the £17 to you not knowing where else to send it since Kinch is dead. As to the future though I will ask you to look upon me as off my share, and not to look upon me as shabby for that, since you have fairly taken to living at Kelmscott, which I suppose neither of us thought the other would do when we first began the joint possession of the house; for the rest I am both too poor and, by compulsion of poverty, too busy to be able to use it much in any case, and am glad if you find it useful and pleasant to use, Yrs. affectly, William Morris.

There is every reason to believe that he intended to drop his side of the tenancy if Rossetti decided to take over the lease; for in that case the respectable cover for Janey living at Kelmscott with Rossetti would have been ended. At the same time he doubtless thought that the threat would be sufficient to dislodge Rossetti, as indeed it was. No decision seems to have been made at once. Rossetti wanted to hang on if he possibly could. He drew in various visitors, Brown and his Emma, Howell, Watts-Dunton (who was now becoming as necessary to him as Howell had been), his mother and the ailing Christina, William and Lucy who noticed how suspicious he was becoming of the servants and others about him. His health was deteriorating, and he turned more and more to his mother. He even had a furnished room in the family house in Euston Road so that he could stay there for the night near to her. The B Js found him changed by 'a sad inertia'. He refused to look at any reviews of his book *Dante and his Circle*, calling them 'the dirt of dogs'. But by July he could hold out no longer. Scott says he had a paranoiac quarrel with some anglers by the river, imagining that they had called insults to him. The local people began talking, and Rossetti retreated to Chelsea, never seeing Kelmscott again. Morris had won in this matter at least. He did not feel well enough off to keep Kelmscott on by himself; but he drew in Ellis as a co-tenant. Ellis shared the place financially till Morris's death, but never seems to have considered himself as more than a lucky visitor there.[6]

In June Morris and B J had gone to Marlborough to look the college over and arrange for Philip Burne-Jones to go there after the summer holidays. At the end of July Morris took Janey and the girls on a tour of Belgium. They went by train from Calais to Tournay, then on to Ghent, but the heat was so heavy that they drove on by road to Bruges through crops and orchards, giving up the project of visiting Antwerp and Mechlin. Perhaps he had hoped that the expulsion of Rossetti would draw Janey towards him again or he may merely have felt that she needed some distraction. But between his fears that she would collapse and the demands of the children he had little time to himself—'no time to myself to think at all: even now they are all here as I write while we are waiting to go out,' he told Aglaia on 24 July. Also they were all badly gnat-bitten. He was installed in the same room at the hotel that Janey and he had had on their honeymoon; and as he went to bed alone there he must have had unhappy thoughts. They were going on to Ypres and then Calais for the channel-crossing. At Eecloo, May recalled, Morris, unable to make himself understood in French or English, shouted at the innkeeper in Icelandic. Perhaps it was this trip that Graham Robertson had in mind in telling us of Janey; 'When she travelled in France, our light-hearted and often beauty-blind neighbours found her appearance frankly amusing and would giggle audibly when she passed by, to the astonishment and rage of Morris, who was with difficulty restrained from throwing down the gage in the cause of his Ladye.'

On his return he went with B J early in August to stay with some customers, the Howards at Naworth Castle, Cumberland, where Canon Dixon was also a guest. Dixon found Ned in poor health, but Topsy 'genial, gentle, delightful, both full of affection'. Rosalind Howard was nervous when Morris arrived with his diminutive carpet bag. She thought of Matthew Arnold in *Culture and Anarchy* with its description of the aristocracy as barbarians:

He was rather shy—and so was I—I felt he was taking an experimental plunge amongst 'barbarians', and I was not sure what would be the resulting opinion in his mind. However he has grown more urbane—and even three hours has worked off much of our mutual shyness—A walk in the glen made me know him better and like him better than I fancied I should. He talks so clearly and seems to think so clearly that what seems paradox in Webb's mouth in his seems convincing sense. He lacks sympathy and humanity though—and this is a fearful lack to me—only his character is so fine and massive that one must admire. He is agreeable also— and does not snub one.

What she felt as his lack of humanity was that element of concentration we have discussed, with its touch of abstraction; it gave him the effect of being uninterested in the person addressed, though in fact he was deeply concerned and observant in his own way. He enjoyed a drive along the border. 'I sniffed the smell of the moors & felt in Iceland again.' Back in London he wrote to Mrs Howard to say how happy he had been. He went on in a way that should have made her realise how far from the mark was her judgment of him.

I hope you will let me come again some time: and that then you will think me less arrogant on the—what shall I say?—Wesleyan-tradesman-unsympathetic-with-art subjects than you seemed to think me the other day: though indeed I don't accuse myself of it either; but I think to shut one's eyes to ugliness and vulgarity is wrong, even when they show themselves in people not un-human. Do you know, when I see a poor devil drunk and brutal I always feel, quite apart from my aesthetic perceptions, a sort of shame, as if I myself had some hand in it. Neither do I grudge the triumph that the modern mind feels in having made the world (or a small corner of it) quieter and less violent, but I think that this blindness to beauty will draw down a kind of revenge one day: who knows? Years ago men's minds were full of art and the dignified shows of life, and they had but little time for justice and peace; and the vengeance on them was not increase of the violence they did not heed, but destruction of the art they heeded. So perhaps the gods are preparing troubles and terrors for the world (or our small corner of it) again, that it may once again become beautiful and dramatic withal: for I do not believe they will have it dull and ugly for ever. Meantime, what is good enough for them must content us: though sometimes I should like to know why the story of earth gets so unworthy. . . .

We see both here and in the March letter on the garden city that he has begun decisively this year to turn outwards and to feel responsibility for the whole human scene. His ideas about history are still vague and confused, but he feels that something should and must be done to tackle the evils of his society. There is still a passive element in his thinking. 'Meanwhile what is good enough for them [the gods] must content us.' But he has taken over the notion of *Ragna rok*, of world end and renewal, from Norse myth and feels that it will somehow assert itself in the pattern of history about him. Things are getting so bad that there must surely come some final confrontation, clash, and new start.[7]

His growing rejection of passivity had shown itself in his personal life in the driving-out of Rossetti from Kelmscott; it now appeared in a determination to reorganise the firm so that it would no longer be held together by his will-power and ceaseless activity, with continual economic troubles and fears of bankruptcy. The strain had become too great. He had feared that it would hold him back, he had said, from his work, his writing; he must have begun to realise, however vaguely, that it would also hold him back from developing the wider application of his ideas. He had every right to ask for a fundamental reconstruction of the firm. Rossetti, Brown, Marshall, Faulkner had long been sleeping partners. Burne-Jones and Webb had indeed carried on doing much design-work, for which they had been paid, but the main responsibility and the drive that kept the thing going was all Morris's work, together with the aid he got from men like Taylor and Wardle. The couple of years after the Franco-Prussian War had seen a boom in English trade and industry, but this year, 1874, things were entering the phase known as the Great Depression, which lasted more than twenty years: that is, through the whole of Morris's remaining lifetime. The worst years were 1879, 1886, 1893, with moments of recovery in 1880, 1882, 1888, 1890. American and German industry was now challenging the British hold on the world market. Though productivity increased, prices were cut and profit-margins lessened as a result of the steady competition. Later, in an address delivered in Lancashire and then in London in 1885, in his socialist days, he realised what it was that had struck the commercial world. The hopes of our capitalists, he says, had been founded

on the assumption that England was to be for ever the one serious manufacturing country in the world, supplying all other countries with manufactured goods and receiving from them raw materials for the non-human machines and food for the human ones to be constantly worked up into fresh goods: the market was to be unlimited, the expansion of production unchecked; changes had happened in the constitution of society before but could never happen again: the heaven of the well-to-do middle class was realised here in England.

In 1874, however, though in no way believing in the heaven of the middle class, he was far from knowing what had begun to hit the country.

What Morris proposed was the winding-up of the firm, the retirement of the non-active partners, and a reconstitution under his own control. He seems to have acted rather tactlessly and thus roused a maximum of resistance. Brown objected and took legal advice; Rossetti supported Brown and Marshall joined him. Brown objected to a friendly discussion. 'As to Morris, I could never meet him again with the least pleasure.' He wanted negotiations left in Watts-Dunton's hands. Rossetti felt that he could both oppose Morris and yet seem to have no personal motive if he insisted on his own share of the assets being allocated to Janey. Morris replied to him in October:

My dear Gabriel, Thanks for the letter. I have no objections to make, but we must settle how the thing can be done, as the money must be vested in trustees.

For the rest, your views of the meeting I think are not likely to be correct in any one point (except that Marshall will certainly be drunk) for I don't think *he* will venture to face the indignant members. I will tell you why tomorrow, which will be worth at least one grin to you, I flatter myself: Webb, Ned and Faulkner have all promised to come: and though Brown refuses, I have asked Watts to attend (which he has promised to do) so as to report what we have to say to Brown. In short, I consider it an important meeting, even if Brown doesn't come. Watts said he would press him to do so. I expect to see Watts to-day, & he may bring news of Brown's being a little more reasonable though I confess I don't expect so.

Brown still insisted that there should be equal shares among the partners, which would have meant that for the original trifling sum each would get some seven or eight thousand pounds. Ned, Faulkner and Webb had no intention of fighting Morris, but the other three stood firm, and in the end they were compensated for the loss of interest at the rate of £1,000 each. The firm then became Morris & Co., with Morris as sole manager.

Rossetti's behaviour was characteristic. He was making a chivalrous gesture while at the same time doing his best to upset Morris; and there was an ambiguous note in thus diverting money from the husband to the woman with whom he had been living. One wonders how Janey could have justified to herself the acceptance of such a gift, yet she seems to have taken the money without a murmur, and later on we find Rossetti arranging payments to her as if she were in need of money. It seems likely that since his breakdown in 1872 he had become impotent. Hall Caine told Bernard Shaw that, in discussing Fanny, Rossetti told him that 'she had been his mistress. He had also told me that she had long ceased to be. In another connection he told me he (as the result of a horrible accident) had been impotent for many years.' That statement was made near the end of his life. We may well doubt the 'horrible accident', of which we hear nothing else, but Rossetti would hardly have made the confession about the impotence if it were not true. The condition may have come on him earlier as his sleeplessness grew worse and he drugged himself with chloral and whisky, but the most likely time seems 1872.

There is no sign of Janey showing any fear or repulsion after his breakdown, though after his death she declared that he had been mad. 'That Gabriel was mad was but too true. No one knows that better than myself. . . .' Later this year we find her staying with Rossetti at Aldwick Lodge, Bognor, where he was finishing off *Astarte Syriaca*. In November he wrote to his mother about books for her, mentioning that the pleasure she had got from *Evelina* was 'very beneficial in giving her strength for the sittings'. As for Morris, we merely hear that he had rheumatism. But on 15 November he wrote to Louie about his translations. He was going on a visit to Cambridge to inspect a window of the firm's in Jesus College Chapel, to read Icelandic with Magnusson, and to attend two dinners. He was still keeping up his drawing, though he dreaded the model day as he used to dread Sunday in childhood. Another sign of his change this year to a more active position was his signature to a letter protesting against restorations of Hampstead parish church, though he was only one among many who signed.[8]

On the first day of 1875 he wrote to Aglaia, now in London, asking if he could call, and saying that he had been ill: 'cold &—liver if I may mention that organ to a lady. I beg to state that I have not the least idea where it lives.' On 4 February he wrote to Georgie from Lichfield where he was spending the day (Sunday) with Thomas Wardle, brother-in-law of George, they had set the blue vat on Saturday and were going to get to work on Monday. That day he was dyeing all the afternoon, 'and my hands are a woeful spectacle'. He adds: 'I lost my temper in the dye-house for the first time this afternoon: they had been very trying: but I wish I hadn't been such a fool.' He was still in a very disturbed state, liable to sudden explosions. Early in March he wrote to Aglaia, of whom he had become very fond, and arranged a visit. He was keen not to miss the spring in the country and meant to go for three days to his mother's place with his illuminating; at the moment he was going off to order new clothes.

I have missed you very much & never expected that it would be so long between the times of seeing you. I went down to my mother's yesterday and stayed there till noon to-day. I was very dull when I went, and expected that it would make me duller; but somehow I found myself much better this morning, and am quite changed now. I can only hope that it will last. I am ashamed of myself for these strange waves of unreasonable passion: it seems so unmanly: yet indeed I have had a good deal to bear considering how hopeful my earlier youth was, & what overweening ideas I had of the joys of life.

Another woman with whom he had a close friendship was Kate Faulkner. We have no record of it in writing, since she lived so close to the works in Queen Square; he could slip in and see her at any time, as we see from the diary which he kept in 1881.

In March the reconstruction of the firm was at last completed, and he decided on a tour of Wales with Faulkner. 'We are going to Shrewsbury, and thence to a college farm of his on the very head waters of Severn and Wye, where we are to have ponies and go over the hills and far away, only for about a week, though.' From Bala, on 5 April, he wrote to his girls about his itinerary along valleys and over mountains. He had gone fishing in the morning despite the rain and caught two trout that they had for dinner. On 7 April he wrote from Towyn to Aglaia, pleased to find that very little English was spoken in that region and that the people were mostly very polite and better mannered 'than the same sort' in England. From Cader Idris he was going to Oxford and then London.

Writing in April to Aglaia from Queen Square on a Monday, he said that since Friday morning, when he visited the Grange, he had been hard at his illuminating. 'I can't help liking to see the page brighten while I am at it. I think I will try to do violence to my inclination & pound away at a poem good or bad before long. I wonder if I have gone stupid & can't though.' We see how worried he is since *Love is Enough* that he has lost his creative force. He wasn't feeling well and wanted very much to see Aglaia. On 17 May he wrote to Murray, who had been getting vellum for him, to ask if he would help out with the Virgil pictures. 'I am up to the neck and trying out designs for papers, chintzes, and carpets, and trying to get the manufacturers to do them. I think we are doing some good things in that way.' This year was designed the paper *Acanthus*, which needed sixteen blocks to do justice to its colour gradations.

Morris spent Whitsun with B J and Faulkner at Oxford, and their adolescent skylarking was revived. Ned wrote to his son Philip:

How we teased Mr Morris on the river! We took our lunch one day, and it was fowl and a bottle of wine and some bread and salt—and Mr Faulkner and I managed to hide the fowl away in the sheet of the sail, and when we anchored at a shady part of the river and undid the basket, lo! there was no fowl. And Mr Morris looked like a disappointed little boy and then looked good, and filled his dry mouth with bread and said it didn't matter much, so we drew out the fowl and had great laughter.[9]

As we have seen, this year he was very uncertain about his direction in poetry. He seems not to have realised the virtues of his first book *The Defence of Guenevere*, and reluctantly let Ellis reissue it in April; no one bothered to find the old erratum slip and the reprint repeated the printer's errors of the original. A month or so later came *Three Northern Love Stories* (mainly revised reprints from the *Fortnightly* and the *Dark Blue Magazine*). He went on slogging at the *Aeneid*, though by his nature not responsive to Virgil's kind of art; but some time, probably after finishing the *Aeneid*, he took up the theme of Sigurd, which he had denounced Wagner for elaborating. Here at last he tried to make an heroic theme his own on an epical scale.

At the same time, partly as a result of his active mood and partly as a result of now having complete control of the firm, he did not do much craft-work, being especially keen to master dyeing. He was determined to reject aniline dyes, made from coal-tar, which had brought about the 'absolute divorce between the *commercial process* and the *art* of dyeing'; and he was able to learn much from Thomas Wardle, who was making his name as an authority on dyes and an expert in treating silk and cotton. For the next two years he was often at Leek, where he and Wardle revived vegetable dyeing as an important industry. The quality of printed textiles had sunk low. The superior firms copied the latest French styles; the firms going in for mass-production in Lancashire and Scotland produced vast quantities of cheap prints to meet the expanding market in Britain's overseas empire, ruining the Indian cotton-weavers with their lovely native designs. Morris turned back to the old Herbals, especially to Gerard's ('the favourite of his boyhood'), and learned there much about old vegetable dyes; he even read Pliny's *Natural History*. He learned methods of producing the four basic colours needed for the art: blue, red, yellow, brown—which could be mixed to beget purple, black, and intermediate shades. He got kermes from Greece through Aglaia, and made a fine red from it; then tried poplar and osier twigs, producing 'a good strong yellow'; walnut-tree roots gave him brown; indigo gave blue. In his 1882 essay he discussed the values of kermes (an insect dye) and the medieval wood dyes grouped under the name Brazil. The wood-dyes, though producing fine colours, were not permanent in comparison with kermes, as he proved by comparing stuffs of the thirteenth and fourteenth centuries (where reds had weakened to a fawn-hue) with tapestries of 1510, where the kermes-reds were still rich. 'I may also note that no textiles dyed blue or green, otherwise than by indigo, keep an agree-able colour by candle-light, many bright greens turning into sheer drab.'

As well as studying old texts, he kept experimenting. Thus, 'I was at Kelmscott the other day, and betwixt fishing, I cut a handful of poplar twigs and boiled them, and dyed a lock of wool a very good yellow.' He was deter-mined to succeed. He told Wardle that he'd give up the side of his business based on textiles if he didn't get 'the soundest and best' dyes. 'However I don't in the least see why I should talk about failing which is after all impos-sible.' He meant to fight on 'and should consider anything that was only tolerable as a ladder to mount up to the next stage—that is, in fact, my life'. He was there speaking the exact truth of himself. For some time however he could not get the printed cottons he wanted, and much stock accumulated.

He told Wardle that his position was awkward 'if we have to be the only persons responsible for the pieces when we have no control over the process of them'. True, Wardle wasn't likely to get back for some time the money he had invested in dyeing and printing. 'For me giving up the dyeing schemes means giving up business altogether, and to give up the printing would be a serious blow to it, especially as last Midsummer our balance showed a loss on that account of £1,023.' At the same time with all the worries Morris deeply enjoyed the experiments and the craftwork. 'An old friend tells the story,' says Crane, 'of his calling at the works one day and, on inquiring for the master, hearing a strong cheery voice call out from some inner den, "I'm dyeing. I'm dyeing, I'm dyeing," and the well-known, robust figure of the craftsman presently appeared in his shirt-sleeves, his hands stained blue from the vat.' On 21 October, writing to Aglaia, he told how he wanted to sit and stare on the pieces of printed cloths hung in the big room, but he had to turn back to his work. 'All this keeps me busy and amuses me very much, so that I may consider myself a lucky man, among so many people who seem to find it hard to be amused.'

Possibly Janey was one of the persons about whom he was thinking as not easily amused. In early November she went to stay with Rossetti at Aldwick Lodge, while Morris stayed alone at Kelmscott amid strong winds and a flooding river, with only bacon and kangaroo meat to eat. Out on the water 'I must say it was delightful; almost as good as Iceland on a small scale'. Janey stayed on with Rossetti till she left to spend Christmas with the family. Then she went back to Aldwick Lodge, and on 26 January Morris was again writing to her about the delight of 'muddling about on the river and floods', with violets, aconites and snowdrops out. While waiting for Janey at Bognor, Rossetti had written *Parted Presence* on enforced separation; an uprooted elm on the lawn reminded him of similar incidents at Chelsea and Kelmscott as evil omens. When Janey left him for Christmas he was miserable and sent Fanny a long account of a 'stupid mess' that occurred; the guests saw that he was tired of them and went after a day or two. He was still hoping somehow to resume his settled life together with Janey.[10] On the last day of the year he wrote to Watts-Dunton with instructions about investing the money from the firm for Janey. That she and he were acting secretively behind Morris's back is proved by the order that the letter to Janey about the form of investment was to be sent, not to her, but care of Rossetti. 'The reasons which might make this more convenient will probably strike you.'

Morris signalised the opening of 1876 by resigning his directorate on the mining company. He wrote to tell his mother. 'I am much better than I have been.' He was now able to sit on his hated top-hat. In January, we saw, he was alone at Kelmscott, with Janey staying at Aldwick Lodge. In March she was still there, with May. Morris had been to Marlborough, to see Philip Burne-Jones. Jenny was with him. They had visited Avebury on a wild stormy afternoon, and perhaps because of the rainy weather Jenny caught a bad cold. 'I am withal in the thick of poetry, blue-vats, and business.' On 18 March from London he wrote again to Janey: 'I won't press you to come back, then: only let me know by return about when you intend coming.' He wanted to get off to Leek and didn't want Jenny left too long parentless. About the same time he wrote to May on his journey, which would take up about a fortnight. At Queen Square the old larder had been fitted up into a makeshift dye-house. From Leek on 26 March he wrote to Georgie: 'My days are crowded with work; not only telling unmoveable Lancashire what to do, but even working in sabots and blouse in the dye-house myself—you know I like that.' He had been on a walk with Wardle, past 'a gim-crack palace of Pugin's', on to Ashbourne Church, which he admired. He was going to Nottingham 'to see the hot vat in operation for flock wool-dyeing: when I was a very youngster, my father's mother, then grown doting, used to promise me a journey to Nottingham, her home, if I were a *very* good boy'. He had been practising weld-dyeing, 'the ancientest of yellow dyes, and the fastest'. Two days later he was writing to Aglaia with more details about his dyeing work.

Mackail gives another letter he wrote from Leek, without mentioning to whom it was written. Perhaps he was writing to Ned; there seems too big a change from the tone of the letter of the 26th for it to be Georgie, though it is barely possible she has written him a depressed note.

Wherein you are spiritless, I wish with all my heart that I could help you or amend it, for it is most true that it grieves me; but also, I must confess it, most true that I am living my own life in spite of it, or in spite of anything grievous that may happen in the world. Sometimes I wonder so much at all this, that I wish even that I were once more in some trouble of my own, and think of myself that I am really grown callous: but I am sure that though I have many hopes and pleasures, or at least strong ones, and that though my life is dear to me, so much as I seem to have to do, I would give them away, hopes and pleasures, one by one or all together, and my life at last, for you, for my friendship, for my honour, for the world. If it seems boasting I do not mean it: but rather that I claim, so to say it, not to be separated from those that are heavy-hearted only because I am well in health and full of pleasant work and eager about it, and not oppressed by desires so as not to be able to take interest in it all. I wish I could say something that would serve you, beyond what you know very well, that I love you and long to help you: and indeed I entreat you (however trite the words may be) to think that life is not empty nor made for nothing, and that the parts of it fit into one another in some way; and that the world goes on, beautiful and strange and dreadful and worshipful.

If the letter were to Ned, we should expect some reference to art and their collaborations. It seems possible then that the recipient was Georgie, and that Morris had now given up all hope of their coming together as lovers. The remark about the world going on reminds one of the unfinished novel, in which Georgie's presence is strongly felt:

... the expectant longing for something sweet to come heightened rather than chastened by the mingling fear of some thing as vague as the hope, that forfills our hearts so full in which, killing all commonplace there making us feel as if we were on the threshold of a new world, one step over which if we could but make it would put life within our grasp—what is it? Some reflex of the love and death going on throughout the world, suddenly touching those who are ignorant of the one, and have not learned [to] believe the other?
    ... Nay whatever there was of sordid about the story had slipped off him and left a pleasant feeling of life active and full of incident and change going on about him, with I know not what of sweeter, of sweetest lurking behind it all; and the little pleasures lying ready to his hand they also were so keenly felt, so full of their own beauty: how happy he was as he strode out into the light. . . .

Such passages, together with phrases in letters like that cited earlier or the remarks to Mrs Howard about the shame of seeing the lost and drunken folk of the streets, give us some idea of the deepening that had gone on in Morris in the years 1869-72. He had been forced to draw back from life and measure with a new depth and fullness what he felt about his place in the world; he had achieved a new detachment and a new intensity of sympathy.

But while Morris was going through this new birth, Rossetti was sinking. Reading young Nolly's posthumous works, he felt that they were an attack on himself; he was afraid that his letters were being read. By late April George Hake wrote to Watts-Dunton for aid. 'Spirits fearfully low and no abatement of suspicions.' He gave instructions that he was to be cremated and not to be buried at Highgate (by Lizzie). He wanted letters at Bognor and Chelsea to be destroyed in the event of his death; he seems mainly to be thinking of Janey's letters to him. The noise of birds upset him, and a man had to be hired to keep birds or any other disturbers away. Janey was ill. He wrote of her to Fanny. 'The visitor whom I was expecting some time back has since been very ill and prevented from coming, and is now again thinking of being unable to come.' He went on hoping, waiting. By mid-June he was 'greatly exhausted' at Bognor, with no Janey, and was thinking again of London. He asked for letters to be sealed. He borrowed almost all the £1,000 he had settled on Janey, and was scared he might have to appear in court when Buchanan proceeded against the *Examiner* for publishing a satire by Swinburne. His poems reflect the feeling that he had lost Janey: *A Death Parting* and *Adieu*. 'And she is hence who once was here.' At last when the Buchanan case had been settled with an award of £150, he felt it safe to go back to Cheyne Walk, in early July.[11]

But this summer a disaster fell on Morris, a blow from which he never fully recovered. Jenny, now fifteen, became epileptic, and he blamed her inheritance from his side of the family. Janey too must have suffered. She seems to have cut herself off from Rossetti, who told Watts-Dunton that not hearing from her was making him 'quite ill and unable to work'. Blunt says that Jenny had been Morris's pride 'for her intellectual faculties'. Shaw tells us: 'Morris adored Jenny. He could not sit in the same room without his arm round her waist. His voice changed when he spoke to her as it changed to no one else.' (Shaw adds his belief that Morris's rages were epileptic and left him humbled and shaken as after a fit.)

Janey took the girls to Deal. Jenny seemed better and on 18 July Morris wrote of his relief; he was proposing to come down for three or more days. The London heat made him long for Icelandic snows. 'I don't feel unwell (and therefore ought to hold my noise, as you very truly say), I am depressed and languid (say lazy) and don't care for my work, at any rate not the bread and cheese part of it.' But he was struggling with *Sigurd*. The *Athenaeum* had sent him £20 for a poem, 'though it was not worth publishing', so he proposed spending the money on carriages at Deal. To Aglaia he admitted: 'My rebellious inclinations turn toward Iceland, though I know it to be impossible.' He managed to spend much of August and September at Kelmscott. While he was driving a party of friends to stay with Crom in his tower at Broadway in the Cotswolds on 4 September, he saw Burford Church being badly altered. He felt that something must be done to save such buildings from destruction and desecration; May says that the sight set him 'to making notes for a letter of appeal for some united action'. Again we see his new active attitude asserting itself. He was further affected by seeing what was being done to Lichfield Cathedral this autumn, when he and Wardle visited it from Leek.[12]

In October he went to Paris to meet Wardle; and when the latter had gone, he searched thirteen shops for old books on dyeing. This month Janey, back from Deal, sat to Rossetti for *Venus Astarte*; and Morris launched himself into politics. He had read of the Turkish atrocities in Bulgaria and was upset by the feeling that England was going to declare war on Russia in support of Turkey. He poured his emotions out in a long passionate letter to *The Daily News*, printed on 24 October. Attacking the Tories as the war-party, he appealed to the Liberals. Characteristically he uses a metaphor of sleep and waking. Three weeks back one might have imagined that the English nation, roused by the accounts of torture and oppression by the Turks, was ready to declare war on them in order to gain for the Bulgarians 'some security of life, limb, and property'. So, 'if I had fallen asleep three weeks ago, and woke up yesterday, I should have expected some such answer to my questions of—For whom? Against whom? and Why?' In fact it is himself who has long been asleep in a Ruskinian dream and who is now jolted awake to the reality of the callous world. He permits himself one gibe at the English: 'we, a peaceful people, not liars (except in trade).' He signs himself: 'William Morris, Author of "The Earthly Paradise".'

He was still far from grasping the complexity of the events into which he now irrupted. The important thing was that his heart and his conscience had been deeply stirred, and that he had made his voice heard. With his deep need to live fully out any position or concept into which he had grown, he could not now but go on exploring the new sphere of interest. He had to match at each step his intellectual effort to understand with a moral effort to carry the resulting ideas out into their fullest actualisation. What he had grasped was the form of exploitation linked with the imperial expansion. He detested the way in which Disraeli was whipping up a war-fever, the new Jingoism as defined in the popular music-hall song: 'We don't want to fight, but, by Jingo, if we do, we've got the ships, we've got the men, we've got the money too!' The money was the key thing. What would the British do with Turkey if she successfully protected her? he asked Faulkner on 15 November:

'Take it ourselves,' says the bold man, 'and rule it as we rule India.' But the bold man don't live in England at present I think: and I know what the Tory trading stock-jobbing scoundrel that one calls an Englishman today would do with it: he would shut his eyes hard over it, to get his widows and orphans to lend it money, and sell it vast quantities of bad cotton.

We see that his sense of the artistic iniquities of the cotton trade has now broadened into a sense of the economic and political exploitations it involved.[13]

In November *Sigurd the Volsung* appeared. Mackail says it was 'but languidly received', though reviewers recognised it 'a noble poem' (Watts-Dunton in the *Athenaeum*), with a style 'more spirited and more virile' (Gosse in the *Academy*), a work that will eventually 'take its place among the few great epics of the English tongue' (anon. in the *Literary World*). The reviewer in *Fraser's* however insisted that a poem which thus 'reflects, with hard, uncompromising realism, an obsolete code of ethics, and a barbarous condition of society, finds itself irreconcilably at discord with the key of nineteenth-century feeling'. Morris had indeed written the work because he felt himself ever more opposed to Victorian feeling, and so he could not expect to be taken to the middle-class bosom. The poem has indeed much vigour and maintains a powerful swell. Inevitably it quite lacks the spare and fierce concision of the *Volsunga Saga*; Morris was trying to use the theme in a way which stayed true to 'a barbarous condition of society' where the code of ethics seemed to him far superior to that of the Victorian world, and which at the same time told the story in a way comprehensible to that world. He had worked hard to draw into his epic a large amount of related material, which he felt would help to strengthen and enrich the expanded version; using the *Lay of Sigrdrifa*, the *First Lay of Gudrun*, the *Snorra Edda*, *Reginsmál*, *Fáfnismál*, the *Short Lay of Sigurd*, and the two Atli lays. For the episode of Sigurd's birth four versions exist; for that of Brynhild's awakening, five; for that of Sigurd's last meeting with her, seven, of which four are important—after rewriting the scene four times Morris got rid of any note of lamentation. His main change in the story as told by the *Saga* was to take over the ending of the *Nibelungenlied*. In the *Saga* Gunnar kills his friend under the stress of irresistible passion; in the poem, as in the Germanic version, his main motive in betraying his friend is in the end the desire to possess the ring.

Here we have the old triadic pattern of two friends in love with the same woman; but perhaps because Morris's emotions are still so raw from his experience of its full working-out between himself, Gabriel and Janey, he feels unable to cope with the theme of a ruthless and overwhelming passion; he puts ambition in its place, as if his conflict with Rossetti had been, not so much for Janey, as on account of their differing ideals. And in fact in the last resort that difference had been the determining element in their relationship. By stressing the effect of gold in breaking up tribal society, he (like Wagner) puts the personal and mythic elements within a true historical perspective. The long swinging lines do not admit of sufficient variation to carry a poem of such length; but apart from this shortcoming Sigurd is indeed a magnificent work. No other artwork of the post-1830 world (apart from Wagner's *Ring*) so powerfully and urgently achieves the heroic note. Amusingly, the antagonistic natures of Morris and Rossetti came out directly in connection with the poem. Rossetti remarked that the dragon-transformation of Fafnir was 'not merely barbarous, but silly', and Morris (says Mackail) 'made a reply which can scarcely be quoted here, but which no one who has heard it is ever likely to forget'.

The part played by the turn to Norse sagas and Iceland in driving Morris to look outwards and to find a pattern of significance in the social and political hurly-burly is well brought out by the conclusion of a summary of northern mythology he wrote about this time:

It may be that the world shall worsen, that men shall grow afraid to 'change their life', that the world shall be weary itself, and sicken, and none but faint-hearts be left—who knows? So at any rate comes the end at last, and the Evil, bound for a while, is loose, and all nameless merciless horrors that on earth we figure by fire and earthquake and venom and ravin. So comes the great strife; and like the kings and heroes that they loved, here also must the Gods die, the Gods who made the strifeful imperfect earth, not blindly indeed, yet foredoomed. One by one they extinguish for ever some dread and misery that all this time has brooded over life, and one by one, their work accomplished, they die: till at last the great destruction breaks out over all things, and the old earth and heavens are gone, and then a new heavens and earth. What goes on there? Who shall, of us who know only of rest and peace by toil and strife: And what shall be our share in it? Well, sometimes we must needs think that we shall live again: yet if that were not, would it not be enough that we helped to make this unnameable glory, and live not altogether deedless? Think of the joy we have in praising great men, and how we turn their stories over and over, and fashion their lives for our joy: and this also we ourselves may give to the world.

Morris now wholeheartedly joined in with the Liberal-Radical agitation against Disraeli. Mass-meetings were held in Trafalgar Square and Hyde Park. A. J. Mundella did a great deal of work in organising the very successful conference held at St James's Hall on 8 December; but Morris played his part in the preparations, and when the Eastern Question Association was brought into being at the meeting he was elected on to its committee. Queen Victoria was scandalised and would have liked to set the Attorney-General on to the speakers. The EQA set itself to issuing tracts; but for the moment the war danger seemed to slacken with the Constantinople Conference. Now for the first time Morris encountered working-class politicians, such as those of the Labour Representation League. These men had lost militancy and a belief in independent working-class action, and had fallen to the Lib.-Lab. level; but the Turkish question brought back something of the old radical internationalism. Morris must have met some of these men, prominent Lib.-Lab. characters such as Broadhurst and Burt. Already he had developed a distrust of Parliament as a middle-class method of government, which seemed by its very nature organised to baffle and deflect the popular will. Hence he had remarked to Faulkner in November, 'I do not feel very sanguine about it all, but it is the only thing that offers at present, and I do not wish to be anarchical: I must do the best I can with it.'

This year he began to act as examiner at South Kensington, and carried on the work till his last illness. In his designs he was now much affected by his discovery and study of medieval woven textiles, especially Spanish and Sicilian, and his style grew more controlled and symmetrical, lacking something of the free flow of his earlier work, but never losing his sense of natural form. This year, 1876, saw the *Honeysuckle* chintz, printed at Leek, made up of honeysuckle sprays with big poppies and fritillaries.[14]

Morris was now close to the fully active integration of his thought and art, and we may glance briefly back at the stages through which he had passed. First came what I have called the garden of happiness and beauty, the forest of independence, of his childhood: a stage which was given depth by his discovery of old crafts and buildings, and his reading of Scott. Secondly came the drama of the fall, the ejection from the earthly paradise, from the warm security of the first phase: a drama centred on Emma, but in fact based on the inner conflict of the family with its merged elements of satisfying union and tyrannical egoism. Thirdly came the achievement of a sense of fellowship through Burne-Jones and the Birmingham group, with schemes for a community of chosen spirits. The first step was taken towards identifying the union of the first phases with worthy and creative activities, and the threatening forces of division with the dehumanising elements in society. Then, with the breakdown of the conventual schemes and the plans for priestly dedication, there arrived the full turning to art: a phase given strength by the hypnotic example of Rossetti, who released the craft-faculty in Morris. Next came his attempt as a married man, with Janey-Guenevere as bride, to use his craft-powers to actualise a medieval paradisiac dream in Red House. Here was the climax of his turning-in on himself, in which, despite a Ruskinian realisation of the need to base craft and art in a society where there could be true happiness in work, he was seeking essentially a personal solution. In the next stages the Ruskinian realisation played an ever greater part and Morris turned outwards. To a considerable extent through economic pressure he founded the firm with his friends and tried to sell to the bourgeois world the sort of products developed for Red House. Now his craft-powers found ever wider fields of expression; but he still laboured under the contradiction that he was seeking to sell to a divided world the sorts of wares that he felt an integrated society would produce. Thus there was at the heart of his activity what we may call a dire conflict between the Rossettian dream and the Ruskinian vision. This conflict poignantly actualised itself in the loss of his wife Janey to Rossetti and the accompanying break-up of Rossetti himself as he, Morris, struggled for a fuller grasp of the vision of integration. Thrown back painfully on himself, he had to fight for a new centre of being: one in which the vision dominated and steadily eliminated the limiting dream. He summoned up afresh the heroic elements which come into his poetry in the days of the hopeful Oxford Brotherhood, and gave them a stronger personal note through his response to the Icelandic sagas. Thus he regained his self-respect and what he called manliness; took a fresh and clearer grip of his life in all its aspects; and looked outwards for ways in which he could link his craft-activity with the struggle for a better world—a world in which the Ruskinian vision could be realised as part of a general way of life. He began with the effort to organise resistance to the desecration of the human heritage embodied in old buildings, and to fight for peace against the war forces which he increasingly saw as linked with the forms of human degradation and exploitation at home.

II

Action on Many Fronts

In January 1877, amid the dyes at Leek, he was writing about the heroic virtues. 'I have been reading the Njala. . . . What a glorious outcome of the worship of Courage these stories are.' He had put off his 'ill temper about the public' and the lack of response to *Sigurd*. 'That was only a London mood.' Matthew Arnold's period as Oxford Professor of Poetry was ending, and Morris was sounded. Mackail says that he was tempted but finally decided to say no. On 16 February he replied to the man who had approached him on the matter; he expressed his gratitude and gratification, but declared that he was not the man for the post. Such a professor should own deep and wide scholarship or be able to lecture with 'ingenious rhetoric', both of which he lacked. Also he thought that the practice of an art rather narrowed the artist with regard to the theory of it. He himself was not a man of letters. (In January he had spoken of 'literature' as 'a beastly French word'.) Janey seems to have been ill, for Rossetti wrote to Watts-Dunton: 'Bad news from Turnham Green is worrying me, but must hope for the best.'

A visit to Tewkesbury, where Morris saw the same desecrating restoration at work as at Burford, led him to write a strong letter to the *Athenaeum*, which brought about the Society for the Protection of Ancient Buildings (SPAB), also known as Anti-Scrape (from the custom of scraping off all weathering so as to leave the stones smooth). He denounced the architects for being, 'with very few exceptions, hopeless, because interest, habit, and ignorance blind them', while the clergy too were hopeless, 'because their order, habit, and an ignorance yet grosser, blind them'. To Lachmere, who put up the conventional defence that the work was meant to 'restore' the minster to its former state (by pulling down later additions and rebuilding them in the style of the earlier parts) he wrote a reply, saying that such restoration was merely forgery, and the stripping of all life from the building. (By this time the firm was refusing any orders for stained glass to go into old churches; though churches of the eighteenth century were not ranked as old.)[1]

In March Morris was taken up with the introduction of a brocader from Lyon into the works; he also 'found time for a little gout'. Janey was not well. On 24 April he wrote to May, 'I am afraid Mama was not much *less* tired than she expected to be.' Rossetti was complaining to Watts-Dunton. 'You know how much anxiety I expressed as to getting no news from the anxious quarter. To-night I have written asking when I can go there, and if silence should still be the result, I shall be quite at a loss. It is making me quite ill and unable to attend to work.' Throughout these later years he cannot bring himself to name Janey in writing to others; he always uses some circumlocation. Sometimes he calls her the divinity or the Divine One.

This spring Wagner was in London. He and Cosima were staying with Dannreuther, the conductor, who was married to Luke Ionides's sister, and Cosima said that she'd like to meet Morris. Morris, invited to dinner, turned and asked if his 'gala-clothes had arrived'. They hadn't, so he asked how he could sit down at the dinner dressed as he was and with his hands dyed blue. However he was induced to sit beside Cosima, 'who was most charming,' says Luke, 'and delighted to have him next to her at table.' We are also told that he went to one of the Albert Hall concerts in May with the BJS and Leighton, while the Wagners sat close by with George Eliot and Lewes; but we know nothing of his reactions. That month he was again taken up with anti-Turk agitation. War had broken out between Russia and Turkey, and he wrote a pamphlet *Unjust War: To the Working-men of England*, which the EQA issued. The remarkable thing about this work is the fact that it is addressed to the workers, not to the middle class who largely made up the association, and the tone of the writing, which prefigures his later socialist positions. He declares, 'We shall pay heavily, and you, friends of the working-classes, will pay the heaviest.' He asks who are the men flaunting the banner inscribed English Interests:

Do you know them?—Greedy gamblers on the Stock Exchange, idle officers of the army and navy (poor fellows!), worn-out mockers of the Clubs, desperate purveyors of exciting war-news for the comfortable breakfast tables of those who have nothing to lose by war. . . . Working-men of England, one word of warning yet: I doubt if you know the bitterness of hatred against freedom and progress that lies at the hearts of a certain part of the richer classes of this country: their newspapers veil it in a kind of decent language; but do but hear them talking among themselves, as I have often, and I know not whether scorn or anger would prevail in you at their folly and insolence:—these men cannot speak of your order, of its aims, of its leaders without a sneer or an insult: these men, if they had the power (may England

perish rather) would thwart your just aspirations, would silence you, would deliver
you bound hand and foot for ever to irresponsible capital—and these men, I say it
deliberately, are the heart and soul of the party that is driving us to an unjust
war. . . .[2]

This turning to the workers would certainly not have occurred without the
contacts he had had with LRL leaders and their propaganda. On 2 May he
wrote to Janey at Kelmscott. Next Monday there was to be a big anti-Turk
meeting at St James's Hall. The firm had now taken over a showroom in
Oxford Street at the corner of North Audley Street. 'Picture to yourself
3 years war and the shop in Oxford Street, and poor Smith standing at the
door with his hands in his pockets! There is a small meeting tonight at the
Cannon Street Hotel: I am going there to swell the crowd.' Perhaps it was
the businessman speaking there about the threat of war; perhaps the comment was meant to stir Janey and make her excuse his enthusiasm. He was
perhaps recalling an LRL handbill which declared that the war policy would
'paralyse our already crippled industry'. Ned was backing Morris in the
EQA, though he was pleased enough when the meeting at St James's Hall was
so crowded that he couldn't get in. All the while the work of the firm was
being carried on. We may take the notes for 18 May left by the son of
Morris's old tutor Guy, who for a while this year acted as his secretary.

Mr Morris slept last night in town, and was up on the move when I arrived. He had
been downstairs and set the new dye-pot at work, ready for him to set an indigo
vat in the afternoon. Kirby's man came and finished fixing the ciphering tubes.
GW and WM talked over Mrs Baring's house in Devonshire: the work we have
proposed to do will certainly take two or three years before all completed: we have
to get our Lyons silk-weaver to work for one thing. WM did a little work to a piece
of embroidery in his room during the morning. I went down into the dye-shop
with WM between 1 and 2 o'clock and helped him to set the vat. He dyed some
blues which he will green on Tuesday next, if all is well, for Dimarco's carpet stuff.
Mr Broadhurst called and saw WM about the Eastern Question.

On 4 June a letter of his appeared in *The Times* protesting against restorations of the choir at Canterbury. On 7 June he replied to the Dean, who has
assumed that SPAB wanted to see old buildings 'reduced to the state of
ruins'.[3] On 10 July he asked Ruskin to let him reprint as a leaflet what had
been said of restoration in *Seven Lamps*. Danger of war against Russia
receded, but Morris joined in the struggle to prevent the Afghan campaign

(aimed against Russia). On 16 August he wrote to Janey to say that next day (Friday), he would be off for Kelmscott with a hamper; he hoped that May would have the right sort of worms ready for his fishing. He had a bonnet for Janey and the BJs were coming on Monday. Rossetti had been forced for health reasons to leave London; he went to Herne Bay for two months. Morris felt that it was safe to build up his own life at Kelmscott, with friends visiting. In October Janey was ill and Rossetti was very worried about the letters in two drawers in the studio; they must have been hers. On 8 October young Guy wrote down:

WM had to see about his packages, which he has to take to Ireland. He started by 8.25 mail train to Holyhead from Euston. He goes to the Countess of Charleville, Tullamore, King's County, to advise her as to the doing up of her house. He has to take with him patterns of carpets, silks, chintzes, etc. He goes to Leek on his way back from Ireland, and will stay there some while, making Tom Wardle look to his dyeing, etc., helping a good deal in it too.

He found Dublin not altogether an ugly town, but dirty and slatternly; the country cottages looked the poorest habitations he had yet seen; at Tulla-more he heard tales of past rebellions. In November Janey and the girls went to Oneglia on the Italian Riviera, where he was to join them in the spring. His letters to them over these months give a full account of his activities in the EQA, SPAB, and at Queen Square, where a poor old Spital-fields weaver had been found to help Bazin. At this phase he assumes that Janey will be interested in his politics. In October there was a fire in the glazier's shop at the back of the works. 'There is a good deal of stained glass destroyed and material for it, but *nothing else*; also we are fully insured: of course there will be a good deal of trouble and loss from the stoppage of business.' He was preparing to give his first lecture, and tried out his voice by reading *Robinson Crusoe* to a group. To write prose and expound his ideas he found a slow and difficult job. The lecture was on the decorative arts, given to the Trades Guild of Learning, in 'a dismal hole near Oxford Street', on 4 December.

He sets out the thesis that since the Renaissance the arts have been ruined by luxury and display, by a barren classicism; a true basis can be found by a return to the traditional yeoman's house and the humble village church. He wants a functional simplicity, with which goes cleanliness and decency. Nature and history are the teachers; as things are, the world is made hideous and inhuman and unhealthy by the ruling commercial interests; and there is no hope of redemption in an élite art. He gives no sign of any realisation of all that is politically and economically entailed in the struggle to bring about the sane world he desires; but his sense of world-end and renewal, stirred by the sagas, and a feeling of deep forces at work in his society, stirred by his experiences in the EQA, convince him that somehow the change will come. 'I hear that I must say that if it does come about, it will be owing to some turn of events which we cannot at present foresee.' For the flood of 'cheap and nasty' wares on the market he blames all classes, but especially the manufacturers; and feels that the only hope lies in the handicraftsmen, who 'have in them the seeds of order and organisation'. He says: 'History has remembered the kings and warriors, because they destroyed; Art has remembered the people, because they created.' From such positions it was inevitable that his political ideas would grow yet more concrete and that he would decide the future of the arts lay with the working class.[4]

On 7 December he wrote to tell Jenny that the lecture 'went off very well, and I was not at all nervous, but made myself well heard'. War threats were coming up again; and on 8 December BJ wrote to Ruskin in Venice for his support. He says that he had thought himself 'a mere outlaw in public opinion. I hope neither Morris nor you will retire wholly again out of such spheres of effort.' On Christmas Day Morris wrote to his girls. He had gone to Much Hadham to spend the day with his mother. 'Edgar & his missis & baby are here, also Isabella & her naval officer, & Ada. . . . Now they are coming in from church, so I shall [have] to give in.' There had been a good meeting of workers on Clerkenwell Green the previous Sunday—meant 'to talk war', but turned the other way. The EQA hoped for a big meeting soon and was issuing a manifesto. On 28 December he wrote to Janey. He was reading the proofs of his lecture. Two glasses of port on Christmas Day had brought on his toe-devil, so he fasted more 'than Henrietta fasted on the day before'. Also, Isabella cut his hair 'in your absence': which implies that usually Janey trimmed it for him.[5]

Now, in the first four months of 1878, Morris gained his crucial education in the field of politics. On 16 January a demonstration was called by the Workmen's Neutrality Committee, the body co-ordinating the LRL and the EQA. The main speakers in the afternoon were the radical professor Thorold Rogers and Joseph Arch, leader of the agricultural workers. Morris in his downrightness remarked that he must face the fact 'that the Court was using all the influences which it possessed'. There were cries of No and Cheers for the Queen; and the chairman called him to order. Morris, writing to Janey, referred to his amiable indiscretion, and said that 'I must confess I have been agitated as well as agitating'; he added that at least the meeting 'refused to cheer the Empress Brown'. In the evening the main meeting came. The roughs, sent to break it up, were kept out through some 'heavy work', and 'the noise of them outside was like the sea roaring against a lighthouse'. They then invaded the overflow meeting in Trafalgar Square but failed to stop the neutrality resolution being passed. Admission to Exeter Hall was by tickets distributed among London trade unions and radical and liberal clubs, and Broadhurst was in charge of the stewards at the door. He had persuaded a fellow stone-mason, organist at a London chapel, to bring a choir of working-class men and women; and Morris had written a song to the tune of *The Hardy Norseman's Home of Yore*: 'Wake, London lads, wake, bold and free!' The song was mediocre, but important in Morris's development; he appealed to the workers from their own class viewpoint and treated them as the inheritors of the national struggle for freedom. Georgie, present with Ned, Faulkner and Crom, wrote to Rosalind Howard, wintering in Italy together with Janey, about Morris's speech: 'It is such a blessing to hear him put truth into straightforward words as no one else does at present, for he is free from the usual forms of public speaking and in fear of no man.' Leaflets of the song had been placed on all the chairs, and a Nonconformist minister read it through; the choir sang it twice; then the whole meeting rose and thundered it out. After each stanza there was a pause for cheers.

Morris felt optimistic. Then on 23 January came news that the fleet had been ordered to sail for the Dardanelles, and Jingoism was active. A meeting on 31 January in Trafalgar Square was broken up by some four hundred workers brought from Woolwich Arsenal in wagons and paid a gratuity for the day's work. 'People on our side had to hide away in cellars & places & get out anyhow.' Janey seems to have feared for his safety. He wrote reassuring her that he was safe in wind and limb. 'I was at very noisy meeting last night down at Stepney, where we had a bare majority. I feel very low & muddled about it.' But he was looking forward to a really big meeting in Hyde Park. The government set about rumours that Constantinople was near falling to the Russians and the Indian Empire in danger. The parliamentary Liberal Party lost its nerve, and Morris was disheartened. On 6 February there was an EQA meeting and it was clear that no help could be expected in Parliament. Morris and some others met at Broadhurst's and talked about the Hyde Park meeting. He and Auberon Herbert had visited

Samuel Morley for money, then spent part of that day and the next lobbying Liberal MPs.

The fleet anchored off the Dardanelles, waiting for Turkish permission to sail through. The Hyde Park project was dropped on account of uncertain weather and fear of the Jingoist roughs. Morris pushed through the idea of a meeting in the largest building in London, the Agricultural Hall. He, Ned, and others each guaranteed £50 towards the cost. Morris and some workers called on Gladstone, who agreed about the meeting, though in fact he was simulating his enthusiasm and refused to speak when Mundella asked him. In Sheffield (Mundella's own constituency) 20,000 inhabitants passed a resolution supporting the government. Gladstone's windows were broken by the Jingoists; Mundella too lost his nerve; Morris was left isolated, with only the LRL and one other man (Chesson) standing firm. He still could not believe that Gladstone had let the cause down, but he was thoroughly disillusioned with the Liberals in general. After various manœuvres by Disraeli, Russia and Turkey signed peace preliminaries. Disraeli called up the Reserves and privately proposed the use of Indian troops to seize ports in the Levant and to take over Cyprus. Morris commented, 'EQA as good as dead.' But the LRL went on with a manifesto and a trade-union petition. The news of 7,000 Indian troops being moved to Malta brought about something of a revulsion of feeling; but in the end, through the Congress of Berlin, Britain gained Cyprus.

Morris's first reaction was one of deep rage and distrust. 'I shall give up reading the Papers, and shall stick to my work.' But the two main lessons he had learned were to stay with him and determine much of his future direction: the feeling that there was something solid and reliable in the organised working class, and a revulsion from the bourgeois parliamentary parties which led him to a complete distrust of Parliament itself for any purposes.

Rossetti had toyed with the idea of going to Italy to be near Janey, but he was not capable of such actions. He contented himself with trying to lower Morris in Janey's ideas by satirical comments on his political work, using the name Odger of a zealous trade unionist.

(27 February) It seems they have been smashing Gladstone's windows: if you were in town, perhaps the air would come in without your throwing the windows open, considering Top's political bias. He is the Odger of the future, my dear Janey, depend on it, & will be in parliament next change.

(1 April) You never say how the business is flourishing in London. Or has Top perhaps thrown trade after poetry, & now executes none but wholesale orders in philanthropy,—the retail trade being beneath a true humanitarian? But no— without a shop he could not be the Odger of the Future!

On 18 March, after advising iron as a medicine, he says, 'I could get you some of that capital forthwith. The dividend (which I mentioned to Watts) has been due for some time & I will take care that it leaves me for you *without fail* in a day or two. I will send it in notes registered.'[6]

On 21 February Morris had gone to Cambridge to speak at the distribution of prizes at the School of Art. The Birmingham Society of Arts had chosen him as their president for the year. In a note to May, he cries, 'I'll go to Iceland.' In early March he was 'lame with gouty-rheumatism, or rheumatic gout. I can't get down stairs, but I find the long room very comfortable.' He had been fishing at Kelmscott with Edgar and Ellis. This month he began house-hunting, hoping to find a new place for Janey to come home to. The house that most attracted him was the Retreat in the Upper Mall, Hammersmith. Janey must have been reporting all his accounts to Rossetti, who at once went to see the place for himself and did his best to put Janey off it. There was a room 'made fearful to the eye with a blood red flock paper and a ceiling of blue with gold stars'. The house was hopelessly damp, as he wrote on 1 April, contradicting Morris and insisting that there was a 'composite swamp in the garden' and a 'frightful kitchen floor', a ladder for kitchen-stairs, no light at all. Morris on the other hand wrote enthusiastically about the garden and the long drawing-room. 'The situation is certainly the prettiest in London.' He had taken Webb to check the drains and look into the question of floods, and the report was favourable. On 2 April he wrote to say that he had arranged to take the house, so that Janey did not have time to protest on the basis of Rossetti's remarks in his letter of the previous day. Morris proposed that Kate Faulkner should come to live with them, but nothing seems to have come of the project.

The house was a plain three-storeyed building of the late eighteenth century, with a row of elms and a towpath leading to the river. Morris was pleased that it was not so far from the Grange, and he tried to win Janey over by saying that they could have much more company there than previously. Rossetti in his attempts to put Janey off tried to suggest that Morris was not thinking of her. He hoped she'd enjoy a proposed visit to Venice where the damps might prepare her somewhat 'for the Hammersmith house, which I really do not think a wise choice, if *you* are the person to be at all considered on the matter'.

Morris had indeed meant to take Janey and the girls on a tour of northern Italian cities, but she now wrote saying that she was too weak for such an ordeal. He however insisted that he would come out if the Howards weren't to bring her home. And if he were once there, why not see Venice and go through the Lombard cities on the way to Milan? 'Don't disappoint my babes too much.' Janey agreed; but when Morris reached Oneglia he was himself crippled by gout. At Genoa he had to be lifted from the carriage and carried; when he tried to stand, he fainted. At Venice he was not much better, and Janey wilted in such a situation. Still, he enjoyed the grass and the birds at Torcello and admired Verona, though disliking Santa Anastasia there. But, what with his illness and the strain he had recently gone through, he was in a distracted state of mind. He wrote to Georgie:

Sometimes it all tumbles into a dream and I do not know where I am. Many times I think of the first time I ever went abroad, and to Rouen, and what a wonder of glory that was to me when I first came upon the front of the Cathedral rising above the flower-market. It scarcely happens to me like that now, at least not with man's work, though whiles it does with bits of the great world, like the Garda lake the other day, or unexpected sudden sights of the mountains. Even the inside of St Mark's gave one rather deep satisfaction, and rest for the eyes, than that strange exultation of spirits, which I remember of old in France, and which the mountains give me yet. I don't think this is wholly because I am grown older, but because I have really more sympathy with the North from the first in spite of all the faults of its work.

He blamed the infernal furnace-heat of Italy for another attack of gout, and he was pleased to escape. On their arrival in England it was Janey who, writing to Rosalind Howard, expressed regret that she couldn't spend another month in Venice. 'I dreamt of myself as a monster in many forms, and hated myself whenever I woke up, my dullness and ill-manners seemed unpardonable, pray forgive me and remember me only as one who loves you.' She considered Jenny restored to health.[7]

On 21 June SPAB held its first annual meeting, with a report on activities. The meetings were at first held in the Oxford Street showroom, with Morris as secretary, but he gave the annual report at Queen Square. Later this year, in November, the society had its own office at 9 Buckingham Street, Strand, with Newman Marks as secretary. As in his April letter to *The Times*,

Morris declared in his report that it was the common assumption any considerations of art must yield if they stood in the way of money interests. A letter from Rossetti to Janey on 1 July gives the first hint of a rift between them:

I can't help saying your letter is no less than a shock to me. Is it possible that mine can have contained anything by which you could really suppose that the question as to your looks influenced in the least my great desire to see you again? That supposition would be contrary to my deep regard for you—a feeling far deeper (though I know you never believe me) than I have entertained towards any other living creature at any time of my life. Would that circumstances had given me the power to prove this: for proved it *wd* have been And *now* you do not believe it.

He goes on to ask if she has taken any cod liver oil lately. On 26 August Morris published a letter in *The Times* attacking the proposal to replace the flat nave-roof of St. Albans Cathedral with a high-pitched one.

Rossetti was often hard put to find anything to write to Janey about and looked round for some amusing anecdote to tell. 'I know you love a laugh.' Janey confessed to a passion for looking on the other side of newspaper cuttings for odd stories. He wanted her to find a drier country place than Kelmscott. On 6 September he asked, 'Have you any plans of going abroad again? You know there is that money at hand to help.' In October he sent her a playlet *The Death of Topsy*, in which he gets rid of Morris in a murder-fantasy and expresses some of the anger he must still have nourished against him for taking over the firm. It is worth citing in full: the subtitle is 'a Drama of the Future in One Unjustifiable Act'.

Scene—London

SCENE I

On one side an Upholsterer's shop, with the name 'Morris and Co.' over the door. On the other side a Grocer's shop. Enter First Young Wardle, carrying a roll of parchment: he goes into the Upholsterer's shop.

1st Y.W. Papa, I've fetched the deed of partnership which Mr Morris sent to be copied.

Wardle (from within). Give it here, my boy.

Enter Second Young Wardle: he goes into the Grocer's shop.

2nd Y.W. If you please, my Mamma wants a pound of your best Coffee.

Grocer (from within). Yes, Sir.

Scene closes as Third Young Wardle is seen going towards a Chemist's shop in the distance.

SCENE II

(St James's Hall)

Topsy is discovered lecturing in Architectural Restoration.

Top (reads). 'Our forefathers had thus reared for us, with superhuman labour, temples worthy of Christian worship,—nay, almost worthy in themselves of some portion of the homage which the worshippers'—*(aside through his teeth,—'I can't have written rot like this'—turns the page to skip, but finding he cannot, goes on)*—'which the worshippers bestowed on that Power which alone could have inspired such mightly achievements.' *(aside, as before, 'I know that damned Ned has stuck it in!'—goes on)*—'Little could those great yet humble ones have dreamed that a too puffed-up posterity'—*(scratches the seat of his trousers, and looks uneasily at the curtain behind him)*—'would have devoted all their efforts only to the defacement of the noble structures bequeathed to their keeping by godlike minds and hands.' *(aside through the curtain,—'I say, Ned, damn you.')*

E. Burne-Jones (from behind curtain). I didn't do it, Top—you wrote it yourself. It's very bad, but go on or the audience will hiss.

(Topsy goes on, lurching a great deal, and at last concludes amid great applause: he bows and goes behind curtain.)

Top. I say, Ned, mustn't they just be fools! I'll pay you out another time, but I must get down to the Wardles, as I said I'd take tea there.

E. Burne-Jones. They always take coffee.

Top. O do they? will you come?

E. Burne-Jones. No thank you. I say, Top, one of the workmen has chalked a large T on your back.

Top. Well, damn you, why don't you rub it out?

(They have now reached the door, and E. Burne-Jones bolts down the street.)

SCENE III

A Private Appartment. Wardle and Madeline seated at a table, with cups & saucers &c.

Madeline. Is the deed signed?

Wardle. Yes.

(A crash without. Enter Topsy.)

Top. I say, I'm very sorry, but I was laying down my hat on a chair outside, and somehow my hand went through it.

Madeline. I pray don't mention it, Mr Morris, it's of no consequence.

Top (to Wardle). I say, old chap, Ned told me just now that someone had chalked a T on my back. *(tries to see it)* Do you see it?

Wardle. No, of course.

Top. Blow that Ned! *(aside through his teeth)* I should like to tread his guts out.

Wardle. He hasn't got any.

Top. O I say, talk about guts—what's become of mine? *(He stands up, and taking the quartern loaf from the table, stuffs it into the waistband of his trousers to show how much room there is,—then pulls it out again and puts it back on the plate.)* There, now you mind you don't call me fat any more.

Wardle. I never did,—I always thought you a fine figure.

Madeline. Mr Morris, you're letting your coffee get cold. George dear, hand the cup.

Top (taking cup from Wardle). All right old chap *(drinks)*. Hullo! how can I have the gripes now that I've got no belly? Hullo! Blow! *(dies)*.

SCENE IV

(Same as in Scene I)

Wardle places a ladder against the Upholsterer's shop, and mounting it erases the name of *Morris* & substitutes *Wardle & Co.*

First Cabman (passing). Hi! Who's the Co.?

Second Cabman (passing). Why, Coffee, in course.

(Topsy is carried out on a stretcher, while *Stennett* is seen passing at the head of a funeral; he stops and gazes intently. *Old Brown* goes by on the top of an omnibus, and turning round, stares in stupefaction at the altered name over the door.)

Emma (from within the omnibus). Did you see that, Ford?

Old B. Yes, Emma *(he raises his eyes and his hands to heaven)*.

(The ghost of Warington Taylor is heard tapping at a Medium's door.)

SCENE V

(The Medium's House)

Mrs Guppy seated at a table of Victorian design, with Ghosts and others. Enter the Ghost of Warington Taylor.

Ghost of Taylor. Topsy you fool, come along. Here's a chance for you. Split on 'em through that table, & let 'em catch it as they deserve.

Ghost of Topsy. Get out, it's beastly rot. Do you think I'm going to believe in bogies merely because I'm one myself? And besides, you don't suppose, you idiot, that I'd talk through a blowed table of such a damned shape as that! *(indulges in language after his kind)*.

Mrs Guppy. That is the very lowest class of spirit of which I ever had experience. May not the essence of such misused humanity rank even below the soulless beasts that perish?—Who shall say? Well, he is gone, my friends,—I dread to think whither. *(She turns to the table)* Shelley, are you there?

Ghost of Percy Bysshe Shelley.

Hi diddle diddle
The Cat & the fiddle—

Mrs Guppy. Hush, my friends, now indeed we shall hear something.

(Curtain)

Rossetti had long been very interested in spiritualism and earlier he had drawn Morris and Janey into a seance, where there was a mysterious light seen by her and others. Mrs Guppy was a famous medium, who once almost converted the sceptical Browning. Bell Scott, in 1869, had noted the incident of Rossetti at Penkill thinking a chaffinch that settled on his hand to be Lizzie's spirit prophesying misfortune; he compared Mrs Guppy with Fanny Cornforth, calling her 'as uncultured and mentally unfurnished as the evil genius of DGR'.

Late in October the Morrises moved into their new house. Rossetti gave Janey most of the furniture he had left at Kelmscott. She in her reply complained of all the work to be done, adding that she herself was doing nothing but feel worn-out and lie awake at nights disturbed by the noise of the river steamers. (Soon Morris installed a loom in his own separate bedroom.) On 8 November Webb wrote one of his jesting letters to Janey:

I saw Morris last night and between the yells & mingled gabble of a full antiscrape meeting he told me you had all safely fled from the little shed on the high road for 'Kelmscott house'!! Lord my dear Janey, what a magnificent title to the house at t'other end of the river. I must take care when I do come to dinner, not to go off to Paddington to the other of that name. . . . Perhaps I may hire a boat one of these moonlight nights at Temple Stairs: and row up to you and sound you a pretty tune off my bassoon—you'll know it's me by the sublimity of the air.

In his desire this year for a thorough reorganisation Morris decided to move his works. When driving with Crom from Broadway he saw old mills at Blockley in the Cotswolds; he liked the place (where notices of the last reduction of wages made before the late eighteenth-century closure were still on the walls) and thought of reviving its traditions. But the area was twenty-five miles from Kelmscott (by pony and trap) and a hundred from London. Wardle insisted on premises near London.[8] So far Morris knew nothing about socialism in any precise sense. 'I was blankly ignorant of economics,' he recalled in 1894. 'I had never so much as opened Adam Smith, or heard of Ricardo, or of Karl Marx.' Oddly, the man who came to his aid at this moment was John Stuart Mill, who published in the *Fortnightly* in February and April 1879 articles entitled *Chapters on Socialism*. In 1894 Morris remembered these articles as attacking socialism in its Fourierist guise, though putting the arguments, 'as far as they go, clearly and honestly, and the result, so far as I was concerned, was to convince me that Socialism was a necessary change'. In fact Mill made no attack, but merely set out the doctrines and asked if they were applicable. He dealt with Owen, Louis Blanc, and Fourier (using passages collected by Considérant). In his *Principles of Political Economy* he also left the issue open; and at some time Morris seems to have read this book. Why Mill had such an effect on him at this moment however was because of the experiences in the EQA and the acquaintance with men of the LRL.

He was still strenuous company at the Sunday breakfasts with the BJs and Ned was fully behind him in his public activities. With the loom installed in his bedroom he was often up at first light to work on it. The first tapestry, the *Cabbage and Vine*, was begun on 10 May; and he kept a diary of his work on it. He completed it by 17 September, sometimes working at it nine or ten hours a day, and missing only two days apart from three intervals when he was out of London. The coach-house and stables adjoining the house were turned into a weaving-room, and carpet looms were built there, later producing the Hammersmith carpets and rugs. In the spring at Kelmscott he wrote, 'Somehow I feel as if there must soon be an end for me of playing at living in the country: a town-bird I am, a master-artisan, if I may claim that latter dignity.' At the same time he was active in the SPAB, keeping his eyes open for cases of outstanding restoration. On 28 June he made his second report, speaking of 'art, the constant companion and expression of the life and aspirations of the world'. His hopes had now grown and he stated his faith that 'we may have an architectural style, the growth of its own times, but connected with all history'. There are here the seeds of the position he was to set out more fully in *Gothic Architecture*, 1889.[9]

Janey was sitting to Rossetti, but with many gaps. He began developing the studies he had made in 1870 for the *Lady at the Window* (also *of Pity*): the lady who found Dante weeping for his lost Beatrice and inspired in him a counterpart of his passion. 'Perchance Love himself set her in my path, so that my life might find peace.' Later in the year he remarked, 'I had written it down a poor thing, but I won't because of the sitter, to whom I owe the best of my art such as it is.' On 14 April he wrote to Janey, 'Long absence & many disappointments have inured me to missing the sight of you, and today at least it was best I should miss it, as the weather is not fit for your being out at any distance.' On 23 May: 'My dearest Janey Really you ought not to be paying my debts—no one can afford that luxury to a friend nowadays. I must see about a settlement.' She had written: 'I am grieved indeed to hear of your bad nights—mine are improving.' She had got used to the river-steamers. In February she had welcomed the return of spring, 'or more correctly the disappearance of the horrible darkness of winter. I can breathe without gasping and you can paint without bad language.' Still, 'my dear old pussy, Jack, succumbed to the cold a few days ago. We buried him in the garden.' Then she says she had begun to chirp too soon about the weather, 'but you know what a babyishly hopeful creature I always am'. Rossetti sent her medicines and prescriptions. 'You don't tell me whether you tried the bottle I sent. I suppose you sniffed and scorned it' (17 June). In July he writes miserably. She was clearly doing very little sitting for him. 'As to sitting again I should be too happy to feel myself of use to any human being, but it is scarcely likely that my back will improve with age. I will not despair yet and you may be quite sure if at all possible I shall let you know.'

In August she went to Naworth in Cumberland to stay with the Howards. She wrote to Rossetti that Kelmscott was out of the question as she felt too ill to cope with an extra house and entertain people. She feared the doctor would send her abroad for the winter. Whenever she sat up, she was subject to fainting fits. (Her invalid condition was shared by many other Victorian ladies, but that indeed stresses the extreme inner division and fear of life which was crushing her. She still had thirty-five years ahead of her.) She consulted Rossetti about her health. What did he think of the 'sea-weed baths at Ramsgate for people of a delicate constitution. One is made in a kind of pie with the sea-weed.' Or perhaps she should go to Italy. 'Could any of that money be got at for the purpose, supposing I could not raise any?'

Morris went with Webb to Salisbury and the old scenes of his college days, such as Oare Hill, 'a place', he told Georgie, 'I remember coming on as a boy with wonder and pleasure'. They got into trouble in the floods on their way back to Kelmscott. Ellis joined him there. 'So I suppose Top is bugging and blaspheming in a boat with him, while he indulges in sonorous British guffaws,' Rossetti wrote to Janey. In early September Morris went up to Naworth, warning Jenny to expect him 'grimy & with a few buttons' off his clothes. Something must have gone wrong, for on the 15th he wrote from Hammersmith to May that he had been 'sorry to miss Mother, but cool reflection of course assured me that there was no chance of doing more than catching my train: apropos of that please remind Mother to tip William (I think) he of the red-head, as I saw nothing of any body at the castle, but one kitchen maid: Such attraction had fat pigs for all the world except Jenny & me.' He had gone off to do business 'in the heavy woollen country' and now gave May instructions to avoid at all costs Willesden Station, where there were few men and those who are there refuse to answer questions. 'The first time I went there I got into the wrong train: the second time I was so exacerbated by the coolness of the officials, that I had to offer to fight the only one I could find; fortunately for me he refused battle.'[10]

However when the girls joined Morris at Kelmscott, Janey went off to visit Crom and his sister. Later she wrote to Rossetti:

I cannot weigh the exact meaning of every word before writing, nor can any human being foresee what construction you will put on the most ordinary phrasing. Surely you know as everyone else does what a violent influenza cold does for one's appearance. You have sometimes refused to be seen under such circumstances and you must pardon a woman if she has the same dislike of being seen with a red nose and the rest.

We see what Webb meant when he rallied her about her claws. She now felt that she could stand up against Rossetti when necessary. (On 8 February 1880 Webb wrote to her: 'Long may you have both teeth & claws (I don't mean that you should show them to me of inordinate length) if only to frighten your foes and protect your friends.')

Morris was feeling rather lost after the excitements of the last year. In October the wrote to Georgie that 'as to poetry, I don't know and I don't know. The verse would come easy enough if I had only a subject which would fill my heart and mind.' His mind was on the social struggle. 'I have seen a many wonders, and have a good memory for them; and in spite of all my grumblings have a hope that civilized people will grow weary of their worst follies and try to live a less muddled and unreasonable life; not of course that we shall see much of that change in the remnant that is left of our days.' Though he was only forty-five he was troubled with fears of age and death. Later he wrote:

I am sitting now, 10 p.m., in the tapestry room, the moon rising red through the east-wind haze, and a cow lowing over the fields. I have been feeling chastened by many thoughts, and the beauty and the quietness of the surroundings, which latter, as I hinted, I am, as it were, beginning to take leave of. That leave-taking will, I must confess, though you may think it fantastic, seem a long step towards saying good-night to the world.

This farewell mood, in which he feels that he no longer has the right to Kelmscott, had been growing on him since 1872, when a deep sense of standing apart and yet feeling the rich and secret movements of the world all round had invaded his consciousness. The withdrawal had as its obverse side an ever-stronger need to enter the full struggle of the world and find his place in it; which involved finding there his comrades and his enemies with a new fullness. The farewell mood deepened his need to achieve union with the earth he loved, not in any simple intuitive way, but by vindicating the earth, by playing his part in a struggle to free it from the polluting, desecrating, and destructive forces that had become dominant. Thus the struggle for peace, for the preservation of ancient buildings, and for a world in which art played its free and rightful part, were all aspects of a single impulse which was now converging on socialism.

This year in the autumn he was drawn closer to the working class by becoming treasurer of the National Liberal League, which had emerged from the EQA period, mainly made up of representatives of the London radical workers. Broadhurst and Howell seem to have meant it to draw together the radical clubs, the trade unions, and some members of the middle class for certain short-term specific democratic reforms. At meetings of the league he first learned to make extempore speeches, which he found difficult. 'When he spoke off-hand,' said a colleague, 'he had a knack at times of hammering away at his point until he had said exactly what he wanted to say in exactly the words he wished to use, rocking to and from the while from one foot to the other.' He was also doing much SPAB speaking against the proposed rebuilding of the west front of St Mark's, Venice. At a meeting in the Sheldonian Theatre, Oxford, he was supported by BJ, who made his one and only public speech. The memorial he drafted was signed by both Disraeli and Gladstone, and he was irritated that he had to deliver it in person to the Italian Ambassador instead of merely posting it to the Italian Minister of Works, 'as to an ordinary mortal'. What really worried him in the whole thing, he told Georgie in November, 'has been all the ridiculous rigmarole and social hypocrisy one has to wade through'. This year he was also one of the scholars who met regularly at the Philological Society.

In November he was busy over the choice of carpets for the Armoury and Tapestry Rooms at St James's, but the funds of the Office of Works did not run to hand-made fabrics. Much thought also was being given to the decoration of the Howard's house at Palace Green, built by Webb. The dining-room was to have panels painted by BJ with the theme of Cupid and Psyche. The work took a long time and two years later the dining-room was not completed. The painter Henry Holiday, returning from the Christmas dance at the Grange, wrote: 'Danced with Mrs Morris . . . and with her daughter May.' At the same time Janey was writing to Rossetti of May that she was 'very tall and excessively delicate: I think she will not drag through a long life. So much the better for her.' (She lived in fact nearly fifty more years.) Rossetti sent Janey the sonnet *Pleasure and Memory* (later *Ardour and Memory*) about the lingering flush on the rose-tree when the roses are gone, when 'flown all joys'.[11]

New Year's Day, 1880, came with a sense of frustration and confusion. He had encountered the idea of socialism, but in an idealistic Fourierist form, and he did not see yet how to link the idea with any consistent struggle, any clear system of theory and practice. 'I am in rather a discouraged mood,' he wrote (no doubt to Georgie), 'and the whole thing seems almost too tangled to see through and too heavy to move. Happily though, I am not bound either to see through it or move it but a very little way: meantime I do know what I love and what I hate, and believe that neither the love nor the hatred are matters of accident or whim.' He felt still that he stood alone, despite his discovery of working-class allies. Tough though he was in certain respects, he was also very sensitive. 'I have had a life of insults and sucking of my brains,' he once said. But his spirits now could not remain depressed. A few months later he was remarking, 'It is a real joy to find the game afoot; that the thing is stirring in other people's minds besides mine, the poetic upholsterer, as Sir Ed. Beckett calls me, meaning (strange to say) an insult by that harmless statement of fact.' He was hurt all the same by the commercial overtones of the term 'upholsterer'. That was why Rossetti, with his acute sense of malice, described him in the Dramatis Personae of *The Death of Topsy* as 'an upholsterer & author of the Earthly Paradise'. A manuscript dated 30 January gives his meditations on the theme of war, 'Our Country, Right or Wrong', and was probably read to some radical group soon afterwards. He states that 'ignorant and unhappy people are dangerous people', and he gives a rather vague account of the socialist future. 'I think of a country where every man has work enough to do, and no one has too much. . . .' In another address of this year (date unclear) he returns to the death of art in a world ruled by money. 'Intellectual riches bred of intellectual poverty and slavery produce scorn, cynicism and despair.' He looks back to the Roman world and contrasts it with that of the barbarians.

Those *barbarians* whom Tacitus looked upon as chiefly of use for destroying each other, so that the civilised world might live on untroubled, it was they who had the fate decreed them of catching up the torch of progress from the dying hands of Rome, it was through them that art and hope lived again, and through them that the very memory of Rome was kept alive: it is with no great feeling of despondency that we read of the latter days of that ancient civilisation, wearing and terrible as the time was to the people of those days; the story can scarcely impress us with its due dramatic significance, since we, wise after the event, see behind all the ruin, the image of the vigorous life of the barbarians, which was once more to lead the world onwards—and whither?

Having felt in every fibre of his being that bourgeois society was hopelessly corrupted by the cash-nexus, the division and fragmentation of labour, he wanted to see it destroyed. But how? Would it generate forces of renewal deep in its own womb, or would it have to be struck down by some new form of barbarism? This problem was to haunt him for some time. Linked with it was his conviction that production for production's sake was an evil linked in every respect with the social system he detested, and that a truly civilised world would consist of people seeing how little they needed, not how much. He could not help looking back to societies of scarcity such as that of Iceland. If the great change could not strike at our world root and branch:

I would we had all together been shepherds or whatnot among the hills and valleys; men with little knowledge, but desiring much; rough men if you please but not brutal; with some sort of art among them, genuine at least and spontaneous; men who could be moved by poetry and story; working hard yet not without leisure; getting drunk sometimes, quarrelling sometimes, even to dry blows; nay if the times were heroic enough sometimes with point and edge: neither malicious nor over soft-hearted; well-pleased to live and ready to die—in short, men, free and equal.

No it cannot: it has long passed over, and civilisation goes forward, swiftly, if unsteadily: and for us, we are here chained to London life by desires, by duties, by necessity: well, if London is no very good place for the pleasures of repose, it is not so ill for the joy of strife.[12]

On 19 February he gave an address, *Labour and Pleasure versus Labour and Sorrow* (later called *The Beauty of Life*), at the prize-giving of the Birmingham Society of Arts at the Town Hall. Here once again he set out his case against his world for its destruction of art and thus of men themselves. 'Have nothing in your houses that you do not know to be useful, or believe to be beautiful.' Architecture, if truly developed, would lead men to all the arts, as it did with earlier men; but it was despised and people were made to live in 'a perfectly shameful way'. The struggle was to find the path leading to 'an Art made by the people and for the people as a joy to the maker and the user'.

Janey and Rossetti were continuing their sad and sick intercourse, out of which they gained much satisfaction. The sonnet that he had sent her at Christmas she ignored till he wrote on 30 January, asking if it was 'conceivable that you put some inconceivable construction upon it?' She replied, 'The truth is I was ill when I received it and would not trust myself to make any remarks on what struck me at first, its extremely woeful character.' (We saw that she was dancing at Christmas but no doubt she collapsed after it.) A little later she remarked of some of his poems: 'You must feel sure how welcome your work always is to me and there is little pleasure left one in this world.' Rossetti, despite his need of her, thought she ought to get away again. 'Your handwriting looked so firm and hopeful when you were at Hastings.' She felt faint when she sat up, so he assured her that he could draw her hands while she lay down. But in April she caught flu and could not come to Cheyne Walk.

The elections early this year had led to a Liberal triumph under Gladstone, whom Morris still respected. The NLL played an important part in rallying the London workers behind Gladstone's slogans of Peace, Retrenchment, Reform; and Morris worked as an electioneer in the campaign for Sir Charles Dilke, aided by BJ and De Morgan. Broadhurst was elected and found himself unable to resist the effects of the flattery he received: he was even in 1884 invited to have a beer with the Prince of Wales at Sandringham in the village pub. Morris wrote to him this year on 4 April, asking 'how to broaden and deepen the stream of radical principle, keeping meanwhile the government both alive and steady, without harassing or frightening it'. But he soon found compromises were liable to erode principle, and later in the year he wrote of the lack of real working-class leaders to make conscious and give leadership to the 'vague discontent and spirit of revenge' of the workers. 'When a man has gifts for that kind of thing he finds himself tending to rise out of his class before he has begun to think of class politics as a matter of principle, and too often he is just simply "got at" by the governing classes, not formally but by circumstances.' Meanwhile the NLL was drawing up a programme of reforms.

In May, Morris held a show of carpets and issued a circular, stating his aim 'to make England independent of the East for carpets which may claim to be considered as works of art'. He also produced twenty-four designs for machine production. In May also he spoke at a SPAB meeting about St Mark's; and in June spoke on behalf of Women's Rights as well as making the annual SPAB report. In the summer BJ records Morris coming on Georgie's birthday:

You would have found him just as if no time had gone by, only the best talk with him is while he is hungry, for meat makes him sad. So it is wise to delay dinner, and get out of him all you can in walks round the garden. He is unchanged—little grey tips to his curly wig—no more; not quite so stout; not one hair less on his head, buttons more off than formerly, never any necktie—more eager if anything than ever, but about just the same things; a rock of defence to us all, and a castle on top of it, and a banner on top of that—before meat—but the banner lowered after that.

He contrasts him with Rossetti, who 'has given it all up, and will try no more, nor care much more how it all goes'. Four or five times a year BJ spent 'a ghostly evening with him, and returned always heavy-hearted'.

In August the Morrises, De Morgan, Crom, and Dick (the Hon. Richard Grosvenor), made a trip 130 miles up the river from Hammersmith to Kelmscott. Morris had hired a small houseboat, *The Ark*; and the party started off in that, with Biffin's men rowing, and Morris and Crom following in a skiff. Morris wrote a detailed account of the delights and misadventures of the journey to Georgie. He and Crom rowed to Kew, then both houseboat and skiff were towed to Twickenham; by ten-thirty they were at Sunbury. The next night was spent at Windsor, and in the morning Dick took them up to Eton. Morris cooked a small meal above Bray Lock, with wasps swarming about an osier-bed and spectators on the bank impeding the tow-rope; they then ran into a regatta at Maidenhead. Morris didn't think much of Cliefden Woods, but loved the view at Cookham Lock. They got through

Marlow Lock, in the dark, skirted a huge weir, and reached their lodgings: 'Crom and I in the Ark close to the roaring water, Dick and De M. in the inn (a noisy one) and the ladies up town, over the bridge.' They looked at Lady Place, Hurley, then went on, with Morris playing 'the cook again a little short of Henley', stuck in the mud at Wargrave, passed Siplake, and halted at Sonning in the sultry night. The goal next day was 'stuffy grubby little Wallingford'. They had all got used to *The Ark*, 'and there was Janey lying down and looking quite at home.' Next day, with Morris cooking another dinner just above Culham Lock, they reached Oxford, where they lodged at the King's Arms. Janey went on by train to Lechlade, while the others rowed up the river to New Bridge. Hay-making was going on, with the hay (mostly sedge) gathered on punts. Night fell and they hung a lantern at their boat's prow. 'Charles was waiting for us with a lantern at our bridge by the corner at 10 p.m., and presently the ancient house had me in its arms again: J. had lighted all up brilliantly.'

After various expeditions around Kelmscott, the party broke up and he returned to London, 'this beastly congregation of smoke-dried swindlers and their slaves (whom one hopes one day to make their rebels)', as he wrote to Georgie, adding: 'though I must admit to feeling this morning a touch of the "all by oneself" independence which you wot of as a thing I like'. In his lecture *Some Hints on House Decoration* (later called *Making the Best of It*), given in London and then in Birmingham, he carried on his message about art, the destructive effects of the cash-nexus, and the need for a different way of life. In December Janey wrote to Rossetti to say that she was thinking of going to Italy with the Howards. Morris had exploded and said that she must pay her own way as he 'can't be owing money to Earl-Kin'. She was going to leave the girls behind to look after him; and in January 1881 she went off as she had said.

In his broodings on the period of 'barbarism' that followed the Roman Empire, Morris was affected by his readings of historians like Stubbs, Freeman, Green, Thorold Rogers; and these readings went on for some time. In 1888 he remarked on the school of historical criticism of the age, which had revealed the egalitarian tendencies still strong in the medieval world, the survival of the customary heritage of the German tribes in feudal institutions. The conviction that in tribal days there had existed powerful elements of brotherhood and equality, despite trends to division and hierarchy, played an important part in stimulating his hope and his belief that such elements could be recaptured and revived on a new level.

Further, around this period, as a result of his deepening love for simple
modes of life which provided the essentials for the enjoyment of the earth
and discarded the accumulation of unnecessary objects and gadgets, he
himself felt an impulse to simplify his styles of design and his whole notion
of furniture and interior decoration. Like architecture, rooms should
express the sort of life we want to lead. All the objects there should give the
effect of being lived in, used, and of welcoming in the person who enters;
there should be in every house no 'signs of waste, pomp, or insolence, and
every man will have his share of the *best*'. (This last quotation comes near the
end of *The Lesser Arts* of 1877; he goes on to say that what he depicts is a
dream 'yet my hope is the greater that it one day will be'. Dreams have come
true and we now 'scarcely think of them more than of the daylight, though
once people had to live without them, without even the hope of them'. He
asks his listeners to help him 'in realising this dream, this *hope*'.) Once after
a lecture one of the audience asked for advice in decorating a kitchen;
Morris said that as a start a flitch of bacon hanging from the ceiling would
do very well.[13]

Again at the New Year, in 1881, Morris felt melancholy; and when one is
just so much subdued, he wrote (probably to Georgie), 'one is apt to turn
more specially from thinking of one's own affairs to more worthy matters;
and my mind is full of the great change which I hope is slowly coming over
the world, and of which surely this new year will be one of the landmarks'.
He hoped that the year would 'do a good turn of work toward the abasement
of the rich and the raising up of the poor, which is all things most to be
longed for, till people can at last rub out from their dictionaries altogether
these dreadful words rich and poor.' In the diary he began this year he
however merely wrote under 1 January, Saturday: 'At home: did a little
pointing at Bells work and coloured that tapestry design. Wind sw, bright
in morning getting dull & wind shifting to se in evening.' (He was an
assiduous observer of the wind and daily set down its direction or changes.)
Typical entries followed:

2nd Sunday. To Grange to breakfast. Ned & Crom to dinner: Allinghams to
supper. Wind se thick & dark: getting thicker towards evening.
3rd Monday. to Richards: talk with Holland about big loom: ordered him to put
on new gear. to Queen Sq: to St. J. to Faulkners. Crom & Richmond here to
dinner. Wind e dullish morning bright in evening.

4th Tuesday. At home: to Grange: then pointing Bells carpet: in afternoon Holland's man for putting new gear to big loom. Edgar takes stock of wools: 1100 & more. Wind NE not cold: dullish.
5 Wednesday. to Brighton & Rottingdean with Ned & back. Wind NE plenty of it: bright sunny day.
6 Thursday. to St. J. to Ellis: to Grosvenor Gallery: to Queen Sq: seeing to dyeing dull red for peacock: to SPAB meeting. Parliament met: Queen's speech very shortly. Wind NE blowing hard: very bright day, frost at night.

On 15 January he spoke at a meeting called to establish the Radical Union; and on the 27th he took part in the first public meeting of the Kyrle Society, with Prince Leopold as chairman. In his speech he said that the society had been founded to fight against carelessness, ugliness, and squalor. We again see how blank he was about the methods for bringing about the kind of society he wanted. Referring to the gulf between the present and the strange future, he said, 'We do not know how to set to work to bridge that gulf full of possible violences and revolutions, and of certain disappointments.' We, with all our longing, 'do not know, outside the ordinary daily duties of our lives, whitherward to turn our hands that we may help that coming day one step forward'. But, 'unless we are to live and die in our discontent there is nothing for it, but to do something, the first things that comes to hand, *to the utmost of our power*'.

The political situation was confused and disturbing. Gladstone was in power, but there was war with the Boers and fighting was going on in Afghanistan, intended to give Russia a setback. Also there was the Irish Coercion Bill, though a Land Act was promising more security to Irish tenants. On 23 February Morris wrote to Janey: 'I can't say I feel any confidence in the Government & only half-confidence in the Liberal Associations: what a pity it is that there is not a proper radical club properly organised for political purposes, who could act speedily at such junctures.' His confidence in the Liberals steadily lessened. Probably through him the NLL added to its demands the insistence that the 'same moral relations' be applied to foreign policy as in private relations. The league also laid stress on the need for reform in the laws on Land Tenure, to prevent land in England or Scotland falling waste through antiquated feudal controls or the depopulation of areas to form deer forests. In the firm Morris was discontented with Wardle: 'Nothing will he do right, & he does write the longest winded letters containing lies of various kinds: we shall have to take to

chintzes ourselves before long and are now daily looking about for premises.'
Edgar, his brother, now working for him, had gone to look at print works at
Crayford, and Morris went himself with De Morgan. He was here in the
region of Red House. The countryside was much spoiled, but 'I saw Hall
Place once more and it made the stomach in me turn round with desire of
an old house'. In March he and De Morgan went to look at print works at
Merton Abbey, some seven miles from Charing Cross: a number of old
weatherboard sheds with red tiles among willows and poplars by a river.[14]

On 3 March he wrote to Janey. De Morgan was about to set up a pottery
works for making lustred tiles and majolica, and was looking at premises at
Hemel Hempstead. He himself was pleased at the Boer victories and was
going next day to Hadham to see various members of the family; he had been
playing at dummy with the girls. His diary shows him calling on Kate
Faulkner. It also brings out how long he worked at each lecture; he took, it
seems, the whole month of February, including eight whole days, for one;
and of another he wrote: ' 'tis to be a short one, but will give me a fortnight's
work, I know.' Janey was suffering from fever, we learn from letters that
Webb wrote to her. On 10 March Morris delivered *The Prospects of
Architecture in Civilisation.* 'Wrote to Janey. to KF & 26 QS, in afternoon.'
He had done three and a half hours' tapestry in the morning. On 16 March
he was at Nottingham, speaking to the Kyrle Society there. 'Entertained at
the house of some good people, whereof the youngers were Ruskinites, &
the elders stiffish religionists: my audience at the castle was polite & attentive; but I fear they were sorely puzzled at what I said.' The town flourished
on 'a perfectly useless luxury: machine lace'. He was enthusiastic about
Merton, where, though the suburb was woeful beyond conception, the
water was abundant and good. In the diary for 26 March he noted that the
political situation was 'unsatisfactory'.

On 8 April Morris had 'pretty much come to the conclusion' with the
owners of Merton Abbey; but he wanted to build kilns for tiles and glass,
so that covenants with regards to chimneys had to be drawn up. On the
19th Webb tells us: 'Morris was in here at lunch-time to-day with a sharp
cold upon him, and he told me that the girls were in a like state.' On
Thursday they had all had a pleasant evening at the Faulkners. We may
compare Morris's diary for the 19th: 'Called Wardle about Merton Abbey &
scare about Webb's demands (he asks £900 & the blocks. We are to offer
£800 & the blocks). did daybook one week. Called Faulk.' Janey returned
home in May. Henry James, who had seen her in Italy, describes her at the

time: 'I didn't fall in love with the strange, pale, livid, gaunt, silent and yet in a manner graceful and picturesque wife of the poet and paper-maker.' She now called again on Rossetti and her letters were business-like, with no opening or end: 'Wednesday, I will come about 12 o'clock then, but I can't, won't wait beyond 1 for my dinner. I can eat anything at that hour, no dainties mind. I can stay all the evening till 9 about. I shall have to call at Ned's on my way back to take up Jenny where she will spend the day.' Rossetti wrote on 15 July, unable to resist belittling Morris: 'I had fancied you might be quite prostrate when I did not hear from you. Watts was enraptured with the enormous democratic obesity of Top. O for that final Cabinet Ministry which is to succeed the *Cabinet d'aisance* of his early years!'

On 7 June the Merton lease was finally signed. Next day Morris went down with Webb, Wardle, and De Morgan to arrange for the alterations. Roofs were raised and foundations trenched and puddled to keep out damp; carpet-looms were built in, vats dug and lined. Poplars were planted round the meadow used for laying out calico prints. He himself set about designing chintzes. On 24 June he made the report at the annual SPAB meeting. In the summer occurred an incident that much affected him. Johann Most, a German exile, had been editing *Freiheit*, which circulated illegally in Germany; he was vain, effervescent, and ultra-left in his propaganda; and when news came of the assassination of Tsar Alexander II, he published an article which Morris described as a 'song of triumph'. He was arrested, probably at the instigation of Bismarck, and sentenced to sixteen months' hard labour. Morris was upset, not because he sympathised with the sentiments of the article, but because for the first time he had come right up against class-justice. He wrote to Georgie:

Just think of the mixture of tyranny and hypocrisy with which the world is governed! These are the sort of things that make thinking people so sick at heart that they are driven from all interest in politics save revolutionary politics: which I must say seems like to be my case. Indeed I have long known, or felt, say, that society in spite of its modern smoothness was founded on injustice and kept together by cowardice and tyranny; but the hope in me has been that matters would mend gradually, till the last struggle, which must needs be mingled with violence and madness, would be so short as scarcely to count.

Jack Williams, later a leader of the SDF, stood outside the Old Bailey while the trial was on, selling an English edition of *Freiheit* with the offending article translated; but he was ignored. A Defence Committee was set up; and by the end of the year there was formed the Labour Emancipation League, the first socialist organisation in London with any effective influence. Morris in the letter cited above went on to say that he found little comfort in SPAB; they had been too late and had too many foes. To be moved to action:

it is needful that a man should be touched with a real love of the earth, a worship of it, no less; and I think that as things go, that is seldom felt except by very simple people, and by them, as would be likely, dimly enough. You know the most refined and cultured people, both those of the old religions and these of the vague new ones, have a sort of Manichean hatred of the world (I use the word in its proper sense, the home of man). Such people must be both the enemies of beauty and the slaves of necessity, and true it is that they lead the world at present, and I believe will do till all that is old is gone, and history has become a book from which the pictures have been torn. Now if you ask me why I kick against the pricks in this matter, all I can say is, first because I cannot help it, and secondly because I am encouraged by a sort of faith that something will come of it, some kind of culture of which we know nothing at present.

So far he is sustained only by 'a sort of faith'. Though he has been much affected by his working-class contacts, he still tends to a middle-class paternalist outlook, as he shows in *The Prospects of Architecture* of this year. He appeals to his class to treat the workers equitably, even if this act of justice will mean loss to them. He still has the position stated in *The Art of the People* (1879): if only the rich would take on a simplicity of life, 'smoothing over the dreadful contrast between waste and want', and thus given 'an example and standard of dignified life to those classes which you desire to raise', then things would move in the right direction, socially and artistically. But slowly this position is being broken down by his growing anger at social and economic injustice, and by his increasing contacts with working-class politics —also by the fact that the first stages of a socialist outlook are emerging among the advanced working-class fighters.[15]

In July Hall Caine became Rossetti's secretary-factotum. He tells us of Janey that she was the only intimate friend of Rossetti whom he did not meet. Whenever she came, Rossetti would write a little note and send it out to him: 'The lady I spoke about has arrived and will stay with me to dinner. In these circumstances I will ask you to be good enough to dine in your own rooms to-night.' Rossetti was preparing his *Ballads and Poems* for publication, and he gave Janey the sonnets to read, vet, and censor if she wished.

He told Watts-Dunton that he hoped 'there may be no adverse view taken. But whatever it is, I must act on it.' Helped by William Michael, he tried to put readers off the scent by mystifications in the dating and by the change of certain words. Dark hair was changed to golden, and *The Love-lamp* became *The Lamp-shrine*. Still Janey was afraid of being recognised. Rossetti re-assured her, 'Every new piece that is not quite colourless will be withdrawn and the book postponed.' She had objected to several of the new sonnets as compromising.

In August again there was an expedition up the river, with Faulkner, De Morgan, and two girls, Lisa Stillman and Bessie Macleod. Morris was somewhat scared of the trip, and he told Georgie that a kind of terror always fell on him when he neared Oxford. 'Indignation at wanton or rash changes mingles curiously in me with all that I remember I have lost since I was a lad and dwelling there.' Violet Hunt, then sixteen, watched the party pass under Sonning Bridge early one morning, Morris 'shouting indecorously worded advice to the other boat', and behind him 'sitting up very stiffly', Janey of the Rossetti paintings, 'ashen-coloured, hair and all, in the sunlight, yet perfectly beautiful' and looking most of all 'like the forlorn lady undone by the miasma of the marshes'. (When Violet, a schoolmate of Jenny, went to tea at Kelmscott House, Janey sat silent and withdrawn on the settle, and all that Violet recalled her saying was, 'There's your milk, Jenny.' She felt that 'she was diffident . . . proudly conscious of a want of mere book-learning' —though we know from the Rossetti letters that she read poetry and made intelligent comments.)

Morris stayed on at Kelmscott, watching the harvest work and the birds, making trips to Lechlade and Cirencester, and keenly fishing. But his mind was on the problem of deep social change. He wrote to Georgie:

How people talk as if there were no wrongs of society against all the poor devils it has driven demented in one way or another! Yet I don't wonder at rich men trembling either: for it does seem as though a rising impatience against the injustice of society was in the air; and no wonder that the craziest heads, that feel this injustice most, breed schemes for setting all to right with a stroke of justice.

He is thinking of hotheads like Most, and cannot yet see a way that is neither theirs nor that of a compromiser like Broadhurst. He goes on: 'All political change seems to me useful now as making it possible to get the social one: I don't mean to say that I myself make any wide distinction between political and social; I am only using the words in the common way.' Georgie wrote to him something about the futility of mere grumbling, especially among friends. He demurred:

It is good to feel the air laden with the coming storm even as we go about our daily work or while away time in light matters. To do nothing but grumble and not to act—that is throwing away one's life: but I don't think that words on our cause that we have at heart do nothing but wound the air, even when spoken among friends: 'tis at worst like the music to which men go to battle. Of course if the thing is done egotistically 'tis bad so far; but that again, how to do it well or ill, is a matter of art like other things.

This last remark of Morris's has been misunderstood. For him art was both a dream and the awakening from dream; it was that which guided and formed men as well as something that they formed; it was something that linked them in all that was deepest in their humanity. So the question of political change was also a matter of art, as distinct from the manipulations, falsifications, and compromises that made up what was considered to be political method.

Rossetti had grown much worse in health and Hall Caine took him in September to Keswick. On the journey back he told Hall Caine about Lizzie and her last note: 'a message that left such a scar on his heart as would never be healed.' He also talked of Janey as his one great love; Caine says that if he were to reconstruct Rossetti's figure out of the impressions of that night, it would be one of 'a man who, after engaging himself to one woman in all honour and good faith, had fallen in love with another, and then gone on to marry the first out of a mistaken sense of loyalty and a fear of giving pain, instead of stopping, as he must have done, if his will had been stronger and his heart sterner, at the door of the church itself'. We can understand how the past had now taken on that pattern in Rossetti's mind, but we may doubt if the matter has been even remotely so clear-cut in 1857–9.

On 13 October Morris spoke on 'Art and the Beauty of the Earth' at Burslem. He set out once more his view of the desecrated and polluted earth, forcibly but as tactfully as he could in the smoky world of the Potteries. He still cannot get rid of the feeling of himself as a middle-class citizen somehow cut off from the common folk however much he feels their lot.

Look you, as I sit at work at home, which is at Hammersmith, close to the river, I often hear go past the window some of that ruffianism of which a good deal has been said in the papers of late. . . . As I hear the yells and shrieks and all the degradation cast on the glorious tongue of Shakespeare and Milton, as I see the brutal reckless faces and figures go past me, it rouses recklessness and brutality in me also, and fierce wrath takes possession of me, till I remember, as I hope I mostly do, that it was my good luck only of being born respectable and rich that has put me on this side of the window among delightful books and lovely works of art, and not on the other side, in the empty street, the drink-steeped liquor-shops, the foul and degraded lodgings. What words can say what all that means?

Only art, he says, can save the people, giving them 'reasonable labour, reasonable rest'. That is art in the Ruskinian sense which he has been developing in more comprehensive ways.

At the start of winter the move into Merton had begun. 'I am in an agony of muddle,' he lamented early in November. 'I now blame myself severely for not having my way and settling at Blockley.' But Wardle told Mackail that Morris could never imagine difficulties till they were on top of him, and had no idea what Blockley would have been like. By Christmas things were going smoothly; and a circular was issued from Oxford Street as soon as the workshops were fully functioning, with a list of the wares to be designed and executed there: painted glass windows, arras tapestry, carpets, embroidery, tiles, furniture, general house decorations, printed cotton goods, paper hangings, figured woven stuffs, furniture velvets and cloths, upholstery.

Morris was now at a crucial point. He had driven the Ruskinian concept of art and work as far as it could go within its own premises. He had insisted in lectures like that at Kyrle Society this year and that at Burslem that only art could save the masses. Yet even in 1877 he had also insisted that the future triumph and liberation of art was involved with political and social changes which under one form or another they all desired. In 1880 he had declared that some day men would come to realise the truth of things 'and cry out to be made men again, and art only can do it, and redeem them from this slavery; and I say once more that this is her highest and most glorious end and aim'. But he kept on attempting to visualise the necessary changes in a Liberal perspective. At the same time, ever since his address to the working class on the 'Unjust War', he had come to feel and understand ever more strongly and clearly the resistances to all real change inextricably lodged in the middle classes, in everyone who accepted the capitalist way of life, however much they might like to see one abused or another curbed. The tension inside his thought and feeling between his Liberal illusions and his realistic sense of the social scene had now reached breaking-point. Last year, in *The Beauty of Life*, he had repeated that if civilisation could not give a share in the happiness and dignity of life to *all* the people, then 'it is simply an organised injustice, a mere instrument for oppression, so much the worse than that which has gone before it, as its pretensions are higher, its slavery subtler, its mastery harder to overthrow, because supported by such a dense mass of commonplace well-being and comfort'. And in *The Prospects of Architecture*, this year, he declared:

It is strange indeed, it is woeful, it is scarcely comprehensible, if we come to think of it as men, and not as machines, that, after all the progress of civilisation, it should be so easy for a little official talk, a few lines on a sheet of paper, to set a terrible engine to work, which without any trouble on our part will slay us ten thousand men . . . and it lies light enough on the conscience of *all* of us; while, if it is a question of striking a blow at grievous and crushing evils which lie at our own doors . . . not only is there no national machinery for dealing with them . . . but any hint that such a thing is possible is received with laughter or with terror, or with severe and heavy blame. The rights of property, the necessities of morality, the interests of religion—these are the sacramental words of cowardice that silences us all!

After such realisations he had either to give up the ghost or take the step into a complete acceptance of socialism.

Incidentally we may note that at a talk, *Some Hints on Pattern Designing*, which he gave to the Working Men's College on 10 December, he brought out that he was not in any way hostile to machines; he was hostile only to the way in which they were employed in an alienated world to dominate men, to divide and fragment them. He recommended machines when the nature of the product made them necessary or when the article could otherwise be made only at the cost of human suffering. In the next chapter we shall find further remarks of his elaborating this position. Here we may merely add that he wanted to use automation in place of unpleasant or repetitive work. 'In cases where art could not be an integral part of the work if it turned out to be necessary work, it would have to be done by machines as nearly automatic as possible.'[16]

12

Into Full Social Action

Early in 1882 he went down with Jenny to BJ's house at Rottingdean. He wrote to Georgie, 'I think I saw more ugly people in Brighton in the course of an hour than I have seen otherwise for the last twenty years: as you justly remark, serves me right for going into Brighton.' They drove to Lewes and he worked at a lecture. Prose kept on causing him much trouble. 'I know what I want to say, but the cursed words go to water between my fingers.' He was very depressed, 'dwelling somewhat low down in the valley of humiliation'.

It sometimes seems to me as if my lot were a strange one; you see, I work pretty hard, and on the whole very cheerfully, not altogether I hope for mere pudding, still less for praise; and while I work I have the cause always in mind, and yet I know that the cause for which I specially work is doomed to fail, at least in seeming; I mean that art must go under, where or how ever it may come up again.

He asked himself: 'Am I doing nothing but make-believe then, something like Louis XVI's lock-making?' About the same time he wrote to George Howard, 'I suppose your election is the North Riding: I haven't seen a paper for four days.' He hoped that he had a good opponent. 'Better to be beaten with a good one than be successful with a bad one. I guess there will be a fine procession of rats before this parliament is over: that will teach us, I hope, not to run the worst man possible on all occasions.'

On 23 January he gave his lecture, *Some of the Minor Arts of Life,* at Birmingham. A problem had come up at Merton, where the water company was threatening to tap the head-springs of the Wandle and thus reduce it to a mere ditch. Morris wrote to Howard for help; thirty-nine other mill-owners on the river joined the protest; and the plan was quashed. He also wrote for a platform ticket for a meeting at the Mansion House dealing with the persecution of Jews in Russia. A letter to Georgie, criticising Swinburne's work as 'founded on literature, not on nature', showed how far he had moved from the position of *The Earthly Paradise*. Swinburne for his part thought Morris had taken a wrong turning into 'all that dashed and blank Volsungery which will end by eating up the splendid genius it has already overgrown and incrusted with Iceland moss'. In March Morris made his testimony before the Royal Commission on Technical Education. He advocated that everyone should be taught to draw as well as to read and write; and he objected strongly at the works presented being judged on their finish. Finish for its own sake was a mere shop-counter look. He wanted artist or craftsman and designer to be the same person. 'Division of labour does a great deal to cheapen goods, but on the other hand I think it does a great deal to deteriorate them.'

Morris has been attacked as inconsistent in organising his own workshops so that there was in fact much division of labour. Apart from his own tapestry and a few trials in other techniques he did not execute his own pattern designs.

He did not even produce the majority of them under his own supervision. All his wall-papers and many of his carpets, silks and chintzes were made by other manufacturers. It is true that in many cases the method used was hand production rather than machinery, but this did not in any way resemble the free handwork of medieval craftsmen. In most of his manufactures Morris used a pre-Victorian process, but it was always organised in the workshop on a serial basis, with different craftsmen responsible for different parts of the sequence and none of them making an individual contribution to the design. The only important exception was in embroidery, although a very limited discretion was also allowed to the glass painters and tapestry weavers . . . Morris and Company was in fact an extreme example of the division of labour in glass work. To begin with, the firm never made its own glass. The white and coloured pot metal was chosen by Morris from Powell's stock. The only colour added by the firm was yellow stain . . . Figures and scenes were designed by most of the partners but the backgrounds in which they were set were designed by either Webb or Morris. (Paul Thompson)

But Morris never set out a principle of complete works executed by a single man. What he believed was that each man should have as all-round a grasp of his craft (and indeed of many crafts); he knew well that in any large-scale matter of production each man or group of men had to have allotted tasks. The art which he considered supreme was at all periods a product of many collaborators working in different fields. What he wanted above all was to break down the division of artist and technician. At Merton he had a number of boys working who were allowed the fullest initiative in carrying out the tapestries for which he set out the designs. He assumed that each one was capable of taking control of the craft. Wardle tells us that at Queen Square he taught William Dearle, 'then a boy willing to adapt himself to anything which gave him a chance of employment. Dearle got on so well that very soon we took on two other boys, Sleath & Knight, as his apprentices'. Then at Merton 'the boys who were still young lived in the house, he gave them board & lodging & a certain weekly stipend'. He did not select any particular boy for a job; he just took the one available, justifying his 'contention that the universal modern system, which he called that of "devil take the hindmost" is frightfully wasteful of human intelligence'. When later he set up a third loom, he took on the first lad he heard of, the nephew of the Merton housekeeper, who turned out an excellent tapestry-worker.

Morris himself had mastered any craft he set others to. He wanted to break down the division of mind and hand. In 1883 he remarked that he wanted division of labour to be reduced to reasonable limits; in 1888, considering the society of the future, he declared that art and literature (which included all forms of craft-activity) would be 'at once sensuous and human', and that 'division of labour would be habitually limited'. Neither in his lectures and essays, nor in *News from Nowhere*, did he attempt to define the precise limits of division which would be acceptable at any phase of a free society. What he insisted on was the problem would be seen in a quite new perspective: what men wanted to make out of their lives in a full and free enjoyment of the earth, and what objects, tools, and machinery they needed to achieve that fullness, in which the bourgeois ideal of endlessly extended production, endlessly heaped-up objects, would have lost all its glamour (based as it was ultimately in capitalism's need for an eternally expanded amount of capital). Though one aspect of his teaching helped the Arts and Crafts Movement into being, the teaching as a whole could not in any sense be reduced to the aims of that movement.[1]

On 9 April 1882 Rossetti died. Writing to Bell Scott, Morris said that his death:

makes a hole in the world, though I have seen so little of him lately, and might very likely never have seen him again: he was very kind to me when I was a youngster. He had some of the very greatest qualities of genius, most of them indeed; what a great man he would have been but for the arrogant misanthropy that marred his work, and killed him before his time: the grain of humility that makes a great man one of the people and no lord over them, he lacked, and with it lost the enjoyment of life which would have kept him alive, and sweetened all his work for him and us.

Later he told Mavor, 'Sometimes Rossetti was an angel, and sometimes he was a damned scoundrel.' We might add that the arrogant element prevented him from struggling to master the medium of paint, so that his work steadily weakened, ending in the gallery of forbidding females, with Janey as the archetypal figure, where the interest is almost wholly one of morbid psychology. His main interest in relation to Morris lies in the way in which, by drawing Morris decisively into the sphere of art, he started him off on the career of artist-craftsman—and in which he then provided the anti-world of Morris, the egoist reduction of what they had once held in common.

On 31 May the Democratic Federation, dominated by the ex-Tory Hyndman, passed a definitely socialist resolution, and the organisation began to look less like what Morris called it (in June this year): 'a sort of Tory drag to take the scent off the fox'. Hyndman, top-hatted and domineering, read *Capital* and became a devoted though highly dogmatic Marxist. By the end of 1882 the DF was considered socialist; during the winter it held conferences to discuss immediate demands that would serve as 'stepping-stones to socialism', and in 1883 it issued its first socialist pamphlet. Meanwhile Morris was questing round for the best group he could find, ready 'to join any body who distinctly called themselves socialists'. But he had to make the SPAB report, he was extremely busy at Merton, and then Jenny fell badly ill, with repeated attacks through the summer and autumn. A sense of gloom and doom weighed him down.

On 5 August he wrote to *The Times* about the Relief Fund for the Iceland Famine. On 23 August he told Georgie that he had been cheered by a visit to the De Morgans at Witley, with a drive among heather, oaks, and a few cornfields. He was somewhat afraid of the 'chance of failure (commercial I mean)' at Merton, and troubled by the evil year: 'the summerless season, and famine and war, and the folly of peoples come back again, as it were, and the more and more obvious death of art'. Also he had himself not been well. He wanted, he said, to go through life, 'not without pain indeed, but with simplicity and free from blinding entanglements'. On 31 August he wrote to May at Rottingdean, 'I had a queer day or two with the Faulkners in Wiltshire, pleasant enough on the whole: one really gets astonished at the vast stretches of downs.' He had been working at Merton, 'only I developed a budding gout in the afternoon'. He was busy on Icelandic relief, then upset to find how wretched was the lot of the Italian peasant. To Georgie he said that he felt ten years older than he did in June. He sold the larger part of his library to gain funds to be devoted to the socialist cause, and on 10 October he spoke on the 'Progress of Decorative Art in England', at Manchester.

He had published *Hopes and Fears for Art*, collecting five of his lectures. To a woman who wrote to him about it he replied:

... I do not like however to be praised at the expense of Ruskin, who you must remember is the first comer, the inventor; and I believe we all of us owe a hope that still clings to us, and a chance of expressing that hope, to his insight: of course to say that one does not always agree with him is to say that he and I are of mankind. As to the machines, the reasonable thing to say of them is that they are like fire, bad masters, good servants: and I fear that in Manchester and thereabouts they are heavy masters enough: I do believe that the day will come when people will be able to recognise this reasonable view of machinery.

Some letters to the family at Bournemouth show him giving advice to the South Kensington Museum on textiles; boxed up at Merton because 'the gout has made another grab at me'; meeting difficulties in printing. 'We are going to get our wheel set straight during the Christmas holidays, so as not to stop work.' But he managed to get to Leek to talk on *Art: A Serious Thing* for the prize-giving at the School of Art there. He is still far from a socialist exposition, but he does say that he trusts there are among the workers men who hope and strive, not to climb up out of their class, but to raise their whole class as a class. 'By such efforts is art more helped if we artists did but know it than by anything else that is done in our days.' He adds that he heartily sympathises with many strikes, 'but when the day comes that there is a serious strike of workmen against the poisoning of the air with smoke or the waters with filth, I shall think that art is getting on indeed'. He had in fact been attending the series of meetings organised by the DF on 'stepping-stones' in the winter 1882–3. The Austrian refugee Andreas Scheu, furniture designer, remembered his first attendance:

One evening the meeting had scarcely started when Robert Banner, the book-binder, who sat behind me, passed me a note. . . . 'The third man to your right is William Morris.' I had never seen Morris before, and looked at once in his direction. The fine, highly intelligent face of the man, his earnestness, the half-searching, half-dreamy look of his eyes, his plain unfashionable dress, made a deep sympathetic impression on me.

Morris had also been reading the books on the land-question by George and Wallace as well as re-reading More's *Utopia*; on 13 November he had written to Jenny that Wallace's *Land Nationalisation* was not such a good book as Henry George's *Progress and Poverty*, 'but there are some nice things to remember in it'. We saw how his emotional sense of something badly wrong with the world had taken a semi-mythic form in the Norse pattern of world-end and renewal; how he hovered between a hope of the fettered spirits of men breaking through into sanity and the resolution to love simply and happily on the earth, and a feeling that some new barbarism would smash an effete and corrupted civilisation, bringing the seeds of a slow regeneration. He was not consistent in his use of the term barbarous or barbarian, at times using it to express the callous and insensitive destructiveness of the bourgeois world, at times using it to express a disruptive force from below that would smash things but would also make renewal possible. How was one to meet such a situation? he had asked himself continually, especially since 1877. Only as he turned wholeheartedly to socialism was he able to answer this question.

On New Year's Day 1883 he was at Merton, with the wheel still not put together again. He was going to sleep there: 'because on Wednesday I have to go to an Icelandic meeting at 12 (noon)'. On 6 January the wheel was going. He wrote to May at Lyme Regis, hoping she'd like their lace. 'Because if only *patricians* may wear it we must give up our manufacturing of it, since there should be no patricians.' A new block had come in for printed dresses, 'and we can dye piece Cotton goods for such like things famously. So, give your orders Ladies, as even the humblest can indulge in these simple articles.' (In these comments we see his growing dissatisfaction with turning out wares only for the richer classes.) He would not come down, he said, till that day next week. We may assume then that he went briefly down to Dorset. On 13 January he joined the DF; his membership card was signed, 'William Morris, Designer'. The same week he was made an honorary fellow of Exeter College, Oxford.

In *The Lesser Arts* he had already expressed the overwhelming joy:

when at last, after many a struggle with incongruous hindrances, our own chosen work has lain before us disentangled from all encumbrances and unrealities, and we have felt that nothing could withhold us, not even ourselves, from doing the work we were born to do, and that we were men and worthy of life.

And he set out his deep emotion of release, after he had made the irrevocable choice, in the passage in *The Pilgrims of Hope* where the hero becomes a communist:

> And now the streets seem gay and the high stars glittering bright;
> And for me, I sing amongst them, for my heart is full and light.
> I see the deeds to be done, and the day to come on the earth,
> And riches vanished away and sorrow turned to mirth;
> I see the city squalor and the country stupor gone.
> And we a part of it all. . . .
> In the days to come of the pleasure, in the days that are of the fight—
> I was born once long ago: I am born again tonight.

This month Morris wrote again about Rossetti to a colleague on the NLL, who had been interested by the posthumous show of the latter's works at the Burlington Fine Arts Club.

I can't say how it was that Rossetti took no interest in politics; but so it was: of course he was quite Italian in his general turn of thought: though I think he took less interest in Italian politics than in English, in spite of his knowing several of the leading patriots personally, Saffi for instance. The truth is he cared for nothing but individual and personal matters, chiefly of course in relation to art and literature, but he would take abundant trouble to help any one person who was in distress of mind or body; but the evils of any mass of people he couldn't bring his mind to bear upon. I suppose in short it needs a person of a hopeful mind to take a disinterested notice of politics, and Rossetti was certainly not hopeful.

Rossetti set off the legend that Morris could only care for people in the mass and never gave a penny to a beggar. We have noted the element of fact behind this comment—the distracted and concentrated aspect of Morris's consciousness; but it certainly was a lie in asserting that he did not feel for individuals. It became however the accepted way of sneering at Morris in art circles. We find it current among the group of Shannon and Ricketts. 'Ross said that at every page in Mackail's Life of Morris he is at some pains to conceal the fact that Morris was hard and selfish.' Ricketts adds that once at Rossetti's everybody agreed on Morris's hardness; Morris was at last impressed and decided to do a good action. So at the next gathering Morris boasted, 'I told a man just now "Excuse me, sir, but your fly is unbuttoned." "If it comes to that, sir," said the man, "so is yours." '

In January 1883 Morris went over to Paris with Armstrong of the South Kensington Museum, to act as an adviser. In his letter to May he mentions that Ellis has just paid the half-yearly earnings of his books; £72 in cash. 'Tell your mother.' Georgie has not been well.

On 22 February a friend, perhaps Crom, describes him at BJ's:

Top came in to breakfast as usual on Sundays: was extremely brilliant as soon as he had shaken off a little dropping of spirits owing to bad news about Jenny: was very angry against Seddon for replacing old Hammersmith church ('a harmless silly old thing') by such an excrescence. He was bubbling over with Karl Marx, whom he had just begun to read in French. He praised Robert Owen immensely. He had been giving an address to a Clerkenwell Radical club—found the members 'eager to learn but dreadfully ignorant'. 'All Socialists are agreed as to education.' Finely explosive against railways. Some imitation Morris wall-paper was 'a mangy gherkin on a horse-dung ground'. Spent the evening at Top's—a long talk on birds: T.'s knowledge of them very extensive: can go on for hours about their habits: but especially about their form.

Morris on joining the DF was, according to Hyndman:

ever too eager to take his full share in the unpleasant part of our public work and speedily showed that he meant to work in grim earnest on the same level as the rank and file of our party.... He was never satisfied unless he was doing things which, to say the truth, he was little fitted for, and others of coarser fibre could do much better than he.... His imposing forehead and clear grey eyes, with the powerful nose and slightly florid cheeks, impressed you with the truth and importance of what he was saying, every hair of his head and in his rough shaggy beard appearing to enter into the subject as a living part of himself.

The comment about working on the same level as the rank and file brings out both Morris's strength and Hyndman's weakness. At the same time we must not idealise the DF as a working-class organisation. Among the leaders Henry S. Salt and J. L. Joynes had been teachers at Eton; Edward Carpenter was Fellow of Trinity Hall, Cambridge; E. Belford Bax was a barrister; Hyndman had been a stock-broker; H. Hyde Champion an artillery officer; and R. P. B. Frost a pupil at Marlborough. We can imagine the effect of such characters selling the socialist *Justice* in Fleet Street and the Strand. Jack Williams recalled: 'There was Hyndman in his immaculate frock coat and high hat; there was Morris, dressed in his usual blue serge suit and soft hat; Joynes in his aesthetic dress; Champion looking every inch the military man; Frost looking every inch the aristocrat; Quelch and myself in our everyday working clothes.' In 1894 Morris was to remark: 'A few years ago the movement was confined to a few persons, of education and of superior intelligence, most of whom belonged by position to the middle classes.' And Bax recalled: 'The Socialism of the eighties and even the early nineties—i.e. the new scientific Socialism of Marx and all that implied—was mainly a middle-class movement. The working classes, to whom in the nature of things the movement ought to have appealed, were largely apathetic and unresponsive in this country for a long time. The work of education in the new social and economic views was mainly done by middle-class men.' In such a situation it was hard to discard middle-class attitudes of paternalism. But Morris threw them off after a while because of the attitudes that Hyndman thought uncalled-for, while Hyndman himself fell into ever worse dogmatism (ending indeed with an acceptance of imperialism) because he saw the workers as a class of slaves who could only be freed from above. 'The leadership, the initiative, the teaching, the organisation, must come from those who are born into a different position, and are used to train their faculties in early life.' (Such a position has nothing in common with Lenin's statement that the working class by itself cannot rise above the level of trade unionism and that the socialist idea must come from middle-class intellectuals; for that presupposes that the idea, entering into the working class, becomes a living force to the extent that it is made their property. Morris, though not putting the issue in these terms, acted on the Leninist principle.)[2]

On 6 March he lectured at the Manchester Royal Institution, dealing with art, wealth, and riches. He took up the theme of art as before, but now made his whole attack far more precise. The enemy was capitalist production with its division of labour under which the worker 'is part of a machine, and has but one unvarying set of tasks to do'. The more he is mechanised, the more valuable is he to the system. The product aims at 'a certain high finish, and what I should call shop-counter look, quite peculiar to the wares of this century'. In human terms such a product involved the degradation of the worker and a deepening class-gulf. Culture itself, language, had been cut in half, with the result of an awful vulgarity, 'which was not in existence before modern times and the blossoming of competitive commerce'. The division in culture must be ended.

I want those who do the rough work of the world, sailors, miners, ploughmen, and the like, to be treated with consideration and respect, to be paid abundant money-wages, and to have plenty of leisure. I want modern science, which I believe to be capable of overcoming all material difficulties, to turn from such preposterous follies as the invention of anthracine colours and monster cannon to the invention of machines for performing such labour as is revolting and destructive of self-respect to the men who now have to do it by hand.

Then Britain will cease to be in part a cinder-heap, in part a game-preserve, and become a 'fair green garden'.

The lecture raised strong protests when reported in *The Manchester Examiner*; and to the complaint that he had dealt with 'another question than one of mere art', he replied that 'the question of popular art was a social question, involving the happiness or misery of the greater part of the community'. He wrote to Jenny that the philistines had been much moved. 'So you see one may yet arrive at the dignity of being hissed for a socialist down there: all this is encouraging. I am now about a lecture for a club in connection with the Democratic Federation; I intend making this one more plain-spoken: I am tired of being mealy-mouthed.' On 14 March he wrote that he had been away from Merton for a fortnight with gout; his lecture had been printed as a leaflet by the DF. (We may note that while he was still struggling as a Liberal for the cause of peace he wrote accounts of his activities to Janey; now that he had turned to socialism he wrote mainly to Jenny.)

On 1 April he lectured at Hampstead and was pleased to find Faulkner in the audience; he told Jenny he was going to speak at Clerkenwell on the 15th. The South Kensington Museum bought the three big pieces of tapestries he had. Ruskin had written: 'You bad boy, why haven't I any bits of glass yet?' On the 15th Morris replied that he had only just got Ruskin's note from Ned, and gave a lengthy account of his glass-work. On Whitsunday he had a large group at Kelmscott House, including Middleton, Benson (architect and designer in metalwork), and Scheu. 'I almost expect to see aunt Emma this week: she has come up to town on what I must irreverently call holy larks.' We see how far distanced he is from the beloved playmate of his early years. He was living what he called to Jenny 'a grass bachelor's life'.

In May he was put on the executive of the DF. 'So I am in for more work. However I don't like belonging to a body without knowing what they are doing. Without feeling very sanguine about their doings, they seem certainly to mean something; money is chiefly lacking, as usual.' So the drain of his resources went on, steadily growing heavier. On 3 May he lectured to the Irish National League, 'Parnellites to the backbone, but dear me! such quiet respectable people.' He told them how much he admired their ancient literature. 'I got my first bundle of sparrow-grass [at Merton] today, but I thought it too small to send to you: so I left it with Kate Faulkner, with whom I teaed this evening.' He had sent Jenny flowers from Axminster, and promised to send a big bunch of wallflowers next day. Janey was ill, for Webb wrote to her on the 16th: 'Your letter did not come to me as quite from the dead, for I had been, a many times, living with you through your great trouble.' Morris was reading Stepniak's *Underground Russia* with admiration. His note of 19 May to Jenny gives some idea of the time he spent getting to and from Merton:

On Tuesday & on Thursday I walked all the way to Merton by Roehampton Lane; really a pleasant walk: I am quite sick of the Underground & I think I shall often walk to or from Merton, it takes a long 2 hours; but you see it is not all pure waste like the sweltering train-business. I came back in an open trap on Tuesday. . . .

By train he had to go from Hammersmith to Farringdon Street, cross the city, and then go from Ludgate Hill to Merton: a journey taking some two hours.

In June the DF issued a manifesto, with Morris among the signatories. He set out his position clearly in a letter to Horsfall, who had been much disturbed; we see how powerfully he had been affected by Marx, how much he had absorbed of *Capital*:

In a few words what I have to say about the manifesto is that, though I may not like the taste of some of the wording, I do agree with the substance of it (or I should not have signed it). This does not however prevent me from agreeing with you that the rich do not act as they do in the matter from malice. Nevertheless their position (as a class) forces them to 'strive' (unconsciously most often I know) to keep the working men in ignorance of their rights and their power.

Where I think I differ from you of the means whereby revolution may be attained is this: if I do not misrepresent your views, you think that *individuals* of good will belonging to all classes can, if they be numerous and strenuous enough, bring about the change: I on the contrary think that the basis of all change must be, as it has always been, the antagonism of classes: I mean that though here and there a few men of the upper and middle classes, moved by their conscience and insight, may and doubtless will throw in their lot with the working classes, the upper and middle classes as a body will by the very nature of their existence, and like a plant grows, resist the abolition of classes: neither do I think that any amelioration of the condition of the poor on the only lines which the rich *can* go upon will advance us on the road; save that it will put more power into the hands of the lower class and so strengthen both their discontent and their means of showing it: for I do not believe that starvelings can bring about a revolution. I do not say there is not a terrible side to this: but how can it be otherwise? Commercialism, competition, has sown the wind recklessly, and must reap the whirlwind: it has created the proletariat for its own interest, and its creation will and must destroy it: there is no other force which can do so. For my part I have never under-rated the power of the middle classes, whom, in spite of their individual good nature and banality, I look upon as a most terrible and implacable force: so terrible that I think it not unlikely that their resistance to inevitable change may, if the beginnings of change are too long delayed, ruin all civilisation for a time. Meantime I must tell you that among the discontented, discontent unlighted by hope is in many places taking the form of a passionate desire for mere anarchy, so that it becomes a pressing duty for those who, not believing in the stability of the present system, have any hopes for the future, to lay before the world those hopes founded on *constructive* revolution.[3]

In June he had made his sixth annual SPAB Report. Two days later he wrote to May at Lyme Regis that he was 'a very little lame, with a very small touch of gout'. On 2 July he and BJ went to Exeter College to dine in hall, taking their places formally as Fellows. (This year BJ painted his *King Cophetua and the Beggar Maid*: the nearest he ever got to a social theme. The point had now been reached where he could follow Morris no longer.) On 10 July Morris spoke at Islington. On 25 July he wrote to Jenny in Hertfordshire, identifying two leaves she had sent him (one was a hornbeam). 'As to that pink flowered plant 'tis called Rest Harrow.' He cautioned her that the manifesto mentioned in *The Daily News* was that of the anarchists. 'We consider them dangerous, for you see they have no programme but destruction.' A friend had sent him some Hampstead paper-cuttings, in which was a reply by Jenny to an attack on his lecture, 'I thank you heartily, especially as it made clear to me that you quite understood what I had been saying.' Janey spent some time at Haworth, for Blunt mentions being specially invited to meet her there in 1883.

On 14 August a letter of his in *The Daily News* attacked the unhealthy condition of the ditch along the towpath from the soap works by Hammersmith Bridge. On the same day he wrote to tell Jenny of a trip he was taking with Middleton to Witney, Burford, Minster Lovell (where he would sleep), then on to Chipping Campden, the Tower, and back to Kelmscott. This summer he told Georgie, 'I haven't had two consecutive hours to call my own since I saw you three weeks ago; my time has been a mere heap of chopped straw.' On 21 August he wrote to her in reply to an effort to draw him back into poetry. 'You see, my dear, there is first of all my anxiety, which I am bound to confess has made a sad coward of me; and then, though I admit that I am a conceited man, yet I really don't think anything I have done (when I consider it as I should another man's work) of any value but to myself: except as showing sympathy with history and the like. Poetry goes with the hand-arts I think, and like them has now become unreal: the arts have got to die, what is left of them, before they can be born again.' Meanwhile propaganda 'gives me work to do, which, unimportant as it seems, is part of a great whole which cannot be lost, and that ought to be enough for me'.

At the end of August he was troubled by the inner conflicts in the DF. 'Some of the more ardent disciples look upon Hyndman as too opportunist, and there is truth in that; he is sanguine of speedy change happening somehow, and is inclined to intrigue and the making of a party; towards which end compromise is needed, and the carrying people who don't really agree with us as far as they will go. As you know, I am not sanguine, and think the aim of Socialists should be the founding of a religion, towards which end compromise is no use, and we only want to have those with us who will be with us to the end. But then again, if the zealots don't take care they will blow the whole thing to the winds; all the more as the religious or theological difficulty is on us, or threatening to be so. . . . I find myself drifting into the disgraceful position of a moderator and patcher-up, which is against my inclination.' Hyndman's idea of a broad organisation working in the parliamentary field as well as others was correct enough; but when allied to what Morris rightly saw as an opportunist streak in his character it had the effect of repelling Morris and intensifying his purist element. At the same time Morris saw that socialism as a religion inevitably made its advocates into a sect, and as a sect it was sure to be rent by 'the theological difficulty'. In acting as moderator his own natural bent to a sort of united front showed itself. The idea of a party which sought to be active in all fields while fighting all the while to preserve its socialist integrity and to spread the socialist idea was hard for Morris at this stage to conceive. He himself goes on to explain one of the main reasons for the sect-position. 'It is obvious that the support to be looked for for constructive Socialism from the working classes is nought.' He saw only a vague discontent and a spirit of revenge. 'What we want is real leaders themselves working men, and content to be so till classes are abolished.' As things were, a gifted worker tended to rise out of his class 'before he has begun to think of class politics as matter of principle, and too often he is just simply "got at" by the governing classes, not formally, but by circumstances I mean'. The problem was socialist education, but that was made more than difficult by the commercial system defending itself against such a development 'in a terrible unconscious way with the struggle for bread, and lack of leisure, and squalid housing—and there we go, round and round the circle still'.[4]

Early in September he wrote the first of the poems later collected as *Chants for Socialists: The Day is Coming*. The poem must have had a strong effect; for the *Christian Socialist* announced next month that it 'was read from the pulpit of at least one London church on the 23rd September, and will be heard from other pulpits during the next few weeks'. In sending it to Georgie Morris tried to answer her objection that education must first change people before a new society could emerge. He argued that 'education will not cure people of the grossest social selfishness and tyranny unless Socialistic principles form part of it'. Meanwhile 'I am sure it is right, whatever the apparent consequences may be, to stir up the lower classes (damn the word) to demand a higher standard of life for themselves, not merely for themselves or for the sake of the material comfort it will bring, but for the good of the whole world and the regeneration of the conscience of man: and this stirring up is part of the necessary education which must in good truth go before the reconstruction of society: but I repeat that without laying before people this reconstruction our education will but breed tyrants and cowards, big, little and least, down to the smallest who can screw out money from standing by to see another man working for him.' On 5 September he wrote a long letter to Scheu, beginning with some advice about dyeing and then giving a brief account of his whole life.

This month he was busy reading Cobbett, fascinated by the downright and earthy character of the man. On 26 October he spoke in support of the DF programme at Birmingham. He had been asked to lecture to the Russell Club, and the hall of University College was lent for the purpose. Faulkner had been one of the intermediaries, as a Fellow of the College, and Morris made it quite clear that he was going to speak as a socialist. Originally both he and Hyndman had been going to speak, but the Master objected to Hyndman. Morris protested, but finally decided to leave the matter in the hands of the club. 'I have undertaken to give my lecture and will not back out of it.' Somehow the authorities could not realise that Morris as a man of means, a manufacturer, a poet, could seriously be a socialist. There had been a growing interest at Oxford in social studies; the idea of university settlements in the East End of London was coming up; Henry George had lectured on land nationalisation. On 14 November the lecture, 'Art and Democracy', was given, under the auspices of the Master, the Wardens of Keble and Merton, and Ruskin, the Slade professor of Fine Arts. Morris set out his thesis that art could not be considered in isolation from society. Art he defined as 'every one of the things that goes to make up the surroundings among which we live'. He attacked the vast and ruthless pollution and desecration going on. Individual artists in such a situation had their minds narrowed and 'their sympathies frozen by their isolation'. The well of art was poisoned at its spring. The destructive force lay in the system of competition in production and exchange; and it must be ended. 'I hold that the condition of competition between man and man is bestial only, and that of association human.' He attacked the conditions forced on the exploited workers and declared that there was plenty of discontent about; the problem was to 'help in educating that discontent into hope, that is into the demand for the new birth of society'. He was speaking as a socialist, warning his listeners that the great change, however delayed, would surely come. He appealed to them to help. 'Organised brotherhood is that which must break the spell of anarchical Plutocracy.'

The Master rose to protest. But Ruskin, as chairman, used his tact and prestige to quieten things down, while insisting that Morris was right. Now Morris was in the news as a socialist, and the attacks began on him for inconsistency in acting as a capitalist while advocating the proletarian cause. He replied to such an attack in the *Standard*. 'We are but minute links in the immense chain of the terrible organisation of competitive commerce, and only the complete unrivetting of that chain will really free us.' From Merton Abbey he wrote to Georgie: 'I have been living in a sort of storm of newspaper brickbats, to some of which I had to reply: of course I don't mind a bit, nor even think the attack unfair. My own men here are very sympathetic, which pleases me hugely; and I think we shall get on much better for my having spoken my mind about things: seven of them would insist on joining the Democratic Federation, though I preached to them the necessity of really understanding it all.' On 16 November he spoke at Wimbledon on 'Art under the Rule of Commerce'; one of the audience protested in *The Times* against his giving of lectures on socialism under misleading titles. On 24 November he spoke on the 'Origin of Decorative Art' at Windsor. On 4 December he repeated his Oxford lecture at the Cambridge Union.

Wardle states that when Morris, disillusioned with the Liberals, 'hoped to organise a strong political party out of the radical elements or out of the trade unions', there were 'meetings in our showroom in Queen Square (in the evenings) to which he invited leaders of the working-men radicals'. He started trying to work out systems of profit-sharing. Wardle comments: 'You cannot have socialism in a corner', and refers to the many small communist societies in the United States. 'Since the buying and selling were both controlled by external conditions, production also was bound to follow them. Mr Morris would gladly have had it otherwise but the problem for him was not to defeat the invincible but to make the best of adverse conditions.' So Morris used piece-work; he listened as to an equal to any worker making an objection or claim; he tried to make salaries proportionate to profits. He worked out a plan of sharing based on Leclaire's experiment. 'The plan was clearly no solution of the question which was occupying Morris, but he adopted so much of it as to give some half dozen of us a direct interest in the business. I pointed out that the expansion of the plan to the whole shop would involve endless book-keeping—a thing he hated.' Once a year at least 'there was a meeting to discuss the balance-sheet and the state of the business'. None of his workers, says Wardle, 'would willingly have joined any other workshop'. (Any surplus he could withdraw, Wardle adds, he seems to have spent on books.)

This year, 1883, was then the decisive year in the development of Morris as a thinker. The political activities of the previous years had brought him to the point where he was able to respond with his whole being to the thought of Marx. He read *Capital* in the French version of Lechâtre (1872–5); and May tells us that he read French with ease. Later in 1887 he reread the work in English. (He stated that he could not read German, but from 1869 he had made much headway with Icelandic and soon mastered the language. 'We all talk nothing but Icelandic together,' he told Aglaia in February 1873. True, he found Anglo-Saxon heavier going when he tackled *Beowulf*. In 1886 he remarked that he could 'only read even Old German with great difficulty and labour'. However, though we must make allowance for his modesty in professions of ignorance, it is unlikely that he could have got through *Capital* in German.) Naturally he found the purely economic sections difficult, and his remarks on this point were taken up by men like Glasier in their efforts to depreciate his role as a Marxist. But their positions have been so thoroughly undermined by the analyses of Edward Thompson and Paul Meier that there is no need here to deal with them. It is beyond question that from 1883 Morris never wavered in his devotion to Marx and that he understood his work in all essentials. He had found at last the vision of history and of human development that made sense of all the issues with which he had been struggling since he first read Ruskin and Carlyle. His work after 1883 is a steady and consistent attempt to clarify and express all that the illuminations of *Capital* meant to him.

Before we turn from 1883 we may glance again at the DF. The pamphlet which it had issued, definitely tying it to Marxism, was called *Socialism Made Plain*. After setting out various radical demands, it proceeded to a forthright attack on the existing system as a form of capitalist monopoly. 'The loan-mongers, the farmers, the mine-exploiters, the contractors, the middlemen, the factory-lords,' turn 'every advance in human knowledge, every further improvement in human dexterity, into an engine for accumulating out of other men's labour and for exacting more and yet more surplus out of the wage-slaves they employ.' As long as the means of production 'are a monopoly of a class, so long must the labourers on the farm, in the mine, or in the factory sell themselves for a bare subsistence wage'.

This analysis provided the basis for the first thorough-going exposition of Marxism by a political group in England; it was repeated with greater clarity and fullness throughout 1883 and 1884 in pronouncements, in articles, in books. Morris was thus actively present from the outset in the development of Marxism as a political instrument in England. Between 1860 and 1880 there was in effect no socialist thought at work in Britain; in its old Owenite form socialism was dead, or at best a plaything in the hands of some ageing eccentrics. When the idea of socialism was suddenly revived from 1883 on, it often came as a revelation and enthusiasts felt that the revolution was waiting round the corner. At the same time there was a tendency to make a dogmatic instrument out of the new and imperfectly grasped doctrine. Hyndman believed in the Iron Law of Wages, which made illusory any gains wrung from the employers; he took an extremely sectarian view of the role of a socialist party; he saw trade unions as representing the aristocracy of labour and thus a 'hindrance to that complete organisation of the proletariat which alone can obtain for the workers their proper control over their own labour'. The trade unions were seen as veiling instead of bringing into the open the antagonism of classes. Hyndman took over from Lassalle, and falsely attributed to the *Communist Manifesto*, the idea that 'opposed to us all other parties form "a reactionary mass" '. Morris was inevitably affected in varying degrees by such conceptions, even though he soon found it necessary to come out in open conflict with Hyndman.

In the new situation of 1883 Morris pioneered in various ways. This year and the following years he did not spare himself in travelling round to address provincial groups. At times the request came from an individual or two or three persons attempting to form a socialist branch; at times from other bodies interested to hear the socialist case. 'At several of these centres he was the first speaker to address a large public meeting on behalf of the new Cause. These lectures were generally well attended: although only 12 people attended the first meeting (addressed by Hyndman and Morris) in Birmingham. Debating societies, Sunday Lecture Societies, Secular Societies, Radical Clubs—all these kept alive public interest in controversial lectures and an audience of up to 1,000 in the seven or eight major cities was not exceptional' (Thompson). In 1883 the DF, taking up from the lead by the Labour Emancipation League, embarked on open-air propaganda. Scheu says that Hyndman opposed Sunday meetings as a continental idea with which the English would not sympathise; but Scheu, Morris, Champion, Banner, Bax and Joynes disagreed and carried the idea through. Till this time only free-thinkers had held regular Sunday meetings out of doors— often in the form of a sort of religious service. By the summer of 1884 the socialists had created a tradition of gatherings in Regent's Park or in Hyde Park by the Reformer's Tree, where literature was sold. Even leading politicians were said to have walked over at times to hear Morris or one of the others. These open-air meetings were one of the most effective forms of early propaganda and gave many workers their first ideas about socialism.[5]

Morris was now in the full swing of his multiple activities, with his lecturing and his work for socialism as dynamic unifying point. For five more years he kept up this tremendous momentum. The cause was now everything. In January his friends grumbled at his preoccupation. 'He can talk about little else, and will brook no opposition.' Vague and amiable chat on the subject became, De Morgan said, less and less possible. On New Year's Day he wrote to Jenny. 'I am off to-day on a sort of roaming journey to London: to see Hyndman first about the DF business: then to Oxford St: then mother; then Faulkners, then Webb, and last the DF meeting in [the] evening; so in a way I have a day's work to do; but really a very grubby & yellow day to do it in.' The DF launched on 19 January *Justice*, the first socialist weekly. Morris contributed a satirical fable. The fowls of the barnyard call a packed meeting to discuss with what sauce they are to be eaten; the bedraggled cock who suggests that he doesn't want to be eaten at all is howled down with cries of 'practical politics'; 'great liberal party!' and so on. Slow stewing was accepted as the least revolutionary form of cookery. There was also an essay signed by Hyndman, Morris, and Taylor, stating that the aim was to show that socialist theory was scientific and that socialism, so far from fomenting anarchy, had as its sole aim the substitution of a beneficient order for the disorder of the existing system. But at the same time discord arose in the committee as to whether or not they should support the parliamentary programme of the Radicals. 'Of course I say no. Mr. Scheu made an excellent speech on my side.' There was a weekly deficit for the paper, which Morris was the only person able to meet. Now it was that street-sales began, in the City and the Strand. (The initial funds had been advanced by Carpenter, but they soon ran out. Engels was not enthusiastic about the leadership; on 16 February he wrote to the Lafargues: 'Hyndman combines internationalist phraseology with jingo aspirations. Joynes is a muddle-headed ignoramus—I saw him a fortnight ago—Morris is all very well as far as he goes, but it is not far.')

Meanwhile on the 16th Morris had given a lecture, *Useful Work versus Useless Toil*, at Hampstead. 'On Friday Mr Joynes is going to lecture to our Merton Abbey Branch. On Monday I go to Manchester and lecture at Ancoats the working suburb, & in the middle of the town to respectabilities on the Tuesday: on the Wednesday I lecture at Leicester; so I have [been] pretty hard at it at present. Give my best love to Granny & Henrietta.' He still feared conflicts with his mother and hid as well as he could from her what he was doing. He told Jenny that he wouldn't send *Justice* to her. 'I fear the element in which you are is altogether too respectable for me to send a copy down there.' At Manchester he delivered *Useful Work* and *Art under Plutocracy*; at Leicester, *Art and Socialism*; on the 27th he spoke in Oxford at the Russell Club together with Hyndman. *Useful Work* he gave nine more times this year: in February at Bradford and Woolwich; in March at Edinburgh and in London (to the Fabians); in April at Bethnal Green; in

July at Hammersmith; in September to the Tottenham Branch of the
SDF; in October at Battersea; in November at Rotherhithe.

In *Art and Socialism* we see that he still thinks primarily of addressing the
middle class and drawing them over to support the cause. How are 'we of the
middle classes, we the capitalists, and our hangers-on', to help the workers?
'By renouncing our class, and on all occasions when antagonism rises up
between the classes casting in our lot with the victims. . . . There is no other
way.' On 26 January he tells Jenny that Hyndman has addressed the Merton
Abbey Branch, with an old Chartist present. 'He said it made him feel 20
years younger.'

Mother is getting better now quickly & will soon be all right: she demands as a
reward for getting well that I should hang the drawing-room with the blue
Windrush as a summer change. I must consent I suppose & salve my conscience
on the grounds of its being an advertisement for the goods.

In *Today* for January he had a poem *The Three Seekers* in which he expresses
his sense of being relieved of the fear of death, the fretting misery of useless
efforts, which had accompanied him through his middle years: there is a
sort of refrain, 'Since I have drawn thee from the dead,' and the conclusion
runs: 'Now life is little, and death is nought, Since all is found that erst I
sought.' The charge that he was an insincere socialist since he lived as a
capitalist had hit him hard; and he was now meditating the sale of his
business (Scheu tells us) so that he could live modestly with his family on
£4 a week. Despite his careless use of money and the way in which he was
accustomed to entertaining friends and retiring now and then to Kelmscott,
he would certainly himself have been happy in many ways with the reduced
income and the more limited sphere of action, but he could not face the
problem of inflicting hardship on the girls, especially Jenny with her bad
health, and of having to force such a system on the unsympathetic Janey,
whose defensive invalidism would certainly have grown very much worse.
We catch a glimpse of his inner struggle in the entry by Cobden-Sanderson,
devoted to the Simple Life, for 16 January:

We told him that he ought to put his principles into practice in his own case: that
his appeal would be much more powerful if he did so. He said he was in a corner and
could not, that no one person could; that, to say the truth, he was a coward and
feared to do so; that there was his wife, and the girls; and how could he put it upon

them? ... Dear old Morris, he would be happier if he could put his ideas into practice.

Cobden-Sanderson, in the pride of his own transformation into a manual labourer, oversimplifies Morris's problems; to have sold the business would not have increased his value to the cause. But we can understand how the question tormented Morris. At Cambridge on 5 February he took part in a debate on socialism as the remedy for 'the present anarchy', and *Justice* reports: 'Mr. William Morris at once rose to reply to the personal question, and to confess that, while not a capitalist in the ordinary sense of the word, he must admit to his own conscience that he was one of a class that lives upon the labour of other people.' On 25 February he wrote one of his rare letters to Janey on his socialist activities. He had been to Bradford and Blackburn and was off to West Bromwich, Birmingham. The Bradford workers 'are pretty comfortable there because all the spinning and weaving is done by women and children. . . . I don't think all my vigorous words (of a nature that you may imagine) shook the conviction of my entertainers that this was the way to make an Earthly Paradise.' In February-March there was a great cotton strike in Lancashire. Macdonald and Williams went up to Blackburn to agitate and prepare the way for a big meeting which was addressed by Morris, Joynes, and Hyndman. Some 1,500 strikers attended, and James Macdonald says, 'Their interest was aroused in the message of Socialism . . . and the meeting was a tremendous success.' Here was the first contact with the broad mass of industrial workers.

On 18 March he wrote to Janey with an account of the first march to Marx's grave. (Marx had died on 14 March 1883.)

I was loth to go, but did not dislike it when I did go: brief, I trudged all the way from Tottenham Court Rd. up to Highgate Cemetery (with a red ribbon in my button-hole) at the tail of various banners and a very bad band to do honour to the memory of Karl Marx *and* the Commune: the thing didn't look as absurd as it sounds, as we were a tidy number, I should think more than a thousand in the procession, and onlookers to the amount, when we got to the end, of some 2 or 3 thousand more I should say. Of course they wouldn't let us into the cemetery, and honoured us with a heavy guard of policemen; so we adjourned to an uncomfortable piece of waste ground near by and the song [the *Internationale*] was sung and speeches made; only diversified by a rather feeble attempt by the hobblehoys to interrupt, which our people checked with the loss of one hat (Mr Williams'); after which we marched off the ground triumphant with policemen on each side of us like a royal procession. Mr Sanderson joined us at the cemetery, and we went home together along with Hyndman all hollow to the last degree, and finished the evening, Dick and Mr Gell and brother being there, with discussion and supper, fairly harmoniously. Well, to-morrow morning early I go to Edinburgh to lecture and shall be back on Friday. All well with business: the new blocker is come and seems a good fellow: we are striking off a fend of 'Wardle' now: item, we are going to begin our velvet-weaving soon, it will be very grand.

Perhaps, with the debate going on in his mind as to whether he should sell the firm, he was making a last effort to interest Janey in his ideas. The *Cray* and *Wandle* chintzes, with the *Wey* of 1883, have a new element of design, an emphatic diagonal effect, which seems to derive from fifteenth-century cut velvet acquired in 1883 by the South Kensington Museum.[6]

The Art Workers Guild was formed this year, uniting artists of all kinds, from painters and architects to printers, bookbinders, cabinet-makers, paper-hangers. A man read papers on his own craft, with the understanding that there was to be no veiling of craft secrets. 'I remember Morris once giving us an evening on paper-making,' says Jackson, 'and bringing his paper-maker, Bachelor, who made a sheet for us in the room, showing how by a dexterous handshake, difficult to acquire and sometimes, strange to say, lost again, the workman secures that interlacing of the linen fibres which makes the durable hand-made article.' (Morris and Bachelor brought good hand-made paper again into vogue: Morris was Master of the Guild in 1892.) This year too was formed the Fabian Society. Shaw wanted a socialist group of a respectable kind, with 'no born poor-men', with 'no illiterate working-men'. He had been repelled by the DF. 'Hyndman's congregation of manual-working pseudo-Marxists could for me be only hindrances.' He drew in Sidney Webb and Sydney Olivier, both Colonial Officer clerks. Thus, no sooner had a serious effort been made to build a Marxist organisation than there came the reformist retort. Morris had read in *Today* the first chapters of Shaw's *An Unsocial Socialist* and had been amused enough to want to make his acquaintance.

On 3 and 10 March at Birmingham he gave two lectures on the 'Gothic Revival'. He stressed the popular element in Gothic.

It was progressive, confident, intolerant, though there was history in every atom of it, it was not conscious of it, was conscious only of exultation in the present and hope for the future. . . . Rough but kindly humour is an essential part of all the Gothic of the N[orth] at least; a wish to scare nobody away by contempt or pride, a feeling as near as may [be] the opposite of that which is the motive feeling of the pedantic art of the Renaissance. . . . It was common to the whole people; it was free, progressive, hopeful, full of human sentiment and humour.

He then traces the decline in the arts and the attempts of the revival to regain the lost qualities.

At first we imitated the outward aspects of it [Gothic] without understanding its spirit much as the Renaissance artists had done with the old classical art, but without infusing any of the spirit of our own times into it as they had done so as to make a living style: even this however is now to a certain extent being attempted owing to the knowledge of history having spread among us till we are beginning to be conscious of the growth and unity of mankind of which I have just spoken.

He thus comes up against the problem which is still with us. Only the ending of the class system, he stresses, can liberate art; at the same time we cannot tamely wait for that moment. Yet 'the spirit of our own times' is inevitably the spirit of the cash-nexus, of fragmentation, and of monopoly; and so the art which most truly expresses this spirit must be the box-architecture fully adapted to the needs of the machine. How then develop in architecture and in all the arts the forms which are both contemporary and revolutionary; which run counter to all the alienating, abstracting, or subjectively narrowed-down tendencies; which struggle for the fully sensuous attitudes of the whole man of a liberated world? The individually whole man is also the man in true dialectical unity with the deepest humanising forces of his world and with nature.

On 1 April Cobden-Sanderson recorded: 'On Sunday we supped with the Morrises. We got off the subject of Socialism for a wonder, and on to the subject of Iceland . . . and Swinburne's estimate, in the Nineteenth Century, of Byron and Wordsworth. Morris was unmeasured in his abuse of Wordsworth: and vastly preferred Byron, whom he admitted, however, to be in the main a rhetorician. We then got on to hero-worship, which Morris denounced.' He could not forgive Wordsworth for his pietism, his moralising of nature. On 1 April Morris himself was giving the lecture *Art and Labour* at Leeds. He dealt briefly with ancient, Byzantine, and medieval society, then with division of labour in his own world. In the socialist future, 'no useless work being done and all irksome labour saved as much as possible by machines made our servants instead of our masters', men would regain pleasure in work. He ended with an appeal to his middle-class audience. This lecture was given again this year in Leicester, London, Manchester, Newcastle, Preston and Glasgow. On 4 April he was driving the same lesson home, with stress on the polluting effects of industrialism, at a picture show in Whitechapel. Eleanor Marx described the speech as splendid, and was delighted with the effects on the self-satisfied ladies and gentlemen. 'It was amusing to note the astonishment not unmingled with irritation of these good people when the poet in very plain prose told them they were not so very superior after all.' On 5 April in *Justice* he published an essay on Henry George, praising him for drawing attention to the land question, but attacking him for being blind to the real enemy of the times, the capitalist. He ignored however the passages in *Progress and Poverty* in which George looks forwards to a society in which the desire for wealth and the fear of need would be ended—passages much in the vein of his own broodings about the future. George too had attacked the division of labour. In *Justice* on 12 April he commented, 'The development of electricity as a motive power will make it easier.' He was thinking of decentralisation, but his remark shows how ready he was to welcome new forms of energy that would, if rightly used, simplify life and production, getting rid of old drudgeries. On 17 April, with Professor Beesly in the chair, Hyndman debated with Charles Bradlaugh the question of socialism, rousing much interest in the secularist and radical movement. Morris's contribution was the poem *All for the Cause*. 'The day is drawing nigh, When the Cause shall call upon us, some to live, and some to die!' The question of profit-sharing was still exercising him and he wrote on 21 April a letter about it to Emma Lazarus (published in the *Century Magazine* 1886).

On 1 June he brought his thoughts on profit-sharing together in a long letter to Georgie. He mentions that last year he made some £1,800, Wardle about £1,200, and the two Smiths (capable men who had been drawn into the management) about £600 each, Debny and West £400. These were the men sharing directly in profits. The colour mixer and the foreman had a bonus on the amount of goods turned out; the other men were on piece-rates or employed as day-workers—most were on piece-rates. The firm's capital was about £1,500. He considered that his earnings were in effect for work done, since the firm would not survive without him or someone like him. However he also got some £120 a year out of his literary works.

Now you know we ought to be able to live upon £4 a week, & give the literary income to the revolutionary agitation; but here comes the rub, and I feel the pinch of society, for which society I am only responsible in a very limited degree. And yet if Janey and Jenny were well and capable I think they ought not to grumble at living on the said £4, nor do I think they would. Well, so far as to my position, which you will see is very different from the ordinary manufacturer's so-called: since he not only gets high pay for 'organising labour' but also claims as a sleeping partner on various absurdly transparent pretexts. On the other hand I admit it would be much easier for me to drop some of my iniquitous over-payment, than for him, because I have personal relations with my men, while his are only machines.

The latter workers, getting more money, would be liable to attempt to set up as small capitalists. Also, there are already some artisans with high wages, but their position does not affect that of the workers in general. Morris goes on to state his belief that the loss of England's monopoly in the world market makes it impossible for a rise in the standards of the whole population. (He here approached the notion of the Iron Law taken over by Hyndman from Lassalle but attached by him to Marx.) If the times were stagnant and without deep conflict he would be content 'to settle down into an ascetic hermit or a hanger-on', but as things are he must obey the call to battle.

On 14 June a Hammersmith branch of the DF was formed, starting with eleven members, one of whom, a Ruskinite, soon left. The committee met once or twice a week, and lectures were given fortnightly or weekly. There were twenty-seven meetings up to the end of the year, Morris attending twenty-one of them; no doubt he was away on propaganda work during the absences. Emery Walker was the secretary and twenty-nine new members were gained in the period.

All the while Hyndman was generating antagonisms by his dictatorial ways. On 22 June Engels wrote to Kautsky:

Hyndman is thinking to *buy up* all the little movement here. . . . Himself a rich man, and in addition having at his disposal resources supplied by the very rich artist-enthusiast but untalented politician Morris . . . he wants to be sole master. . . . Hyndman is a skilful and good business man, but a petty and hard-faced John Bull, possessing a vanity considerably in excess of his talent and natural gifts. Bax and Aveling have most excellent intentions, but everything has gone to pieces, and those literateurs alone cannot do anything. The masses still will not follow them.

Engels was substantially right in these comments from a purely political viewpoint; but he never understood and appreciated Morris. He was now nearing the age of sixty-four, and since 1870 had been living in a fine house in Regent's Park Road. It was easy for him in his last years to look out on a confused world where nobody in the English scene had anything like his rich and acute store of political experience and understanding; the nickname used by intimates like Eleanor Marx and Aveling, the General, brings out clearly enough the way in which from his remote tower of observation he liked to lay down the law, even if what he said was for the most part eminently sensible. Also nicknamed the Grand Lama of Regent's Park Road, he lacked the deep concern of Marx for the moral and the aesthetic issues which burns through the early *Economic and Philosophic Manuscripts*. Marx knew much of Goethe and Heine by heart; year after year he read *Aeschylus* in the original; he never ceased studying Shakespeare; he also loved Dante, Cobbett, Burns. The Marx family had a cult of Shakespeare, and his three daughters knew much of the plays by heart; they used to sing the songs and recite the satirical poems of Burns. Marx, one feels, would have fully appreciated Morris and his contribution, and it was unfortunate that he died just as Morris was turning to socialism. Engels could only see the limitations in Morris's medievalism; and if he had ever glanced at his poems (that is, *The Earthly Paradise*) he saw nothing there but Victorian sentimentality. He judged all Morris's positive qualities through the belittling focus of his political errors or confusions in the first years of his self-education as a socialist.

Bax was an odd character, an extremely intelligent man who produced the first serious critiques by an English Marxist; but he had his fads and his prejudices, obsessed by the joyless philistinism of the middle classes, the deadly form taken by the family and the hypocritical use of religion. Absentminded, lacking a sense of humour or proportion, he yet was far better equipped than Morris to grasp the philosophic aspects of Marxism, its historical method, in its full range of applications. On his weak side, 'his articles on imperialism keep on plunging off after the spectacle of hypocrisy, rather than the fact of exploitation. When the Trafalgar Square Riots took place Morris—on the front page of *Commonweal*—was wrestling with the essential political implications of the outbreak, while in the inner pages Bax was having the time of his life using the incident as a text for a very long and triumphant article on the importance of the event as an "exposure of the abject cowardice of the English middle classes *en bloc*".' (Edward Thompson)

Dr Edward Aveling, a Fellow at University College, London, had begun as a secularist and exponent of Darwinism. Reading *Capital* early in 1884, he accepted Marx as a scientist to be linked with Darwin; but he looked on Marxism as the exposition of a set of clear-cut economic laws, not as an historical method. Morally he was a very dubious character. Shaw, who depicted him as Dubedat in *The Doctor's Dilemma*, said that 'he seduced every woman he met, and borrowed from every man'. Eleanor Marx was caught by his charm and driven to suicide.[7] She had wanted to be an actress, sharing her father's passion for Shakespeare, but when he died she had to take a post in a boarding-school. She soon was drawn into the socialist movement, writing notes on the international situation for *Today*, working with Engels on her father's papers, and this year becoming a member of the Federation's Council. Aveling, though separated from his wife, was still married, and he and Eleanor lived openly together in a free marriage. Morris was among her supporters. Eleanor had one of the finest of characters, sensitive, loyal, passionately concerned for the social cause, but also for all that made for truth, kindliness, and comradeship in personal relations.

Morris, Bax, and Aveling, then, made up a remarkable trio, but we can understand why Engels did not see how they could give an effective leadership against Hyndman, building a genuine mass-party.

On 1 July at the SPAB yearly meeting Morris read a paper on Architecture and History. On the 9th he wrote to Scheu in Edinburgh about arguments over next year's International Conference with Antwerp as its site. He hated having to be 'politic' in such squabbles; but despite Hyndman 'I cannot yet forgo the hope of our forming a Socialist *party* which shall begin to act in our time, instead of a mere theatrical association in a private room with no hope but that of gradually permeating cultivated people with our aspirations.' On the 11th he spoke on Textile Fabrics at the International Health Exhibition, South Kensington Museum. On the 16th he wrote to Scheu about a big meeting held by Burns and Williams in Hyde Park. Arrangements were being made to follow up next Sunday. Money should have come in from the Marylebone Branch, but hadn't, 'Perhaps 'tis my bourgeois blood, but this un-straightness on money matters discourages me very much.' On the 18th he wrote again about the dissensions in the Federation:

If I have any influence amongst our party (if party it be) it is because I am supposed to be straight and not to be ambitious, both which suppositions are, I hope, true; and feel sure that any appearance of pushing myself forward would injure my influence, such as it is, *very much*; therefore I will not secede for any mere matter of tactics however important I may think it, unless I am positively driven to it; but if I find myself opposed on a matter of principle ... I will secede if I am driven to it by the opposition embracing the false principle; and in that case of course will join any men if they be only two or three, or only yourself to push the real cause. Meantime I know enough of myself to be sure that I am not fit for the rudder; at least not yet; but I promise to take my due share in all matters, and steadily to oppose all jingo business; but if I can with coolness, or I shall be bowled over, since I have not got hold yet of the strings that tie us to the working-class members; nor have I read as I should have.

We see there that he could not be accused of lack of self-knowledge as to his position in the movement.

At the Hyde Park meeting on the 23rd, called by the London Trades Council, radical feeling was strong. The main question was the role of the House of Lords, with the Liberal veteran Bright calling for a severe limitation of its powers of veto. The Federation set up its own stall and was joined by the Labour Emancipation League. Hyndman in his speech attacked Fawcett, and Burns then attacked Bright. The workers were enraged, and there was a violent scrimmage. We see that socialists had merely a few dozen staunch supporters. They stood out against the working-class Liberalism that the mass of workers were defending. In so doing they could be accused of undue sectarianism; but they were probably right in deciding that a definite stand was needed at this moment if the working class were to be made conscious of their own main interests. Sam Mainwaring, engineer, later described one stirring phase of the struggle. The socialist banners had been torn and broken up, and many socialists were being run off to the Serpentine.

Morris fought like a man with the rest of us, and before they had us half way to the water we had succeeded in making a stand, and I remember Morris calling on Burns to finish his speech. Being on ground level, and our opponents still fighting, Burns said he wanted something to stand on. That day we had only our first pamphlet, 'Socialism Made Plain', of which Morris had a large bag-full at his side. These he placed on the ground in a heap, and Burns mounted and continued his speech, while Morris, and a dozen of us, were fighting to keep back the more infuriated of the people. Some of our friends found fault with Burns for using language to irritate the crowd, but Morris's opinion was that they would have to be told the truth, and that it was as well to tell them first as last.

In a letter to a young poet, Robert Thompson, on the day after the fight,

Peacock and Dragon woven woollen 1878

Compton design, last of Morris's wallpaper designs

Honeysuckle chintz design 1876

Pages from Kelmscott Chaucer

Eve and the Virgin Mary, drawing for stained glass by Morris,
Middleton Chinet 1864

we see how his ideas were clarifying. 'You must understand 1st that though I have a great respect for Ruskin, and his works (beside personal friendship) he is not a Socialist, that is not a *practical* one. He does not expect to see any general scheme ever begun: he mingles with certain sound ideas which he seems to have acquired instinctively, a great deal of mere whims, deduced probably from his early training of which he gives an amusing account.' There can be no Socialism 'unless the State, or people rather, has made up its mind to take over for the good of the community *all the means of production*: i.e. credit, railways, mines, factories, shipping, land, machinery, which are at present in the hands of private monopolies'. Any partial scheme carried out 'side by side of the ordinary commercial competition is doomed to fail just as the co-operative scheme is failing', at the same time the fight for the reduction of the working day is of supreme importance; and 'it would at once become an international affair'. He now speaks with the voice of the workers, not as a middle-class man appealing to his fellows to help the workers up.

We cannot turn our people back into Catholic English peasants and Guild craftsmen, or into heathen Norse bonders, much as may be said for such conditions of life: we have no choice but to accept the task which the centuries have laid on us of using the corruption of 300 years of profit-mongering for the overthrow of that very corruption: commerce has bred the Proletariat and uses it quite blindly, and is still blind to the next move in the game, which will be that the Proletariat will say: We will be *used* no longer, you have organised us for *our own use*.

Education and organisation of the workers are the means to be used.

Resistance to Hyndman had been growing stronger in the DF. Losing his place as president in July, he nominated Morris, who declined. Eleanor, Aveling, and Joseph Lane, now on the committee, intensified the struggle against him; and he in turn looked on Eleanor and Aveling as emissaries of Engels, foreign intruders in British socialism. Bradlaugh, on the strength of some financial 'irregularities' in the accounts of the Secular Society, demanded Aveling's expulsion, and Hyndman thought the moment was opportune to drive Aveling off the SDF executive; but Morris thought he should stay on. Morris himself was reaching the end of his patience with Hyndman. 'I have done my best to trust him, but cannot any longer.' On 13 August he wrote to Scheu an account of a troubled meeting with himself in the chair. 'I am afraid we are but at the beginning of our troubles: I tried to do as well as I could; but am not up to much as a Chairman: however will learn.' The veering and confused states through which he was passing are shown by his comment on the programme: 'I am sorry to say I could not hinder two ineptitudes creeping into it; Disestablishment moved by Aveling: and the Irish matter by Frost (Aveling supported this also); at any rate it was better than the old one, and is not parliamentary.' Yet the Federation had expressed, with Morris's complete support, its strong backing for the cause of Irish independence and had played some part in the agitation. Now however Morris was against the question being included in the programme, and the Hammersmith Branch followed up by resolving that any Federation statement on it or the disestablishment of the church was 'superfluous'. (Both questions were prominent in radical agitation.) Also about this time the Hammersmith Costermongers, threatened by the Board of Works with loss of their kerbstone markets, were loudly protesting, and Morris wrote in support of their claims in *Justice*, while telling Scheu, 'We, the SDF, have been helping them and gaining credit and recruits.' Yet he does not seem to have realised the importance of such fights for limited aims.[8] During this period (August–September) the policy-changes in the Federation led to a change in its name; it became the Socialist Democratic Federation.

Morris at the same time put off any consideration of Parliament as a setting for serious struggles by Hyndman's attitudes. Hyndman at moments was all for stepping-stones and palliatives as a way of rallying discontent; at others he poured scorn on them and saw himself as an irresistible agitator who could build up a strong enough workers' party to force the government to carry out his demands by threats and pressure. He had hopes of acting as a sort of Parnell of the proletarian cause, holding a balance of power and compelling the Liberals and Tories to toe his line.

The strain on the SDF executive increased, with Hyndman holding fast to editorship of *Justice* (financed by Morris) and defying the efforts of the others to bring the periodical under the control of the executive. The breaking-point came over the Edinburgh branch, which Scheu had been strenuously building up. A Scottish Land Restoration League had been formed in Glasgow after the Highland clearances which turned off the crofters to make room for stags and grouse; on its executive was John Bruce Glasier, a young architectural student. Scheu aimed at creating a Scottish Land and Labour League, affiliated to the SDF, and this excellent scheme was at once seen by Hyndman as a blow to his authority. He started intriguing to bring Scheu down. Morris in the midst of these conflicts felt his lack of secure theory. 'I feel myself weak as to the Science of Socialism on many points; I wish I knew German, as I see I must certainly learn it.' He added, 'Then, I want statistics terribly: you see I am but a poet and artist, good for nothing but sentiment.' Such self-deprecating remarks have been taken all too seriously. In fact he was doing his best to grapple with the Science of Socialism, both for the purposes of immediate politics and for the deepening of his sense of history.

He had been asked to lecture to the Edinburgh Philosophical Society, but they cancelled the request when they learned he meant to speak on socialism. 'Didn't see the connection between art and Socialism—Yah!' On 1 October the London *Echo* editorially put Morris in his place. 'Judging him by the company he keeps, he would disturb the foundations of Society in order that a higher artistic value may be given to our carpets. . . . We are a manufacturing nation. We produce in order that we may sell to other countries. . . . The first thing is to exist; then to exist on as much comfort as possible; then to provide ourselves with luxuries.' He replied that he had been acting as an entirely convinced socialist, in full sympathy with the SDF's aims. The *Echo* retorted: 'We believe that Mr. Morris contributes 1s a week towards enlightening the world as to the aims of the Social Democratic Federation.' The attempts went on for long to deride Morris as a poet who didn't understand what he was doing; a capitalist who inconsistently denounced other capitalists.

He was re-reading Blake, writing more socialist poems, some of which were set to music and sung at Art Evenings organised by the SDF. Later we find Bernard Shaw at such evenings playing piano duets with Annie Besant and Kathleen Ina; and Morris and Aveling gave readings. The Hammersmith branch had its own choir, singing at Kelmscott House and trained by Gustav Holst, who lived nearby. In December Morris went up to Scotland. He was scheduled to speak at Greenock and Edinburgh—*How We Live and How We Might Live*—but we have no record of the speeches being made; however Glasier tells us of an extempore talk in the Glasgow branch rooms and *Art and Labour* in St Andrew's Hall. Glasier speaks of his lion-like head, 'not only because of his shaggy mane, but because of the impress of strength of his whole front', his restless hands, his way of reciting the speech with moments of pause when he explained a point in a man-to-man sort of way. 'Our minds seemed to gain a new sense of sight, or a new way of seeing and understanding why we lived in the world.'

Morris had learned in Edinburgh through the League's chairman, the Rev. John Glasse, something of Hyndman's interference in events there.

After the Glasgow meeting (under the auspices of the Sunday Lecture Society) he went to the room over a warehouse in Gallowgate where the branch held meetings, and found the comrades badly disturbed by the London quarrel. Nettled by the secretary, Nairne, he is said by Glasier to have cried, 'To be quite frank, I do not know what Marx's theory of value is, and I'm damned if I want to know.' This is totally at variance with everything else he ever said, and with the whole tenor of his ways as a socialist, and may be taken as a distortion of the scene built up in Glasier's mind over the many years before he wrote his memories, wanting at all costs to make Morris out as a non-Marxist. Possibly Morris said something like, 'One doesn't need to know Marx's theory of value to know that our system is one of heartless exploitation.'[9]

On his return to London an anti-Hyndman group was formed: Morris, Eleanor, Aveling, Bax, Lane, Mainwaring, Robert Banner, and Clarke, joined by Mahon, who had come from Scotland with evidence of Hyndman's intrigues. On 16 December the first show of strength was made. A motion to expel Clarke was rejected by nine votes to seven. On Hyndman's side were Champion, Quelch, John Burns, James Murray and Burrows. On the 18th Morris reported to Janey: 'On Tuesday next we move confidence in Scheu, and the paper *Justice* is to be handed over to the executive under a joint editorship excluding Hyndman: if these are carried I don't see how the beggar can stay in the Federation. All this is foul work: yet it is a pleasure to be able to say what one thinks at last.'

Morris hated this sort of in-fighting among men who should have been able to find a common basis. The argument on Tuesday, the 23rd, 'came off to the full as damned as I expected. . . . It was a piece of degradation, only illumined by Scheu's really noble and skilful defence.' For the rest it was all 'mere backbiting, mixed with some melancholy and to me touching examples of faith'. However he expected to be out of the painful mess by Saturday, the 27th. He says that his group had decided to let Hyndman keep the name of the SDF 'and try if he can really make up a bogie of it to frighten the Government, which I really think is about all his scheme; and we will begin again quite clean-handed to try the more humdrum method of quiet propaganda'. On Friday he tried in a letter to Allingham to outline his view of the contradictions of the existing state of things, but showed a vastly oversimplified notion of what was going to happen in the near future. The Revolution was at hand. 'England will go first—will give the signal, though she is at present so backward. Germany with her 700,000 Socialists is pretty near ready,' and so on. (Soon afterwards Allingham spoke to Tennyson of Morris and his views; Tennyson cried, 'He's gone crazy!')

The Saturday meeting did bring about the final break. Hyndman had packed the room with his noisy adherents, while members of the LEL were kept outside. (A minor issue was the status of this affiliated body, the reality of the branches that Lane claimed, the money contribution it should make, and the question of its control. Hyndman may have had some valid points to make in this relation, and the question of the LEL must have strengthened his suspicions of Scheu's Scottish League.) Speakers not on the executive all took Hyndman's side. Morris wrote to Scheu his views of the speakers. Champion spoke well, but not to the point; Burrows disgracefully incited to personal violence against Mahon; Banner spoke badly and not to the point; Mainwaring began well, but rather broke down; Lane spoke cleverly, sensibly and damagingly; Aveling spoke briefly and well; Hyndman gave 'a crafty and effective speech, mostly lies in form, all lies in substance'. The vote gave the dissidents a majority of ten to eight. But then, instead of moving the ejection of Hyndman from the executive, Morris rose and read out the prepared resignation of the majority.

On the morning of the 27th Aveling and Morris called on Engels, at his suggestion, to discuss their future actions. They had in fact decided on what next to do, and even had ready the name for a proposed weekly paper, the *Commonweal*. Engels said that 'we were weak in *political* knowledge and journalistic skill', and suggested that the paper should start as a monthly; Morris reluctantly agreed. (In his letter to Scheu he seems to be apologising for having submitted to Engels and his advice. 'Though I don't intend to give way to Engels, his advice is valuable.' Then he explains circuitously that he does mean to give way. Probably he and Scheu were both keen on a weekly and Morris disliked to admit that he had been overborne. Scheu admired Engels, but he was an old Viennese leftist and anti-parliamentarian, and never seems to have been asked to visit Engels.) Two days later Engels wrote an account of the discussion to Bernstein.

Those who resigned were Aveling, Bax and Morris, the only honest men among the intellectuals—but men as unpractical (two poets and one philosopher) as you could possibly find. In addition, the better of the known workers. . . . They want to act in the London branches; they hope to win the majority and then let Hyndman carry on with his non-existent provincial branches. Their organ will be a little monthly journal. Finally, they will work on a modest scale, in proportion to their forces, and no longer act as though the English proletariat were bound to act as soon as a few intellectuals became converted to Socialism and sounded the call.

The morning after the split Morris had hired 'very humble quarters for the Socialist League', he told Georgie. He meant to inaugurate the new society next evening. (He was writing from Merton with a view of the winter garden and the workers spreading chintzes on the bleaching ground outside: 'something of a consolation'.) He was feeling unhappy at the dissensions and recalled how about a week before he had visited Edward Carpenter at Millthorpe, Chesterfield. 'I listened with longing heart to his account of his patch of ground, seven acres: he says that he and his fellow can almost live on it. . . . While I think, as in a vision, of a decent community as a refuge from our mean squabbles and corrupt society; but I am too old now, even if it were not dastardly to desert.' He wrote to Scheu, 'I will never tell you in my letters that I am in bad spirits even when I am. But in truth I am now in good fair working spirits, not very sanguine but quite determined and not at all dejected.'

Was Morris right in his tactics? Hyndman's whole career showed the correctness of the estimate of his character made by Morris and the others, and some sort of break certainly had to come. The question was whether Morris was right to secede, and we may well consider that he took the wrong step. Bax warned him against the resignations, but Morris was the one who stood out for that step. He tried to argue that 'the alternative would have been a general meeting, and after a month's squabble for the amusement of the rest of the world that cared to notice us, would have landed us first in a deadlock and ultimately where we are now'. But in fact if he and his friends had known how to handle the situation there would have been no need for a deadlock. We must remember that the rank and file of the SDF had no idea whatever of the conflicts that had been going on, and the haste with which Morris tackled things had the effect of repelling the honest members of the executive who still believed in Hyndman. The refusal to submit to a general meeting, where the anti-Hyndman group could have put their case and taken the rank and file into their confidence, seemed to make them the intriguers who were afraid of full daylight on their positions. Hyndman, a clever tactician, at once seized the advantage and issued a counter-statement calling a general meeting, opening the council's minutes to inspection, and expressing the view:

that in leaving the control of the Executive Council in the hands of a minority accused by them of not acting in accordance with the principles of Socialism, the majority have not fulfilled their duty to those who elected them to the Council.

Morris, in his fear and revulsion from prolonged personal disputes in public, had thus made the split as damaging as could be to the young socialist movement. However it must be added that Engels does not seem to have noticed this crucial point. To Bernstein he merely said that the majority had resigned from the executive 'because the whole Federation was really nothing but a swindle'; a remarkably unbalanced statement. And Eleanor wrote to her sister at the end of December, 'Oh dear! is not all this wearisome and stupid! But I suppose it must be gone through with. I comfort myself by recalling the long Schweitzer-Lassalle-Liebknecht quarrel in Germany, and the Brousse-Lafargue split in France. I suppose this kind of thing is inevitable in the beginning of any movement.' Paul Lafargue, however, noted the mistaken tactics; on 5 February 1885 he wrote to Engels from Paris: 'Everyone here is very surprised that after having the majority our friends have resigned instead of throwing out the minority.'

But whatever political errors of judgment Morris might have committed, these years, 1883–4, had plunged him right into the mid-stream of the young socialist movement and brought him both theoretically and practically up against the question of the working class. On the theoretical side he had grappled with *Capital* and mastered many essential points of Marxist historical method; on the practical side he had learned how to take his place in the direct struggles of the workers, to know and feel them as persons as well as abstractions in economic or artistic theory. One aspect of this latter turn was the interest that appeared this year in the actual factory conditions of work and in the ways in which those conditions could be bettered and finally made acceptable to a socialist world.[10]

13

The Socialist League

The new League, founded on 30 December 1884, had its offices at 27 Far-ringdon Street. Morris was still hoping to issue *Commonweal* as a weekly, but had to admit: 'paying for *Justice* has somewhat crippled me, and I shall have to find money for other expenses of the League at first. . . . Faulkner will give us £100 also which is something.' The paper was an eight-page news-sheet costing a penny; Morris was editor, but control was in the council's hands. The first issue appeared in early February. On 10 January the *Saturday Review* had jeered at Morris for leaving poetry which he understood for politics 'of which he knows nothing'; he denounced profit-mongers, but made not 'the least attempt to pour his capital into the lap of the Socialist Church, or to divide his profits weekly with the sons of toil who make them'. The middle classes, which in 1883 had ignored the socialists and in 1884 had at most discovered derisively that a few crackpots were using socialist terms, this year began to realise that something more serious was happening, and to feel that there might be a threat looming to their property. The Liberty and Property Defence League (called by Morris the Liberty to Plunder Defence League) claimed 400,000 members and affiliates this year and poured out leaflets and pamphlets. After briefly relaxing its grip, the trade depression had returned; and the working class had been stirred by radical agitation. Under the third Reform Act the franchise had been much extended. The Socialist League was only a week old when Joseph Chamberlain made the first of New Democracy speeches in Birmingham, with an effort to expand the reforms he had carried through in his hometown so as to embrace the nation. Morris, regarding this situation, felt that a new anti-socialist grouping of Liberals, Tory Democrats, and Radicals was about to appear; but he also foresaw a 'patriotic' front of Tories and diehard Whigs, which would produce 'a party not only reactionary, but of such portentious priggishness and stupidity, that it will be of great service to the cause of the people'. And he and Bax in a few months were saying that the word socialist would be taken up demagogically by the reactionaries to disguise the new mechanism of resistance, which Morris was to call the Policy of Force and the Policy of Fraud—a mixture of repression and (where necessary) concession to obstruct and confuse the struggle for socialism.

Morris's League had its Provisional Council, but no members. J. L. Mahon, the secretary, was reduced to writing to the SDF with a request for a list of their branch secretaries' addresses. However, in a few weeks several affiliations came about, from London branches, from the LEL, branches at Leeds and Oxford, and the Edinburgh Land and Labour League. Some council members wanted an immediate denunciation of Hyndman and the SDF rump; Scheu wanted a manifesto against 'the party of Jingoism and Boss-ship at Westminster'; Tom Maguire declared, 'A dignified silence just now counts for nothing against the Jesuitical activities of pronounced opponents.' But the council itself, apart from the dislike of Morris (and probably also of the Avelings) for a violent internal fight waged in the public eye, was in accord on the reasons for the split and the nature of the new policy. On 8 January Morris, in an interview with the *Daily News*, set out what was probably a viewpoint on which all would have agreed: the need to build a party of cadres to carry out intensive agitation and education among the masses. 'It goes without saying that a great proportion of these instructors and advisers would be working men.' Hyndman he blamed for arbitrary rule, for 'political opportunism tinctured with Jingoism'. Behind this line of policy there was probably counsel from Engels, who wrote later (January 1886) to Sorge: 'The whole movement here is a phantom, but if it is possible to draw into the Socialist League a kernel of people who have a good theoretical understanding, much will be gained for a genuine mass movement, which will not be long in coming.'

However, the statement issued by the seceders on 13 January had a much narrower perspective, a stronger purist note, a failure to work out an effective policy of alliances. Indeed all alliances were seen as weakening, as diluting the purity of revolutionary fervour; any connection with the parliamentary system was denounced as opportunism, as a sure way of corrupting or disarming the socialist fighter. Behind the outlook lay the belief that what was needed was the group issuing well worked-out instructions and propaganda, and that at any moment there would be a complete crisis of the system, leading to spontaneous and misery-provoked uprisings. For the next few years Morris was wholly in the grip of these ideas. The concept of educating the workers through struggle, through a succession of interlinked struggles aimed at raising their standards of living and giving them confidence, was nowhere present. He was helped in maintaining his positions through his close contact with many of the workers in the League, men like Lane, Kitz, Mainwaring. They had seen so much suffering and squalor in the East End, such callousness and hypocrisy in the middle and upper classes, that they had complete scepticism as to the possibility of using any existent governmental forms for socialist purposes; they saw the State as indelibly and unchangeably oppressive. Morris with his realisation of the implacable resistances in the exploiting classes to any transformations of society found his attitudes closely akin to theirs.

In the early days the League's provisional council adopted a draft constitution which we may take to have been mainly the work of the Avelings, with Engels's advice behind it.

1. Forming and helping other Socialist bodies to form a National and International Socialist Labour Party. 2. Striving to conquer political power by promoting the election of Socialists to Local Governments, School Boards, and other administrative bodies. 3. Helping Trade-Unionism, Co-operation, and every genuine movement for the good of the workers. 4. Promoting a scheme for the National and International Federation of Labour.

The preamble stated: 'While fully sympathising with and helping every effort of the wage-earners to win better conditions of life under the present system, the Socialist League aims at abolishing the Capitalist and Landlord class.' If the League had stuck to these principles, its history would have been very different. But in estimating the difficulties of men like Morris in holding fast to such conceptions we must understand how weak still was the working-class movement at the time. The members drawn to a socialist or revolutionary position were still mostly isolated individuals. Later Morris recalled how such men 'were there by dint of their special intelligence, or of their eccentricity; not as working-men simply'. He remembered how a friend had once said: 'We are too much a collection of oddities.' The situation was soon to change, but for the moment it was hard to strike socialist roots in the working-class organisations or in the heavily industrialised areas.

Morris himself was uneasily aware of his own weaknesses. He wrote to Joynes: 'I feel miserably uncomfortable at having any leadership put upon me, but I hope I shall be able to do whatever is necessary.' But who else was there? Bax was too unpractical and ready to quarrel; Aveling had his doubtful qualities and was very busy; Eleanor was too young and inexperienced; none of the available workers was suitable. The League had no chairman; Morris was treasurer (till Webb took over that role) and editor; the secretary, paid for full-time services, was an executive official rather than a leader. Morris found that he could not evade the task of checking decisions, advising branches, and trying to provide a steady coherent policy.

The purist line appeared already in the February statement by Mahon to the Leeds branch that if it joined the League it must reject 'the political opportunism and State Socialism of the SDF', which implied the abandonment of all local or parliamentary electioneering. The branch accepted this position. By 20 February three new branches were being started in London; at Hammersmith they were setting up a reading-room; some 200 people had come to a meeting at South Place; Aveling started a series of lectures; the LEL formally joined the League; Faulkner (Morris's loyal follower, who came with him into socialism as into all other things) brought over the radical association in Oxford. On the other hand the SDF had had a meeting of the unemployed, with some 5,000 attending. 'But yet no good: very likely it will lead to some relief works being started, but that won't bring people any nearer Socialism.' Morris went up with Aveling to talk at Oxford, speaking in a room in Hollywell, he told Georgie, 'just opposite where Janey used to live—Lord, how old I am!' The meeting ended with one of the opponents letting off a stink-bomb.

This month Khartoum had fallen and the League fought hard against the prevalent mood of Jingoism, distributing a thousand copies in London of a strongly worded leaflet:

Citizens, if you have any sense of justice, any manliness left in you, join us in our protest against the wicked and infamous act of brigandage now being perpetrated for the interest solely of the 'privileged' classes of this country; an act of brigandage led up to through the foulest stream of well-planned hypocrisy and fraud that has ever disgraced the foreign policy even of this commercial age....

Clear denunciation of imperialism rather than the winning of allies was the motive force here as in other lines of propaganda. On 24 February the Peace Society called a meeting, with Burt in the chair, but the speeches were weak and evasive, so that the League proposed a rider to the general resolution, stressing that the Sudanese war was aimed at extending the fields of capitalist exploitation and the Sudanese victory 'was a triumph of right over wrong won by a people struggling for freedom'. It was enthusiastically carried. When however it was put forward at later meetings, it met more opposition, though it was carried. (We see the change in Morris's sense of fellowship in that the rider describes the meeting as 'consisting mainly of working men'.)[1]

He was meeting much vilification. Last year in *Art and Socialism* he had warned those he was trying to convert that they must be ready for a painful time:

You will at least be mocked and laughed at by those whose mockery is a token of honour to an honest man; but you, I don't doubt it, will be looked on coldly by many excellent people, not *all* of whom will be quite stupid. You will run the risk of losing position, reputation, money, friends even: losses which are certainly pin-pricks to the serious martyrdom I have spoken of; but which none the less try the stuff a man is made of.

Now on 3 March he wrote to Scawen Blunt, 'As a Socialist I think I stink in people's nostrils.' One of the trials he had to bear was the fact his socialism was the final touch driving Janey away from him. Shaw tells us:

I knew that the sudden eruption into her temple of beauty, with its pre-Raphaelite priests, of the proletarian comrades who began to infest the premises as Morris's fellow-Socialists, must be horribly disagreeable to her . . . and as one of this ugly rag-tag-and-bobtail of Socialism I could not expect her to do more than bear my presence as best she might.

She had all the aloofness and snobbism of someone who had come up from the lowest working-class levels to a high genteel status, and her sense of superiority had been subtly strengthened by Rossetti. We find later that Morris, too loyal to speak of the antagonism publicly, in effect admitted it when he wrote to Scheu, 'I shall be by myself,' and 'There will be no one to object to you as I am alone with the girls at present'.

On 10 March, in a letter to an Oxford subscriber, he shows how he was relying on a sudden extreme crisis of capitalism to bring about the revolution: '. . . As one studies the question more on the one hand, and on the other sees more of the workers, the more one is disinclined (if one is honest and noticing) to fix any date or to hurry matters at all: because the economical march of events will be the thing which will help us in the long run. Preaching won't turn men into revolutionists; but men driven into revolutionary ideas may be educated to look to the right aims instead of mere folly—that's our real business in spite of any appearances to the contrary.' He had begun writing episodes of the poem that turned into *The Pilgrims of Hope*, and publishing them in *Commonweal*. A letter to May shows that he had no clear idea of the structure of the poem as it was to develop, but felt the need to find some theme for expressing his new experiences among the working class. On 21 March Cobden-Sanderson recorded that he 'thought my work too costly; book-binding should be "rough"; did not want to multiply the minor arts(!); went so far as to suggest that some machinery should be invented to bind books.' No doubt Cobden-Sanderson's idealistic approach to the solution of social problems made him particularly sharp; but his words bring out how far he was from any simple arts-and-crafts position.

We have seen how Morris, Bax, and the Avelings had begun the Socialist League with Engels's blessing. Paul Lafargue refers to them as '*nos amis*' and Eleanor as 'our people'. On 31 December she had said that the General had now promised them his aid. She took over the task of arranging the international contacts for the League. Morris wrote a letter, also signed by Aveling, to Wilhelm Liebknecht with a request for articles. Mahon was told to let Engels have four copies of the first issue of *Commonweal*, which he was to send to Liebknecht, Bebel, Sorge and Bernstein. Among the pamphlets that Morris and Bax hoped to publish was one by Engels, *Cheap Goods*. The second issue of *Commonweal* included an important essay of his, *England in 1845 and in 1885*, which analysed the movement of prosperity following the decline of Chartism with the growth of crisis as the world-monopoly was lost. (It has been noted that Engels at points writes much in the idiom of Morris: 'New markets are getting scarcer every day, so much so that even the negroes of the Congo are now to be forced into the civilisation attendant upon Manchester calicoes, Staffordshire pottery, and Birmingham hardware.') The essay had a deep effect on Morris, who in an address given in July, *The Depression of Trade*, took up many of its lines of argument. Indeed already in a talk given late in March he shows how impressed he had been.

Janey and the girls had been for some time at Bordighera in Italy. On 1 April Morris wrote with news. There had been Commune celebrations. 'Eleanor Aveling was the best I think.' He had been talking at Croydon and elsewhere and was feeling somewhat nervous at the project of moving a socialist rider to the resolution at a peace-meeting under the aegis of the redoubtable orator Bradlaugh. In fact when he spoke next day at the meeting against the Sudanese war, Bradlaugh cut him short after two minutes and there was a furious argument. Morris gave way, and his seconder had a few words; then Annie Besant opposed and Burns tried to fight his way to the platform. The rider was rejected. Three weeks later the League had its own meeting with Morris in the chair and Burns and Champion of the SDF among the speakers. Comrade Shaw, billed to speak, had objections to the resolutions and remarked: 'I am G. Bernard Shaw, of the Fabian Society, member of an individualist state, and therefore nobody's comrade.'

In April Morris was in Scotland. On the 24th he read passages of his own poetry in Glasgow, then gave lectures on the next two days, ar... on the 27th spoke at Chesterfield, with Carpenter as the chairman. He wrote to Georgie about the north country, ' 'tis the pick of all England for beauty, I fared to feel as if I must live there, say near Kirby Stephen, for a year or two before I die: even the building there is not bad; necessitous and rude, but looking like shelter and quiet.' In the train he had read Richard Jefferies's *After London* with its account of the breakdown of the existing civilisation, London turned into a poisonous swamp, and the countryside once more thick with forests. Here was a picture of the fall back into barbarism which had long haunted his imagination. 'Absurd hopes curled round my heart as I read it.' Carpenter tells of him arriving with the book, which delighted him 'with its prophecy of an utterly ruined and deserted London'. He read page after page out with glee 'that evening as we sat round the fire'. The centre of England is a vast lake and on it occur the adventures of the hero Felix Aquila. Here certainly is the source of Morris's romance *The Water of the Wondrous Isles*; indeed *After London* underlies all the later romances, stirring as it did the ideas and imagery which Morris had put into his early prose-tales, and providing a new and enlarged sphere of reference. It has passages about gardens and houses of simple wooden construction, and an idyllic folk, the Shepherds, which struck deep into Morris's predilections. The fact that Jefferies has no hope of any future beyond what he depicts did not matter; he himself could add the further interpretations—'absurd hopes'. He was clearly thinking of the book when on 13 May he wrote:

I am in low spirits about the prospects of our 'party', if I can dignify a little knot of men by such a word. Scheu is, I fear, leaving London again, which is a great disappointment to me, but he must get work where he can. . . . I have more faith than a grain of mustard seed in the future history of 'civilisation', which I *know* now is doomed to destruction, and probably before very long: what a joy it is to think of! and how often it consoles me to think of barbarism once more flooding the world, and real feelings and passions, however rudimentary, taking the place of our wretched hypocrisies. With this thought in my mind all the history of the past is lighted up and lives again to me. I used really to despair once because I thought what the idiots of our day call progress would go on perfecting itself: happily I know now that all that will have a sudden check—sudden in appearance I mean— 'as in the days of Noë'.

We must recall that Marx did not see any necessary progress into socialism; the future could also hold a new barbarism. But he was not using the latter term in the positive sense that Morris lends it. He was thinking rather of a massive use of state power and ideological deception to prevent the socialist resolution as capitalism reached the limits of its contradictions. On 27 May Morris wrote to Georgie about the depressing effect of incursions into the East End; he had been in Stepney: 'some twenty persons in a little room as dirty as convenient and stinking a good deal. It took the fire out of my fine periods, I can tell you: it is a great drawback that I can't *talk* to them roughly and unaffectedly. Also I would like to know what amount of real feeling underlies their bombastic revolutionary talk when they get to that. I don't seem to have got at them yet—you see this great class gulf lies between us.' His lecture was: *Work, as It Is and as It Might Be*. Amid all his socialist activities he did not forget SPAB. On 30 May he spoke against the demolition of churches at York; and on 4 June gave the opening speech as chairman at the annual meeting.[2]

The SDF was spreading the story that the League was composed of middle-class men with no real interest in the workers, not socialists at all but anarchists and revolutionists, all at loggerheads with each other and only held together by Morris. Scheu, Lane, Bax and others were always ready for hostilities with the SDF, though Morris did his best to prevent such conflicts, and Burns and Williams co-operated with the League on issues like free speech. In the provinces the London quarrels had little reverbera-tion, except in Glasgow. In June the League had new premises in Farringdon Road. In *The Architect*, in accord with his view that the new life should be closely linked with an historical sense that preserved continuity in all the vital aspects of art, Morris suggested that churches should neither be left to decay nor turned to commercial purposes; they should 'be used for parish purposes, schools, or something of that kind'. On 11 June the League had an evening of entertainment for which he wrote a *Prologue*, in which he pleaded that the struggle for the new life of fellowship and freedom should penetrate every moment of their life. 'Let the cause cling About the book we read, the song we sing, Cleave to our cup and hover o'er our plate, And by our bed at morn and even wait. Let the sun shine upon it; let the night Weave happy tales of our fulfilled delight! The child we cherish and the love we love, Let these our hearts to deeper daring move; Let deedful life be sweet and death no dread, For us, the last men risen from the dead!' The art of the socialist is then one in which every value, every aspect of form and content, has been transformed by a new concrete concept of human unity. On the 28th he lectured both in the morning and evening at Northampton.

On 5 July the League held its first annual conference. The membership amounted to only a couple of hundred. At the meeting the draft constitution drawn up early in the year was defeated: which meant the rejection of the line advocated by the Avelings (and Engels) and the triumph of Morris's purism. In *Commonweal* Morris set out his objection to parliamentarian legislation—'the doctor trying to heal his patient by attacking the symptoms and letting the cause of his disease alone'—and all forms of 'palliation' which confused the issue. In his Manifesto he set out at length the Marxist view of class struggle, the contradictions between monopoly ownership and increasingly socialised forms of productions, the effects in degrading the working class and spoiling their lives: the terrible brutality among them 'which is indeed but the reflection of the cynical selfishness found among the well-to-do classes, a brutality as hideous as the other'. Commodity production was to be seen in 'the crowd of criminals who are as much manufacturers of our commercial system as the cheap and nasty wares which are made at once for the consumption and the enslavement of the poor'. He then went into the changes which would come about under socialism, the social and moral changes which would accompany the common ownership of production and distribution. He attacked, as limited or distorting panaceas, Co-operation ('competitive co-operation for profit'), Land Nationalisation by itself, or State Socialism.

On 11 July he spoke on the Hopes of Civilisation, at Manchester; next day, at Oldham, on the Depression of Trade. On the 13th he spoke at an Oldham open-air meeting in defence of free speech—the Manchester Socialist Union, then being harassed by the local police, supported him. Next day he spoke extempore at Desborough. At Oldham he declared, 'I have lived through and noted the most degrading epoch of public opinion that ever happened in England, and have seen the triumphant rule of the swindler in private and public life, the rule of hypocrisy and so-called respectability, begin to shake and totter.' He expanded his thesis on the lines of Engels's *Commonweal* essay and Bax's on Imperialism versus Socialism, which dealt with colonial wars, and their relation to the new concentration of capital. In a lecture given a few months later he developed his argument more cogently, pointing out that commercial wars were no new thing, but that there was a new quality, a new intensity, about the way in which they were now being fought; and he stressed that the inevitable result of this phase was a clash between the conquering imperialist powers as the available areas for exploitation lessened. The imperialists were risking 'wars which may or indeed must in the long run embroil us with nations who have huge armies and who no more lack the "resources of civilisation" than ourselves.' Then Britain would no longer be crushing 'barbarous countries', but would be faced by rivals with equal destructive powers.

In the Notes that Morris and Bax added to the Manifesto there is an important passage; they are forecasting the second stage of socialism (communism) when commodity production and the forms of distribution connected with it no longer exist:

Finally, we look forward to the time when any definite exchange will have entirely ceased to exist; just as it never existed in that primitive communism which preceded Civilisation.

The enemy will say, 'This is retrogression not progress'; to which we answer, All progress, every distinctive stage of progress involves a backward as well as a forward movement; the new development returns to a point which represents the older principle elevated to a higher plane; the old principle reappears transformed, purified, made stronger, and ready to advance on the fuller life it has gained through its seeming death. . . . The progress of all life must be not on the straight line, but on the spiral.

Behind this passage there lies no doubt many discussions with Bax, and probably others both Bax and Morris had with Engels. The terms of the statement strongly suggest the hand and mind of Morris. Here for the first time in Marxist writing is the clear statement of movement by spiral and not by the simple straight line. There was a sketchy reference to the idea in Engels's *Socialism Utopian and Scientific* (with a version in French by Paul Lafargue in 1880), but not in the clear form of the Manifesto. Not till the *Dialectic of Nature* was published in 1925 was there a definite statement, though again brief and schematic, of the spiral of development by Engels in print. True, Lenin independently arrived at the idea in his *Materialism and Empiriocriticism* of 1908, but it is to Morris in the Manifesto that we must look for the first effective enunciation of the principle of spiral development and its applications. Why Morris so enthusiastically and firmly took hold of the idea is plain. It enabled him at last to solve the conflict in his mind between Barbarism and Civilisation; he saw now that the values and qualities he so strongly liked in the barbarous world were those that would be regained on a new and more stable level through socialism, with their elements of violence and disequilibrium eliminated. The door was now opened to his later romances and indeed to the whole distinctive contribution he made to Marxist thought.

On 19 July Morris must have enjoyed the Revolutionists' Excursion to Epping Forest, sponsored by the International Club, at which he spoke in the open air. On the 26th he spoke again in the open air, at Victoria Park, for the League. Tom Mann was there:

He was a picture on an open air platform. The day was fine, the branches of the tree under which he was speaking spread far over the speaker. Getting him well in view, the thought came, and has always recurred when I think of that first sight of Morris—'Bluff King Hal'. I did not give careful attention to what he was saying, for I was chiefly concerned to get the picture of him in my mind, and then to watch the faces of the audience to see how they were impressed.

Passers-by on the fringe remarked, 'Poverty, eh, he looks all right, don't he?' But the workers applauded him heartily.[3]

On 5 August he gave a speech dealing with the recent revelations by W. T. Stead about prostitution, especially of children, in London. He also probably spoke on the theme in a Hyde Park demonstration on the 22nd. And he gave other speeches this month at Stratford, Hoxton, and Hammersmith. In September he spoke again in Manchester as well as in London. For some time there had been trouble in London with the police. On 9 May they had attacked the International Club in Stephen's Mews; they broke windows, destroyed or carried off various pieces of property, and arrested members of the club. A Defence Committee was formed with Morris as treasurer. The police began arresting socialists for 'obstruction'. Kitz was arrested in August at Stratford, but the case was dismissed; and the centre of persecution became Dod Street in Limehouse, where radicals and religious speakers had long been used to speak. The League and the SDF collaborated, and the Defence Committee was turned into a Vigilance Committee backed by the Fabians and the strong East London United Radical Club. On 20 September, Sunday, there was a large crowd addressed by Hyndman and a radical at one end of the street, and by Mahon and Kitz at the other. After the meeting had been declared closed and the crowd was dispersing, the police launched a violent attack, making arrests. Next day eight men were brought up at the Thames Police Court before a magistrate Saunders. Aveling and Eleanor gave evidence on behalf of the accused, and stated that they had spoken and would continue speaking in the street. The police especially pressed the case against Lyons, and at least one of them was later shown to have told lies. Lyons was sentenced to two months and the others given the choice of a forty-shilling fine or a month in jail. The spectators in court, who included Morris, cried *Shame* and 'a rush of police was made' at them. Aveling states that they 'commenced an assault upon all and sundry', and particularly on Eleanor. Morris, 'remonstrating at the hustling and thumping, became at once the chief thumpee. There has rarely been seen anything more brutal than the way in which two or three able-bodied young men fell upon the author of what one of the newspapers called the "Paradise League".' When Morris threatened to summons the police, he was himself arrested. Two hours later he was placed at the bar on the charge of disorderly conduct. A policeman declared that he had struck him on the chest and broken the strap of his helmet; Morris denied that he had raised his hands and said that he was prepared to bring a charge of assault against the man. The *Daily News* reported:

Mr Saunders: What are you?
Prisoner: I am an artist and a literary man, I believe pretty well known throughout Europe.
Mr Saunders: I suppose you did not intend to do this?
Prisoner: I never struck him at all.
Mr Saunders: Well, I will let you go.
Prisoner: But I have not done anything.
Mr Saunders: Well, you can stay if you like.
Prisoner: I don't want to stay.

Next Sunday, thirty to fifty thousand people turned up in Dod Street, and Aveling, Hyndman, Shaw, Burns and radicals spoke. The police kept away. The Sunday following Morris spoke at a meeting that welcomed Jack Williams of the SDF on his release. There was considerable publicity about his appearance in court, and he detested such matters. However he used the occasion to write letters, when the press attacked him, in support of Lyons. Shaw describes him as 'desperately uncomfortable at a police court, going bail for some of the comrades. I found him rubbing it all off by reading *The Three Musketeers* for the hundredth time or so.' He adds: 'He had nothing of the bully in him in spite of his pathological temper, and when physical courage came under discussion said: "I am a funkster; but I have one good blow in me." ' The police persecutions went on for some time, in the provinces as in London, and Morris all the while carried on as bailsman, witness, speaker, commenter in *Commonweal*.[4]

In October he spoke to the Working Men's College and the Marylebone branch of the League, probably also at Hammersmith and Peckham. On the 16th he wrote to Scheu. He had just got back from Preston, where he'd addressed the socialists. 'The people there are a little better than last year; but very wooden. I think of making some arrangement for a stumping tour of the North in early spring next—make a fortnight of it.' He wasn't sure if he could go to Victoria Park next Sunday. 'I can't get rid of my sciatica and now I have a cold to boot.' On the 26th his gout was so bad that he couldn't put foot to ground. 'I am wheeled to the dining-room & back here on the sofa.' There had been a good meeting in Hyde Park. On the 31st he told Georgie, 'Till yesterday it has been a month of wheeling me.' He was afraid of having acquired lazy habits, which included novel-reading. 'I don't think it comes from my knocking about to meetings and the like, but rather from incaution as to diet, which I really must look after. You see, having joined a movement, I must do what I can while I last, that is a matter of duty. Besides, in spite of all the self-denying ordinances of us semi-anarchists, I grieve to have to say that some sort of leadership is required, and that in our section I unfortunately supply that want; it seems I was missed last Monday, and stupid quarrels about nothing took place, which it was thought I could have stopped. All this work I have pulled upon my own head, and though in detail much of it is repulsive to the last degree, I still hold that I did not do so without due consideration.' He already foresaw the League's collapse. 'On the morrow of the League breaking up I and some half-dozen must directly begin a new organisation.' But he had faith in the stability of the movement and he felt only 'hopeless loathing' for the existing society. Ideas about the future were needed, though in the details he did not find any great confidence.

For some time he had been working on a version of the *Odyssey*, the heroic story of a man who has lost his home and seeks to find his way through countless obstacles. In October *Commonweal* announced that they would publish an article by Engels on the second part of *Capital*; but what appeared in November was a demolition of a pirated and bad version of *Capital* published in *To-Day*. On 20 November Morris had in the *Daily News* a letter attacking the attempt by the Dons to demolish 'the few specimens of ancient town architecture which they have not yet had time to destroy, such, for example, as the little plaster houses in front of Trinity College. . . .' We see that he wanted humble vernacular buildings to be saved as well as the large edifices. On 27 November he wrote to Jenny from Rottingdean where he had been playing cribbage, draughts, and backgammon with Janey, 'Now I am going for another hobble up and down in the sun while it lasts.' On 3 December, still at the seaside, he was carrying on with the *Odyssey* in bad weather. The wind had blown down London smoke to spoil what sunlight had appeared. 'Had oysters to supper last night, and all the delicacies of the season.' He had already forgotten his remarks about diet. On 26 December he wrote to Ellis: 'As to the British working man, to say truth— he could hardly be faster asleep than he is now. . . . I sometimes fear he will die asleep, however hard the times grow, like people caught frozen.' The counterpart of a baseless belief in the revolution waiting round the corner was the tendency to underestimate the true potential of the present.

Despite all his socialist work Morris managed to keep in touch with the firm, its problems and programme. This year A. L. Lazarus bought Littler's printworks near Merton Abbey, where he began printing Paisley silks and art-nouveau designs. Between 1885 and 1887 Morris made the *Woodpecker* and *Forest* tapestries, the latter for Luke Ionides with flowers by Dearle and lion, hare, fox, peacock by Webb. After 1885 most designs for chintzes and wallpapers were done by Dearle and May Morris, who had thoroughly absorbed Morris's methods.

November and December had seen increasingly bad relations with the SDF. That organisation had put two candidates, taking advantage of the new Reform Act. Williams and Fielding stood for Hampstead and Kennington; they polled 27 and 32 votes respectively. Worse, it leaked out that they had been supported by Tory Gold and that Hyndman had called on Chamberlain with threats of more candidates opposing the Liberals unless he promised to support the Eight Hours Bill. Scheu was now convinced that Hyndman was a Tory or Liberal-Reactionary agent; Bax drafted a resolution (at which Morris vainly protested) repudiating 'the tactics of the disreputable clique concerned on the recent nefarious proceedings'. Otherwise Morris kept comments out of *Commonweal*. But SDF members who thought Hyndman guilty only of an error in tactics resented the SL's attitude at a moment when they were being generally laughed at and abused. There were indeed seceders among the SDF, but few of them joined the League. In the elections the League had issued a leaflet by Morris (reused whenever there were elections) advising workers not to vote at all.

If we compare the account written by Morris to Carruthers of these events with that by Engels to Sorge and Bernstein it seems certain that they had been closely discussing things. In one of Engels's letters there is even the phrase: 'as Morris says'.[5]

On 2 February 1886 he replied to a questionnaire by the *Pall Mall Gazette* as to his favourite books. His list was composed of the Bible, Homer, Hesiod, the *Edda*, *Beowulf*, the *Kalevala*, *Shahnemeh* and *Mahabharata*, folktales (headed by Grimm and the Norse tales), Irish and Welsh traditional poems, Herodotus, Plato, Aeschylus, Sophocles, Aristophanes, Theocritus, Lucretius, Catullus, Plutarch's *Lives*, *Heimskringla*, Icelandic Sagas, the Anglo-Saxon Chronicle, Dante, Chaucer, *Piers Plowman*, the *Nibelungennot*, Danish and Scotch-English Border ballads, Omar Khayyam, other Arab and Persian poetry, *Renard the Fox*, the best rhymed romances, *Morte d'Arthur*, *The Thousand and One Nights*, Boccaccio, the *Mabinogion*, Shakespeare, Blake ('the part of him which a mortal can understand'), Coleridge, Shelley, Keats, *The Pilgrim's Progress*, several Defoe works, Scott, Dumas, Hugo (the novels), Dickens, Borrow, More's *Utopia*, Ruskin, Carlyle, and Grimm's *Teutonic Mythology*. Many of these are works or authors we should expect; some are surprises; for example, Plato and the Greeks. He adds that he hates Milton for his cold classicism and Puritanism. Scott and Dickens he specially praised.

On 8 February a group of Tory Free Traders called a meeting in Trafalgar Square, and the SDF called a counter-demonstration of the unemployed. Both bodies met in the Square, and the SDF speakers (who included Hyndman, Burns, Williams), with Sparling of the SL, gave wild speeches of which Morris and Engels did not approve. At the end the socialists led the crowd up Pall Mall for a second gathering in Hyde Park. Gentlemen in the clubs jeered; the unemployed replied by throwing stones and breaking windows. There was much damage and looting, from which Morris's Oxford Street shop escaped. There was much panic, with rumours of the East End marching through the fog to the West, and shops put up shutters. The

Mansion House Fund for the unemployed rose with remarkable speed, especially as there were unemployed demonstrations in Norwich, Birmingham and elsewhere, with riots in Leicester. Charity organisations multiplied. The socialist leaders thought they had really sparked off 'the first skirmish of the revolution', as Morris put it, and for some weeks the tension continued. On 21 February the police viciously attacked a huge demonstration called by the SDF. *The Times* reported that the police were 'compelled to draw their batons and use them without mercy on all who encountered them'.

A garbled account of a speech by Morris appeared in the *Daily News* on 11 February and attributed to him such statements as that the SDF was a dangerous body. Morris at once replied with a complete repudiation of the report. Above all he would not have made such remarks 'when members of the Social Democratic Federation are threatened with prosecution for accidents that accompanied their performance of a duty which I myself have frequently to perform'. The day before he had written to Glasse that he regarded the affair 'as an incident of the Revolution', though he disapproved of a policy of riot:

all the more as I feel pretty certain that Socialists will one day have to fight seriously because though it is quite true that if labour could organise itself properly the enemy could not even dream of resisting, yet that organisation could not possibly keep pace with the spread of discontent which will accompany the break-up of the old system.

He wrote a reassuring letter to the worried BJ, which ended, 'I wish I was not so damned old. If I were but twenty years younger! But then you know there would be the Female complication somewhere. Best as it is after all.' Twenty years back would have been 1866 when he was in the first pangs of the break with Janey and struggling to found the firm. Does he mean that his domestic situation then was too difficult to have made possible his turn to socialism, or is he merely thinking in a vague way that if he were in his early thirties again he would be unable to accept his present state of sexual privation? To Georgie he unburdened himself of his political anxieties: 'I have often thought we should be overtaken by the course of events—overtaken unprepared I mean. It will happen again and again; and some of us will cut sorry figures in the confusion.' To Ellis he wrote about his work on the *Odyssey*: a difficult task because of the meaningful simplicity of the original.

In March he set out in *Commonweal* his view of the riots. He saw them as a flicker of revolution and called even more strongly for socialist education as the only way of preparing for a serious crisis. 'We *must* hope that a strong party can be so educated.' Palliative measures might well result from the riots; also it was possible that the socialists would be suppressed, 'practically at least, if not formally'. However, 'Opinion which must be suppressed is Revolutionary . . . the Socialist Party will become a political force when all these things happen.' His respect for Marx was shown by his objections when Annie Besant in an article called him 'prolix and pedantic'. She agreed for the footnote in question to be cut out. On 18 March he met the anarchist Kropotkin at the meeting commemorating the Commune. 'I like him very much; had a long talk with him yesterday evening at a gathering of the SDF' (24 March). On the 20th Engels wrote to the Lafargues that fortunately the League was sleeping for the moment:

Our good Bax and Morris, torn by the desire to do something (if they knew but what!) are restrained only by the circumstance that there is absolutely nothing to do. Nevertheless they have far more truck with the anarchists than is desirable. Their fête on the 18th was held in common with the latter, and Kropotkin spoke at it—rubbish so I am told.

The years 1885–7 saw much agitation for Irish Home Rule. The SL, while supporting the radicals on the issue, insisted that the only true hope lay in socialism with an international perspective. In January 1886 its leaflet supported independence but made the main point: 'You must be free from RENT!' An April leaflet argued that independence alone would bring no freedom to the people. This month Morris thought the question of enough importance to warrant a visit to Ireland, making a night-crossing and arriving at Dublin on 9 April. He spoke that day on the Aims of Art, and next day on the Political Outlook in the afternoon, with the opening speech on a debate about Socialism in the evening. There was nearly a riot when someone turned out the gas-lights. On the 13th he spoke on Socialism for the Dublin branch of the League. He liked the cosy shabbiness of Dublin and had a pleasant day in the Wicklow mountains. On the 14th he arrived back in London and next day wrote that he was going to Leeds and Bradford. On the boat he translated some fifty lines of Homer. At Bradford on the 18th he spoke on 'Socialism', and next day at Leeds on the 'Present and Future of the Working Classes' (a revision of his lecture on the 'Dawn of a New Epoch'). On the 24th, from Kelmscott House, he wrote to Glasier on the question of the family under socialism (raised by Bax). He said that one thing was clear: 'In opposition to the present bourgeois view, we hold that children are *persons*, not *property*, and so have the right to claim all the advantages which the community provides for every citizen.' For his part, 'being a male man, I naturally think more of the female man than I do of my own sex.' But child-bearing made women dependent at times, and 'it would be a poor economy setting women to do men's work (as unluckily they often do now) or vice versa'. But there should be an absolute equality of condition between the sexes. On the 29th Engels wrote to Liebknecht that both Bax and Morris were strongly under the influence of the anarchists. 'These men must pass through this *in corpore vile*'—that is, must live through the experience and come out the other end. 'They will get out of it somehow, but it is certainly fortunate that these children's ailments are passing before the masses come into the movement. But so far they are obstinately refusing to come in.' They won't be brought in by sermons.[6]

In May, Morris was rather exhausted. 'Rebellion is getting quite fashionable now; I shall join the Quakers.' He dislikes contention, and 'a very little self-deception would have landed' him among the moderates. 'But self-deception it would have been.' He wrote in *Commonweal* that Ireland would probably have 'to go through the dismal road of peasant proprietorship before they get to anything like Socialism.' This month the periodical turned into a weekly. An editorial by Morris and Bax, looking back at Hyndman's tactics, declared that 'the rudest and most unsuccessful attempts at revolution' were better than 'periods of quietude' inculcating in the workers 'a dull contentment'. On the 16th and 17th he spoke three times at Birmingham, and probably went on to speak at Leeds. On the 21st he wrote to Janey from Kelmscott House about a dream of the previous night:

We were all together in the High-street near the end of River Court Road, and watching shooting stars which were red & green & yellow like the lights on the new Hammersmith bridge, when all at once one fell to earth in the middle of the road and we all bolted for fear it should burst like a shell; taking it rather coldly though: why the deuce should one dream such nonsense? Mother seems well.

This is the one case where he tells us of an actual dream of his. The coloured stars seem derived from the lights on the bridge, which would have wavered in the water. The fear-element may derive from his feeling that arrests and persecutions were likely soon to come the way of resolute socialists; the lightburst, connected with water, would then probably have links with imagery of what is called the birth-trauma. Note the immediate transition to his mother; he goes on to ask Jenny to write to her granny on her birthday, Monday next. If this conjecture is correct, we see perhaps a link of his own explosive outbursts with birth-traumatic experience (as indeed on general grounds we would assume), with the revolution felt as the supreme explosion, the final demolition of the obstacles to the Earthly Paradise.

Letters to Jenny give us much of the information about his June movements. On the 2nd he wrote that he had had somehow to find West Ham Police Court to pay the fines for Leaguers arrested at Stratford (£5 17s.). 'I am busy lecturing all this week, and have plenty of regrets for Kelmscott and your dear company; but what will you: it is part of the day's work.' On the 2nd he gave two speeches in Hyde Park. On the 3rd Binning resigned. He stated that meetings of the council were disorderly; the League lacked discipline or serious organisation, and was dominated by a London faction. He feared it would 'degenerate into a mere Quixotic debating society for the discussion of philosophical fads. I care not how angelic may be the theories of Anarchists or Anarchist-Communists. I contend that the real solid basis of the Revolutionary movement is the economic question'—that is, taking part in the day-to-day struggle for wages, conditions, and so on. On the 5th, Morris wrote, ' 'Tis all meeting and lecture, lecture and meeting, with a little writing interspersed.' He had been to the Grange, for the birthday of Georgie's daughter Margaret and found her 'ever so old, 20 actually, just think'. And he had been watching the Hammersmith and Merton gardens. On the 8th had been the SPAB annual conference; and on the 11th he spoke on Whigs, Democrats, and Socialists at a Fabian Conference on political action. On the 15th he said that the Saturday before last he had spoken at Stratford at 'the disputed place', but the police ignored him, then the next Saturday Mowbray was arrested. 'We are not going to give it up however yet, but shall try to get the Radicals to go into it heartily.' On Saturday he himself had spoken at Hyde Park. 'I was quite nervous about it, I don't know why; because when I was speaking at Stratford I was not nervous at all, though I expected the Police to attack us.' On Sunday the League had had its annual conference, sitting all day. 'May and I getting home about 11.30 p.m.' As he wasn't a delegate, he didn't have to speak. The main subject in dispute was the constitution with its decision against parliamentary action; but those who wanted to alter it lost the day. Nineteen branches were represented, and of the five who did not send delegates, only one (Stratford) seems to have been inactive. No figures of membership were published, but in April Engels had told Bebel that at best the SDF and the SL did not have more than 2,000 paying members between them, nor their papers 5,000 readers. The League probably had half the readers and some six to seven hundred members. On the day after the conference the Leaguers had an outing to Box Hill and Dorking. 'I regret to state that in the town generally we were taken for a detachment of the Salvation Army.' But 'I am rather enjoying myself to-day after the last two days' excitement, in being quietly at home on a nice fresh day, though I am obliged to work very hard.'

But a few days later he was in Scotland. On the 22nd he spoke in Arbroath, then next day at Edinburgh, and after that at Glasgow, going on to Dundee, and speaking on the 27th and 28th at Glasgow again and at Bridgeton. He was pleased to find Arbroath 'in fact Fairport of "The Antiquary" '. In July in *Commonweal* Morris again analysed the Irish question after Gladstone's defeat in the election. After attacking the 'shuffling and intriguing self-seekers' who stood for parliament, and the voters who thought they'd fulfilled the duties of citizenship by casting a vote, he prophesied a fresh attempt to divide the Irish into moderates and irreconcilables 'like the familiar demon in the old fable, cut by his unhappy employer into two unmanageable devils'. The League strongly opposed the new coercions brought in by the Tories, while still holding that independence was irrelevant to the key issues of the class struggle. In *Commonweal* for 17 July Morris reviewed Shaw's *Cashel Byron's Profession*. Praising Shaw for his power of indicting 'our sham society', he saw the heroine as a mere 'embodiment of the author's view of life', while the other characters were alive. The scenes were depicted clearly and accurately, 'more after the manner of a painter than a dramatic writer', but they were each isolated, 'lacking the power that accumulation gives'; the story rather left off than reached an end. But the contemporary novel in general failed to attain what Scott and Dickens now and then touched: 'the unity and completeness of a great drama.'

This month the question of freedom for open-air meetings again came up. Mainwaring and Williams were arrested and committed for trial. 'When we all thought,' said Mainwaring, 'that a long term of imprisonment would be the result, he [Morris] volunteered to speak in the interval between the committal and trial; and when reminded of the general impression that imprisonment would be the result, he simply said: "Well, it will be another experience, and we must not allow fear of consequences to interfere with our duty." '

Next week he took his stand in the debated Bell Street, where speakers had carried on unchecked for years. A chief inspector made his way through the crowd and told Morris to stop. Morris refused, and had his name and address taken. He then remarked that 'the middle and upper classes were enabled to live in luxury and idleness on the poverty and degradation of the workers. There was only one way in which this state of things could be altered—society must be turned downside up.' He appealed to his listeners to prepare for the great social revolution, and was then summoned for obstruction. He and Mainwaring came up in court on the same day. The magistrate said that Morris as a gentleman would at once see, when it was pointed out to him, that such meetings were a nuisance and would desist from taking part in them. So he fined him a shilling. Williams and Mainwaring were each fined £20 and bound over with a surety to keep the peace for twelve months; on refusing to pay the fine they were jailed for two months.

After the Bell Street decision the Marylebone branch merely moved their meetings to a new site. Morris was busy throughout August:

I had a brisk day yesterday, though tell your mother, no policeman's hand touched my sacred collar. I went from the Grange to Walham Green where we had a good little meeting attentive and peaceable, back then to Grange & dinner and then away Eastward Ho to Victoria Park rather sulky at having to turn out so soon after dinner. Though Victoria Park is rather a pretty place with water (dirty though) and lots of trees. Had a good meeting there also spoke for nearly an hour altogether in a place made noisy by other meetings near, also a band not far off. Whereby I was somewhat hoarse for our evening lecture which was Shaw's not mine, and very good. . . . The garden looks nice and smells so now the N wind no longer blows across—not Araby the blest, but Brickfields the t'othered. I have been hard at work all day long at an article. Did another & lots of Homer all Saturday.

He was at last getting on fast with the *Odyssey*. On 18 August Engels complained to Bebel that there were as many sects as heads; the SDF had at least a programme and a certain discipline, but no mass-support. The League was passing through a crisis. Morris

has fallen headlong over the phrase 'revolution' and become a victim of the anarchists. Bax is very talented and understands something—but after the fashion of philosophers has concocted his own form of socialism which he takes for the true Marxist theory and does a lot of damage with it. However, this is an infantile disease in his case and will pass, it is only a pity that this process is being gone through in public. Aveling is forced to work so hard for his daily bread that he is not able to do much studying; he is the only one I meet regularly.

It follows that he was seeing the other two now and then.

Morris was doing his best to patch up the break between the SDF and the SL. He approached the SDF with the proposal for a joint meeting, to welcome Williams back on his release from prison, to be held on 29 August in Trafalgar Square. Hyndman replied that he would always be pleased to have Morris as a speaker at SDF meetings—he made several attempts to draw Morris away from the League—but he refused any co-operation with the League, making a number of charges; that Leaguers had tried to break up SDF branches in Hull, Croydon, Hackney, and now Clerkenwell, in the 'meanest and dirtiest' ways; that Mahon, now at Leeds, and Aveling had continually vilified SDF members in the 'American and other foreign Press'. He made no mention of the collaborations between men of the two bodies, as when Williams and Mainwaring both spoke at Bell Street, and so on. Morris thought the charges 'preposterously petty'. He asked, 'Why will people quarrel when they have a serious end in view?' He saw Hyndman 'stiff and stately, playing the big man' in 'a Wolf and Lamb business'. In Glasgow also the conflicts between the two groups went on. With this sort of thing going on, it was understandable that little thought had been given to the whole question of working in the trade unions and of finding out what were their problems and what the conditions under which their members worked. Bax had written *An Address to Trade Unions*, which consisted mainly of an historical account and a brief exposition of socialism. Binning wrote a more direct and useful pamphlet in August this year; but only *The Factory Hell* by the Avelings was likely to come home to the workers.[7]

After the breakdown of the attempts to work with Hyndman, Morris wrote: 'I went to Merton yesterday and worked very hard at patterns and found it amusing.' He was now in the ninth book of the *Odyssey*. 'How jolly it would be to be in a little cottage in the deep country going on with that, and long walks interspersed—in the autumn country, which after all I love as much as the spring.' After four days at Kelmscott he felt 'sulky at being dragged away' on 7 September. He was still much concerned with police matters, young Tom Wardle being committed for trial; the League was hoping for an alliance with the Temperance speakers. 'I think we shall beat the police in the long run after all.' But he still had time to study the autumnal garden. On the 17th he spoke 'against the Party of compromise' at a meeting called by the Fabians at which socialists representing various London societies met at Anderton's Hotel to discuss the formation of a British Socialist Party. On the 26th and 27th he spoke at Manchester; on the 28th at Sheffield. By the end of the month he was in Edinburgh to give an address. He told Georgie that he had done 110 lines of Homer and was reading versions of Russian Epic Songs, while the smoke hung low over the city. This month a long strike of miners began in Lanarkshire and Northumberland. The League's standard strike leaflet argued that strikes were 'a waste of time and energy', bringing suffering on the men and their families and useless 'as a means of permanently bettering' conditions; the strikers should stop 'a hopeless fight' and join the socialists. Such propositions show how sadly the League had fallen out of the real struggle in its efforts to maintain a purist attitude. They also help to explain the irritable comment by Engels on 13 September to Laura Lafargue: 'Morris is a settled sentimental Socialist; he would be easily managed if one saw him regularly a couple of times a week, but who has the time to do it and if you drop him for a month, he is sure to lose himself again. And is he worth all the trouble even if one had the time?' We see again that Engels was seeing him now and then though not a couple of times a week.

In October Morris spoke on the 11th at Norwich and on the 18th at Reading, as well as at least eight times in London. On the 17th he expounded his views on sex and marriage to Faulkner, who had written to him on the subject (recently broached in the *Christian Socialist* and *Commonweal*). He considered that in a free and equal society all persons would be free to unite or part as they were impelled; all remnants of the attitudes that treated people as things would be ended. 'But I should hope that in most cases friendship would go along with desire, and would outlive it, and the couple would still remain together, but always as free people. In short artificial bolstering up of natural human relations is what I object to, though I admit that to make some ceremony or adornment of them is natural & human also.' He seems here to be thinking of his own situation. He considers that in a socialist world 'public opinion would leave people free; though once more I believe that it would without violence and in some way that I cannot foresee, take care of the decencies; that it would adorn the subject in such a way as its knowledge of the great art of living would bid it.' Thus he is far from a nihilistic-anarchist position which, by its egoist and atomistic notion of people, sees freedom as simply a matter of endless predatory satisfactions on the part of the individual, with no sense of the fuller unions needed for the flowering of human personality. Morris says that he feels new centres of being will emerge, in which the basis of union and separation will be different from anything we know—even though we may in a way intuit them through all that is most truly and deeply human in us. How far he had developed from the prevailing dualism of body and spirit, which appears equally in conventional Victorian morality or the Swinburnean defiances, may be read in his remarks on mating:

Copulation is worse than beastly unless it takes place as the outcome of natural desires and kindliness on both sides: so taking place there is even something sacred about it in spite of the grotesquery of the act, as was well felt by the early peoples in their phallic worship. But further man has not been contented with leaving the matter there, mere animal on one side, inexplicably mysterious on the other; but has adorned the act variously as he has done the other grotesque act of eating and drinking, and in my opinion he will always do so. Still if he were to leave off doing so, I don't think one ought to be shocked; there will still remain the decent animalism plus the human kindliness: that would be infinitely better than the present system of venal prostitution which is the meaning of our marriage system on its legal side; though, as in other matters, in order to prevent us stinking out of existence, real society asserts itself in the teeth of authority by forming genuine unions of passion and affection.

By 'real society' he means the living element of concrete production, with its manifold co-operative and uniting aspects, which carries on all the while inside the alienating and abstracting forces of division, exploitation, de-humanising property values, money. Here he shows the sort of thinking that pervades Marx's early manuscripts of 1844.

On the 29th he wrote to Jenny that on Tuesday (2 November) he was off to Lancaster, with Preston for the next day. He spoke on 'Socialism, the End and th Means', and the 'Dawn of a New Epoch'. 'Back again on Thursday and if I possibly can I will come down on Friday evening or Saturday morning, but must be in town again in time for the meeting on Monday.' As he wrote:

A beautiful bright morning & quite warm to-day. I feel almost inclined to walk to Merton, but am afraid I can't spare the time. I have finished the 10th Book of Odyssey now & shall certainly do 12 books before the year is out. It really would be rather convenient for me to have a little gout in order to do some literary work.

I am going to start getting my *Pilgrims of Hope* in order, so as to make a book of it:
I shall add and alter a good deal though.

Pilgrims had been appearing at intervals in *Commonweal* since 1885; he had
begun it without any clear idea and gone on packing into it elements from
his own experience in the socialist struggle, at the same time trying to re-
interpret that experience in terms of a worker awakening to the realities of
his world. An anachronistic element crept in through his drawing his material
from the struggles of the 1880s and yet making the events work up to the
outbreak of the Paris Commune. At the same time he could not help bringing
in the basic triadic pattern which we continually find in his expressions. The
hero of the poem is estranged from his wife, yet they seek to keep up
appearances before others. 'But indeed as a wedded couple we shrank from
the eyes of men. As we dwelt together and pondered on the days that come
not again.' The wife has a lover, and the trio go to take part in the Commune,
where the hero survives but the other two are killed. We thus have the
pattern of the very earliest poem by Morris that we know, transposed into a
realistic situation. He meant, as we learn above, to revise and augment the
poem, but he never returned to it. The poem then was very hastily written;
but the strong emotion that went to its making gives it a vitality all its own
and makes it the most important poem of contemporary narrative in
England during the nineteenth century (after Byron's *Don Juan*). For all its
roughnesses it succeeds in reviving the emotion at discovering the cause of
socialism and human unity, and in communicating much of the deep impulse
carried on through the wearying day-to-day struggle. It is thus the first
imaginative work in English which truly breaks through the class barriers
into a new level of human realisation. It antedates the work of Gorky and
other pioneers of socialist realism.

On 1 November he wrote to the *Pall Mall Gazette* against the proposal
for a Professorship of English Literature. Here he expressed the scepticism
he always felt about literary criticism. He said that he would not object if the
aim was to teach literary history or philology; it was criticism he distrusted.
He suggested a chair of medieval archaeology instead of the proposed one.
This month a subcommittee of the League was set up to attempt to settle
the disagreement on the question of parliament: Mahon and Lane against,
and Bax and Binning for, participation in matters connected with parliamentary action. No common viewpoint was reached, and the attitude
towards the agitation for the Eight Hours Day was also divided. By late 1866

the conflicts of the two factions on the council went on all the while. In November *A Dream of John Ball* began to appear in *Commonweal*. Morris is said to have suggested to a Leaguer the writing of a serial story on Wat Tyler. The man refused on the grounds of a lack of the epic faculty, and Morris (according to Sparling) shouted, 'Epic faculty be hanged for a yarn! Confound it, man, you've only got to tell a story.' A few days later he brought along the first instalment of *John Ball*. About this time the lecture-room at Hammersmith was offered to speakers of many varying outlooks. Yeats, living at Bedford Park with his family, often came to the coach-house on Sunday evenings and was one of those invited to stay on for supper. He mentions having met there Walter Crane and Emery Walker very often, Shaw and Cockerell less constantly, and once or twice Hyndman and Kropotkin. 'There, too, one always met certain more or less educated workmen, rough of speech and manner, with a conviction to meet every turn.' Of Morris he said, 'You saw him producing everywhere organisation and beauty, seeming almost in the one instant helpless and triumphant; and people loved him as children are loved.' Morris was 'the one perfectly happy and fortunate poet of modern times. His intellect, unexhausted by specula-tion of casuistry, was wholly at the service of hand and eye, and whatever he pleased he did with an unheard of ease and simplicity, and if style and vocabulary were at times monotonous, he could not have made them otherwise without ceasing to be himself.' Once at supper he dispraised the houses he had decorated: 'Do you suppose I like that kind of house: I would like a house like a big barn, where one ate on one corner, cooked in another corner, and in the fourth received one's friends.' On 25 November, May, writing to Shaw, remarked: 'The "damned bourgeois branch", as Leaguers have been pleased to call the Hammersmith Branch, is going to have a party on Jan. 1st.'[8]

On 1 December Morris wrote to Glasier that it might be necessary for socialists to go into Parliament on the verge of a revolution—so as to capture the army or shake their confidence in the legality of their position. 'At present it is not worth while even thinking of that, and our sole business is to make Socialists. I really feel sickened at the idea of all the intrigue and degradation of concession which would be necessary to us as a parliamentary party, nor do I see any necessity for a revolutionary party doing any "dirty work" at all. . . .' But he asked about the lock-out and strike in Dundee. 'Can any of our friends do anything there?' On the 12th he spoke on 'Early England' at Hammersmith, and wrote to the *Pall Mall Gazette* about a bad distortion of his remarks as reported. The *Gazette* had made him say of the Germanic tribes invading Britain that 'the civilisation they spread was commercial, and their chief characteristic therefore was vulgarity'. What he had said was that the Romans brought in 'the great tax-gathering machine called civilisation', whereas the society that begot *Beowulf* 'breathed the very spirit of courageous freedom'. On the 25th *Commonweal* published a resolution of the League's council protesting against the British government's brutal actions against the struggle of the Irish peasant for 'a larger share of the product of his labour'. Any actions, legal or illegal, by the Irish people against English oppression were perfectly justified.

If we consider the position that Morris had now reached, we see that he had thoroughly assimilated Marx's concept of surplus value and of the contradictions at work inside bourgeois society. He did not merely repeat generalisations. In *Dawn of a New Epoch* (1885) he carried his analysis into the distribution of surplus value among the different branches of capital and touched on the question of ground-rent and landed property. In *Misery and the Way Out* he dealt with variations in the value of labour power. Following Marx and Engels, he tried to unbare the mechanism of capitalist production and the inner contradictions taking the form of crises and man-made famines. Both in his addresses and his *Commonweal* articles we can see the effect of definitions and formulations studied in *Capital*, the *Communist Manifesto*, and other works by Marx or Engels. He kept on trying to extend and deepen his grasp of Marx's central ideas. He was indeed one of the few Marxists who have understood, as Marx did, that in political economy we deal not only with forces outside men's control—the exploiting side of production, in which alienation and reification are concentrated—but also with the very life process of men, in which what is produced and re-produced is not merely commodities, but is men themselves and nature.

He had grasped deeply the dialectical nature of development, the spiral form and the leap into new levels. For his old scheme of barbarism into civilisation into barbarism he had substituted the scheme of barbarism into civilisation, with a resulting climax of conflict and contradiction in which there could be a lapse into a new form of barbarism or a resolution on a higher level. In that resolution what was positive in the earlier barbarous phase was regained, but in a stable way made possible by the intervening advances in production and social organisation. He now totally rejected the negative aspects of barbarism, and had gone far to get rid of certain mechanistic views and ideas of spontaneity. That is, he no longer believed that the point of breakdown and renewal would come about of its own accord, as the result of social and economic forces operating without the intervention of the human will; and he no longer trusted in a spontaneous or automatic release of new potentialities through the breakdown.

Not that he has wholly got rid of the mechanistic and spontaneous elements in his thoughts and emotions. He still feels that capitalism is going to grind to a halt or to a point of unworkable confusion and the result will be a mass-uprising of some kind. But he realises that a crucial role is going to be played by the extent to which socialist ideas have been disseminated among the masses and gained a grip upon them. But because of his incorrect estimate of the length of life still stretching ahead for capitalism, and because of the lack of any forms of militant organisation among the workers at all adequate to the coming tasks, he is driven back on the notion of education divorced from day-to-day participation in every aspect of the social struggle; and he finds himself at the mercy of certain anarchist or semi-anarchist ideas and attitudes, even though he rejects anarchism on a political level and realises the need for certain forms of persisting organisation. To understand Morris's position we cannot stress too much the backwardness of organised labour in the early 1880s. For instance Tom Mann was the first British worker since the days of Benbow, Smith, and Morrison (1832-4) to make socialism the inspiration of militant trade unionism. He soon clashed with Hyndman:

He criticised me severely for my championship of the trade unions. What were these precious unions: By whom were they led? By the most stodgy-brained, dull-witted, and slow-going time-servers in the country. To place reliance upon these, or to go out of our way to conciliate them, would be entirely wrong. . . . The meeting endorsed Hyndman's views.

John Burns in *Justice*, 3 September 1887, insisted that the only class-war recognised by the skilled workers was that between themselves and the labourers. We see how hard it was for Morris, despite his strong sympathy for striking miners or Irish peasants, to move to any broad strategies of the class-struggle. He could not but feel a strong sense of fellowship with such workers as Kitz. 'Like most of our East-Enders he is somewhat tinged with anarchism and perhaps one may say destructivism: but I like him very much. I called on the poor chap at the place where he lived, and it fairly gave me the horrors to see how wretchedly off he was; so it isn't much to wonder at that he takes the line he does.'

However, he had thoroughly absorbed from Engels and Bax, as part of the spiral concept of development, the idea that socialism would go through two phases, in the first of which, despite the common ownership of the means of production, the state and its machinery would survive, and in the second of which the state would have withered away and only the element of free association remain. He accepted the need for the first phase, but kept his enthusiasm for the second one (communism). He felt much affinity with Kropotkin, whom he invited to Kelmscott House. Kropotkin's anarchism put little emphasis on violence, direct action, destruction; he was concerned primarily with what had held men together throughout history and would flower in a society without compulsions. He never gave the least support to the anarchists troubling Morris in the League; and indeed in an unsectarian way he favoured any movement breaking down class-society. All sincere socialists, he said, agreed that the expropriation of capital must occur in the coming revolution. 'Then every struggle that prepares this expropriation should be unanimously upheld by all the socialist groups, to whatever nuances they belong.' Morris seems to have taken from him the idea that under communism there would be a federal system based both on locality and on work.

But however he rejected anarchism as a political guide for the revolution and the first phase of socialism, his purism, much strengthened by revulsion from Hyndman's opportunism, swung him over to a position in which he could not effectively combat the anarchists like Kitz in the League. The latter more and more brought in dissension and disruption, and he had no leadership to give which might have developed the basis of unity through coherent action.[9]

14

Climax

In early January 1887 the League tried to get the SDF and the Radical clubs to join in a demonstration for Irish independence and the abolition of land-lordism. The SDF declined on the grounds that agitation on behalf of English workers would better help the Irish. On the first day of the year Morris spoke at Hammersmith on the 'Origins of Ornamental Art', and the next day he again delivered his talk on 'Early England', to the Fabians, and took the chair in the evening for a lecture by Annie Besant. Thus he began a year even yet busier than the last, about which we know a great deal because of the diary he kept for a large part of it. He remarked to Jenny that it 'may one day be published as a kind of view of the Socialist movement seen from the inside, Jonah's view of the whale, you know'. We are enabled to see his continual round of lectures, open-air meetings, committees and discussions. The record opens on 25 January:

I went down to lecture at Merton Abbey last Sunday: the little room was pretty full of men, mostly of the labourer class: anything attacking the upper classes directly moved their enthusiasm; of their discontent there could be no doubt, or the sincerity of their class hatred: they have been very badly off this winter, and there is little to wonder at in their discontent; but with few exceptions they have not yet learned what socialism means.

Next day he was at the South Kensington Museum, looking at late fabrics from Egypt that showed the transition to the Byzantine style. 'The contrast between the bald ugliness of the classical pieces and the great beauty of the Byzantine was a pleasing thing to me, who so loathe all classical art and literature.' In the evening he spoke at the Hammersmith Radical Club against the Highland evictions of crofters. So he goes on till mid-June, with a strenuous period in the North: two speeches at Glasgow on 3 April, one at Dundee next day, then a lecture on 'Monopoly' at Edinburgh on the 5th, on 'Socialism and the Labour Struggle' at Hamilton on the 7th, on the 'Ways and Means to Socialism' at Paisley next day, lectures on the two following days again at Glasgow. On the 11th he spoke three times for the Northumberland Miners, at Blythe, Horton, and Ryton Willows. Two days later he was speaking in London against the Irish Coercion Bill once more.

His notes show how eagerly and thoroughly he looked at the places and at their workers, their way of life and their forms of response to the socialist call. But his purist attitudes deterred him from seeking the points at which the League and the workers could unite in organised action, so that all concerned might deepen their understanding of socialism through struggle and in the process form a coherent and powerful party. Instead he wanted to find workers who had arrived somehow at a complete grasp of socialism and all that it entailed; and as he found very few such, he continually felt depressed.

They seemed to me a very discouraging set of men, but perhaps can be got at somehow: the frightful ignorance and want of impressibility of the average English workman floors me at times. [Hammersmith]

The sum of it all is that the men at present listen respectfully to Socialism, but are perfectly supine and not inclined to move except along the lines of radicalism and trades unionism. [Chiswick]

This audience . . . quite mixed, from labourers in their Sunday lounge to 'respectable' people coming from Church: the latter inclined to grin: the working men listening attentively trying to understand, but mostly failing to do so. [Open-air meeting]

Amongst the woeful hovels that make up the worse (& newer part of Mitcham . . . I doubt if most of them understood anything I said. . . . I wonder if people will remember in times to come to what a depth of degradation the ordinary English workman has been reduced; I felt very downcast. . . .

March 20th. The annual meeting of our Hammersmith Branch came off: a dead failure, as all our meetings except open-air ones have been lately. I lectured in the Chiswick Club Hall and had a scanty audience and a dull. It was a new lecture [*Monopoly*], and good, though I say it, and I really did my best; but they hung on my hands as heavy as lead.

He was now often finding himself in the rough-and-tumble of things, becoming a known figure. A small boy swinging on an iron gate at Hammersmith called, 'Have a ride—Morris.' Then someone in a covered greengrocer's cart hailed him as Socialist and Morris. At Victoria Park a Cockney shouted after him, 'Shakespeare—yah!' At Coatbridge a cashier from the ironworks told the steel-workers that they had been listening to 'one of the leading men of literature and art to-day', and Morris replied, 'After all, my friend, I wish to remind you that it is just the sort of way that Diogenes and Christ, and for all we know, Homer and your own Blind Harry the Minstrel, used to get their audiences.' A cheapjack tried to sell linoleum and wallpaper, 'the newest and best designs on the market, fit to make the homes of the working-class vie with the palaces of princes', while a Salvation Army band blared and a drunken Irishman wanted to put Morris right on Home Rule. 'All this we did by star and furnace-light, which was strange and even dreadful.'

More important, in Northumberland for the first time he came in contact with the organised workers engaged in a fierce struggle. At Hamilton, Morris had arrived after the miners had given in, and the branch of the League formed there during the strike was in a bad way. Everyone was depressed and the lecture had 'rather a chilly feeling over all'. But he does not seem to have drawn any lessons from the big progress made in the period of militancy, and the lack of response that followed the defeat. Then came his experiences in the Northumbrian collieries. He was met at Newcastle on 10 April, Sunday, by Mahon and Donald, and they happened to meet Hyndman, 'who I suspect was not over-pleased to see me, as the SDF have been playing a rather mean game there', trying to bag the miners instead of keeping to the agreement that neither it nor the SL should use the situation for sectional advantage. Next morning they set off for the mines. While Mahon went on with the preparations, Morris and Donald stayed at a miner's cottage in Seghill. Morris was impressed by his host, who had lost one eye and had the other damaged in a mine accident, and who was a kindly intelligent man speaking with 'that queer Northumbrian smack'. Though the houses were woeful things and the whole district 'just a miserable backyard to the collieries', the house where he stayed, and the others he passed, were 'as clean and neat as a country cottage'.

They went on to Blyth by train, and there Morris climbed on to a trolley and made an extempore speech to the crowd who greeted them. He spoke for forty minutes, then they walked on through the dreary villages, '& that terrible waste of endless back-yard', with a strip of bright blue sea on their left. After some three miles they met a contingent with band and banner, and marched on, now some 2,000 strong. A six-mile march brought them to the meeting-field, with thousands coming in from all the mining villages around. They spoke from a wagon: Mahon, Morris, Hyndman, then Donald. Morris found before him a new kind of audience, 'orderly & good-tempered', but strong and sure in their responses. They threatened to put the reporters out unless they promised to put down everything in the speeches. When a reporter remonstrated, the miners' spokesman told him they had had experience of the bogus reports in the papers. The reporters agreed to give a full and accurate report. 'But only in the case of the *Newcastle Chronicle* was it fairly kept.' Morris noted the large number of women present, who were warmly involved. The front ranks of the miners squatted on the ground, so that the others could see and hear better; and Morris, much moved, had the scene indelibly imprinted on his mind—the desolate earth, the intent faces, 'the bright blue sea forming a strange border to the misery of the land'.

The speaker's plank on the wagon was 'rather perilous'. Morris wanted to avoid it and come round to the front, but some of the men at the side shouted, 'If yon man does na stand on the top we canna hear him!' So Morris got up on to the plank and someone below provided a notice-board on a pole for him to lean on. 'It was very inspiriting to speak to such a crowd of eager & serious persons. I did pretty well and didn't stumble at all.' He made a passionate attack on the conditions of life and work among the workers. 'That was not the life of men. That was the life of machines. That was the way in which the capitalists regarded them. . . . If the present labour system were to continue no theologian or parson need trouble himself to invent another hell. That would be perfectly good enough for all purposes. (Hear, hear, and laughter.)' He stressed the need for men to rebel against such a situation. 'War was the condition of their lives as against their masters (Cheers). War was the condition of the masters' lives both as against the men, and against everyone of their own class also. What he preached to them was what the Socialists always had to preach. Not war—peace.' When the workers were everywhere organised and called for socialism, the masters might give in. But 'if there was such a thing as a general strike, he thought it possible that masters of society would attack them violently—he meant with hot shot, cold steel, and the rest of it'. But he believed that in such a crisis the soldiers and sailors, faced with the resolute will of the people, 'would not dare to obey their masters. They would cry, "Give us work: let us all be honest men like yourselves".' Then he urged his audience to realise that nothing short of socialism would be victory. But at the same time he declared, 'And yet every skirmish in the road and every attack on the position of the masters brought them nearer. They must go on until all the workers of the world were united in goodwill and peace upon earth. (Loud cheers).'

Back in London Morris got the sl council to agree to a Hyde Park meeting in support of the miners, but he also found 'one of the usual silly squabbles about nothing'. Next Sunday, speaking at Beadon Road, he 'couldn't help contrasting our Cockneys much to their disadvantage with the northerners'. Sadly, the League was being rent by ever more hopeless discords and confusions at the moment when deep and widespread struggles were beginning among the workers.

On 22 January *A Dream of John Ball* had reached its final instalment in *Commonweal*, and Morris was securely launched on the final phase of his career as an imaginative writer. In the Peasants' Revolt of 1381 he saw the culmination of the brotherly and communal elements in the medieval world, inherited from tribal days and never destroyed by all the feudal oppressions and hierarchical divisions. *A Dream* may be criticised for oversimplification. In fact the social conflict expressed by the Revolt was very complex; there was no such fight between the peasants and the lords as that which is described, and so on. But we are dealing with a dream-parable, not with an historical novel, and for his purposes Morris is justified in concentrating on what he feels to be the key-aspect of the uprising, that fraternal element which has kept on reasserting itself through history at moments of crucial upheaval, but which at any given moment is entangled with a host of partial and limited viewpoints and aims. The tale richly and warmly succeeds in what it sets out to do: to express those aspects of brotherly association to which Morris deeply responded in medieval society, and to set these aspects in a dream-perspective which is also a dialectical vision of human struggle and growth. Earlier we saw the great importance to Morris of the dream-focus with its release of deeply-buried symbolism and its shifting patterns that brought out links of thought and emotion that were clouded in the everyday consciousness. Here he brilliantly succeeds in re-creating this dream-method of his in terms of his new socialist world-view. What gives the final validity to the vision, vindicating fully the aesthetic system that Morris has built up, is the concluding section, where John Ball and Morris himself talk in the church, each man a dream-figment to the other, and yet, taken together, embodying a complete grasp of the essential forces in history. Morris's effort to explain to Ball what has happened to men in the five

centuries following the Revolt, and Ball's effort to reach up out of the
medieval categories of thought into the bourgeois situation, create a strange
and powerful criss-crossing of ideas and reactions, which evoke richly the
sense of what has concretely happened to men and continues to happen and
will continue, until all that is deepest in Ball's medieval sense of man and in
Morris's struggle to re-create a sense of human wholeness in the night of
darkest alienation have united in a final assault on the citadels of division.
How fully Morris had realised the nature of Marxist dialectics is brought
out by the passage in which he says:

I ... pondered how men fight and lose the battle, and the thing that they fought
for comes about in spite of their defeat, and when it comes turns out to be not what
they meant, and other men have to fight for what they meant under another name.

He must have been discussing the spirals and ironies of history with Engels.
It can hardly be an accident that in the latter's *Ludwig Feuerback*, published
later this year, there is a passage on the relation between the aims of individuals and the total movement in which they play a part, which concludes:

the ends of the actions are intended, but the results which actually follow from
these actions are not intended; or when they do seem to correspond to the end
intended, they ultimately have consequences quite other than those intended.[1]

In the dialogue of Ball and the Guest, Morris may well have been recalling
Southey's *Colloquies* (possibly read at Oxford) in which there is the long
argument of More and Montesinos, a medieval man and an exponent of
nineteenth-century ideas. But whereas in the *Colloquies* we merely have an
abstract argument between two men of different viewpoints, in *John Ball* we
meet the concrete dialectics of history, each man speaking out of the heart
of a totally different situation, with all the anguish of the human condition
implicated in the desperate attempt to understand one another.

Morris had been working again at Marx. On 15 February he wrote in his
diary: 'Tuesday to Bax at Croydon where we did our first article on Marx:
or rather he did it: I don't think I shall ever make an economist even of the
most elementary kind: but I am glad of the opportunity this gives me of
hammering some Marx into myself.' His deprecatory comments on himself
as an economist must not be taken to refer to his keen and constant interest
in the dialectic of historical materialism in Marx, his thorough assimilation
of its principles.

During this year May and Henry Halliday Sparling, who had been working on *Commonweal* as co-editor, fell in love and wanted to get married. On 14 April Morris tells Jenny: 'May has gone with Sparling to exhibit that young man to your Granny.' And Janey wrote to Rosalind Howard in June: 'May's love affair has not progressed since you saw the lovers. They are as much in love as ever, & no nearer marriage as far as one can see. May rightly insists on employment being found by her fiancé before she marries, and I strongly uphold her.' This month the first volume of his *Odyssey* appeared.

Meanwhile the troubles in the League went on growing. Lane had read in April at a council meeting his extremely leftist *Anti-Statist, Communist Manifesto*; but the vote went against printing it. It declared for the abolition of the state in every form and variety, for atheism, for free love; and it forecast a bloody revolution, though rejecting anarchist propaganda-by-deed (theft, arson, dynamite) together with all forms of political and industrial struggle. Trade Unions were 'little better than Benefit Societies', and the only course open to socialists was educational propaganda. Though Morris voted against the Manifesto, he failed to see that Lane's positions were in many ways the logical result of his own anti-parliamentarianism; they were a caricature of it, but nevertheless a warning of what his purism could lead to. Supporters of Lane's ideas included Faulkner, Kitz, and Slaughter of Norwich. Morris in desperation tried to form a centre-group able to reconcile the disputants; Lane and Kitz did not consider themselves anarchists, but their ideas could not but breed anarchism. On the side favouring parliamentary action were young Donald, an intellectual from Edinburgh, Bax (who failed to make any theoretical contribution to the argument), and Aveling (whose reputation was fast growing more tarnished, unknown to Engels). Bax's branch, Croydon, tabled a motion at the annual general conference, amending the constitution of the League to include the sentence: 'Its objects shall be sought to be obtained by every available means, Parliamentary or otherwise.' Events like the strikes of the miners had made many Leaguers more inclined to political activity in industrial matters, but most of the leftists were ready to unite against any acceptance of Parliament. The question of Parliament was quite theoretical, since no socialist had the remotest chance of getting near Westminster, while the attitude to such matters as the Eight Hours movement and the Unemployed urgently needed clarification. Yet it was the parliamentary issue which seemed the main point of principle, and Morris replied to the Croydon resolution by having a counter one sent in by Hammersmith. His resolution was meant to be conciliatory, asking for the issue to be deferred for a year; but it spoiled this intention by going out of its way to state that the main work of the League 'must always be steadily educating the people in the principles of Socialism'. In reply to some doubts on the part of Glasse he wrote to him on 23 May that when the movement was strong enough he believed that it would put members into Parliament, but 'as rebels, and not as members of the governing body prepared by passing palliative measures to keep "Society" alive. But I fear that many of them will be drawn into that error by the corrupting influence of a body professedly hostile to Socialism, & therefore I dread the parliamentary period (clearly a long way ahead at present) of the progress of the party: and I think it will be necessary always to keep alive a body of Socialists of principle who will refuse responsibility for the action of the parliamentary portion. . . .' He thought the League could constitute such a body of principle.

He was contemplating the need to resign from the League if he were defeated. He gave up seeking tactics of conciliation and sided strongly with the anti-parliamentarians. If the parliamentarians won, he meant to walk out and 'invite you [Glasier] & some few honest men to form a new organisation'. Mahon, a parliamentarian, who had been seeking to build a North of England Socialist Federation, now brought in a third resolution, doubtless drafted with Engels's aid, which attempted to set out in as unsectarian a way as possible the policy of working in all and any organisations with the aim of permeating them with socialist ideas; of taking part in all contests, parliamentary, municipal, and the like; of organising the people into a Socialist Labour Party. 'While we share the common aspirations of the wage-earners to win better terms from capitalists, we steadily insist that their complete economical emancipation can only be effected by transforming the society of to-day into a co-operative commonwealth.' The Croydon branch withdrew its resolution in favour of that of Mahon. It was unfortunate however that Mahon's resolution was brought in abruptly at the last moment.

At the Conference Morris withdrew the Hammersmith resolution when it failed to win unanimous support. An anti-parliamentary resolution from Glasgow, unsupported by Morris, was rejected. Mahon then pressed on with his resolution. Morris and Faulkner made a sharply anti-parliamentary amendment, and after long discussion won the day by seventeen votes to eleven. Their opponents then refused to stand for the council.

Next day they held a private meeting and organised a definite faction within the League, with treasurer and secretaries. They decided to join the Labour Emancipation League (affiliated to the SL) and use it as their base.

Engels reported the situation in a somewhat different form to Sorge: 'Our people now want to organise the provinces, and after three or four months to call an extraordinary congress to overthrow the decision.' No doubt he knew from Mahon and other sources the new possibilities opening up for socialist groups in the mining and other industrial areas. In fact Mahon, Donald, and others had been given the job of building things up in North England and Scotland.

The aims of the faction were excellent; but their methods could only appear to Morris and his friends as underhand and disloyal. Further, by walking out of the council they handed it over to the leftists or anarchists. They thus ensured the breakdown of the League. Morris had a considerable basis for his complaint on 2 June to Glasier: 'If they are right, time will show it and they will be able to have their way without breaking up the League.' The faction also set about implementing their own policy in a hasty way that laid it indeed open to the dangers which Morris had prophesied:

not least the dangers of personal corruption, either by political ambition or by the vanity bred in the individual leaders who each felt that they themselves alone understood the correct line of advance for the movement, and that its future was bound up with their own influence. The years between 1887 and 1893 were to provide a melancholy series of illustration of the personal degeneration or political confusion of individuals not subject to the support, correction, and discipline of a *party*—John Burns, H. H. Champion, Aveling—but no more forcible illustration can be found than in the actions of that ceaseless propagandist, J. L. Mahon. (Edward Thompson)

Morris felt the need to set out his own position on the debated matters more fully than he had yet done. In July, after giving at least six open-air speeches, he delivered on the 31st at Hammersmith *The Policy of Abstention*. He argued at length that parliament as a democratic institution was the great capitalist myth, and that unless any representative of the workers went there purely as a rebel he would be corrupted or used to hand out 'what concessions may be necessary for the ruling class to make in order that the slavery of the workers may last on'. He condemned everything whatever that tended to mask the irreconcilable opposition of capitalist and worker, or to confuse it, weakening the popular force and giving a new lease of life to reaction. He suggested that it might be useful to create a truly popular centre outside Parliament, 'call it the labour parliament if you will', which could have its own deliberations and send out its own decrees to the people, using the weapons of the strike, co-operation, and the boycott, and all the while educating people in the administration of their own affairs.

All this while he had the firm, the family, and his literary work also to take up much of his attention. A letter from Ellis (who had been staying at Kelmscott) to Bell Scott on 17 July suggests that Janey was feeling miserable and showing it:

If I thought his opinions on the relations of the sexes in old days were the same as he professes to hold now—why then, you might believe anything—as it is I am quite inclined to forget old histories—whatever fault if any attached to the poor lady in question I fear she has had and has ample room and cause for repentance and regret and has rather a sad time of it now all things considered.

In August Janey wrote to Rosalind to ask if she might go up to Naworth. 'I want so much to have a little bright life before the dreary winter sets in.' At the moment

May is away at Kelmscott Manor alone learning cooking & how to live on a few shillings a week. She is bent on marrying without waiting till her future husband gets employment. I have said & done all I can to dissuade her, but she is a fool, and persists.

According to Blunt, Morris disapproved of the marriage. 'He had a strong, affectionate heart and had centred his home affections on his two children.' Blunt was not a good interpreter of Morris's emotions; we have no evidence as to how Morris acted with regard to May and Sparling. Perhaps he did not like to oppose overtly Janey's obvious dislike of a son-in-law with no income or prospects. He certainly must have gained over these years much comfort from his daughters' interest in politics, and must have been proud of May's activities. Earlier this year, at the Hyde Park demonstration against the Irish Coercion Bill, Blunt made a speech, noting that 'there was a second platform for Morris's section, and I saw May Morris on their cart like a French revolutionist going to execution'. With Morris's strong views on the right of everyone to live their own life, he can hardly have stood in the way of May's marriage, even if he did not think Sparling likely to make a good husband.

On 25 August he wrote that he had finished the *Odyssey*. 'And I'm not over-inclined for my morning preachment at Walham Green, but go I must, as also to Victoria Park in the afternoon. I had a sort of dastardly hope that it might rain. Mind you, I don't pretend that I don't like it in some way or other, when I am on my legs.' In September he was at Kelmscott and felt once more the sense of deep creative joy. 'I had three very good days at Kelmscott: once or twice I had that delightful quickening of perception by which everything gets emphasised and brightened, and the commonest landscape looks lovely; anxieties and worries, though remembered, yet no weight on one's spirits—Heaven in short. It comes not very commonly even in one's younger and brighter days, and doesn't quite leave one even in times of combat.' He set to work on a small play or interlude to be acted at Farringdon Road for the benefit of *Commonweal*. Also, he was beginning to realise that his real opponents in the movement were not the pro-parliament faction in the League, but the Fabians, led by Shaw, with their reformist positions.[2]

On 16 October the play, *The Tables Turned, or Nupkins Awakened*, was performed. Shaw said he'd never attended such an overwhelmingly successful first night. The theme was the prosecution of a Leaguer for obstruction and incitement to riot, in the court under Mr Justice Nupkins. Morris took the part of the Archbishop of Canterbury, and May and Sparling also acted; Janey slipped into the room just before the curtain went up, 'austere, handsome, pale'. The Archbishop was a witness, saying that he took a cab to Hammersmith to see for himself what a socialist meeting was really like, and the speaker complained that it was 'damned hard lines to have to speak to a lamppost, a kid, and an old buffer'. Tennyson also testified that he attended a League meeting in disguise:

They sat and smoked, and one fool was in the chair, and another fool read letters; and then they worried till I was sick of it as to where such and such fools should go and spout folly the next week; and now and then an old baldheaded fool and a stumpy little fool in blue made jokes, at which they all laughed a good deal; but I couldnt understand the jokes—and came away.

The trial under the hectoring Nupkins was interrupted by the singing of the *Marseillaise* and the advent of the revolution offstage. In the second part, Nupkins was in the fields, afraid of arrest as a rogue and vagabond. Mary Pinch (May Morris) entered and spoke of the pleasant hot late-summer morning with the wheat nearly ready for cutting and the river low and weedy. 'All that pretty picture of plenty that I told you about on that day when you were so hard upon me has come to pass, and more.' She bade

Nupkins come along to see 'the pretty new hall they are building for the parish; it's such a pleasure to stand and watch the lads at work there, as merry as grigs'. And Nupkins in a lawyerless world had to dig up potatoes as a temporary penance.

The work was a slight jest, but it broke new ground in the creation of agitprop. Morris was doubtless stimulated in pioneering with this form by the thought of medieval popular plays: hence his name for it of interlude. The second part has its interest as a first sketch of the dream-prophecy he was to elaborate in *News from Nowhere*.

Two days later a letter of his appeared in the *Daily News* protesting at police brutality against demonstrations of the unemployed. The *News* had stated that the police were to be commended in their efforts to maintain order and that the demonstrations were 'soon like to try the patience of the public'. Morris referred to the episode of the Chicago anarchists on 3 May 1886 when the police had fired on a peaceful demonstration of strikers, killing six and wounding several more. On 4 May a protest meeting was again attacked by police and someone threw a bomb that killed a policeman and wounded others. Seven leading anarchists were arrested, though no serious attempt was made to implicate them in the bomb-throwing, and five were condemned to death. On 26 October Morris at Kelmscott wrote to May, 'I suppose I must come back for the council meeting on Monday, as we seem to be approaching another crisis, and I cannot allow myself to be made a cat's paw of. I suppose Harry told you how beautifully I kept my temper last Monday.'

Despite the police-harrying the unemployed had kept on with their demonstrations and by November they were gathering daily in Trafalgar Square, while hundreds of them slept at night in the streets. On 8 November the Commissioner of Police banned all further meetings in the Square on the grounds that it was Crown property; and the press supported him. On the 12th *The Times* praised the judicial murder of the Chicago anarchists, since juries in America 'draw no distinction between incendiaries of the platform and the Press, and the men who do their dirty work'. The paper looked enviously towards the States where the police carried revolvers and used them 'without mercy when they see signs of resistance'. Such firmness set an example for the handling of disorders in Ireland and nearer home. Morris at once wrote to the *Pall Mall Gazette*, proposing a Law and Liberty League, to defend the right of free speech. W. T. Stead and others supported him. The Federation of Radical Clubs and the Irish called for a demonstration in the Square on 12 November in protest against coercion and the treatment of the jailed

M.P. O'Brien. On Saturday the Commissioner gave further orders that no organised procession was to be allowed to approach the Square.

Hundreds of thousands of men made for the meeting-place on Sunday, with the police attacking and dispersing them. The Square itself was guarded by ranks of policemen four deep, and mounted police with batons rode down any gathering group. The few men who managed to push through were clubbed down. Behind the police were three hundred soldiers with fixed bayonets, each man with twenty rounds of ammunition. In support was a battalion of Life Guards. Three demonstrators died as a result of injuries, and two hundred were taken to hospital; no doubt there were many other wounded men who feared to go and be treated.

Morris marched with the SL contingent from Clerkenwell Green. He and Annie Besant addressed the marchers on the need to resist all attempts to gag free speech. 'They must press into the Square like orderly people and good citizens.' The contingent, into which gathered a SDF branch and other groups, was some 5,000 strong. But when they reached Seven Dials, the police, rushing out of side-streets, attacked them in the rear and on both sides. Morris, with Shaw, had been in the middle, but, expecting trouble, had gone on to the head of the column.

It was all over in a few minutes: our comrades fought valiantly, but they had not learned how to stand and turn their column into a line, or to march on to the front. Those in front turned and faced their rear, not to run away, but to join in the fray if opportunity served. The police struck right and left like what they were, soldiers attacking an enemy, amid wild shrieks of hatred from the women who had come from the slums on our left. The band-instruments were captured, the banners and flags destroyed, there was no rallying-point and no possibility of rallying, and all the people composing our strong column could do was to struggle into the Square as helpless units. I confess I was astounded at the rapidity of the thing and the ease with which military organisation got its victory. I could see that numbers were of no avail unless led by a band of men acting in concert and each knowing his part.

The same sort of tactics were used to break up other columns of marchers. The police had things so well in hand that Morris was surprised to see the Life Guards form up in the south of the Square and march to St Martin-in-the-Fields, headed by a magistrate who read the Riot Act. The crowd cheered the soldiers as well as hooting at them: 'I think under the impression that they would not act as brutally against the people as the police: a mistaken impression, I think, as these gorgeous gentry are just the helmeted flunkies of the rich and would act on their orders just as their butlers and footmen would do.' He thought the socialists had been taught a lesson in street-fighting. Morris was very lucky, or the police had instructions to ignore him. Cunninghame Graham, on reaching the Square with Burns and Hyndman was clubbed and dragged along by the hair. He recounted many deeds of extreme brutality—a woman asking a police inspector or sergeant about her child was knocked down by him—and adds that the houses and hotels all round were crowded with well-dressed women who cheered and clapped whenever 'some miserable and half-starved working-man was knocked down and trodden under foot'. *The Times* exulted at the police behaviour and said that the demonstrators were made up of 'all that is weakest, most worthless and most vicious in the slums of a great city', apart from 'a small band of persons with a diseased craving for notoriety'. It reported great rejoicing all over London on the following day.

The following Sunday the police galloped about the Square and chased odd groups of bystanders. In Northumberland Avenue a young man, Alfred Linnell, was ridden down and died soon after. For his funeral on 18 December Morris wrote *A Death Song*, printed and sold at a penny, with a woodcut by Crane, for the benefit of Linnell's children. A vast procession moved from Soho to Bow Cemetery, with Morris among the pall-bearers. He wrote: 'There was to me something aweful (I can use no other word) in such a tremendous mass of people, unorganised, unhelped, and so harmless and good-tempered.' At the grave he said that 'our friend who lies here has had a hard life, and met with a hard death. We are engaged in a most holy war, trying to prevent our rulers making this great town of London nothing more than a prison.' He felt sure the lesson had been learned. 'We should begin tomorrow to organise for the purpose of seeing that such things shall not happen again.'

For his role in the funeral he was much attacked by the press, but as a result he became a familiar and beloved figure among the workers all over England. Burns and Graham were each sentenced to six weeks' imprisonment at the Old Bailey; and Morris went on taking an active part in the agitation for free speech. It is often said that his experiences had disillusioned him, but nothing could be further from the truth. The lesson he did learn was that his dreams of some vast uprising of the dispossessed were mere fantasy. 'Up to this time,' Bax tells us, 'he had more or less believed in the possible success of a revolutionary outbreak on the part of the populace of our great cities.' At the time Bax was away in Zürich at the German Social-Democrats'

Congress. Morris wrote to him saying 'that he had always recognised the probability of any scratch body of men getting the worst of it in a rough-and-tumble with the police, not to speak of the military, yet he had not realised till that day how soon such a body could be scattered by a comparatively small but well-organised force'. When Bax was back in London, Morris made the same point in talking about the day in detail. But his brooding on the problem did not mean that he had slackened in his revolutionary ardour; it merely meant that he realised the need to think over the question of tactics again from the ground up. The man who was scared and disillusioned was Shaw, who lost the last remnant of his faith in people, in the idea that 'there was a great revolutionary force beginning to move in society'. Though he and Morris remained friends till the end, Shaw now turned definitely to a political course opposed to that of Morris.[3]

In November the second part of the *Odyssey* was published. Sparling and May had now come together, despite all Janey's forebodings. On 21 December, Morris was writing to Glasier on the need to get back to the work of socialist education after all the excitements. In late 1887 there had come up the project of exhibition by the Arts and Crafts Society. Morris had had nothing to do with the society's foundation, though its organisers owed much to his teaching and example. He was doubtful about the success of the show; and thought that the things in it, apart from some work by Crane and Burne-Jones, would be amateurish. For the rest 'our customers can come to our shops to look at our kind of goods'. So far from being interested in a return to crafts as a panacea he poured scorn on those who clung to the idea. He saw no way of redemption there, though he welcomed such developments as the Arts and Crafts movement as a protest against the vulgarisation of the whole of life and as one sign among others of the unhealthy state of our culture. They deserved consideration and encouragement, and could help to maintain memories of the past that were necessary elements for the life of the future. The intelligent craftsmen who had once made existence tolerable, in the midst of wars and ceaseless troubles and uncertainties, could one day provide again an element of happiness.

He consistently looked on as degenerate a society in which a few persons were considered fine artists while the rest of the people had no link with art. In *A Factory as It Should be* (1884) he had concluded by setting out how he imagined the workers of the future using their spare time, which would have become considerable: this spare time

I have supposed that some would employ in perfecting themselves in the niceties of their craft, or in research as to its principles; some would stop there, others would take to studying more general knowledge, but some—and I think most—would find themselves impelled towards the creation of beauty, and would find their opportunities for this under their hands as they worked out their due quota of necessary work for the common good; these would *amuse* themselves by ornamenting the wares they made, and would only be limited in the quantity and quality of such work by artistic considerations as to how much or what kind of work really suited the wares; nor, to meet a possible objection, would there be any danger of such ornamental work degenerating into mere amateurish twaddle such as is now being inflicted on the world by the ladies and gentlemen in search for a refuge from boredom. . . . Our workers, therefore, will do their artistic work under keen criticism of themselves, their workshop comrades, and a public composed of intelligent workmen.[4]

1888 was in many ways an anticlimax after the previous year with its many exciting events. The plans of the parliamentary faction in the League to build its own base had rather fallen flat. Engels had advised its members to leave the League; but the Avelings and the strong Bloomsbury branch stayed in. In the autumn *Commonweal*'s circulation had gone up slightly and the struggles round Trafalgar Square brought the two sections together; but the progress made was trivial in comparison with the needs and possibilities of the situation. By early 1888 the gains were lost; and the provincial branches broke down or weakened. The League still held some ground in Manchester, but had failed in the cotton-towns which were left to the SDF. Already in 1887 Morris had noticed that the Glasgow branch tended to draw in petty-bourgeois characters, with a few non-typical workers (self-educated poets and the like), while ordinary industrial workers turned to the SDF. This tendency increased, and after 1888 only Leeds and Bradford had a strong group of militant workers—partly through the chance of Tom Maguire emerging as leader, a highly intelligent man, who was a poet with a clear grasp of the class-struggle, and partly through the admiration felt for Morris. Such branches were not kept in the SL ranks because they had any anti-parliamentary views.

The League thus in general failed to realise the resurgence of mass-activity and the mood of the industrial workers. Those workers were gaining definite industrial and political objectives, which made them ready to listen to socialist arguments; but they did not want the latter in the abstract, unrelated to their immediate problems. In such a situation the anarchist influence on the SL council could not but grow. The leaders were Mowbray, a tailoring worker who had served nine months for addressing a group of Norwich unemployed that later sacked a butcher's shop, Fred Charles (F. C. Slaughter) also of Norwich, David Nicoll, an excitable young intellectual, Tochatti, another tailoring worker, H. Davis and Tom Cantwell. They had taken over from the old leftists such as Lane.

In February it seemed that the spirit of the November struggles might be regained. On the 19th Morris went early in the morning to Pentonville Gaol to welcome Burns and Cunninghame Graham on their release. In the evening he helped to serve tea at a social held in their honour, which the Irish and the Radicals joined. Next evening there was arranged a great meeting, with Michael Davitt, Irish leader, in the chair; the speakers were to be O'Brien (whose imprisonment had been the occasion for calling the demonstration of 13 November), Annie Besant, Burns, Graham, W. T. Stead, Hyndman and Morris. All went well till Hyndman stood up. He made an unprovoked attack on the twelve Radical MPs who had accepted seats on the platform. The meeting broke up in fights and general disorder. Morris had not given his speech. Thus ended the unity brought about in the struggles of 1887.

Morris had written an attack in *Commonweal* on practical socialism. He must have felt the strength of the reply made by a worker whose letter was printed on 25 February and who remarked that it was easy for the well-off to scorn the struggles for bettering the living conditions of the workers. In March he wrote to Georgie that he thought things would stay quiet till October or November and then start simmering again. He was reading Tolstoy's *War and Peace* 'with much approbation but little enjoyment', and yet 'with a good deal of satisfaction'. He remarked:

I am not in a good temper with myself: I cannot shake off the feeling that I might have done much more in these recent matters than I have; though I really don't know what I could have done: but I feel beaten and humbled. Yet one ought not to be down in the mouth about matters; for I certainly never thought that things would have gone on so fast as they have done in the last three years; only, again, as opinion spreads, organisation does not spread with it.

His perception of the situation was correct enough, but he still could not put his finger on the main flaw in his own attitudes and methods.

This month *John Ball* appeared as a book. Morris was certainly feeling a heavy financial strain through his generosity to the movement: rent for premises, the *Commonweal* deficit, charges for leaflets, publications, salaries. Early in 1888 he had to find £1,000 for damages in a libel action. He had been forced to neglect the firm, and he had his ailing and complaining wife as well as the epileptic Jenny to consider. No wonder that he could do nothing to help May and Sparling. (How great the pressure was may be gauged from the fact that at Whitsun 1889 he was compelled to withdraw his salary-guarantee of £1 a week from the League.)

In later March he was in Scotland, speaking on the 21st at Kilmarnock on 'Monopoly'; next day in the open-air at Edinburgh; on the 24th at West Calder; on the 25th at Glasgow on 'Art and Industry in the Fourteenth Century'; on the 26th, again at Edinburgh, on the 'Society of the Future'; then the next two days at Dundee and Aberdeen. At Glasgow there had been snow with flakes as big as your fist, and at the mining-town of West Calder a boy was sent round with a bell to announce the meeting.[5]

At the annual conference of the League in May, Morris in his fear of reformists threw himself into the arms of the anarchists. The rival factions issued circulars; and Morris himself acted dubiously in offering money to the Glasgow branch (that is to Glasier) so that it could pay off its arrears and be in a position to send delegates, while there is no evidence that he made the same offer to Leeds, which was taking the parliamentary side and was also in arrears. (We have no proof that he lent or gave the money to Glasier, but he was ready to do so.) Worse, he seems to have come to regard Donald and his friends as tainted in aims and motives as well as policy. On 20 May at the conference the argument went on for nearly twelve hours. The Bloomsbury resolutions were thrown out. The Hammersmith amendments, which ignored the parliamentary issue and merely called for 'cordial co-operation' (as against formal federation) with other socialist groups, were accepted. Morris then 'made a deeply earnest appeal', Glasier tells us, 'for unity and good-will'. The parliamentarians again refused to serve on the council, which as a result was composed of leftists with the two anarchists, Tochatti and Charles. Morris seconded a resolution asking the council 'to take steps to reconciliate or, if necessary, exclude the Bloomsbury Branch'. As he and Glasier went home to Hammersmith on the bus, he admitted: 'We have got rid of the parliamentarians, and now our anarchist friends will want to drive the team.' But he thought he had council and *Commonweal* safe for another year. A week later he wrote that they had suspended, not dissolved, the Bloomsbury branch. The charges were that some members belonged also to the SDF and that Mahon, conducting a 'largely political' propaganda in the

North, had acted as election-agent for Keir Hardie in Mid-Lanark. But, sadly, the occasion of the branch's suspension lay in the fact that its members had 'sold publicly in the streets' an illustrated squib deriding Morris. (He was shown as a sandwichman bearing the slogan: No number of mere administrative changes until the workers are in possession of all political power would make any real approach to Socialism. The sentence was from the League's Manifesto.) Soon an independent Bloomsbury Socialist Society was formed and a few days later the LEL (Hoxton) disaffiliated itself. On 9 June *Commonweal* published a new policy statement, drafted by Morris, which repeated the old position.

It seemed that Morris's contacts with the Northumbrian miners had soon lost all effect. He was further than ever from any sense of what was going on in the industrial areas. The League ignored the important Mid-Lanark election fight except to censure Mahon for taking part in it. By July Morris was beginning to feel some doubts. He wrote to Georgie:

I am a little dispirited over our movement in all directions. Perhaps we Leaguers have been somewhat too stiff in our refusal of compromise. I have always felt that it was rather a matter of temperament than of principle; that some transition period was of course inevitable, I mean a transition involving State Socialism and pretty stiff at that. . . . But then in all the wearisome shilly-shally of parliamentary politics I should be absolutely useless: and the immediate end to be gained, the pushing things a trifle nearer to State Socialism, which when realised seems to me but a dull goal—all this quite sickens me. . . . Yet on the other hand I sometimes vex myself by thinking that perhaps I am not doing the most I can merely for the sake of a piece of 'preciousness'.

In August he went to Norwich, on the 12th speaking twice in the Market Place and giving a lecture in the evening with Faulkner in the chair. Next day he again spoke twice in the Market Place, and in the evening took the chair for a lecture by Annie Besant. In London on the 19th he spoke in the open-air at Weltje Road in the morning, and in the evening lectured from notes on Mommsen and Roman history. During August he marched through Richmond with the Leaguers, with band and banners, to the Park, where he joined in a foot-race, reaching home 'rather tired'. He also went to Birmingham to see about a new window. Later in the month he went down to Kelmscott and stayed there as much as he could until the end of October, working at a new romance, *The House of the Wolfings*, busy also with SPAB, the firm, and *Commonweal*. Still in September he did open-air speaking at

Hammersmith, Battersea Park, Fulham, and was scheduled to read poetry at an entertainment for the Yarmouth Free-Speech Fund at the International Club. In October he seems only to have given open-air speeches on the 14th and 21st.

At Kelmscott he was regaining his inner balance. 'The nights have been fine, and the moon rises her old way from behind the great barn.' And 'I saw an owl last night come sailing along, and suddenly turn head over heels and down in the grass; after a mouse I suppose: such a queer action I never saw.' He needed this feeling of being close to the earth and to elemental life in order to write his romance. He was happy in the wildflowers along the river: 'the long-purples & willow herb, and the strong-coloured yellow flower very close and buttony', and 'a very pretty dark blue flower: I think mug-wort, mixed with all that besides the purple blossom of the horse mint & mouse ear & here and there a bit of meadow-sweet belated'. In his recoil from the confused inner-party struggle, entangled as it was with his preachings of socialism, he turned to the dream-picture of tribal society, which he now saw in the light of the spiral-concept of history. He wanted to summon up the warm heartening feeling of that society as the pledge for the regaining of brotherhood on a new level. He explained the theme and form of his new romance succinctly in a letter of 17 November:

It is a story of the life of the Gothic tribes on their way through Middle Europe, and their meeting with the Romans in war. It is meant to illustrate the melting of the individual into the society of the tribes: I mean apart from the artistic side of things that is its moral—if it has one. It is written partly in prose and partly in verse: but the verse is always spoken by the actors in the tale, though they do not always talk verse; much of it is in the Sagas, though it cannot be said to be performed on their model.

A note to one of his daughters in early September shows the sort of difficulties he got into through being hard up, trying to live in some respects in a working-class way, and yet having to humour Janey's middle-class standards. 'To confess and be hanged I went 2nd class to Kelmscott with your mother: we did not like to be scrowdged.' We see that he had taken to travelling 3rd class on the trains. In October Faulkner, his most faithful follower, was struck down by paralysis; he lingered on for another three years. Webb, who had also followed Morris into socialism, was ill through much of 1887–8, but he had now become treasurer of the League. A letter of 14 September to Jenny shows him hard at work for the firm. He had been to Tilbury to 'see about things' for a ship of the Orient line to Australia. 'We had already done some carpeting for these ships.' He was going to Holland Park 'to call on our decoration'. In October he went through 'the wilds of Surrey' to Hundhead to deal with a client.[6]

In November, on the 1st he spoke on Tapestry and Carpet Weaving at a gallery in Regent Street for the Arts and Crafts Society; on the 10th he made a speech welcoming Mrs Parsons, widow of one of the executed Chicago anarchists, at a meeting sponsored by the combined London socialist and anarchist groups, with Cunninghame Graham in the chair; and next day spoke in Hyde Park at a Bloody-Sunday memorial demonstration sponsored by the same groups. The day after that he took the chair at yet another memorial meeting in Store Street Hall, and the next day he spoke in the open air at Clerkenwell Green. On the 18th he gave two lectures at Nottingham; and on the 28th spoke at the farewell meeting for Mrs Parsons. Naturally the celebrations of the Chicago anarchists tended to strengthen the hand of the anarchists on the League council. Lucy Parsons was a striking woman: 'Indian with a touch of negro,' says Morris, 'but she speaks pure Yankee. I was much tickled by her indignation at the barbarous and backward means of communication in London.'

He had now become interested in typography, mainly through the influence of Emery Walker, and he discussed the format of *The House of the Wolfings*, which went to press in early December. In that romance he had gone back behind the sagas to the Germanic world of purer tribalism. He wanted to regain the heroic note. The emotions that had stirred him among the Northumbrian miners, on the march to Trafalgar Square, during the funeral procession of Linnell, were demanding an outlet; and they found it in this picture of folk still at a level of communal organisation. These folk are in conflict with the Romans, who represent class-society, enslavement, money, individual power-lust; and though, as with *John Ball*, there is no question of a detailed historical reconstruction, Morris seizes on what he rightly feels to be the key-element in tribal society, the binding kindred-force. Despite archaic touches in the diction, there is gusto, a surging energy, a warm coloration in the tale.

Early in December Morris spoke at Manchester, Bolton, Blackburn, Liverpool, Rochdale, and then later at Nottingham. He realised that the League was in a bad way. On 15 December he wrote to Glasier, 'The Anarchist element in us seem determined to drive things to extremity and break us up if we do not declare for anarchy—which I for one will not do.'

He thought that 'the only thing to be done is to go on steadily trying to strengthen local bodies'. He was distressed as always by the dissensions. 'I find that living in this element is getting work rather too heavy for me.' He spent the time over Christmas 'doing patterns for stuffs', and at the end of the year went to see his mother at Hadham, finding her 'in very good spirits but very deaf'.

As we have seen, various seeds sown by Morris were now bearing fruit. The Art Workers Guild of 1884 had been followed by the Arts and Crafts Exhibition Society, and lesser associations such as Home Arts, or Cottage Arts Societies, or Village Industries were coming up. The Arts and Crafts Society had succeeded in holding its exhibition; and once it got under way, he gave it his support. From now on his various teachings on art were to have a steadily extending effect in all fields of design, including that of architecture.

In the autumn Morris had published a collection of seven socialist lectures with the title *Signs of Change*. The review in the Fabian *To-day* was significant in setting the key of denigration that was to be used for many a long year in order to divert attention from Morris's consistent Marxism. The Fabians considered that Wicksteed and Shaw had overthrown Marx's theory of value; they were doing their best to debunk the idea of the class struggle—or rather to admit that there had been struggles of the oppressed in the past while denying that such struggles had relevance to contemporary Britain. Hyndman and Aveling were the authorities they had to tackle on the question of Marxist economics; but in Morris they had an adversary not so easy to knock down. Besides the breadth of his achievement in the arts and literature, there was the prestige in the socialist movement he had achieved through his proved devotion and the fact that his Marxism dealt with life as a whole, with historical development and the function of art. The only way was to avoid a head-on collision and to belittle him. So the Fabian reviewer set about treating Morris as a well-meaning eccentric who didn't really understand what the whole thing was about. 'His utterances on the platform are apt to smack too much of the "hare-brained chatter of irresponsible frivolity". When such deliverances are made to a Socialist audience, who knows him and who overlooks the eccentricities of the lecturer in the liking for the man . . . the amount of harm done is a minus quantity. But when he takes to publishing his views it is a different matter; for many of them are such as . . . to render Socialism a subject of mockery to sane men and women.' And so on.[7]

1889 was rather like 1888 for Morris, with the League running ever more down. On 21 January he wrote to Glasier: 'The truth must be faced, that the "Communists of the League" are in a very weak position in the Socialist party at present. We have been much damaged both by parliamentaries & Anarchists, & I don't think we are strong enough to run a paper; although, numbers apart, there is something to be said for us. You see John Burns has got something of his desire—rather him than me in the position—ugh.' Burns had been elected as a Lib.-Lab. on to the London County Council. On the same day, writing to Jenny, Morris took a more sympathetic attitude to Burns's election:

On the whole the London election has been a great blow to the reactionists; though I don't suppose that the County Council can do much directly as they are now constituted: yet they may become Socialist in feeling, and so make a rallying-point for a kind of revolt against the Parliament. In Paris, you know, the *tendency* of the Municipality is decidedly Socialist, and do such things as voting substantial sums of money to men on strike, and so forth.

He adds that Kropotkin had been at the house. 'Sitting with us in the dining-room after the lecture he told us many interesting though sad things about our comrades in Siberia & the prisons.' On the 29th he had written about twenty pages of a new tale, *The Roots of the Mountains*. 'This time I don't think I shall drop into poetry, at least not systematically. For one thing the condition of the people I am telling of is later (whatever their date may be) than that of the Wolfings. They are people living in a place near the Great Mountains.' Morris again wanted to build a heartening picture of a people in close and happy relation to the earth, farmers and craftsmen, who settle all questions in the Folkmote. The enemy that they face are the enslaving Huns. One satisfaction that he found in this romance and those that followed was the depiction of a heroine who was as unlike the precious Pre-Raphaelite dream-woman (Janey) as possible. He had begun such portrayals with Clara in the 1872 novel; but now he could carry on with full verve. We meet the Bride with her red hair and lips thin rather than full, 'hardy and handy and lightfoot: could swim as well as any, and show well in the bow and wield sword and spear: yet she was as kind and of great courtesy'. A girl who was a 'good animal' as well as a staunch comrade. The development of his daughter May certainly helped a great deal to clarify this image of free young womanhood. May was a very handsome girl with a striking presence. A diarist of the eighties mentions her at a private view at the Grosvenor Gallery, where most of the pictures were by Watts: 'She was dressed like the pictures of Raphael. The dark red velvet cap suited her style of beauty, and she was the observed of all observers, and it was pleasant to look at her.' On the 30th the *Daily News* printed a letter from Morris against a scheme for memorials in Westminster Abbey. 'If some evil fate does compel us to continue the series of conventional undertakers' lies, of which the above-mentioned brutalities [monuments already there], in all their loathsomeness, are but too fitting an expression, surely now that we have learned that if they are necessary they are still ugly, we need not defile a beautiful building with them.'

On 10 February he spoke on the 'Society of the Future' at Glasgow, and on the following two days on 'Gothic Architecture' and on the 'Arts and Crafts of To-day'; on the 13th he lectured on 'Equality' at Edinburgh, and on the 14th talked on art education at Macclesfield School of Art and Science. In the Arts and Crafts lecture he repeated his spiral-concept of history; the existing failure of the arts merely represented a period of negation out of which a new birth would come about. On 1 March he spoke to the Fabians on the theme: How shall we live then? He sets out his general ideas of a free world. 'Decentralisation and equality of condition are the necessary concomitants of my ideal of occupation: but I am not clear as to whether they should be looked on as the cause or the effect of the state of things foreshadowed by that ideal.' A primary condition of the communist society is that 'we live like good animals', enjoying the full exercise of the body in work and all the normal functions of life. The division of hand and mind must be broken down. The great urban conglomerations and the factory-districts must disappear. The big cities are merely the 'counting houses of commerce; the jobbing houses of officialdom; the lairs for the beasts of prey big and little that prey upon the follies and necessities of a huge mass of people who have no time to find out what they want. . . . I do not deny lastly that they are the camps to which the soldiers of revolution must flock if they are impelled to do anything to further their hopes before they die.' The machines of the future will be 'as nearly automatic as possible'. In this lecture he goes even further than he did in his letter to Jenny in his comments on the LCC elections. 'The Tories themselves, driven on I believe by a blind fate, have given us in the County Councils the germs of a revolutionary local opposition to centralised reaction.' Most of his old friends had now gone: Faulkner stricken down, Joynes ill and retired, Bax in the SDF, the Avelings, Binning and Fred Lessner gone with the Bloomsbury branch, Scheu now travelling for Jaeger and becoming disappointed in the workers.[8] In April a discussion on Communist-Anarchism was opened in *Commonweal*. Some resolutions of the Spanish Anarchists were cited with sympathy. In May Morris replied, saying that he was a Communist and recognised no 'rules derived from *a priori* ideas of the relation of man to the universe'. All communistic life will grow 'from these two things, the equality of condition and the recognition of the cause and effect of material nature'. He totally rejected anarchism. 'If freedom from authority means the assertion of the advisability or possibility of an individual man doing what he pleases always and under all circumstances, this is an absolute negation of society and makes Communism . . . impossible.' Even in communist society there could be differences of opinion that had to be settled by the vote and authority of the majority, though, as far as possible, this authority would take the form, not of force, but of that something 'made up of the aspirations of our better selves . . . the *social conscience* without which there can be no true society'. In one point, however, he admitted agreement with the anarchists in ultimate aims; he too wanted decentralisation and a system based on small communes.

In May he went into Wiltshire on SPAB business; and on the 13th, after a letter to Georgie about the trip, he wrote to Glasier that he had read Bellamy's *Looking Backward* as he had promised to lecture on it. 'Thank you. I wouldn't care to live in such a cockney paradise as he imagines.' Indeed he was outraged at the picture of a future which was based on further mechanisation, on the rendering of all the present vulgarities and dependences on commodity-production an eternal condition of man, with social life itself become a highly regimented and centralised system with all the free play of creativeness driven out of it. But his irritated reading of Bellamy's book, which had had a great success, together with his lectures on the future and his arguments with the anarchists, had the effect of making him feel the need to elaborate his own notion of communist society in concrete terms. Thus came the impulse to write *News from Nowhere*.

On 15 June he was writing to Glasier, worried about the nearing annual conference and expecting an attempt to put on the council a majority 'of hobbledehoys who call themselves anarchists and *are* fools', and for whom Kitz as secretary was not left enough. If they succeeded, he would walk out. However the conference turned out to be tame and dull; there were now delegates from only twelve branches as compared with the twenty-one of 1888. Still, the anarchist group on the council was strengthened, and Morris had for support only Webb, Sparling (who was not too reliable), and two of the Hammersmith branch. But the SDF was also in a bad way, with Hyndman's sectarianism and dictatorial ways obstructing any effective participation in the New Unionism and the Eight Hour agitation.

On 3 July, at the twelfth annual meeting of SPAB, Morris repeated his faith that 'the greatest side of art is the art of daily life which historical buildings represent', and that 'what romance means is the capacity for a true conception of history, for making the past part of the present'. On Midsummer Day he was at Kelmscott, happy in the haymaking. 'The country is one big nosegay, the scents wonderful, really that is the word; the life to us holiday-makers luxurious to the extent of making one feel wicked, at least in the old sense of being bewitched.'

In July came the one great experience of the year. An International Socialist Working-Men's Congress was being called in Paris—opposed by Hyndman. It was to be the foundation of the Second International. Morris and Kitz were the League's delegates nominated by the council, while several branches sent their own delegates. There were delegates from all European countries and from America; Morris found their 'earnestness and enthusiasm' very impressive, but he was annoyed at bad organisation and careless behaviour—the Parisian delegates chatting loudly as soon as the French speeches were over, so that Eleanor and other translators could not be heard. There was not enough time to discuss resolutions as too many speakers had gone on past the permitted time. Several anti-parliamentary resolutions, including one by Kitz, were never discussed. The committee chose Morris to make the report from England; German Marxists predominated on it and there can be no doubt that by now he had a high prestige in the international socialist movement. Edward Carpenter describes his speech:

After the glib oratorical periods of Jules Guesde and others, what a contrast to see Morris . . . fighting furiously there on the platform with his own words (he was not feeling well that day), hacking and hewing the stubborn English phrases out—his tangled grey mane tossing, his features reddening with the effort! But the effect was remarkable. Something in the solid English way of looking at things . . . made that speech one of the most effective in the session.

Keir Hardie, at Morris's own insistence, made a second report on the parliamentary side. As the main matters discussed were labour legislation and the Eight Hour Day, what Morris had to say was outside the general range of the arguments. What inspired him was rather the social events and the informal meetings, where he felt a deep spirit of international fraternity. And afterwards he decided that the real use of such occasions was as demonstrations.

On the last day, when Morris, with Kitz and Tarleton, was visiting his beloved Rouen, Dr Merlino, an Italian anarchist from London, caused trouble when his lengthy resolution did not come up for discussion; he was ruled out of order and forcibly expelled. The delegates of the SL who were present walked out with him; and Morris felt out of loyalty to his comrades that he should register a formal protest. Merlino, who had wanted some such incident, went on vociferating about suppression of opinion, joined by Kitz and others; but Morris refused to take part in the uproar. During the period leading up to the Congress Morris seems to have been much in contact with Engels. Paul Lafargue did a great deal of work in organising the event, and he mentions Morris in his correspondence with Engels: 'Morris is full of ardour for the Congress, it's necessary to warm him up and make use of *Commonweal*' (26 May), and 'I'll write to Morris' (2 June).[9]

Back in London Morris found himself again in the midst of the arguments with the anarchists as to how differences in a communist community would be dealt with; as ever he insisted on a social as opposed to an individualistic attitude. Something of a relaxed mood had settled on him as he felt released from day-to-day urgencies. The situation in the League had more or less got beyond his control; he was recognising to some extent the need for broad participations in all fields of struggle, but this was not a matter in which he could or would take a leading role. He had not in the least weakened in his socialist passion, but he was seeing things in a longer perspective. He expressed this emotion in his moving essay *Under an Elm-Tree; or Thoughts in the Countryside*, in *Commonweal* on 6 July. Here he broods over the midsummer landscape, 'one huge nosegay', and sees in it all the marks of men's long struggle to be free and enjoy the earth, the oppressions and the liberations when 'the new White Horse would look down on the home of men as wise as the starlings, in their *equality*, and so perhaps as happy'. Then came the great Dock Strike late in August. At Kelmscott he had not realised its significance, but on arrival in London he found a ferment of excitement at the League. He himself still tended to see such events as important 'chiefly as showing such a good spirit on the part of the men', and expected them to be beaten. He thus did not foresee the victory that came about on 16 September, or the part played by the strike in helping to extend trade-unionism among the unorganised or unskilled and to build up a new militancy. But he was in many ways learning fast. On 21 September in *Commonweal* he wrote that the dockers[10] had shown

qualities of unselfishness and power of combination which we may well hope will appear again before long. . . . They have knocked on the head the old slander against the lower ranks of labour, and shown that . . . these men can organise themselves at least as well, and be at least as true to their class, as the aristocracy of labour. No result of the strike is more important than the effect it will have as a blow against class jealousy among the workers themselves.

This changed attitude was carried on into an October statement by the SL council: 'Members of the League do not in any way compromise their principles by taking part in strikes', though they were asked 'not to let the revolutionary propaganda suffer thereby'. These remarks still lagged far behind the practice of men like Maguire, but were an advance. There was still no awareness, as there was on the part of Engels, that a rebirth of the working class was going on and the key-problem was to help in building the organisations of the workers, giving them leadership and direction, and stirring their consciousness of the nature of capitalism through coherent struggle.

Morris found time to write a letter to the *Pall Mall Gazette* on the subject of restorations of Peterborough Cathedral (19 September). And he was growing more and more interested in typography. *The House of the Wolfings* had been printed at the Chiswick Press under his supervision; he got the Press to use the Basle type, an early nineteenth-century recutting of a sixteenth-century original, for trial pages. The title-page, set in capitals and including several lines of verse, was unlike those of any trade-printed books of the time. In *The Roots of the Mountains* he carried these experiments further, and declared the book the best-looking one since the seventeenth century (says Cockerell). After it he had to take up printing himself if he was to carry his ideas further.

On 10 October he wrote that the night before he had finished *The Roots* a second exhibition of the Arts and Crafts Society had been held, and this time he was quite happy about it.

I have been to Oxford Street and Merton, and find business good: the girls were hard at work on the yellow carpet, but had not done very much to it yet. I was busy at pointing all the day. The tapestry is going on well, though not very fast. We have sold the 'Peace' exhibited at the Arts and Crafts for £160, which I am glad of. As for the Exhibition, I think it will be a success: the rooms look very pretty; and there are a good many interesting works there.

At the end of October there came the Art Congress at Edinburgh. On the 29th he spoke on the 'Art of Dyeing' at a meeting of workers in the Museum of Science and Art; next day on the 'Arts and Crafts of Today', to the Applied Art Section, and in the afternoon chaired a meeting; on the 30th he chaired the general conference, at the National Portrait Gallery. On 1 December he spoke to the Edinburgh SL on socialism, and next day on the 'Origins of Ornamental Art'. On the 3rd he chaired a talk by Crane at Glasgow. Earlier he had written to Glasier, 'You had better arrange with Glasse about my day in Glasgow, always remembering that I shall want to go South to the pock-pudding as soon as I can; for my business needs me sorely,' adding his best wishes 'even for the wicked of your branch, let alone the good like yourself'. Walker and Cobden-Sanderson, as well as Morris and Crane, had spoken at the Congress. 'On the whole the working men were good and attentive, and stood our Socialism well, in fact seemed to relish it.' But he had found things rather dull, stuck in the chair 'hour after hour listening to men teaching their grandmother to suck eggs'. However, 'since the Tory evening paper here declares that Crane and I have spoiled the Congress, you may imagine we have not let all go by default'.

In mid-November *The Roots* was published, a few copies being bound in one of his own chintzes. On 21 November he wrote to Ellis that he thought of designing a chintz for his next book, and of having it calendered to keep dirt off. The lack of good handpress men made it difficult to develop printing as he'd like to see it. 'I really am thinking of turning printer myself in a small way; the first step to that would be getting a new font cut.' He and Walker had been discussing Jenson as a model.

The branches of the SL were breaking up. This autumn the Edinburgh branch amalgamated with the local branch of the SDF, and, with other survivors of Mahon's work to bring about the Scottish Land and Labour League, formed the Scottish Socialist Federation. Of the other still-existent branches some were under anarchist control (Glasgow, Leicester, Norwich, Yarmouth), the rest had taken a parliamentary position (Leeds, Bradford, Manchester, Aberdeen), apart from a few scattered groups at Walsall and elsewhere. Maguire at Leeds had shown how a lead could be given to militant workers. In November, the Builders' Labourers' Union, having won a strike, was strongly entrenched; five thousand gas-workers had demonstrated and were organised for the hard struggles soon to come; the tailoresses had approached Maguire, who had helped them to form a union of fifteen hundred members—600 of whom were striking. In October Maguire and his comrades had helped to form a branch of the Gasworkers' Union after a demonstration of 9,000 stokers and their sympathisers. At Bradford the Leaguers were learning fast from Leeds. Group after group of unskilled workers came to Maguire for help and advice. But such developments in the provinces did not affect the London Leaguers, with the result that men like Maguire found the name of the League an obstacle rather than an aid. *Commonweal* had been displaced by new journals more closely linked with the new struggles, such as Keir Hardie's *Miner* or the *Labour Elector*.

15

Last Years

On 11 January 1890 Morris began publishing *News from Nowhere* in *Commonweal*; the instalments went on till 4 October. The arguments and experiences he had been through, together with his indignation at Bellamy's utopia in which bourgeois society was seen as perpetuating itself with its contradictions miraculously removed, had had the effect of making him want to set out as concretely as possible his ideas as to what the struggle was all about. In his account he made his supreme use of the dream-systems that meant so much to him. The depth and strength with which he felt the bitter pervasive conflicts of his world drove him to attempt to get past them in fantasy while at the same time controlling his fantasy at every point as much as he could by his Marxist understanding. At the end of his first day in the free society the Guest relaxes:

Here I could enjoy everything without an after-thought of the injustice and miserable toil which made my leisure; the ignorance and dullness of life which went to make my keen appreciation of history; the tyranny and the struggle full of fear and mishap which went to make my romance. The only weight I had upon my heart was a vague fear as it drew toward bed-time concerning the place where I should wake on the morrow: but I choked that down, and went to bed happy, and in a few moments was in a dreamless sleep.

On 25 January he printed in *Commonweal* a long review of *Fabian Essays*. He pointed out that Sidney Webb's error was to 'over-estimate the importance of the *mechanism* of a system apart from the *end* to which it may be used'. Webb himself seemed 'to enjoy all the humiliations of opportunism, to revel in it'; he ignored the class-struggle and saw only state-regulations of industry and the like.

He is so anxious to prove the commonplace that our present industrial system embraces some of the machinery by which a Socialist system *might* be worked ...

that his paper tends to produce the impression of one who thinks that we are already in the first stages of socialistic life.

Morris analysed how Webb ignored the transitional period that began in the sixteenth century and involved the driving of the people off the land. 'The transition is treated of by Karl Marx with great care and precision under the heading of the "Manufacturing Period".' By omitting it Webb was able to drop all consideration of the characteristic nature of capitalism and its exploitations, and to deal only with a generalised phenomenon, industrialism.

This year he still carried on open-air speaking, but not to the extent of the previous years. On 2 February he was at Leicester, giving his lecture, *How shall we live then?* On 11 March he spoke on the 'Class Struggle' there and on the 25th at Leeds, with Maguire officiating at the meeting. A few weeks later the branch broke up. Maguire had given steady leadership in the gas-strike, which had burst into flares of violence, including a battle of strikers and their wives against soldiers and police. The response of the anarchists in the League had been to cause as much trouble as possible, with 'all kinds of personal attacks and insinuations' (said Maguire); then, after playing little or no part in the strike, they 'attacked not only the League but ourselves, and finally told the people that no policy should be entertained but physical force'. In Manchester Leonard Hill, young like Maguire and also very capable, was also helping to build the new unionism. In London two groups of ex-Leaguers were trying to gain control of the movement of unskilled workers and lead it. We see then that the League had done much to build men who were now doing their best to develop the situation, though Morris by his purism had shut himself out and made it impossible for the League as a whole to keep together and give a united support to the struggling workers.

Meanwhile he went on with his effort to find ways of getting a Press going. In February a splendid tapestry of the Adoration of the Kings was completed for Exeter College Chapel. In the spring Morris wrote a romance, *The Story of the Glittering Plain* (published in four issues of the *English Illustrated Magazine*, June to September). Here he returned to the quest-theme. Hallblithe goes seeking his beloved carried off by sea-rovers. He is misdirected to the Glittering Plain, but his beloved is not there; instead he finds a parody of the true Earthly Paradise, everything seems fine and there are no conflicts, but there is also no fellowship. (From one angle this is Bellamy's phoney utopia.) Trapped there, Hallblithe cries, 'I seek no dream, but rather the end of dreams.' Here then we have the falsifying dream of a mock-harmony in contrast with the dream that awakes into a fuller reality, as in *News from Nowhere*.[1]

A letter to Glasier on 19 March shows how well aware Morris was of the derelict state of the League:

> I am now paying for the League (including paper) at the rate of £500 a year, and I cannot stand it; at Whitsuntide I must withdraw half of that, whatever may happen: which will probably be the end of Commonweal followed by the practical end of the League. A little while ago this would have seemed very terrible, but it does not trouble me much now. Socialism is spreading, I suppose on the only lines on which it could spread, and the League is moribund simply because we are outside those lines, as I for one must always be. But I shall be able to do just as much work for the movement when the League is gone as I do now.

The anarchists wanted to make the paper ever 'more revolutionary', writing the articles themselves, 'which they can't do', a little blood and thunder without meaning: 'which might get *me* into trouble but couldn't hurt them.' The last article by John Sketchley, the old Chartist, who had contributed striking factual studies of capitalism, appeared in April; *News from Nowhere* carried on; and July–August saw the text of Morris's lecture on the Development of Modern Society. Otherwise the anarchists took over.

On 5 April he wrote to Janey: 'We met some Conservancy men going up the water in a big punt this morning: which makes me uneasy, as I fear their bedevilling the river; they are a crying example of the evils of bureaucratic centralisation.' How deeply he felt about the work of the Conservancy in destroying the willows is shown by the fact he introduces it into both *John Ball* and *News*. On the 12th and 13th he gave three lectures at Liverpool. When the question of May Day came up, the League made a big error. The council decided to celebrate May 1st (when the German workers were to demonstrate) in opposition to the decision of the London Trades Council to hold their meeting on the nearest Sunday, 4 May. Thus they split the movement. They gathered some thousands at Clerkenwell Green on the Thursday, while on the 4th more than a hundred thousand massed in Hyde Park. The League thus turned away from the mass-movement, and when the sixth annual conference was held on 25 May only fourteen delegates attended. The anarchists dominated in all matters and elected their group solidly on to the executive; Morris was isolated in a corner with Webb and two Hammersmith members. The new council threw Morris and Sparling out of the editorship of *Commonweal*, putting Kitz and Nicoll in their place. Morris

realised that the end had come; while the others were exultantly exchanging
ultra-leftist phrases, he scribbled flower-patterns on his agenda-paper till he
could bear it no longer, threw himself back in his chair, and growled, 'Mr
Chairman, *can't* we get on with the business? I want my TEA!' The meeting
broke up at ten. The Hammersmith group went home on the underground.
'The wind's in the West,' said Morris as they watched the lights and the
traffic on the Thames from the embankment; 'I can almost smell the country.'
May says that 'he found himself musing on the subject-matter of discussion,
but still discontentedly and unhappily. "If I could but see a day of it," he said
to himself; "if I could but see it!".' We feel in his words the impulse that had
driven him into writing *News from Nowhere*.

In between the two sad dates of May Day and the AGM, on 12 May, there
had been an entertainment to raise money for *Commonweal*, and Morris made
his second and last appearance as an actor. The play, given in a hall in the
Tottenham Court Road, was *The Duchess of Bayswater and Co.* On 10 June,
writing to Georgie, he has nothing to say of the League, but tells of four out-
ings (two of them on business): to Chislehurst, Stanmore, Lincoln (on SPAB
matters), and Kelmscott. Ten days later: 'I am steadily at work, reading my
own poems, because we are really going to bring out a one-volume "Earthly
Paradise" this autumn. Some people would say the work was hard. "The
Glittering Plain" I have finished some time, and begun another.' He was con-
ferring with Quaritch about the publication of a Saga Library; by 8 July six
letters of the type he was designing had been done. In the note on his aims in
founding a Press he stated:

What I wanted was letter pure in form; severe, without needless excrescences;
solid, without the thickening and thinning of the line which is the essential fault
of the ordinary modern type, and which makes it difficult to read; and not com-
pressed laterally, as all later type has grown to be owing to commercial exigencies.
There was only one source from which to take examples of this perfected Roman
type, to wit, the works of the great Venetian printers of the fifteenth century, of
whom Nicholas Jenson produced the completest and most Roman characters from
1470 to 1476. This type I studied with much care, getting it photographed to a
big scale, and drawing it over many times before I began designing my own letter;
so that though I think I mastered the essence of it, I did not copy it servilely; in
fact, my Roman type, especially in the lower case, tends rather to the Gothic than
does Jenson's.[2]

The day he wrote excitedly about the Saga Library and the new fount, he was scheduled to take the chair at the yearly celebration of the International Workingmen's Club. A strike of postmen was going on. Mahon, Donald, and Binning had been trying to organise postal workers, but the strike at Mount Pleasant failed and scores of workers were victimised. On 7 July Morris opened a discussion on 'The Present Strikes of Police, Postmen & Guards' at Hammersmith. He had in effect withdrawn from action on the executive of the League, and the last of his *Notes on News*, which he had been contributing to *Commonweal* fairly regularly for over five years appeared on 26 July. He did not however make any formal break. No doubt he did not like to desert the few supporters who still hung on in the provinces, and *News from Nowhere* had still some time to run in *Commonweal*; but above all he did not want to give an effect of personal chagrin at having been ousted from *Commonweal*. (He would have recalled that an important issue in his break with Hyndman had been the control of *Justice*.) Further he must have shrunk from making an irreversible decision and abandoning a society of his own founding, for which he had worked so hard.

However the anarchists were making things more and more difficult for him. The articles in *Commonweal* grew irresponsibly wilder. Nicoll called for barricades in the No Rent Campaign, which would hold the law at bay for weeks. Kitz hailed the police-strike with the announcement that 'the whole Government machine is going to pieces'. Even the practical middle class, he said, were asking, 'Are we on the verge of a Revolution?' Samuels lamented that no corpses of blacklegs had been left after the attacks at Leeds. Morris wrote to Nicoll: 'I must say that I think you are going too far: at any rate further than I can follow you. You really must put the curb upon Samuels' blatant folly, or you will *force* me to withdraw all support.' He added that he looked on Nicoll as 'a sensible and friendly fellow' and that what he wrote was meant to be private. 'Do your best not to drive me off. For I do assure you that it would be the greatest grief to me if I had to dissociate myself from men who have been my friends so long and whom I believe to be at bottom thoroughly good fellows.'

On 3 August the council called a Revolutionary Conference, at which six London and four provincial branches were represented, with several groups of foreign refugees. 'All red-tapeism and quasi-authoritarianism were banished.' That is, the office of chairman was abolished. The aim was United International Action if a European Crisis occurred. Mowbray said that in a crisis 'the first thing to do was to fire the slums and get the people into the West-end mansions'. Kitz declared that they should preach to the thieves, the paupers, and the prostitutes. Malatesta advocated the seizure of property in general. Pearson of the Freedom Group wanted 'individual guerilla warfare. . . . We should recognise individuality.' Kent of Sheffield Sociality Society wanted to know where the gatling guns and the like were kept 'so that we might find them when wanted'. Nicoll wanted a general strike, which 'would mean the streets thronged with desperate hungry crowds ready for anything, and that would mean the Revolution'.

On 15 August Morris wrote to *The Times* against some proposed restorations in the church of Stratford-on-Avon. He had decided that a reprint of Caxton's *Golden Legend* should be the first large book of his Press. About the same time the futility of the League anarchists was shown by the way they were chased away by dockers at a demonstration into which they intruded their revolutionary propaganda.[3]

On 4 October *News from Nowhere* reached its last instalment. To summarise this work would be to summarise all the ideas that we have seen gathering strength and scope in Morris. *News* is a highly personal work, based on the dream-mechanism that we had so often to discuss, and bringing to a triumphant resolution all Morris's deepest inner conflicts; it is also a magnificent effort of objectification, translating into direct images all that he had most thoroughly thought out of human needs and aspirations. The journey up the river is the final and complete version of the journey which he sketched out in the unfinished novel of 1872, the quest for love and satisfying earth-roots; it is also the movement into origins which by the spiral turn becomes the movement into a new phase of being. Morris is above all concerned with an imaginative realisation of how people would feel and behave if the existing pressures of division—class division and labour-fragmentation —were ended, if the division of town and country were ended, if the all-round approach of the whole man was substituted for the maimed and limited attitudes of alienated or self-divided man. He would have been the first to admit that much of the coloration and terms were idiosyncratic, the result of his own love of the communal and craft elements in medieval life; but he could have argued that the sympathetic and intelligent reader should be able to see beyond these limiting aspects into the universal truths he was attempting to expound. He takes rather a holiday moment of his communist society; we are given glimpses of factory-buildings where new forms of energy are used and which we assume use the highly developed kinds of automation he spoke of elsewhere. But he is not concerned to elaborate these aspects of the new society or the ways in which forms of association operate in the productive and social spheres. Here we touch on one of the gaps in the book: but he would doubtless have said that he preferred such gaps rather than having elaborated pictures of systems that time would be sure to show up as insecurely based. Bellamy's utopia had increased his aversion from such attempts to imagine the future; he felt that the composer of worthwhile utopias must concentrate on the more purely human aspects. While admitting that his position was generally correct in all that, we may still argue that he has carried his own preoccupations too far and failed to solve the conflict between the good animal elements of the freed men and women, and their forms of association, which would also involve their forms of art and science, and of scientifically exploring natural process.

He is aware of this weakness in his depiction and tries to get over it by suggesting that the society he describes is one of a period of rest, of peaceful and happy stabilisation, which may be followed by new and unprecedented forms of struggle or search. He asks, 'What is to come after this?' The old man laughs, 'I don't know; we will meet it when it comes.' The spirit of something like unrest—or perhaps one should say the unquiet sense of something new striving to be born, though as yet not near its time—is suggested above all by the character of Ellen. At the same time Morris expresses through her his fear that the new society, if it does not thoroughly understand the past and the reasons for the creation of class-society, will bring miseries down on its head through illusions, through the advent of new competitive individualities. 'Who knows? happy as we are, times may alter; we may be bitten with some impulse towards change, and many things may seem too wonderful for us to resist, too exciting not to catch at, if we do not know that they are but phases of what has been before; and withal ruinous, deceitful, and sordid.'

There is indeed a real problem here. If Marx was right, a genuinely new society can be born *only when commodity-production ends*, and with it division of labour, money, market-systems, and alienation in all its many shapes and forms—above all the alienation from nature. Morris is one of the extremely few thinkers who have tried to realise at all fully what such a situation implies. It certainly implies the end of all systems of production for production's sake (which repose finally on the need for capital to renew and multiply itself); it implies a situation where all poverty has indeed been abolished, but above all where men are able to understand just what they do need in order to live a truly satisfactory life as the good animals of an accepted earth. In the world where commodity production has ended, we have neither maximum production nor zero-growth; we have instead a society where people, freed from fear, are able to realise how *little* they need in order to achieve fulfilment and happiness. These problems are now beginning to come up for us all, not as the philosophical problems they were for Marx and Morris, but as problems of necessity in a world where men seek to make an infinite use of finite sources of energy and productive materials. The greatness of Morris, as of Marx, lies in the fact that he realised the urgency of such issues, not as the result of practical problems connected with energy-resources, but wholly from his understanding of the human essence, of the wrong being done to men and women by a fragmenting and alienating society, of the possibilities that opened up as soon as the wounds of division were healed. For the same reason he followed up the understanding of Marx that the blind development of production and science could have disastrous results. Marx said: 'Cultivation, when it progresses in a primitive way and is not consciously controlled . . . leaves deserts behind it.' Morris, coming at a later phase of industrial expansion, realised that uncontrolled productive activity begot pollutions and destructions of the environment in an ever-increasing virulence. The society which 'restored' and destroyed its cultural inheritance, he discovered, was a society which poisoned the very earth itself.

He then sets out the proposition in *News* that a society which has swept away the dynamic of capitalism (the accumulation of capital for the expansion or intensification of commodity-production) has reached a position of equilibrium with nature. There was something of this equilibrium in early tribal societies, but insecurely and imperfectly achieved because at any moment the balance might be badly disturbed (by famine, drought, disease and so on) to the detriment of the human group. By the spiral-turn, communist society, as shown in *News*, has re-achieved the harmonious relation with nature without any fear of regression; there is established a stability which is unlike anything in previous human history. That is the point which Morris is seeking to make. What baffles him is to define just what are the forms of growth and movement inside this new condition of stability and harmony. But, he would say, the essential thing is that new condition, which we can understand in so far as it represents a negation of all forms of competition, of conflict, as such things have been known so far. What is harder to grasp is the positive aspect, the new kind of creativeness, which would emerge out of the negation—the negation of the negation. However, we can at least ensure that we do not present this new creativeness in a phoney form, as a sort of vastly enlarged control of mechanisms of power; for such a form is only a lunatic reflection of the tendencies of our own day. Hence the way in which Morris in *News* keeps himself strictly to the simplest relations of men and women with one another and with work. He feels that if he truly captures the spirit of the new harmony, the happy balance of man and nature, the rest can be left unstated—since in any event we have no terms at our disposal to state it.

Ellen is the culmination of Morris's attempt to create the kind of woman he admired, the anti-Janey, who had many of the elements of Georgiana Burne-Jones, but who became yet stronger and bolder as his socialist ideas developed. His account of how the revolution came is based on his experiences of the 1880s, but he has learned a fair amount of caution about thinking that the crucial changes lay round the corner. However, he still thinks, as other Marxists did, that the main struggles would come about through the sharpening of the contradictions of bourgeois society at the great centres of production. What he sets out is a picture not unlike what actually happened in 1926 with the General Strike, if we can imagine the conflicts there driven to their full conclusion. The fact that things worked out in 1926 very different from the events in *News* brings out the extent to which Morris and others underestimated the expansive possibilities of the system they detested, the vastly greater area of manœuvring for the State that was to emerge. But Morris's account still has great force and shows his firm grip on the essentials of social struggle; and his insight into the middle class which already by the 1870s he had seen as 'a most terrible and implacable force', enabled him to prophesy the rise of Fascism in the epoch of imperialist decay, the counter-revolution of the Friends of Order.

Three days after the last instalment of *News*, Morris wrote to Glasier: 'I have been down at Kelmscott (where Ellen vanished, you know) off & on for some weeks now.' He had not been well and had needed a rest—'not that it was not full of work though'. He felt that he should go back to London for socialist propaganda, though he felt out of key with the turn 'towards unideal & humdrum "gradual improvement", i.e. towards general deadlock and break up. That's all right of course but it goes slow; and meantime I sometimes feel rather sick of things in general.' In an interview with *Cassell's Saturday Journal* he stressed his debt to Marx and said nothing of the League's dissensions. Questioned as to the split, he merely said that there was argument as to the precise social system of the future and the best means of attaining it. 'But these are matters which will work themselves out as we go along.' Asked by Hyndman to write again for *Justice*, he said that he had decided no form of journalism suited him. 'I want to pull myself together after what has been, to me at least, a defeat.' But with Glasier he discussed the possibility, at some future time, of a paper embracing all sections of socialist opinion. For the moment there was only speaking and lecturing. Still, he could not resist making an attack on the Salvation Army, *Workhouse Socialism*, printed 1 November, and two weeks later wrote an essay, *Where are We Now?*

But the complete break had to come. In November he and the Hammersmith branch withdrew to form the Hammersmith Socialist Society. He had contracted his system to its base and made no further attempt at large-scale organisation. He went on with his Sunday morning meetings at the foot of Hammersmith Bridge or at the corner of Weltje Road, made trips to Victoria Park on Sunday afternoons, and gave lectures or listened to someone else in the coach house. Crane designed a new banner, which May worked. Emery Walker was the society's secretary. Meanwhile the replies to *Where are We Now?* brought out how untenable Morris's position in the League had become. Mowbray declared that a determined few with 'gatlings, hand-grenades, strychnine, and lead' could paralyse the exploiters. People could carry dynamite round in their pockets and 'destroy whole cities and whole armies'. Creaghe of Sheffield suggested that 'every man should take what he requires of the wealth around him, using violence whenever necessary'. Writing to Glasier, Morris said that the walking-out had been sudden, and admitted that the expulsion of the Bloomsbury branch had ensured the dominance of the anarchists. 'I feel twice the man since I have spoken out. I dread a quarrel above all things, and I have had this on my mind for a year or more. But I am glad it is over at last.' But 'don't be downcast, because we have been driven to admit plain facts. It has been the curse of our movement that we would lie to ourselves about progress and victories.'

On 9 December he was forcing himself to write a manifesto for the new society. 'I had so much rather get on with my Saga work.' He particularly attacked the idea 'of the complete independence of every individual, that is, of freedom without society'. But with anarchism he also still repudiated parliamentarianism. On the 11th he was at Cambridge, speaking for SPAB. He continued lecturing till his last year, but much less than he had done in the 1880s. His main socialist activity lay in his keeping the Hammersmith room a lively centre for exposition and debate. H. G. Wells, then a science student, recalled the days when for him socialism was a splendid new-born hope. 'Wearing our red ties to give zest to our frayed and shabby costumes we went great distances through the gas-lit winter streets of London and by the sulphureous Underground Railway, to hear and criticise and cheer and believe in William Morris, Bernard Shaw, Hubert Bland, Graham Wallas and all the rest of them, who were to lead us to that millennial world.' Morris 'used to stand up with his back to the wall, with his hands behind him when he spoke, leaning forward as he unfolded each sentence, and punctuating with a bump back to position'.

A worker, Muncey, recalled that 'what he could not stand was smug respectability and cant. If an opponent came forward, however illiterate but with honest purpose, Morris was delighted; he was just the reverse with hypocritical criticism'. Rowley said, 'It was delightful to watch his patience when the same old questions were asked by labouring men, or his vehemence when flooring some well-to-do jobber—often a mere rentier, who assumed he was advocating robbery.' The artist Pennell noted his thick curly hair massed over his forehead and always in confusion because when excited he ran his fingers through it. Once he was so enraged at an opponent that he 'worked himself up to the verge of apoplexy, calling his opponent every possible bad name, lost his voice in the process and did not recover it all evening'. (Pennell as Whistler's friend was probably not very sympathetic.)[4]

The new manifesto was accepted on 2 January 1891. It rejected parliamentarianism as well as anarchism, and proposed socialist propaganda by lectures, street-meetings, and publications. But there was no attempt to set the society up as the sole source of socialist truth. Anyone, not only locals, could join. This month the printing press was installed in a cottage rented close to Kelmscott House. Morris began buying old books once more. In an article in *New Review* he reiterated his concept of art as something involved with life at every point, with all the moments of living. Most of his attention was now being given to the Press. A room upstairs in the cottage had been fitted with racks, cases, imposing stone; in another was the second-hand Albion handpress. Sparling remarks: 'Except for the change from wood to iron, and substitution of levers for screw, this press was essentially similar to Caxton's.' But late in February Morris was stricken down by gout complicated by kidney disease. He was told that henceforth, says Mackail, 'he must consider himself an invalid to the extent of husbanding his strength and living under a very careful regimen.' No man was ever less suited to carry out such advice. But he was in a bad way: 'My hand seems lead and my wrist string. . . . Yes, 'tis a fine thing to have some interesting work to do, and more than ever when one is in trouble.' He was suffering from the accumulation of extreme nervous strain as well as from his careless ways of living; at home he had the unhappiness of an aloof unloving wife, the anguish of Jenny's fits, and abroad he had had the ceaseless struggle for the cause, which in many ways seemed to have so sadly miscarried. In mid-March May wrote to Glasier that worry about Jenny 'had terribly upset my father's nerves'. Sparling said that he even talked about dying.

On 2 March the first sheets of his romance, *The Story of the Glittering Plain*, were run off. He and Jenny had gone to recuperate at Folkestone, where he was working at ornamental borders and floriated initials. By 27 March he was feeling better. By April he was back at his work; but from May to July he spent much time at Folkestone. However he was able to attend the May Day celebrations (on 3 May), this time at the mass-meeting. He spoke, with Aveling as chairman on the platform. Cunninghame Graham, Shaw and Harry Quelch (of the SDF) also spoke, and Engels had a seat with them. Here at last was the united front so much desired by Morris but not in an organised form.[5]

The Glittering Plain had been finished on 4 April, two hundred copies of which were published in May. For the second book from the Press he had collected a number of his shorter poems as *Poems by the Way*; he included his socialist pieces. By the end of May the Press was moved to larger premises in the same street, a part of an old family mansion now occupied by a photo-engraving works. Among the compositors was Binning of the League days. At the end of July he wrote to Georgie: 'I am ashamed to say that I am not as well as I should like, and am even such a fool as to be rather anxious—about myself this time.' He and Jenny had climbed on the downs above a sea-fog. 'It looked like Long Jokull (on Iceland), only that is glittering white and this was goose-breast colour. I thought it awful to look on, and it made me feel uneasy, as if there were wild goings on preparing for us underneath the veil.' To Aglaia he said that it 'looked as if the world was newmade almost'. He was on the eve of a tour of northern France with Jenny, which took up three weeks; he found the countryside there as lovely as he had remembered, and gave himself up 'to thinking of nothing but the passing day and keeping my eyes open'. He wrote several letters to Walker, Webb, Janey, which showed how happily and keenly his eyes were at work.

On 23 September he wrote to Jenny at Kelmscott about the printing of *Poems by the Way*. He had also had a specimen copy of Volume II of the Saga Library. 'I shall probably bring along a copy of the cheap "Glittering

Plain", and the cheap "Poems by the Way" will soon be out. So you see, my own, that if it doesn't rain "blue elephants" it may almost be said to rain new books of mine. Do you know, I do so like seeing a new book out that I have had a hand in. Mr Prince is also getting on with the new fount of type. . . .' On 2 October he opened a show of Pre-Raphaelite paintings in Birmingham. He described the school as sharing a love of nature with Gothic art, and adding a romantic quality through the work of Rossetti and Burne-Jones; he praised their revolt against academic art and declared that when artists were consciously telling a story their work becomes more beautiful. (Since he opposes the Pre-Raphaelites to the academics, he does not mean by 'telling a story' the use of anecdotal motive; he means that the art is fully and imaginatively absorbed in the human force of some significant action.) Two days later he lectured twice at Manchester, on 'Socialism up to date', and on 'English and French Cathedrals'.[6]

He still spoke when he could at Hammersmith Bridge, to an audience of some 300. At the seventy-five business-meetings of the branch between January 1891 and June 1892 he attended forty. In October the branch took some first steps towards supporting a candidate from the Chelsea SDF in the School Board elections, but the relations were later broken off. The branch had been selling the *Labour Leader* (of Keir Hardie) and then Burgess's *Workman's Times*. This month it started issuing a small four-page monthly of its own. In November Morris was thinking of the Press publishing all his own works, meaning to begin with *Sigurd*. The printing of the Interminable, as the *Golden Legend* had come to be called, was getting on. At Christmas he was busy at one of the several romances that he started and then dropped, losing interest or finding himself too busy. This year a young girl, Floss Gunner, fourteen years old, entered the Morris household. In 1965 she gave her memories of Morris. 'His head was always so much buried in his work that I don't think he'd notice a little thing like me.'[7]

In February 1892 the Press reprinted Ruskin's chapter on the 'Nature of Gothic'. Morris wrote: 'To some of us when first we read it, now many years ago, it seemed to point out a new road on which the world should travel. The lesson that Ruskin teaches us is that art is the expression of man's pleasure in his labour.' He went on building up his splendid collection of thirteenth-century manuscripts and early printed books. In February disaster fell on the anarchists. Auguste Coulon, in the pay of the police, had been for some time doing his best to provoke trouble with the slogan, 'No voice speaks so loud as Dynamite.' He was one of the leaders under whose influence *Commonweal* in late 1891 had been calling for theft, train-robbery, murder, looting of warehouses, and indiscriminate terrorism. In time even Nicoll grasped what had been happening: 'Coulon understood his trade.' Several anarchists were arrested and Coulon disappeared. Sentences of ten and five years were passed on four men, two of whom had made a bomb which they thought was destined for Russia. Nicoll wrote an article in *Commonweal* which could only be interpreted as incitement to kill the judge who had done the sentencing. The paper's office was raided, and Nicoll and Mowbray were arrested. To enable Mowbray to attend the funeral of his wife Morris came before the court and entered into surety for him for £500. At the same time in the *Hammersmith Socialist Record* (May) and in his lecture on Communism (February next year) he stressed that he saw only perversity or madness in 'a war of violence', in the attempt of a small minority to terrify a vast majority into accepting something which they do not understand, by spasmodic acts of violence, mostly involving the death or mutilation of non-combatants.

On 25 February he wrote from Kelmscott to Jenny about the garden. 'I have lost two things; first my brushes (for drawing), second my cold.' The day before Webb had written to Janey about the death of Faulkner and the broken-down state of Kate after the strain of three and a half years' nursing of her brother. 'You who have had a sore time of it will understand, I am sure.' He always had a strong sympathy for Janey, perhaps feeling that the rough and obsessed side of Morris had played its part in bringing about the break between them.

On 7 March Morris completed an essay for SPAB on Westminster Abbey, the vigorous summation of his long struggle against 'restorations'. The day before he had written to Glasier: 'I sometimes have a vision of a real Socialist Party at once united and free.' He was beginning to see the virtues of a broad struggle in all areas where the conditions of people were at stake. On the LCC elections he says, 'It is certainly the result of the Socialist movement, and is a Labour victory. . . . Of course, I don't think much of gas-and-water Socialism, or indeed of any mere mechanical accessories to Socialism; but I can see that the spirit of the thing is bettering, and in spite of all disappointments I am very hopeful.' On the 25th he commented to Watts-Dunton on the anti-artistic aspect of the contemporary Briton. 'I think, because he has gone further through the mill of modernism; some survivals of the old artistic spirit still cling in a queer paradoxical way to Frenchmen

& Germans: to Englishmen none, unless they have gone through the mill and come out at the other [end].' At moments his old energy returned to him. On 9 April, after telling Jenny about the almond-blossom, the hyacinths, and the old chestnut-tree, he adds, 'happening to be awake at 6 a.m. I went & got my book and wrote several pages of the story. . . .'

In April, writing in the *Record*, he at last recognised the educative effect of the day-to-day struggle:

The conduct of the labour war under its present purblind guidance and weak organisation will teach the workers by blind necessity. Their very mistakes will force them into looking into the facts of their position; their gains will show how wretchedly they live still; their losses will show them that they must take the responsibility of their labour and lives on their own shoulders.

So in the end they will arrive at a socialist consciousness. In June, dealing with the sufferings among the miners and their families in Durham and Cleveland, he expressed regret, not for the strike, but for the lack of socialist leadership. The old attacks against him as a rich man kept on coming up. In July the *Primitive Methodist Quarterly Review* declared that 'This modern Moses of Socialism prefers the ease and luxury of commercial Egypt to the arduous and risky labour of leading the hosts to their promised land.' But such abuse was futile. The socialist movement knew that Morris was incorruptible.

In these last years, from 1892 to 1896, Morris stood *above* the movement—not in the sense of standing apart from it, but in the sense of comprising in his own person a point of unity above the divisions. He could write for the *Labour Prophet* (the organ of the Labour Church) although it was known that he had no interest in religion; or for *Liberty* without being accused of returning to Anarchism; or for *Justice* without bringing down on himself an attack from the Labour Leader; or he could lecture to the Fabians without being accused by Hyndman of treachery to the cause. This was in part, it is true, because he was no longer so closely engaged in the day-to-day struggle of the movement. But this very disengagement meant that he could work for the unity he so much desired with better effect. (Edward Thompson)

We may add that his previous entanglement with the day-to-day politics, whatever errors or limitations it may have involved, gave him now the moral force with which he could speak for the whole movement.

Much of this summer he spent in London, so as to be close to the Press.

In August he invited Sydney Cockerell to Kelmscott for a week. The first night Cockerell was too shy to pass through Morris's room to reach his own bedroom and slept on the sofa of the Tapestry room. He was taken round to the Great Coxwell barn and local churches, and in the evenings he and Morris played whist or twenty-questions with Janey and Jenny. This month, writing in the *Record* on the General Election, Morris repeated his scorn of Parliament, an institution to prevent things being done, a mess of 'cowardice, irresolution, chicanery, and downright lies in action', and insisted on the need to keep always a socialist aim in mind: 'equality political and economic. When the workers understand that this is their true aim, every step they take will be a real gain, never to be taken from them.'

He was thinking of translating *Beowulf*, and enlisted the aid of the scholar A. J. Wyatt. By mid-September the *Golden Legend* was finished and Burne-Jones had begun his drawings for the edition of Chaucer which was taking shape in Morris's mind. In October, Cockerell was again at Kelmscott and was invited to catalogue the library at Hammersmith at a salary of two guineas a week. Morris insisted on a thorough job and often sent Cockerell to the British Museum to check details. On 11 October he wrote to Glasier: 'I must say no to the art lecture: it is with the greatest difficulty that I can get to you at all, and I must cut it as short as I possibly can.' He was amused at the fuss going on as to who would succeed Tennyson as Poet Laureate. 'Bet you it is offered to Swinburne. Bet you he takes it.' But to his vast surprise he found that he himself was the candidate being considered. He replied by suggesting instead a court poetaster, the Marquis of Lorne. Some hints of what was going on reached the newspapers, and Blatchford sent a *Clarion* reporter to interview Morris.

'The very idea!' he replied. 'As if I could possibly accept it. A PRETTY PICTURE I should cut: a Socialist Court Poet!' And his laugh was good—exceedingly good to hear.

In October the Press completed Caxton's *Historyes of Troye*, with initials and ornaments by Morris. Quaritch did the publishing; but Morris now decided to publish as well as print. He was working at *Beowulf*. Janey was in bad health and in November he took her over to Bordighera and then rushed back to watch over Jenny. The Independent Labour Party was emerging in the North, and in December the Hammersmith society debated whether it was now desirable to form a Socialist Federation. Agreeing that it was desirable, they made approaches to the SDF and the Fabians; and on the 18th a subcommittee, which included Morris, was set up 'to promote the alliance of Socialist organisations in Great Britain'. Morris advocated, not a merging of bodies, but an alliance of autonomous groups. Despite his dislike of the theatre he went to the first night of Shaw's *Widowers' Houses*. Cockerell adds: 'In the evening W.M. was at a party of Walter Crane's (in dress clothes).' The modern theatre Morris classified as a hopelessly bourgeois form; he wanted popular and festival forms, arguing that actors should wear masks and that scenes and costumes should be simple and symbolic. In Italy we find him heartily enjoying a performance at Florence. The main actor was 'said to be one of the best Stentorella [Stenterello] men acting, he was got up as a fine gentleman and making love to everyone all round, his face was admirable with the half mask. . . .' He could not approve of Shakespeare in the proscenium theatre with productions destroying the original pattern by attempting naturalistic settings and connections. 'Shakespeare's genius has consecrated by its poetry and insight what was really a very bad form of drama.' (Shaw made his own version of this viewpoint in his dramatic criticisms in the *Saturday Review*.)

At Christmas Sparling wrote, 'We are all here at Kelmscott . . . except Mrs Morris, who had to go to Italy for the winter. Shaw is also here, musing himself by pasting into a scrap-book all the Press-notices of his play.' Morris, after vainly trying to get Shaw or Sparling to join him, had gone off to try for a pike. 'He is extremely well & hearty.' On the 27th Morris wrote to Joynes. 'This is the first time that I have been here in mid-winter and I think I rather enjoy the frost as a change; though not so much as I should have done 40 years ago.' Shaw was happy 'because (as he sleeps with his window wide open) his water-jug is frozen deeper than any one else's'.[8]

With 1893 we find him working on *Beowulf*. The Press was going well. Early came Caxton's *Reynard the Foxe* in Troy type, then in February two books in Golden type, Shakespeare's poems and *News from Nowhere*. Next came Caxton's *Order of Chivalry* with Morris's verse translation of *L'Ordene de Chevalerie*, a thirteenth-century poem which may have underlain Caxton's treatise: here the Chaucer type was used. Then came Cavendish's *Life of Wolsey* and in April Caxton's *Godefroy of Boloyne*, the first book both printed and sold at the Kelmscott Press. In all, fifty-three books were printed, in some 18,234 volumes; mostly the prices were high, but a few cost as little as 2s. 6d.

In mid-January the Hammersmith Society was following up the idea of a socialist alliance, and on 10 February it was resolved to call a conference of all socialist societies. Five delegates were appointed from Hammersmith, five from the Fabians, five from the SDF. Morris was chairman; and he and Shaw were appointed to draw up a manifesto, which was issued on May Day. Later Hyndman claimed it as his work; in fact it seems certainly a joint work of Morris and Hyndman, with very little of Shaw. There are none of the Fabian equivocations; instead there was a strong call for co-operation among all socialists, with a definite programme of immediate steps on which to campaign (Eight Hour Day, Prohibition of all Child Labour, Equal Pay for Equal Work, Minimum Wage in State Services, Abolition of Swearing; Universal Male and Female Suffrage; Payment for all Public Service), and with the recommendation that all socialists unite 'into a distinct political party with definite aims, marching steadily along its own highway'. By July the Fabians withdrew from the committee. Morris had wanted to draw the ILP in, but Hyndman and his followers were flatly hostile to the new party. As if to bring out the Hammersmith attitude, Keir Hardie and another ILPer were asked to speak on their aims in February and March. In Morris's lecture, *Communism*, of this year, he fully accepted immediate measures helping to raise the living standards of the workers, 'give form to vague aspirations', train workers in 'organisation and administration'. He naturally added that 'this education by political and corporate action' must be supplemented by ceaseless education as to the aims and nature of socialism. Last year he had been revising with Bax the series of articles which they had written for *Commonweal* on Socialism from the Root up; now they were published in book form as *Socialism; Its Growth and Outcome*. Though there is perhaps too long an historical introduction for a short work and not enough backing up of the generalisations by examples drawn from the everyday experiences of workers, the statement is a clear and strong exposition, with a central place given to Marx and Engels, and with a new emphasis on the importance of industrial struggle and on the need for a vital interrelation of theory and practice. Socialism would not appear as the result of some catastrophe, but through slow and complex struggle. The victory of revolution would not be the 'complete establishment of Communism in a day', but the creation of an administration with a conscious and definite aim 'to prepare and further, in all available ways, human life for such a system'.

There was much delay over the Chaucer through the problem of getting BJ's designs cut in wood. In June Morris went to Oxford in an attempt to save the medieval statues round the base of the spire of St Mary's; but his motion was heavily defeated in Convocation. In July Glasier was in London on his honeymoon, and both he and his wife spoke at Hammersmith, the latter on the 'Dearth of Joy'. She mentioned Rossetti as exemplifying the moral and intellectual enfeeblement of literature and art, turning from the real pangs and troubles of people to 'merely aesthetic griefs and pains'. Glasier says that he was afraid that Morris would dissent at this stricture on Rossetti, as he himself had once roused Morris's fury by deprecating Burne-Jones; and he was relieved when Morris declared his thorough agreement.

In August, in a letter to Walker, Morris said that he was still hoping 'to see a due Socialist party established'. In an interview in the *Daily Chronicle* (9 October) he said that in a socialist world things like his big tapestries would be public property, hung in town halls and the like. In the same paper (10 November) he wrote a letter on the Deeper Meaning of the Struggle, once more denying that art could be kept vigorously alive 'by the action, however energetic, of a few groups of specially gifted men'. The best way to help a vital art into birth was by actions such as those of the miners.

No one can tell now what form that art will take; but as it is certain that it will not depend on the whim of a few persons, but on the will of all, so it may be hoped that it will at last not lag behind that of past ages, but will outgo the art of the past in the degree that life will be more pleasurable from the absence of bygone violence and tyranny, *in spite* and not *because* of which our forefathers produced the wonders of popular art, some few of which time has left us.

He was referring to the great coal lock-out of this autumn. He had done his best to get a joint statement of support for the miners drawn up; but Blatchford, consulted, said that the latter would not read or understand it. So it was not published. In December Tochatti, one of the anarchists whom Morris had liked, asked him to write something for his *Liberty*. Morris replied that he could not write anything for an anarchist periodical, in view of the murders or attempts at murder by anarchists over the last couple of years, unless an express repudiation of such acts was made—acts that could bring 'nothing but disaster to the cause of liberty'. Tochatti published the repudiation, and Morris allowed him to print *Why I am a Communist* both in *Liberty* and then as a pamphlet. (Morris wrote another article for him in May 1895.)

Morris did not do much work in the provinces this year. Sometime in

January he spoke at Ancoats, Manchester, on 'Town and Country'; on 10 October he spoke twice at Manchester, on 'Printed Books' and on the 'Dangers of Restoration' with special reference to Westminster Abbey; on 10 December he was at Burnley, lecturing on 'Waste' and on 'What Shall We do Now?' On 23 December he wrote to his mother, thanking her for some stands and dishes, and Henny (Henrietta) for a neck-kerchief. The sun was shining into his room and Jenny sat by him reading a paper.[9]

He had not entirely given up designing for wallpapers. In 1890 he did his *Hammersmith*; this year his *Lechlade*; and next year he was to do the *Spring Thicket*. His efforts to encourage original work among his workers had had such success that he was able to say of a piece of tapestry shown at the Arts and Crafts this year:

The people who made it—and this is by far the most interesting thing about it— are boys, at least they are grown up by this time—entirely trained in our own shop. It is really freehand work, remember, not slavishly copying a pattern . . . and they came to us with no knowledge whatever. . . .

In January 1894 he wrote two articles aimed at furthering the cause of unity. In the *Labour Prophet* he declared that 'our business at present seems to me to preach Socialism to non-Socialists and to preach unity of action to Socialists'. He observed:

The tendency of the English to neglect organisation till it is forced upon them by absolute necessity, their ineradicable personal conceit, which holds them aloof from one another, is obvious in the movement. The materials for a great Socialist party are all around us, but no such party exists. We have only the scattered limbs of it; we are divided into various organisations, which . . . stand in the way of *organisation*, since they are all afflicted with some degree of narrowness. . . .

In *Justice* he argued that you cannot start with revolt. 'With the tremendous power of modern armies, it is essential that everything should be done to legalise revolt.' The events at Featherstone, when Yorkshire miners were fired on by soldiers in 1893, proved that the army would shoot people down 'without hesitation so long as there is no doubt as to the legality of their doing so. Men do not fight well with halters round their necks, and that is what a revolt now would mean'. The immediate need was to create a strong party, 'a party with delegates in the House of Commons, which would have complete control over those delegates'. At the same time he attacked anarchism as 'a social disease caused by the evil conditions of society', and saw those who believed in anarchism pure and simple 'as being diametrically opposed to us'.

Blatchford in the *Clarion* was calling for Morris to assume his rightful position in the leadership of the ILP. But Morris could not do this, mainly because of his lack of physical resilience since 1891. He would not become a mere figurehead and he simply did not now possess the strength to take up the role that Blatchford demanded. Such work as he could do was restricted to London and the kind of activities to which he was accustomed. Also, he still shrank from getting himself too closely involved with parliamentary work or the like, however much he now recognised the necessity of it. He had for a while his doubts about Hardie 'because of his seeming absorption in mere electioneering tactics', though he came to feel that his fight for the unemployed 'has had something great in it'. Blatchford he 'rather liked the looks of'. As he told Leatham of Aberdeen, now in the SDF, 'you must let a man work on the lines he really *likes*. No man ever does good work unless he likes it: evasion is all you can get out of him by compulsion.' However, he went so far as to speak for George Lansbury, SDF candidate at Walworth in a February by-election.[10]

On 21 February he spoke twice at Birmingham. On 11 March he spoke twice at Manchester, at the Free Trade Hall and near the Ship Canal in the open air. He declared that he had been wrong, and Hyndman right, in coming out for a policy of political objectives or palliatives. 'We are now hand in glove.' On May Day he spoke from the SDF platform. A drawing by Crane shows him stick-supported on a wagon wreathed with greenery. In *Justice*, 16 June, in *How I Became a Socialist*, he stressed the importance of cultural matters for the socialist movement and made some jesting comments on his difficulties in grappling with *Capital*. Such passages must be seen in their context; he was thinking of the doctrinaire and bleakly mechanistic attitudes of the SDF and wanted to suggest that perhaps after all there was more to learn from Marx, whose meanings did not lie so easily on the surface.

At Whitsun he went on a holiday to Northern France. Late in July he testified at the trial of Tom Cantwell, once on the League council and *Commonweal* compositor, who had been charged with 'soliciting the murder of members of the royal family' through selling a pamphlet which defended the anarchist killing of Carnot in France, near Tower Bridge while the Prince and Princess of Wales were opening the bridge. On 8 August the printing of the Chaucer at last began. Morris spent much of the autumn at Kelmscott. He was now feeling much weaker and could seldom take long walks or spend days at fishing. Late in September, on a walk, while his companions perched on a gate to rest, he sat on the roadside with his legs straight out. 'I shall sit on the world.' Mackail tells us:

Two days later, on a Sunday morning in Buscot Wood, he talked for some two hours on end on the principles of conducting business, with all his old keen insight and fertility of illustration. It was noticeable how he seemed to speak of the whole matter as, for himself, a past experience. One of the visitors at Kelmscott that week was Sir Edward Burne-Jones's little grandson, in whose favour Morris discarded any prejudices which he might have against other children than his own; for outside of his own family he was not a lover of children and seldom took any notice of them.

He was working hard at borders and initials for the Chaucer. Early November he was back in London, where the first elections under the Local Government Act of 1894 were being held. On 14 December he wrote to Georgie, who was standing at Rottingdean:

Well now. I hope you will come in at the head of the poll; and I hope we shall beat our Bumbles. No one here can even guess how it will go. I daresay you think me rather lukewarm about the affair; but I am so depressed with the pettiness and timidity of the bill and the checks and counterchecks with which such an obvious measure has been hedged about, that all I can hope is that people will be able to keep up the excitement about it till they have got it altered somewhat. However, I shall go and vote for my twelve to-morrow morning, but I am lethargic and faint-hearted.

A week later he wrote to thank her for the circular she had sent to her electors: 'as good as the subject admits'. She had won. 'Here they beat us properly; though I don't think, all things considered, that it was so bad, as we polled about half of what they did.' In all London the middle class had voted against them. 'They have an instinct, which they can't resist, against any progress in any direction. Item, they are very fearful lest the rates should be raised on them; as they certainly will be, whoever is in. We did better with the Guardians' election, getting eight out of twelve.'

The campaign for unity had received a rebuff from Hyndman, who rejected a new approach from the ILP, though the Hammersmith Society welcomed it. Late in the year Morris finished his *Beowulf,* one of his least successful productions. During this winter his mother died. He told Georgie: 'Tuesday I went to bury my mother: a pleasant winter day with gleams of sun. She was laid in the churchyard close by the house, a very pretty place among the great wych-elms, which, if it were of no use to her, was softening to us. Altogether my old and callous heart was touched by the absence of what had been so kind to me and fond of me. She was eighty-nine, and had been ill for nearly four years.'[11] Early in 1895 Morris was working on the *Heimskringla* with Magnusson, taking up the version he had begun over twenty years before. Looking back at the elections, he felt that the enthusiasm felt by some of his colleagues on capturing a part of the Liberal vote was 'tommy-rot', leaving him cold. The third hand-press was turning out a selection of Coleridge, to be followed by editions of Keats and Shelley. We have the notes he made on 30 March for a talk to be given next day on 'What We Have to Look For'. He goes at some length into the question of reformism, of limited objectives with no perspective of deep-going change. Confused as the labour movement still seems, he feels inherent in it 'a spirit of antagonism to our present foolish wasteful system' and 'a sense of the unity of labour as against the exploiters of labour which is the one necessary idea for those who were ever so little conscious of making towards Socialism'. As a sign of the true response to ideas of socialism he points to the great response gained by Comrade Blatchford's *Merry England.* Again he expresses his hopes for a united party. This year when Glasier saw him for the last time, he asked many questions about the ILP, Hardie, and the movement in the North. At the end, laying his hand on Glasier's shoulder, he said, 'Ah, lad! if the workers are *really* going to march—won't we all fall in.'

All the evidence then shows that Morris was as devoted to the cause in his last years as he ever was. But because of his failing health from 1891 on, which slowed down and limited his activities, the word went round in intellectual circles that he was disillusioned and losing heart. Such stories were sure to spring up among groups who did not understand him or who felt in various confused ways a certain sense of shame or affront at his rejection of the artist's claim to a special or privileged position, above the struggles of the people.

By April there were changes in the system of holding Kelmscott. The old owner of the Manor Farm had died and Morris lent the son £6,000 so that he could buy the whole estate of 275 acres, while agreeing to renew Morris's lease for another twenty years. Thus in effect the estate was mortgaged to

Morris. In April, Morris was in the manor house, enjoying the spring flowers. By the end of the month he had finished his *Heimskringla* and a new romance, *The Water of the Wondrous Isles*, and was hard at work defending Peterborough Cathedral from vandalism. On 9 May the *Daily Chronicle* published a letter coming to the rescue of Epping Forest against the 'experts'. He summed up: 'We want a thicket, not a park.' He had heard of the tree-felling and gone with Webb, Walker, Ellis, and Cockerell on a long walk through the woods, from Loughton to Chingford, during which they 'laughed and talked and enjoyed every moment'. On May Day he was once more on the SDF platform. In *Justice* he again drew the contrasts between the reformist and the revolutionary ways. The crux of the matter lay, he said, not simply in the improvement of conditions but rather 'in the change of position of the working classes'. That is, the question was not one of bettering conditions from above, but of implicating the workers in action so that the partial aim in time became the comprehensive one of achieving a new kind of society. During May, Morris, Walker, Carruthers and Cockerell spent a week in northern France. At Beauvais Morris knocked Cockerell up at 7 a.m. to help in buying a thirteenth-century manuscript he had noticed going cheap in an old curiosity shop. Late in the month it was found that a number of the Chaucer sheets had been discoloured through some error in the preparation of the ink. The yellow stain could be removed, they found, by careful bleaching in the sun, but it was not till late in the autumn Morris was satisfied that the stain would not reappear. On 1 June in *The Times* he again took up the question of monuments in Westminster Abbey. In July he revisited Suffolk, staying in particular at Blythborough, while the second haycrop was being taken in in the marshland valley. He also took up with the Thames Conservancy Board the proposal to rebuild the lock-keeper's cottage at Eaton Weir.

His romance *The Wood Beyond the World* had been published. The *Spectator* review, he told Georgie, had interpreted the book as 'a Socialist allegory of Capital and Labour! It was written with such an air of cock-certainty that I thought people might think that I had told the reviewer himself; so I wrote a note to explain that he was wrong.' In the note he called the work 'a tale pure and simple, with nothing didactic about it. If I have to write or speak on social problems, I always try to be as direct as I possibly can be'. But that did not mean the story had no meaning at all. It tells how Walter leaves home because of the infidelities of his heartless wife. He has a vision of a horrible dwarf, a beautiful woman, and her handmaid.

He sails away and later has the same vision. He and his ship are driven on to a strange country where he feels impelled to go inland through the mountain cleft. There he meets the maid, who is under the magical power of the woman. He may not even touch her for fear that the woman will know and will destroy them both. The woman herself is tiring of the lover she has taken, and is ready to inveigle Walter. He has to pretend love, embrace her, tell ceaseless lies, waiting till the maid has matured her counter-magics, which bring about the woman's death. The pair flee and are caught by the Bearfolk, who take the maid among her flowers to be a goddess. (The maid here supplants the woman, who had previously been worshipped.) The lovers reach a city where through a strange custom Walter is chosen king. He opens all the prisons and succours the needy.

Without any simple identification of the woman with Janey and the maid with Georgie, we feel that Morris has here packed all his deep revulsion from the life of lies and semi-lies that he has lived domestically for so many years. The story powerfully presents the way of life in which the false-face has taken control and the individual has to live an anguished existence, torn between his human and his alienated self. A true devotion to love provides the way out, but in the deadly conflicts there is no easy escape; the cruelties of an alienated world pervade all relations, all forms of struggle. The end is not that of *Love is Enough*, the total enclosure in the fantasy of some perfect and consuming personal love; the lovers find their final release by winning their place in the town where compassion and justice are the primary needs.

In one sense Morris had been driven back in on himself after 1890–1. He had a deep sense of failure and yet as deep a sense of belonging to a movement which could not betray him and which would yet bring to fulfilment all that he had dreamed of a free and happy earth. He resolved this inner conflict on the one hand in his work for a united movement and on the other hand in the romances in which he turned back to his partly-suppressed personal life, used old themes of harassed and ultimately triumphant love, and at the same time finally harmonised these themes with his social feelings and aspirations. These last romances, from *The Wood* to *The Sundering Flood*, belong thus to a different dimension than did *John Ball* and *News*, *The House of the Wolfings* and *The Roots of the Mountain*, where the dominant factor was the social vision, the attempt to grasp and define concretely the elements of brotherhood and equality leavening past and future societies.

Here we may glance at the three romances he wrote after *The Wood*: *Of Child Christopher and fair Goldilind* (completed on the Press, 25 July 1895),

The Well at the World's End (2 March 1896), and *The Water of the Wondrous Isles* (printed after his death). *Child Christopher* was based on the medieval *Havelok the Dane*. A child-king is deprived of his heritage by a treacherous counsellor, but escapes being murdered and grows up obscure. He marries a young queen, whom another evil counsellor had meant to betray by marrying her off as bidden to the strongest and comeliest of men—not realising that Christopher is other than of humble birth. The lovers finally triumph. The tale becomes a courtly romance, with rebel barons, outlaw heroes, knightly encounters in a land of forests cleared here and there for abbey churches, cathedral towns, royal cities. The central episode deals with a sort of Robin Hood, the unjustly-banished Jack of the Tofts, who dwells in the wasteland. With Jack's help Christopher regains his kingdom, and establishes a rule of justice and equity. 'It was to him as if he had gotten a wound when he saw as much as one unhappy face in a day.'

The Well is a quest-tale, Ralph seeks the waters of wisdom from the well at the world's end, and realises that happiness lies at home in Upmeads, to which he returns, to guard it 'and see my children growing up about me, and lie at last beside my fathers in the choir of St Lawrence'. He passes through a succession of shepherding down-lands, wastes, forests, towns (each with a different character). One is a cheaping town, another an ideal medieval town under a beloved abbot, a third is prosperous and war-minded, with liberties steadily undermined, a fourth shows full class-division, 'a city planned in a spirit of dedication but completed in egoism and greed'.

The Waters of the Wondrous Isles has a strong magical element. It deals mainly with the girl Birdalone; the adventures of her and her companions are thus epitomised: 'They lived without shame and died without fear.' Birdalone as a baby was stolen by a witchwife and taken to a clearing beyond the wood of Evilshaw. She grows up under the harsh training of the witchwife, to which however is added the kindly wisdom of the woodmother Habundia. She is a strong girl, lovely and compassionate, ready for any job of work. She escapes on a magic boat and comes to the isle of Increase Unsought (a hell of spontaneous plenty where no one can find any work); there she meets three lovely women separated from their speech-friends by guile and spell. Her role in reuniting the lovers takes up much of the tale. In one episode she goes to a medieval town, the City of the Five Crafts, where for five years she lives by the needle, is taken into the guilds, and supports herself and her apprentices.

We may say that after 1890 Morris realised the limitations of the forms in which he had been trying to wage the struggle; he saw at the same time that the period of conflict ahead was to be much more complex and prolonged than he had thought. He turned to the romances in which magical elements often play their part and the quest-pattern is dominant: as if he felt that he must go yet deeper into the nature of history, of man's relation to nature, and grasp the fundamental pattern revealed in all individual and collective experience. So he discovered in various ways what we may call the structure of tribal initiation-ritual, in which the initiate, becoming for the moment the culture-hero of his people, goes through various tests, ordeals, phases of withdrawal into solitude, and so on, until he finds his way through into a new life. In ritual myth the triumphant emergence was often expressed as a marriage.

Morris can have known little if anything of the actual rituals of primitive life; but he gained his sense of the deep underlying patterns from his response to folktales and folk-culture, to the Germanic and Greek epics, and so on. He intuitively realised the basic patterns under relatively more developed and varied applications in the tales and poems; and thus was able to use them in his own way in the romances. We may note too that often we meet in symbolic forms the movement from one level of social organisation to another. Thus, in *The Wood*, the breakaway from the system of magical powers (which represent the alienating forces operative at all social levels short of complete and stable brotherhood) leads on to the pre-agricultural tribal folk of the Bears. Their system in turn leads on to the medieval city, which the hero transforms into a society of brotherly love. There is always the rejection of the false utopia for the life of struggle that leads on ultimately to a truly human world. *The Sundering Flood*, where the egalitarian attitudes are most strongly expressed, exists in a form that Morris would have filled out more if he had lived; in his last months he had to dictate it to Cockerell.

One aspect that makes the stories difficult to read is the element of archaic diction, which for Morris represented the return to a popular style, but which in fact cuts them off from popular response in his own world. Here he belongs to a group of advanced anti-bourgeois writers of the later Victorian world, writers who felt the need to turn away from conventional values and speech-forms. (Already in 1853 BJ noted of Ruskin: 'He transcends himself in diction, more Saxon pure and simple than ever.') With Hopkins, Doughty, and Barnes, Morris wanted to Saxonise the language. These writers sought to get a new sort of concreteness and directness into their work and looked for kindred forms to the medieval world. Both Hopkins and Barnes wanted to adopt the tricks of Welsh prosody, especially the *cynghannedd*, into their verse; and Hopkins said of Barnes's use of Dorset dialect that the poems charmed him 'by their Westcountry "instress" '. But Morris, who had enough to say of artists trying to solve the general artistic problem by individual innovations or single-handed efforts, failed to realise that language could not be revitalised by returns to archaic forms such as he attempted; the problem was to build on what elements of strength and imaginative force still resided in the speech and song of his own world. However, once one sets oneself to reading the stories, after a few pages the force of the narrative takes charge and one no longer bothers about the diction. Yeats found them so fascinating that he savoured every word and didn't want them ever to end. So far then from representing any escapist or withdrawing element in Morris the romances show his obstinately continuing effort to plumb the deep recurring patterns of human experience and to relate them in turn to the structure of history in which they have played a dynamic role of transformation. They reveal yet one more attempt on his part to grasp fully what the spiral concept of development implied.[12]

In August he wrote to Georgie from Kelmscott. He had been depressed at the sight of an old barn near Black Bourton with a new zincked iron roof. The struggle against destructive vulgarisation seemed hopeless, though he meant to keep on with SPAB. 'Now that I am grown old and see that nothing is to be done, I half wish that I had not been born with a sense of romance and beauty in this accursed age.' He also felt that he had been wrong 'when I have been "hurt" and (especially of late years) have made no sign, but swallowed down my sorrow and anger'. He should have acted as some of his Icelandic heroes did, gone to bed and stayed there for a month or two. 'But I admit it wants to be done well.' His strength was definitely failing.

Languor insensibly stole over him. 'It is sad,' Sir Edward Burne-Jones wrote in autumn, 'to see his enormous vitality diminishing.' He was less ready for any active expeditions, and began to suffer from sleeplessness. . . . He found that the clipping of a yew dragon which had been for some years in progress under the gable of the tapestry-room at Kelmscott was too fatiguing a task for him. His country walks became shorter in their range, and fishing was almost given up. . . . Even writing began to be a fatiguing task. (Mackail)

In September and October he returned to a number of socialist activities, so as to give the lie to the rumours that he was losing interest. The Hammersmith Society took up the subject of united action again, but Hyndman rejected the plea. On 30 October, at the request of Hines, old Leaguer and chimney-sweep, Morris inaugurated the Oxford Socialist Union at an enthusiastic meeting. On 28 December he made his last open-air speech, at the funeral of Sergius Stepniak (killed by a train), in a foggy drizzle outside Waterloo Station. A speaker had claimed Stepniak for Fabianism. Morris replied to the slander. 'This is a lie—to suggest that Stepniak had ceased to be a revolutionary. He died as he had lived, a revolutionary to the end.' And on 9 January 1896 Morris told an American correspondent, 'I have *not* changed my mind on Socialism.'

Meanwhile, on 4 October he had written to the *Daily Chronicle* against the restoration of Rouen Cathedral, and on 26 November on behalf of the Almshouses built after designs by Wren in Mile End Road; again on 13 December about Peterborough. In late November he had gone down to Rottingdean for quiet, with Rashdall's book on medieval universities and *Pride and Prejudice*. He was anxiously waiting for the completion of the Chaucer. The last of Burne-Jones's eighty-seven pictures was done two days before Christmas, and the same week Morris began *The Sundering Flood*. The theme here was of a deep river sundering two lovers; May says that it was taken from an Icelandic novel. Osberne and Elfhild can only talk across the river at one point where the gorge narrows. Then war in Westdale carries her off. He must go south if he is ever to find her again. His quest is ended after years, when he has reached the city where the river runs into the sea. Among the episodes is that of the lesser crafts rising against the greater, with craftsmen and commoners affirming the rights of the workers. Morris is here looking back to one of his favourite moments of medieval history: that of the struggles in Ghent. The monopoly of the older guilds is broken and folk learn that they need no king. In Wethermel, where Osberne succeeds, Morris builds a picture of stubborn freedom and direct simple living.[13]

On 3 January he was at the SDF New Year's meeting in Holborn Town Hall. He was welcomed with tumultuous applause. Lansbury moved a resolution of international fraternal greetings, and Morris seconded. The time was that of the Jamieson Raid and he turned to the theme of imperialism.

The Boers had stolen their land from the people it belonged to; people had come in to help them 'develop' their stolen property, and now wanted to steal it themselves. (Laughter and cheers.) The real fact, however, that we had to deal with was that we lived by stealing—that was, by wasting all the labour of the workmen.

On 5 January 1896 he gave his last talk in the clubroom at Hammersmith, on the theme of unity. Next day his diary tells us: 'Could not sleep at night: got up and worked from 1 to 4 at Sundering Flood.' On the 7th he sent his last poem to Georgie: *She and He*, a dialogue in a farewell mood. The beloved is splendidly married; the poet sets out on shipboard. The theme thus links with that of the quest-departure in the romances and helps us to see how Georgie was merged with the sought and lost heroine. On 18 January Hyndman revealed openly the imperialist taint which Morris and Engels had detected in *England for All* in 1883; the SDF executive called for naval expansion; claiming that the navy was not an anti-democratic force. On 31 January Morris spoke for the last time in public, to the Society for Checking the Abuses of Public Advertising.

In February he was still longing for the Chaucer to be finished, and was working on a new romance, *Kilian of the Closes*. After another stay at Rottingdean he was found to be suffering from diabetes, with complicating conditions. 'I don't feel any better: so weak.' (*Kilian* dealt with the conflict of medieval craftsmen with a tyrannous lord who imposes heavy taxation. At last the craftsmen feel that they must revolt, though they are unprepared for war, which 'was not their mystery'. The Porte had followed the policy of appeasement between the two sides, with unhappy results. Clearly Kilian was to come forward as champion of the craftsmen, bringing to a head what had been done by 'all the fathers of the Kindred before him, and their doughty trustiness and their hot blood and wise hearts'. The story shows that Morris was going to be more concerned with the inner life of the characters than in other romances. Kilian at a windy March sunset sits in his hall, turning over uncheery thoughts. 'The night drew on and seemed entering the wall from the grey world without as if it would presently tell him that there should never be another day.') BJ was disturbed. 'Morris has been ill again—I am very frightened—better now, but the ground beneath one is shifting, and I travel among quicksands.' He had been upset when in midbreakfast Morris paused and leant his forehead on his hand. The last time he went out with Morris was to the Society of Antiquaries to see some illuminated manuscripts, but Morris was too weak to concentrate on them for more than five minutes at a time. The news of his nearing death must have spread wide; Liebknecht wrote from Germany: '*Au revoir*, dear Morris! My wife, who translated your splendid *News from Nowhere* sends her love.'

By late April he must have known that his end was near. Mackail insists that he always had a 'haunting fear of death, to a degree which would be called morbid in any less imaginative nature'. Cockerell says even now 'he avoided all talk of death, and even when those about him knew from the doctors that he was beyond hope of recovery, we strove to persuade him that he was better—and he was anxious to believe it'. Re-flooring had been going on at Kelmscott Manor since late 1895. On 17 April Webb wrote to the flooring company to say that he hoped the new wood floors would be laid soon as the doctor was sending Morris down on the 22nd. On the 27th Morris wrote from Kelmscott to Webb: 'I don't seem to mend a bit, am weak and balley-achy. Let that pass.' But he could still enjoy the flowers and the apple-blossom. He wrote to Georgie also about the flowers. 'I have enjoyed the garden very much, and should never be bored by walking about and about in it.' He was doing a little drawing and writing. This year was produced the *Compton* paper, probably his finest, a luxuriance of poppies, tulips, honeysuckle, speedwell and pimpernels.[14]

For the special issue of *Justice* on May Day he wrote an eloquent essay, which gains poignancy from the circumstances of its writing. 'Waste of material, waste of labour. . . . Waste, in one word, of LIFE.' The day of re-birth will come.

Anything less than that the capitalist power will brush aside. But that they cannot; for what will it mean? The most important part of their machinery, the 'hands', becoming MEN, and saying, 'Now at last we will it; we will produce no more for profit but for *use*, for *happiness*, for LIFE.'

He had composed this essay at Kelmscott. Back in London on 6 May he found that all the Chaucer illustrations were printed and the title-page block was ready for approval. Two days later the book was done. Near the end of the month he spent a few days at Blunt's Newbuildings Place. On 2 June the first pair of Chaucers came from the binder. Most of this month he spent at Folkestone; but the sea air did him no good, and the ribbon-development along the coast infuriated him. He was near a state of nervous prostration and his condition was worsened by news of his friend Middleton's death. Still he strolled about the harbour and on the Leas; and one fine day he went to Boulogne and back with Cockerell. Friends kept coming down to see him, the BJs, Ellis, Blunt, Walker and others. Early in July he returned to London and saw his doctor. 'He thought me a little better (I'm not), and ordered me a sea voyage.' He felt too weak to do any work, he told Wyatt.

He went on a sea-trip to Norway with Carruthers on 22 July. But he was weary and restless all the time. In his disordered state he thought the rope-coils on the decks were serpents preparing to crush the life out of him. (We are told the obsession stayed with him till Mary de Morgan, nursing him near the end, managed to cure him of it. 'You have rid me of the coils,' he told her.) In Norway, depressed by the melancholy firths, he could make no excursions. He stayed at Vadsö, near North Cape, a week, and then sailed back to England. However, Carruthers told May that he joked with other passengers and liked to have his deck-chair set near the youngest and prettiest of the women. From Norway he had sent a telegram of greetings to the International Socialist Workers' Congress in London, at which Keir Hardie and Tom Mann gave fraternal addresses, but which was finally dominated by the anarchists.

On 18 August he reached Tilbury. He wrote at once to Webb:

My dear Fellow, I am back. Please come and see me. I saw Thrundhjem—big church, terribly restored, but well worth seeing: in fact, as beautiful as can be. It quite touched my hard heart. Yours affectionately, W.M. P.S. Somewhat better, but hated the voyage; so glad to be home.

He wanted above all to get to Kelmscott, but in a day or two he felt too ill to travel. He wrote to Jenny:

Dearest own child, I am so distressed that I cannot get down to Kelmscott on Saturday; but I am not well, & the doctors will not let me; please my own dear forgive me, for I long to see you with all my heart. I hope to get down early next week, darling. I send you my very best love & am Your loving father W.M.

It was to Jenny, not to Janey, that he turned in this dire moment. Tom Wardle wrote asking him to try the pure Derbyshire air at Swainslow; in a dictated reply Morris said that he was now too weak to walk over his own threshold; but he asked if the Manifold wasn't the river that Wardle once carried him across on his back—'which situation tickled us so much that, owing to inextinguishable laughter, you nearly dropped me in. What pleasant old times those were.' The last few lines of *The Sundering Flood* were dictated to Cockerell on 8 September. A few days before, he wrote in his own hand to Georgie at Rottingdean: 'Come soon, I want a sight of your dear face.' With Ellis he was working at a selection of Border Ballads. The project of the *Morte d'Arthur*, illustrated by BJ, had to be dropped. Congestion of the left lung had set in and refused to go. A general organic degeneration went steadily on. The tenderness and quick response, which Mackail says had always been part of his nature, had got out of control. On one of her last visits Georgie found he burst into tears when something was said about the hard life of the poor. He longed to hear some medieval music. Arnold Dolmetsch brought a pair of virginals to Kelmscott House. The pieces that Morris liked best were a pavane and a galliard by William Byrd. He broke into a cry of joy at the opening phrase, and after the music had been repeated he was too deeply moved to hear any more. Benson brought some thirteenth-century manuscripts from the Dorchester House library. Morris could only look at them a few minutes at a time, but they gave him much delight.

Webb, the BJs, Emery Walker, Cockerell and Mary de Morgan tended him devotedly. On 29 September he said that he felt better. The weather was fine and they took him out in a bathchair, into Ravenscourt Park. He said that he was so little tired he felt able to do some walking. At 4.45 Cockerell went to the post and on his return found him upstairs with blood streaming from his mouth. Ellis was with him. They helped him down and put him to bed. Four days later, at 11.15 on 3 October, he quietly died. Almost his last words were, 'I want to get mumbo jumbo out of the world.' Janey, May, Georgie, Mary de Morgan were in the room. Mary and Walker went to Kelmscott to break the news to Jenny.

The burial took place on the 6th in Kelmscott churchyard, with south-westerly winds at gale force. The low-lying meadows were flooded and the noise of water was everywhere. Four countrymen in moleskins carried the body to an open hay-cart festooned with vines, alder, and bullrushes, and a bay wreath lay on the coffin of unpolished oak with wrought-iron handles. The mourners followed the cart down the dripping lanes. The church was decorated inside for harvest-festival; the vicar of Little Faringdon, who read the service, had been at Marlborough with Morris. Among the mourners were Burns, Jack Williams, Crane, Kropotkin, the BJs, workers from Merton Abbey, members of the Art Workers' Guild, Webb, Walker, Ellis, Arthur Hughes, Richmond, Cockerell, Cunninghame Graham. But there were many thousands of workers all over England who joined in the mourning. Fred Charles, still serving his sentence over the Walsall Case in Portland Gaol, met Edward Carpenter with tears in his eyes. Alf Mattison, engineer of Leeds, tells us: 'Well do I remember that grey October morning, when— amid the rattle of riveters' hammers [and] the whirl of machinery . . . a fellow shopmate, who shared my admiration for William Morris, shouted the sad news to me through the tube-plate of a boiler ... that he, the inspirer of my youthful ideals, had passed away.' Muncey, postal worker and Leaguer, wrote later, 'The greatest man that ever lived on this planet.' Blatchford in the *Clarion* made the most adequate statement:

I cannot help thinking that it does not matter what goes into the *Clarion* this week, because William Morris is dead. . . . He was our best man, and he is dead. . . . I have just been reading the obituary notices in some of the London papers, and I feel sick and sorry. The fine phrases, the elaborate compliments, the ostentatious parade of their own erudition, and the little covert sneers at the Socialism Morris loved: all the tawdry upholsteries of these journalistic undertakers seems like desecration. . . . Morris was not only a genius, he was a *man*. Strike at him where you would, he rang true.

Janey went to stay for six months in Egypt with the Blunts. Her health became better, and she was even ready to talk. Will Rothenstein says that he found her, not the noble silent figure of legend, but serene, interested, 'an admirable talker, wholly without self-consciousness'. But she could still be the silent sphinx. Dorothy, daughter of Robert Steele, tells me that as a schoolgirl she was sent once with books to May Morris at Hammersmith. 'Mrs Morris was dressed in black, seated in a chair; she did not speak or show by any sign that I was in the room.' Her letters to Cockerell bring out how practical and business-like she was. When the Hammersmith house was sold, she retired to Kelmscott, though she often stayed with Morris's sister Emma at Lyme Regis. In her later letters to May and Mary Murray she appears much more likeable than in her earlier years. 'I was so glad you enjoyed yesterday, it was one of the most wonderful I ever remember. I was tempted to go out after tea and saw such a sunset with the harvest moon rising in the other direction, the men working in the cornfields, many of them on the wains showing clear against the sky, a most lovely picture altogether, it made me feel happy & grateful.' Words that might have been written by Morris himself. She lived on till 1914. Georgiana died in 1920; May Morris in 1938.[15]

16

Some Conclusions

At the outset of this study we examined what appeared as the basic motivation of Morris, his constant attachment to the garden and forest of his childhood, which held for him the imagery of beauty and of freedom. All his life he clove to that imagery, while at the same time driving ahead to find ways and means of actualising the essence of the earthly paradise, of building a secure world of brotherhood and joy accessible to all men. Thus he had to find the childhood-dream inside history and then struggle to refashion history so that it led to that dream in a fully socialised form. Throughout there was an extreme tension between the personal dream and the vast range of reality which had to be related, understood, subdued, and transformed. But the dream was not lost or perverted in the difficulties of adjustment to society, nor was the grasp on reality lost or perverted in the struggle to find what elements in other people harmonised with the dream and made the actualisation possible. The pattern at one level remains very simple; at another it grows increasingly complex. The constricting or fettering forces are step by step identified with the elements in society that obstruct or distort the struggle of men to grow ever more human; the imagery of things desired is extended to take in all that truly develops and enriches people. Thus the personal aspects are steadily purged of their limitations, their more idiosyncratic colorations and connections; yet throughout the process the deep original dynamic persists. Morris's life thus shows both a remarkable unity and a wide series of enlarged and varying meanings, in which the original pattern, despite all the strains put upon it, covers effectively more and more of life, finally achieving a comprehensive judgment of his world.

Something of this kind of development will no doubt be found in the life of every significant creator; but with Morris the tension between the original pattern and the range of experiences that it orders and illuminates is surprisingly clear. One is tempted to say that, apart from Marx, there is no creative mind of the nineteenth century which reveals that kind of tension with such purity, force, and sustained drive. For Morris the adventure of freedom is also always a realisation of beauty and a communion with the earth; and so the liberation of the human essence is aesthetic as well as social. It involves always the re-creation of art as a vital activity pervading all aspects and moments of life. Here the positions of Morris merge with those of Marx, which see the division of labour and commodity-production at every point bringing about an alienation of the individual from his own body, from sensuous activity and self-realisation. But whereas these ideas remain theoretical with Marx, with Morris as an artist there is the unceasing effort to actualise them in the struggle to link art-activity organically with political and social aims. Not in the form of subordinating art to those aims as a propagandist vehicle, but in a complex effort to bring art once more to the centre of being and action. The arc of growth between the early poems and romances on the one hand, and *News from Nowhere* and the later addresses on the other—between the first craftwork under Rossetti's influence and the expansion of the firm into all areas of design in the productive sphere—is something that is quite without parallel elsewhere.

In saying that, one is not claiming a pre-eminent place for Morris as an individual artist. One has only to think of Balzac, Dickens, Tolstoy, Dostoevsky, of Turner, Courbet, Cézanne, of Beethoven, Wagner and many other great creative figures of the century, to see that his significance lies in a different sphere from theirs. From the outset he refused to make the outstanding individual artist the criterion of a period's art or of the ultimate values of art. He was a new kind of artist, a new kind of thinker; and despite his roots in Ruskin his sole fellow was Marx. His art in some respects looked backward, to the medieval world (and behind that to the art-craft of tribal society); but in its working-out it involved both an attack on the industrial world and a struggle to transform that world into something quite different, which belonged to the future.

He was an artist whose works required a communal basis, and that basis was totally lacking. No one knew better than he that it could not be the work of a single man or of any group of men; and yet unless he was to give up the ghost—something that a man of his temperament could not possibly do—he had to keep on struggling to produce the kind of art that satisfied him, setting against contemporary values the values that alone seemed to him to matter. That meant an acceptance of the existing situation as providing the basis from which to start, but no further. From the basis thus given the movement must always be one of transformation, with the present realised in terms of a spiral movement that included both past and future. From his mid-twenties the conflict between his childhood imagery of freedom and joy, and the denying or perverting world, was merged with the conflict between a world where art was degraded or made the property of an élite, and the world of his imagination in which art was a happy part of common life, informing all activities. What prevented the world of his imagination from becoming rootlessly subjective was the extent to which on the one hand it was based on a deep understanding and sympathy of the artwork of periods when the division of labour was still embryonic, and to which on the other hand it ultimately reposed on what concrete labour existed in his own period, despite the alienating divisions and abstractions. The proof of the concrete basis of his imagination came as he moved from the championship of joy-in-work to the full political and social struggle which alone could have as its aim the achievement of brotherhood and the ending of commodity-production.

Morris was thus always ready to test out the validity of his imaginative vision by seeking to put it into action, and herein lies his greatness. For with every fresh extension of activity he gave the vision deeper roots; and what had begun as the weak romanticising of the first poems to Emma ended as the richly-based concepts of *News from Nowhere*. Morris had very little philosophic discipline; he had to advance step by step in a close link of theory and practice. Ruskin gave him his first coherent ideas of a comprehensive kind: the belief that art and work had once been harmoniously united, and that they still ought to be, despite the general movement towards degradation and mechanisation. During the 1860s he tried to bring about the harmonious union in his own work and in that of his associates. The fact that this effort was made by means of a group, in which he dominated, brought out ever more strongly the limits to which such an effort was subjected by the pressures of his society. The struggle to extend the work without undue compromise forced him into ever greater antagonism towards those pressures. The feeling that the productive worker was fettered artistically and morally by the manufacturers widened into the conviction that there was a hopeless contradiction between socialised production and individual or monopoly ownership of the means of that production. Such a contradiction could not go on merely deepening; it must lead to a point of revolutionary break in which the socialising elements would triumph. Then there would arrive once more a communal situation in which a universally shared tradition of art-work would again become possible, necessary. Morris knew that the new community, the new art would not come about overnight; he accepted the position that the state would carry on for a while, and with it the market of commodity-production; and he knew that during such a phase the communal bases that he wanted would be limited in various ways. But, like Marx and Lenin, he believed that the transitional phase would not last long and would be directed towards eliminating, as quickly as was possible, the division of labour, commodity-production, money, state-power. (He could not foresee the longdrawn survival of imperialist forces side by side with socialist societies, and the resulting arrest or distortion inside the latter of the forces making for the death of the state. He would have been a severe critic of all such delays and distortions, while recognising the new potentialities of brotherly and egalitarian living.)

The points to be made here are (a) the logical coherence of the steps that led him from the fantasies of *paradis enfantins* to socialism (b) the fact that he was the only thinker or artist of the nineteenth century who reached Marxism by the inner logic of the positions from which he began, and who did so because of his inability to halt at half-measures or half-realisations (c) the fact that for these reasons there was no question of a conversion to Marxism; rather he arrived at Marxism through the dynamic impulsions of a quest that could accept no other point of rest. He lacked the philosophic discipline and training, the sense of mathematical logic, which carried Marx both into the ideas of 1844 and into *Capital*. But he had the positive qualities of his defects: a practical approach, an unfailingly concrete sense of people and their needs, of art in its full integration with the life-process. And so, from his own angle, he arrived at the same fundamental concepts as those that had guided Marx. He owned a clear sense of the living relations of man and nature, of nature and art: a sense that at the outset began from Ruskinian bases but always had behind it the understandings that Marx had set out in 1844:

The *human* essence of nature exists only for *social* man; for only here does nature exist as the *foundation* of his own *human* existence. Only here has what is for him his *natural* existence become his *human* existence and nature become man for him. Thus *society* is the unity of being of man with nature—the true resurrection of nature—the naturalism of man and the humanism of nature both brought to fulfilment.

Up to 1882–5 Morris had based himself wholly on a British tradition that began with Adam Smith, went on through the Scottish thinkers to Coleridge, then on to Carlyle and Ruskin. This tradition recognised the effects of the division of labour under industrialism and gradually sought to find and advocate an alternative way of life, in which wholeness might be regained. With Ruskin the revolt went as far as it could in purely aesthetic and moral terms; but his failure to understand the situation in terms of political economy (which was seen only as the instrument of the market-lords) led to a changing series of utopian or reactionary recipes for a better world. With Morris the final step was taken. With him the British tradition merged with the European; the moral and aesthetic revolt merged with the great philosophic tradition carried on from Bruno and Spinoza into Goethe and Hegel, and lifted to a new level of comprehension by Marx.

The final step involved the discovery and absorption of Marx, and the realisation of the proletariat as the sole revolutionary force capable of breaking through all the existing contradictions. But because of the angle from which he approached the issues, the moral and aesthetic aspects were never lost or obscured inside the political. Marx himself never forgot for one moment what he had learned in his 1844 formulations; always for him the ultimate aim was the ending of the division of labour and of commodity-production. But his readers, concerned with the immediate political and economic struggles, were almost all able to see only the elements in his work directly dealing with political economy. Morris then, for all his weaknesses, must be seen as the first Marxist who grasped in its fullness the nature of revolutionary change—indeed, apart from Lenin, almost the only one who never lost or diluted his sense of the vital unity of the political, economic, aesthetic and moral factors. It is of interest that about the same time as Morris turned to Marxism in England there was born in Russia the group called the Liberation of Labour (September 1883), largely on the initiative of Plekhanov. He began the Marxist analysis of culture, but without the active element inherent in Morris's positions.

Thus, Morris, far from being an incidental by-product on the edge of the movement, lies at its heart and has a contribution to make which sets out many crucial matters not to be found elsewhere. These mainly concern the process by which the divisions and mutilations of self-alienated man may be overcome. The key-thing is the restoration of work to the centre of human life as a creative and joyous activity. The concept of liberated work is always present in Marx; but with Morris it gains a new force, a new depth and concreteness, because his whole life was an effort to link art and life, art and productive process. The day-to-day struggle in both artistic and political fields involved a ceaseless struggle to reformulate the concept in terms of the deepened experience thus brought about. The utopia in the sense of an imagined future became more and more a necessary part of the immediate struggle, and was freed from the arbitrary and the subjective elements of the old utopias. What was desired was what was realised as emerging from the struggle as new human potentialities. Marx had avoided utopian pictures because he knew that one cannot legislate for the future; he restricted himself to generalisations of what could not but emerge as the negation of the negative aspects of his world: the ending of money, of the state and its bureaucracy, of commodity-production and the division of labour. But Morris, approaching the same issues as an artist, felt the need to concentrate more on the positive effects of freedom from the old alienating forces. 'A reflection from the peace of that future will illumine the turmoil and trouble of our lives, whether the trouble be seemingly petty, or obviously tragic; and we shall, in our hopes at least, live the lives of men.' The man of an alienated world can catch, through consistent struggle, glimpses of what life would be like without alienation; and these glimpses indeed are a necessary product of the impulse that drives him on, the intuition and hope of wholeness. At the same time Morris knew as well as Marx that there could be no question of legislating for the future. Hence the way in which in his lectures or in *News* he keeps to general aspects, though seeking at the same time to conjure up the human essence of the liberation in concrete images.

Marx and Engels were aware of the disastrous effects on nature that a society of commodity-production was liable to inflict; but for Morris, with his concrete sense of the immediate situation and of the forms that must resolve its conflicts, the awareness of this destructive tendency was central. It was strongly alive in his Ruskinian period, as he saw men losing all joy in work and at the same time wrecking what visible signs remained of the ages when that joy had been vitally present. As he watched the destruction and desecration of the art-heritage, he also realised that nature was being spoiled, trampled, polluted by the competitive society all round him. His anger drove him on to understand just what the society was that did not merely permit such evils, but had at its heart the need to perpetuate them. When he moved on to join in the fight against war, he realised that in war was the same destructive and competitive spirit as that he had deplored in trade and industry at home. Having gone so far, he found it only a simple step to move on to socialism. Thus at the core of his socialism was the struggle against pollution and the destruction of the environment. He was pioneering a century ago in the comprehension of problems which have risen into the general consciousness, and even then imperfectly, only in the 1970s.

He also always stressed the insensate waste of the competitive world. Linked with the question of earth-pollution there has come up in our day that of the reckless waste of materials and energy-sources—a question made all the more acute by the increasing needs of an expanding world-population in housing, food, and so on. Large numbers of desperate solutions, mostly with little chance of adoption, have been put forward by the belatedly-disturbed ecologists. Some of these may have value as interim palliations; and no doubt a sane world-society would find its energy-sources in sun, wind, and water, which alone are self-renewing and unpolluting. But Morris already knew that the only way in which the destructive tide could be turned was by the ending of commodity-production and all competitive systems.

Hence the enormous relevance of *News from Nowhere* today, while it seemed largely an amiable fantasy and little more in the period between 1890 and 1970. Only for those who can throw off the spell of an idea of progress based on ever-increased production is it possible to see any rational or happy future for mankind. And what we now have to realise painfully, in a darkening world of pollutions, alienations, and production-for-production's-sake, is something that Morris was saying all the time. The details he gives of the way his future people enjoy themselves and express their deeply-satisfying communion with the earth, are derived from his own idiosyncratic positions; but the essence of what he says about happiness, stability, work, brotherhood, harmony with nature, freedom in association, has nothing arbitrary about it. As we saw, there are still problems to be explored in this situation, which *News* ignores or only glances at; but we may claim that Morris seriously and illuminatingly deals with matters that no one else (apart from Marx in his generalisations) has recognised at all: how men and women would live, feel, and think when the pressures of division have ended and all the old forms of movement inside society are gone with them. In such a situation there is only man set over against nature in dialectical connection; a balance of an unprecedented kind has been achieved, and with it a new relation of individual and social whole. We are helped to some extent by looking back at tribal societies, but the new world-society is on such a different scale and endowed with such different powers that we cannot draw any simple analogies. All mumbo-jumbo is gone. There is a new transparency in the relations of men with one another and with nature, expressed in a new kind of art that embraces all forms of living. (It would be expressed also in a new kind of science, and in the breaking-down of the division of art and science, but that is one of the aspects which Morris omits.)

We see then how his concept of work and art provided his revolutionary fervour and threw a richly heartening light into the human future; it enabled him to integrate his aesthetic, moral, social, and political thought and practice in a way that makes his contribution both allied to Marx's positions and complementing them. But of equally great importance were the immediate effects of his struggle to put the concept into action. Through the work of the firm and his lectures on art, society, and craftwork, he sent out a large series of radiating influences which made his activity as a designer quite unlike that of anyone else in his world. It is not merely a question of the virtues of his own particular designs and of the designs by men like Webb whom he influenced; it was rather a matter of the total impact of his ideas and practices on his own generation and those that have since followed it. He played an important part, directly and indirectly, in bringing to birth a wide range of organisations, such as the Arts and Crafts Movement, the Century Guild of Macmurdo and Horne, the Guild of Handicraft of Voysey and Ashbee, the St George's Art Society, and the like. We have seen that he had many predecessors as well as contemporaries sharing his ideas and enthusiasms in varying degrees; and many of these men made contributions of their own. But it was Morris who drew together the most vital elements in the world of art-and-craft design and gave them new force and significance, so that he reacted powerfully on the situation which had created him, and thus transformed it. Nor was his impact limited to Britain; as it spread it affected the main European centres. (At the Central Art Institute in Warsaw in 1952 I found a serious and intelligent effort being made to co-ordinate peasant-crafts and industrial design. I remarked how William Morris would have enjoyed the institute, and Mme Telakowska, who had done the main work in founding it, smiled and said that she had studied under a disciple of his.)

In design-work in general, ranging from carpets and textiles to architecture and book-printing, it was not so much any particular idea or system of his that counted. It was the total impact, the devotion and thoroughness of his attitude, his mixture of an historical sense with a feeling for the contemporary world, his respect for materials, his insistence on the relation of form and function. Thus his work led on to the Bauhaus and to multiple modern developments. Nor is the significance of his impact lessened by the fact that so many of the later practitioners, while in different ways looking back to him as the father of the modern movement, in fact turned his ideas upside down. What he had developed out of the quest for a new organic art, they used for devising forms adapted to the machine-world and expressing it. In a sense they betrayed his message. His protest against minor-forms of box-architecture led on to the vast and brutalised exploitation of box-forms under the name of functionalism. His attacks on the intellectualised architectural systems of the Renaissance preluded an exclusion of all human considerations from a mathematically-conceived set of geometrical forms; and so on. (Expressionist reactions against abstract machine-forms still do not embody his ideas; for they reveal a wilful or individualistic attitude, as far as ever from a human architecture rooted in communal ways of life.) But we must not make the mistake of seeing the parodies or inversions of his ideas, applied in the service of the alienated world of commodity-production, as having the last word. Morris's ideas live on, helping to reveal the abstractions for what they are, and stimulating afresh the adventure into a truly human world. This fresh impact of his ideas has been noticeable in the last few years. Here, as in the political field, his ideas are not worn-out or exhausted. Rather they are only now at last beginning to come into their own. They will play, we may dare to prophesy, an ever-larger role in bringing about the sort of future of which he so passionately dreamed.

Thus, we may say of his furniture and decorative schemes there was a steady development 'from the dark richness of Red House to the white simplicity of Clouds and Standen'. In his early turning to Gothic he was turning to a sort of 'primitive simplicity'. In his lectures,

Morris, probably without anticipating how he would be understood, was calling for a much more drastic purging of the Victorian interior, for an economic and modern simplicity. He could do this because he was not merely concerned with art furniture, but with society as a whole, and was as fearless in his approach to each. This is the key to his lasting reputation in the history of furniture design. There are few of his pieces or decorative schemes which made an important contribution to the stylistic development of the period, and much Morris work is distinctly conservative in spirit. Nevertheless, all his design has a fundamental integrity, a respect for material, and a quality of workmanship, which conveyed more than any characteristics of style. . . . His example gave dignity to these crafts, and encouraged younger architects to take up similar work. His call for simplicity sprang from this same integrity and has proved an equal inspiration. (P. Thompson)

Thus, while looking back to the organic past, he impacted on the contemporary world and on the succeeding generations, who made partial and at times mechanistic applications of his ideas, but at the same time he produced a critique of such applications and set out values that in turn are preparing the ground for an art which is both organic and modern.

One final comment. In a world where alienation, pollution, and destructive forces have increased so enormously since Morris's day, there may seem almost no point of contact between the problems and the possibilities then and those now facing us. It is easy to feel a naïvety in many of his professions of faith and hope, in the programme that he sets out for men in revolt against the dehumanising forces. Difficult as he saw the achievement of such a programme, his problems now appear as almost trifles next to those posed by a technological expansion he could not foresee. The distortions and pollutions which he saw as solely the work of a bourgeois world have now invaded the socialist lands; the set of resistances we face is incomparably more entangled and entrenched than anything he knew. But once we establish contact with the living core of his ideas, we find them in all ways relevant to our situation; indeed far more relevant than ever they were in the past. If the earth is not to be a radioactive waste, it will surely become something like Morris's garden and forest.

Notes

Morris's works and activities were so extensive, and the amount of discussion to which they have led is so large, that one could annotate an account of his life almost indefinitely. I have here kept to essential sources, which in turn give further references and details, and which can be added to by means of the Bibliography. The following abbreviations are used:

Ball, John Ball in Nonesuch edition; BJ, Burne-Jones; CR, Compton-Rickett; CW, Collected Works; *Cweal, Commonweal*; D, Doughty; DGR, Rossetti; ET, Edward Thompson's *Life*; F, Faulkner's *Critical Heritage*; GG, R. G. Grylls's *Portrait of Rossetti*; H, Hammersmith; J, Journal of WM Society; M, Mackail; *Mem., Memorials of Burne-Jones*; MM, May Morris (1); *News*, Nonesuch edition; Nons., Nonesuch; PH, Philip Henderson; RW, Ray Watkinson; WM, William Morris; WMR, William Michael Rossetti.

Lemire gives a full list of lectures, speeches, etc., with details of place, etc., and with references as to publication, etc. There has then been no need to repeat such details here. For letters there is Henderson's collection (L here, plus page), and the collections in the BM Additional MSS. The main sets are: letters from Morris to Janey, 45338; to Jenny, 45339; to May, 45341; Webb's letters to Janey or the girls, 45342; DGR's to Janey, 52333AB. As the letters are arranged in chronological order, there is no need for complicated references. Wardle's account is in 45350.

I CHILDHOOD

1. Sheltons went back to Henry S., mercer of Birmingham, under Henry VII. Firm: Harris, Sanderson, and Harris; later Sanderson & Co. Moved to 185 King William St. Reading: MM ii 613, cf. Shaw, *ib.* ii p. xxxiii; *News* 28. Area: L184, L363, *News* 16, L305, *News* 64, M. i 6, CW i 319 and xvi 68.

2. MM ii 613, *News* 16, MM ii 614 and 613. BM 45331–2 (12); *News* 127, 132, 135, 145, 175, 189f. Medieval survivals in early 19th c., Eggar, Chandler ch. 2.

3. M ii 343; Yeats (1) 178f; CR (1) 55–7, cf (2) 157–63; Richmond Papers 318; Watts-Dunton (1) 487; G (1) 162; Clutton-Brock 188; Noyes 20; Grey 57; W.

Clarke (in Lee) 13. Fury: CR (1) 35–7 etc. 1876: M i 329 (to Janey at Deal). Scolding: MM ii 612f, M i 22–5.

4. G (1) 46; *Ball* 238. 1822: CW xxii 254. MM i 250; CW xxii 87–91 (1880); *News* 130; L62. In general, Meier 605–11; note link with *Barnaby Rudge*, start of ch. iv; Nons. 558; CW xxii 91, 116; MM i 155; M i 143; *Mem.* i 212; L382 etc. Burns: CR (2) 163. 1884: Nons. 640f, 583; Meier 607, *Justice* 12 April 1884; MM ii 179 and 305. Visual sense: Meier 378–80.

5. Nons. 545. Scott: Meier 144. Afraid: M i 8. *Ruined Castle*, BM 45298 (32a). Novel, BM 45328 (10, 38, 15); *News* 197.

6. M ii 335; L184; MM ii 613. Webb: BM 45342 (59). Sunday: J ii (2)8. London: MM i 193. Also MM 615, M i 10; Blunt i 283; L320; *News* 95, cf. 94 (fairytales). But note children hardly at all in *News*: Meier 768.

7. ET (3) 3f; CW vi p. xiii–xiv; Meier 770f; *News* 76; Meier 773–83, education under communism, relation to Rousseau, 1886: MM ii 466; 1883: Jackson 129; *Cweal*, MM ii 305f. Crest: M i 12f. Note Ruskin and his Pig, which he linked with St Antony of Padua.

2 BOYHOOD

1. *Mem.* i 9f. College: James (4). Architect, Blore; Fleuss, drawing and German classes. Prospectus after public meeting 1 July 1842. Watson: Wiles 12f; G (1) 134; L3, M i 18, 22.

2. J. ii (3) 5; M i 17. Tortures: *Hist. of M. Coll.* by A. G. Bradley etc.; B. Gardner, *Public Schools* 1973. Blunt 231f. To Master: *Marlburnian* 1894, 187. Pugin: 'I wish to pluck from the age the mask of superior attainments so falsely assumed. . . .'

3. Some project between WM and Emma: L3. Desertion M i 24f; Mackail Notebook, Walthamstow; Le Bourgeois (1).

4. Riot: James. Diary of B.T.G.W. Somerset. Ruskin paid for the nomination of a pupil to M.C.: BJ and Millais sent sons there; WM and BJ executed a work in the new chapel. An asst. master says of riots, 'Despite the disorders, work has continued as usual and latterly has shown a great improvement.'

5. Guy was friend of Canon Dixon. Chairs: M i 26. Great Exhibition: F. S. Ellis, *J.R. Soc. of Arts* xlvi 618, cf. BJ's horror, 1854 (*Mem.* i 101), material and structure 'unnecessarily rigid and mechanical'. Paris: L163. Family: Walthamstow MS 106–9; PH 19f; Blunt L148; Isabel: J ii (1) 38 refs. Owen: A. L. Morton (3) 209f. My book on Dickens for Fanny. See correspondence *TLS*, August to November 1974, on Brothers and Sisters; no one there glimpses the reasons as I sketch them.

3 OXFORD

1. *Mem.* i 75f; M i 29. Walthamstow MS J 189.

2. M i 33; Butterfield 42; *Mem.* 1 93, 65; M i 35f.

3. B J born 23 Aug. 1833, his mother dying within a week; his father a carver and gilder; the school rebuilt 1834 by Barry. Early 1852 B J met the Macdonalds, the father a Wesleyan minister appointed 1850 to the Birmingham circuit: *Mem.* i 54, 65f. Dixon: M i 43–6; Morris compares *Oriana* with S. Russian ballads. Faulkner: *Mem.* i 75. For Smith etc. see J.L. *Meredith.*

4. *Mem.*; 87–9; Butterfield 41. M i 46f, *Mem.* i 76–9, 88f. The Pembroke group were interested in Carlyle, De Quincey, Thackeray, Dickens, Mrs Gaskell. Dixon gives date 1854–5, but seems to go back to 1853. Harry Macdonald also now in group. Dixon later Canon of Carlisle and friend of Hopkins; Crom became head of United Services School, Westward Ho!: Kipling, *Stalky and Co.*

Digby also wrote *The Broad Stone of Honour*; Ruskin said that it was he 'from whom I first learned to love nobleness', cf. his ideas on obedience and dangers of republics and democracy in *Fors*: Grennan 28; Chandler 155ff.

5. Poem: MM ii 276–82; BM 45298A; Effie's letter 16 Oct. 1921. Restoration: *Stones* ch. iv (v. Scott). 1854: *Mem.* i 99, Meier 185; the earlier citation seems given by Georgiana 1853, but must be 1854.

6. *Mem.* i 60, 63, 77f, 91, letter 81–5, Ruskin 92f; ET 55; May 133. B J had seen a Cistercian Monastery in Charnwood Forest, Grennan 26. Note first Anglican Sisterhood near Christ Church, founded by Pusey, with much effect on Christina Rossetti; Maria R. later joined All Saints's Sisterhood. Young Englanders (14 years after Southey's *Colloquies*) try to raise funds for Anglican Sisterhood, recalling his wish for English Beguines and Sisters of Charity. Maurice, Furnivall, Hughes, Kingsley found Working Men's College in Gt. Ormond Street; idea leads to many other things, University Settlements and Extension Movement. WEA etc.

7. Rouen: M i 48; *Mem.* i 103; M i 64f. Grennan ch. 1; Chandler ch. 5, for Young Englanders. *Mem.* i 103–5; Harry Macdonald gone up six months before with scholarship; C. Price at Brasenose in Oct.

8. Dickens: ET 71. *Mem.* i 106–8 (Faulkner); 102f, visiting old friend of Newman, 99; sports, M i 65g. poem, 51f CW xxi. M i 53–7; Meier 35f.

9. M i 58; war, *Mem.* i 109f; Smith joins, Magazine: *Mem.* i 89–91, M i 71 and 115, also 68 (Tennyson vol. of 1830). Letter: M i 69; for Fra Angelico cf. *Kisses.* RA: *Mem.* i 101.

10. Helplessness: Clough, ET 55. Grennan 15. Fragmentation: ET 67–9, Walth. MS (free translation from *Capital* in French); Page Arnot (4).

11. *Mem.* i 112. Tales: ET 53f; Hoare 33–7; Grennan 32. B J's stories, *Mem.* i

134f. Trip: M i 71–9, *Mem.* i 114, dating of *Frank's Sealed Letter*, M i 79 Jackson ch. V for Scott; 13th c., 55f and 65; attitudes to Ruskin 71; conflict over Gothic and classical in Whitehall, 72. V. le Duc had illusion of exact restoration: E. Wind, *Art and Anarchy* 1963 163f; Corbusier, *Quand les cathédrales étaient blanches* 1937.

4 ARCHITECT AND ARTIST

1. *Mem.* i 115–17; M i 8of. Malvern: M i 82 (Worcester, *Mem.* i 117). Letter 29 Sept.; to mother 83–6.

2. More on group: *Mem.* i 117–19. DGR cut, M i 87, *Mem.* i 121f. Fulford: *Mem.* i 88f, 'a great relief to Topsy'. Magazine: M i 9of, Buxton, F. 22–33, Grennan 31. Cracroft studied law (Trinity, Camb.), later contrib. to *Westminster Rev.* under Mill; pub. *Essays on Reform* etc. Lushington also studied law. Healey married Sept., and soon left for India. Street: Chandler 212.

3. Magazine pp. 443 and 559. M i 100–3, *Mem.* i 130–4. Street's: M i 103–5. Norman Shaw took over from Webb, 1858. RA: *Mem.* i 153; ET 73f, 91. Hunt: *Mem.* i 139. Topsy: ET 76f. DGR also drew WM as Lancelot for Moxon's Tennyson; Blessed D., *Mem.* i 153, PH 73. Furnivall p. xxv, 20.

4. Street: PH 55. Embroidery: ET 129, PH 55f, BM 45341.

5. 1891: MM i 304f, ET 84f. Stephens in *Germ* IV on Modern World, ET 82. WM on PR's: Meier 145–9. Politics: Grennan 34.

6. Note DGR's *Last Confession*, man changing from parental to sexual feeling. *Found:* K. Nield, *Prostitution in Victorian Age* 1974. Note *Mem.* i 189, BJ rescuing whore from roughs.

7. M i 106–8; *Mem.* i 134f (WM takes Turner's *Rivers of France*). Loved works include *Alice and the Angel, Col. Quagg's Conversion* from *Household Words*. Oxford: *Mem.* i 150, sister 141, Healey 144f, Faulkner Fellow of Univ. Coll. 2 June, entered New Coll. in Oct. Move: M i 112–14, *Mem.* i 147. BJ and glass: *Mem.* i 154 and MM i 15. Winston, RW 49–41. Alfred Stevens designed stoves and grates.

5 OXFORD UNION AND JANE BURDEN

1. See M i 110, DGR to Bell Scott, Feb. 1857. Mother: M i 111. Mary later Mrs Nicholson, i 169–72, GG 120, M i 122; put musical box under his pillow; street-organs, *Mem.* i 172f.

2. Jane: Troxell (1) 4; Tristram theme in glass, 5 years later, at Harden Grange, and water-colour in A. and A. Brown on Lizzie: 'thinner and more deathlike and

more beautiful and ragged than ever', WMR (3) 29. Ruskin *Mem.* i 147, PR show 157; WM plants tree, 157. Ruskin PH 62f, 66. The Museum, only building with R.'s principles and supervision, is very ugly.

3. Ridge: *Mem.* i 160. Val Prinsep, *Mem.* i 161f. Stunner at inn at Godstow. Pouring buckets of water on BJ and DGR; DGR spoils costly lapis lazuli. His voice, 'a kind of sustained musical drone or hum, rich and mellow, and velvety, with which he used to dwell on and stress and prolong the rhyme-word and sound-echoes', S. Colvin. DGR shocks BJ, ET 78. Burden: Mackail Notes 30 June 1897, Walth. J 163–6; Mackail to Cockerell, Sept. 2898, BM 32734. Pre-Celt, see Angeli 211, 'rather shy'. Swan, eccentric friend of DGR; Bowen later president of Union; Hill, later ed. Boswell's Johnson; Bennet, succeeded Bowen as president. Swinburne at Balliol, Jan. 1856, had already written on Iseult Blanchemains. Watts on the Union: D 234. BJ and DGR once made a pointless rush to London and back. Ruskin on Union: WMR (3) 193. Swinburne made scene at having to listen to paper by Acland on sewage. Dinners: M i 128f, *Mem.* i 166f.

4. Embroidery: M i 129 puts it here. Painting on beam at Drawda Hall, 23 High St., see Tunstall, Goodwin (1) 29. BM: J ii (1) 2. DGR carving capital: Lethaby (1) 24, M i 129. Satire: Goodwin (1). Cooke in 1857 at Adelphi in *My Poll and My Partner Joe.* In general: H. Hunt (1), Goodwin, H. A. Morrah.

6 MARRIAGE AND RED HOUSE

1. Picture: Troxell (1) 5. *Defence:* B. Forman 35–7, M i 131–5, Faulkner (1) 6f, 31–49 and PH 75. Effect Tennyson's *Idylls*, M i 136. Browning's influence: M I 132f. See JL (1) 7–11. Use of primary sources: Grennan 35.

2. Bessy: L50; BM 52470, Cockerell to May 5 Dec. 1915, also Janey to C. at V. and A., Meier 58; Cockerell intro. reprint Mackail 1950 p. vii. See D 374–6; Mrs Bell Scott, 'not an Englishwoman certainly'; WMR, 'created to fire' DGR's 'imagination', BJ *Mem.* i 187, 183, 176f (party). Club: 190 and M ii 198f for Carlyle, rules etc., Brown's furniture designs refused. Idealisation: *Mem.* i 169.

3. Trip: PH 77f, Lethaby 73, Fanny and Boyce: his diary, D 251–3. BJ moved to studio, corner Russell Sq. and Howland St.; Swan took Red Lion Sq., *Mem.* i 189. House Plans in V. and A. *Scenes:* MM 393f (pocketbook 1862), M i 166f.

4. *Mem.* i 191, 193f. Fulford, after leaving set, now back, writes to Miss Price. Illusions, ET 197. Janey: *Mem.* i 195f. Gothic: Jackson 72ff. Fanny: D 253f.

5. Upton: remains of Augustinian Priory near. Architects: CW xii 321f. Webb: Girouard fig. 10, his sketch of Butterfield's school at Gt. Bookham, Surrey, drawn 1861–2. Red House: Vallance (1) 49; Pevsner (1) 65; Girouard; Casson; Brandon-Jones 250ff; *Mem.* i 208–12; M i 139–44; PH 79–81. Serge: Dufty 4; dresser had links with W. Burges; Walls, BJ did 3 of intended 7 panels. DGR to Norton 'more

a poem than a house', but 'an admirable place to live in'. (Walls not properly prepared.) Embroidery: M i 218; Bessy taught at R. School of Art Needlework in 70s. Janey and DGR: D 250, 258f, Boyce 15 Oct. 1859 and 3 days before Christmas.

6. D 254, 684 (Middleton). Note sonnet *After French Liberation of Italy* based on whore's embrace; drawing, *Mary Magdalen at door of Simon the Pharisee.* Volunteers: Jackson 81. In Aug. Fanny married a waster Hughes. Brown's tale of Lizzie's intended elopement with Swinburne: Ford 248–51, D 275. DGR and Lizzie contemplate adopting small girl: D 280. Mrs Scott, 1860, heard Georgiana sing *Greensleaves* and saw Janey who dwarfed 'all we little women', Packer 155. Move: M i 159, *Mem.* i 208–12, MM i 315f. Guests: Hughes once rode down, Morris rode part of way back to London. 'We laughed because we were happy', *Mem.* i 160. Lizzie: CR (3), Troxell (2) 8, 'all people who are at all happy or useful seem to be taken away', Lizzie, June 1861.

7. *Unto This Last:* K. Clark (1) 264f; Harrison 96–101. Morris later wanted to print it, but found too many weaknesses. Firm: *Mem.* i 213, M i 145, Watts-D. (1).

8. Firm: esp. RW; Pevsner (1); Floud; PH 86–8. SK: Jackson 50, Lethaby 391 (Middleton carried on from Cole). Crane (1) 51–3; ET 123–6.

7 THE FIRM

1. Birth: M i 161, *Mem.* i 222f, D 277–80, Lizzie's child dead two or three weeks before, M i 147f; *Mem.* i 223. Marshall did designs of George and Dragon in glass. Fulford and Dixon now clergymen, Crom in Russia three years, Harry M. in America. Circular: M i 151f, PH 89f. For draft of trade letter after SK exhibition: BM 45336 (26v–28). Opposition: Vallance 58; RW 37: ET 124f. Fire: M i 161f, *Mem.* i 227f. Booby trap: *Mem.* i 226. BJ very ill, Dec. DGR taken up with Blake through Gilchrist: Gilchrist 111. Thomas Keighley protests in name of Gabriele against the son taking *Vita Nuova* as autobiography and Beatrice as a real person. Lizzie: Oct. 61 at Red House: Troxell (2) 8; DGR *Fam. Leers* ii 169 (prob. now the other letters and the wall-painting).

2. M i 152, 155. Capital 'an infinitesimal of the second order', Faulkner, *ib.* 157. Lizzie's poem: GG 89. Faulkner: M i 157f, *Mem.* i 249. April, Boyce takes Chatham Place rooms, DGR cannot go back. SK Exhibition: Anon (9), PH 93, RW 37. May 15th, BJ with Ruskin to Italy; June DGR abroad, GG 94–9. Churches: PH 96f; Sewter, for WM's glass, MM i 15ff, PH 99. Morris's work: L168f, ET 127, Shields 98. Two trends, RW 37–8. Citations: MM i 244–51; CW xxii 175–205 and 270–94. Lethaby (2); ET 136f.

3. Flowers: MM i 25; Sewter; RW 37f; Lethaby (2) and (1) 62; ET 137. Cheddleton is near Leek, Staffs. No sign of interest in Ruskin's new works, trouble through essays in *Frazer's*: ET 236. DGR parties: GG 99ff. Furniture: Webb and Brown:

Lethaby 19, Aslin 56; WM, see RW 53–5, P. Thompson, ch. 3. Elegant rush seated chair by DGR; Sussex chair 1866; later catalogues full of Queen Anne period tables and cabinets, despite WM's scorn of 18th century. Way of work: cf. Courbet. Costing: RW 35. Wardle, 2 Nov. 1875 (V. and A. MSS); Meier 55. Birt: Wardle in BM 45350(11). Middleclass: Meier 58, including letter to Brown (Huntingdon Lib. MSS). Miners, ET 50.

4. M i 162, *Mem.* i 277. In Feb. BJs at Winnington, he working at Good Women. Faulkner: M i 175, *Mem.* i 276f. BJ's bogey-drawings, *Mem.* i 272f (at school he drew devils). Glass: Sewter (3) 24–6; P. Thompson, ch. 6. Papers: RW 45; P. Thompson, ch. 4. De Morgan: M i 223f. WM and cooking, love of onions, women no good at cooking or clothes. DGR's *Music*, 1864, and series of *Morte d'Arthur* by BJ, etc.

5. M i 193f; buys Boccaccio's *De Claris Mulieribus* (1473). Littlehampton, M i 163, *Mem.* i 278–80. BJ imitates famous preachers. BJs helped: *Mem.* i 282; DGR in Paris (on painters) 283.

6. Jan. BJs move, *Mem.* i 288f; WM gives Persian carpet and Dürer engravings. 'Our Bohemian days are over now.' Poynter takes their old rooms. March: Georgie's sister marries J. Lockwood Kipling; Brown has show of coll. works. Party, *Mem.* i 291–3 (Christina and Mrs Scott do not come as it is Passion Week). Queen Square: mouldering statue of Queen Anne in centre (gone): M i 174f, PH 104f. Cockerell, ET 134.

7. Taylor: *Mem.* i 290f, M i 168–70, 175f; RW 35; J i (2) 6–10; Lethaby (1); Letters V. and A, reserve case 35. Altar cloth: ET 287, G 56. *Mem.* i 294. Louie Macdonald (later Baldwin) used to help. Move: heavier furniture left in Red House. People eyeless: Meier 57, M ii 93; ET 153ff. Morris takes cinder-heap image from *Our Mutual Friend*; note that he turns to Dickens for social symbols. (Q. Sq., see *Times* 12 May 1928, later history.)

8. M i 178ff, ET 144–54, MM i 401, PH 113–19, *Prologue*: ET 145f, M i 188 (bad taste). Late 1865 Browns to 37 Fitzroy Sq. where Emma becomes successful hostess. Conway notes Janey there 'not less remarkable for grace than for height'. Brown's glass-work; Sewter (6).

9. RW 52 for examples. Repeats: RW 50, paper 52. His scholarship ET 135; Lethaby 137, 220. Wardle (2) 1; PH 99f. Politics: ET 232; Allingham diary 149. For designs: lecture on Pattern Designing, RW 52.

10. J. i (1) 22, for SK Green Dining Room. L22 to Campfield, 'Burn this letter'. 1866 was Panic Year, says DGR, who however did well and opened bank account; painted Beatrice in a 'death trance' (Boyce), Tour: *Mem.* i 301–4. Wardle (2) 2. Glass: RW 35, Wardle: 'Morris often regretted that he was not able to make the glass himself.' SK: M i 176. For St James's see Mitchell for all details and dates. Webb: PH 108. MacShane, clerk, now doing the books; Taylor satisfied. Psyche: M i 222f.

Morris said (according to Blunt) on 29 May 1896 that he sold his shares and his relations thought him 'both wicked and mad', but there is no evidence he sold them till they were more or less worthless. He was probably ashamed of the whole thing. Note how euphemistically he tells Scheu about his taking over the firm: 'the firm broke up, leaving me the only partner'.

8 NORSE FORTITUDE

1. Critics: see Faulkner. ET 183 on Morley's criterion. WM: M i 185. *Jason*, after 2nd edition, transferred to Ellis, who agreed to publish *Earthly Paradise*: M i 195. Summer M i 186–8, *Mem.* i 304.

2. D 349, 616; after 1877 Alexa drops out, models are Janey and Mrs Stillman (who appears after 1874): D 346. DGR at Lymington in autumn. BJS: M i 192, *Mem.* i 306f; they stay 30 years, fine old mulberry on lawn. Illustrations: PH 113f. Guy: M i 191f. No interest shown in Ruskin's *Time and Tide* (one of his worst books).

3. Ellis: M i 193–5. Only decoration the title-page woodcut. Party: GG, 117f. WMR: Angeli 117, ET 232. *E.P.*, M i 195f, 266f. Chaucer: 197f. WM refers to Icelandic sagas, Border Ballads, Froissart; on Keats, 200. ET 162–4, 186–9 (reception of *E.P.*), F79–151, PH 114, 117ff. Bright: ET 164.

4. PH 124; *Mem.* ii 2f, 67; D 365f; Webb to the girls, 31 Oct. Magnusson: CW vii pp xvif, xxxiif, xliii, ET 216f. PH 135f. MM i 639f. Browning's letters: MM i 641f. DGR: GG 125. *Pandora* painted spring and autumn 1869.

5. M i 201. Maria Z., DGR (2) ii 685, PH 125. DGR (2) ii 688, F 173–5. DGR (2) 708: 750 lines a morning. Swinburne: F 196–8; he and DGR admired *Gudrun*. H. James: Lubbock i 16–19. Janey: Mrs Stillman as 'Mrs Morris for beginners'. *Grettis*: M i 201, ET 216f, 220–3, 225–7, MM i 445–96; Swannel 17–20; Hoare 54f; L186; PH 136–8. *Gudrun*: PH 136f, finished by June. Envoi: BM 45347.

6. DGR sonnets: D 348, 389, 391. Pandora sonnet in mid-March. Ems: M i 203, L26–9; GG 126, 121, 131. Troxell (2) 85–7 and 114–16f; PH 128–31 (Lizzie as chaffinch).

DGR still sends 'Love to Top' etc. Austin: F 93–100. Webb, 17 Aug. 'Dunn said —Gabriel was pretty cheery.'

7. On *E.P.*, Swinburne and DGR, PH 131, F 195; Ruskin, CW xxxvii 3. Taylor: Le Bourgeois (2). *Volsunga*: CW vii p. xviii; Haseall. *Pall Mall*: 105–7, 109 F (Simcox). Union: M i 124f. DGR: wombat as Top, Troxell (2) 92. From now on WMR in editing was careful to delete most refs. to Janey. Romantic idea of exhumation: D 417, 302.

8. DGR: 18 Feb. PH 140; review M i 209, L33. Chaucer, L34; family, L33. Illumination: M i 208, 276–8, PH 144f; J i (1) 5f. Stress shown in portrait, PH 145.

Wardle: RW 23. Madeleine Smith married W. 1861, died later in N.Y. under new name.

9. DGR: D 427, GG 135. Stillmann on DGR and Morris: PH 143. Chloral: D 430f, 690f; WMR (2) 157. Sonnets: D 691, 685; 'golden hair' supplants 'rippling hair' etc. Marie Stillman, D 434f, L34; she became friend of Janey. L34, Watts, Bessy, Aglaia. Watts: M i 213, PH 138.

10. Mrs Howard (later Lady Carlisle): Webb and WM decorated her house, Kensington, 1868. Visit: E. V. Lucas 35; ET 210. Gosse late summer 1870 or early 1871. Also D 453–5, PH 122. DGR paints her as Marianna.

11. L34, Janey ill; L35, ET 19, scared at new clothes, the children. *E.P.*, M i 201f, ET 189f, L37, F 119–51. BJ wants to do public wall-painting; feels old, *Mem.* ii 13; breaks with Ruskin; is attacked for indecency, ii 11f.

12. Poems: Goodwin. A Book of Verse: V. and A., RC.AA 17; BM 45298A; *Studio* 1934 97; RW illust. 80; *Mod. Philol.* lx 1965 340f.

9 KELMSCOTT AND ICELAND

1. M I 215–18; Wardle on ability to turn at once from one thing to another. Reads first page of book and knows if he wants to read more. Cooking and eating, M i 223f; sees self as Tristram, Sigurd, or as Joe Gargery, Mr Boffin. 220f. DGR: Troxell (2) 99. *Academy*: ET 205.

2. R. Church in *Apex One* (2 Feb. 1974) for Chapman. No sex: D 460. Ionides: PH 185. Commune: ET 234f, JL (5). *Mem.* ii 17.

3. M i 225–39; L41; *News* 186–90, ET 212; Dufty 28.

4. Love: ET 818–20 (Bodl. Lib.); *Cweal* Sept. 1885; *Socialism: Its Growth* etc. M i 235f. CW viii p. xxvi. DGR: ET 20, M i 274, GG 145. Tapestry room: PH 149.

5. Purkis, Bushell, J i (1) 7–12. Revised Journal for Georgie: M i 242. L186; ET 22. DGR: PH 159. Southey of Iceland: Grennan 11.

6. L45. Visit to Wimbledon: M i 273f. J ii (2) 7. Mouse: M i 274f. Watts-D. (1). D 533–8. ET 198. Blunt saw Kelmscott as 'extremely primitive' 1889. D 470f.

7. Poems: Goodwin; ET 195f; PH 116–22; Le Bourgeois (1). First title for *Wanderers* was *Fool's Paradise*. DGR: D 369, Hall Caine 200f. DGR: D 487–91—his fear of attack, warned Swinburne about *Poems and Ballads*, objected to his sonnets against Nap. III, Troxell (2) 201. Feud with Buchanan went back to days when he took over from him an edition of Keats, etc. In Oct. BJ in Italy.

10 THE HEROIC VIRTUES

1. M i 280. J ii (2) 7, L46. Buchanan in March in *St Paul's Magazine*: D ch. xi,

Grigson in *Encounter* Nov. 1961. Novel: L46. Janey: GG 152–5 Webb: BM 45342; Le Bourgeois (who relates poem to Emma): PH 165. Buchanan said he was encouraged by Tennyson and Browning; DGR saw *Fifine at the Fair* as attack on him (indeed it dealt with his type of inner split). Buxton F. defended DGR in *Tinsley's Mag.*

See Fredeman's important documentation of Rossetti's breakdown and also of his relations with Janey at this period, drawn largely from Scott's letters. This work finally leaves no doubt as to the fact that Janey and DGR were lovers in the full sense of the term. One interesting point in that DGR seems to have felt that Buchanan had penetrated his secret when he remarked that his House of Life 'is probably the identical one where the writer found "Jenny" '—Jenny identified with Janey.

2. L47, PH 165f; L48, fears letters 'stupid'. *Omar* done 16 Oct., M i 278f, PH 145. DGR: suicide theme of Arria, visit by Scott and Hake, Dec., carpenter against draughts.

Book: F 204–10. Now often at Faulkner's, M i 217. Glass: J i (1) 24.

3. L51: M i 289f; Meier 56; PH 169–71; ET 203. 'Don't be alarmed for any domestic tragedy; nothing has happened to tell of and my dullness comes out of my own heart.' Aglaia was in Athens. WM had never cared for Q.Sq. but the empty rooms struck a chill in him. DGR: Dunn brought a model for *Ligeia Siren* (orig. a nude), and Alexa Wilding came several times. May was used for an angel. June: Christina and Mrs R. at K.

4. Letter, 1 April 1873(?). Italy: M i 293, PH 171–3, *Mem.* ii 35–8. At Norton's, complained of feeling old, hair greying. Reply to Bliss about Rome, M i 293. L55–6. Aug. *Academy* on WM, ET 185. Iceland: M i 292, ET 219, L58, PH 173f. 'It is all like a kind of dream to me, and my real life seems set aside till it is over.' DGR: D 558f, changes at K., bit by dog, afraid of Fanny who was jealous of Alexa.

5. L58, ET 219, PH 175, M i 296–8 (old lady from Somerset). J ii (2) 7. Doesn't expect to return. L59, M i 301, CW xxii p. xxxii–iv, PH 177, wants to settle down as 'really industrious man'. M i 299–301. Christmas: *Mem.* ii 46 (Poynter married to G.'s sister). CW xxii p. xxix.

6. Troxell (1) 7f, D 562. J ii (3) 24f, letters to Murray. DGR weakens in summer. Maria joins sisterhood 1876. Ellis: see his few entries in Visitors' Book 1889–1902, esp. May 1–4, 1896. Garden City: L61, M i 302f, Meier 607, ET 232, PH 177. See E. Howard, and F. J. Osborn (Country-Belt); P. Thompson 62–5. R. Unwin, planner of Hampstead Garden Suburb and Lechworth Garden City, contributed to *Cweal* and supported SL in 1890s.

7. He had been at Bruges with Fairfax Murray, 3 Oct. 1870, now finds entry in book at Hospital of St John; surprised, though only 2 years before. L62, M i 304 to mother, PH 179f. E. V. Lucas 35; L63; PH 183. World-end: Meier 354f, Grennan, Litzenberg (2) 184, M: 333f. *Sigurd*: Goode, Hoare, D. J. Gray, P. Thompson.

8. M i 305–8, PH 183–5, depression ET 346, Troxell (2) 71f. Meier 741; D 567; BM 50531, f34 (impotent) 24 Sept. 1928. Next year also Janey at Bognor. Stillman says DGR still hears voices of his enemies. J ii (2) 8. Work: PH 191. Union: Goodwin 26–8.

9. L64–7 on dull Lichfield. Vellum-troubles, M i 319.

10. Dyeing: M i 311f, PH 191–3, Aardle M i 312–15, ET 129f. Floud; PH 191. Essay on Dyeing as Art 1889; bad materials, M i 311. Also ET 130, Crane (3). Herbals, PH 194, Loom: ET 130, Marillier (2) 16, *J. Derbyshire Arch. Soc.* 5 April 1893. Mommsen: *Mem.* ii 55f. Only a fragment of DGR letter to Janey 1875. Swinburne: M i 323. Oxford Union, 5 November. DGR has show at Grosvenor Gallery, D 603f; M ii 69ff.

11. L73, plans to take up his M.A. L73–5, embroidery, poetry; M i 327f, George Eliot. To whom? (not Kate or Aglaia): H; 327f.

12. GG 171 thinks *Near but Far Away* now written to Janey; PH 201f. Shaw (7). L78f, dullness. L79, Janey. L79f, to Aglaia, Sept., speaks of Wagner's 'instructive great work'; he may be being polite as she was sister-in-law to E. Dannreuther, translator of W.'s prose works, but he may have changed his mind through knowing more. DGR, summer movements, GG 169f, back to London, end of Aug. for next twelve months. Restoration: M i 340, ET 266, PH 323f.

13. PH 194f, Turks, L80–3; stimulated by letters of Freeman. Buxton F 83 on meeting WM at work on *Aeneid* in Underground. Maria R. dies in Nov.

14. Sigurd: F 230–67, Hoare, Wahl, M i 330–5, ET 227–9; P. Thompson 181–6, PH 203–6. EQA, ET 247–50, PH 211, M i 348. To Faulkner: 'I know the Russians have committed many crimes', etc. Examiner, M i 374, ii 49. Work: PH 188f.

II ACTION ON MANY FRONTS

1. M i 335, L84. Professorship: M i 336f, P. Thompson 146. SPBA: M i 339–46, L85, ET 230f, 266, 172f (Ruskin), 270, Jackson 37, L87f, PH 232–6 (Tewkesbury). Salisbury Cathedral, last old church for which glass was made (1878).

2. L86f, Mrs Holiday, embroidery; PH 188, 191; P. Thompson, 108–11. M i 351. Carlyle: L87, M i 345f; Meier 162f. Weaving: L89, PH 229f, letter to May 24 April 1877; in general, P. Thompson ch. 5 (patterns in textiles). Cosima: M ii 79–81, PH 205f, G. Haight 502. Manifesto: M i 348–50, PH 211–13, Meier 59f, ET 231, 249–52. Wardle on EQA: PH 211.

3. ET 251f. Manifesto 11 May. Meeting of 4 May, M i 350. BJ was at mass-meetings, Trafalgar Sq. and Hyde Park, joined EQA and backed Morris, protesting that politics should be swept away 'if God would send a besom'. Cf. *Mem.* ii 73f. Guy: M i 353–7 for June, July, 20–1 Sept., 8 Oct. DGR relapsed in May. Guy went to Oxford to take orders.

4. June 13th to Jenny at Hardwick (there with Emma 20 years before). L93 Ruskin. Fanny, GG 173, Janey's letters: Pedrick 208. L94–7, Mrs Holiday, also L1oof. In Oct. BJ found village of Rottingdean, decided to make it a second home; bought 2 owls at Brighton, *Mem.* ii 81. Ireland: M i 357–9, L94. Lecture: ET 248f, 287, 291, 296, 265f, M i 359, Meier 354f, *Mem.* ii 605, PH 238–40. Published by Ellis and White; in collection, *Hopes and Fears for Art*. DGR: D 599–610; to Jenny, 19 Nov.

5. L101, 104 to Mrs H. 'My mind is so perversely unarchitectural . . . I prefer the many-coloured work on the cotton.' L101–2, Gilbert and Sullivan. To K. for a few days. BJ, *Mem.* ii 73f. War-fears; M i 350f, ET 262, 297 for Marx and Disraeli. Anticlericalism: Meier 38.

6. Jan.: L106f, MM ii 468–70, M i 350, L109, ET 255–62. Hoarseness: ET 255, MM ii 604. Broadhurst, etc.: ET 81–4, 229; Armitage (3) 181–4. L111; to May, 25 Feb. 1878.

7. L112 to Janey; Arnold on Equality. House: L111–17, PH 217–19, M i 371f. On 25 March at Hadham, hair cut 'in the presence of my Kinswomen & the parrot'. L119, Aglaia. Letter to *Times*, 17 April '78, on City Churches, PH 237. DGR on damp of house as preparation for Venice, PH 219. Reading Finlay and Hugo: to Jenny 18 and 27 March. To Murray, J. i (3) 27. Venice: PH 222.

8. MM i 112–19; PH 236. On 6 June to Allingham on St Albans. *Death of Topsy*: I omit Dramatis Personae, text follows the copy sent to Janey, postmark 17 Oct. 1878, BM Deposit 4798; his first copy is in Ashley MSS 1412. Stennett is 'a Carpenter and Undertaker'.

Seances: *Mem.* ii 331; GG 103, 127; D 395; Pedrick 98–103. Watts-D. trying to get DGR to write: *Fam. Letters* i 367f. Whistler-Ruskin case, BJ a witness. Meier 183. Work: M i 373f, PH 228.

9. MM ii 77 (*Justice* 1894); H. Jackson (3) 145, Nons. 637; Fritzsche and Meier 250–4; CW xii p. ix–x. *Mem.* ii 90f. Loom: M i 373, 375. L127 to *Athenaeum* as to sagas, stressing role of Magnusson. SPAB, L128; MM i 119–24; ET 273, 279f; Meier 694; Nons. 492. Janey: Troxell (2) 73.

10. GG 178f; D 608, replicas of the Blessed Damozel, Naworth: PH 222f, GG 211f; PH 223f. Trip: letter to Jenny 23 Aug. Lectures 1879: LeMire 235 (Feb., April).

11. GG 180f, Oct., M ii 1f, ET 306, PH 255. NLL, ET 299f; M ii 7; Furnival 10. Palace Green: M ii 52–6. DGR, Christmas: GG 212, 181 (sonnet). To Ellis on fishing: M i 2. Barbarians: Meier 356–9. Work: PH 229–31.

12. M i 23f, ET 294, MM ii 53–62 (30 Jan.), other 1880 addresses, MM ii 63, LeMire 236f. Spring, Janey and DGR: GG 181. Arnold on Equality: MM ii 69.

13. Elections, ET 299f, MM ii 72. May, carpets, PH 230. Georgie's birthday: *Mem.* ii 106. DGR contacts: PH 223f, GG 212, 237, 181, PH 258f. August, estimates for St James's. Kelmscott: M ii 14–16. L139 (24 Aug.) on *Orchard* carpet. Work:

PH 187, 256; M ii 7. BJ jesting protest at bad pay: *Mem.* ii 105f; Kate F., *ib.* 110–12, also WM's hate of pianos, RW 69ff. Smith partners, PH 397.

Historians: Meier 160ff; Grennan; H. Jackson (3) 212, CW, xvii 319. Simplification: P. Thompson 75, 80f; Meier 622f. Refs.: Nons. 583, Macmillan 218 and 113, Nons. 513, 516; CR (1) 30f.

14. 1881 Diary gives details day by day, e.g. 22 Jan. sees Janey off by boat to Boulogne, etc. M ii 24, L143. Kyrle Soc., MM i 192–7. St James's: M ii 30. NLL: ET 302 (address 20 Jan. 1882). L145, work at Palace Green, PH 224, M ii, 45, 54–6. Janey: GG 182, L143f, Feb. letters. MM ii 581, ET 301f. Merton: M ii 34, PH 275–80.

15. Lectures, ET 290. L147f, more on politics. H. James: Lubbock, i 80. Janey letter: GG 185, George Howard won Cockermouth Division. WM meets Oscar Wilde: PH 271. Most: M ii 25–7, MM i 583, ET 307, 329–32; Bax (1) 42; Barker 36; *Marx-Engels Sel. Corr.* 391. Illusions: Meier 61–3; H. Jackson (3) 261, Nons 535f; Macmillan 195f, 198 etc. Still in 1882 speaks as bourgeois.

16. Hall Caine 141f; sonnets, GG 184f, Ashley MS A 1964 (37f). Trip M ii 16–19, PH 264–7; BM 45407; V. Hunt, MS at Needham Cool., Cambridge. Fishing: PH 268f. M ii 26f ('art'). DGR's book out, Oct., *Mem.* ii 116f. Carlyle and his liver: M i 28f.

Hints on Pattern-Designing: CW xxii, Meier 487–90, MM ii 584; Sparling 41. Letters: 3 Nov., heavy carpet; 28 Nov. *Daily News* on Ashburnham House; 10 Dec., *Athenaeum*, on High Wycombe Grammar School; M ii 54, L154f. To May, 10 Dec. at Rottingdean; he is going down, Thursday or Saturday, 'like a proper City-man'. Work: glass, J i (1) 27.

12 INTO FULL SOCIAL ACTION

1. M ii 66–70, PH 282f, L156, ET 288, *Mem.* ii 123. Tapestry: Meier 625, PH 280f. M ii 77, MM ii 616; simplicity, Meier 623f. Love of doing every aspect of work, Meier 517, MM ii 623, RW 53, P. Thompson 85, 191. Floud (2) for misunderstanding. Jews, PH 285, L157. Swinburne, PH 283f. Wilde, ET 187, 23 Feb. repeated 1879 address in series sponsored by SPAB. Merton: L159, M ii 70–2; up river with Wardle. St James's completed, March. Royal Commission LM ii 48–50, ET 131f, Meier 499, 516f, MM i 209, 211, 220; H. Jackson (3) 163. Wardle, BM p. 20f; 1883, H. Jackson (3) 129; 1888, MM ii 466.

2. DGR dies: *Mem.* ii 117, PH 260, Minto, ii 319, Mavor i 201. WM: ET 306f. To May, 12 June, to May on Hadham, hay-making; 23 Aug. on Carlyle. L161, Ellis. Oct., Library sold: M ii 87. L161–2, to Mrs Howard. To May, 16 Nov., Tennyson an old fogey, Dr Morgan and elections for school board, Borrow. *Hopes and Fears*: Buxton F. 98f, MM ii 584. Speech: LeMire 50f. Scheu: M ii 95f (making it early

1883), see Scheu iii ch. 6. St George: ET 338, 307, Meier 276. WM in 1880s: ET 119. Work: RW 69ff.

3. M ii 89. Joins DF, ET 308, 353f, Meier 306, 67, CW xxii 269. BJ and glass, *Mem.* ii 128f. Tapestries: PH 280ff, M ii 100f. DGR: GG 239, Mii 82f, Ricketts (2) 26 Sept. 1902. Paris: to May, 25 Jan. (she still in Dorset), L163. Feb. to see Ashburnham MSS in BM; M ii 97f (to Horsfall), PH 306, ET 308, 354. Middleclass, ET 345. DF: Meier 65; Williams; Tzuzuki 26–8, 92, 140–2, 270; ET 348; Bax (1) 173–82, 71f; WM, Liberty Feb. 1894; G 29. Slave-class: Meier 66f; Hyndman (5) 432f.

4. L165, to *Manchester Examiner*. L171, trials at meetings. May: Meier 71 n2; BM. 50541 (49f). Ellis and fishing, May M ii 101. Letters to Maurice: M ii 162–9, sets our case more weakly than to Horsfall, H. George and poor woman and son. L179, Cobbett. Kelmscott: Dufty 3. George: M ii 102, 109f, Meier 160 (history). L180, dyeing still a good sport. M ii 110f, letter late Aug. Religion: Meier 31–9; Christian Socialists, ET 364.

5. M ii 112f, ET 364, L182, working at 'lecture & chintz-patterns hard'. L183 to Scheu on himself. Hyndman asked him to join DF; Bax said asked him on to executive: ET 362n. To May, 16 Oct., SPAB and going to Kelmscott, cf. M ii 114; 23 Oct., lecture at Oxford and Hyndman speaking. Cobbett: ET 354, Meier 149–51, also sv his Index. 27 Oct. Glasier writes of WM in Glasgow weekly. Oxford: M ii 117–20, 134, LeMire 239, PH 300–5. Meier 183f, J ii (1) 3f, ET 309, 459f. Swinburne refuses, gives poem to *Today*: L191, PH 308f. *Today* taken over by Bax and Joynes. Fear of socialism: M ii 119, PH 305. Willesden: J ii (3)17. Profit-sharing: MM ii 603–6, Wardle to Cockerell 24 Aug. 1898; BM 45350 (29–31).

Capital: Meier 306, MM ii 606. German: Meier 309. Notes: ET 67f. *Socialism Made Plain*: ET 386f. Hyndman: Torr 174, 180, 183, 199. TUS, ET 390. Letter to Rowley, 2 Dec., glad he shocked respectables. BJ: ET 374f, PH 305f, J i (1) 23 (Viking subjects). *Erewhon*: M ii 90. Boston Fair: RW and Buxton F. 192. Macmurdo: RW 71f. LEL, ET 331. Open-air work, ET 362f. Designs card: PH 307.

6. M ii 120f. *Justice*, ET 365. Carpenter and simple life: M ii 128, PH 292, 319–21, ET 137f, L193 (Cobden-S. and vegetarianism). Lectures: L193, LeMire 240–5. To Leicester: ET 371. Art and Socialism: Ancoats, ET 311, 291, 378, Meier 63, 69. L194, Manchester. Poem, ET 312. Cambridge: Meier 74–6. Lancashire: ET 366, S. Macdonald (3). Allingham: L169f, ET 383. M ii 123, Faulkner and Oxford branch. Group active: ET 367. Champion, son of a general resigned commission because of 1882 Egyptian war. Chintzes: PH 311, Floud. Women workers at Merton: *Spectator*, 2 Nov. 1883.

7. Guild: M ii 198, MM i 83f, Meier 579f, Jackson (3) 218, 247, Shaw: Stokes 16. H. George: Meier 177–82. Gothic Revival, 'cheap and nasty', LeMire 83. LeMire lists 51 speeches (some announced, no proof of delivery) for 1884. Art show: Eleanor in *Today*, May 1884, 388; *Justice*, 24 May RA 'wild jumble' of inanity.

Bradlaugh: MM ii 102f. What WM would have to give up, 2 servants etc., PH 325, ET 368–73. To Young Poet; L195, 201, 204; Meier 238f. More on profit-sharing: L196f, M ii 135–9, PH 322–5, ET 371–4, MM ii 603, Meier 76f; WM calls self a mere hanger-on of the capitalist class.

Hyndman and Radicals: ET 394. Hammersmith branch: ET 393, BM 45, 891, M ii 124f. Engels, *Labour Monthly*, Sept. 1933; ET (2). Bax, ET 438f. Aveling, ET 428–31, MM ii 226, PH 315, Bernstein 203f, 162, 164; Salt 80.

8. 1 July, SPAB report has ref. to 'great man' (Marx): CW xxii 311. *Art and Labour* (Leeds, 1 April) dealt with div. of labour: LeMire 114 for WM and Iron Law, also *Cweal* 3 Aug. 1889. 6 July, lecture at H., *ib.* 242. 9 July, L201f, Scheu, Bradlaugh, Annie Besant. 18 July, L203f, students and 'damned religion'. 19 July, Engels: ET 398. Hyde Park, L208. Mainwaring: *Justice*, Jan. 1897, ET 382. Irish, costermongers, ET 393; L221f, H. minutes.

Functionalism in *Textile Fabrics*: PH 245f. SDF strains: ET 400f. WM feels old, Aug. to Scheu. On RA in July, M i 121–3, Meier 598, 694, 567, WM sees the aim of painting: vision, combination of colour and form; representation of place or person; mastery over material—i.e. unity, realism, craft.

9. ET 294f. Meier 643, ET 368f. Art-evening: PH 311; WM read Passing of Bryn-hild at Hall in Hart St., Bloomsbury, 21 Nov. L217 sees no hope of legal limitation of labour-day. Contrast ET 389. Hopes of near revolution (Meier 153, Grennan 153) but in 1889 saw a century needed. Blake: Meier 148f Sept. letters L213, ET 421 (end of break with Brown). Shaw and SDF: ET 584. Error of G (17 Nov.), Meier 64 n3. This year, interest in actual factory conditions, Meier 512ff, leading to *Factory as it should be, Useful Work* (Nons. 619); M ii 129. Lectures include: *Misery and the Way Out, Iceland, How We Live.*

10. ET 410f, 354; Meier. SDF conflict: ET 412ff, 401 (Engels); L220–9, MM ii 593. Engels: *Lab. Monthly*, Oct. 1933. Eleanor: Meier 841. Hyndman to WM on *Justice*, 28 Dec., ET 377, BM 45345. Reform Act this year. Wilde, PH 246. Sketchley's book, ET 321f; Broadhurst, ET 300, MM ii 72.

13 THE SOCIALIST LEAGUE

1. Meier 78f, M ii 132f, ET 368. Bourgeois, ET 422f. By 1866 there was also the Loyal and Anti-Socialist League of GB and Ireland. Forecast: ET 424–6. League: ET 445. Left workers: ET 450. Draft constitution: ET 448f. Oddities: BM 45334. Joynes: MM ii 172. Khartoum: ET 455. *Cweal*, PH 322, ET 451–3. Liebknecht: Meier 842. To May, 20 Feb., Jenny has attack. Aveling: ET 896. Oxford, Meier 79, profit-sharing. Donkey-race: L232. See letters to Fred Henderson: ET 875–85.

2. Trials: Meier 70, Nos. 644, ET 368f, M ii 98f, 117–20, Kocmanova 9. Blunt: V. and A. MSS. Faulkner at Oxford, Meier 843. Shaw: MM ii p. xxiv, Meier 70.

Scheu: L258, also 23 Nov. 1889, CIISG, Amsterdam. Engels: Meier 333–5. Style: ET 453 n2. Also BM 45334, MM ii 311, notes on propaganda, BM 45345. Peace-meeting, 2 April, ET 456f; *Daily News* 3 April; *Cweal* April. Jefferies: M ii 144, Meier 107–14, 353f, 13, to Georgie. BJ still anti-war: *Mem.* ii 148. Letter to Engels, Meier 843 (? 1885). 27 May, M ii 145, ET 467, 484, PH 328f, 331. Wilde: PH 246. Gissing in *Demos*: ET 405.

3. ET 477f. *Architect*, 6 June 1885, 339; Meier 595. Poem: M ii Lectures at H., L233. Manifesto: ET 849–57, Meier 278 (George), 690 (spiral). Meier 691–4. Saint Simonians saw civilisation cyclic and progressive, with oscillations of organic and critical ages, but moving to Golden Age. But this is still idealistically vague. M i 140, MM ii 170. Imperialism: ET 454f, BM 45333. July tour, L237; *Pall Mall* scandals. Tom Mann (1) 48f, ET 364. 17 Aug. L238. H. branch, ET 496f. Middle-class appeal till 1886, Meier 68f. Influence of past thinkers (Babœuf, Saint-Simon, Comte, Fournier: Meier 244–6. Fournier on div. of labour, 263f. Prologue, *Socialists at Play* (11 June), MM ii 625.

4. To May, 8 Sept., Rottingdean. Police: ET 467–71, M ii 146–8, PH 331–4, L239 (to Birmingham). Dialogue: I follow corrections by Robert Steele in his copy of Mackail (in my possession). SDF: ET 470, *Cweal* Nov. 1885, ET 477, BM 45345. Shaw (7). Poem by H. D. Traill in *Sat. Rev.* on how 'faction's poison drugged his poet-sense', ET 187f.

Gissing, ET 470, 494, 497, 778, 822. Work: PH 326, MM ii 188f, ET 499f, 465. New opposition: ET 425, *Cweal* July 1885, MM ii 194. Struggle with anti-religion, Meier 40. Cockerell, J. i (2) 28. Penny pamphlets: Buxton F. 120f. Joynes's version of Marx's *Wage, Labour and Capital* by the Modern Press that did Morris's *Art and Socialism*; also Jaynes's *Socialist Rhymes* and *Socialist Catechism*.

5. Oct., Meier 835–40, notes for *Justice and Socialism*. L239f; SDF, and wish that Scheu was in business with him. L240: like to see desert of Egypt. L241, to Georgie. Engels: ET 452f, Meier 335.

May and workers: Meier 71. L244, Gimson. Dec. ET 484; Mackail's Notebooks. Maguire's work: ET 391. SDF: ET 478–80. Engels: ET 478, 447.

6. Riot: M ii 151, PH 336–40, Torr 226–38, ET 480–2, L250f. Glasse: ET 483, Page Arnot (1). Aveling in *Cweal*, March 1886, on 'revolutionary change' as alone of use. Annie B., BM 45346 (9 March), ET 898. Engels: PH 317, Meier 335–9, Bünger, 84, ET 435, his influence. Also *Lab. Monthly* Nov. 1933. *Odyssey* started Feb. G letters, 184. Branches: ET 492–4. Eight Hour Day: Torr, 214, 216–21.

7. *Cweal*, ET 462, 486, PH 323f. Later Sparling was joint editor. Dream: ludicrous analysis, PH. List of socialist thinkers in *Cweal*, 12 June, Meier 242. June, AGM, ET 488f, M ii 159, L256. July, Ireland, ET 457f. Trial, PH 340–2, ET 472–8, M ii 161–3, *Cweal* 24 July; remark to lady, PH 340. L257, PH 341, 14 Aug. to Jenny. L258, ET 476. Mainwaring's speech: *Cweal* 21 Aug. Quarrels: M ii 162f, PH 344, ET 477f, 486f. Binning, ET 474. July sales *Cweal*, ET 500, 488. Mahon, ET 489, 525.

Emma Lazarus visit, prob. July: *Gazette J. Lewis Partnership*, 17 March 1962. To Scheu, 20 and 26 Aug. L288f. H. branch: ET 496f, 369.

8. 7 Sept. M ii 166, meets Powell (also of Walthamstow). 17th, fight in hotel, letter to Jenny; leaflets ET 513, Oct. lecture L260, 13th and 16th. To Faulkner, in Bodleian, ET 818–20. *Pilgrims of Hope*; M ii 168, Morton (4) 19–21, PH 343; Buxton F. 125, *A Short Account of the Commune of Paris* (Socialist Platform, no. 4) by Bax, Victor Dave, WM, 2d, 1866, Meredith quotation on verso. (No. 3 was the Avelings' *Factory Hell.*) Parliament, ET 525. Ball M ii 168. Yeats (1); his elder sister embroidered under May. May: BM 50541 (80). L259 to Bell Scott, loss of reputation, great day coming. Webb's masterpiece, Clouds, done 1877–86: P. Thompson 80. Birmingham: ET 493.

9. L262, ET 489, branch formed; weakness, ET 490f, 498. St Clerkenwell Green, LeMire 260. Mann: Torr 207. Kitz: BM 45345, Meier 284; 3 Feb. 1885 to Joynes. Kropotkin to May: BM 45345, Meier 283–7; Arnot (2) 60; L263; CW xxp. xxi, MM ii p. xvi. Meier suggests Kropotkin in turn affected by Morris. Gissing, ET 497, WM: ET 499–502, Carruthers 897, Avelings in USA 437, Loyal League, 423. WM poses the two views of Barbarism: Meier 369f; Lenin on anarchists, CW (Russian) v 377f; Meier 463f. Marx: Meier, 345. Lemire gives 18 lectures, speeches, this year 1886 (17 probably given, but no account, only announcement).

14 CLIMAX

1. ET 458. Diary: BM 45335, M ii 168–80, PH 345ff, ET 506ff. 17 March, Commune Anniversary, tried to be 'literary and original', ET 511, cf. to Jenny, 18 Feb. 1887. Hamilton: ET 515, Cweal 16 April. Northumbria: L271–4, ET 512–25, Cweal 16 and 23 April, *Newcastle Chronicle* 12 April 1887, Discord in SL: ET 525–39. *Ball*, see Index ET, Engels, ET 836f (on dramatisation). 27 Jan. to G on staying power, ET 506. Norwich group: ET 595; worried Cweal becomes monthly again, 508. 3 Feb. to Aglaia, growing interest in working-class conditions. Well known: PH 348–50, Coatbridge, Glasier. Need for unity: Cweal 5 Feb. M ii 180f, *Odyssey*; 26 Feb. to Ellis on socialists going into parliament. Easter, Hyde Park, against Coercion Bill. ET 459: 'There was a second platform for Morris's section, and I saw May Morris on their cart like a French revolutionist going to execution' (Blunt). Medieval king as oppressor: *A King's Lesson*, cf. preface to R. Steele's *Med. Lore*, etc. Naworth: Castle Howard Collection.

2. Sparling: PH 350. SL: ET 526–39, 537 (LEL), 536, 538 (Engels). Abstention: ET 539–551; MM ii 434–52. Sept. at K., M ii 187. Fabians: ET 545, MM ii p. xx, ET 586f. *Odyssey*: PH 358f. Jingo Jubilee, ET 365–8, N. of England Fed., 551f; People's Palaces, Meier 585.

Summer, river party to Hampton Court with Janey, the girls, Aglaia. 'Janey was too tired' to help: M ii 185–7. Mahon rejoins SDF, taking with him remnants of N. of Eng. Soc. Fed., ET 561f. L275, 25 Sept., Scheu and Shaw argue on parliament, Shaw agrees to act in Interlude, but doesn't. More letters, ET 545, Arnot (1) 7f, L276.

3. Play: M ii 187f, PH 359f. Janey: E. Rhys 205. Chicago: ET 592–4, Torr 159f. (Morris on George as traitor: Meier 278f.) Bloody Sunday: M ii 190–3. ET 568–88, Torr ch. xv, PH 361–8, West 34–47; Briggs (3). Effects: Stokes (1) 15, ET 583–7. L. and L. League: ET 581. Funeral, G 190. Further: ET 583, Bax (1) 87f, Vallance (1) 339.

WM and drama; M ii 188f. Mahon in Oct., ET 556f; unemployed demonstrations 569, woman with flag 575, WM's advice to marchers 574.

4. G 190, Arts and Crafts: RW, Meier 508f, M ii 202f, PH 187, *Mem.* ii 171, Sparling 50f, ET 812, WM at work. Letter to Sharman, ET (2) 4. Letter, 26 Nov. to May. Looks back at EQA days. *Cweal* 7 Jan. 1888. To Glasse, 9 Jan., etc., Arnot. Blunt in jail in Ireland, M ii 203f, L278. Glasgow branch, ET 596f, Mahon 552f, Kier Hardie 599. To Bainton, L182–9, Meier 48; to G, 16 and late April. Squabbles, ET 588f.

SL: ET 595f, 549–51; prisoners released, Feb., ET 582f, L178f. Worker's letter: Meier 73f, March, L280, ET 589. May: ET 611. *Signs of Change* published, May, M ii 205. Scotland L281f. Speeches this year: 105 (probable 17).

5. May: L289, 291. G. 191, ET 597, G 43ff. Fabians, ET 628–32; Engels, ET 871, 472. June, ET 613–15, 562f, (Cobden-S.) 645; *Cweal* 18 June. July, L291, ET 599, 548f, 599. L292, G 193, M ii 206, PH 369; L292, PH 369. August, Norwich, ET 602, R. Groves 100f, L284, *Cweal* 25 Aug.; at K., M ii 210–2. L293f, M ii 206, ET 606f, Emery Walker at K., PH 371f, L297. 24 Aug. to Jenny on flowers. L294, Hadham; M ii 208, L295f, PH 370, M ii 219, L298, G 194, depressed. Sept., M ii 211, L299, with Walker and Janey to Bampton. 14 Sept., drive with Janey. *Cweal* sales, ET 608. To Georgie: PH 372. 8 Oct., fishing, Tom Sawyer; 17 Oct., Alma Tadema's house. Faulkner: M ii 215.

6. Troubles over Lucy Parsons, ET 595. *Echo*: Meier 74. 8 Nov., Cobden-S. Journals. Mahon, ET 564, Typography: M ii 212f, L305, RW 57ff. Swinburne: M ii 213–15. L305, to Stanmore near Harrow about tapestry. In Manchester stays with J. H. Watts, impressed by number and enthusiasm of SDF rank-and-file, ET 613. Still conscious of wealth, Meier 82. Spalding's book, ET 340; monopoly and imperialism, 605f. L304 on Bloomsbury branch. This year, Art Congress in Liverpool.

Mote-founding as climax in later romances, Chandler 229; Herder on German freedom and communal property etc. 126, 221–5. Morris exploded when a German professor wrote innocently asking for his sources.

7. Fabians: ET 628–30. Speeches during 1888: 94 (probable 11).

8. Westminster Abbey, L309f, agrees with mons. in St Paul's. Spiral: Meier 692f; Jackson (3) 241f. To *Daily News*, 17 April, L311. Lethaby: L312, MM i 3f.

Feb., Mahon and Engels, ET 871f, 615f, 617–19. How shall we live then? Meier (2). End of big towns: Meier 18 n2; MM ii 461. System of federations: Meier 18.

March, at K., M ii 219f, decides not to kill Bride in *Roots*, but make her marry the Brother. Friends: ET 610, finance 611. May: Partingdon 158. 25 March, to Laura Lafargue on poems, Meier 843, 340. Easter: M ii 220f, PH 371, sad over willows.

9. April L313, lecture slides. G 202, anarchists 'ranting revolution' in the streets. Engels and Mahon, ET 871, Democratic Club, 873. ET 638–40, MM ii ch. xii, *Cweal* 18 May, 17 Aug. 1889. May, in Wilts, M ii 221f. Bellamy: M i 244, Morton (3) 24f, Meier 114–41. Midsummer, M ii 222f. Congress: ET 624f, 639f; Hyndman and French Possibilists. Carpenter in *Freedom*, Dec. 1896; Meier 340. Merlino turned up with same resolution at Possibilists.

10. Dockers: M ii 223–6, Torr ch. xvii. Visit to Yarmouth, ET 619–21. L316 to Jenny, Manifesto, M ii 224, Torr 301. Builders' labourers at Leeds strike while he is in Paris, ET 621. Summer at K., PH 372, Blunt. Engels, 17 Aug., Morris as puppet of anarchists. Letter to May, 1, 17 Aug. Coal Porters' Union, ET 652. WM on dockers, *Cweal* 21 Sept. 1889. 10 Oct. M ii 266. L280, L3191 G 300. Art Congress: M ii 225f, L319f, G 84ff. Typography: Walker, neighbour, was partner in photo-engraving firm and learned in print-matters. *Roots*: M ii 227f. SL, ET 648–50. Peterborough L317. Dec., profit-sharing in *Cweal* 14 Dec. 393, Meier 79. Engels, ET 691, 668 (bourgeoisification). Struggle, LCC and ILP, M ii 320. M ii 228f, to Mother. Glass: J i (1) 22; Yeats: P. Faulkner (3) 19. BJ sees Impressionists as doing 'unfinished works', *Mem.* ii 188; still Sunday breakfasts, 193f, then to open-air speaking. Citations from Ruskin's *Fors* in *Cweal*, Meier 232f, also 237. Speeches during 1889: 63 (probable 12).

15 LAST YEARS

1. Fabians: ET 615–18, L288. Feb. to Glasse: Arnot. Leeds: ET 651, 601, G 201, L321. L. Hall: ET 652. Merton: Smith brothers take over Merton as managers. 8 March, on Christianity: Meier 30, 40f.

2. March, L321; April L322, state of things. *Cweal*, a couple of slight things by G., ET 659. Thames: Meier 451, BM 45338; Nons. 266, 184; Blunt, *Diaries* 24; MM ii 620, Stirling (2) 315f. May Day, ET 654f. Engels to Sorge 19 April, AGM: ET 654–6, PH 376, Tom Barclay (2), MM ii 321–4, Sparling to Steele, 2 June 1890, BM 45345, Play: M ii 231, PH 376. Quaritch, L324, M ii 247. Press: M ii 247f. Verses for BJ *Mem.* ii 204. Quarrel with G over BJ, G 50f (also on Huckleberry Finn, 52f). AGM, SPAB: 25 June. On 1 June at H. on effect of socialist movement on Imperial politics.

3. Postmen: ET 652, LeMire, 11 June. To May, 20 June at K., fishing. *Cweal*, ET 656, L324. Conference: *Cweal* 16 Aug. 1890, ET 658f. August: L235, M ii 248f. Docks: *Cweal* 30 Aug., ET 680. Sept., Press, M ii 249–51, L326f. MM i 663f, to Walker on a drive.

4. *News*: he wrote as it went along, see letter to Nicoll. Nons. 169, 182, 185; mill or factory with garden all round, 183. Oct. at K., L328, M ii 251, working on *News*, on 16th to London. Casell's: ET 660. Branch: M ii 232–7, circular 238–40. H branch had 120 members, ET 662, effects 661, new paper 678, others 679. *Cweal* after break, 678. Also L328f, Oct., and Dec. He paid off all debts to end of 1890, leaving plant, type, copyright of *Cweal* to League council. To Hyndman, L231; on Press, 31 Dec. L331. Manifesto, M ii 240. Cockerell on SPAB, J i (2) 28. Abortive experiment, Gunnlaug Saga, M ii 252. In general, RW 57–66; Orchard PH 281. Kropotkin's *Mutual Aid*, 1890, Meier 287f. Utopia: see Meier, esp. 373–97; WM reads bits at meetings, 386, mobilising effect 389 etc. Meier on WM and his ideas of the two stages, 419–74; productive forces, 475–509; beauty in daily life 589–615; pollution, 615–40. Speeches 1890: 34 (probable 5).

H. room, ET 642–7; J ii (2) 9–13; M ii 251f, G 111f. Pennell (2) i 158f. rage, Workers: Meier 80–2. Homage of Kitz, *Freedom*. May 1916. Yeats 183f. Reviews of *News*, Faulkner 339–55.

5. New manifesto: ET 670f, 676. Press: M ii 253–6. Paper, PH 267f. Atmosphere: ET 673. Old books: M ii 253f, L335, ET 675. Ill, ET 671f. May Day: Meier, 340 ET 675; 2 May, visit to Hythe, L338. Feb., SL ends, ET 677, 678–80; 5 Feb. to *Times*, Westminster Abbey, L335. March, Engels on Hyndman, ET 691.

6. Poems: M ii 257f; Faulkner 356–62. Boutalls, PH 392. M ii 260, flowers. L339, to Georgie and Aglaia. France: L340, M ii 262–4, L341, 345, MM i 661–70. At K., M ii 265f, J i (1) 16. PRS: Meier, 157, 694, M ii 270–4, MM i 239f, PH 396.

7. Ruskin: Meier 184–6, MM i 89, BM 52751, V. Meynell (1) 31, 59f. Meetings, ET 675; papers sold, 676. Press: M ii 276, ET 673f, only one outside job. Character: M ii 267f, Meier 750–60.

Embroidery: M ii 268f, dyes PH 386f. Architects Bill: letter of protest. More objective on medievalism, MM i 196–310; ancient buildings, MM ii 269. Speeches 1891: 12 (probable 2). K. Press: McLean; Sparling; Cockerell (2) Leatham; H. Jackson (1); Tschan; Balston: MM i 310 and 244; *Philobiblion* vii 1934, 4.

8. Anarchists, ET 680–7. A Socialist Co-op. Fed., M ii 237. Elections ET 687f, April, 677, attacks. Meier 64 n7. 26 Jan. on woodcuts of Gothic Books to Soc. of Arts. New fount: M ii 278. Books bought: M ii 279f, PH 399f. Cockerell, L350; V. Meynell (2), PH 499, M ii 282. Cockerell in 1894 sec. to K. Press. Whitsun, with Alf Matthison of Leeds, ET 690. Summer, Blunt at Merton, PH 373. 11 Oct. to G., L351—did he go? Poet Laureate: *Clarion*, 19 Nov., Sparling 7, M ii 287, ET 693. Bordighera, L352, 18 Nov. to Jenny, on landscape. Alliance: ET 694f. Theatre: Ibsen, PH 405. To Jenny, Firenze. Sparling (Radford MS) 24 Dec., ET 717, PH 401.

M Master of Art Workers Guild. About London, ET 718. Speeches 1892: 7 (probable 2).

9. Manifesto: ET 695–7, Meier 458. Weakness: unity arranged from above, not forged by struggle; Shaw admitted later his bitter hostility. ILP, ET 699; first conference at Bradford, Jan. 1893. *Beowulf*, L352, Wyatt supplies translation. WM reads his version to BJ Sunday mornings. *Socialism*, ET 708–11, Meier 270f, M ii 289. Oxford, L354; B. H. Jackson. G 131–4. Books, PH 408f. Scheu, German version of *Ball*: L355. Deeper Meaning, L355, ET 720f, 'a survival of the organic art of the past'. Oct., Brown dies, *Mem.* ii 239f. Miners: L. Thompson 97, ET 700, MM ii 519–21. Maguire: ET 702f; Wilde, PH 446; Jackson calls, his book 247. Burnley, also at Ancoats meeting in Jan. with Town and Country. 1893: 15 speeches (probable 1). Printing: P. Thompson, 142–5.

10. ET 397, 133; Vallance 121.

11. *Justice*, ET 687, 711f, *Labour Prophet*, 700, 705–7. *Justice*, 17 Jan., ET 711f, 687. K. Hardie, G 137, ET 712. Feb. letters, 357f, Swinburne, *D. Chronicle* (Westminster Abbey). Lansbury: ET 713f, *Justice*, 24 Feb.; Leatham, MM ii 340. Feb. *Liberty*, Meier 462f.

16 June, *Justice*, ET 713, Meier 82f, Nons. 655 (Huxley usurping place of Homer, tribute to Carlyle and Ruskin). Cantwell, ET 528, 596, 684f. Chaucer, M ii 306, PH 407–10, L360. M ii 307f. Town and Country, M ii 301. Local elections, M ii 308, ET 712f, tommy-rot, 713, also H. Society, M ii 308f, BM 45410 (15 Feb.). July, M ii 312 and 282, L359, L358, Wise, Bainton. L360f, MM i 672f, Nov. L362, MM i 495f. Lethaby: RW 75, 77. Maguire ET 703. Speeches 1894: 9 (probable 1).

12. Coleridge, PH 412, with M ii 311f. 11 March L363 to Scheu on minutebooks of SL, same day to Glasse, Arnot. Books: M ii 311f, PH 408. Maguire dies: ET 703f. Estate: M ii 312; PH 413; Dufty. May owned manor-house and most of village. Peterborough, M ii 313f. Southwold: had written *Oct.* for *E.P.* there, with Janey and girls, after DGR had been there. Review, L369–71. M ii 316. L371, 374, tapestry. Quest: Meier 761. Romances: talk by C. Oberg, 9 May 1974 to WM Soc.

13. United action, ET 701, 721. Stepniak: Arnot (1) 21, *Times* 30 Dec. 1895, ET 721f. Floods at K., Nov., PH 413; at Rottingdean. Dec., M ii 322. Shaw's *Sanity of Art*, Stokes 17. Wilde, Cockerell, TLS 3 Feb. 1950. BJ *Mem.* ii 262, 265, 269f. Speeches 1895: 13 (probable 1).

14. New Year: *Justice* 11 Jan. 1896. Diary, BM 45411. *He and She*; J i (2) 15–17; CW xxi. *Mem.* ii 322f. 'I like Punch', 279. Fear of death: Meier, 758–63. M i 215, 73f. Cockerell to May: BM 52740 (200). *Mem.* ii 278, plan for Hill of Venus, 'Prose looks blacker in the page and fills up better.' Right of way at K., PH 413f. Books, M ii 323f. Compton: PH 397, RW 52. Books L382, M ii 327f. BJ scared of bawdry, PH 423, L383, Cockerell. H. Society, ET 725, M ii 331. Well, Buxton F. 184–8. Glass: J i (1) 27.

15. MM ii 361–3, ET 724f. Norway, L384. Coils, PH 424, 451, Stirling 146.

Carruthers, BM 45350. Aug. 9, B 140. Music: May played on lute and sang early music. Death: Cockerell diary, Blunt, Cobden-S. 12 Sept. Funeral: ET 727, A. S. Tschiffely, *Don Roberto*; Fredeman (3); Mackail Notebooks Walth. MSS J 163–6. Hughes said: 'Mrs Morris very broken down, May bearing up well, but poor Jennie weeping piteously.' Lethaby 195; Mackail ii 345–8. Cunninghame Graham, *Sat. Rev.* 10 Oct. 1896. Tributes, ET 729–31. H. branch, ET 728f; Rothenstein, *Men and Memories* 1931 i 288. May: April 1918 letter of Ricketts to T. Lowinsky says he was once 'snubbed by Mrs Morris, then a magnificent elderly woman. Shannon and I even presented her with a mechanical toy-bear'. Cockerell: V. and A. Reserve Case JJ 34. Lyme Regis: Effie's notes. Janey's last letter mentions visit by WM to IOM.

Bibliography

All English works are printed in London unless otherwise stated; all French in Paris.

Aldred, G. A., *Pioneers of Antiparliamentarianism* (Glasgow, 1840). Allingham, H., with D. Radford, ed. William Allingham's *Diary*, 1907. Anon (1) '*A Plain Tory*': *Justice for England, or, How to Fight Socialism*, 1893 (2) *Quarterly Rev.*, cxc July–Oct. 1899, 487–512 (3) *Portfolio*, May 1894 (4) *Pre-Raphaelite Drawings*, Arts Council, 1953 (5) *Romantic Art in Britain, 1760–1860*, Philadelphia–Detroit, 1968 (6) *W. H. Hunt*, Arts Council, 1969, M. Bennett (7) *Ford Madox Brown*, Liverpool etc., 1964 (8) *J. E. Millais*, Liverpool/London, 1967 (9) *Exhibit. Victorian and Edwardian Dec. Art*, V. and A., 1952, arranged P. Floud (10) *Athenaeum* 10 Oct. 1896 (Obit., Watts-Dunton). Archer, M., *Country Life*, 1 April 1965 (PR painted furniture). Armytage, W. H. G., (1) *Heavens below*, 1961 (Ruskin's Guild) (2) *Yesterday's Tomorrows*, 1968 (3) *A. J. Mundella*, 1951. Arnot, R. P., (1) *Unpublished Letters* (to Glasse) 1951 (2) *WM, the Man and the Myth*, 1964 (3) *Bernard Shaw and WM*, 1957 (4) *WM A Vindication*, 1934. Ashbee, C. R., (1) *An Endeavour toward the Teaching of J. Ruskin and WM*, 1901 (2) *Craftsmanship in Competitive Industry*, 1908 (Essex House Press). Aslin, E., (1) *The Aesthetic Movement*, 1969 (2) *Nineteenth Century English Furniture*, 1962 (3) *Apollo*, Dec. 1962 (Godwin and Japs). Aveling, E., *Labour Prophet*, Sept., 1895.

Bainton, G., *Letters on Socialism by WM*, 1894. Baldwin, A. W., *The Macdonald Sisters*, 1960. Ball, A. H. R., *Selections Prose Works WM* (OUP, 1931). Balmforth, R., *Some Socialist and Political Pioneers of the 19th Century*, 1900. Balston, T., *Private Press Types* (Camb., 1951). Barclay, Tom, (1) *The Rights of Labour according to J. Ruskin*, 1856 (2) *Memoirs and Medleys: The Autobiography of a Bottle-Washer* (Leicester, 1934). Bardoux, J., *Le mouvement idéaliste et social dans la litt. anglaise aux XIXe s.*, 1901. Barling, E., (1) *Gaz. of J. Lewis Partnership*, xliii, 7 Oct. 1961, 839 (Standon) (2) *ib.*, xliv, 17 March 1962, 158–60. Bate, P. H., *The English Pre-R. Painters*, 1899. Baum, P. F., (1) *DGR's letters to Fanny Cornforth* (Baltimore, 1940) (2) *DGR: an analytical list of MSS in Duke Univ. Lib.* (Duke U.P., N. Carolina, 1931). Bax, E. Belfort, (1) *Reminiscences and Reflections of a Mid and Late Victorian*, 1918 (2) *A Short Account of the Commune of Paris*, 1886 (3) *The Religion of Socialism*, 1887. Beazley, E., *Archit. Rev.*, cxxx, Sept. 1961, 167–72. Beer, Max., *A History of British Socialism*, 1940. Bell, Mackenzie, *Christina Rossetti*, 1898. Bell, Malcolm, ed., *B.J.: a Record and a Review*, 1898. Bell, Q., *Victorian Artists*, 1967. Bellas, R. A., *Diss. Abstracts*, xxii, 1961, 857f. Bennet, Mary, *Apollo*, lxxvi, Dec. 1962, 748–53 (PRs and Liverpool Prize). Benson, A. C., (1) *Rossetti*, 1904 (2) *Memories and Friends*, 1924. Bernstein, E., *My Years of Exile*, transl. B. Miall, 1921. Biber, A. R., *Studies in WM's Prose Romances* (Griefswald, 1907). Blatchford, R., (1) *The Sorcery Shop*, 1907 (2) *My Favourite Books* (pref. dated 1900). Bliss, T., *Jane Welsh Carlyle*, 1950. Bloomfield, P., (1) *WM*, 1934 (2) *R. Soc. of Arts J.*, 1934. Blunt, W., *Cockerell*, 1964. Blunt, W. S., *My Diaries*, 1932 (2nd ed. one vol.). Boase, T. S. R., *English Art 1800–70* (Oxford, 1959). Bøe, Alf, *From Gothic Revival to Functional Form* (Oslo, 1957). Boyce, G. P., *Extracts from G.P.B.'s Diaries*, Old Water-Colour Soc.'s Club, xix, 1841. Bradley, A. G., *Hist. of Marlborough College*, 1896. Brandon-Jones, J., *Victorian Architecture*, 1963. Briggs, Asa, (1) intro. *Selected Writings of WM* (suppl. G. Shanklin), 1968 (2) *Victorian People*, 1965. Briggs, R. C. H., (1) *Handlist of Public Addresses of WM*, 1961 (2) J i [4] 2–22 (3) J i [1] 29–31. Broadhurst, H., *The Story of his Life: From a Stonemason's Bench to Treasury Bench*, 1901. Brockway, A., *Socialism over Sixty Years: The Life of Jowett of Bradford*, 1946. Brookes, G. H., *The Rhetorical Form of Carlyle's Sartor Resartus* (Univ. California, 1973). Brooke, A. Stopford, *Four Victorian Poets*, 1908. Buckley, J. H., (1) *The Pre-Raphaelites* (N.Y., 1969) (2) *The Victorian Temper*, 1952 and 1966 (3) *The Triumph of Time* (OUP, 1967). Bünger, S., *F. Engels und die brit. sozialist. Bewegung*. Burges, W., *Art Applied to Industry* (Oxford, 1965). Burgess, J., (1) *Pall Mall Gaz.*, 9 Feb. 1886 (2) *John Burns*, 1911. Burne-Jones, G., *Memorials of Edward B.J.*, 1904. Burns, J., *Our History*, no 16, Winter, 1959. Burrough, B. C., (1) *Connoisseur*, Aug. 1969 (Gimson) (2) *ib.*, Sept. 1969 (Ashbee) (3) *ib.*, Oct. (Lethaby) (4) *ib.*, Jan. 1970. Burt, T., *Thomas Burt: An Autobiography*, 1924. Butterfield, *WM*, 1934.

Caflesch, M., *WM, Der Erneurer der Buchkunst* (Bern, 1960). Caine, Hall, (1) *Recollections of Rossetti*, 1928 (2) *Recollections of DGR*, 1882. Calder, G. J., *The Writing of Past and Present* (Yale, 1949). Cardwell, D. S. L., *Brit. J. for Hist. of Science Soc.*, June 1963 (dyes). Carpenter, E., (1) *My Days and Dreams*, 1916 (2) *Freedom*, Nov. 1896 (3) *Towards Democracy*, 1883. Carpenter, Niles, *Guild Socialism* (N.Y., 1922). Carnall, G., *R. Southey* (OUP, 1960). Carriere, E., (1) *L'art dans la démocratie*, 1904 (2) *Écrits et pages choisis* (2nd ed.) 1907. Carroll, Owen, *Everyman*, 23 Sept. 1933. Carruthers, J., (1) *Socialism and Radicalism*, 1894 (2) *Communal and Commercial Economy*, 1883. Cary, E. L., *WM, Poet, Craftsman and Socialist*, 1902. Cassidy, J. A., *PMLA*, March 1952, no 2, lxvii, 65–94 (Buchanan). Casson, H., *Listener*, 1 Oct., 1953. Chadwick, O., ed., *The Mind of the Oxford Movement* (Stanford, 1960). Chandler, A., *A Dream of Order*, 1971. Chevrillon, A., *La pensée de Ruskin*, 1909. Clark, Kenneth, (1) *Ruskin Today*, 1967 (2) *Gothic Revival*, 1928 (3) *ib.*, enlarged, (N.Y., 1950). Clutton-Brock, A., *WM: his work and influence*, 1914. Cobden-Sanderson, T. J., *Journals*, 1926. Cockerell, S., (1) *An annotated list of all the books printed at the K. Press*, 1898 (2) *A Note by WM on his Aims in Founding the K. Press*, 1898 (3) J i [2] 6–10 (4) *Listener*, 27 Nov. 1947, 24 April, 1 and 15 May (5) Intro. *Cat. of Exhib. of Works of WM* (Manchester, 1908). Cole, G. D. H., (1) ed., *WM Stories* etc., 1944 (2) *Revaluations*, 1931 (3) *WM as a Socialist*, 1960 (4) *A Hist. of the British Working Class Movement*, ii, 1926. Colebrook, F., *WM, Master Printer* (Tonbridge Wells, 1897). Collins, H., and C. Abramsky, *K. Marx and the British Labour Movement*, 1965. Collingwood, W. G., *Life of J. Ruskin*. Compton-Rickett, A., (1) *WM: a Study in Personality*, 1813 (2) *I Look Back*, 1933. Conway, Monecure, *Travels in S. Kensington*, 1882. Cook, E. T., *Life of J. Ruskin*, 1911. Crane, W., (1) *WM to Whistler*, 1911 (2) *An Artist's Reminiscences*, 1907 (3) *Scribner's Mag.*, July 1897 (4) *Die neue Zeit*, 1896, 133ff (5) *Ideals in Art*, 1905. Crow, G., *WM, Designer*, 1934, *Studio*, Winter No.

Davidson, J. Morrison, *The Annals of Toil*, 1899. Dawtry, F., *A Few Notes on WM* 1936–7, in *Labour's Northern Voice*. Day, L. F., *Easter Art Annual*, 1899. Dearden, J. S., *Apollo*, lxxviii, Dec., 1960, 190–5, and lxxiv, June, 1961, 171–8. Digby, K., *The Broad Stone of Honour*, 1929. Doughty, O., (1) *A Victorian Romantic, DGR*, 1949 (2) with J. R. Wahl, *Letters of DGR* (Oxford, 1965) (3) *English Miscellany*, xi, 175–209, Rome. Douglas, J., *T. Watts-Dunton* (N.Y., 1906). Drinkwater, J., (1) *WM: a Critical Study*, 1912 (2) *Prose Papers*, 1917 (WM and State) (3) with H. Jackson, *Speeches in Commem. of WM*, 24 March 1934. Dufty, A. R., *Kelmscott*, 1969. Dunlap, J. R., *N.Y. Public Lib. Bull.*, lxiv, Oct. 1960, 534–47=*Shavian* ii, Feb. 1961 (Shaw and Typog.). Dunn, H. T., *Recollections of DGR and his Circle*, 1904. Dupont, V., *L'utopie et le roman utopique dans la litt. anglaise* (Cahors, 1941). Earland, A., *Ruskin and his Circle*. Eastlake, C. L., (a) A *History of the Gothic Revival*, 1972 (2) edition by J. M. Crook (Leicester, 1971). Eckhardt, W. von, *Horizon*, iv, Nov. 1961, 58–75. Eggar, J. A., *Remembrances of Life and Customs in G. White's, Cobbett's and C. Kingsley's Country*, 1924. Ellis, F. S., *J. of Soc. of Arts*, 27 May 1898. Elton, G., *England Arise*, 1931. Eshleman, L. W., *A Victorian Rebel* (N.Y., 1940) (see Grey). Evans, H., *Radical Fights of Forty Years*, 1913.

Fairbank, A., J i (1) 5f (Calligraphy). Fairman, F., *The Principles of Socialism Made Plain*, with pref. by WM, 1888. Farley, F. E., *Scandinavian Infl. in Eng. Romantic Movement* (Boston, 1903). Faulkner, P., (1) *W.M. The Critical Heritage*, 1973 (2) *WM and W.B. Yeats*, 1962 (3) J i [3] 18–23 (4) *Threshold*, iv, Jan. 1960, 18–27 (5) J ii [1] 9–12. Fern, A., *Graphic Design*, N.Y. Mus. Ind. Art, 1960 (WM and Art Nouveau). Ferrez, B., *Recollections of A. N. Welby Pugin*, 1861. Fielding, Una, J ii [3] 2–5 (May). Floud, P., (1) *Penrose Annual*, liv, 1960 (2) *Listener*, 7 Oct. 1954, and 14 Oct. (3) *Tributes to P. F.* William Morris Soc. 1960 (4) with B. Morris, *CIBA Rev.* no. 1 1961, 21–3 Basle (chintzes) (5) *Archit. Rev.*, July 1959 (6) *WM* at V. and A. with intro. by P.F., 1958 (7) *Penrose Annual*, 1958 (Voysey papers). Ford, Ford Madox, *Mightier than the Sword*, 1938. Forman, H. Buxton, *The Books of WM*, 1897. For his forgeries, *Quaritch Cat.* no. 926, 1973. Forsyth, P. T., *Religion in Recent Art*, 1901. Franklin, C., J ii [2] 14–18 (K. Press). Fredeman, W. E., (1) *Pre-Raphaelites*, 1965, Harvard, a Bibliographical Study (2) *Burlington Mag.* cii, Dec. 1960, 523–9 (PRs in caricature) (3) J ii [1] 28–35 (4) *Prelude to the Last Decade: Dante Gabriel Rossetti in the Summer of 1872* (reprinted from the John Rylands Library Bulletin, 1971). Freemantle, A., *The Little Band of Prophets* (Fabians, 1960). Fritzsche, G., *WM's Sozialismus und anarchist. Kommunismus* (Leipzig, 1927). Fuller, R., *WM, Selection and Commentary* (OUP, 1956). Furneaux, Jordan, R., (1) *Medieval Vision of WM*, 1960 (2) *Victorian Architecture*, 1966. Furniss, H., *Some Victorian Women*, 1923. Furnivall, F. J., *A Volume of Personal Record*, 1911, biog. by J. Munro.

Gaul, V., *Scottish Field*, cviii, Jan. 1961, 55–8 (Penkill). Gaunt, W., (1) *The PR Dream*, 2nd ed., 1943 (2) *The PR Tragedy*, 1942 (3) *The Aesthetic Adventure*, 1957. Gilchrist, H. H., *Anne Gilchrist*, 1887. Girouard, M., *Country Life*, 16 June, 1960. Glasier, Bruce (1) *WM and the Early Days of the Soc. Movement*, 1921 (2) *Socialism in Song* (Manchester, 1919) (3) MSS, Mus. Walthamstow. Gooch, G. P., *History and Historians of the 19th c.*, (2nd ed.) 1952. Goode, J., in J. Lucas, *Lit. and Politics in the 19th c.* Goodwin, K., J ii [3], 1968, 24–31. Gordon, W. K., *Diss. Abstracts*, xxi, 1961, 3781–2. Gould, F. J., *Hyndman, Prophet of Socialism*, 1928. Graham, Cunninghame, *Sat. Rev.*, 10 Oct., 1896. Gray, D. J., *Boston Univ. Studies in English*, v, Spring 1961, 1–17. Grennan, M. R., *WM Medievalist and Revolutionary*, 1945. Greville, F. E., see Warwick, Countess of. Grey, L. E., *WM Prophet of England's New Order*, 1949. Grierson, G., *A Choice of WM's Verse*, 1969. Grierson, J., *Isabella Gilmore*, 1968. Groves, R., *Sharpen the Sickle*, 1949. Grylls, R. G. (Lady R. Mander), (1) *Portrait of Rossetti*, 1965 (2) *Connoisseur*, cxlix, Jan., 1961, 2–11 (3) ed. V. Hunt (2). Gunner, Floss, *Isis*, no. 1500, Nov., 1965. Guyot, E., *L'idée socialiste chez WM*, 1909.

Haight, G., *G. Eliot*, 1968. Hake, T. G., (1) *Memories of Eighty Years* (2) *Life and Letters of T. Watts-Dunton*, 1916, with Compton-Rickett. Hale, J. R., *The Evolution of British Historiography*, 1967. Hall, A. V., *WM and Main Street* (Univ. Washington, 1922). Harrison, F., *J. Ruskin*, 1902. Harrison, M., with B. Waters, *Burne-Jones*, 1973. Hart-Davis, R., ed., *Letters of Oscar Wilde*, 1962. Hascall, D. L., J ii [3] 18–23 (Volsungs). Headlam, S. D., *The Socialists' Church*, 1907. Healy, C., *Confessions of a Journalist*, 1904. Helmholtz, A. A., *The Social Philosophy of WM* (Duke Univ., 1927). Henderson, A., *G.B. Shaw, his Life and Work*. Henderson, P., (1) *WM*, 1952 (2) *WM*, 1967 (refs. made to this issue) (3) *The Letters of WM*, 1950. Hicks, T., *Figures of Transition* (N.Y., 1940). Hilton, T., *The Pre-Raphaelites*, 1970. Hoare, D. M., *The Work of Morris and Yeats in relation to early saga lit.*, 1937. Hobson, J. A., *J. Ruskin, Social Reformer*, 1898. Holiday,

H., (1) *Reminiscences of my Life*, 1914 (2) *Stained Glass as an Art*, 1896, illustr. by BJ (3) *The Artistic Aspects of E. Bellamy's Looking Backward*, 1890, Guild and School of Handicrafts, Trans. i. Holland, B., *Memoir of Kenelm Digby*, 1919. Holman-Hunt, Diana, *My Grandmothers and I*, 1960. Holman-Hunt, H., (1) *The Story of the Pictures on the Walls* etc., 1906 (2) *Pre-Raphaelitism and the PR Brotherhood*, 1905 (3) *Chambers Enc.* sv Pre-Raphaelitism (4) 19, 13 ed. of (2) and N.Y. reprint, 1967. Howard, Ebenezer, *Garden Cities of To-Morrow*, ed. F. J. Osborn, Intro. L. Mumford, 1945 (also 1965). Howell, G., *Trade Unionism New and Old*, 1891. Howitt, Mary, *An Autobiography*, 1889. Hubbard, E., *A WM Book* (N.Y., 1907). Hudson, D., *The Forgotten King*, 1960 (PRs). Hueffer, F. M., (1) *Ford Madox Brown*, 1896 (2) *Ancient Lights and Certain New Reflections*, 1911. Hulse, J. W., *Revolutionists in London*, 1970. Hunt, Violet, (1) *The Wife of Rossetti*, 1932 (2) J ii [3] 6–17. Hyndman, H. M., (1) *The Coming Revolution in England*, 1884, reprinted from *N. American Rev.*, Oct., 1882 (2) *The Historical Basis of Socialism in England*, 1884 (3) SD tract no. 1 (4) *The Record of an Adventurous Life*, 1911 (5) *Justice*, 15 March, 1884 (Iron Law) (6) with Morris, *A Summary of the Principles of Socialism*, 1884 (7) *Reminiscences*, 1911 (8) *Further Reminiscences*, 1912 (9) *England for All*, 1881. Hyndman, R. T., *The Last Years of H. M. Hyndman* (N.Y., 1924).

Ikeler, A. A., *Puritan Temper and Transcendental Faith* (Ohio Univ., 1973). Ingram, J., *Life of Oliver Madox Brown*, 1883. Ionides, Luke, *Memories* (Paris, 1925), privately printed. Ironside, R., and Gere, J., *PR Painters*, 1948. Irvine, A. L., J ii [2] 3–5.

Jackson, B. H., *Recollections of T. G. Jackson* (OUP, 1950). Jackson, Holbrook (1) *WM Craftsman and Socialist*, 1926 (1st ed., 1908) (2) *Three Papers on WM* (with Hewitt and Shand), 1934 (3) *On Art and Socialism*, essays and lectures by WM, intro. H. J., 1947. Jackson, T. G., *Modern Gothic Architecture*, 1873. James, L. Warwick, (1) *The Kennet*, Winter, 1950, 9–14 (2) *ib.*, Spring, 1951, 9–12 (3) *ib.*, Summer, 1951, 14–16 (4) *ib.*, Winter, 1951, 11–15 (5) personal communication. Jarrett, D., *Age of Hogarth*, 1974. Jeffereys, J. B., ed., *Labour's Formative Years*, 1948. Jowett, E. W., *What Made me a Socialist* (n.d.), see Brockway.

Keith, A., *The Nazarenes* (OUP, 1964). Kent, W., *John Burns: Labour's Lost Leader*, 1950. Kocmanova, J., (1) *Philologica Pragensia*, no. 3, 1960 (on WM's poetry) (2) *Brno Studies in English*, ii, 1960, 113–48 (3) *The Aesthetic Purpose of WM in the Context of his late Prose Romances*, *ib.*, 1960, 75–146 (4) *The Poetic Maturing of WM* (Prague, 1964). Kropotkin, P., (1) *The Conquest of Bread*, 1974 (Penguin Press, 1972) (2) *Mutual Aid*, ditto, both ed. O. Avrich. Kuster, E. C., *Mittelalter und Antike bei WM* (Berlin, 1928). Lahor, J., (1) *L'art pour le peuple à défaut de l'art par le peuple*, 1902 (2) *Les habitations à bon marché et un art nouveau pour le peuple*, 1904. Landow, G. P., *The Aesthetic and Critical Theories of J. Ruskin*, Princetown. Lang, C. Y., (1) *The PRs and their Circle* (N.Y., 1969) (2) *The*

Swinburne Letter Book, Yale. 1959–62, Lawrence, E. P., *Henry George in the British Isles* (Michigan, 1957). Lazarus, Emma, *Century,* July, 1886. Leatham, J., *WM Master of Many Crafts* (Turiff, 1896). Le Bourgeois, J., (1) unpublished lecture to WM Soc., 1973 (2) *Durham Univ. J.,* March, 1974, 203–5. Lee, F. W., ed., *WM Poet Craftsman Socialist* (N.Y., 1891). LeMire, E. D., (1) *Unpublished Lectures of WM*, 169, Detroit (2) J i [3] 3–10 (Whistler and WM). Leno, D., *Christian Socialist,* 1 Jan. 1885. Lessner, F., *Sixty Years in the SD Movement,* 1907. Lethaby, W.R., (1) *Philip Webb*, 1935 (2) *WM as Work-Master,* 1901. Lewis, C. S., *Rehabilitation and Other Essays* (OUP, 1939). Lilienthal, T. M., *A WM Press Goes West* (Berkeley, 1961) (Morris's Albion). Lindsay, Jack, (1) *WM Writer,* 1961 (2) *Charles Dickens,* 1950 (3) *WM, Selected Poems* (Grey Walls Press, 1948) (4) *George Meredith,* 1956 (5) *Modern Quarterly* (Commune and Writers), July 1954. Litzenberg, K., (1) *Rev. of Eng. Studies,* xii, Oct., 1936 (2) *The Social Philosophy of WM and the Doom of the Gods*, Michigan, *Lang. and Lit.,* x, 1933, 183ff (3) *Contributions of Old Norse Lang. and Lit. to the Style and Substance of WM*, Michigan, *L. and L.,* x (4) *Scand. Studies and Notes,* xiii, no. 7, Aug., 1935 (5) *ib.,* xiv, no. 3, Aug., 1936 (Heimskringla) (6) *ib.,* xiv, no. 2, May, 1936 (Edda) (7) *WM and Scand. Lit.: A Bibliog. Essay* (Wisconsin, 1935). Lockhead, M., *The Victorian Household,* 1964. Lowe, W. F., *Museum J.,* V. and A., lx, Aug. 1960, 121f. Lubbock, P., *The Letters of Henry James,* 1920. Lucas, E. V., *The Colvins and their Friends,* 1928. Lucas, F. L., *Eight Victorian Poets* (OUP, 1920). Lumet, L., (1) *L'art pour tous,* 1904 (2) Journal of that name, editor.

Maas, J., *Victorian Painters,* 1969. Maccoby, S., *English Radicalism 1853–86,* 1938. Macdonald, James, (1) *Justice,* Jan. 1914, (2) *ib.,* 11 July, 1896 (3) *ib.,* 23 Feb., 1884. Macdonald, Jean, *Guide to Red House,* 1960. McDowell, G. T., *Scand. Studies and Notes,* 1921–3, no. 7, 151–68 (Volsunga Saga). McEntee, G., *Social Catholic Movement in GB* (N.Y., 1927). Mackail, J. W. (1) *Life of WM,* 1901 (2) Notebooks, WM Gallery Walthamstow (3) *WM Address,* 1901 (4) *Parting of the Ways,* 1902 (5) *WM and his Circle* (Oxford, 1907). McLean, R., (1) *Victorian Book Design,* 1963 (2) *Modern Book Design,* 1958. Macleod, R. D., (1) *WM without Mackail,* 1934 (2) *WM as seen by his Contemporaries* (Glasgow, 1958) (attempt to blackguard Morris). McMinn, N. L., *The Letters of WM to the Press,* 1928 Diss., Northwestern Univ. Madsen, St. Tschudi, (1) J i [4] 34–40 (Munthe) (2) *The Sources of Art Nouveau* (Oslo, 1956). Magnusson, E., *Camb. Rev.,* 26 Nov., 1896. Malcolmson, R. W., *Pop. Recreations in Eng. Society 1700–1850,* 1973. Mâle, E., *The Gothic Image: Religious Art in France of the 13th c.,* 1961. Mann, Tom (1) *Tom Mann's Memories,* 1923 (2) *Daily Worker,* 24 March, 1934 (3) *Our History,* no. 26–7, Summer–Autumn, 1962. Marillier, H. C., (1) *DGR, an Illustrated Mem. of his Art and Life,* 1899 (2) *History of Merton Abbey Tapestry Works,* 1927 (3) *The Morris Movement* n.d. privately printed (1931) (4) *The Liverpool School of Painters,* 1904. Mason, H. J. L. J., *Architect,* 19 Feb., 1915, 172ff (WM craftsman). Mattison, Alf, *Tom Maguire: a Remembrance*. Maurer, O., in *Nineteenth Century Studies*, ed. Davis etc. (Cornell, 1940). Mavor, J., *My Windows on the Street of the World*, 1923. Meier, P., (1) *La pensée utopique de WM*, 1973 (2) *Internat. Rev. of Social Hist.*, xvi, 1971, pt 2 (3) *La Pensée*, no. 156, April, 1971, 68–70 (4) *Nouvelles à Nulle Part*, 1961. Meynell, V., (1) *Friends of a Lifetime: Letters to Sir S. Cockerell*, 1940 (2) *The Best of Friends*, 1956. Millais, J. G., *Life and Letters of Sir John E. Millais*, 1899. Minto, W., ed. *Autobiographical Notes of Bell Scott*, 1892. Mitchell, C., *Archit. Rev.*, Jan., 1947 (St James's Palace). More, P.M., *Shelburne Essays*, 7th s., 1910, 95–118, N.Y. Morrah, H. A., *The Oxford Union*, 1923. Morris, B., (1) *Handweaver and Craftsman*, xii Spring, 1961, 6–11, 54f (2) *ib.*, xii, Fall, 1961, 18–21 (3) *Vict. Embroidery*, 1962 (4) *The Saturday Book*, no. 22, ed. J. Hatfield, 1962 (Art Nouveau). Morris, May, (1) *WM Artist, Writer, Socialist* (Oxford, 1936) (2) ed. CW, 1910. Morris, William, see Index for his books. Bibliographies, Buxton Forman, Temple Scott (1897), LeMire etc.; Richard Bennet etc. (Cat. of MSS and Early Printed Books from the Lib. of WM, 1907). WM Soc. publications: *The Typographical Adventure of WM*, 1957, *Work on WM*, 1962. *WM and the K. Press* (Brown Univ. Providence, 1960). His preface to *Arts and Crafts Essays*, 1893, essay with J. H. Middleton, on mural decoration, in *Enc. Brit.* xvii, 1884. Morrison, Stanley, *Four Centuries of Fine Printing*, 1924. Morton, A. L., (1) *The English Utopia*, 1952 (2) *The Matter of Britain*, 1968 (3) *The Life and Ideas of R. Owen*, 1964 (4) *Three Works by WM*, 1954 (5) *Political Writings of WM*, 1973. Muir, W. M. Pattison, *Oxford and Camb. Rev.*, 1909, vii, 37–60 (romances). Mumby, L. M., *Zeits. f. Anglistik u. Amerikanstik*, x, 1962, 56–70. Mumford, L., (1) *N.Y. Rev. of Books*, 23 May, 1968 (2) *The Story of Utopias* (N.Y., 1922) (3) same (N.Y., 1962) (4) *Brief Lives*, ed. Louis Kronenberger (1972). Muncey, R. A., *The Leaguer*, Oct., 1907. Murray, C. Fairfax, *Connoisseur*, cl, July, 1962, 158–62. Muthesius, S., *The High Victorian Movement in Architecture*, 1973.

Nettlau, M., Docs. coll. by M.N., Internat. Inst. of Social Hist., Amsterdam (SL 1885–8, letters Lane, Kitz, Barker, WM, Shaw, Scheu). Nevinson, H. W., *Clarion*, 24 March, 1934. Nicoll, J., *The PRs*, 1917. Noyes, A., (1) *WM*, 1908 (2) Intro. Everyman *Early Romances of WM*, 1907. Nordby, C. H., *The Infl. of Old Norse Lit. upon Eng. Lit.* (Colombia N.Y., 1901).

Osborn, F. J., *Town and Country Planning*, Spring, 1945.

Packer, L. M., (1) *Christina Rossetti*, 1953 (2) *Western Humanities Rev.*, xvi, Summer, 1962, 243–52 (Ellis and Rossettis). Paden, W. D., *Register of the Mus. of Art*, Univ. of Kansas, ii, no. 1, Nov., 1958. Parrott, T. M., with W. Thorp, *Poetry of the Transition 1850–1914* (N.Y., 1932). Paton, J., *Proletarian Pilgrimage*, 1935. Peardon, T. P., *The Transition in English Hist. Writing* (N.Y., 1933). Pease, E. E., *History of the Fabian Soc.*, 1916. Peck, W. G., *The Social Implications of the Oxford Movement*, 1933. Pedrick, Gale, *Life with Rossetti*, 1964. Pelling, H. M., *The Origins of the Labour Party 1880–1900*,

(2nd ed.) 1965. Pennell, E. R. and J., (1) *The Life of J. McNeill Whistler*, 1909 (2) E.R. alone, *Life and Letters of Joseph Pennell* (Boston, 1929, London, 1960). Perrine, L., *Philol. Q.*, xxxix, April, 1960, 234–41. Peters, R. L., ed., *Victorians on Lit. and Art.*, (N.Y., 1961). Pevsner, H., (1) *Pioneers of the Modern Movement*, 1936 (2) *Archit. Rev.*, Oct., 1968 (3) *RIBA Journal*, 19 March, 1957 (Morris's views) (4) *Ruskin and Viollet-le-Duc*, 1971 (5) *Archit. Rev.*, Jan., 1952. Phelan, A. A., *Social Philosophy of WM* (Duke Univ., 1927). Pierson, S., *Marxism and the Origins of British Socialism* (Cornell, 1973). Prinsep, Val C., *Mag. of Art*, 1904. Pugin, A. W., (1) *Contrasts*, 1836 (2) *An Apology for the Revival of Christian Architecture in England*, 1843 (3) *The True Principles or Pointed in Christian Architecture*, 1853 (4) reprint of (1) 1971 (5) of (2) 1971 (6) *Present State of Eccles. Architecture in England*, 1971 reprinted (7) reprint of (3) 1971. Punde, H., *DGRs Einfluss auf die Gedichte des Jungen WM*, 1920 (Diss. Univ. Breslau), summary printed 1922. Purkis, J., *The Icelandic Jaunt*, 1962.

Raven, C. E., *Christian Socialism*, 1920. Rawson, G. S., *WM's Political Romance 'News from Nowhere'*, Diss., Univ. Jena, 1913, Borna-Leipzig Noska, 1914. Reynolds, G., *Victorian Paintings*, 1967. Rhys, E., *Everyman Remembers*, 1931. Richmond, Sir A., *Twenty-six Years, 1879–1905*, 1961. Richmond, Sir W. Blake, *Leighton, Millais, and WM*, 1898. Ricketts, C., (1) with L. Pissarro, *De la typographie et de l'harmonie de la page imprimé: WM et son influence dans les arts et metiers*, 1898 (2) *Self-Portrait, Letters and Journals*, ed. C. Lewis, 1939 (3) *Observer*, 14 Oct., 1928. Robertson, W. G., *Time Was*, 1931. Roe, F. W., *The Social Philosophy of Carlyle and Ruskin* (N.Y., 1921). Roebuck, G. E., *Some Appreciations of WM*, 1934. Rosenberg, J. D., *The Darkening Glass*, 1963. Rossetti, Christina, *The Family Letters of C. G. Rossetti*, 1908 (2) *The Poetical Works*, Memoir by WMR, 1904. Rossetti, D. G., (1) *DGR Painter and Poet*, R. Acad. Arts, Jan., 1973 (2) *Letters*, ed. O. Doughty and J. R. Wahl, 1965–67 (3) *Paintings and Drawings of DGR*, V. Surtees, (Oxford, 1931) (4) *The Rossetti–Macmillan Letters*, ed. L. M. Packer (Camb., 1963). Rossetti, W. M., (1) *DGR: his Family Letters*, with a Memoir, 1895 (2) *DGR as a Designer and Writer*, 1889 (3) *Ruskin: Rossetti: Pre-Raphaelitism*, ed. 1899 (4) *Some Reminiscences*, 1906 (5) *Fine Art Chiefly Contemporary*, 1867. Rowley, C. (R. Gilderoy), *Fifty Years of Work without Wages*, 1912. R.R., *Adelphi Mag.*, Oct., 1933 (Marx, WM, Hardie). Ruskin, J., (1) *Works*, ed. E. T. Cook and A. Wedderburn, 1902–12 (2) *Diaries*, ed., J. Evans and J. H. Whitehouse (Oxford, 1956–9). Ruyer, R., *L'utopie et les utopies*, 1950.

Saintsbury, G., *Corrected Impressions*, 1895. Salt, H. S., *Seventy Years among Savages*, 1921. Sambrook, J., (1) *A Poet Hidden: Life of R. W. Dixon*, 1962 (2) *Études anglaises*, xiv, Oct.–Dec., 1961, 331–8. Sanders, W. S., *Early Socialist Days*, 1927. Savarit, J., *Tendances mystiques et esotériques chez DGR*, 1961. Scheu, A., *Umsturzkeine* (Vienna, 1923). Schmidt-Kuensemueller, F. A., *WM und die neuere Buchkunst*, 1955. Scott, Temple, *Bibliography of Works of WM*, 1897. Scott, W. B.,

Autobiographical Notes, 1892. Scott, W. Dixon, *Primitiae* (Liverpool, 1912). Scudder, V. D., *Social Ideals in English Letters* (Boston, 1923). Sewter, A. C., (1) *Archit. Rev.*, cxxvii, March, 1960, 196–200 (2) *ib.*, Dec., 1964 (3) J i [1] 22–8 (4) *J. of British Soc. of Master Glass-Painters*, xii, 1960–1, 419–24 (5) *Apollo*, lxxvi, Dec., 1962 (6) J ii [2] 19–29 (7) *The Stained Glass of WM and his Circle* (Yale, 1974–5). Shagrin, B., *Anglo-Soviet J.*, xxi, 1960. Sharp, W., (1) *Atlantic Monthly*, Dec., 1896 (2) *DGR*, 1882 (3) *Papers Critical and Reminiscent*, 1912. Shaw, G. B., (1) *Morris as I knew him*, 1966 (2) App. to Pease (3) Intro. MM ii (4) *Sanity of Art*, 1895 (5) Pref., 1st ed., *Quintessence of Ibsenism* (6) *Ruskin's Politics*, 1921 (7) *Observer*, 6 Nov., 1949. Shields, F., *Life and Letters of Frederick Shields*. Shine, H., *Carlyle and the Saint-Simonians* (Baltimore, 1941). Simpson, W. J. P., *History of Anglo-Catholic Revival*, 1932. Sinclair, W., *Fortnightly Rev.*, xciv, 1910, 723–35 (WM Socialist). Sizeranna, R. de la, *Ruskin et la religion de la beauté*, 1897. Skelton, Sir J., *Table Talk of Shirley*, 1895. Sketchley, J., (1) *A Review of European Society*, with preface by WM, 1884 (2) *To-Day*, July, 1884. Soutter, F. W., *Recollections of a Labour Pioneer*, 1923. Spargo, J., *The Socialism of WM* (Westwood, Massachusetts, 1906). Sparling, H. H., (1) *The K. Press and WM Master-Craftsman*, 1924 (2) *Man versus Machinery*, 1888. Spanton, W. S., *An Art Student and his Teacher in the Sixties* (F. Murray), 1927. Staley, A., *The PR Landscape* (OUP, 1973). Stedman, J., *Opera News*, xxiv, 20 Feb., 1960, 8f, 23 (WM, Wagner). Stephens, F. C., *DGR*, 1894. Stevenson, L., *The Pre-Raphaelite Poetry* (OUP, 1973). Stillman, W. J., *Autobiography of a Journalist*, 1901. Stingle, R., *Assn. Canadian Univ. Teachers of English Report*, 1960, 4–10 (WM, symbols, not allegory). Stirling, A. M. W., (1) *The Richmond Papers*, 1926 (2) *William De Morgan and his Wife*, 1922 (3) *The Merry Wives of Battersea*, 1956. Stokes, E. E., (1) J i [1] 13–18 (2) J i [3] 22–30 (3) J. ii [2] 5–8. Summerson, J., (1) *The London Building World of the Eighteen Sixties*, 1974 (2) *Victorian Architecture* (Columbia, 1971). Sussman, H. L., *Victorians and the Machine* (Harvard, 1968). Swann, T. B., *Wonder and Whimsey* (Francestown N.H., 1960). Sypher, W., *Rococo to Cubism in Art and Lit.*, N.Y.

Tatersall, C. E. C., *History of British Carpets* (Benfleet, 1934). Thompson, E., (1) *WM Romantic to Revolutionary*, 1955 (2) *ib.*, 1961 (3) *The Communism of WM*, 1965. Thompson, L., *Robert Blatchford*, 1951. Thompson, P., (1) *The Work of WM*, 1967 (2) *Past and Present*, April, 1964. Thorne, W., *My Life's Battles*, 1925. Thornton, A. P., *The Imperial Idea and its Enemies*, 1959. Tinker, C. B., with C. P. Rollins, *WM as Poet* (Stanford, 1937). Torr, Dona, *Tom Mann and his Times*, 1956. Townshend, Mrs, *WM and the Communist Ideal* (Fabian tract no. 167), 1912. Trappes-Lomax, M., *Pugin, a Medieval Victorian*, 1933. Triggs, O. L., [1] *WM: Craftsman, Writer and Social Reformer*, c. 1902, Chicago (2) *Chapters in History of Arts and Crafts Movement*, c. 1902, Chicago. Troxell, J. C., (1) J ii [1] 4–8 (2) *Three Rossettis* (Harvard, 1937). Tschan, A., *WM* (Bern, 1962). Tsuzuki, C., (1) *H. M. Hyndman and British Socialism* (OUP, 1961) (2) *The Life of Eleanour Marx*.

Tunstall, E. A., and A. Kerr, *Burlington Mag.*, lxxxii, Feb. 1943, 42–7. Turner, Ben, *About Myself*, 1930.

Vachon, M., *Les Musées et les écoles d'art en Angleterre*, 1896. Vallance, A., (1) *WM: His Art, his Writings, and his Public Life*, 1898 (2) revised 1909 (3) *The Art of WM*, 1897. Vaughan, C. E., *Bibliographies of Swinburne, Morris, and Rossetti* (Oxford, 1914). Vidalenc, G., (1) *WM*, 1920 (2) *Mercure de France*, 1 July, 1911.

Wahl, J. R., *No Idle Singer*, inaugural lecture, Univ. of Orange Free State, Cape Town, 1964. Wardle, G.Y., (1) *Notes and Queries*, 9th s. 22 Dec., 1900, 495b (WM, man of business) (2) BM Addl. MS 45350. Warwick, Countess of, *Houses and Haunts of WM*, 1912. Waterhouse, P., *Archit. Rev.*, iii, iv, 1898. Watkinson, Ray, *WM as Designer*, 1967. Watts-Dunton, T., (1) *Athenaeum*, 10 Oct., 1896 (2) *English Rev.*, Jan. 1909 (3) *Old Familiar Faces*, 1916. Webb, B. and S., (1) *History of Trade Unionism*, 1894 (1a) 2nd ed. 1923 (2) *Industrial Democracy*, 1897 (3) S. alone, *Socialism in England*, 1890. Webb, P., *Cartoons for the Cause 1886–1896*, 1896. Weekley, M., *WM*, 1934. Weevers, T., *Neophilologus*, xlvi, 1962, 210–12 (accentual verse). Wells, H. G., *Experiment in Autobiography*. Werner, A., *Kenyon Rev.*, xxii, Summer, 1960, 392–407 (Solomon). West, Alick, *A Good Man Fallen among Fabians*. Whitehouse, J. H., *Ruskin Centenary Addresses* (OUP, 1919). Whitley, C., *Lord John Manners and His Friends*, 1905. Wilenskin, R. H., *J. Ruskin, an Intro.* (N.Y., 1933). Wiles, H. V., *WM of Walthamstow*, 1951. Wilkes, J. A., J ii [2] 9–13 (K. House). Williams, Jack, *Justice*, 15 Jan., 1914. Wood, H. T., *The Story of the R. Soc. of Arts*, ed. G. K. Menzies, n.d.

Yeats, W. B., (1) *Autobiographies*, 1926 (2) *Essays* (N.Y., 1924) (3) *If I were Four and Twenty* (Dublin, 1940). Young, L., *T. Carlyle and the Art of History* (Pennsylvania, 1939).

Index

Index